Blender®

ALL-IN-ONE

by Jason van Gumster

for
dummies®
A Wiley Brand

Blender® All-in-One For Dummies®

Published by: **John Wiley & Sons, Inc.,** 111 River Street, Hoboken, NJ 07030-5774, www.wiley.com

Copyright © 2024 by John Wiley & Sons, Inc., Hoboken, New Jersey

Published simultaneously in Canada

For general information on our other products and services, please contact our Customer Care Department within the U.S. at 877-762-2974, outside the U.S. at 317-572-3993, or fax 317-572-4002. For technical support, please visit https://hub.wiley.com/community/support/dummies.

Wiley publishes in a variety of print and electronic formats and by print-on-demand. Some material included with standard print versions of this book may not be included in e-books or in print-on-demand. If this book refers to media such as a CD or DVD that is not included in the version you purchased, you may download this material at http://booksupport.wiley.com. For more information about Wiley products, visit www.wiley.com.

Library of Congress Control Number: 2024933364

ISBN: 978-1-394-20404-5 (pbk); ISBN: 978-1-394-20406-9 (ePub); ISBN: 978-1-394-20405-2 (ePDF)

SKY10070012_032024

Contents at a Glance

Contents at a Glance

Table of Contents

Introduction

Welcome to *Blender All-in-One For Dummies*, your introduction to one of the most well-known free programs for creating 3D computer graphics. With Blender, you can create characters, props, environments, and nearly anything else your imagination can generate. And it's not just about creating objects. You can set them in motion, too. Tell a story in an animation, walk people through a world of your own creation, or add a special effect to some video footage. It's all possible. They still haven't quite designed a way for Blender to give you a foot massage if you've had a bad day, but in all seriousness, it's difficult to imagine a task in computer animation that you can't do with Blender. And just think: the developers of Blender have included all these features in a package you can download for free and run on nearly any computer. Crazy!

Blender sits at a very unique position in the world of 3D computer graphics. In the distant past, to get into 3D modeling and animation, you had only a few options, and most of them were too expensive, too limiting, or — *ahem* — too illegal for people just trying to see what this whole 3D thing was all about. Blender circumvents all those issues because it's free. And not just zero-cost free, but freedom Free. Blender is open source. A world full of developers and users regularly contribute code and documentation to this project, adding enhancements and improvements at a mind-boggling pace.

Of course, 3D computer graphics is a complex topic, and all software of this type is dense with buttons, options, settings, and unique ways of working. Perhaps more than any other program like it, Blender has carried a pretty heavy reputation for being difficult to understand. Blender wasn't typically viewed as software for beginners. But, with every new release, it gets better and better. Of course, there's still a lot in there. That's why this book exists. If I've done my job right, this book will help get you started at a sprint. *Blender All-in-One For Dummies* is not just a book on using Blender. Sure, I explain why things in Blender work in their peculiar Blenderish ways, but I also make a point to explain core principles of 3D computer graphics as they are relevant. There's no use in being able to find a button if you're not really sure what it does or how it works. My hope is that with this combined knowledge, you can actually take advantage of Blender's unique traits to create your own high-quality 3D art as quickly and efficiently as possible. Perhaps you can even become as addicted to it as I have been for the last 25+ years!

About This Book

Blender is an extremely complex program used for the even more complex task of producing high-quality 3D models and animations. In fact, Blender's capabilities have expanded so much since in the three years since *Blender For Dummies, 4th Edition* was released, we couldn't just do a new edition; we had to make it an All-in-One! That said, I can't cover every single feature and button in this powerful tool. For a more comprehensive manual, refer to the excellent online documentation available through Blender's website at `https://docs.blender.org/manual`.

Because I want to bring you up to speed on working in 3D space with Blender so that you can start bringing your ideas to life as soon as possible, I focus on introducing you to the fundamental "Blender way" of working. Not only do I show you *how* something is done in Blender, but I also often take the time to explain *why* things are done a certain way. Hopefully, this approach will put you on the fast track to making awesome work, and also allow you to figure out new parts of Blender on your own when you come across them.

Throughout the book, I refer to the Blender community. Blender's user community is probably one of its most valuable assets. It really is a feature all its own, and I would be remiss to neglect to mention it. Not only do many members of the community create great work, but they also write new code for Blender, write and edit documentation, and help each other improve. And understand that when I make reference to the Blender community, I include you in that community as well. As of right now, you are a *Blenderhead* — a fellow Blender user and, therefore, a member of the Blender community.

Blender is a truly *cross-platform* program running on Linux, Windows, and macOS. Fortunately, not much in Blender differs from one platform to another. However, for the few differences, I'll be sure to point them out for you.

Foolish Assumptions

I've written this book for two sorts of beginners: people who are completely new to the world of 3D and people who know a thing or two about 3D but are completely new to Blender.

Because of the various types of beginners this book addresses, I tend to err on the side of explaining too much rather than too little. If you're someone who is already familiar with another 3D computer graphics program, such as Maya, Cinema 4D, Houdini, or even an earlier version of Blender, you can probably skip a number of these explanations. Likewise, if you're a complete newbie, you may notice that I occasionally compare a feature in Blender to one in another package. However, that comparison is mostly for the benefit of these other users. I write so that you can understand a concept without having to know any of these other programs.

I do, however, make the assumption that you have at least a basic understanding of your computer. I assume that you know how to use a mouse, and I *highly* recommend that you use a mouse with at least two buttons and a scroll wheel, and that you've configured your operating system to enable the middle- and right-click buttons on your mouse. You *can* use Blender with a one- or two-button mouse or even a laptop trackpad, and I provide workarounds for the unfortunate souls in that grim state (*cough* . . . Mac users . . . *cough*), but it's certainly not ideal.

An exception is if you're using Blender with a drawing tablet like the ones produced by Wacom. Blender is accessible to tablet users and quite useful for tasks like drawing and sculpting. Of course, even though tablets are much less expensive these days than in the past, not everyone has one. For that reason, I focus primarily on using Blender with a mouse, although I will occasionally point out where having a tablet is helpful. Because Blender makes use of all your mouse buttons, I stipulate whether you need to left-click, right-click, or middle-click. And in case you didn't already know, pressing down on your mouse's scroll wheel typically accesses the middle mouse button. I also make use of this cool little arrow (⇨) for indicating a sequence of steps. It could be a series of hotkeys to press, menu items to select, or places to look in the Blender interface, but the consistent thing is that all these items are used for steps that you need to perform sequentially rather than simultaneously. For things that have to be done simultaneously like hotkey combinations such as Ctrl+Z for undo, I use a plus symbol (+).

I also assume that you're working with Blender's default settings and theme. You can customize the settings for yourself (in fact, I still use the presets from previous releases of Blender; 20 years of muscle memory doesn't go away easily), but if you do, Blender may not behave exactly like I describe in the book. For that reason, I focus mostly on accessing features through the menu system rather than using hotkeys. Hotkeys are meant to be customized, but the menus in Blender remain a consistent way of accessing features. Bearing in mind the point about Blender's themes, you may notice that the screenshots of Blender's interface are lighter in this book than you see onscreen. If I used Blender's default theme colors, all the figures in the book would appear overly dark. So for the last edition of this book

I created a custom theme with lighter colors that shows up better in print. Since then, that theme has actually been incorporated with Blender and ships with it. If you like the look of it, you can enable the "Print Friendly" theme from the Themes section of Preferences.

Icons Used in This Book

As you flip through this book, icons periodically appear next to some paragraphs. These icons notify you of unique or valuable information on the topic at hand. Sometimes that information is a tip, sometimes it's more detail about how something works, sometimes it's a warning to help you avoid losing data, and sometimes they're images that match icons in Blender's interface (there's a *lot* of them). For the icons that aren't in Blender's interface, the following are descriptions of each icon in this book.

This icon calls out suggestions that help you work more effectively and save time.

This icon marks something that I think you should try to keep in mind while working in Blender. Sometimes it's a random tidbit of information, but more often than not, it's something that you'll run into repeatedly and is, therefore, worth remembering.

Working in 3D can involve some pretty heavy technical information. You can usually work just fine without ever having to know these things, but if you do take the time to understand it, I bet you dollars to donuts that you'll be able to use Blender more effectively.

This icon doesn't show up often, but when it does, I definitely recommend that you pay attention. You won't blow up your computer if you overlook it, but you could lose work.

Blender is a fast-moving target. Quite a bit has changed since the previous edition of this book. These icons point out things that are new or different in Blender so that you can get to be at least as effective (and hopefully *more* effective) with the current version as you were with past versions. Also, because this book focuses on the 3.6 LTS release of Blender, there are some differences that appear in more recent releases. I use this icon to let you know of those as well.

Beyond the Book

Blender All-in-One For Dummies includes the following online goodies only for easy download:

>> **Cheat Sheet:** You can find the Cheat Sheet for this book here: www.dummies. com/article/technology/software/animation-software/blender/ blender-for-dummies-cheat-sheet-208646/, or by going to www. dummies.com, typing **blender** in the search box, and clicking Explore Articles.

>> **Extras:** I keep and maintain a website at blenderbasics.com with additional resources. I have a whole bunch of tutorials, both in written and in video format, specifically for readers of this book. Also, Blender's a big, fast-moving program. I do my best on that site to chronicle changes in Blender that affect the content of this book (and perhaps share a new tip or two as well).

Where to Go from Here

Wondering where to start? The easy answer here would be to say "Just dive on in!" but that's probably a bit too vague. This book is primarily intended as a reference, so if you already know what you're looking for, flip over to the table of contents or index and start soaking in the Blendery goodness.

If you're just starting out, I suggest that you merely turn a couple of pages, start at Chapter 1, and enjoy the ride. And, even if you're the sort of person who knows exactly what you're looking for, take the time to read through other sections of the book. You can find a bunch of valuable little bits of information that may help you work more effectively.

Regardless of how you read this book, though, my one hope is that you find it to be a valuable resource that allows you to flex your creative muscles and, more importantly, have fun doing it.

1

Wrapping Your Brain Around Blender

Contents at a Glance

Chapter **1**

Discovering Blender

I n the world of 3D modeling and animation software, programs have traditionally been expensive — like, thousands-of-dollars-and-maybe-an-arm
expensive. That's changed a bit over the years, with software companies moving to more subscription-based ways of selling their programs. The entry cost is
lower, but paying each month can still add up pretty quickly. There are *some* valid
reasons for the high prices. Software companies spend millions of dollars and
countless hours developing these programs. The large production companies that
buy this kind of software for their staff, make enough money to afford the high
cost, or hire programmers and write their own in-house software.

But what about us, you and me: the little folks? We are the ambitious dreamers
with big ideas, high motivation . . . and tight budgets. How can we bring our ideas
to life and our stories to screen, even if only on our own computer monitors?
Granted, we could shell out the cash (and hopefully keep our arms) for the expensive programs that the pros use. But even then, animation is a highly collaborative
art, and it's difficult to produce anything in a reasonable amount of time without
some help.

We need quality software and a strong community to work, grow, and evolve with.
Fortunately, Blender can provide us with both these things. This chapter is an
introduction to Blender, its background, its interface, and its community.

Getting to Know Blender

Blender is a free and open source 3D modeling and animation suite. Yikes! What a mouthful, huh? Put simply, Blender is a computer graphics program that allows you to produce high-quality still images and animations using three-dimensional geometry. It used to be that you'd only see the results of this work in animated feature films or high-budget television shows. These days, it's way more pervasive. Computer-generated 3D graphics are everywhere. Almost every major film and television show involves some kind of 3D computer graphics and animation. (Even sporting events! Pay close attention to the animations that show the scores or players' names.) And it's not just film and TV; 3D graphics play a major role in video games, industrial design, scientific visualization, and architecture (to name just a few industries). In the right hands, Blender is capable of producing this kind of work. With a little patience and dedication, *your* hands can be the right hands.

REMEMBER

One of the things that makes Blender different and special compared to similar 3D software is that it is freely available without cost, and that it's *free and open source* software.

Being free of cost, as well as free (as in freedom) and open source, means that not only can you go to the Blender website (www.blender.org) and download the entire program right now without paying anything, but you can also freely download the source or the code that makes up the program. For most programs, the source code is a heavily guarded and highly protected secret that only certain people (mostly programmers hired by the company that distributes the program) can see and modify. But Blender is open source, so anybody can see the program's source code and make changes to it. The benefit is that instead of having the program's guts behind lock and key, Blender can be improved by programmers (and even non-programmers) all over the world!

Because of these strengths, Blender is an ideal program for small animation companies, freelance 3D artists, independent filmmakers, students beginning to learn about 3D computer graphics, and dedicated computer graphics hobbyists. It's also being used (if a bit clandestinely) more and more in larger animation, visual effects, and video game studios because it's relatively easy to modify, has a very responsive development team, and no need for the headache of licensing servers.

Blender, like many other 3D computer graphics applications, has had a reputation for being difficult for new users to understand. At the same time, however, Blender is also known for allowing experienced users to bring their ideas to life quickly. Fortunately, with the help of this book and the regular improvements introduced in each new release of Blender, that gap is becoming much easier to bridge.

Discovering Blender's origins and the strength of the Blender community

The Blender you know and love today wasn't always free and open source. Blender is actually quite unique in that it's one of the few (and first!) software applications that was "liberated" from proprietary control with the help of its user community.

Originally, Blender was written as an internal production tool for an award-winning Dutch animation company called NeoGeo, founded by Blender's original developer and the current head of the Blender Foundation, Ton Roosendaal. In the late 1990s, NeoGeo started making copies of Blender available for download from its website. Slowly but surely, interest grew in this less-than-2MB program. In 1998, Ton spun off a new company, Not a Number (NaN), to market and sell Blender as a software product. NaN still distributed a free version of Blender, but also offered an advanced version with more features for a small fee. There was strength in this strategy, and by the end of 2000, Blender users numbered well over 250,000 worldwide.

Unfortunately, even though Blender was gaining in popularity, NaN was not making enough money to satisfy its investors, especially in the so-called "dot bomb" era that happened around that time. In 2002, NaN shut its doors and stopped working on Blender. Ironically, this point is where the story starts to get exciting.

Even though NaN went under, Blender had developed quite a strong community by this time, and this community was eager to find a way to keep their beloved little program from becoming lost and abandoned. In July of 2002, Ton provided a way. Having established a non-profit organization called the Blender Foundation, he arranged a deal with the original NaN investors to run the "Free Blender" campaign. The terms of the deal were that, for a price of €100,000 (at the time, about $100,000), the investors would agree to release Blender's source code to the Blender Foundation for the purpose of making Blender open source. Initial estimations were that it would take as long as six months to one year to raise the necessary funds. Amazingly, the community was able to raise that money in a mere *seven weeks*.

Because of the Blender community's passion and willingness to put its money where its metaphorical mouth was, Blender was released under the GNU General Public License on October 13, 2002. With the source in the community's hands, Blender had an avalanche of development and new features added to it in a very short time, including somewhat common features like Undo (a functionality that was conspicuously missing and highly desired since the initial releases of Blender by NeoGeo).

Over two decades later, the Blender community is larger and stronger than ever. Blender itself is a powerful modern piece of software, competitive in terms of quality with similar software costing thousands of dollars. Not too shabby. Figure 1-1 shows screenshots of Blender from its early days to the Blender of today.

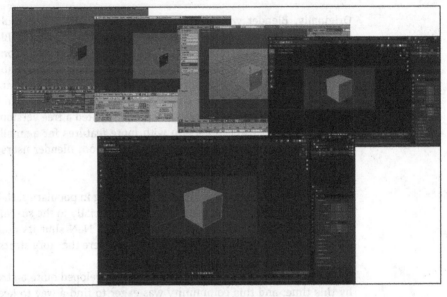

FIGURE 1-1:
Blender through the years: (from left to right) Blender 1.8, Blender 2.46, Blender 2.72, Blender 2.83, and the Blender of today (bottom).

Understanding Blender release versions

Multiple releases of Blender come out over the course of a year. As of this writing, typically three releases come out each year. One of those releases is always a long-term support, or *LTS* release. Most 3D software doesn't have such a high-paced release schedule. As Blender has gotten more popular, it's been put to work in a bunch of large organizations: big studios, enterprise environments, and manufacturing facilities. These companies don't actually update their software to new versions all that frequently and prefer to only update for critical bug fixes or security patches.

This approach makes sense. Using the example of large feature-length animated films, those productions often take three years or more to complete. If you're in the middle of producing a multi-million dollar production like that, it's more important to have a stable, predictable tool than to have the latest and greatest new features (with all of the associated bugs and changes that may accompany that feature). Likewise, the process of creating educational material can sometimes be just as time-consuming. For example, this book is scheduled for release in the first part of 2024. I started working on this book in April of 2023. Three different versions of Blender were released in that time.

It's for these kinds of long schedules that the Blender developers decided to mark certain releases as LTS releases. Those releases of Blender get bug fixes and security updates for two years following their release to ensure that there are stable versions of Blender available for people who are using it for production or creating documentation. Everyone else can stick to the regular, more frequent releases and take advantage of the latest and greatest features when they come out.

For this book, I try to split the difference. The majority of the content in these pages is focused on features that are available in Blender 3.6 LTS. However, sometimes new features are just too cool to skip talking about. So there are a few moments in this book where I cover a feature that's in Blender 4.0. I'll be sure to make you aware of it when I cover those features, so no worries there.

Making open movies and games

One of the cool things about the programmers who write Blender is that many of them also use the program regularly. They're writing code not just because they're told to do it, but because they want to improve Blender for their own purposes. Many of Blender's developers started as artists who wanted to make Blender do something it wasn't able to do before. Part of the programmers' motivation has to do with Blender's open source nature, but quite a bit also has to do with the fact Blender was originally an in-house production tool, built for artists, based on their direct input, and often written by the artists themselves.

Seeking to get even more of this direct artist feedback to developers, the Blender Foundation launched "Project Orange" in 2005. The project's purpose was to create an animated short movie using open source tools, primarily Blender. A team of six community members were assembled in Amsterdam, in the Netherlands, to produce the movie. Roughly seven months later, *Elephants Dream* premiered and was released to the public as the first *open movie*. This means that not only was it created using open source tools, but all the production files — 3D models, scenes, character rigs, and so on — were also released under a permissive and open Creative Commons Attribution license. These files are valuable tools for discovering how an animated film is put together, and anyone can reuse them in their own personal or commercial work. Furthermore, if you don't like *Elephants Dream*, you're free to change it to your liking! How many movies give you that luxury?

Due to the success of the Orange project, Ton established the Blender Institute in 2007 for the expressed purpose of having a permanent space to create open movie and game projects, as well as provide the service of training people in Blender. Since then, the Blender Institute has churned out open projects every couple of years. Like with *Elephants Dream*, both the final product *and* the production files for each project are released under a permissive Creative Commons license. More recently, the Blender Institute has spun off a separate entity, the Blender Animation Studio, a Blender-based animation studio with the goal of producing and releasing a feature-length animated film.

With the completion of each of these projects, the functionality and stability of Blender significantly increased. Much of the content of this book wouldn't even exist without these projects. For example, Chapter 6 in Book 4 covers using Blender's Grease Pencil objects to do 2D animation in 3D space. All the content in Chapter 2 in Book 5 is focused on the *Compositor*, a way of combining and enhancing still images and animations. In fact, nearly all of Book 4 is devoted to features that were enhanced or directly added for one of these open projects.

All these projects continue to exhibit the strength of the Blender community. Each of them was financed in large part by DVD presales (and now Blender Cloud subscriptions) from users who understand that regardless of the project's final product, great improvements to Blender are the result, and everyone benefits from that.

Joining the community

Congratulations! As a Blender user, you're a part of our community. You're joining a diverse group that spans all age ranges, ethnicities, professional backgrounds, and parts of the globe. We are a passionate bunch: proud of this little 3D program and more than willing to help others enjoy using it as much as we do. Have a look at the supplemental website for this book, blenderbasics.com, for a list of invaluable community resources, not only for discovering the intricacies of using Blender, but also for improving yourself as an artist.

You can find innumerable opportunities for critique, training, discussion, and even collaboration with other artists, some of whom might also be Blender developers. I've made quite a few good friends and colleagues through the Blender community, both through the various community websites and by attending events like the annual Blender Conference. I go by the name "Fweeb" on these sites, and I look forward to seeing you around!

Getting to Know the Interface

Probably one of the most daunting aspects of Blender for newcomers and seasoned 3D professionals alike has been its unique and somewhat peculiar interface. For a long time, the interface has arguably been the most controversial feature Blender has had. In fact, at one time, merely calling the interface a feature would raise the blood pressure of some who tried using Blender in the past, but gave up in frustration when it did not behave as expected.

Although the interface wasn't the primary focus, the interface updates to Blender added in the 2.5 series of release made great strides toward alleviating that frustration, and the improvements continue through to today. In fact, Blender's interface is more welcoming to newcomers than ever before. As a small example, when you first launch Blender, the "splash image" provides you with some quick setup options to configure Blender to your liking right from the start. If you're more familiar with other programs' hotkeys and mouse behavior, you may want to try using the "Industry Compatible" shortcuts. If you're a long-time Blender user like me, you may choose the Blender 2.7X shortcuts. This book is written with the assumption that you're going with the default choices in this splash screen. Figure 1-2 shows the splash image you're presented with when you start Blender for the first time.

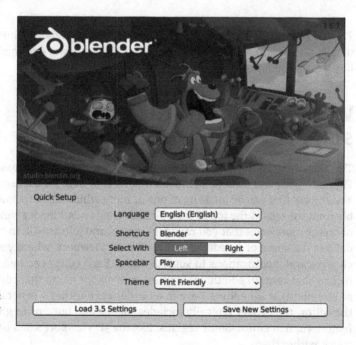

FIGURE 1-2: The Blender splash screen.

If you click anywhere other than the splash screen, the splash screen goes away, and you're greeted with Blender's default General workflow template in the Layout workspace, shown in Figure 1-3. If you're looking at the interface for the first time, you may think it appears pretty daunting. However, the purpose of this book is to help you get the hang of Blender (and its interface) with minimum pain.

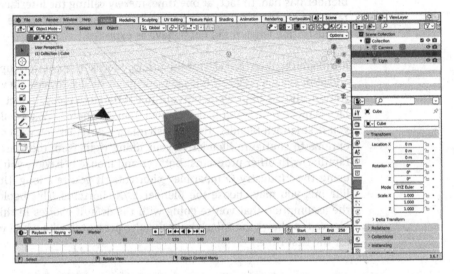

FIGURE 1-3:
The default
Blender interface.

This book explains some of the design decisions in Blender's interface and ultimately allows you to be productive with it. Who knows, you might even start to like it and wonder why other programs don't work this way!

Working with an interface that stays out of your way

The first thing to understand about Blender's interface is its basic organization. Figure 1-3 displays a single Blender window. Your base Blender session consists of a *workspace* that can be made up of one or more windows. Workspaces are accessible from the tabs at the top of each Blender window. A Blender window can consist of one or more *areas* that you can split, resize, and join at will. In all cases, an area defines the space of an *editor*, such as the 3D Viewport, where you actually make changes and modifications to your 3D scene. Each editor can include one or more *regions* that contain additional features or tools for using that editor. An example of a region that all editors have is a header region that's generally at the top of the editor; the header typically includes menus and buttons to give you access to features in that editor. Some regions, like the 3D Viewport's Sidebar, have *tabs* and *panels* within them.

Figure 1-4 illustrates the hierarchical breakdown of the building blocks in Blender's interface.

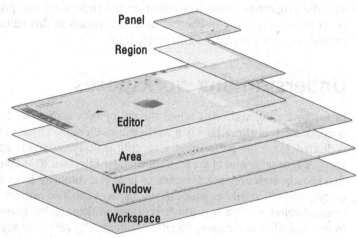

Panel

Region

Editor

Area

Window

Workspace

Knowing this organizational structure, the next important thing to know is that Blender is designed to be as *non-blocking* and *non-modal* as possible. Areas in Blender never overlap one another (non-blocking), and using one feature of Blender typically won't restrict you from using any of the others (non-modal). As an example, if you want to change the material on a 3D object in some other software packages, they may spawn a dialog or sub-window. This dialog is an overlapping window that not only blocks things behind it from view but, in some cases, also prevents you from making any changes to your file. This scenario isn't the case with Blender. In Blender, the Shader Editor never gets in the way of the 3D Viewport unless you explicitly want it to.

REMEMBER

At first, working in a non-blocking, non-modal interface may seem to be really restrictive. How do you see different types of editors? Can you see them at the same time? Everything looks like it's nailed in place, so is it even possible to change anything? Fortunately, all these things are possible, and you get the benefit of never having your view of one area obstructed by another. Having an unobstructed workspace is a great way to be able to see at a glance what's going on in your file. Furthermore, if you absolutely *need* multiple windows that can overlap, you can have them. For example, you might have two computer monitors that are different sizes, and you'd like a full-sized Blender window in each. I show you how to do this later in this chapter in the "Duplicating an area to a new window" section.

TIP

Even Blender's interface is written using a 3D software library. You're doing 3D in 3D! One of the notable benefits of being written this way is that many parts of Blender's interface allow you to zoom in on them. Try it! Hover your mouse cursor over the Properties editor (the editor on the right side) and press Numpad Plus (+) or Numpad Minus (-). You can make the panels in this editor much larger or smaller than they are by default. Pretty cool!

Understanding workspaces

In the preceding section, I noted the set of tabs across the top of the Blender window. Each of these tabs is a *workspace* in Blender. Think of a workspace as a dedicated space for performing a specific task. Functionally speaking, a workspace is a preset layout of areas in the Blender interface. This layout and the editor that goes in each area are designed to help you complete the task to that area as quickly and efficiently as possible. Workspaces can also control which mode your selected object is in when you switch to that workspace. For example, if you switch to the Sculpting workspace, Blender automatically sets your selected object to be in Sculpt mode.

REMEMBER

It's easy to make the mistake of thinking that each workspace is "locked" and that you can't make any changes to it. That's far from the truth. In fact, with a little bit of effort, you can make any workspace look and behave like another one. I've done full projects without ever leaving the Layout workspace; I just rearrange the editors and areas to match whatever thing I am trying to do. That's not a great habit to get into, though. Workspaces are there so you don't have to do as much of that rearranging, and you can spend more of your time making cool stuff rather than fiddling with the size of your editor areas.

Blender ships with 16 different workspaces built into your starting .blend file (listed in alphabetical order):

>> **2D Animation:** Yes! You *can* do 2D, hand-drawn animation in Blender using Grease Pencil objects. This workspace is designed to help you do that faster. You can find out more about animating with Grease Pencil in Book 4, Chapter 6.

>> **2D Full Canvas:** Think of this workspace as a kind of "focus mode" for 2D drawing in Blender. The Blender window is populated with a single area that has a 3D Viewport. It's an open canvas for you to work with no distractions.

>> **Animation:** The Animation workspace is the place to go for access to editors used in a standard 3D animation workflow. Have a look at the chapters in Book 4 for more on animating in Blender.

>> **Compositing:** Compositing is the art of mixing image data together to generate a new image. That task is best completed from this workspace; see Book 5, Chapter 2.

>> **Geometry Nodes:** The ability to use a node-based interface to generate procedural models is one of the newest features added to Blender in recent years. You can do so much with this feature, a whole workspace was added to Blender for you to use it. See Book 2, Chapter 5 for more on using Geometry Nodes.

>> **Layout:** The Layout workspace is the default "home base" where most people start working in Blender. It's a solid general purpose workspace that you can use for most 3D work. The name "Layout" comes from the layout step of traditional animation pipelines where an artist blocks in a scene and sets basic timing and placement for the characters and camera in that scene.

>> **Masking:** The Masking workspace is typically used when you're using Blender for visual effects (VFX) tasks. VFX often requires artists to create and animate masks to either isolate or hide visual elements in a shot, so Blender has a workspace dedicated to this task. See Book 5 for more on using Blender in VFX.

>> **Modeling:** This workspace looks quite a bit like the Layout workspace, but without the Timeline at the bottom of the window because that's not as necessary when making 3D models. All of Book 2 covers the general topic of modeling, but most of your time in this workspace is going to be in Chapters 1 and 2 of that book.

>> **Motion Tracking:** If you want to seamlessly integrate 3D graphics into video, you need to use a process called *motion tracking* to get the movement of the camera in your 3D scene to match that of the physical camera that shot the video. Blender has a built-in motion tracker, and this workspace is designed to help take the most advantage of it. You can find out more about motion tracking in Blender in Book 5, Chapter 3.

>> **Rendering:** At some point, it's likely that you'll want to take your 3D model or animation and convert it to a still image or a video file that you can share with others. The process of converting your 3D scene to those formats is called *rendering,* and this is the workspace where you monitor that process. There's more on rendering in Book 3, Chapter 4.

>> **Scripting:** In addition to all the graphical things Blender can do, it can also run custom blocks of code that you (or someone else) can write called *scripts*. These scripts can be little simple things to automate monotonous tasks, or they can be full-blown applications in their own right that just happen to live in Blender. The Scripting workspace is where you can develop these scripts. Book 6, Chapter 2 helps you get started with this complex, yet time-saving skill.

>> **Sculpting:** Most 3D modeling these days starts with sculpting rather than manually pushing around vertices. The Sculpting workspace gives you the fastest access to Blender's sculpting tools so you can get your models created quickly. Sculpting is covered in more depth in Book 2, Chapter 3.

>> **Shading:** If animation is what brings life to a 3D model, then shading is what gives it style. The *shading* or *surfacing* of a model can make it look realistic, cartoony, or completely out of this world. The entirety of Book 3 involves shading and working with the Shading workspace.

>> **Texture Paint:** As part of the surfacing process, many models have custom images, called *textures*, applied and painted to the surface of their geometry. The Texture Paint workspace is the best place to get this work done. Have a look at Book 3, Chapter 2 for more on this topic.

>> **UV Editing:** Before you can paint a texture on a mesh, you need to go through a process of describing how that flat 2D image is applied to the mesh. That process is called unwrapping, and the UV Editing workspace is work you do that work. See Book 3, Chapter 2 for more on unwrapping and working with UVs.

>> **Video Editing:** Blender's primary purpose is to make 3D art. However, you can also use it to arrange sequences of video to build more complex movies. The work of editing those videos happens in the Video Editing workspace. See Book 5, Chapter 1 for more on video editing in Blender.

Also, it's worth noting that you're not just limited to these workspaces that I've just listed. Because a workspace is just a preset layout, you can create your own if you'd like. Notice that there's a little plus (+) icon to the right of the last workspace tab. Click this icon and Blender provides a menu of each of the available workspaces so you can add one to your active .blend file. If you look at the last item in that menu, it's labeled Duplicate Current. Click that menu item, and Blender creates a new workspace that's identical to the one you were just in. If you double-click the workspace tab for your new workspace, you can rename it something of your liking. Now you can adjust the size of your areas and the editors that live within them to build out your own custom workspace. See the "Resizing areas" section later in this chapter for more on how to do that.

Blender workflows

When working in 3D, there's not just one single process to go through to get from idea to the final deliverable thing, be it a model, a really cool still image, or a complete animation sequence. The production pipeline is actually made up of a sequence of processes. The workspaces described in the previous section each represent one of those process sequences. If you chain those together, you get a *workflow*, sometimes referred to as a *pipeline*. As an example, consider the process of modeling a 3D character. That process typically looks something like this (don't worry if you don't understand the details in these steps; we'll cover them in more detail throughout the book):

1. Start with concept art in the form of a 2D drawing.

2. Sculpt the character's geometry in 3D.

3. Retopologize the character to prepare it for texturing and rigging.

Looking at each of those steps and thinking about the workspaces in the preceding section, it's easy to imagine doing the concept art step in the 2D Animation workspace, sculpting in the Sculpting workspace, and then retopologizing in the modeling workspace . . . and in that order. That's a workflow.

The Blender development team knows that this is how people typically work, so they created a bunch of workflow templates that ship with Blender by default. Humorously, the workflow I described above isn't one of them. However, like with workspaces, you can also create your own workflows also called *application templates*. The process for that is a little bit more involved than creating your own workspaces, so I've included that as its own follow-along tutorial on this book's supplemental website, `blenderbasics.com`. That said, the workflows that ship with Blender are pretty helpful. You can see them by navigating to File ⇨ New in Blender's topbar menu. The submenu that appears gives you a list of workflows that you can choose from:

>> **General:** This is the default workflow that Blender launches with, starting you in a Layout workspace and then from left to right you have workspaces for Modeling, Sculpting, UV Editing, Texture Paint, Shading, Animation, Rendering, Compositing, Geometry Nodes, and Scripting. This workflow is loosely based on the pipeline used to produce animated movies, though with additions like the Geometry Nodes workspace, it's a bit more general purpose.

>> **2D Animation:** As the name indicates, this workflow template is meant to facilitate the creation of 2D animation with Grease Pencil objects. The workspaces in this workflow are 2D Animation, 2D Full Canvas, Compositing, and Rendering.

>> **Sculpting:** The Sculpting workflow has workspaces only for Sculpting and Shading. Part of the reason for this is because there are jobs in 3D just focused on sculpting and not much else.

>> **VFX:** If you're going to be doing visual effects work like motion tracking or compositing, then it's worth checking out the VFX workflow, which has workspaces for Motion Tracking, Masking, Compositing, and Rendering.

>> **Video Editing:** Like the Sculpting workflow, the Video Editing workflow has only two workspaces by default, Video Editing and Rendering, and for much the same reason.

Resizing areas

Regardless of the type of editor that's contained in an area, you modify and change all areas in a Blender window the same way. To change the size of an area, left-click the border between two areas and drag it to a new position. This method increases the size of one area while reducing the size of those that adjoin it. If you have only one area in your Blender window, it's exactly the same size as that window. To resize it, you need to either adjust the size of its parent Blender window or split a new area into that space, as covered in the next section.

Splitting and removing areas

While working in Blender, you may find that the workspace you're in isn't quite what you need to work efficiently, but you don't need as extravagant a change as a whole new workspace. Sometimes you may just need an additional 3D Viewport, or you may want to see the Image Editor in addition to the 3D Viewport.

To create either of these layout changes, you need to *split* an existing area into two. You can split or join areas by right-clicking the border between two areas and choosing either Split Area or Join Area from the menu that pops up. Most editors also have a View ⇨ Area submenu that provides you options for splitting. However, there's a faster way. It's a little tricky to get used to, though. Look at the corners of any area. Notice how the corners are rounded and when you move your mouse cursor near them, the cursor changes from the standard pointer to crosshairs. These are the area's *corner widgets*, and they're a shortcut for splitting and joining areas. To split any area into two, follow these steps:

1. **Left-click one of the corner widgets and drag your mouse cursor away from the area's border and into the area.**

2. **Drag your mouse cursor left or right to split the area vertically.**

   Dragging it up or down splits the area horizontally.

As you drag your mouse, the areas update in real time so that you can see the result of the split while you're working.

TIP

If you decide that you actually don't want to split the area, you can cancel the operation by right-clicking or pressing Esc.

If you want to remove an area, the process is similar. Rather than splitting an area in two, you're joining two areas together. So instead of left-clicking the corner widget and dragging your mouse cursor *away* from the area border, drag it *towards* the border of the area you want to join with. This action darkens the area your mouse is in to indicate which area you want to remove.

When I work in Blender, I find myself constantly changing the screen layout by splitting and joining new areas as I need them.

Duplicating an area to a new window

In addition to splitting and joining areas, you can use an area's corner widgets to duplicate that area into a new Blender window of its own. You can move that window to a separate monitor (if you have one), or it can overlap your original Blender window. And within this new Blender window, you can split the duplicated area into additional ones as you like. This area-duplication feature is a slight violation of Blender's non-overlapping principles, but the benefits it provides for users with multiple computer screens make it very worthwhile.

To take advantage of this feature, follow these steps:

1. **Shift+left-click one of the corner widgets in an area and drag your mouse cursor away from it in any direction.**

    This step duplicates the area you clicked in and creates a new Blender window to contain it.

    You can also achieve this effect from the header menu of some editors by choosing View ⇨ Area ⇨ Duplicate Area into New Window.

TIP

2. **Close the additional Blender window by clicking the close button that your operating system adds to the border of the window.**

Customizing headers

All editors in Blender have a horizontal region called the *header* that usually runs along the top of the editor. The header usually features specialized menus or buttons specific to the editor you're using. Here are some ways you can customize the header:

» **Hide the header.** If you right-click the header, you get a menu with the Show Header check box that you can use to toggle the visibility of the header. When the header is hidden, what remains is only a small down-arrow icon in the right corner of the editor. If the header is at the bottom of the editor, the arrow icon points up and appears at the bottom right of the editor. Left-click this icon and the header reappears.

>> **Scroll the header's menus.** There will be occasions while working that you make an area too narrow to show all the menus and buttons in it. No worries. All headers in all of Blender's editors are scrollable. If you have a narrow area where parts of the header are obscured, hover your mouse cursor over the header and scroll your mouse wheel to slide the contents of the header left and right. You could also middle-click and drag the header to do the same thing.

>> **Hide menus in the header.** Of course, maybe you don't want to be constantly scrolling the contents of your header. You'd rather just save space by hiding the menus. Right-click the header and toggle the Show Menus option to collapse the menus for that header down to a single button with an icon of three lines (sometimes called a *hamburger menu*).

>> **Change the location of the header.** You can also change the location of the header to either the top or bottom of the editor it belongs to. To do so, right-click the header and choose Flip to Top (or Bottom, depending on where your header currently is).

>> **Hide or show Tool Settings.** This one is specific to any editors with a Tool Bar, such as the 3D Viewport, the Image Editor, or any of the Node Editors. If you right-click the header for these editors, there's an additional check box that you can use to toggle the visibility for settings on your active tool and regain a bit of screen real estate.

Maximizing an area

When working in Blender, you also occasionally need to maximize an area. Maximizing an area is particularly useful when you're working on a model or scene, and you just want to get all the other areas out of your way so you can use as much screen space as possible for the task at hand.

To maximize any area, hover your mouse cursor over it and press Ctrl+Spacebar. You can toggle back to the tiled screen layout by either pressing Ctrl+Spacebar again or clicking the Back to Previous button at the top of the window. These options are available in the header menus of nearly all editor types by choosing View ⇨ Area ⇨ Toggle Maximize Area. You can also right-click the header and choose Maximize Area from the menu that appears. If the area is already maximized, then the menu item will say Tile Area.

You may notice another option in the View ⇨ Area menu, Toggle Fullscreen Area. This option gives you even more screen space by hiding the menus and workspace tabs at the top of the Blender window. The hotkey to toggle this is Ctrl+Alt+Spacebar.

TIP

The menu that is a pie

There's another feature of Blender's user interface that's worth mentioning. That feature is called pie menus. Contrasted with the more conventional linear, list-type menu, a *pie menu* lists your menu options radially around your mouse cursor. This setup has a few advantages:

>> **Each menu item has a much larger click area.** With a typical list-type menu, after you find the menu item you want, you need to precisely click a relatively small area. Having a small click area can be especially frustrating if your primary input is with a pen tablet like many artists have. With a pie menu, your mouse cursor only needs to be in the general area around your menu selection (its slice of the pie). Because you don't need to be as precise with your mouse, you can navigate menus faster with less stress on your hand.

>> **Menu options are easier to remember.** As humans, we tend to naturally think about things spatially. It's much easier to remember that a thing is up or left or right than to remember that it's the sixth item in a list of things. Because the menu items are arranged in two-dimensional space, pie menus take advantage of our natural way of recalling information. Also helpful for memory is the fact that any given pie menu can only have as many as eight options.

>> **Selecting menu items is a *gestural* behavior.** A *gestural interface* relies on using mouse movement to issue a command. Pie menus are not purely gestural, but by arranging the menu items spatially, you get many of the same advantages provided by gestures. Most valuable among these advantages is the reliance on muscle memory. After working with a pie menu for an extended period of time, selecting menu items becomes nearly as fast as using hotkeys, and for essentially the same reasons. You're no longer thinking about the direction you're moving your mouse cursor (or which key you're pressing). You've trained your hands to move in a specific way when you want to perform that task. Once you get to that point (it doesn't take very long), you'll find that you're working very quickly.

TECHNICAL STUFF

Before you get too excited about pie menus, they have a couple of limitations:

>> Pie menus are basically limited to a maximum of eight menu items. (It's possible to have more items, but if a pie menu has more than eight items, it becomes cluttered and the speed and memory advantages are lessened.) Blender has a number of very long menus; therefore, they don't all translate nicely to the pie menu model. This means that some menus will be pies and others will not. Hopefully, as development continues on Blender, these menus will migrate to being more pie-like.

>> Some pie menus aren't enabled by default. A number of hotkeys are bound to pie menus already, but you can enable even more as add-ons from Preferences. (Read more about Blender add-ons in Chapter 2 of this book.)

The process of enabling additional pie menus is easy:

1. **Open User Preferences (Edit ⇨ Preferences) and go to the Add-ons section.**

2. **On the search field on the upper right of the window, type pie menu.**

   The add-on list should have one choice available: 3D Viewport Pie Menus.

3. **Enable the pie menu add-on you want by left-clicking its check box.**

   Additional pie menus are now enabled.

That's it! By default, Blender automatically saves what you set in Preferences, so additional pie menus will be automatically enabled each time you start Blender in the future.

To try out pie menus, you don't have to actually enable any add-ons at all. With your mouse cursor in the 3D Viewport, press Ctrl+Tab to show the Mode pie menu. You should see a menu like the one in Figure 1-5. Throughout this book, you'll see what each of these modes can be used for. The point here is to recognize pie menus and know how to use them.

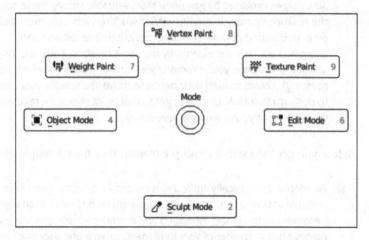

FIGURE 1-5:
Your first pie (menu)!

With the menu still visible, move your mouse cursor around the screen. Notice that the highlighted area of the circular slice indicator at the center of the menu points to your mouse cursor. Also notice that as you move your mouse cursor, individual menu items highlight when you enter their slice of the menu. This highlighting is how you know which menu item is currently ready to be picked. Press Esc to close the menu without selecting anything.

You can choose menu items in a pie menu in two ways:

>> **Press, release, click:** This can be considered the standard method:

1. *Press and release the hotkey that activates the menu.*

   In this example, press and release Ctrl+Tab.

2. *Move your mouse cursor to your desired menu item's slice.*

3. *Choose that menu item by clicking anywhere within its slice.*

   The current active slice is indicated by the circular slice indicator at the center of the menu, as well as the highlighting of each menu item as your mouse cursor enters its slice.

>> **Press, hold, release:** I think of this method as the fast way.

1. *Press **and hold** the hotkey that activates the menu.*

   In this example, press and hold Ctrl+Tab.

2. *Move your mouse cursor to your desired menu item's slice.*

3. *Release the hotkey to choose that menu item.*

Even without enabling any add-ons, pie menus are still used throughout Blender's interface, so it's worth getting used to them. One of the advantages of the add-ons is that they enable you to configure which hotkeys have an associated pie menu, so you can disable some of those pies if you'd like.

IN THIS CHAPTER

» **Familiarizing yourself with Blender's windows**

» **Working in three-dimensional space**

» **Using the regions in the 3D Viewport**

» **Adjusting Blender's interface to fit the way you work**

Chapter **2**

Understanding How Blender Thinks

It's time to get intimate with Blender. No, I don't mean you need to start placing scented candles around your computer. I mean that this chapter's focus is a detailed introduction to Blender's interface and how you can start finding your way around in it. First of all, it's pretty important to have an understanding of the various types of editors that Blender has and how to access them. These editors are the gateways and tools for creating whatever you want.

With the knowledge of what you can do with these editors, the next thing is actually building those creations. To do so, you need to understand how to work in a virtual three-dimensional space, and specifically, you need to understand how Blender handles that space. I also cover these topics in this chapter.

Menus in Blender

There's a somewhat unique quirk of Blender's menus. Because editors and their headers can literally be just about anywhere in a Blender window, depending on how you've split it, menus will either roll down or up from wherever you click, depending on where there's the most available space. Furthermore, the menus are designed to help you by keeping the distance you need to move your mouse cursor as short as possible. In practice, this means that when you open a menu from an editor's header near the bottom of the Blender window, it flows upward with the first menu item at the bottom, closest to your mouse cursor. When you open a header menu near the top of the Blender window, it flows downward, and the first item is at the top.

For floating menus like the Add (Shift+A) menu in the 3D Viewport (covered in Book 1, Chapter 4), the behavior is a little bit different. Those menus always list the first item at the top; *however*, Blender remembers the last item you picked in any of these floating menus and automatically places that item under your mouse cursor. Again, this is for speedy workflow. The idea is that if you chose one menu item last time, it's likely that you want to pick it again this time. To reduce the distance you have to move the mouse cursor, Blender facilitates this notion by jumping directly to the last menu item you chose.

Looking at Editor Types

In many ways, Blender isn't so much one program as it is a bunch of different programs sharing the same interface and access to the same data. Thinking of it this way, each of Blender's editor types is kind of its own little program in a Blender area.

In fact, there's a much greater emphasis on having Blender's workflow cater to users familiar with other specific applications. So, for example, if you're familiar with common interfaces for non-linear video editors, Blender's Video Editing workspace will make use of many of the same interface paradigms that you're used to. Likewise for the Animation or Sculpting workspaces. The Blender developers have worked very hard to balance Blender's internal consistency with the expectations of people migrating from other applications.

That said, once you're in a workspace, you still have the ability to re-organize and adjust it, adding and removing areas and editors as you see fit. As noted in the Book 1, Chapter 1, a Blender area can contain any editor type. You can see what editor types are available by left-clicking the button on the far left of that editor's header. Figure 2-1 shows the menu that appears when you press this button.

Each editor type serves a specific purpose, but you can organize them into four basic categories, as shown in the menu: general editors, animation editors, scripting editors, and data editors. The following subsections give you an overview of each editor, organized by category.

FIGURE 2-1:
The Editor
Type menu.

General editors

The editors covered in this section are usually the most common way of interfacing with objects in your 3D scene and actually creating things in Blender.

TIP

You may notice that the same hotkey combination gets listed for multiple editors. The reason for this re-use of hotkeys is because those editors often get used together in a particular workflow or have a similar work paradigm, so having the same hotkey allows you to quickly toggle or shuffle through those editors.

These are editors you use to make things in a Blender scene:

» **3D Viewport (Shift+F5):** Arguably the most-used editor in Blender, the 3D Viewport shows you the three-dimensional view of your model or scene and provides access to many of the tools you can use to modify it.

» **Image Editor (Shift+F10):** With the Image Editor, you can do basic image editing, masking, and digital painting.

» **UV Editor (Shift+F10):** To apply images to the surface of your 3D objects, you often need to go through a process called *unwrapping* to edit the texture coordinates for your models (see Book 3, Chapter 2). The UV Editor gives you the bulk of the tools necessary to complete that process.

» **Shader Editor (Shift+F3):** Blender has a node-based editor for creating and modifying materials and textures. Both Cycles and Eevee, Blender's two integrated render engines, make heavy use of the Shader Editor for materials and lighting.

Book 3 covers materials, textures, and lighting extensively.

» **Compositor (Shift+F3):** Similar to the Shader Editor, Blender uses a node-based system for *compositing* or mixing images after they've been rendered. To find out all about the Compositor, have a look at Book 5, Chapter 2.

» **Texture Node Editor (Shift+F3):** The Shader Editor is a great place to generate materials for your 3D objects, but sometimes you need a specific interface for building textures. That's what the Texture Node Editor is for.

Think of it as a Compositor of image data *before* you render. I get into the Texture Node Editor a little bit in Book 3, Chapter 2.

 » **Geometry Node Editor (Shift+F3):** One of the newest features added to Blender since the last edition of this book is Geometry Nodes. With Geometry Nodes, you have *procedural* control of 3D objects, all the way down to the geometry that they're made of. It's like visual programming for 3D objects, and the Geometry Node Editor is where all of that work happens. You can find out more about Geometry Nodes in Book 2, Chapter 5.

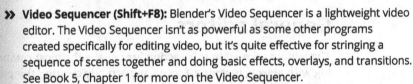 » **Video Sequencer (Shift+F8):** Blender's Video Sequencer is a lightweight video editor. The Video Sequencer isn't as powerful as some other programs created specifically for editing video, but it's quite effective for stringing a sequence of scenes together and doing basic effects, overlays, and transitions. See Book 5, Chapter 1 for more on the Video Sequencer.

 » **Movie Clip Editor (Shift+F2):** The Movie Clip Editor is the primary go-to editor for Blender's motion tracking features. *Motion tracking* is a process where the software analyzes moving parts of a video in an effort to relate them to 3D space. With video that's been successfully motion tracked, you can integrate 3D models into recorded video. Have you ever wondered how they get computer-generated monsters to look like they're in the same room as living actors? Motion tracking! Book 5, Chapter 3 is all about motion tracking in Blender.

Animation editors

The following editors relate specifically to animation (detailed information on using these editors can be found in Book 4):

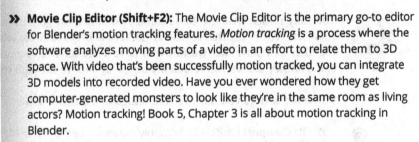 » **Dope Sheet (Shift+F12):** The Dope Sheet is where you create and adjust your overall animation using actions or keying sets. You can use *actions* to animate all of a character's movement in a scene, or you can mix them together in the Nonlinear Animation Editor. *Keying sets* give you the ability to group together a bunch of different animatable attributes.

» **Timeline (Shift+F12):** If you're working on an animation, the Timeline editor offers you a convenient way to quickly jump from one moment in your animation to another as well as play back the animation. You can also do some simple keyframe editing from this editor.

» **Graph Editor (Shift+F6):** Blender's Graph Editor shows a graphical representation of animatable attributes in your scene as they change over time.

 » **Drivers (Shift+F6):** Drivers are a bit of an advanced rigging topic. Simply put, drivers give you the ability to control one animatable parameter with the values of another. For example, you could control the Z-axis rotation of one object with the Y-axis location of another. The Drivers editor is what you use to map and define that relationship. Go to Book 4, Chapter 2 for full details on using the Drivers editor.

 » Nonlinear Animation: The Nonlinear Animation (NLA) editor allows you to mix pre-animated actions on a single character (such as mixing a waving hand animation with a walking animation to have your character walk and wave their hand at the same time).

Scripting editors

The following editors are useful for automating tasks within Blender (see Book 6, Chapter 2 for more on using these editors):

 » Text Editor (Shift+F11): Blender's integrated Text Editor is not only handy for keeping notes about your scenes and models, but once you become a more advanced user, it's also a convenient place to write and test your own Python scripts and material shaders in Blender.

 » Python Console (Shift+F4): The Console is a pretty handy editor that's more often utilized by advanced users to help write custom Python scripts. It's a "live" console where you can use the Python language to directly issue commands to Blender.

 » Info: The Info editor displays basic information about your scene. It also serves as a reporting space where warnings and errors are logged. This can be used to figure out what happened if a feature doesn't work as expected.

Data editors

The following editors are particularly useful for working with data that you want to pull into Blender or that already exists within your Blender session:

 » Outliner (Shift+F9): The Outliner gives a hierarchical view of all the objects in your scene along with the ability to see how they're related to one another. In complex 3D scenes, the Outliner can be used to more easily select objects and make simple edits, like naming and parenting. It's also the best tool for manipulating collections (see Book 1, Chapter 4) and your scene's View Layers (see Book 5, Chapter 2).

 » Properties (Shift+F7): You can manipulate nearly all the different attributes for your scene and the objects within it via this editor. You can find out more about this topic later in this chapter in the section "Understanding the Properties editor."

» **File Browser (Shift+F1):** This editor allows you to look through the files on your computer. It also allows you to look at the innards of your Blender projects to see how things are structured or for linking to other projects.

NEW
FEATURE

» **Asset Browser (Shift+F1):** In the past, Blender users would make use of the File Browser to build and navigate libraries of models and other assets that they've created for re-use in their Blender projects. Since the release of Blender 3.0, however, there's now the dedicated Asset Browser editor that you can use to create and manage asset libraries much more comfortably. Book 3, Chapter 4 has more information on working with the Asset Browser.

NEW
FEATURE

» **Spreadsheet:** When Geometry Nodes were being developed for Blender, it became apparent that there was a need for an editor to help more clearly understand what's being procedurally generated by a node network. For this reason, the Spreadsheet editor was added to Blender. Have a look at Book 2, Chapter 5 for the full story on Blender's Spreadsheet editor.

» **Preferences:** Also available from the Edit menu in Blender's top bar, the Preferences editor allows you to customize how you interact with Blender.

Understanding the Properties Editor

After the 3D Viewport, the Properties editor is probably the second-most used editor type in Blender. You use buttons and values in this editor to modify the attributes of your scene and elements within it. Because this editor can manipulate so many parts of a scene, it's broken down and organized into a series of subsections known as *contexts*.

TIP

You can access each of the various contexts by using the tabs along the left side of the Properties editor. It's worth noting here that these contexts are ordered logically from large contexts (such as Scene Properties) to progressively smaller contexts (such as Object Data Properties) as you go down from the top. It's also good to know that the available contexts in the Properties editor can change depending on what your active selection is in the 3D Viewport. For example, if you have a camera object selected, the Modifiers tab of the Properties editor isn't visible (because modifiers can't be applied to cameras). The following list describes each subsection of the Properties editor:

» **Tool:** Blender uses the concept of *active tools* where you can select a tool to work on something in your scene. I cover this more throughout the book, but for the time being, it's worth it to know that this tab of the Properties editor is where you can find settings and controls for whatever tool you have active. This context is also where you can manage customizations for your current workspace, covered later in this chapter.

 » **Render:** The Render context has controls that determine what the final output of your scene will look like when you decide to render it to an image or video. Book 3 covers these properties in more depth.

 » **Output:** Whether you render to a still image, a sequence of images, or a video, Blender needs to know how that image data should be saved to your hard drive. The Output tab of the Properties editor is where you set those parameters.

 » **View Layer:** You can organize the output of your scene in *view layers,* useful for compositing different render outputs into a final image (see Book 5, Chapter 2). The properties in this context give you control over organizing your render layers.

 » **Scene:** The properties in this context dictate the nature of your scene, including things like the active camera, units of measurement, and the strength of gravity if you're using simulated physics.

 » **World:** The buttons and values in the World context control the environment that your scene is built in. They have a large influence on the final output of your scene.

 » **Collection:** In Blender, you can organize the objects in your scene to be members of one or more *collections.* The Collection tab of the Properties editor is where you can manage attributes of a collection.

» **Object:** Any object in your scene is going to have its own set of properties that you can modify. The Object context allows you to make changes that affect an object as it relates to the scene.

» **Modifiers:** A lot of work goes into building 3D models, so it's to your benefit to take advantage of your computer and have it do as much work for you as possible. Let it take care of boring procedural steps like mirroring parts of your object or making it smoother while you focus on the more interesting steps in the process. Modifiers are great tools to facilitate these kinds of healthy shortcuts and allow for more advanced uses in animation. This tab is where you manage those modifiers. You can find out more about modifiers in Book 2, Chapter 2.

NEW FEATURE

» **Effects:** The Effects context is available only for Grease Pencil objects. Effects are similar to modifiers in that they're procedural ways of tweaking the look or behavior of an object. Unlike modifiers, though, Grease Pencil effects can influence more than just the geometry of those objects. They can also affect how they're rendered. Have a look in Book 4, Chapter 6 for more on Grease Pencil objects and effects.

» **Particles:** In computer graphics, particle systems are often used to create special effects or manage the behavior of groups of objects. This context of the Properties editor is where you manage particle systems in Blender. Working with particles is a pretty advanced topic. Book 4, Chapter 5 gives you a brief introduction to the possibilities that they have.

» **Physics:** In the spirit of making your computer do as much work for you as possible, having the computer simulate physical behavior in your objects is sometimes helpful. It lends realism to animations and can often help you work faster. The Physics tab gives you controls for simulating physics on your objects. See Book 4, Chapter 5 for more on these topics.

» **Constraints:** When working in 3D — particularly with animation — it's often useful to constrain the properties of one object to that of another. Constraints automate parts of your scene and help make it much more manageable. Book 4, Chapter 2 goes into constraints more deeply.

» **Data:** Buttons and values in the Data context, sometimes referred to as the *Object Data* tab, change slightly depending on what sort of object you've selected, but their primary purpose is to give you the ability to work with the fundamental structural elements of your object.

TIP

"Object Data" is a generic term. Think of this context as properties based on what you've got selected. Even the icon for Object Data Properties changes depending on your selection. For example, if you have a camera object selected, the Data tab would hold camera properties, and the icon for this section looks like a camera. If you have a curve object selected, the icon looks like a curve, and on support forums, some users may refer to it as the Curve Properties tab.

» **Bone:** The Bone context is available only if your active selection is an Armature object. Armatures, sometimes called skeletons in other programs, are used for animation in Blender, and they consist of a set of bone sub-objects. The Bone tab of the Properties editor is where you can adjust attributes of a specific bone that you've selected in the armature.

» **Bone Constraints:** Similar to the properties in the Constraints tab, this context helps you manage constraints. The difference, however, is that this subsection is available only if your active selection is an Armature in Pose Mode, and it's for managing constraints on bones rather than objects. Chapters 2 and 3 in Book 4 cover constraints and the use of constraints on bones.

» **Material:** The controls in the Material context of the Properties editor allow you to dramatically change the appearance of objects in your scene. Book 3, Chapter 1 goes into this context in much more detail.

>> **Texture:** You can use textures built in this context as custom brushes when painting and sculpting in Blender. This context is where you can edit those textures. You can find out more on texturing brushes (and your 3D models!) in Book 3, Chapter 2.

REMEMBER

Throughout this book, I frequently refer to the tabs of the Properties editor by the name of that tab context, followed by the word "Properties." So I may refer to the Output tab of the Properties editor as "Output Properties." It's a fast way of referring to that context, and it doesn't require always writing it out the long way. As a handy reminder, if I'm mentioning that context in a sequence of steps, I show the icon for that tab in the margins.

Navigating in Three Dimensions

The 3D Viewport is probably the most-used editor in all of Blender. The purpose of this section is to guide you in understanding how to wield this part of Blender like a virtual 3D ninja!

All right, so perhaps I am a little over the top with the whole ninja thing, but hopefully this section takes you at least one or two steps closer to that goal.

Orbiting, panning, and zooming the 3D Viewport

When trying to navigate a three-dimensional space through a two-dimensional screen like a computer monitor, you can't interact with that virtual 3D space exactly like you would in the real world, or as I like to call it, *meatspace*. The best way to visualize working in 3D through a program like Blender is to imagine the 3D Viewport as your eyes to this 3D world. But rather than thinking of yourself as moving through this environment, imagine that you have the ability to move this entire world around in front of you.

The most basic way of navigating this space is called *orbiting*. Orbiting is the rough equivalent of rotating the 3D world around a fixed point in space. In order to orbit in Blender, middle-click anywhere in the 3D Viewport and drag your mouse cursor around.

Occasionally, you need to keep your orientation to the world, but you'll want to move it around so that you can see a different part of the scene from the same angle. In Blender, this movement is called *panning*, and you do it by holding Shift while middle-clicking and dragging your mouse cursor in the 3D Viewport. Now when you drag your mouse cursor around, the world shifts around without changing the angle that you're viewing from.

The third way of navigating 3D space is when you want to get closer to an object in your scene. Similar to working with a camera, this movement is called *zooming* the view. In Blender, you can zoom in two ways. The easiest method is by using your mouse's scroll wheel. By default, scrolling forward zooms in and scrolling back zooms out. However, this method doesn't always give you fine-grained control, and, even worse, some people don't have a mouse with a scroll wheel. In these cases, you can zoom by holding Ctrl while middle-clicking in the 3D Viewport. Now, when you drag your mouse cursor up, you zoom in, and when you drag your mouse cursor down, you zoom out. If you prefer to move your mouse horizontally rather than vertically for zooming, you can adjust this behavior in the Navigation section of Preferences.

TECHNICAL STUFF

For the pedantic among us, you may notice that the use of the word "pan" isn't an accurate reflection of what panning is in meatspace. When working with a traditional film or video camera, *panning* is the act of horizontally rotating the camera, like when capturing a panorama (the origin of the word *pan*). Unfortunately, this word has been re-appropriated in computer graphics to generically mean moving along a plane in 3D space. Likewise, zooming in Blender isn't exactly like zooming in a real camera; it's more like moving the whole camera closer or farther away from the subject. It makes me sad, but that's just the way things are.

TIP

If you happen to be working with a mouse that doesn't have a middle mouse button or you work with a pen and tablet interface, you should go to Preferences under Input and enable the Emulate 3 Button Mouse check box. With this check box enabled, you can emulate the middle mouse button by pressing Alt+left-click. So orbiting is Alt+left-click, panning is Shift+Alt+left-click, and zooming is done with Ctrl+Alt+left-click. Table 2-1 has a more organized way of showing these hotkeys.

TABLE 2-1 **Keyboard/Mouse Keys for Navigating 3D Space**

Navigation	Three-Button Mouse	Emulated 3-Button Mouse
Orbit	Middle-click	Alt+left-click
Pan	Shift+middle-click	Shift+Alt+left-click
Zoom	Ctrl+middle-click	Ctrl+Alt+left-click

Blender has some additional navigation controls in the upper right corner of the 3D Viewport. You can see them in Figure 2-2 as the four icons and mini navigation axes. These controls are particularly helpful when working in Blender with a drawing tablet, but they're also handy if you just don't want to use the keyboard as much while working. The following list describes how each control works:

TIP

>> **Navigation mini-axes:** This unique widget not only shows you the orientation from which you're viewing your 3D scene, but it also gives you immediate control over orbiting the view. Click and drag on these colored axes to orbit your view just like you would by middle-clicking.

As an additional bonus feature, if you click any of the circles at the extent of any of these axes, Blender automatically gives you a view of your scene as if looking down that axis. This method is a very quick way of seeing the front, side, and top views of an object you're making.

>> **Zoom control:** Click and drag this icon to zoom in and out of your scene. Just like Ctrl+middle-clicking, move your mouse cursor up to zoom in and down to zoom out.

>> **Pan control:** Click and drag this icon to pan the view. This is the same as Shift+middle-clicking and dragging anywhere in the 3D Viewport.

>> **Camera view toggle:** Click the camera icon to toggle between your normal user view of the 3D scene and the view from the perspective of your camera object.

>> **Perspective/Orthographic projection toggle:** Click this icon to switch between perspective and orthographic views. The *orthographic* view of a 3D scene is similar to how technical drawings and blueprints are done. If two objects are the same size, they always appear to be the same size, regardless of how far away from you they are. This view is ideal for getting sizes and proportions correct in your models, especially if they're based on blueprints or technical drawings. The *perspective* view is more akin to how you actually see things. That is, objects in the distance look smaller than objects that are near you.

Changing views

Although using the mouse to work your way around the 3D space is the most common way to adjust how you view things, Blender has some menu items and hotkey sequences that help give you specific views much faster and more accurately than you can do alone with your mouse.

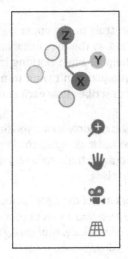

FIGURE 2-2:
Navigation
controls at the
top right of the
3D Viewport give
you fast mouse-
based control
over how you see
your 3D scene.

The View menu

On occasion, you want to know what a model looks like when it's viewed directly from the front, side, or top. Blender has some convenient shortcuts for quickly switching to these views. Aside from the navigation controls in the upper right of the 3D Viewport, the most obvious way to change views is to use the View ⇨ View-point menu in the 3D Viewport's header, as shown on the left of Figure 2-3. This menu lets you choose a variety of angles, including the top, front, right, and the view from the active camera in your scene.

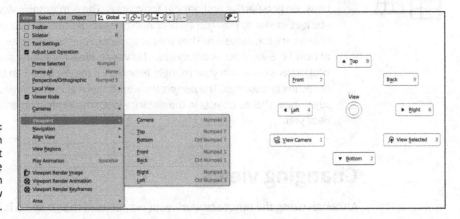

FIGURE 2-3:
The View menu in
the 3D Viewport
(left) and the pie
menu version
of the View
menu (right).

TIP

You can also use pie menus, as described at the end of Book 1, Chapter 1, for an even faster menu to change views. With your mouse cursor hovered over the 3D Viewport, press Tilde (~). When you press this hotkey, a pie menu appears under your mouse cursor. The options in this pie menu are conveniently arranged for changing views. Move your mouse cursor up to change to top view, down for bottom view, left and right for their respective views, and so on. It's really incredibly fast. It feels almost like you're flinging the 3D Viewport around in front of you. On the right side of Figure 2-3 is the pie version of the View menu.

Behold the power of the numeric keypad!

The View menu and navigation controls are certainly helpful, even with the pie menu, but you can change your view in an even faster way: the numeric keypad. Each button on your keyboard's numeric keypad (if your keyboard has one) has an extremely fast way of changing your viewing angle in the 3D Viewport. Figure 2-4 is an image of the numeric keypad with an indication of what each key does.

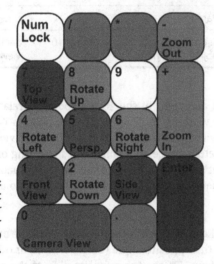

FIGURE 2-4:
The numeric keypad is your ultimate tool for navigating 3D space.

If the image in Figure 2-4 doesn't quite work for you as a reference, Table 2-2 shows what each key does in a table-based format.

In Figure 2-4, notice that the hotkeys are arranged in a way that corresponds with how you would expect them to be. Top view is at the top of the keypad at Numpad 7. The front view is accessed at Numpad 1, and if you move to the right on the keypad, you can see the right side view by pressing Numpad 3. Because it's the view you render from, the active camera is the most important and, therefore, gets the largest key at Numpad 0. Pressing Numpad 5 is a quick way to toggle between orthographic and perspective views.

REMEMBER

If you're ever unsure about what view you're looking from, have a look in the upper left corner of the 3D Viewport. The first line tells you the view angle and whether you're looking at it in perspective or orthographic view.

TABLE 2-2 Hotkeys on the Numeric Keypad

Hotkey	Result	Hotkey	Result	Hotkey	Result
1	Front	Ctrl+1	Back	+	Zoom in
2	Orbit back	Ctrl+2	Pan down	-	Zoom out
3	Right side	Ctrl+3	Left side	/	Toggle local view
4	Orbit left	Ctrl+4	Pan left	.	View selected
5	Perspective/ Orthographic				
6	Orbit right	Ctrl+6	Pan right		
7	Top	Ctrl+7	Bottom		
8	Orbit forward	Ctrl+8	Pan up		
0	Camera view	Ctrl+0	Set active object as camera	Ctrl+Alt+0	Set user view as camera

REMEMBER

The notions of what is left and right in the 3D Viewport are relative to you, *not* the object or scene you're working in. That is, if you model a character who's facing you from the front view, pressing Numpad 3 (right side view) shows your character's *left* side. This setup can be a bit confusing in writing or conversation, but while you're working, it's really not much of an issue. I actually tend to think of the right and left side views as *side view* and *other side view* to avoid confusing myself.

Here is where the numeric keypad shows its real power. With the numeric keypad, you can just as easily view the opposite angle (bottom, back, or other side views) as you can the standard views. To see the opposite side of the standard views, press Ctrl while hitting the corresponding Numpad key. For example, if you want to see the bottom view, press Ctrl+Numpad 7.

Now, maybe you got a little bit excited and hit Ctrl+Numpad 0 to see what the opposite of the camera view is and had some unexpected results. Ctrl+Numpad 0 does something entirely different than pressing Ctrl in combination with the other Numpad numbers. The Ctrl+Numpad 0 hotkey actually allows you to treat any selectable object in Blender as a camera, with the view looking down the object's local Z-axis. You can also access this functionality from the View menu at View ➪ Cameras ➪ Set Active Object as Camera. If you're confused, take a quick look at the beginning of the next chapter for more explanation on local and global coordinate systems. The ability to treat any object as a camera may seem like a strange feature to have, but it can be really helpful for doing things like aiming lights and checking the line of sight of an object or a character.

Another cool thing you can do with Numpad 0 is to quickly snap the camera to your user view. For example, say that you've been working on a 3D model for a while from a certain angle, and you want to see what the model looks like in a render from that specific angle. Rather than try to grab and rotate your camera to get close to this same angle, you can simply press Ctrl+Alt+Numpad 0 or choose View ⇨ Align View ⇨ Align Active Camera to View, and the camera jumps directly to where you're viewing your model. I find myself using this hotkey sequence quite a bit when I'm creating my models. Sometimes it's just easier to change your user view and snap your camera to it than it is to aim the camera how you want it.

The numeric keypad also gives you the ability to navigate your scene like you might normally do with your mouse. You use the 8, 4, 6, and 2 keys on the numeric keypad. Numpad 8 and Numpad 2 orbit the view towards and away, respectively, whereas Numpad 4 and Numpad 6 orbit it left and right. By default, Blender does these rotations in 15-degree increments, but you adjust this amount to be more fine or coarse in Preferences in the Navigation section with the value labeled Rotation Angle. Orbiting with the Numpad is a nice way to get a quick turntable view of a scene, particularly if you have your View rotation set to Trackball in Preferences. You can also pan the view by pressing Ctrl in combination with any of these buttons. For example, Ctrl+Numpad 4 and Ctrl+Numpad 6 pan the view left and right. You can even zoom the view by using the Numpad Plus (+) and Numpad Minus (−) keys.

Two more useful hotkeys are on the numeric keypad: Numpad Slash (/) and Numpad Dot (.). These keys are somewhat more esoteric than the other keys, but they definitely come in handy.

Of the two, I tend to use Numpad Slash the most. Pressing Numpad Slash (/) toggles what Blender calls *Local View*. Basically, Local View hides everything in your scene except for the object or objects you've selected. Local View is really helpful for temporarily isolating a single object or set of objects in a complex scene so that you can work on it without anything else getting in your way.

The Numpad Dot (.) hotkey also comes in handy when you want to focus on a specific part of your scene. Pressing Numpad Dot (.) centers the objects you've selected in the 3D Viewport. Centering is particularly useful if you've rotated or panned everything out of sight, and you want to bring your selected objects back into view.

One other key worth mentioning, although it's not exactly on the numeric keypad, is the Home key. Whereas using Numpad Dot (.) brings your selected objects into view, pressing Home zooms your view back until all objects in your scene are visible in the 3D Viewport. Home is a very convenient key for getting an overall idea of what's going on in your scene.

Understanding How
Blender Thinks

Ways to see your 3D scene

Aside from changing the angle from which you view your 3D world, you may also want to change how the world is shown in the 3D Viewport. In particular, I'm referring to what is called the *viewport shading*. By default, Blender starts in the Solid shading type, which shows your models as solid 3D objects, lit by the studio lights you can set in Blender's Preferences under Lights. You can change the viewport shading from the 3D Viewport's header by clicking any of the Viewport Shading buttons, as shown in Figure 2-5.

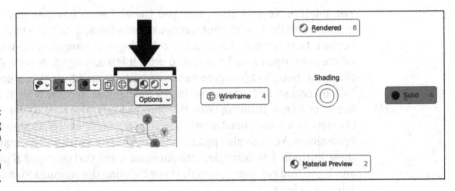

FIGURE 2-5:
Viewport shading types from the 3D Viewport's header (left) and from a pie menu (right).

There are four possible viewport shading types:

» **Wireframe:** This viewport shading type shows the objects in your scene as transparent line-drawings. The wireframe viewport shading type is a good, quick way to get an idea of the structure of your models. And because Wireframe is a bunch of lines, Blender doesn't have to worry about shading and, therefore, doesn't tax your computer's processor as much. On older computers, Blender is a lot more responsive using Wireframe than any of the other viewport shading types.

» **Solid:** Solid is the default viewport shading type that Blender starts with. Solid is usually the standard mode for working in Blender. It's the shading type that allows you to focus on just the geometry of your model without being distracted by materials or scene lighting.

» **Material Preview:** Blender's Material Preview viewport shading type attempts to faithfully show you what your object looks like when textured and lit. Do note that the default behavior is not to use the lighting from your scene; instead, you have the option to light your scene using an assortment of different lighting scenarios defined by *high dynamic range images*, or HDRIs.

» **Rendered:** As you might expect, this viewport shading type renders your scene in the 3D Viewport from whatever arbitrary perspective you want.

Depending on the complexity of your scene, this is a great way to get a very accurate preview of your final rendered images.

Fair warning: the Rendered viewport shading type can be extremely slow when using the Cycles renderer. It's much more responsive when using Eevee. See Book 3, Chapter 1 for more on the differences between Cycles and Eevee.

You can also change viewport shading types by pressing Z to reveal a shading pie menu. The options here are the same as the shading types described in the previous paragraph. The only difference is that they're faster to access by using the pie layout. Figure 2-5 has the pie menu of viewport shading types on the right side.

You may also notice that if you have more than one 3D Viewport window, they don't all have to have the same viewport shading type. You can see the wireframe of your model in one editor while adjusting the lighting using the Shaded draw type in another.

Selecting objects

The fastest way to select objects in the 3D Viewport is to move your mouse cursor over the object and left-click. Shift+left-click another object, and it's added to your selection set. Shift+left-click it again, and it's removed from the selection. If you want to select all the objects in your scene, you can do so quickly by pressing A or by choosing Select ⇨ All from the 3D Viewport's header menu. You can deselect all objects by pressing Alt+A or choosing Select ⇨ None.

Shift+selecting actually works regardless of what active tool you have chosen in the Toolbar.

Using Blender's selection tools

That said, when you first open a Blender session with the General workflow template, the 3D Viewport in the Layout workspace defaults to having the Select Box tool active. This isn't the only selection tool available, though. If you left-click and hold your mouse button on the Select Box tool's icon in the Toolbar, Blender presents you with the following options:

» **Tweak:** The Tweak tool isn't only a selection tool, though it works pretty well that way. Left-click selects and Shift+left-click adds to selection, just as you might expect. However, if you left-click and drag your mouse cursor on an object, you can immediately start moving that object, tweaking its location in 3D space.

>> **Select Box:** This is the default selection tool. Left-click and drag your mouse cursor in the 3D Viewport to draw a rectangle from where you click to where you release your mouse button. Anything within that box is selected. Shift+left-click and drag to add to your selection. Ctrl+left-click and drag to remove from your selection set.

>> **Select Circle:** This tool is sometimes called *brush select* because selection is a lot like painting. Any *object origin* (the small dot that's typically at the center of an object) that you run your mouse cursor over while holding down the left mouse button is selected. Shift+left-click and Ctrl+left-click work like they do with the Box Select tool. You can change the size of your Circle Select's "brush" by adjusting the Radius value in the Tool tab of the Properties editor.

>> **Select Lasso:** The Select Lasso tool allows you to draw an arbitrary shape in the 3D Viewport using left-click and drag. Any object origin within the shape you draw is selected. Shift+left-click and Ctrl+left-click work like they do with the preceding two selection tools.

The selection tools I just mentioned are also available without going to the Toolbar, so you can still select large groups of vertices without changing your active tool. They operate a little bit differently from the dedicated Toolbar tools:

>> Box Select is activated by pressing B. Then you can left-click and drag your mouse cursor to add to your selection. Deselection is done with middle-click and drag or with Shift+left-click and drag. Get out of Box Select by right-clicking or pressing Esc.

>> Circle Select is activated by pressing C. In this case, you can quick change the radius of your selection brush by scrolling your mouse wheel.

>> To use Lasso Select functionality, Ctrl+right-click and drag your mouse cursor around the vertices you want to select. Anything within that selection region is added to your selection. Ctrl+Shift+right-click and drag to deselect the objects that you're lassoing.

REMEMBER

Although the hotkey approach to these selection tools is a much faster way to work than constantly going to the Toolbar to switch tools, you do lose the ability to navigate the 3D Viewport while selecting with them. So if you're doing a complex selection that requires you to move around your scene, the dedicated tools are probably the better way to go.

And, of course, all these selection tools also work in Object mode. Figure 2-6 shows what the various selection tools look like when in use.

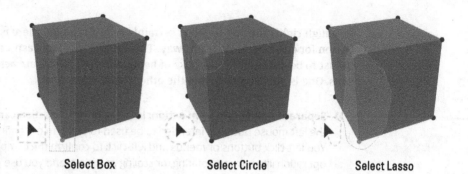

FIGURE 2-6:
Border Select,
Circle Select, and
Lasso Select.

Select Box **Select Circle** **Select Lasso**

TIP

For a slightly faster way to switch between dedicated tools, you can use the Shift+Spacebar hotkey combination to open a little Toolbar menu next to your mouse cursor. Figure 2-7 shows what this menu looks like.

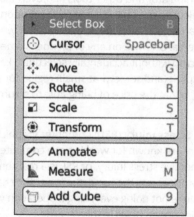

▶ Select Box	B
Cursor	Spacebar
Move	G
Rotate	R
Scale	S
Transform	T
Annotate	D
Measure	M
Add Cube	9

FIGURE 2-7:
You can open
a little Toolbar
menu near your
mouse cursor
by pressing
Shift+Spacebar.

Why right-click select?

There's a little history here that's worth taking a page or so to explain, especially if you go looking for help online and find older Blender tutorials. It might be surprising, but how you select objects used to be one of the most controversial design decisions in Blender's interface. It used to be that we selected with right-click. In fact, this way of working is still an option you can choose to use.

So why in the world did older versions of Blender have right-click to select as the default behavior, and why is it still an option? Left-clicking was bound to placing Blender's 3D cursor. I talk more about the 3D cursor later in this chapter, but in the meantime, you're probably thinking, "But *why*?"

Although right-clicking to select certainly seems strange, there is actually a good reason for choosing to do it this way. This design decision wasn't made at random or just to be different for the sake of being different. There are actually three reasons. One is philosophical, and the other two are practical.

>> **Separating selection from action:** In the right-click selection paradigm, the left mouse button is intended to be used to perform or confirm an action. You left-click buttons or menus and left-click to confirm the completion of an operation like moving, rotating, or scaling an object, and you use it to place the 3D cursor. Selecting an object doesn't really act upon it or change it. So right-click is used to select objects as well as cancel an operation before it's completed. This setup is a bit abstract, but as you work this way, it does actually begin to make sense.

>> **Prevention of accidental mis-clicks:** A functional example would be interacting with the 3D manipulator and other tools (as covered in Book 1, Chapter 3). If action and selection are on the same mouse button, it's quite easy to accidentally move an object using the 3D manipulator when you only meant to select, and vice versa. Likewise on any of Blender's time-based editors, it was difficult to scrub without accidentally selecting a keyframe. As of Blender 2.80, there's an explicit (and somewhat small) region for scrubbing, so this is less of an issue now, but at the price of being able to scrub anywhere in the editor.

>> **Prevention of Repetitive Stress Injury (RSI):** Computer graphics artists like 3D modelers and animators are known for working at a computer for insanely long stretches of time. Repetitive stress injury, or RSI, is a real concern. The more you can spread the work across the hand, the lower the chance of RSI. By making it so that you're not doing every single operation with the left mouse button, the right-click option helps in this regard.

REMEMBER

Bottom line, the right-click-to-select paradigm really is a nice, efficient way of working in 3D space, but it takes time to get used to it. Although this book is written with the default left-click behavior in mind, I encourage you to try out right-click selection by enabling it in the Keymaps section of the Preferences editor. It feels a little weird at first, but it's a faster, safer way to work for me.

Taking advantage of the 3D cursor

"Okay," you say, "What's with this funky crosshair in the middle of my 3D Viewport? It seems pretty useless."

That crosshair is the 3D cursor. It's a unique concept that I've seen only in Blender, and this design is anything but useless. The best way that I've found to understand the 3D cursor is to think about a word processor or text editor. When you add text or want to change something in one of those programs, it's usually done with or relative to the blinking cursor on the screen. Blender's 3D cursor serves pretty much the same purpose, but in three dimensions. When you add a new object, it's placed wherever the 3D cursor is located. When you rotate or scale an object, you can do it relative to the 3D cursor's location. And when you want to snap an object to a specific location, you do it with the 3D cursor.

There are three primary ways to move the 3D cursor in your Blender scene:

>> **Shift+right-click:** If you Shift+right-click anywhere in the 3D Viewport, Blender places the 3D cursor directly at that location, oriented with its axes towards you. This means of placing the 3D cursor is super-fast, but you're limited in orientation options because it uses only the same orientation as the one you're using to look into the 3D Viewport.

>> **Sidebar View tab:** If you press N while in the 3D Viewport, Blender reveals its Sidebar region along the right side of the editor area. If you go to the View tab in this region, you should see a panel labeled 3D Cursor. From the Location and Rotation value fields in this panel, you can accurately adjust the position and orientation of the 3D cursor.

>> **Cursor tool:** Along the left side of the 3D Viewport is Blender's Toolbar. The second tool from the top looks like the 3D cursor. When you choose to activate this tool, you can place the 3D cursor anywhere in your scene with a simple left-click. That in itself is nice, but the real benefits of using this tool are the options you get in the Tool context of the Properties editor. Of particular interest is the Orientation drop-down menu. By default, this menu is set to View, reflecting the same behavior you get when Shift+right-clicking. However, you can change to any of the following options:

- **None:** If you choose None as your orientation, Blender just keeps the 3D cursor at whatever orientation it's currently using.

- **View:** This orientation type is the default behavior. The 3D cursor simply points at you through the 3D Viewport.

- **Transform:** Choosing the Transform orientation option tells Blender to have the 3D cursor share the same orientation as set in the Transform Orientation menu in the 3D Viewport's header. By default, that menu is set to Global, but other options are also covered in the next chapter.

- **Geometry:** The Geometry option is extremely handy while modeling. If you left-click to place the 3D cursor on an object in your scene, not only will Blender place the 3D cursor there, but its orientation will also adjust to match the surface geometry of that object. This feature is most useful when trying to place an object so it looks like it's naturally protruding from an object's surface.

Figure 2-8 shows the 3D Viewport's Sidebar region as well as the Tool context of the Properties editor where you can have these controls over your 3D cursor.

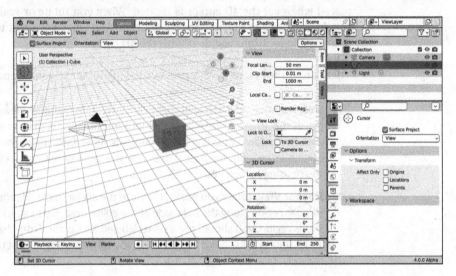

FIGURE 2-8:
You can control the position and orientation of your 3D cursor from the Sidebar in the 3D Viewport, as well as the Tool tab of the Properties editor when the Cursor tool is active.

In terms of adjusting your 3D Viewport, you can use the 3D cursor as a quick way to recenter your view. Simply place the 3D cursor anywhere in the 3D Viewport by Shift+right-clicking. Now press Shift+C. This hotkey combination relocates the 3D cursor to the origin coordinates of the 3D environment and then brings all objects into view. The Shift+C hotkey combination is like pressing Home with the added benefit of moving the cursor to the origin.

In Book 1, Chapter 3, I cover the topic of moving, scaling, and rotating objects. Usually, you want to use Blender's default behavior of doing these operations relative to the median point of the selected objects. However, you can also perform any of these operations relative to the 3D cursor by pressing the Period (.) key on your keyboard and choosing 3D Cursor from the pie menu that appears. Alternatively, you can select 3D Cursor from the Pivot Point menu in the 3D Viewport's header. Figure 2-9 shows the two menus you can use for changing your pivot point. The default behavior is Median Point.

The 3D cursor is also very useful for *snapping* or moving a selection to a specific point in space. For a better idea of what snapping means, hover your mouse over the 3D Viewport and press Shift+S. A pie menu like the one in Figure 2-10 appears.

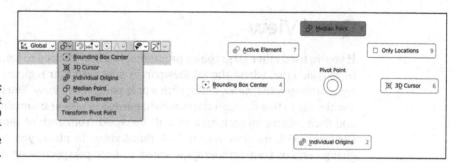

FIGURE 2-9:
The Pivot Point menu in the 3D Viewport's header (left) and as a pie menu (right).

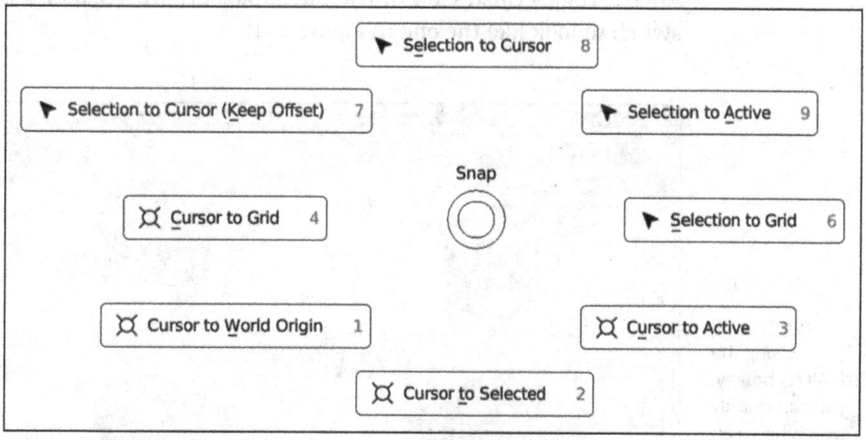

FIGURE 2-10:
The Snap menu.

Through this menu, you can snap your selected object to a fixed coordinate on the grid in the 3D Viewport, the location of the 3D cursor, or to the center of the grid, also known as the *world origin* of the scene. You also have the ability to snap the 3D cursor to the middle of multiple selected objects, a fixed location on the grid, or to the active object in the scene. This method is an effective way to move an object to a specific point in 3D space, and it's all thanks to the little 3D cursor.

Extra Features in the 3D Viewport

A handful of additional features in Blender's 3D Viewport are worth mentioning. They can be classified as productivity enhancers, learning aids, or comfort features for users migrating from other programs. This section outlines a few of these features.

Quad View

If you've used other 3D graphics programs, you may be used to something referred to as *Quad View*, where the 3D Viewport is split into four regions: top, front, and right orthographic views, along with a user perspective view. You *can* create a layout similar to this through the somewhat arduous task of manually splitting areas and then setting up each area as a 3D Viewport from each of those perspectives. However, with no clear way to lock those views in place, you could very easily change one of your orthographic views to user perspective on accident. Fortunately, there's a better way. Go to the 3D Viewport's header and choose View ⇨ Area ⇨ Toggle Quad View or use the hotkey Ctrl+Alt+Q, and your 3D Viewport will switch to look like the one in Figure 2-11.

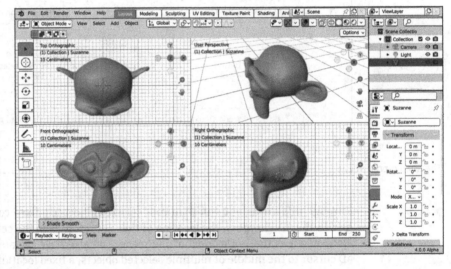

FIGURE 2-11:
Using the Ctrl+Alt+Q hotkey, you can quickly switch between Blender's regular viewport and a Quad View viewport like some other 3D programs have.

REMEMBER

When toggling back to Full View from Quad View, Blender always jumps back to whatever angle you're viewing from in the user perspective view quadrant.

Regions

In the Book 1, Chapter 1, I briefly describe regions as areas in an editor that give you additional tools specific to that editor. In fact, you've already had exposure to a couple types of region in this chapter: the header, the Toolbar, and the Sidebar. This section focuses on the latter two in more detail.

Flanking either side of the 3D Viewport is a Toolbar on the left, and on the right is a region for modifying the properties of the 3D Viewport, referred to as the Sidebar.

The Sidebar

You can toggle the visibility of the Sidebar by choosing View ⇨ Sidebar in the header or by pressing N (for iNformation) while your mouse cursor is in the 3D Viewport. In fact, quite a few editors in Blender have a Sidebar. And with the exception of the Text Editor, which uses Ctrl+F (because it would be annoying if the Sidebar popped up every time you typed an N in the Text Editor), you can consistently open all of them by using the N hotkey.

In the 3D Viewport, the Sidebar serves three primary purposes, each designated by a specific tab:

>> **Item:** From the Item tab, you can directly modify your selected object by typing in explicit location, rotation, and scale values within the Transform panel.

>> **Tool:** The Tool tab has much the same content you would see in the Tool context of the Properties editor. This tab is particularly useful if you're working with a maximized 3D Viewport (Ctrl+Spacebar). I tend to use it a lot when sculpting and painting.

>> **View:** The View tab is dedicated to customizing your 3D Viewport. From here, you can control features like the viewport camera (which is different from the scene camera), the location and orientation of the 3D cursor, and the collections that are visible in the 3D Viewport. Chapter 4 of this book has more on working with collections. The View tab is also where you can control annotations in the 3D Viewport. There's more on annotations later in this chapter.

The Toolbar

The Toolbar is located along the left side of the 3D Viewport. You can toggle its visibility by choosing View ⇨ Toolbar in the 3D Viewport's header or by using the T hotkey.

The Toolbar allows you to have a workflow similar to other computer graphics applications where you first select a tool and then use that tool to act on an object or selection. Depending on what mode you're in (Edit mode, Object mode, Sculpt mode, and so on), you will have a whole bunch of tools or only a handful.

Tool Settings

Specific to editors that feature a Toolbar, there's an additional space at the top of the header referred to as the Tool Settings region. This area of the header is where you see some of the specific settings available for whatever tool you choose in the

Toolbar. You can toggle the visibility of the Tool Settings region by choosing View ⇨ Tool Settings in the 3D Viewport's header menu.

The controls in Tool Settings are really handy, but they're also available in the Sidebar and the Active Tool tab of the Properties editor. Personally, I tend to hide Tool Settings to save screen space, but if you're used to programs like Photoshop or Krita, you may find the Tool Settings region more familiar.

The Last Operator panel

There's an additional quasi-region in the 3D Viewport that's extremely useful. At the bottom left of the 3D Viewport is the Last Operator panel. If you've just opened Blender, you won't see this panel at all (because you haven't done anything yet). However, if you perform an action in Blender — also known as an *operator* — like moving your selected object or adding a new object, this panel updates to display values relevant to that operator. Using this panel, you can perform a quick, rough operation and then tweak it to be more precise. For example, if you add a UV Sphere to your scene (Add ⇨ Mesh ⇨ UV Sphere), Blender adds a UV Sphere object to your scene at the location of the 3D cursor with 32 segments and 16 rings. Using the Last Operator panel, you can not only adjust the location of your new sphere, but you can also modify the number of segments and rings it has. You can see more on how the Last Operator panel is used in Book 2, Chapter 1.

TIP

Depending on the last action you do in Blender, the Last Operator panel can sometimes take up quite a bit of space, so you may choose to leave it collapsed. However, it can be annoying to constantly move your mouse back to the Last Operator panel just to expand and collapse it. Fortunately, there's a faster way. You can access the Last Operator panel by pressing F9. Upon doing so, a "floating" Last Operator panel appears under your mouse cursor. Figure 2-12 shows the floating Last Operator panel after adding a UV sphere to the scene.

WARNING

You should note that the Last Operator panel is relevant only for the last operation you actually performed. It's not a construction history, and it doesn't persistently remain in memory after you perform subsequent operations. For example, if you add a UV Sphere and then immediately rotate that sphere, there's no way for you to adjust the number of segments and rings in it from the Last Operator panel. Even if you undo the rotate operation, those Last Operator values won't return (after all, Undo is another operation). The Last Operator panel relates to the last thing you did — no more, no less.

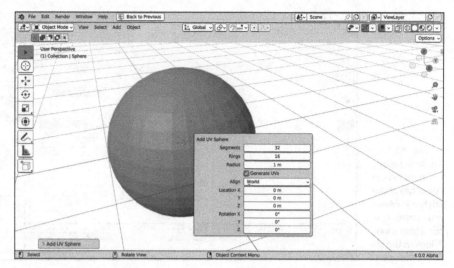

FIGURE 2-12:
You can open a floating Last Operator panel by pressing F9.

Collaborating (with others and yourself) with annotations

If you're making anything big with 3D computer graphics like a movie or a video game, you're most likely going to be collaborating with other people. 3D computer graphics in general, and animation specifically, is an extremely collaborative art form. Otherwise, it would take forever to get anything completed. If you're working with other people, it's often useful to be able to pass notes to each other within the context of your work so you can give helpful feedback or let the next person in the pipeline know why you did something. In fact, this can even be useful if you're working solo. I leave notes to myself all the time in my .blend files as reminders so I don't have to mentally keep track of every random design decision I made while working.

Blender's annotation feature gives you the ability to leave these kinds of notes in your .blend files, right in the editor you're working in. The controls for annotations are at the bottom of the View tab of the Sidebar. Expand the Annotations panel, and you should see a button labeled New. Click that button and the panel will expand to look like what's shown in Figure 2-13.

The list box can hold multiple layers of annotations. By default, Blender prepopulates this list box with a single layer named Note. To the left of the layer is a color swatch that dictates the color of any annotations on that layer. Add and remove layers by using the plus and minus buttons to the right of the list box. Below the layer list box is a Thickness slider that controls the thickness of any annotations you make on that layer.

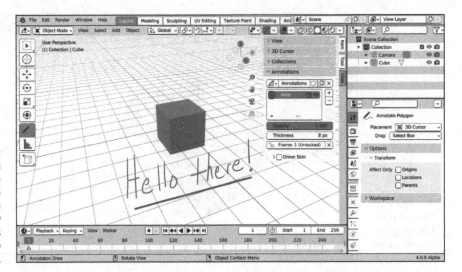

FIGURE 2-13:
The Annotations
panel in the
View tab of the
Sidebar is where
you control how
your annotations
look in the 3D
Viewport.

The easiest way to make a new annotation is to use the Annotate tool in the Toolbar. Activate this tool by clicking it, and you're instantly able to start writing and drawing in your 3D Viewport on your active annotation layer. If you hold down your left mouse button while clicking the Annotate tool in the Toolbar, you also get options to draw lines, polygons, and erase.

For faster access to annotating, you don't have to use the Annotate tool. You can just hold down D while left-clicking and dragging your mouse cursor in the 3D Viewport. This action gives you quick access to Annotate's draw tool and lets you add marks on whichever annotation layer you have active in the Sidebar.

Technically, you can even animate your annotations (for giving feedback on animated work). You just need to scrub forward on the Timeline and make a new annotation mark. Your annotations will update on playback as you change to those frames. You can adjust the timing of your annotations from the Timeline or the Dope Sheet.

You can actually make quite detailed and intricate animations using annotations alone. However, if you're going to try and do full-blown 2D or 2.5D animation, I suggest you use Blender's Grease Pencil objects instead. They're more powerful and way better-suited for the job. See Book 4, Chapter 6 for more on animating with Grease Pencil.

Don't know how to do something? Hooray for fully integrated search!

Blender has a search feature that's fully integrated into Blender's interface. The benefit here is that if you know the operation you want to perform but don't know where to go in Blender's interface to access it, you can simply search for that operator and perform it immediately. How's that for awesome?

The fastest way to access Blender's integrated search feature from any editor is to press F3. A blank menu with a search field at the top appears. From here, simply start typing the name of the operator you want, and Blender updates the menu with search results that match what you've typed. Furthermore, if a hotkey is associated with that operation, it shows up to the right of the operator name in the menu so that you can remember the hotkey in the future. As an example, open the search menu (F3) and type **save**. As you type, the menu updates with operations within Blender that relate to saving.

Using the integrated search feature is a great way to familiarize yourself with the way Blender works, even more so if you're migrating from another program. In that case, you know the terminology for what you want to do; you just have to find out how Blender does it. Figure 2-14 shows Blender's integrated search menu.

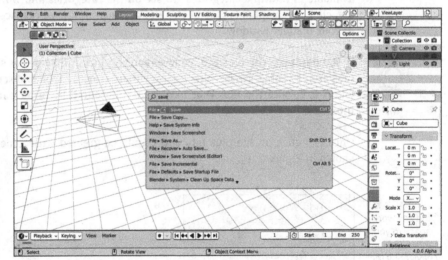

FIGURE 2-14: Blender's integrated search menu is a great way to get familiar with Blender's operators.

Customizing Blender to Fit You

You can tweak Blender's screen layout, known as a *workspace*, to virtually any configuration you can imagine. However, Blender's customization features go much deeper than just readjusting the areas in a Blender window. With a little time and effort, you can completely overhaul Blender to be as comfortable a work environment as possible. This ability to customize is especially useful for people who are migrating to Blender from other 3D graphics programs. I won't say that you can make Blender behave exactly like any of these other programs, but sometimes little things like using the same keyboard shortcuts help make the transition smoother.

REMEMBER

Although this section gives you the means to completely bend Blender's interface to your will, bear in mind that unless otherwise specified, this book relies on the default settings that ship with Blender. Unless you can remember your customized behaviors, it may be more helpful to use Blender's default settings (File ➪ Defaults ➪ Load Factory Settings).

Using preset workspaces

You can make a variety of workspaces depending on the sort of work you're doing. By default, Blender comes with a variety of preset workspaces broken up into five major categories: General, 2D Animation, Sculpting, VFX, and Video Editing. Each category has two or more workspaces to choose from, with a few workspaces available in multiple categories. To see all the categories and workspaces available, click on the plus (+) tab at the end of the series of workspace tabs at the top of your Blender window.

TIP

If you don't see the plus tab, your screen resolution may be set such that all the tabs aren't visible. Hover your mouse cursor over the tabs and scroll your mouse wheel to expose the tabs that have gotten obscured by other parts of Blender's interface.

Once you click on the plus tab, you should be greeted with a menu like the one shown in Figure 2-15.

FIGURE 2-15:
Add any workspace to your Blender window by navigating the menu invoked by clicking the plus icon at the end of the workspace tabs along the top of the Blender window.

The following sections give a quick breakdown of each workspace per category.

General

These workspaces are the most common in a general 3D animation workflow.

>> **Animation:** The Animation workspace gives you a screen layout with an assortment of editors that allow you to animate in your 3D scene efficiently. See Book 4 for more on using this workspace.

>> **Compositing:** Compositing is the art of mixing images (or, more commonly, sequences of images, like in videos) so they look like a single integrated image. This workspace is where you can do everything from simple color adjustment to adding balls of electricity to a character's hands. Book 5, Chapter 2 has more on compositing in Blender.

**NEW
FEATURE**

>> **Geometry Nodes:** Blender's procedural system for creating and modifying geometry is called *Geometry Nodes*, and because this approach to working in 3D is quite different from other ways of modeling and editing, this appropriately named workspace is dedicated to this kind of work.

>> **Layout:** In 3D animation, the *layout* stage is where you block in your scene and figure out how your characters and camera are positioned relative to each other and their environment. It's where all your scene planning starts, so it makes sense that this workspace is the default one that loads when you first launch Blender. The screen layout for this workspace is a good general-purpose place to start any 3D project.

>> **Modeling:** Unless everything in your scene is supposed to be simple cubes and spheres, you're going to want to have more complex-looking characters, props, and environments. The modeling workspace is an ideal workbench for building your 3D creations. Book 2 gets heavily into modeling and using this workspace.

>> **Rendering:** Once you've gone through the process of building out and animating your scene, you're likely interested in sharing the results. Not everyone has a copy of Blender (but they could, it's free!), so the common practice is to *render* that scene to image or video. From the Rendering workspace, you can focus on refining those final output images, getting Blender to produce the highest quality output in the shortest possible amount of time. Book 3, Chapter 4 covers rendering in more detail.

>> **Scripting:** Scripting in this case doesn't refer to writing screenplays (though you could technically use this workspace for that. I have!). Instead, in this case, scripting is the process of writing little snips of code to automate steps in your process and generally make your life in 3D more pleasant. See Book 6, Chapter 2 for more on writing scripts in Blender.

>> **Sculpting:** Modern 3D modeling tools have evolved to the point that they're almost like working with digital clay. This way of working is much more

familiar to artists with a traditional art background and Blender, being a modern 3D application, totally supports this approach. Use the Sculpting workspace to digitally sculpt your 3D assets. See Book 2, Chapter 3 for more on sculpting in Blender.

>> **Shading:** The default materials in nearly any 3D application are flat and boring. It's up to you to provide realism and interest to your objects' surfaces. Book 3, Chapter 1 covers the tools necessary to go through this process, and the Shading workspace is a critical part of that workflow.

>> **Texture Paint:** Whereas shading covers general material properties like roughness and reflectivity, texture painting is where you can really add a lot of detail and explicit color to your objects. The Texture Paint workspace is designed to make this process as straightforward as possible. See Book 3, Chapter 2 for more on working with textures.

>> **UV Editing:** For the most part, hand-painted textures are flat images. Like the longitude and latitude lines on a globe, you need a coordinate system to map the pixels of your flat image texture to the surface of your object. That process, called UV mapping, is covered in Book 3, Chapter 2 and makes use of the UV Editing workspace.

2D Animation

Blender has become a full-fledged 2D animation tool in addition to being the "Swiss Army chainsaw" of the 3D world. These workspaces give a 2D animator the best possible work environment that Blender can offer. See Book 4, Chapter 6 for more on animating in 2D in Blender.

>> **2D Animation:** This workspace very much resembles the Layout workspace used in 3D animation. The primary difference is that the 3D Viewport is configured to look more like a blank canvas than a 3D environment, and the rest of the layout is geared for animating.

>> **2D Full Canvas:** This workspace is similar to the 2D Animation workspace, but it's more of a distraction-free approach. The drawing area in the 3D Viewport is maximized, and every other area in the Blender window is either removed or minimized as much as possible.

>> **Compositing:** Animation is animation. Eventually you're going to be mixing images together. This workspace is exactly the same as the Compositing workspace previously described.

>> **Rendering:** Similarly, whether you're animating in 2D or in 3D, your output from Blender needs to be rendered. This workspace is the same as the Rendering workspace already described.

Sculpting

Digital sculpting has become *the* way that the majority of 3D assets are created. If your primary interest is in digital sculpting, then Book 2, Chapter 3 and the two workspaces in this section are the ones you most want to focus upon.

>> **Sculpting:** This is the same workspace described previously. This workspace is just easier to find than digging into the General menu.

>> **Shading:** If you're sculpting, then you're also probably interested in customizing the surface of your sculpted work, so the Shading workspace (just like the one already described) is quite handy to have at the ready.

VFX

Visual effects, or *VFX* for short, is the art of taking existing footage — often captured with a camera, but it could also be animation footage — and modifying it to achieve a particular effect. Maybe you want to make a daytime scene look like it's happening at night, or perhaps you want to put a dragon in footage of your front yard. That's all VFX and the workspaces in this section are tuned to getting that job done well. Book 5 goes into more detail on Blender's VFX tools.

>> **Compositing:** This workspace is the same as the one used in the General category as well as the 2D animation one. Compositing is at the heart of VFX work, so it makes sense to include it among this group.

>> **Masking:** If you're mixing footage, be it live-action or animated, chances are good that you will have to hide or otherwise remove something from the shot, be it the strings on a puppet or an entire house in a neighborhood. You do this with masking, and because you're dealing with moving images, it's a more involved process than you might be used to if you've only ever done something like that in a single image editor like GIMP or Photoshop. So Blender has a whole workspace dedicated to masking.

>> **Motion Tracking:** In VFX, you're dealing with moving images. To make your 3D assets seamlessly integrate, it's useful to track the movement in your footage. Blender has a built-in motion tracker, which gives you the ability to track the location of the video camera in 3D space as well as the movement of objects on screen. This workspace is tuned to help you use the motion tracker as effectively as possible.

>> **Rendering:** As with most work that you produce in Blender, it has to be rendered to output files that you can share. This workspace is the same one that has been described previously.

Video Editing

If you're creating animations in 3D or 2D, chances are good that you're not doing a single shot in isolation. It's more likely that you're interested in chaining a series of animated sequences in a particular order with a specific timing as a means of telling a story. That's the nuts and bolts of video editing and the two workspaces in this category.

>> **Rendering:** This workspace is the same one described in preceding sections. Once you finish editing your video, you need to output the results to a video file of its own. The Rendering workspace is the best place to go through that process.

>> **Video Editing:** This is the workspace where you can do the actual work of editing video footage, whether it comes from external files captured by a camera or directly from Blender scenes. See Book 5, Chapter 1 for more on Blender's video editing tools.

Blender workflows

The main categories described in the previous sections — General, 2D Animation, Sculpting, VFX, and Video Editing — are more than just categories for nesting workspaces. They're also Blender *workflows*, sometimes referred to as *workflow templates*. When you start a new Blender project with File ⇨ New, that project can be one of those five workflow types. Each workflow can be considered as a bundle of workspaces, with the workspace tabs along the top of the Blender window arranged in the basic order you would go through for that workflow from start to finish. Blender's default behavior is to launch with the General workflow template and put you in the Layout workspace, because layout is one of the first steps in a general 3D animation process.

TIP

In addition to clicking on a workspace tab to use it, you can cycle through workspace tabs by pressing Ctrl+Page Up and Ctrl+Page Down.

REMEMBER

The workspace tabs at the top of the Blender window are arranged in an order that reflects the common steps in a workflow. However, that may not be the way you do things. Right-click any tab and Blender provides you with options to put the tab at the front or back of the list, duplicate it, or remove it altogether. As of this writing, you can't reorder tabs by dragging and dropping, but hopefully that feature will come in future releases of Blender.

Creating a new workspace

To create a new workspace, left-click the plus tab at the end of the series of workspace tabs and choose the workspace that most closely matches the screen layout you want to work within. From here, you can make the changes to create your own custom workspace layout. For example, you may want to create a 2D painting workspace or a multi-monitor workspace with a separate window for each of your monitors.

Customizing your new workspace

When you create a new workspace, there are a lot of ways you can customize that workspace. It's not just about changing the editors and the size of the areas in that workspace. There's more you can do!

The first thing you should do after creating a new workspace is give it a name that corresponds to the activity you're trying to do in that workspace. Rename any workspace to another name you want by double-clicking its tab.

TIP

I find that renaming workspaces is a good practice, even with the default workspaces. Those names work reasonably well for most situations, but as I work, I tend to customize a workspace to the point that I'm using it for something quite different from its original name. So in that case, I'll often rename the workspace to better reflect what I'm doing. Get used to the idea of naming everything in your projects. Trust me, being in the habit of using a reasonable name makes life infinitely easier. It's especially true when you come back to an old project, and you need to figure out what everything is.

The rest of the customizations for your workspace actually live in the Tool tab of the Properties Editor. Within that context is a panel with the name Workspace. Expand that panel, and you'll see the following options:

>> **Pin Scene:** When you start getting into complex Blender projects, you may find yourself creating multiple scenes in a single .blend file. For example, you may have multiple shots in an animation, each with its own scene, and then one more empty scene that you use for ordering these shots in the Video Sequencer. By default, Blender keeps the same active scene across all workspaces. However, if you enable the Pin Scene check box for a workspace, it assigns (or *pins*) the scene to that workspace. Then every time you switch back to that workspace, Blender automatically switches to the pinned scene.

>> **Mode:** Using this drop-down menu, you can tell Blender to automatically switch to a particular mode on your selected objects when you change to this workspace. For example, the Sculpting workspace uses this feature so that whenever you switch to that workspace, your selected object is automatically put into Sculpt mode to save you a few extra keystrokes.

>> **Filter Add-ons:** Although there are a lot of incredibly useful Blender add-ons out there, sometimes they can get cluttered or take over Blender's interface in a way that may not be particularly helpful. If you enable the Filter Add-ons check box, Blender disables all the add-ons you have enabled for the current workspace. Then, using the list below the Filter Add-ons check box, you can selectively enable which add-ons you actually want to see in your custom workspace.

TIP

When adjusting the layout of your workspaces, the menus and buttons in the header of an editor can be obscured or hidden if the area is too narrow. This scenario happens particularly often for people who work on computers with small monitors, but it can sometimes happen on high resolution, or *HiDPI*, 2k, and 4k screens. In this case, you can do three things:

>> **Right-click in the header area and toggle Header ⇨ Show Menus.**

The menus are collapsed into a single button with an icon consisting of three lines, sometimes called a *hamburger menu*. This frees up a little bit of space, but on smaller monitors, it may not be enough.

>> **Hover your mouse cursor over the header region and scroll your mouse wheel.**

If any parts of the header are obscured, you can scroll them in and out of view.

>> **Middle-click the header and drag your mouse left and right.**

The contents of the header move left and right so that you can bring those obscured buttons into view. I personally like this approach because it feels more direct.

Setting new defaults

If you've fully customized your Blender environment, you might want to have your changes be your own personal defaults when you first launch Blender. You need to save a new *startup file*. This is basically a template file that Blender uses to store the preferred environment that you want to start in. For example, say your primary interest is 2D animation and you want Blender to always launch with the workspace tabs for that workflow; follow these steps:

1. **Start a new Blender session in the 2D Animation workflow by choosing File ⇨ New ⇨ 2D Animation.**

2. **Choose File ⇨ Defaults ⇨ Save Startup File to set this workflow as your default work environment the first time you launch Blender.**

When you use the Save Startup File feature, Blender saves your current settings, workspaces, and even 3D scenes to a special .blend file called startup.blend that gets loaded each time Blender starts. So any models you have in the 3D Viewport and any changes you make to other workspaces are saved, too. Fortunately, if you've made a mistake, you can always return to the default setup by choosing File ⇨ Load Factory Settings and re-create your custom layouts from there.

TIP

This behavior of saving a special startup.blend file is fine for setting up custom workspaces, but it has no influence on changes you make in Preferences (such as custom hotkeys or themes). Those kinds of changes are automatically stored separately when you make them. Your startup file doesn't have any effect on changes made in Preferences (see the next section for more on configuring your preferences in Blender). This way, you can store custom workspaces without overwriting more important settings like keymaps and preferred add-ons.

Setting user preferences

This section on user preferences is by no means comprehensive. The number of options available in Blender's Preferences editor is mind-bogglingly large. My intent here is to introduce you to the editor itself. Have a look on this book's supplementary website (blenderbasics.com) for setting some of the most useful and relevant options in the Preferences editor. For specific details on every single button, see the online documentation available at https://docs.blender.org/manual.

Of course, the first question is, "Where exactly *are* the controls for user preferences?" Well, the Preferences editor is just like any other editor in Blender and can, therefore, appear in any area you want by using the Editor Type menu in the header region of any editor. (For more information, see the section "Looking at Editor Types," earlier in this chapter.) Of course, you can also choose Edit ⇨ Preferences, and Blender creates a new window just for the Preferences editor. Although creating a separate window is a bit of a violation of Blenders non-overlapping philosophy, it is sometimes nicer because you don't have to replace or split any of your existing areas to get a Preferences editor. Also, it's unlikely that you'll be modifying your preferences frequently while working on a Blender project, so the chances are low that this overlapping window will get in your way.

TIP

If you choose Edit ⇨ Preferences, and you don't see a new window with the Preferences editor, your Blender window may be in a full-screen state, and your operating system's window manager may not be allowing the window with Preferences to sit atop that full-screen window. To get around this issue, toggle off the full-screen view by choosing Window ⇨ Toggle Window Fullscreen.

REMEMBER

By default, Blender automatically saves any changes you make in the Preferences editor so they'll persist to the next time you launch Blender. If you don't want this auto-save behavior, click the button with the three-line icon (sometimes called a *hamburger menu*). You'll get a menu that includes a toggle option for Auto-Save Preferences. Click that menu item to toggle it off. With auto-save disabled, you manually choose to save them as your personal defaults by clicking the Save Preferences button at the bottom of the Preferences editor next to the hamburger menu.

Using custom event maps

Blender has one of the most customizable event systems of any application I've worked with. An *event system* is required for a complex program to interact with you and me, the users. Each time you press a button or move your mouse, it registers with the program as an *event*. The program then handles the event by performing an action of some sort. As an example, moving your mouse registers as an event, which then triggers your computer to perform the action of updating the location of the mouse cursor on your monitor.

Blender provides the ability to customize the event system to suit your needs, mapping events to a wide variety of possible Blender operations. Don't like using a particular hotkey in Blender's default configuration? You're free to change it. And that's just the start!

The majority of the Keymap section in Preferences (Edit ➪ Preferences) is devoted to modifying how events are handled within Blender. This list of events is particularly daunting, and you can easily get lost among all those expanding and collapsing categories of events. Fortunately, you can modify how events are handled in a much easier way, and you don't even have to use the Preferences editor if you don't want to. Instead, you can follow these steps:

1. **Find the operator you want to bind in Blender's menu system.**

As mentioned earlier in this chapter, an operator is a thing that Blender does; it's the thing that happens when you click a menu item in Blender's interface. As an example, say that you want to change the hotkey for saving a project from Ctrl+S (the current hotkey) to Ctrl+W, the hotkey used in older versions of Blender. You can find this operator by going to the menus at the top of your Blender window and choosing File ➪ Save. Go to that menu item, but *don't click it* yet. Just hover your mouse cursor over it and proceed to the next step.

2. **Right-click the menu item for the operator and choose Change Shortcut from the menu that appears.**

In this example, choose File ➪ Save, right-click it, and choose Change Shortcut. Blender prompts you for a new hotkey.

3. **When prompted, use the new hotkey that you want to assign to the operation.**

In this case, you press Ctrl+W.

Congratulations! Your new hotkey is assigned!

Figure 2-16 shows this process in action.

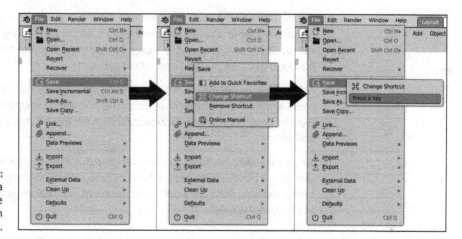

FIGURE 2-16:
Customizing a
hotkey sequence
directly from
Blender's menus.

WARNING

As of this writing, Blender doesn't warn you if you attempt to assign a hotkey that has already been bound to another operator. Blender simply double-binds the hotkey, favoring default behaviors over custom ones. Blender's interface will still say your custom hotkey is assigned to the desired action, but it just won't work as expected. Currently, the only way to get around this problem is to make sure that your desired hotkey isn't already assigned.

Of course, for ultimate control, the Keymap section of Preferences is really the way to go. As daunting as this section may appear, it's actually pretty easy to use. The most effective way to use the event editor is to use the search feature, a text field with a magnifying glass icon:

1. **In the search filter field, type all or part of the operator you want to customize and press Enter.**

The listing below updates with Blender's best guesses for the operator you're looking for. Alternatively, you can just drill down through the categories until you find the event you want. Using the previous example, you might type "save" in this field to find the Save Blender File operator.

If you don't know the name of the operator, you can search by the hotkey it uses. Left-click the drop-down menu to the left of the search filter field. You can choose between Name (the default) to search by operator name or Key-Binding to search by hotkey.

2. **Modify the event you want to change.**

Changing an actual event is much like the process used to add hotkeys to menu items. It works like so:

(a) *Use the Type of Event Mapping drop-down menu displayed to the right or the operation name to stipulate whether the event is coming from a keyboard, mouse, text input, or some other source.* For example, if you're adjusting a hotkey, make sure that you've set it to Keyboard.

(b) *Left-click the Type of Event field that comes after the Type of Event Mapping menu.* It will either be blank or already have an event in it. Upon doing so, Blender prompts you for your new custom event (hotkey, mouse click, and so on).

(c) *Set the event with the action you want assigned to it.* For example, if you're changing a hotkey, simply enter the key combination you want to use. If you decide that you don't want to change the event, just click anywhere outside of the Event Type field.

While you're editing your events, you might notice that a Restore button appears at the top of the section you're working on. At any time, if you decide that you want to revert to the system defaults, click the Restore button. Everything goes back to the way it initially was.

You can also use this interface to activate and deactivate events, delete events, and restore them to their initial values. Furthermore, if you expand the event's details by left-clicking the triangle to the left of the operation name, you have even more advanced controls.

Customizing the event system can be a pretty involved topic, so if you're really interested in making extensive changes, it's to your benefit to play with the event system editor in the Keymap section of Preferences a lot and make heavy use of the Restore buttons so that you can get Blender back to its defaults if something messes up.

After you have your events customized, you can save them to an external file that you can share with other users or simply carry with you on a USB drive so that your customized version of Blender is available wherever you go. To do so, click the Export button at the top right of the Preferences editor. A File Browser opens, and you can pick where you want to save your configuration file. The configuration is saved as a Python script. To load your custom configuration, it's possible to load your script in Blender and just run it. However, simply using the Import button at the top of the Preferences editor is much easier.

Speeding up your workflow with Quick Favorites

As you work more and more with Blender, you may find that there are certain operators that you use frequently. However, perhaps you don't want to go through the hassle of finding a free hotkey to use as a custom event. Well, dear artist, Blender has a special feature just for you: the Quick Favorites menu. The Quick Favorites menu is your own custom menu that you can populate with the tasks you perform most frequently in Blender.

To access the Quick Favorites menu, press Q. By default, you get an empty menu that tells you that there are no menu items found. Of course, you're certainly going to want to start adding things to this menu. The process for adding menu items to Quick Favorites is much like creating a custom keymap:

1. **Use Blender's menus to navigate to the operator you want to add to the Quick Favorites menu.**

2. **Right-click the menu item you want to add and choose Add to Quick Favorites.**

And there you go! In just two steps, you've added an operator to your Quick Favorites menu. If you ever want to remove an item from your Quick Favorites menu, just call up Quick Favorites (Q), right-click the menu item in question, and choose Remove from Quick Favorites.

REMEMBER

The Quick Favorites menu is context sensitive, so you can effectively have different Quick Favorites available in each editor. For example, if you put Add Marker in the Quick Favorites menu of your Timeline, that menu item won't appear when you invoke Quick Favorites from the 3D Viewport.

WARNING

As of this writing, there's no easy way to re-order your Quick Favorites menu. Items get added to this menu on a first-come, first-served basis. So if you added a menu item to Quick Favorites early on and want it at the bottom of Quick Favorites, you'll need to remove it first and then re-add it.

Chapter **3**

Getting Your Hands Dirty Working in Blender

B lender is built for speed, and its design heavily emphasizes working as quickly and efficiently as possible for extended periods of time. On more than one occasion, I've found myself working in Blender for 10 to 15 hours straight (or longer). Although, admittedly, part of this ridiculous scheduling has to do with my own minor lunacy, the fact that I'm able to be that productive for that long is a testament to Blender's design. This chapter gets you started in taking full advantage of that power. I cover the meat and potatoes of interacting with three-dimensional (3D) space in Blender, such as moving objects and editing polygons.

If you've worked in other 3D programs, chances are good that a number of Blender concepts may seem particularly alien to you. Although this divide is reduced with each update, to quote Yoda, "You must unlearn what you have learned" in your journey to become a Blender Jedi. If you've never worked in 3D, you may actually have a slight advantage over a trained professional who's used to a different workflow. Hooray for starting fresh!

Grabbing, Scaling, and Rotating

The three most basic ways of changing an object in a 3D scene are called *transfor-mations* by mathematicians. When you see technical documentation, transforms are described using the following terms:

>> Change location using *translation.*

>> Change size using *scale.*

>> Change rotation using *orientation*.

In Blender, the terms are a little bit more straightforward. Rather than use the mathematical terms of translation, scale, and orientation, most Blenderheads use the terms *grab*, *scale*, and *rotate*, respectively. Other programs might use the term *move* in place of grab or *size* in place of scale. Whatever you call them, and what-ever program you use, these three operations place any object in 3D space at any arbitrary size and with any arbitrary orientation.

Differentiating Between Coordinate Systems

Before you bound headlong into applying transformations to your objects, you need to understand how coordinate systems work in 3D space. All coordinate sys-tems in Blender are based on a grid consisting of three axes:

>> The *X-axis* typically represents side-to-side movement.

>> The *Y-axis* represents front-to-back movement.

>> The *Z-axis* goes from top to bottom.

This grid system with axes is referred to as the Cartesian grid. The origin or center of this grid is at the (0,0,0) coordinate. The difference in the coordinate systems within Blender lies in the way this grid is oriented relative to a selected 3D object. Figure 3-1 shows the Transform Orientations roll-out in the 3D Viewport header when you left-click it as well as the corresponding pie menu that you can see by pressing the Comma (,) hotkey.

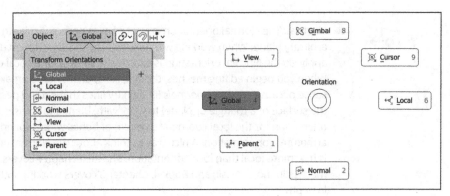

TIP

If you're coming from another 3D program, you may find the way Blender handles coordinates a bit disorienting. Blender uses what's known as a "right-handed, Z-axis up" convention. Some programs (such as Cinema 4D and Maya) have the Y-axis representing vertical movement and the Z-axis going from front to back. And still other programs have either Z or Y as the vertical axis, but oriented in a left-handed convention. Currently, you can't change the coordinate system in Blender to match any of these programs, so the right-handed Z-up system is one thing that migrating users need to get used to.

As Figure 3-1 shows, you can choose from seven orientations: *Global*, *Local*, *Normal*, *Gimbal*, *View*, *Cursor*, and *Parent*. Working in any of these coordinate systems gives you absolute control of how your object lives in 3D space. Depending on how you'd like to transform your object, one orientation may be more appropriate than the others. Blender also gives you the ability to create custom orientations. That topic is covered later in this chapter.

**TECHNICAL
STUFF**

The following list describes details of the six possible orientations:

>> **Global:** You see this orientation of Blender's base grid in the 3D Viewport. In many ways, the Global orientation is the primary orientation to which everything else relates, and it's the base coordinate system described at the beginning of this section. The Z-axis, marked in blue, runs vertically in the space. The Y-axis is marked in green, moving along the front-to-back line, and the X-axis is in red, along the side-to-side line. The origin is located directly at the center of the grid.

>> **Local:** In addition to the Global orientation, each 3D object in Blender has a local coordinate system. The base of this system isn't the same as the Global coordinate system's base. Instead, this coordinate system is relative to the center point, or origin, of your object. The *object origin* is represented by the orange dot usually located at the center of your 3D object. By default, when you first add a new object in Blender, its Local coordinate system is aligned to the Global axis, but after you start moving your object around, its Local coordinate system can differ greatly from the Global orientation.

Getting Your Hands Dirty
Working in Blender

CHAPTER 3 **Getting Your Hands Dirty Working in Blender** 73

>> **Normal:** The Normal orientation is a set of axes perpendicular to some arbitrary plane. When working with just objects, this description doesn't really apply, so the Normal orientation is exactly the same as the Local orientation. When you begin editing meshes, though, Normal orientation makes more sense because you have *normals* (imaginary lines that extend perpendicular to the surface of a triangle or plane) to work with. Blender also uses the Normal orientation for the local coordinate system of bones when working with armatures for animation. A nice way to think about the Normal orientation is the "more local than local" orientation. The next chapter covers editing meshes in more detail, and Book 4, Chapter 3 covers working with armatures in depth.

>> **Gimbal:** When you rotate an object about its X-, Y-, and Z-axes, the angles about those axes are known as Euler (pronounced like *oiler*) angles.

Unfortunately, a side effect of using Euler angles is the possibility of running into *gimbal lock*. You run into this problem when one of your rotation axes matches another one. For example, if you rotate your object 90 degrees about its X-axis, then rotating around its Y-axis is the same as rotating about its Z-axis; mathematically speaking, they're *locked* together, which can be a problem, especially when animating. This orientation mode in Blender helps you visualize where the axes are, to avoid gimbal lock.

>> **View:** The View orientation appears relative to how you're looking at the 3D Viewport. Regardless of how you move around in a scene, you're always looking down the Z-axis of the View coordinate system. The Y-axis is always vertical, and the X-axis is always horizontal in this orientation.

>> **Cursor:** In the previous chapter, I cover the use of Blender's 3D cursor for adding objects and using it as a reference when modeling. You can also use the 3D cursor's orientation as a reference transform orientation by selecting this option from the Transform Orientations roll-out.

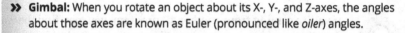

>> **Parent:** If your selected object is the *child* of another object, its local coordinate system may differ from that of the *parent* object. However, there may be situations where you want to transform that child object using the parent's coordinate system. Choose this transform orientation to accomplish that task.

All these coordinate-system explanations can be (please forgive the pun) disorienting. An easy way to visualize this concept is to imagine that your body represents the Global coordinate system, and this book is a 3D object oriented in space. If you hold the book out in front of you and straighten your arms, you move the book away from you. It's moving in the positive Y direction, both globally and locally. Now, if you twist the book to the right a few degrees and do the same thing, it still moves in the positive Y direction globally. However, in its local orientation, the book is moving in both a positive Y direction and a negative X direction. To move it in just the positive local Y direction, you move the book in the direction in which its spine is pointing.

To relate this concept to the View orientation, assume that your eyes are the View axis. If you look straight ahead and move the book up and down, you're translating it along the View orientation's Y-axis. Gimbal orientation would be if you rotate the book 90 degrees toward you, rotating about its X-axis. Then its Y- and Z-axes are locked together. For a clear reference, the 3D manipulator in Figure 3-2 shows the difference between the coordinate systems.

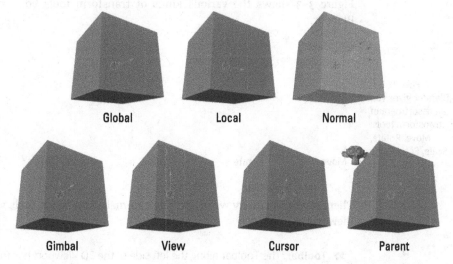

Global   Local   Normal

Gimbal   View   Cursor   Parent

FIGURE 3-2:
The Global, Local, Normal, Gimbal, View, Cursor, and Parent coordinate orientations.

REMEMBER

The last object you select is the *active* object. If you use the Local, Gimbal, Normal, or Parent orientations and select multiple objects, the transform operations happen relative to the active object's orientation. An exception to this is if you have the Transform Pivot Point menu set to Individual Origins, then the orientation of the active object is ignored.

TIP

You can quickly change the coordinate system you're using by using the Comma (,) hotkey to invoke a Transform Orientation pie menu.

Transforming an Object by Using Tools

In Blender's default configuration, there doesn't appear to be a clear way to grab, scale, or rotate whatever you have selected. In other 3D applications, there are object *gizmos*, *widgets*, or *manipulators* that give you onscreen controls for transforming objects. Blender has them as well. In Blender, they're *gizmos*, and they can be activated by tools.

REMEMBER

In all transform orientations under Blender, red represents the X-axis, green the Y, and blue the Z. If you think about the primary colors for light, a handy way to think of this is XYZ = RGB.

Activating transform tools

Figure 3-3 shows the various kinds of transform tools you have available in Blender.

FIGURE 3-3:
Blender gives you
an assortment of
transform tools:
Move, Rotate,
Scale, Scale Cage,
and Transform.

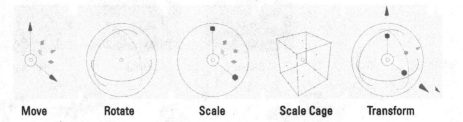

Move   Rotate   Scale   Scale Cage   Transform

There are two primary ways that you can make transform tools visible in the 3D Viewport:

>> **Toolbar:** The Toolbar along the left side of the 3D Viewport has four buttons for tools dedicated to transforming your objects. They're located just below the Cursor tool. In order from top to bottom, they are as follows:

- **Move:** Also referred to as grabbing or translating. You get a set of colored axes at the origin of your object. Click and drag on the arrow of any axis to move your selection along it. Click and drag one of the squares between two axes, and you can move your selection along the plane formed by those axes.

- **Rotate:** Choose this tool, and you get a set of colored circles around your selected object's origin. Click and drag one of the colored circles to rotate your selection about that axis.

- **Scale:** The default behavior that you get when you select this tool is a set of axes that look and behave very similar to those for the Move tool. However, if you hold down your left mouse button when selecting this tool, you get access to another tool called the Scale Cage. With that tool, a box-shaped "cage" appears around your selection. Click and drag any point on the cage to scale in that direction.

- **Transform:** The Transform tool is a general-purpose tool that allows you to move, scale, or rotate without changing tools.

The advantage of using the transform tools in the Toolbar is that you have quick access to them with a mouse, and their icons make it very clear what they do. Also, the Toolbar is the only way you can activate the Scale Cage tool. The downside of the tools in the Toolbar is that they can only be activated one at a time. If you want to move your object and then rotate it, you have to constantly go back to the Toolbar to change tools. This is alleviated somewhat with the general Transform tool, but that often shows more than you really want. Furthermore, to use any of these tools, you have to stop using another tool (like any of the Select tools or any of the assorted tools available in Edit mode).

>> **Show Gizmos menu:** There's another option to give you the ability transform your selection in the 3D Viewport. The Show Gizmos menu in the header of the 3D Viewport, as shown in Figure 3-4, has a section devoted to object gizmos containing check boxes for Move, Rotate, and Scale. They're all disabled by default, but if you enable any one of them, you'll get a control gizmo that looks just like the corresponding one you get when activating one of the transform tools in the Toolbar. There are two distinct advantages to activating object gizmos this way:

- **Multiple activation:** You can activate any combination of gizmos. If you want to see just the Move and Rotate gizmos, enable those check boxes. Enable them all and you get the same as the Transform tool. Or, as is the default, you can disable them so they're not in your way at all.

- **Always active:** A key feature of the gizmos approach is that they're always there, regardless of what tool you're using in Object or Edit mode. This approach saves you time because you're not always switching between tools just to move your selection around (and then trying to remember what tool you were using before moving). Generally speaking, this means you end up working faster.

The only real downsides of the Show Gizmos menu approach is that enabling and disabling gizmos is slightly slower because it requires an additional click to expand the Show Gizmos menu, and you don't have access to the Scale Cage tool for scaling.

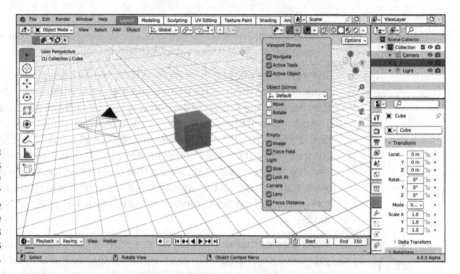

FIGURE 3-4:
The Show Gizmos
menu in the 3D
Viewport's header
gives you the
ability to activate
transform gizmos
so they're always
available.

Using transform gizmos

General usage for the object gizmos is described in the preceding section; however, there are some additional nuanced controls that you have while transforming your selection in the 3D Viewport.

TIP

Notice that when you have the Move, Rotate, or Scale gizmos active, a white circle appears either around the origin of the gizmo or all the way around the gizmo. Refer to Figure 3-3 if you need a refresher. This white circle control allows you to transform your object relative to your current view angle (except for Scale, which allows you to uniformly scale on all axes). For example, you can move a selected object in the XY plane of the View orientation by left-clicking and dragging this circle with the Move gizmo active. This convenient shortcut prevents you from having to continually switch orientation modes for the manipulator.

You can use the Ctrl and Shift keys while transforming to have more control. Move in fixed increments with default settings by holding down Ctrl. Hold down Shift while transforming an object to make adjustments on a finer scale. Hold down the Ctrl+Shift key combo while transforming to make adjustments in smaller fixed increments. Interestingly, these same modifier keys also work when using any of Blender's value input fields.

This fixed-increment control is similar to (though not exactly the same as) the basic *snapping to the grid* or *increment* snapping found in other 2D and 3D applications. Blender also offers the ability to snap your selected object to other objects (or parts of them), called *snap targets*, in your scene. Choices for snap targets are *Increment, Vertex, Edge, Face Project, Face Nearest, Volume, Edge Center,* and *Edge*

Perpendicular. You can snap directly to the 3D scene's grid by toggling the Absolute Grid Snap check box. You choose which snap target you want to use by left-clicking the Snapping menu in the 3D Viewport's header, as shown in Figure 3-5.

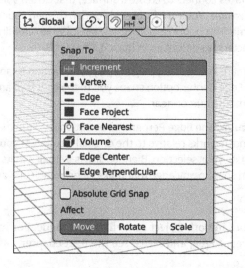

Holding Ctrl while transforming is actually a way to *temporarily* enable snapping behavior based on a chosen snap target. However, you may prefer snapping to be the default behavior (so you don't have to hold down Ctrl). You can enable snapping by left-clicking the magnet icon next to the Snapping menu in the 3D Viewport's header or by using the Shift+Tab hotkey. This option tells Blender to snap as default and that holding down Ctrl then temporarily disables snapping.

Here are the different available types of snap targets in Blender:

>> **Increment:** In Blender's default behavior, your selection is snapped to fixed increments of Blender's base unit.

>> **Vertex:** The vertex is the fundamental element of a mesh object in Blender. Using this target, the center of your selection snaps to vertices or points (for curves and armatures) in other objects or the same object.

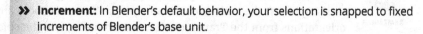

>> **Edge:** The line connecting vertices is referred to as an *edge.* Select this target to snap your selection to edges in objects of your scene.

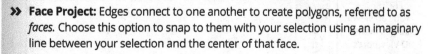

>> **Face Project:** Edges connect to one another to create polygons, referred to as *faces.* Choose this option to snap to them with your selection using an imaginary line between your selection and the center of that face.

>> **Face Nearest:** This option is similar to Face Project in that you're snapping to faces, but it's subtly different. Rather than relying on an imaginary projection line, this choice just picks the nearest point on the surface of a face.

>> **Volume:** When faces connect to create a surface, that closed surface is referred to as a *volume.* You can choose this option to snap your selection to an object's volume. This option is particularly useful when creating a rig for animating characters, as described in Book 4, Chapter 3.

>> **Edge Center:** Whereas Edge snapping snaps your selection to any close point on an edge, the Edge Center option snaps you to the center of an edge that you move your mouse cursor near.

>> **Edge Perpendicular:** The Edge Perpendicular option is a little tricky to wrap your head around. It works relative to the original location of your selection. When you translate your selection, Blender draws a small X at its original location. You can snap to any edge that makes a perpendicular angle with that X.

Snapping targets work in both Object as well as Edit mode. For more information on Edit mode, vertices, edges, and faces, see the next chapter.

TIP

You can quickly change snap modes by using the Shift+Ctrl+Tab hotkey combination.

You can observe the changes made to your object in real time by looking in the 3D Viewport's header as you transform it. Figure 3-6 shows how the header explicitly indicates how much you're changing the object in each axis.

TIP

REMEMBER

Transform operations are consistent across all manipulator modes in Blender, so you can apply any of these methods of interacting with the Translate manipulator in the Rotate and Scale manipulator modes. Don't forget that you aren't limited to working in just the Global coordinate system. You can choose any of the other six orientations from the Transform Orientation menu, and the object gizmos adjust to fit that orientation.

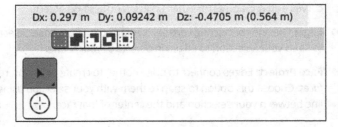

FIGURE 3-6:
You can view changes in the 3D Viewport's header.

Creating Custom Transform Orientations

In addition to the seven base transform orientations described earlier in this chapter, you can also define custom transform orientations that are relative to how something else in your scene is oriented. This feature is most commonly used in Edit mode while modeling on mesh objects. There's more on Edit mode in the next chapter, but here's an example use case. Imagine that you're modeling an angled support for a shelf of some sort. That support's Local coordinate system defines which way is up so it can be easily positioned.

However, what if you want to move some object (maybe a model of a nail) relative to the angle of that support? You can select one of the faces on that support and get its Normal coordinate system, but that coordinate system goes away after you go back to Object mode. It would be really great if you could use that face's coordinate system to get the angles you need. With custom transform orientations, you can

1. **Select the object or component that has the orientation you're interested in using.**

    In the example, I said a face on a mesh, but it could be an edge, a control point on a curve, or an object.

2. **From the Transform Orientations roll-out in the 3D Viewport's header, left-click the plus (+) icon in the upper right to create a new custom orientation.**

3. **Your new custom orientation is added to the bottom of the Transform Orientation's roll-out and can be selected whenever you need it.**

TIP

By default, your custom transform orientation will take the name of whatever you had selected. If it was a face, the custom transform orientation will be named Face. If you used the orientation of the default cube in the Blender scene, then the custom transform orientation would be named Cube. You can rename a custom transform orientation by selecting it from the Transform Orientations roll-out and editing the text field at the bottom. Click the X icon next to that text field to remove the custom transform from your .blend file.

Saving Time by Using Hotkeys

Many Blender users find that the transform gizmos obstruct their view too much when working, so they never enable them or even use the transform tools from the Toolbar. But wait, with the gizmos gone, how do I transform my objects? I'm glad you asked. Enter one of the most powerful features of Blender: hotkeys.

Part of the beauty of Blender's hotkeys is that they take a lot of pressure off of your mouse hand and shorten the distance of mouse-based operations. The accumulation of these little time-saving actions is what makes using hotkeys so powerful.

Transforming with hotkeys

You can access nearly every piece of major functionality in Blender with hotkeys. Transforms are no exception. One of the other terms for moving in Blender is *grabbing*. That naming has specific significance as it pertains to hotkeys. To see what I mean, follow these steps to Grab/Move your object:

1. **Select the object you want to move.**

2. **Press G.**

   Congratulations! You moved your object.

3. **Confirm the move by left-clicking or pressing Enter.**

   Cancel by right-clicking or pressing Esc.

REMEMBER

To rotate your object, press R. Scale it by pressing S. See a pattern here? Quite a few of Blender's default hotkeys are easy to remember. Most of them just use the first letter from the operation in question. And just like when using the gizmo, the familiar Ctrl, Shift, and Ctrl+Shift keypresses for snapping and fine adjustments still apply.

TIP

Also, because Blender tries to maintain consistency throughout its interface, you can use these hotkeys in more than just the 3D Viewport. For example, the same grab and scale operations work when you edit keyframes and motion curves in the Graph Editor. How's that for convenient?

REMEMBER

In addition to emphasizing efficiency, Blender is designed to allow you to work for as long as possible while incurring the least amount of repetitive stress. For this reason, relatively few operations in Blender require you to hold down a key. Typically, you press and release a key to begin the operation; you confirm its completion by left-clicking with your mouse or pressing Enter. To cancel the operation instead of confirming, right-click or press Esc. In fact, this keyboard combination even works on some operations that require you to hold down a button. For example, if you try to split an area (left-click and drag a corner widget) and then decide you don't actually want to split it, you can right-click or press Esc while adjusting the boundary between areas; the operation stops.

Hotkeys and coordinate systems

By default, your transformations all happen in the View coordinate system when you use hotkeys. So no matter how you're viewing the scene, you're working in the XY plane of the 3D Viewport.

Suppose, however, that you want to grab your object and move it in the global Z-axis. You use a sequence of keypresses to do this action. Follow these steps to grab an object and move it to the global Z-axis:

1. **With your object selected, press G.**

   You're now in Grab/Move mode.

2. **Without canceling this operation, press Z.**

   A blue line should appear that indicates the global Z-axis. Your object is locked to move only along that line. If you press Y, your object moves only along the global Y-axis, and pressing X constrains it to the global X-axis.

Pretty neat, huh? This method of using a sequence of hotkeys works with rotating and scaling as well (for example, R ⇨ Z rotates around the global Z-axis and S ⇨ X scales along the global X-axis).

What about any of the other orientations? That's easy too. All you need to do is set the orientation you want from the Transform Orientations roll-out as described earlier in this chapter. Even though you're not using gizmos to transform your selection, Blender still pays attention to the choice you've made in this menu. After you choose your preferred transform orientation, just use the standard G ⇨ X/Y/Z hotkey sequence to move your object along the corresponding axis in that transform orientation.

TIP

Again, this method of using a sequence of keypresses works with scaling and rotation as well. Keying the sequence R ⇨ Y rotates around your chosen orientation's Y-axis and S ⇨ Z scales along your chosen orientation's Z-axis.

TIP

If you keep your transform orientation set to Global, there's a shortcut to transforming on the local axis. Just press that axis hotkey a second time. That is, if you're using the Global transform orientation and you want to move your selection along the Local Z-axis, press G ⇨ Z ⇨ Z. Likewise, if your transform orientation is set to Parent (for example) and you want to use the Global coordinate system, the G ⇨ Z ⇨ Z hotkey sequence will move your object along the Global Z-axis.

One of the more powerful features of the transform gizmos is the ability to work in a plane rather than just one axis. You can work in a plane with hotkeys as well. Use Shift plus the letter of the axis that's perpendicular to the plane you want to move in. For example, to scale your object in the global XY plane, press S ⇨ Shift+Z. For the global YZ plane, press S ⇨ Shift+X. This same methodology also works for the Grab operation (though, not for the Rotate operation because rotating around a plane doesn't make much sense).

Table 3-1 shows most of the useful hotkey sequences for transforming your objects assuming you're in the Global transform orientation.

TABLE 3-1 **Useful Hotkey Sequences for Transformations**

Grab	Scale	Rotate	Orientation
G	S	R	View
G ⇨ Z	S ⇨ Z	R ⇨ Z	Global Z-axis
G ⇨ Y	S ⇨ Y	R ⇨ Y	Global Y-axis
G ⇨ X	S ⇨ X	R ⇨ X	Global X-axis
G ⇨ Z ⇨ Z	S ⇨ Z ⇨ Z	R ⇨ Z ⇨ Z	Local Z-axis
G ⇨ Y ⇨ Y	S ⇨ Y ⇨ Y	R ⇨ Y ⇨ Y	Local Y-axis
G ⇨ X ⇨ X	S ⇨ X ⇨ X	R ⇨ X ⇨ X	Local X-axis
G ⇨ Shift+Z	S ⇨ Shift+Z	N/A	Global XY plane
G ⇨ Shift+Y	S ⇨ Shift+Y	N/A	Global XZ plane
G ⇨ Shift+X	S ⇨ Shift+X	N/A	Global YZ plane
G ⇨ Shift+Z ⇨ Shift+Z	S ⇨ Shift+Z ⇨ Shift+Z	N/A	Local XY plane
G ⇨ Shift+Y ⇨ Shift+Y	S ⇨ Shift+Y ⇨ Shift+Y	N/A	Local XZ plane

TIP

An even faster way to constrain to axes involves using the middle mouse button. As an example, select an object and grab (G) it. Now move your mouse in roughly the direction of the X-axis and then middle-click. A red line should appear through your object's origin, and the object should be locked to moving along that line, constraining you to that axis. The same thing works in both the Y- and Z-axes. For an even more interactive way of constraining axes, hold down your middle mouse button while you're grabbing. All three axes appear, and your object locks to one of them as you bring your selected object closer. I absolutely *love* this feature.

Numerical input

Not only can you use hotkeys to activate the various transform modes, but you can also use the keyboard to explicitly input exactly how much you would like your object to be transformed. Simply type the number of units you want to change after you activate the transform mode.

As an example, suppose you want to rotate your object 32 degrees around the global X-axis. To do so, press R ⇨ X ⇨ 32 and confirm by pressing Enter. Translate your object -26.4 units along its local Y-axis by pressing G ⇨ Y ⇨ Y ⇨ -26.4 ⇨ Enter. These steps can be a very quick and effective means of flipping or mirroring an object because mirroring is just scaling by -1 along a particular axis. For example, to flip an object along the global Z-axis, press S ⇨ Z ⇨ -1 ⇨ Enter. For consistency, these numerical input operations are also available when using the 3D manipulator.

Blender also has the ability to use mathematical equations as part of the numerical input system. This system is called the Blender's advanced numerical input system. To take advantage of this feature, press the Equal (=) key before entering your numerical input. As an example, say you have a model of a car that's 4.6 meters long, and you want to move it along the Y-axis by 6 car lengths. Sure, you could do the math in your head (or with a calculator, if necessary), but it's even easier to let Blender handle the math for you by pressing G ⇨ Y ⇨ =4.6*6 ⇨ Enter. This advanced numerical input system even allows for simple math functions and constants, such as sine, cosine, and pi (π). So, if you find that you need to rotate an object about its X-axis by the cosine of 2π (that's 1°, by the way), you could use the following key sequence: R ⇨ X ⇨ =cos(2*pi) ⇨ Enter. If you're coming from an industrial design or architecture background, this is an immensely useful feature.

Other Ways to Transform Objects

Blender gives a wide variety of ways to move your objects around. In fact, there are two other places in Blender's interface where you can perform transform operations on your selected objects: the Sidebar in the 3D Viewport and the Object tab in the Properties editor.

Why so many ways to do the same thing? Really, it depends on workflow. Blender does a bunch of different things in 3D space and is therefore used by all kinds of people in different contexts. So it's useful to have different ways to do the same thing. Organic modelers may only care about rough units or the position of objects relative to one another and may not want to have gizmos cluttering their 3D View, so they may be just fine with using hotkeys. Animators are used to having mouse-based controls on their rigs, so perhaps they're more comfortable using gizmos. People with a more technical background may have a greater interest in the exact numbers associated with transforms. They may prefer to use the Item tab in the Sidebar or the Object context of the Properties editor.

The Sidebar

One way to explicitly translate, scale, and rotate your object is through the Sidebar region (see Book 1, Chapter 2) of the 3D Viewport. To reveal the Sidebar, go to View ⇨ Sidebar in the 3D Viewport's header, or press N while your mouse cursor is in the 3D Viewport. The Sidebar sits along the right side of the 3D Viewport, and the Item tab of the Sidebar includes a Transform panel that allows you to explicitly enter numerical values (and simple math expressions) for Location, Rotation, Scale, as well as general Dimensions for your selection.

Object Properties

Similar to the Sidebar in the 3D Viewport, the Object tab of the Properties editor has a Transform panel. This panel has all the same basic transform values for your selected object, with one major exception: There are no Dimensions values. Those values are available only from the Sidebar.

When in Object mode, the values in the Sidebar and Object Properties don't change depending on which coordinate system you've selected. Location and Rotation are always in the Global orientation, whereas Scale is always in Local.

REMEMBER

Chapter **4**

Working in Edit Mode and Object Mode

When working on a scene in Blender, your life revolves around repeatedly selecting objects, transforming, editing, and relating them to one another. You regularly shift from dealing with your model in Object mode to doing refinements in Edit mode.

This process isn't only for modeling but also for most of the other heavy tasks performed in Blender. Therefore, you can reuse the skills you pick up in this chapter in parts of Blender that have nothing to do with 3D modeling, such as animating, rigging, compositing, and motion tracking. Even if you don't know how to do something, chances are good that if you think like Blender thinks, you'll be able to make a successful guess.

Making Changes by Using Edit Mode

Moving primitive objects around is fun and all, but you're interested in getting in there and completely changing the primitive objects that ship with Blender (described in detail in this chapter) to match your vision. You want to do 3D modeling. Well, you're in the right place. This section introduces you to Edit mode, a concept that's deeply embedded throughout Blender for editing objects. Even though this section is focused mostly on polygon modeling, also called *mesh editing*, most of the same principles apply for editing curves, surfaces, armatures, and even text.

When you understand how Blender thinks, figuring out unknown parts of the program is much easier.

Switching between Object mode and Edit mode

In Book 1, Chapter 3, you do just about everything in Object mode. As its name indicates, Object mode is where you work with whole objects. However, Object mode isn't very useful for actually changing the internal structure of your object. For example, select the cube in the default scene. You know that you can turn it into a more rectangular shape by scaling it along one of the axes. But what if you want to turn the cube into a pyramid? You need to modify the actual components that make up the cube. These changes are made by entering Edit mode.

There are a handful of different ways you can get to Edit mode. To get there by menu, left-click the Interaction Mode drop-down in the 3D Viewport's header. It should say Object Mode right now, because that's the mode you're currently in. From the drop-down menu, select Edit Mode (see Figure 4-1). Be aware that if you're working with an object other than a mesh, such as an armature, the contents of this menu may vary slightly to relate more to that object. However, most objects have some sort of Edit mode.

FIGURE 4-1:
On the left, the Mode button allows you to switch between Object mode and Edit mode for a selected object. On the right, the mode selection pie menu.

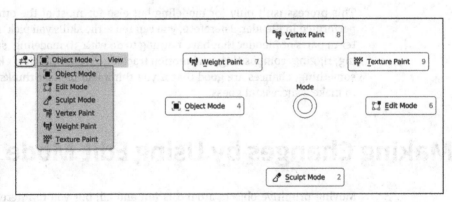

TIP

Of course, Blender also has a hotkey to enter Edit mode. Actually, technically speaking, the hotkey toggles you between Object mode and Edit mode. Pressing Tab is the preferred way to switch between modes in Blender, and it's used so frequently that Blender users often use Tab as a verb and say they're *tabbing into* Edit or Object mode. This language is something you come across fairly often in Blender user forums and in some of Blender's online documentation.

TIP

A slightly better approach, in my opinion, is to use pie menus. Press Ctrl+Tab to open a pie menu with the option of many modes. It isn't quite as fast as toggling with Tab, but it can be pretty fast if you use the hold hotkey ⇨ drag mouse cursor ⇨ release hotkey method of using the pie menu. More importantly, you get the added benefit of easily choosing other modes. Figure 4-1 also shows the Interaction Mode menu in the 3D Viewport's header and the Mode pie menu.

TIP

There's another means of entering Edit mode that's really quite handy: You can use Blender's workspaces to your advantage. By default, Blender launches in the Layout workspace is a decent general purpose workspace you can use to get a lot done. However, the Layout workspace isn't specifically geared for modeling. If you switch to the Modeling workspace (click the Modeling tab at the top of the Blender window), Blender automatically toggles Edit mode for your selected objects.

As Figure 4-2 shows, the Modeling workspace doesn't really look all that different from the Layout workspace. It's basically the same area configuration, minus the Timeline at the bottom and with a little more space for the Properties editor. That said, there's a lot of value in using the right workspace for the job. A good workflow would be to select the object you want to work on in the Layout workspace and then jump over to the Modeling workspace (you can get there by hotkey using Ctrl+PageDown) to edit the components of your model in Edit mode. And after you're done, you can pop back over to the Layout workspace (Ctrl+PageUp) to pick another object to work on in Object mode.

Selecting vertices, edges, and faces

Regardless of how you get into Edit mode, once you're there, the cube changes color and dots form at each of the cube's corners. Those dots represent components of your mesh called *vertices*. There are actually three core component types when working with meshes:

>> A *vertex* is a point in space and a core building block of a mesh object.

>> The line that forms between two vertices is an *edge*.

>> A *face* is a polygon that has been formed by three or more connecting edges.

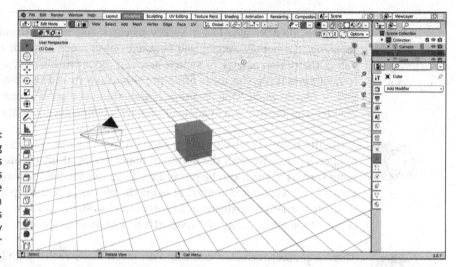

FIGURE 4-2:
The Modeling workspace gives you quick access to Edit mode and a screen layout that's more specifically geared for modeling.

For polygon editing, you can use three different types of Edit modes, sometimes called *selection modes*: Vertex Select, Edge Select, and Face Select. By default, the first time you tab into Edit mode, you're in Vertex Select mode.

Two visual cues in the Blender interface clue you in to what selection mode you're using. First, for Vertex Select mode, you can see the individual vertices in the mesh. Second, as Figure 4-3 shows, three new buttons appear in the 3D Viewport's header while you're in Edit mode. The button on the left (it has an icon of a cube with a dot over one corner) is enabled, indicating that you're in Vertex Select mode.

FIGURE 4-3:
The Edit mode Select buttons.

To the right of the Vertex Select button is a button displaying an icon of a cube with a highlighted edge. Click this button to activate Edge Select mode. When you do, the vertices are no longer visible on your mesh. Clicking the last button in this block, which has an icon of a cube with one side marked in solid, activates Face Select mode. When Face Select mode is active, vertices aren't visible, and each polygon in your mesh can be selected as a single unit.

Now, you may notice that the selection mode buttons are blocked together, kind of like they can be used together. That's because they can! In any given Edit mode session, you can have multiple selection modes active at the same time. Simply Shift+left-click the selection mode buttons to get this functionality, called *Combo*

Select. Some Blender modelers like to have Vertex Select and Edge Select modes active at the same time to speed up their workflow. This combined selection mode gives them immediate control at the vertex and edge level, and you can easily select the faces by Box-selecting across two edges.

Blender also has some handy hotkeys for quickly switching between vertex, edge, and face selection. They're the numbers 1, 2, and 3 across the top of your keyboard (*not* the Numpad!). A handy mnemonic to help you remember which key belongs to which selection mode is to remember how many vertices make up each one. A vertex is a single unit, so the hotkey for Vertex Select is 1. It takes two vertices to make an edge, so the hotkey for Edge Select is 2. And a face consists of three or more vertices, so the hotkey for Face Select is 3. You can activate Combo Select by holding Shift while pressing any of these hotkeys (for example, if you're in Vertex Select and you also want to be in Edge Select, press Shift+2). Figure 4-4 shows the default cube in each of the select modes as well as a Combo Select mode.

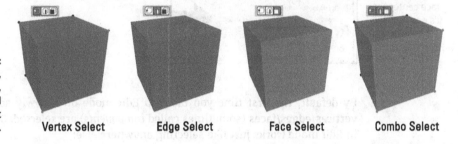

FIGURE 4-4:
Vertex Select,
Edge Select,
Face Select, and
Combo Select
modes.

Vertex Select   Edge Select   Face Select   Combo Select

TIP

As Figure 4-4 shows, it can be a little bit tricky to tell at a glance whether you're in Edge Select or Face Select. To make things a little more clear, I recommend that you enable face centers (sometimes called *face dots*) in the Viewport Overlays roll-out menu in the header of the 3D Viewport. Expand the menu by clicking the down arrow that's to the right of the Viewport Overlays icon, and you should see a menu like the one in Figure 4-5.

NEW FEATURE

Because the Viewport Overlays roll-out is so large, starting in Blender 4.0, an additional Mesh Edit Mode Overlays roll-out appears when you're in Edit mode. This roll-out is the new location of the check box for enabling the display of face centers.

This menu is large, but about halfway down, under the label of Mesh Edit Mode, there are a series of check boxes. One of which is a check box somewhat vaguely labeled Center. Enable that check box, and you should see a small dot appear at the center of your faces while you're in Face Select mode. That should give you a bit of a visual cue to indicate which mode you're in.

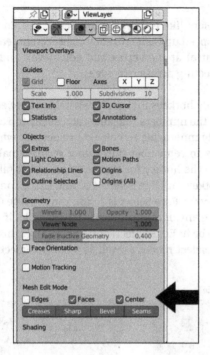

FIGURE 4-5:
Use the Viewport Overlays roll-out menu to enable face centers so it's easier to tell what selection mode you're using.

By default, the first time you tab into Edit mode on a newly added object, all vertices/edges/faces (sometimes called *components*) are selected. Selecting things in Edit mode works just like selecting anywhere else:

>> Left-click any component to select it.

>> Select and deselect multiple components by Shift+left-clicking them.

>> Select all components by pressing A.

>> Deselect all components by pressing Alt+A or clicking in an empty space in the 3D Viewport.

>> Use one of the select tools from the Toolbar as described in Book 1, Chapter 2.

 If you're using Blender's default settings, you can't see through your model. You can't select the vertices, edges, and faces on the back side of the model unless you orbit the 3D Viewport to see those vertices or drop into wireframe viewport shading. (Press Z to open the Viewport Shading pie menu.) On occasion, however, you may find it useful to see (and select) those hidden vertices while in one of the other viewport shading types. To do so, click the Toggle X-ray button. Located to the left of the viewport shading types block in the 3D Viewport's header, this button has an icon of a cube with a dotted line of its back face visible through it. By default, the Toggle X-ray toggle is disabled but you can click this button to reveal the vertices, edges, and faces on the back of your model. The hiding of those rear vertices is often referred to as *backface culling,* and it's incredibly useful when you're working with complex models. For faster access, you can press Alt+Z.

Understanding ngons and their limitations

TECHNICAL STUFF

In the past, faces in Blender and other applications were limited to only three-sided and four-sided polygons, often referred to as *tris* (pronounced like *tries*) and *quads.* Since that time, Blender — like many other programs — gained support for something called an *ngon* that can have a virtually limitless number of sides. The name "ngon" comes from the fact that it's a polygon with an arbitrary number of sides, represented by the variable "n" . . . aren't mathematicians fun?)

Ngons are a fantastic help when modeling 3D meshes. However, there are still some limitations. For example, an ngon cannot currently have a hole in it — not on its own, at least. As Figure 4-6 shows, to get a hole, you need to have two faces. There need to be edges that connect from the inner ring of vertices to the outer ring.

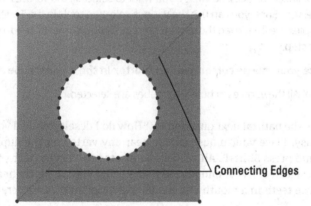

FIGURE 4-6: Ngons in Blender can't have holes in them.

Connecting Edges

It's best to think of ngons as a process tool. On any mesh that's likely to be used in animation (like a character model) or included in real-time environment like a video game, the finished mesh should be composed of only tris and quads. In fact, most detailed character models are made almost completely with quads and an occasional triangle, and all 3D geometry is reduced to triangles when it gets to your computer hardware. An exception to this rule of thumb might be for architectural models or models intended to be rendered as still images. Because those meshes won't be deformed by something like an armature or a lattice and they don't have to work in a game engine, sometimes you can get away with leaving ngons in them.

Working with linked vertices

Another handy way to select things in Edit mode is by selecting linked vertices. *Linked vertices* are a set of vertices within a mesh that are connected by edges. In order to understand linked vertices better, go through the following steps:

1. **Select your default cube in Blender and tab into Edit mode (or switch to the Modeling workspace).**

    All the vertices are selected. If not, press A.

2. **With all the vertices selected, choose Mesh ⇨ Duplicate from the 3D Viewport's header or press Shift+D to duplicate your selection.**

    Blender creates a copy of your selection and automatically switches to grab mode, allowing you to immediately move the duplicate set of vertices, edges, and faces.

3. **Use your mouse to move your new cube off the original and confirm your placement by left-clicking or pressing Enter.**

    None of the vertices in the original cube are selected. Each cube represents a set of linked vertices. So what if you want to select all the vertices in the original cube, too? Sure, you can use the various selection tools in the Toolbar, but on complex meshes, even those tools can get cumbersome. Instead, move to the next step.

4. **Place your mouse cursor near any vertex in the original cube and press L.**

    Blam! All the vertices in both your cubes are selected.

Of course, the natural next question is, "How do I deselect linked vertices?" That's just as easy. Place your mouse cursor near any vertex on the duplicate cube you created and press Shift+L. All vertices connected to the one near your mouse cursor are deselected. I've found myself using L and Shift+L pretty heavily when trying to place teeth in a mouth I've modeled. These hotkeys are *very* handy.

Quite a few more selection options are available to you when working with meshes. I describe these selection methods in detail in Book 2, Chapter 1.

While you're in Edit mode, you can work only with the current selected objects. You can't select and manipulate other objects while you're in Edit mode. That said, it *is* possible to have more than one object in Edit mode at the same time. Simply select multiple objects and tab into Edit mode as you normally would with just one object. The only caveat is that this works only on objects of the same type. If, for example, you have a mesh and a metaball selected, only one of them (typically the last one selected) will go into Edit mode when you press Tab.

Still Blender's No. 1 modeling tool: Extrude

Besides transform operations (see Book 1, Chapter 3), the most commonly used modeling tool in Blender is the Extrude operator. In meatspace, *extrusion* is a process whereby some material is pushed through a shaped hole of some sort. When you were a kid, did you ever cut out a shape in cardboard and force clay or mud or Play-Doh modeling compound through it? If so, you were extruding. If not, you certainly missed out on a good solid five to ten minutes of fun (but don't worry, it's never too late to start).

In 3D, extrusion follows a similar concept, except you don't have to create the hole to extrude through. Instead, that shape is determined by your selection, and you can extend that selection in any direction. Follow these steps to extrude:

1. **Select the object you want to edit.**

2. **Tab into Edit mode or switch to the Modeling workspace.**

3. **Select the vertices, edges, or faces you want to extrude.**

   Use any of the selection methods listed in the previous section.

4. **Extrude your selection in one of several ways:**

   - **Vertex, Edge, or Face menus in the 3D Viewport's header.**

     Quite sensibly, because the Extrude operator is used so frequently, it's the first choice in each of these menus. Do note that Blender will extrude only the components associated with the menu you use. So even if you have a whole face selected, if you choose Vertex ⇨ Extrude Vertices, Blender extrudes only the vertices in your selection rather than the whole face. Most frequently, you'll probably want to use Face ⇨ Extrude Faces.

   - **Extrude tool.**

     When you tab into Edit mode, the Toolbar on the left side of the 3D Viewport expands with a whole mess of additional tools you can choose from. Near the top of these added tools, of course, is the Extrude tool. Actually, that button is the home of a few different extrusion tools, which I cover later in this section. The default tool for extrusion is Extrude Region, and it has an icon like the one to the left. When you choose this tool, a yellow gizmo appears on your mesh: a plus sign in a circle with a line to your selection. Left-click and drag that gizmo to extrude your selection in the direction it's pointing.

   - **E hotkey.**

     The E hotkey is by far the fastest way to extrude in Blender. When you press E, your selection is extruded, and Blender automatically puts you in grab mode on your newly extruded parts. This means all your constraint hotkeys still work as well. Want to extrude your selection along the global X-axis? Press E ⇨ X, and off you go! If you have a face selected, your new extrusion is constrained to move only along its normal. If you don't want this constrained behavior, middle-click your mouse (without moving it) and the constraint is removed, allowing you to freely move your extrusion around.

There are advantages and disadvantages to Blender's extrude operator leaping directly into grab mode when you use the hotkey approach. The advantages are that you have all the transform functionality, such as axis-locking, snapping, and numerical input, immediately available to you. The disadvantage is that, because of this autograb behavior, if you cancel the operation by right-clicking or pressing Esc, the newly extruded vertices, edges, or faces are still there, just located in exactly the same place as the vertices, edges, or faces that they originated from.

For this reason, if you cancel an extrude operation, make sure that your duplicate vertices, sometimes called *doubles*, are no longer there. A quick way to check is to press G after you cancel your extrusion. If it looks like you're extruding again, you have doubles.

You can get rid of doubles in a variety of ways:

>> **If the canceled extrusion operation was the last thing you did, undo it by pressing Ctrl+Z.** This solution usually is the quickest.

>> **If you still have the doubles selected, delete them.** You can activate the delete operation with hotkeys (X or Del), choosing to Mesh ⇨ Delete ⇨ Dissolve Vertices in the 3D Viewport's header. If you use the Delete hotkey, you see a menu where you decide what elements of the mesh you want to delete. In this case, you choose Dissolve Vertices. By choosing the Dissolve operation, you remove those extra vertices without losing the face that they created.

>> **If you're unsure whether you have doubles from previous canceled extrusions, use Blender's special Merge Vertices function:**

1. **In Edit Mode, select all by choosing Select ⇨ All from the 3D Viewport's header or pressing A.**

2. **Right-click in the 3D Viewport and choose Merge Vertices ⇨ By Distance.**

   With this operator, Blender removes all doubles from your mesh. You can also find this option in Vertex ⇨ Merge Vertices ⇨ By Distance in the 3D Viewport's header, as well as with the Alt+M hotkey.

WARNING

If you have Blender's mesh auto-merge feature enabled (it's disabled by default but can be enabled in the Tool tab of the Properties editor within the Options panel), you might expect that duplicate vertices automatically are removed/merged if you have a canceled Extrude operation. This isn't the case. Those extruded vertices will remain in place until you move them, so don't assume that you're automatically safe from having doubles when auto-merge is enabled.

Looking at the Toolbar, if you click and hold on the Extrude tool's icon, you have more than one Extrude tool available to you. Your choices are as follows:

» **Extrude Region:** The default Extrude tool is Extrude Region. It works exactly as described earlier in this section. Click the gizmo to extrude your selection. Once extruded, you can tweak your extrusion's position and rotation using regular transform tools.

NEW FEATURE

» **Extrude Manifold:** This is an interesting variation of Blender's extrude functionality. It often happens that when you're modeling mechanical components, sometimes called *hard surface modeling*, you end up extruding over or near existing geometry, and you have to do a lot of clean-up work to remove overlapping geometry, add vertices at intersections, and adjust the positions of neighboring vertices. The Extrude Manifold tool is designed to handle all that grunt work for you. It generally works just like the Extrude Region tool, with more functionality.

» **Extrude Along Normals:** Every component in a mesh has a *normal*, an imaginary line that sticks out orthogonally from that vertex, edge, or face. This tool is most useful when you have multiple faces selected in your mesh. It keeps the components of your selection joined like with the Extrude Region tool, but each face in the new extrusion moves along its own normal. To use this tool, just click and drag in the 3D Viewport, and your selection will extrude accordingly. If you enable the Offset Even check box in the Tool tab of the Properties editor, this extrusion tool is very helpful for architectural and hard surface modeling. Book 2, Chapter 1 has more on normals and the different approaches to modeling.

» **Extrude Individual:** The Extrude Individual tool works like Extrude Along Normals, but your extruded components aren't connected as a cohesive unit. Instead, in the case of faces, each face in your selection extrudes on its own along its own local normals.

» **Extrude to Cursor:** This tool gives you the fastest way to make a long series of extrusions. Say you're modeling tree branches or the profile of a wine glass. The Extrude to Cursor tool is the way to go. Simply click in the 3D Viewport, and your selection extrudes right to that point. If you hold down your mouse button, you can tweak the position of your extrusion as you go. Working this way is particularly useful when you're doing a series of extrusions, one right

Working in Edit Mode
and Object Mode

TIP

after the other, such as when you're roughing out a shape by "drawing" with vertices and edges.

Technically, this tool's feature is also available outside the tool system. While in Edit mode, if you Ctrl+right-click in the 3D Viewport, whatever you have selected is extruded to that location.

For some simple examples of how to make a model using the extrude operator, visit the tutorials I've placed on www.blenderbasics.com.

Modeling organically with Proportional Editing

Often, when you're modeling organic objects or objects with smoothly curved surfaces, such as characters, creatures, or sports cars, you may find yourself pushing and pulling a bunch of vertices to obtain that smooth surface. You can simplify this process by using Blender's *Proportional Editing* feature.

If you come from another 3D package, you might recognize proportional editing as being similar to the *soft select* feature. You activate proportional editing by left-clicking the Proportional Editing button, which looks like two gray concentric circles in the 3D Viewport's header. The hotkey for this operation is O. Now when you perform a transform operation, a circle appears around your selection. Your transformation influences any vertices that are within this circle with a gradual falloff.

You can adjust the influence circle used by proportional editing by scrolling your mouse wheel or pressing Alt+Numpad Plus (+) and Alt+Numpad Minus (−). Additionally, you can control how gradual the falloff is by using the Proportional Editing Falloff roll-out next to the Proportional Editing button in the 3D Viewport's header, or by choosing one of the options that appears in a pie menu when you press Shift+O.

The Proportional Editing feature in Blender has one more useful option. On complex meshes, you may want to use proportional editing on one set of vertices that are connected to each other but not to other nearby vertices in the same mesh. For example, say that you've modeled a character with their hand at their side near their leg, and you'd like to smoothly edit their hand and pull it away from the leg without having to gradually adjust the vertices of the arm. Proportional editing is the perfect tool for this job. However, when you try to use proportional editing as described in the previous paragraphs, other leg vertices are within the influence circle, and you end up moving those unintentionally. Wouldn't it be great if proportional editing could understand that you only want to move the hand? Well, I have good news: It can! Expand the Proportional Editing Falloff pull-down menu in the 3D Viewport header and enable the Connected Only check box. Alternatively, press Alt+O. With the Connected Only option enabled, proportional editing adjusts only vertices connected to each other within its influence area. Neat, huh?

Proportional editing works in Object mode as well. This capability can be really handy, but it can sometimes yield undesirable results if you want to use this feature only while in Edit mode. For this reason, double-check your 3D Viewport's header before performing a transformation to see whether proportional editing is enabled.

Understanding Datablocks: Fundamental Elements in a Blender File

A lot of the features of Blender depend on understanding how Blender files are organized. Your `.blend` file is really a database of interrelated blocks of data, or *datablocks*. Datablocks are used throughout both Blender's interface and its internal structure, so understanding how they work and how you can take advantage of them goes a long way to understanding Blender itself. Nearly every critical element in Blender is stored in a type of datablock, from workspaces and scenes to objects and animations.

Datablocks in Blender are linked together to form a database that efficiently describes what's in your `.blend` file, and you have the ability to control how some of this linking happens. For instance, you can link datablocks and let them share information. As an example, say that you've created an excellent wood material, and you want to have two objects — a table and a chair — look like they're both made of the same wood. Well, rather than re-create that exact same material for each object, you can simply link both object datablocks to the same material datablock. Your computer uses less memory, and, more importantly, you have less work to do. And because datablocks are used throughout Blender, this same concept works in all kinds of situations: sharing textures between materials, sharing particle systems between objects, and even sharing worlds between scenes. You can even share datablocks between `.blend` files. It's an incredibly powerful feature of Blender, and I refer to datablocks a lot throughout this book.

Adding to a Scene

There's got to be more to life than that plain default cube, right? Indeed, there is. Blender offers a whole slew of *primitives*, or basic objects, to build from.

Anytime you add a new object in Blender, the origin of that object is located wherever you place the 3D cursor.

Adding objects

To add a new object to your scene in Object mode, you can use the Add menu in the 3D Viewport's header. However, I find it faster to hover my mouse cursor over the 3D Viewport and use the Shift+A hotkey combination. The menu that appears is the same as the Add menu at the top of the editor but you don't have to move your mouse as far to make a selection. Whichever way you choose to invoke the menu, you're given the option of a wide variety of primitives to put into the scene. You have the following choices:

» **Mesh:** Meshes are polygon-based objects made up of vertices, edges, and faces. They're the most common type of modeling object used in Blender. Book 2, Chapter 1 goes into high detail on modeling with meshes. The majority of other types of primitives listed here are covered in Book 2, Chapter 4.

» **Curve:** Curves are objects made up of curved or straight lines that you manipulate with a set of *control points*. Control points are similar to vertices, but you can edit them in a couple of ways that vertices can't be edited. Blender has two basic forms of curves, Bézier curves and NURBS (Non-Uniform Relational B-Spline) curves. You can also use curves as paths to control other objects.

» **Surface:** A surface is similar to a mesh, but instead of being made up of vertices, edges, and faces, surfaces in Blender are defined by a set of NURBS curves and their control points.

» **Metaball:** Metaball objects are unique primitives with the cool ability to melt into one another and create a larger structure. They're handy for a variety of effects that involve blobby masses, such as clouds or water as well as quick, rough, clay-like models.

» **Text:** The text object allows you to bring typography into your 3D scene and manipulate it like other 3D objects.

» **Grease Pencil:** Grease Pencil objects are an advanced version of Blender's annotation feature that you can use to make 2D images and animations. Book 4, Chapter 6 has a ton more on using Grease Pencil objects.

» **Armature:** Armature objects are skeleton-like structures that consist of linked bones. You can use the bones in an armature to deform other objects. Bones are particularly useful for creating the puppet-like controls necessary for character animation. There's a lot more detail on armatures in Book 4, Chapter 3.

» **Lattice:** Like armature objects, you can use lattices to deform other objects. They're often used in modeling and animation to squash, stretch, and twist models in a non-permanent way.

 » **Empty:** The unsung hero of Blender objects, Empties don't show up in finished renders. Their primary purpose is merely to serve as a reference position, size, and orientation in 3D space. This basic purpose, however, allows them to work as very powerful controls.

 » **Image:** Image objects are special kinds of Empties that can be used for background and reference images while you work.

 » **Light:** Light objects are necessary for lighting your scene. Just like in the physical world, if you don't have any light, you don't see anything.

 » **Light Probe:** Light probe objects are specific to Blender's Eevee renderer. They're used to capture indirect lighting and provide more realism to scenes rendered in Eevee. See Book 3, Chapter 3 for more information on how to use light probe objects.

 » **Camera:** Like real-world cameras, camera objects define the location and perspective from which you're rendering your scene.

 » **Speaker:** You can use a speaker object in your scene to create immersive 3D sound.

 » **Force Field:** In the simplest terms, a *force field* is an Empty that acts like the source of some physical force such as wind or magnetism. Force fields are used primarily with Blender's integrated physics simulation. I briefly touch upon force fields in Book 4, Chapter 5.

 » **Collection Instance:** A collection is a set of objects you define as being related to each other in some way. The objects in a collection don't have to be the same type. Collections are handy for organization as well as appending sets of objects from external files.

WARNING

When adding new objects, be aware of whether you're in Object mode or Edit mode. If you add while in Edit mode, then your add options are limited to the type of object you're editing. That is, if you're in Edit mode on a mesh, you can add only new mesh primitives. Also, your new object's data is joined with the object you're editing. If you don't want the object data to join, make sure that you tab back to Object mode before adding anything new.

Meet Suzanne, the Blender monkey

Many 3D modeling and animation suites have a generic semi-complex primitive used for test renders, benchmarks, and examples that necessitate something a little more complex than a cube or sphere. Most of these other programs use the famous Utah teapot as their test model.

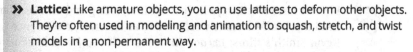

Blender has something a little more interesting and unique. Blender has a monkey head that's affectionately referred to as Suzanne, a reference to the ape in two of Kevin Smith's films: *Jay and Silent Bob Strike Back* and *Mallrats* (close to the end). You can add Suzanne to your scene by pressing Add ➪ Mesh ➪ Monkey. If you look through the Blender community's forums and much of Blender's release documentation, you see Suzanne and references to her all over the place. I happen to know that she's even shown up in an official U.S. patent. Even the annual awards festival at the Blender Conference in Amsterdam is called the Suzanne Awards. Suzanne is a very important monkey. Figure 4-7 shows a test render featuring Suzanne.

FIGURE 4-7:
Suzanne!

If you absolutely *must* have a teapot as your test mesh, you can have that, too. It's in the Extra Objects add-on for meshes. Enable this add-on by going to the Add-ons section of Preferences (Edit ➪ Preferences) and looking in the Add Mesh category. Once enabled, you can find the teapot in the Add menu (Add ➪ Mesh ➪ Extras ➪ Teapot+).

TIP

Joining and separating objects

In the course of creating models for your scenes, you may need to treat separate objects as a single one or break the parts of a single object into their own distinct objects — for example, you may accidentally add a new primitive while you're still in Edit mode. Of course, you can simply undo, tab into Object mode, and re-add your primitive, but why act like you made a mistake and go through all those extra steps?

There's another way. When you add a new primitive while in Edit mode, all the elements of your new primitive are selected, and nothing from your original object is selected. If only there were a command that would let you break this primitive away from the container object and into an object of its own. Fortunately, there is. While in Edit mode, choose Mesh ⇨ Separate ⇨ Selection, and your new primitive is separated into its own object. You can also access this function by hotkey (P ⇨ Selection).

Tab back into Object mode and select your new object. Its origin is located in the same place as its original object's origin. To put the origin of your new object at its actual center, choose Object ⇨ Set Origin ⇨ Origin to Geometry in the 3D Viewport's header. This Origin to Geometry operation checks the size of your object and calculates where its true center is. Then Blender places the object's origin at that location.

You can also specify that the object's origin be placed wherever your 3D cursor is located by choosing Object ⇨ Set Origin ⇨ Origin to 3D Cursor.

A third option is similar to Origin to Geometry, but it moves the object's content rather than the origin itself. Perform this operation by choosing Object ⇨ Set Origin ⇨ Geometry to Origin.

As expected, you can also join two objects of the same type into a single object. To do so, select multiple objects. You can practice using the Box Select or Lasso Select tools, or you can simply Shift+click objects to add them to your selection. The last object you select is considered your *active object* and is the object that the others join into. With your objects selected, join them by choosing Object ⇨ Join from the 3D Viewport's header or by using the Ctrl+J hotkey combination.

REMEMBER

You can join objects of the same type only. That is, you can join two mesh objects, but you can't join a mesh object with a curve object. It's possible to get around this by converting objects to be the same time (Object ⇨ Convert to). However, using parenting or collections (discussed later in this chapter in the section "Discovering parents, children, and collections") may be more appropriate.

Understanding the difference between joins and booleans

This is a bit of a terminology thing. If you've never worked in 3D computer graphics before, you might expect that a join operation on two objects would result in a single, *connected* mesh. That's not quite how it works. Earlier in this chapter, I explain that an object can consist of both linked and unlinked elements. There's no requirement that, for example, all the vertices in a mesh object are linked by faces and edges. When you join two separate objects using Object ⇨ Join, you're really just bundling them into the same object datablock. You aren't changing any of the component mesh data.

To actually merge meshes into a single linked unit, you need to take one of the following approaches:

>> Edit the mesh data manually — merging vertices and creating new edges and faces as necessary.

>> Use a *Boolean* — an operation that does a logical (for example, *and, or, intersection*) combination of two meshes.

   In Blender, Booleans are done with a modifier. Modifiers are covered in more detail in Book 2, Chapter 2.

>> Use Blender's remeshing capabilities, either using the Remesh modifier as covered in Book 2, Chapter 2, or the Remesh operator in Sculpt mode, as covered in Book 2, Chapter 3.

Creating duplicates and links

In the section "Working with linked vertices," earlier in this chapter, an example involved duplicating your selected vertices by using Mesh ⇨ Duplicate. As you may expect, this operation also works in Object mode (the hotkey is the same — Shift+D — but the menu item is slightly different at Object ⇨ Duplicate Objects). This duplication method is great if you intend to take an existing object and use it as a starting point to model another, more individualized object by tweaking it in Edit mode. However, suppose you want your duplicated object to be identical to the original in Edit mode. And wouldn't it be nice if, when you do go into Edit mode, your changes happen to the original *as well as* to all the duplicates? For duplicated objects that you have to edit only once, you want to use the power of *linked duplicates*. Linked duplicates are objects that share the same internal datablocks.

REMEMBER

Linking objects, in this case, is different from the linked vertices described earlier in this chapter. The fact that the same word is used in a couple different ways can be a bit confusing, but there's a mnemonic that can help you keep things straight:

>> Linked vertices (as described earlier in the chapter) are specific to Edit mode.

>> Linked objects (as described in this section) are specific to Object mode.

Linking data between objects

Linked duplicates are similar to what other programs call instance copies. The process to create a linked duplicate is pretty straightforward:

1. **Select the object you want to duplicate.**

2. **With the object selected, choose Object ⇨ Duplicate Linked from the 3D Viewport's header or use the Alt+D hotkey combination.**

   From here, the behavior is just like regular duplication.

   The object is automatically in grab mode.

3. **Place the object with your mouse and confirm its new location by left-clicking or by pressing Enter.**

You can use a few methods to verify that this duplicated object is, in fact, a linked duplicate. The easiest way is to tab into Edit mode on the original object or on any of the duplicates. When you do, any changes you make here immediately and automatically update all the other objects. Figure 4-8 shows three linked duplicates of Suzanne being simultaneously modified in Edit mode.

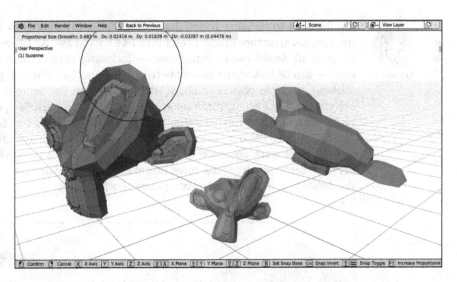

FIGURE 4-8: Editing duplicated Suzannes!

A second way to verify the linked status of duplicates is to look in the Object Data tab of the Properties editor. At the top of this panel, look at the top datablock field. This datablock field gives the name of the mesh datablock that your active object is using. In this case, that mesh datablock is named, appropriately, Suzanne. To the right of the name is the number of objects linked to this datablock. In other words, this number is the count of your linked duplicates. In the case of Figure 4-8, the number is 3. If your datablock is linked to only one object, also known as having one *user*, then there's no number at all. Figure 4-9 shows how this panel looks when one of the Suzannes in the previous figure is selected.

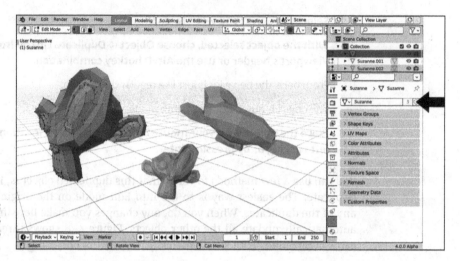

FIGURE 4-9:
Three objects are sharing this datablock.

TECHNICAL STUFF

Another way to visualize linked data in Blender is to consider that Blender treats the internal structure of its .blend files like a database. As I cover earlier in this chapter, all datablocks in your scene — including objects, materials, and mesh data — can be linked and shared between one another. The real power comes in allowing multiple objects to share with each other. For example, you can have objects share materials, mesh data, actions, and even particle systems. And different scenes can even share objects! Taking advantage of this feature not only reduces the size of your .blend files, but it can also seriously reduce the amount of redundant work you have to do. Figure 4-10 shows a data schematic for the previous scene involving the three linked duplicates of Suzanne. You can see how the datablocks in that scene relate to one another.

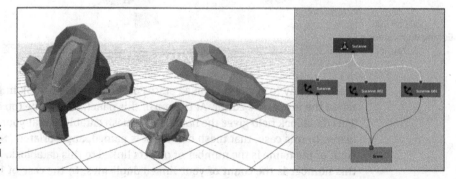

FIGURE 4-10:
A data schematic of linked Suzannes.

So say that you've been using Blender for a while without knowing about linked duplicates, and your .blend file is rife with redundant mesh data. Is there a way to get rid of those regular duplicates and make them linked duplicates? Of course! Follow these steps:

1. **Select all the objects that you want to share the same data.**

   Use any of the selection tools available to you (Box, Circle, Lasso, and Shift+click). All the objects must be of the same type, so you can't have a mesh object and a curve object share the same datablock.

2. **With each desired duplicate selected, add to your selection (Shift+click) the object with the datablock that you want to share with the others.**

   This step makes that last-selected object the active object.

3. **Choose Object ⇨ Link/Transfer Data ⇨ Link Object Data from the 3D Viewport's header menu or press Ctrl+L to open the Link/Transfer Data menu.**

   Kerplooie! All the selected objects now link to the same internal data.

Figure 4-11 shows the preceding process, using a bunch of cubes and a Suzanne object.

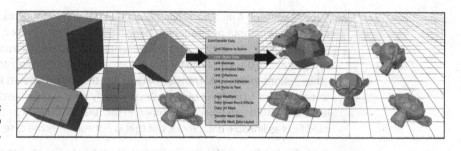

FIGURE 4-11:
Linking cubes to Suzanne.

You probably noticed that the Link/Transfer Data menu had some other interesting options. Following is a description of what each one does:

>> **Link Objects to Scene:** If you have multiple scenes in your .blend file, you can make those scenes share the same objects. This option reveals another menu with all the scenes in the file. By choosing a scene, the object or objects that you selected have linked duplicates created in that other scene.

>> **Link Object Data:** This option is the one you used in the preceding example. Object Data links the internal data — be it a mesh, a curve, a lamp, or nearly any other object — of the selected objects to the internal data of the active object. For this option to work, all the selected objects must be of the same

type. This is the only option where having objects of the same type is important.

>> **Link Materials:** Choosing this option causes all the selected objects to share the same material settings. For more information on materials, see Book 3, Chapter 1.

>> **Link Animation Data:** This option relates directly to animation. It's the set of keyframes that describe the motion of an animated object, called *actions*. (Book 4, Chapter 4 has more information on actions.) Choosing this option causes all your selected objects to share the same actions as the active object.

>> **Link Collections:** In the "Discovering parents, children, and collections" section of this chapter, you see how Blender allows you to organize your objects into collections. Choosing this option puts all the selected objects in the same collection.

>> **Link Instance Collection:** One cool thing about collections is that you can generate them as duplicated instances in a few ways. Choosing this option allows multiple objects to share the same instance collection.

>> **Link Fonts to Text:** This option is specific to text objects. If you want to change the font on a bunch of text objects at the same time, it can be a pretty tedious manual process. However, by choosing this option, you can quickly set the same fonts for all selected text objects.

>> **Copy Modifiers:** A *modifier* is an operation that Blender performs on your object's data without permanently changing that data (see Book 2, Chapter 2). Modifiers allow you to have very complex models that are still manageable, while retaining the simple editability of the original data. Unlike most of the other options in the Link/Transfer Data menu, this option doesn't link the same modifier to multiple objects. What it really does is copy the modifier and its settings from one object to another. In the future, you may be able to treat modifiers as linkable datablocks, but that is not currently the case.

>> **Copy Grease Pencil Effects:** This option is specific to Grease Pencil objects (see Book 4, Chapter 6). Grease Pencil objects can have *effects*, which are similar to modifiers. And like modifiers, this operation doesn't link effects between Grease Pencil objects. Instead, it copies effects from one Grease Pencil object to the other.

>> **Copy UV Maps:** UV maps (covered in Book 3, Chapter 2) are used for mapping a 2D image to the surface of your 3D object. You can share UV coordinate layouts between multiple 3D objects that share the same mesh topology (objects that have the same number and connections between vertices, but not necessarily the same vertex positions).

Like modifiers, this doesn't really link datablocks; it actually copies the UV layout from one mesh to the other. If you edit the layout after that, it only has an effect on the active object.

>> **Transfer Mesh Data:** Mesh objects in Blender can have a variety of different kinds of additional data associated with the core geometry. These data could be vertex groups, UV seams, vertex colors, smoothness values, plus a whole lot more. There are situations where you sometimes want to transfer that data, as best as possible, from one mesh object to another. This operation is how that's done. The actual use of this operator is a bit of an advanced topic, so it's more than I can cover in this book, but there are two keys to using this feature correctly:

- Overlap your meshes. The more your meshes cover the same physical space, the more accurately the data layers will transfer from one to the other.

- Use the Last Operator panel. This feature doesn't work unless you tell it what data you want to transfer. You tell Blender what that data is from the Last Operator panel.

>> **Transfer Mesh Data Layout:** This operator is similar to Transfer Mesh Data, but instead of trying to copy the actual data, it just copies the layers that hold that data so you have consistency in the name and number of layers between objects.

Unlinking datablocks

Of course, if Blender has a way to create links and duplicates, you'd logically (and correctly) think that you can convert a linked duplicate into an object with its own, non-shared datablock. In Blender, this process is called giving that datablock a single user.

The reason for the *single user* terminology goes back to how these datablocks are tied together. From the perspective of the datablock, each object that's connected to it is considered a user. Refer to Figure 4-11: Each Cube object is a user of the Suzanne datablock. By choosing to use the Make Single User operator, you're effectively telling Blender to duplicate that datablock and make sure that it connects to only a single object. To make an object have single user data, select the object you want and then choose Object ⇨ Relations ⇨ Make Single User in the 3D Viewport's header. You see a menu with the following options:

>> **Object:** Use this option when you have an object linked to multiple scenes and you want to make changes to it that appear only in the specific scene that you're currently working on.

>> **Object & Data:** For cases like the preceding example with the linked Suzanne meshes where you have a linked duplicate that you'd like to edit independently of the other meshes, choose this option. Doing so effectively converts a linked duplicate into a regular duplicate.

>> **Object & Data & Materials:** If you have an object that is not only sharing internal object data with others, but also sharing material settings, choose this option, and both those datablocks are duplicated and singly linked to your selected object. Using this option is a pretty good way to make sure that your selected object isn't sharing with any other objects at all.

>> **Materials:** In cases where you no longer want to share materials between objects, choosing this option makes sure that your selected object has its own material settings independent of all the other objects.

>> **Object Animation:** This option is the inverse of the Make Links ⇨ Animation Data option. If your selected object is sharing actions with any other objects, choosing this option makes sure that it has actions of its own.

>> **Object Data Animation:** This option is similar to Object Animation; however, it applies only to values that you've animated in the Object Data context of the Properties editor.

REMEMBER

Another way to make object data a single user is to use the datablock buttons in Blender's interface. In Figure 4-9, the number 3 is highlighted showing that three objects share that particular datablock. If you left-click that number, you make that a single user datablock. This little button shows up in many places throughout the Blender interface. The datablocks that it operates on vary with context (for example, seeing this button in the Material tab of the Properties editor means that it's working on a material datablock; seeing it in the Dope Sheet means that it's working on actions, and so on), but it always means the same thing: Create a datablock like this one that has only the selected object as its user.

There is one other way to make object data a single user: Use the Outliner. Right-click an object data entry and choose ID Data ⇨ Make Single User from the menu that appears. There are a few datablocks (such as material actions) where this is the only clear way to make them single user.

Discovering parents, children, and collections

Working in 3D, you may encounter many situations where you'll want a set of objects to behave like a single organizational group. Now, if the objects are all the same type, you can join them into a single object, but even with the L and Shift+L linked selection operations in Edit mode, this approach can get unwieldy. Joining them into a single object requires you to tab into Edit mode each time you want to work with an individual item. That's not very efficient, and it doesn't give you the flexibility of working with different kinds of objects as a single unit. The better way to organize your objects is with parent-child relationships or with collections.

TIP

Blender has the ability to have multiple objects in Edit mode at the same time. This feature certainly helps when trying to model an object consisting of multiple parts, but even with this handy feature, there are times when parenting and collections are a better course of action.

Establishing parent-child relationships between objects

Creating parent-child relationships between objects or *parenting* in Blenderese, organizes the objects hierarchically. An object can have any number of children, but no object can have more than a single parent. To make an object a parent, follow these steps:

1. **Select the objects you want to be children.**

   They don't have to be of the same type.

2. **Make your last selection (the active object) the object that you want to become the parent.**

3. **Choose Object ⇨ Parent ⇨ Object in the 3D Viewport's header menu or use the Ctrl+P ⇨ Object hotkey combination.**

   After you confirm the operation by left-clicking or pressing Enter, Blender adds a dotted line from the origin of each child object to the origin of the parent. Now when you select just the parent object and perform a transform operation on it, it affects each of its children. However, if you select a child object and transform it, none of the other children or the parent object is influenced.

TIP

A good mnemonic device for remembering the correct order for selecting objects when you want to create a parent-child relationship is to think of the order people get off of a boat when they're abandoning ship: "Children first!"

Parenting is a great way to organize a set of objects that have a clear hierarchy. For example, say that you've modeled a dinner table and the chairs to go around it. Now you want to place that table and chairs in a room, but the room is scaled much smaller than the table and chairs. Rather than select, scale, grab, and move each object into place, you can parent each of the chairs to the table. Then you can just select and transform the table. When you do so, all the chairs transform right along with it, as if they were a single object! Woohoo!

To clear a parent relationship, the process is only two steps:

1. **Select the child object that you want to remove from the hierarchy.**

2. **Choose Object ⇨ Parent ⇨ Clear Parent in the 3D Viewport's header or press Alt+P to clear the parent relationship.**

If you use the hotkey, you see a pop-up menu with three options:

- **Clear Parent:** This option removes the parent-child relationship between your selected object and its parent. If the parent object was transformed after the parenting took place, the cleared child jumps back to the position, scale, and rotation that it was in before it was parented.

- **Clear and Keep Transformation:** This option behaves the same as Clear Parent, except any transformations that were made while the selected object was a child are applied. This means that the cleared child does *not* snap back to its original pre-parented state. Aside from the dashed relationship line between the former child and parent disappearing, nothing should appear to change in your 3D scene.

- **Clear Parent Inverse:** This option is a bit tricky to understand. It actually does not remove the link between the selected child object and its parent. Instead, it basically clears the parent's transformation from the child. Clear Parent Inverse is handy for situations where you've transformed an object before parenting it, and you want it to relate to the parent as if it had not been transformed prior to parenting. To be honest, I don't use this option very often, but it's certainly good to have around when you need it.

TIP

Another quick way of parenting within Blender is from the Outliner. The fastest way is by holding Shift while you drag and drop one object to another in the Outliner. Of course, if you find that you're doing a lot of parenting, it may be annoying to keep holding Shift. You can eliminate this annoyance by changing the Outliner's display mode. By default, the Outliner uses the View Layer display mode. To change its display mode, click the Display Mode drop-down menu at the top of the Outliner. In this case, you want to choose the Scenes display mode. Now, from the Scenes display mode of the Outliner, you can left-click the icon of any object and drag it over the name of another object in the Outliner (essentially dropping it in like copying a file into a folder on your computer's file browser). That action automatically creates a parent-child relationship between the two objects. On complex scenes, this is an extremely handy trick.

TIP

Many game engines and other 3D applications have a notion of grouping that's very different from how Blender works. They tend to treat all members of a group as a single unit, regardless of which one gets selected. They also tend to treat groups hierarchically; an object can only belong to one group (in turn, that group can be a member of another group, but the base object is still only a member of one). In fact, this behavior is a lot more like Blender's parenting. To mimic this behavior more seamlessly, follow these steps:

1. **Create an Empty object near the center of your "grouping" of objects and display it as a cube (Add ⇨ Empty ⇨ Cube).**

2. Adjust the size of the Empty from the Last Operator panel (it's the Radius value) to roughly include all the objects in your grouping.

3. Name the Empty something clever to indicate the grouping's name.

4. Make all objects you're grouping a child of the Empty (select each object, select the Empty, Ctrl+P ⇨ Object).

With this bit of legwork done, you can select the Empty's cube outline to transform your whole grouping. Even better, your grouping will be hierarchically organized in the Scenes display mode of the Outliner. Many game-engine export scripts properly recognize and translate this structure to their native means of grouping.

Creating collections

Of course, under some circumstances, parenting doesn't make sense for organizing a set of objects. A good example is a lighting setup that you want to adjust and reuse. Sure, you can rationalize that perhaps the key light is the most important light and, therefore, should be the parent, but that logic is a bit of a stretch and doesn't make much sense in more complex setups. You could also add an Empty to the scene and parent all your lights to it. That solution works, but what if you wanted to make a duplicate instance of that light rig?

For these cases, Blender's *collections* feature is ideal. You may not be aware of this, but if you've been working in Blender, you've been using collections all along. Fire up a new Blender session and have a look at the Outliner. You should see something like what's shown in Figure 4-12. By default, all Blender sessions start with two collections: a Scene Collection that binds objects to a particular scene in your .blend file, and a general collection — named Collection — within that scene. All the default objects (the cube, camera, and light) are part of the collection.

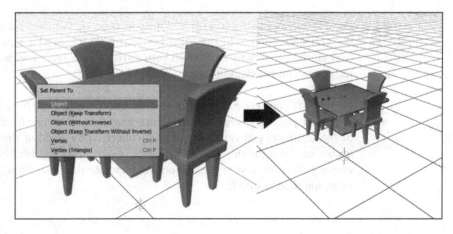

FIGURE 4-12: The Outliner is where you manage collections. Four chapters into this book, and you've been using them all along!

REMEMBER

If you're coming from another 3D application, you might think of collections like groups or layers, but they're so much more than that in Blender. Collections are not only a great way to organize your scenes, but they're also an integral part of other processes in Blender such as instancing and compositing.

Even with just the one collection in your scene, there are a few things you may want to do from the Outliner. For the first thing, I *strongly* recommend that you rename your collection to something that makes sense to you. Nothing is more confusing than opening an old project and seeing your collections named Collection, Collection 1, Collection 2, and so on.

To rename a collection, double-click its name in the Outliner and type the new name you'd like to use. You can't do this with the scene collection, but any collection within the scene is fair game.

Looking back at Figure 4-12, notice also that the collection has a check box to the left of its name and an eye icon to the right of it. Both these controls seem to have a similar effect on the objects in the 3D Viewport, but in application, they're used very differently. The check box is specific to how the collection relates to your current view layer used when rendering and compositing (see Book 5, Chapter 2 for more on view layers). If you disable the check box, that collection is basically disabled for this part of your scene. The eye icon will also hide the objects from your scene if you click on it to disable it, but the difference is that those objects aren't disabled, they're just not currently visible in the 3D Viewport.

To test the difference between these two controls, disable one and then render your scene (Render ⇨ Render Image). Then re-enable it and disable the other before rendering again. You should notice that when you disable the check box, nothing appears when you render, but when you click the eye icon to close it, your objects in the collection still appear when you render.

TIP

For a faster way to control the visibility of collections in your scene, you can use the Collections panel in the View tab of the 3D Viewport's Sidebar. That panel lists all the collections enabled in your current view layer and provides you with toggles to control visibility.

Playing with one collection is fun and all, but it's when you have multiple collections that you can really see this feature sing. From the View Layers display mode of the Outliner, you can create a new collection by clicking the New Collection button on the right side of the Outliner's header. Clicking this button adds a new empty collection to your scene. You can populate that collection by dragging and dropping objects into it.

Of course, you're not always working in the Outliner. Sometimes the Outliner is hidden or you're working with a maximized 3D Viewport (Ctrl+Spacebar) and you don't want to shrink it just to see the Outliner. Fortunately, you can also manage collections from the 3D Viewport. The easiest way to create a new collection from the 3D Viewport is to move one or more objects to it. Follow these steps:

1. **Select all the objects you want to include in the new collection.**

As an example, say you want the lights in your scene to be in their own collection, so you start off by selecting all your lights.

2. **Choose Object ⇨ Collection ⇨ Move to Collection or use the M hotkey.**

A secondary menu appears with a list of your current collections in your scene. Choose the menu item at the top that says New Collection. A pop-up will appear where you can name your new collection. In this example, you might choose to name that collection Lights. After you confirm the collection's name by clicking OK, all your selected objects are moved to your new collection.

Looking in the Outliner, you should now see that your selected objects (in this example, your lights) are no longer in your original collection, but in your newly added one. You can also go to the Object tab of the Properties editor and look in the Collections panel to see what collections an object belongs to.

Actually, this is an important point that highlights another example of how collections and parenting differ. Whereas an object can have only one parent, it can be a member of any number of collections. Let me write that again for emphasis. *An object can belong to multiple collections.*

You might find yourself wondering what possible uses there could be for having objects be members of multiple collections. The simple (but not easy) explanation is scene organization. This is especially true as your scenes become more and more complex. You may have a scene full of foliage. Each tree, flower, and shrub is part of a corresponding collection, each named "trees", "flowers", and "shrubs". Now say you're doing a little physics simulation on that scene, and you only want the tallest trees and shrubs to be affected by that wind force. You wouldn't want to pull your trees and shrubs from their collections to a collection called "physics". It would be much better if those trees and shrubs could be members of both collections.

If you choose the Object ⇨ Collection menu, you have a number of options:

» **Move to Collection (M):** This menu item invokes the operator used in the preceding example. Whatever objects you have selected get moved to another collection, either pre-existing or new.

>> **Link to Collection (Shift+M):** This operator is similar to moving your selection to a collection, but it does so without being removed from any collections your selected objects are already members of. This is how you get an object to be part of multiple collections.

>> **Create New Collection (Ctrl+G):** This option is always available and creates a new collection, adding your selected objects to it. Be warned, though. As of this writing, when you add a new collection with this menu item, it doesn't show up in the Outliner, even though you can plainly see it in the Object tab of the Properties editor. For the time being, I'd suggest that you avoid using this menu item.

>> **Remove from Collection (Ctrl+Alt+G):** This option is always available, and choosing it removes the selected objects from any collections they may be a member of. Removing all objects from all collections doesn't delete those collections while your Blender session is still active.

>> **Remove from All Collections (Shift+Ctrl+Alt+G):** This is a quick shortcut to remove the selected objects from all the collections they may be a member of.

>> **Add Selected to Active Collection (Shift+Ctrl+G):** To use this feature, you need to pay attention to which object is your active object (hint: it's the most recent object you've selected). Then any objects you have selected become members of all the collections your active object is a member of.

>> **Remove Selected from Active Collection (Shift+Alt+G):** Choose this option, and all your selected objects (including the active object) are removed from any collections in the active object.

TIP

In addition to having objects as members of multiple collections, you can also nest collections within each other to give yourself a bit of a hierarchical organization. The easiest way to nest collections within one another is through the Outliner. Simply click and drag one collection into another, and then that collection and all the objects in it becomes a member of the collection you moved it into.

Using collections

You can actually use collections for more than just organizing your scene. They're also a pretty incredible tool for sharing data between .blend files and even making scenes in one file more efficient. A big part of this ability comes from a feature in Blender called *collection instances*. Recall that earlier in the chapter, I say that linked data between objects is sometimes called instancing in other 3D applications. While that's true, collection instances are even closer to that phenomenon. Basically, you can add a copy of all the objects in a collection to your Blender scene all in one shot. Even better, that collection instance *does* act like a single object, similar to groups in other applications.

It's easiest to understand how this works with an example. So, first create a simple scene with a new collection by following these steps:

1. Start a new Blender session in the General workflow template (if you already have Blender open, choose File ⇨ New ⇨ General).

2. Add a mesh cone to the scene (Add ⇨ Mesh ⇨ Cone).

Assuming you haven't moved the 3D cursor, the cone should be inside the cube.

3. Move the cone up the Z-axis.

You can use the Move tool or press G ⇨ Z to move it up. Your scene should look a little bit like your cube has a dunce cap.

4. Add the cube to your selection by Shift+left-clicking it.

5. Add your cube and cone to a new collection (Object ⇨ Collection ⇨ Move to Collection ⇨ New Collection).

Name the collection something memorable, like "dunce cube", and click OK.

Now that you have a collection, you can start doing things with it. The first option at your disposal is creating an instance of that collection. Follow these steps:

1. Place the 3D cursor somewhere in the 3D Viewport (Shift+right-click).

It doesn't really matter where at this point, as long as it's not at the origin where your original objects currently live.

2. Go to Add ⇨ Collection Instance in the 3D Viewport's header.

You should see your new collection (in this example, the one named "dunce cube") listed there.

3. Click the menu item for your collection to add an instance of it at the location of the 3D cursor in your scene.

You can repeat the previous steps as many times as you'd like to create multiple instances of your collection. These collection instances are selectable as single objects, and when you transform or otherwise edit the original objects in that collection, those changes are reflected in every instance.

There are more controls for your collection in the Properties editor. If you select your collection in the Outliner, the Collection tab should appear in the Properties editor. This context gives you more fine-grained control over the behavior of your collection. I get into some of these features in other parts of this book. The Restrictions panel is most related to view layers and compositing (Book 5, Chapter 2), and the Line Art panel relates to non-photorealistic rendering (covered briefly in Book 3, Chapter 1). The most relevant panel to this chapter, however, is the Instancing panel. From this panel, you can offset the geometry within your instance relative to the collection instance's origin.

TECHNICAL STUFF

Technically speaking, a collection instance is really just an Empty object in Blender with some extra settings preconfigured to display your collection at the location of the Empty. You can confirm this by making your own collection instance by hand, using the following steps:

1. **Place the 3D cursor somewhere in a vacant part of your scene (Shift+right-click).**

2. **In the Outliner, select the default Collection.**

   This step ensures that your Empty isn't a member of the collection that you're trying to instance.

3. **Add a new Empty object (Add ⇨ Empty ⇨ Plain Axes).**

4. **In the Object Data tab of the Properties editor, expand the Instancing panel and click the Collection button.**

   The panel should expand with more options.

5. **From the Collection datablock drop-down, choose your new collection (in the previous example, that would be the collection named "dunce cube."**

   Immediately, the objects from your collection appear at the location of your Empty object.

Now you know a little bit more about the inner workings of Blender. Neat, huh?

Selecting with parents and collections

When you're using parenting and collections, you gain the ability to rapidly select your objects according to their groupings. Choose Select ⇨ Select Grouped or press Shift+G, and you see a menu with a variety of options:

>> **Children:** If you have a parent object selected, choosing this option adds all that object's children to the list of selected objects while deselecting the parent object.

>> **Immediate Children:** Similar to selecting all children, except this option traverses down the hierarchy by one step only. Children of children are not added to the selection.

>> **Parent:** If the object you've selected has a parent object, that parent is selected.

>> **Siblings:** This option is useful for selecting all the children of a single parent. It does not select the parent object, nor does it select any children that these sibling objects may have.

>> **Type:** This option is useful for making very broad selections. Use Type when you want to select all lights or all meshes or armatures in a scene. This option bases its selection on the type of object you currently have as your active object.

>> **Collection:** Use this option to select objects that live in the same collections. If an object is in multiple collections, any objects that share any collection with your selected object are added to the selection.

>> **Hook:** If you've added *hooks*, which are objects that control selected vertices or control points in an object, this option selects them. You can find more information on hooks in Book 4, Chapter 3.

>> **Pass:** Similar to layers, objects may have a Pass Index value that is useful for compositing and post-production work in Blender. Choosing this option selects any objects that share the active object's Pass Index value. You can find more information on passes and the Pass Index in Book 5, Chapter 2.

>> **Color:** This option allows you to select objects that have the same color, regardless of whether or not they link to the same material datablock.

>> **Keying Set:** *Keying sets* (covered more in Book 4, Chapter 1) are used for organizing a group of objects and properties for animation. They're properties that all have keyframes set at the same time. This option selects all objects that share the current object's keying set.

>> **Light Type:** This option is similar to the Type option, though it's specific to lights. If you currently have a light selected, choosing this option also selects any lights of the same type (such as Spot, Point, Area, and so on).

Saving, opening, and appending

Quite possibly the most important feature in any piece of software is the ability to save and open files. Having quick access to saving and opening files was especially useful for early versions of Blender, which lacked any sort of undo function. Blender users learned very quickly to save early, save often, and save multiple versions of their project files. One beneficial side effect of this history is that Blender reads and writes its files *very* quickly, even for complex scenes, so you rarely ever have to wait more than a second or two to get to work or save your project.

To save to a new file, choose File ⇨ Save As from the main header or use the Shift+Ctrl+S hotkey combination. One strange thing you may notice is that

Blender doesn't open the familiar system save dialog that Windows, Mac, or Linux uses. This is for a couple reasons. Because Blender uses its own File Browser interface, you can be guaranteed that no matter what kind of computer you use, Blender always looks and behaves the same on each platform. As another point, the Blender File Browser has some neat Blender-specific features that aren't available in the default OS save dialogs.

Take a look at the File Browser shown in Figure 4-13. The header for this editor features an assortment of buttons for navigating your hard drive's directory structure and filtering the files shown. If you've used the file browser that comes with your operating system, most of these buttons should be familiar to you. The options in the side region on the left of the File Browser are there to give you shortcuts to various locations on your computer's hard drive.

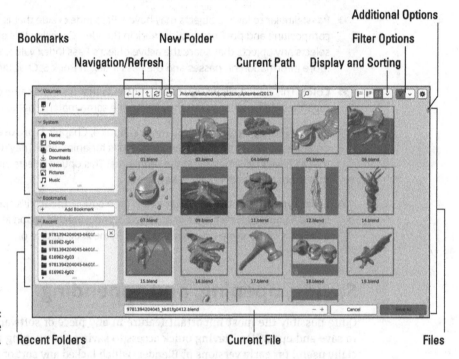

FIGURE 4-13:
The Blender File Browser.

The largest portion of the File Browser is devoted to actually showing files and folders. The topmost text field in this region is the current path on your hard drive to the folder/directory you're currently viewing. At the bottom of the File Browser is the text field for the actual name of your file. In this field, type your project's name. Pressing Enter or clicking the Save As button at the bottom right corner saves the file for you. Between the header and Current File text field is a list of the files in the current folder. Figure 4-13 shows the Blender File Browser and labels the various buttons in it.

By default, Blender pops up the File Browser as a child of the main Blender window. Although this behavior is familiar if you use other applications, it breaks the general non-blocking philosophy of the Blender interface. If you want to retain the single-window approach, you can go to the Interface section of Preferences (Edit ⇨ Preferences), and within the Temporary Editors sub-section, you can set File Browser to Maximized Area rather than its default of New Window.

Saving after the first time

After you save your `.blend` file once, saving gets much quicker. To do a fast save while you're working, choose File ⇨ Save or, even faster, press Ctrl+S.

On larger projects, however, you may not want to continually overwrite the same file. In those cases, it's sometimes more favorable to save progressive versions of your project as you work on it. You can open the File Browser and type a new name for each version — but it's slow. Often, when people save versions of a project file, they usually append a number to the end of the filename (for example, `file1.blend`, `file2.blend`, `file3.blend`, and so on). Blender knows this habit and aims to help you out.

The ultra-fast way is with the following hotkey sequence: Shift+Ctrl+S ⇨ Numpad Plus (+) ⇨ Enter. Pressing Numpad Plus (+) while in the File Browser automatically appends that number to your filename for you. And if the file already has a number, it increments it by one. For logical consistency, pressing Numpad Minus (–) decrements that value. How's that for speedy? If you prefer to use your mouse, you can also perform the same function in the File Browser by left-clicking the Plus (+) and Minus (–) buttons after the filename text field. In Blender 4.0, you can access this feature even faster using File ⇨ Save Incremental.

Opening a file

Opening a `.blend` file is a straightforward task. Choose File ⇨ Open or press Ctrl+O. The File Browser opens again and allows you to choose which file you want to load. To load the file, left-click the filename and click the Open Blender File button in the upper right corner. If you have a large monitor and don't want to move your mouse that far, or you're just interested in speedy shortcuts, you can quickly select and open a file by double-clicking it.

Appending from an external file

Now, what if you have a model of a really excellent character saved in one `.blend` file, and you'd like to bring it into a scene that you've been working on in another `.blend` file? Wouldn't it be convenient if you could bring that character in and not have to remodel it from scratch? Of course it would! This capability is precisely what Blender's Append feature is for.

To append an item from an external file, click File ⇨ Append. The File Browser opens, but now when you click on a .blend file, you can actually drill down into its structure. You can select any datablock in the file and bring it — as well as anything it's linked to — into your project. So if you select an object, you append that object, its object data (mesh, curve, and so on), any materials and textures it may have, and any animation linked to it. If you want to append just a material or texture, you can do that, too!

TIP

Appending works very well. However, on large projects it often makes more sense to reference, or *link*, an asset rather than fully copy it in with appending. Blender allows you to make a reference that points to the datablock in the original file by clicking File ⇨ Link. It works just like appending, but instead of copying the data-block into your .blend file, you're merely making a reference to that datablock in the other file. I like to call this reference a *linked appendage*. The advantage of a linked appendage is that any changes you make to the original file are automatically updated in the file that links to it. These updates are really quite handy in large projects where you have a variety of models, materials, and other resources that you'd like to use over and over again. This way of working is fantastic for large collaborative projects like animated short films.

TIP

If you've read through this chapter, you may have noticed that the term "link" is used in three very different ways within Blender. You have linked vertices in Edit mode, linked duplicates in Object mode, and now linked assets between .blend files. It can be a bit confusing. However, if you think about it in terms of scope and context, that can help you keep things organized in your mind. The following mini-table tries to illustrate.

Scope	Link Type	Other Common Term
File/Asset	Linked appendage	Linked object or linked data
Object mode	Linked duplicate	Instance copy
Edit mode	Linked vertices	Connected vertices

When a collection is made to a linked appendage, the linking file creates an Empty and binds the collection reference to that as kind of a child, known as a collection instance (I briefly touch on collection instances earlier in this chapter in the "Discovering parents, children, and collections" section). With this scheme, you can successfully transform and even animate your linked collection. For a lot more on linking and appending, have a look at Book 6, Chapter 1.

The moral of this story: If you're appending with links, it's probably in your best interest to create a collection in the original file and create a linked appendage to that collection from your new file. Using links to collections in external files is the primary way artists use assets on medium-to-large animation projects.

2
Creating Detailed 3D Scenes

Contents at a Glance

Chapter 1

Creating Anything You Can Imagine with Meshes

Polygon-based meshes are at the core of nearly every piece of computer-generated 3D artwork, from video games and architectural visualization to television commercials and feature-length films. Computers typically handle meshes more quickly than other types of 3D objects like NURBS or metaballs (see Book 2, Chapter 4), and meshes are generally a lot easier to control. In fact, when it comes down to it, even NURBS and metaballs are converted to a mesh of triangles — a process called *tessellation* — when the computer hardware processes them.

For these reasons, meshes are the primary foundation for most of Blender's functionality. Whether you're building a small scene, creating a character for animation, or simulating water pouring into a sink, you'll ultimately be working with meshes. Working with meshes can get a bit daunting if you're not careful because you have to control each vertex that makes up your mesh. The more complex the mesh, the more vertices you have to keep track of. Book 1, Chapter 4 gives you a lot of the basics for working with meshes in Edit mode, but this chapter exposes handy Blender features that help you work with complex meshes without drowning in a crazy vertex soup.

Pushing Vertices

A *mesh* consists of a set of vertices connected by edges. Edges connect to each other to form faces. (Book 1, Chapter 4 covers this in more detail, along with how to work with each of these mesh building blocks.) When you tab into Edit mode or switch to the Modeling workspace on a mesh, you can manipulate that mesh's vertices (or edges or faces) with the same basic move, rotate, and scale tools that work on all objects in the 3D Viewport, as well as the handy extrude tool. These actions form the basis for 3D modeling, so much so that some modelers refer to themselves as *vert pushers* because sometimes it seems that all they do is move little points around on a screen until things look right.

Of course, modeling has more to it. You actually have a choice between three primary methodologies when it comes to modeling:

>> **3D sculpting and retopology:** This approach to modeling has taken hold of the 3D computer graphics world to the point that it's now the dominant method in which 3D models are created. The process works like this: Using specialized sculpting tools in 3D software, you start by creating a model with no regard at all for *topology* or how the vertices, edges, and faces are arranged in your mesh. And Then after arriving at the form you want for your model, you *retopologize* (retopo for short), creating a second mesh with cleaner topology based on the shape and form of your sculpt. The retopo step uses a combination of specialized retopo tools and the traditional modeling methods described in the following bullets. Initially, this technique may sound like you're doing double the work, but it almost always produces better results and is a much more comfortable way to work for artists with a traditional art background. See Book 2, Chapter 3 for more details on this technique.

>> **Box modeling:** As its name indicates, *box modeling* starts with a rough shape — typically a box or cube. By adding edges and moving them around, the artist forms that rough shape into the desired model. Bit by bit, you refine the model, adding more and more detail with each pass.

This technique tends to appeal to people with a background in traditional sculpture or carving because the processes are similar. They're both primarily subtractive in nature because you start with a rough shape and bring about more detail by cutting into it and reducing that shape's volume. If you need to add more volume to the mesh outside of the initial box shape, you select a set of edges or faces and extrude or pull them out. If you need to bring part of the mesh in from the initial box shape, you select those edges or faces and either extrude inward or just pull them in. Box modeling is a great way to get started in modeling, but you run a danger of ending up with really blocky models if you aren't careful about how you move your edges around.

>> **Point-for-point modeling:** Point-for-point modeling consists of deliberately placing each and every vertex that comprises the model and creating the edges and faces that connect these vertices. The process is actually not as bad as it sounds. You can think about point-for-point modeling like drawing in three dimensions. And as you may expect, this technique appeals to people who come from a drawing background (or control freaks like me!). The advantage of this method is that you can control the final look of your model, and you're less inclined to end up with a boxy shape. However, some beginner modelers fall into the trap of getting too detailed too quickly with this technique, so you have to be careful.

The especially cool thing is that Blender supports all three of these basic modeling techniques so you can use any one of them. Or, even better, you have the freedom to take a hybrid approach and combine them as needed while you work. Figure 1-1 shows the difference between a rough human head started with box modeling techniques, a point-for-point method, and sculpting.

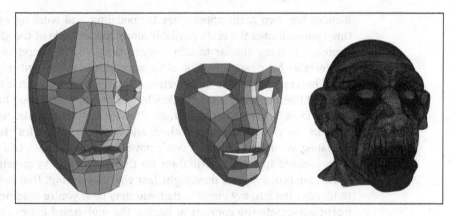

FIGURE 1-1:
From left to right, box modeling, point-for-point modeling, and sculpting a simple human head.

REMEMBER

Regardless of all the tools covered in this chapter, remember that one of Blender's most powerful modeling tools is the humble Extrude operator, as covered in Book 1, Chapter 4. In fact, the vast majority of your modeling workflow in Edit mode can be covered with just a few operators:

>> **Extrude (E):** As covered in the previous chapter, you can use the various Extrude operators in the Vertex, Edge, and Face menus to extend geometry from existing components in your mesh.

>> **New Edge/Face from Vertices (F):** If you select two vertices and press F (or choose Vertex ⇨ New Edge/Face from Vertices), Blender creates an edge between those vertices. If you select three or more vertices and run the same operator, Blender creates a face or an ngon from those vertices.

>> **Duplicate (Shift+D):** Any geometry you have in your object can be duplicated with the Shift+D hotkey combination or by choosing Mesh ⇨ Duplicate. From there, you can do further extruding and face or edge creation.

>> **Delete (X):** The variety of delete and dissolve features available when you press X or choose Mesh ⇨ Delete is amazingly large. The biggest thing to remember is that Delete operators completely remove components, whereas Dissolve operators try to remove components between linked vertices.

>> **Connect Vertex Path (J):** If you have two vertices on the same face that aren't already connected by an edge, you can explicitly add that edge by pressing J (as in *join*) or by choosing Vertex ⇨ Connect Vertex Path.

All the other modeling operators and tools in Blender are basically more convenient ways of chaining these basic operators together.

Getting familiar with Edit mode tools

Blender has two main approaches to modeling and working in 3D in general. One approach uses the tools available along the left side of the 3D Viewport. This approach is more similar to other applications and is, therefore, typically more comfortable for new users. The other approach is almost entirely based on keyboard hotkeys and mouse movements. Although this approach is often faster with a skilled Blender user, it often takes longer to learn. The good news is that both are available. Whereas in the past, an effective Blender modeler would be required to make use of all manner of hotkeys and "finger gymnastics" to make a model, the latest versions of Blender don't have that requirement. Of course, the older hotkey-based approach is still there for those of us who've grown to love it for its direct, unobtrusive, and downright fast way of working. However, if you're new to Blender (which, my guess is that you may be if you're reading this book), you might appreciate the comfort of having the tool-based approach available. This section focuses on that approach.

TIP

When you tab into Edit mode or switch to the Modeling workspace, the 3D Viewport's toolbar expands to provide you with a wide assortment of tools for mesh editing. In fact, depending on the size of your computer screen, there may be more tools there than you have screen space to see. You could certainly use your mouse's scroll wheel to scroll up and down the whole Toolbar, but that approach could get really annoying, especially if you happen to be working with a pen-based tablet interface. Fortunately, there's a workaround. If you move your mouse cursor to the rightmost edge of the Toolbar, you should notice that the mouse cursor changes to a pair of arrows pointing left and right. Click and drag from there, and you're able to expand the width of the Toolbar. If you pull to the right about double the size of the Toolbar, you'll get two columns of tool buttons. Pull even farther and the Toolbar goes back to being a single column, but with text descriptions of each tool. For working on smaller computer screens, I recommend using the two-column variation. Figure 1-2 shows the expanded versions of the Toolbar when in Edit mode.

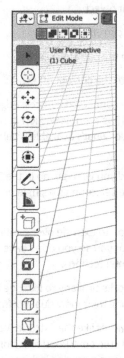
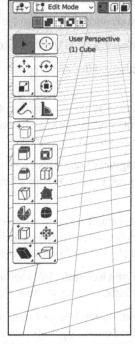
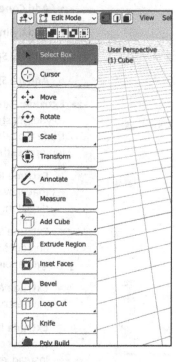

FIGURE 1-2:
You can expand the Toolbar in Blender's 3D Viewport by clicking its border and dragging to the right.

If you notice, the tools in the Toolbar have a color coding. Tools with a green accent are tools that add geometry to your mesh, whereas tools with a violet accent modify existing geometry. I go into detail on a few frequently used tools later in this chapter, but the following is a quick list of all the mesh editing tools available to you in the Toolbar.

NEW
FEATURE

>> **Add Primitive:** Although you can add primitive objects to your object using the Add menu in the 3D Viewport, the Add Primitive tools give a more pleasant visual interface for adding these geometric forms. When you choose any of these tools, a small grid appears under your mouse cursor in the 3D Viewport. The cool thing is that this grid doesn't just snap to the XY plane of the global coordinate system. It also snaps to the surface of any other object in the 3D Viewport so you can "grow" your primitive from the surface of that other object. All these tools work by first left-clicking and dragging to draw a rectangle that defines the base dimensions of the primitive. When you release your mouse button, you can define the height of the primitive object. Hold

Shift while working to make a primitive with even proportions. Hold Alt while working to grow from the center of the primitive rather than a corner. You have the option of adding any of the following primitives:

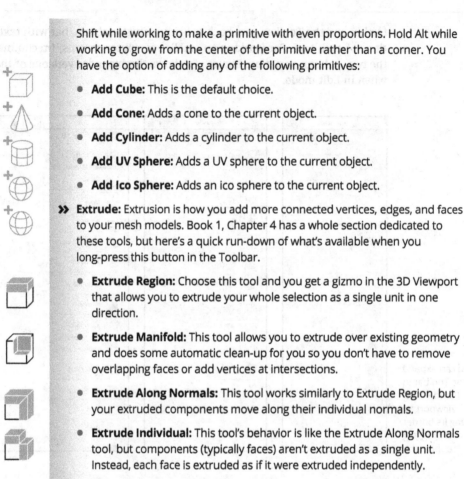

- **Add Cube:** This is the default choice.

- **Add Cone:** Adds a cone to the current object.

- **Add Cylinder:** Adds a cylinder to the current object.

- **Add UV Sphere:** Adds a UV sphere to the current object.

- **Add Ico Sphere:** Adds an ico sphere to the current object.

» **Extrude:** Extrusion is how you add more connected vertices, edges, and faces to your mesh models. Book 1, Chapter 4 has a whole section dedicated to these tools, but here's a quick run-down of what's available when you long-press this button in the Toolbar.

- **Extrude Region:** Choose this tool and you get a gizmo in the 3D Viewport that allows you to extrude your whole selection as a single unit in one direction.

- **Extrude Manifold:** This tool allows you to extrude over existing geometry and does some automatic clean-up for you so you don't have to remove overlapping faces or add vertices at intersections.

- **Extrude Along Normals:** This tool works similarly to Extrude Region, but your extruded components move along their individual normals.

- **Extrude Individual:** This tool's behavior is like the Extrude Along Normals tool, but components (typically faces) aren't extruded as a single unit. Instead, each face is extruded as if it were extruded independently.

- **Extrude to Cursor:** With this tool, your selection is extruded as a single unit, but directly to the location of where you click your mouse cursor in the 3D Viewport.

» **Inset Faces:** Whereas your typical extrude operation adds more faces to your model and then automatically lets you move them around, the Inset Faces tool is more like extruding and immediately scaling to add geometry within a selected set of faces. There's more detail on using the Inset Faces tool later in this section.

» **Bevel:** There's no such thing as a perfect edge in meatspace. Just about every corner has at least some amount of *beveling* or rounding to it. The Bevel tool is an excellent way to give your models that added realism. See the section "Rounding your corners by beveling" for more on working with the Bevel tool.

>> **Loop Cut:** As described later in this chapter, *loops* in a mesh are a continuous path of vertices, edges, or faces along the surface of your mesh. Blender's loop cut tools give you the ability to add more geometry along these loops.

- **Loop Cut:** The Loop Cut tool is the base tool for adding loops to your mesh. When you select it and move your mouse cursor over your mesh, Blender provides a little preview of the potential route of new vertices and edges added by your loop cut.

- **Offset Edge Loop Cut:** There's no previsualization for this tool, but if you click and drag on an existing edge loop that you've already selected, this tool creates a new edge loop on either side of it.

>> **Knife:** Blender gives you two tools for cutting arbitrary shapes into your mesh. There's more detail on them later in this section, but here's a quick rundown of the basics of each:

- **Knife:** Choose this tool and your mouse cursor changes to look like a precision craft knife. With this tool active, you can basically draw arbitrary shapes on the surface of your mesh, and Blender will add the necessary geometry to make that happen.

- **Bisect:** Whereas the Knife tool allows you to cut geometry into the surface of your mesh, the Bisect tool gives you the ability to add geometry *through* your mesh, as if cutting it with a plane with whatever orientation you'd like.

>> **Poly Build:** When you first activate the Poly Build tool, it may seem like you can't do very much with it. Clicking in the 3D Viewport just adds a single vertex. However, don't be deceived. The Poly Build tool is actually an incredibly useful tool for retopologizing sculpted geometry. There's more on retopo and the Poly Build tool in Book 2, Chapter 3.

>> **Spin:** There's more on the Spin tools later in this chapter, but the gist is that these two tools allow you to grow geometry from your selection in a radial way. One key tip for these tools: You'll get the best results by using the Cursor transform orientation.

- **Spin:** Think of the Spin tool like a very fancy variant of the Extrude Region tool. With this tool, you can quickly generate a series of evenly spaced extrusions along the shape of an arc.

- **Spin Duplicates:** Whereas the Spin tool is like extruding radially, the Spin Duplicates tool is like making copies of your selection and arranging them radially. You can use this tool to quickly make things like the petals of a flower or tickmarks on the face of an analog clock.

» **Smooth:** Rather than think of these as smoothing tools, I prefer to think of them as vertex tweak tools. They don't create any geometry; they just adjust the position of the geometry you've selected in your model.

- **Smooth:** Click and drag in the 3D Viewport, and Blender does a smoothing operation on your selected vertices, trying to distribute the vertices evenly in your selection.

- **Randomize:** In contrast with the Smooth tool, the Randomize tool shifts the vertices in your selection to give them a more random distribution, often making the surface of your mesh more rough looking.

» **Slide:** The slide tools move your selected geometry along the surface of your mesh. They're an excellent way to adjust your geometry without drastically deforming the general shape of your mesh.

- **Edge Slide:** With one or more selected edges, you can use the Edge Slide tool to move those edges along their adjoining faces.

- **Vertex Slide:** The Vertex Slide tool is similar to Edge Slide, but it works at the vertex level, sliding your selection along their adjoining edges.

» **Shrink/Fatten:** These two tools work a little bit like scaling, but they use a slightly different frame of reference.

- **Shrink/Fatten:** When you use the Shrink/Fatten tool, you're moving all your selected faces along their local normals. I sometimes like to think of this tool as an "erosion/accumulation" tool because that's a bit like how it feels when you use it on a whole mesh.

- **Push/Pull:** The Push/Pull tool is similar to Shrink/Fatten, but with a bit of a nuanced difference. It's like a compromise between Shrink/Fatten and Scale. Like Shrink/Fatten, this tool moves all of your selection a uniform distance. However, like Scale, you can choose the reference point that the selection is moving relative to (such as the median point of the selection or the location of the 3D cursor). This tool can be quite useful when working on mechanical models.

» **Shape Deformation:** The two tools in this button area are most useful for modifying the overall shape of your selection.

- **Shear:** This is the default tool that you see. With it activated, you get a gizmo that lets you move the components in your selection parallel to a plane that intersects them. In 2D shapes, shearing is a quick way of changing a rectangle into a parallelogram.

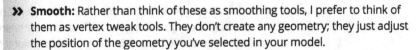

- **To Sphere:** I tend to use this tool a lot more frequently than the Shear tool. With this tool active, you can click and drag in the 3D Viewport and Blender pushes the vertices in your selection to make their shape as sphere-like as possible.

>> **Rip:** In 3D mesh modeling, when you *rip* a selection from the mesh, you're partially disconnecting it and creating new geometry based on your selection. If you have a string of edges selected and you rip them, it almost feels like you're unzipping that part of the mesh. Blender has two main rip tools:

- **Rip Region:** When you use this tool on a selection in the 3D Viewport, you basically create a hole between your formerly selected vertices and your newly ripped ones.

- **Rip Edge:** The Rip Edge tool operates similarly to the Rip Region tool, but instead of leaving a hole in the gap between old and new vertices, Blender keeps that space filled with new faces. In that way, the Rip Edge tool is like a combination of the Extrude tool and the Poly Build tool.

When working with tools from Blender's Toolbar, pay close attention to the status bar at the bottom of the Blender window. Blender uses that space to display mouse and hotkey hints on how to use the tools when they're activated.

Adding geometry by insetting

In the preceding section, I introduced you to the Inset Faces tool. Simply put, an *inset* on a face is similar to extruding that face and scaling it inward. What goes on under the hood is slightly more involved. The benefits of insetting rather than scaling become much more apparent when you start working with complex shapes. Have a look at the model shown in Figure 1-3. On the left is the result you get when extruding and scaling, whereas on the right you can see what happens when insetting. In short, insetting gives you a much more even border because the new vertices move along their normals relative to their old position instead of simply scaling down to a single point.

FIGURE 1-3:
Insetting (right) creates a nicer border on a complex shape than just extruding and scaling (left).

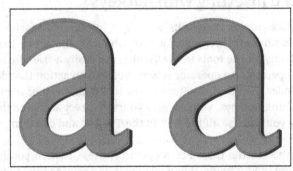

Using the Inset Faces tool

The gizmo for the Inset Face tool, if you can call it that, is simply a circle around your selected faces in the 3D Viewport. When you activate this tool by clicking on it in the Toolbar, not much of anything changes in the 3D Viewport. However, if you look at the status bar at the bottom of the Blender window, you get some hints about how the tool works. You have four basic controls:

>> **Select:** If you left-click on your mesh, you can select components of your mesh as if you had the Select tool active.

I suggest you work in Face Select when using the Inset Faces tool. The tool will still work in the other selection modes, but it's faster to select the faces you want to inset if you're in Face Select.

>> **Inset Faces:** When you left-click and drag within the Inset Faces circle gizmo, that action triggers the Inset Faces operator to start working. Drag toward your selection to inset farther. Drag away from your selection to bring your new geometry closer to the edge that generated it.

>> **Rotate View:** One of the benefits of using a tool-based workflow is that you retain the ability to navigate the 3D Viewport (as described in Book 1, Chapter 2) while you work. Even with the Inset Faces tool active, you can middle-click and drag to orbit around your scene, Shift+middle-click to pan, and use your mouse's scroll wheel to zoom.

>> **Call Menu:** While you work with the Inset Faces tool, a context menu is always available. Open it by right-clicking in the 3D Viewport. This menu gives you quick access to other modeling operators while you still have the Inset Faces tool active.

Advanced insetting with hotkeys

The Inset Faces tool is great in its own right, but there's a faster way to access the Inset Tool's functionality, regardless of whatever the active tool is. You can use hotkeys. Nearly all the tools in the Toolbar are really a friendly interface wrapped around an operator. An operator is what you call an action that does something in Blender. Under the hood, the Inset Faces tool makes use of Blender's Inset Faces operator. Using hotkeys, you can give yourself direct access to the operator without pulling your mouse all the way to the Toolbar and changing tools.

To directly access the Inset Faces operator, press I when you have one or more faces selected in Edit mode. When you press and release the I hotkey, Blender puts you in a kind of Inset Faces mini-mode where you can immediately inset your selection by moving your mouse cursor. You don't have the ability to navigate your scene or call a context menu while in this mini-mode, but you do have access to a few other handy features of the Inset Faces operator:

>> **Thickness (move your mouse cursor):** While in the Inset Faces operator's mini-mode, moving your mouse cursor around allows you to adjust the thickness of the border that insetting creates.

>> **Confirm (Enter or left-click):** When you've gotten your inset to the place you want, left-click or press Enter to confirm the operation and hop out of the mini-mode.

>> **Cancel (Esc or right-click):** If it turns out that you don't really want to inset anything at all, you can right-click or press Esc to get out of the Inset Faces mini-mode.

>> **Depth (Ctrl):** This functionality is a convenient feature of the Inset Faces operator. If you hold down Ctrl while moving your mouse cursor, you can move your newly inset faces along their normals. With this feature, you're not limited to keeping your inset faces in the same plane as the faces they originated from. You basically get an extrude operation built-in for free!

>> **Outset (O):** Sometimes, what you really want is the ability to *outset* your selected faces or create a border around your selection rather than inside it. Press and release O while in the Inset Faces mini-mode, and you gain the ability to make an outset of your selection.

>> **Boundary (B):** Quite often, when you're insetting faces, you're doing that on a *closed mesh* or a mesh that forms a solid volume. However, on occasion, you may have a mesh with *open edges* or edges that don't have any neighboring faces, also known as *boundary edges*. In those situations, the Inset Faces operator might give you some pretty funky results trying to inset those open edges. Press and release B while in the Inset Faces mini-mode to toggle whether you want insetting to work on boundary edges.

>> **Individual (I):** Sometimes when you work, you don't want to inset your whole selection of faces as a single unit, but instead, you'd rather inset each face in your selection individually. In a way, it's kind of similar to the difference between the Extrude Region and Extrude Individual tools. In the case of the Inset Faces operator, though, they're both packed into the same place. Press and release I while in the Inset Faces mini-mode to toggle whether you want to inset a region or each face individually.

TIP

You can see the available options of direct-access operators like Inset Faces by looking at the header of the 3D Viewport while you're working.

TIP

All the hotkeys I just described are *also* available when you're using the Inset Faces tool. Blender just doesn't tell you that you can use them. So, for example, if you have the Inset Faces tool active and you decide you want to add depth to your inset faces while you work, just hold Ctrl after you left-click and drag to start insetting. You don't have to choose between the operator and tool. You can use both!

Cleaning up ugly geometry by merging

WARNING

Be careful when you inset on very complex shapes, though. It's very easy to get ugly intersecting faces (especially at corners) if you inset too far without paying attention to what you're doing. That intersecting geometry can give you all kinds of problems down the road when you begin adding materials to your mesh, and especially when animating.

If you get these kinds of nasty intersections, don't worry too much. It's not overly difficult to clean them up. The most straightforward approach is to use Blender's merge operator. Assume you took the mesh in Figure 1-3 and inset it too far. You'll end up with a couple problem areas, like the ones shown in Figure 1-4.

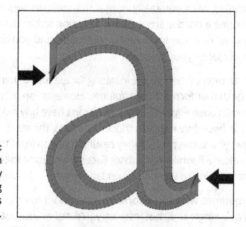

FIGURE 1-4: Insetting can cause ugly overlapping intersections at corners.

To fix these intersection issues, I recommend using Blender's Merge operator. You can find it in the 3D Viewport's menu at Mesh ⇨ Merge. Alternatively, you can invoke the Merge operator by using the M hotkey combination. In either case, Blender provides you with a submenu that gives you the following choices:

>> **At Center:** This option is always available. When you choose this menu item, all your selected vertices merge to a single one at the median point of that selection. This option is a good default choice if you're unsure about which one you want to use.

» **At Cursor:** There are times when you want to merge vertices at a very specific location that isn't the median point of your selection or the location of any one of your vertices. In that case, you want to choose the At Cursor option. With this option, all your selected vertices merge at the location of your 3D cursor. When you use this option, I suggest you place your 3D cursor first, and then run the Merge at Cursor operator.

» **Collapse:** In Book 1, Chapter 3, I cover the concept of having multiple parts within a single object, sometimes called *mesh islands*. If you have a mesh object with a few different islands in it and you choose the Collapse variant of the Merge operator, each island is merged into a single vertex.

» **At First:** This option is available only if you're in Vertex Select, but its functionality is easy to understand. If you select a series of vertices and run this operator, all those vertices will be merged at the location of the first one you selected. This option may not be visible in the menu if you mass select a bunch of vertices all at once (because in that case, there was no first vertex).

» **At Last:** Like At First, this variation of the Merge operator is available only in Vertex Select and visible only if you have an active vertex (the last vertex you select; it should be highlighted brighter than the others). When you choose this operator, all your selected vertices merge at the location of your active vertex.

» **By Distance:** In Book 1, Chapter 3, I also introduce the concept of *removing doubles* or merging a bunch of vertices that are in the same location (or near each other within a certain threshold). That kind of behavior is what you get when you run the Merge by Distance operator.

With a minute or so of quick selecting and merging, you can take those messed up corners from Figure 1-4 and clean them up so they look like the ones in Figure 1-5.

FIGURE 1-5:
Clean corners on
your inset, thanks
to the power
of the Merge
operator!

Cutting edges with the Knife

You can also add geometry to your mesh by cutting into it using the Knife tool. Blender's Knife tool gives you the powerful ability to add arbitrary vertices, edges, and faces on the surface of your mesh objects. Usually, the Knife tool is used as a starting point for another modeling operation you do after it. For example, maybe you have a wall, and you want it to look like there's a hole with a bunch of cracks in it. You might use the Knife tool to draw the shape of the hole and those cracks before extruding or deleting the faces for that hole. Figure 1-6 gives an illustration of this example.

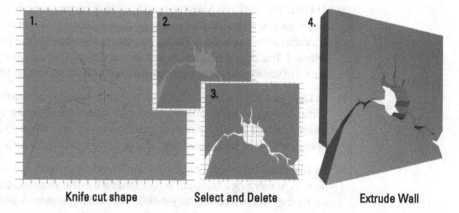

FIGURE 1-6:
Using the Knife tool, you can prepare your mesh for other mesh operations like extruding.

Knife cut shape   Select and Delete   Extrude Wall

Using the Knife tool

When you select the Knife tool from the Toolbar, your mouse cursor changes to look like a precision crafting knife. Similar to the Inset Faces tool, you can navigate the 3D Viewport while this tool is active, and you have quick access to a context menu by right-clicking. However, once you left-click anywhere in the 3D Viewport, you enter a Knife mini-mode (kind of like the Inset Faces mini-mode that you get when using the I hotkey in Edit mode). You can still navigate the 3D Viewport when that happens, but your mouse's right-click gets new functionality. The following list is all the functions you have available in the Knife tool's mini-mode:

>> **Cut Edges (left-click):** By left-clicking and dragging your mouse cursor in the 3D Viewport, you can draw across the edges you want to cut. If you just left-click and release without dragging, you can define locations for new vertices in your mesh and the Knife automatically generates the edges between them.

While you're making cuts, watch the red and green squares that appear along your cut line. These represent the vertices that the Knife will create once you confirm:

- Red squares are vertices that will definitely be created.

- Green squares are a pre-visualization of these new vertex locations.

They show only when you're in the middle of a specific cut.

>> **Navigate (middle-click):** Even in the Knife tool's mini-mode, you can still navigate the 3D Viewport (orbit, pan, and zoom) with your middle mouse button.

>> **Confirm (Enter/Spacebar):** When you finish cutting with the Knife, press Enter or Spacebar to confirm your cuts (the latter is faster because your hand is already closer to Spacebar than Enter).

>> **Cancel (Esc/Right-click):** To quit the Knife mini-mode without performing any cuts at all, either right-click or press Esc.

>> **Close Cut (Double left-click)/New Cut:** You can perform multiple separate cuts while in the Knife mini-mode. If you double-click, you can start a new cut anywhere else on your current mesh.

>> **Midpoint Snap (Ctrl):** If you hold Ctrl while making your cuts, you're telling the Knife that you want new vertices to be placed at the midpoint of any edge your cut line crosses. If you're drawing straight cut lines with the left-click-and-release method, you can see the planned location of your new midpoint vertices as green squares.

>> **Ignore Snap (Shift):** By default, Blender snaps the Knife to an edge if your mouse cursor is near it. However, there are occasions when you need to precisely place a new vertex near but not directly on an edge. In those cases, the default snapping behavior can be particularly frustrating. If you hold Shift while using the Knife, the default snapping behavior is temporarily disabled.

>> **Angle Constraint (A):** Occasionally, you need to make a cut that's perfectly horizontal, vertical, or at a 45° angle (relative to the view axis). Press and release A to toggle the Knife's ability to constrain your cuts to these axes.

Try to avoid holding down A for the angle constraint feature; otherwise, you may notice that your cut line jitters erratically. This is because the angle constraint feature is conflicting with snapping.

>> **Cut Through (C):** In some instances, you may want the Knife to cut through both sides of a mesh with the same cut line (for example, if you're modeling a four-post bed and you want to add a cut at the same height on all four posts). If you press C while in the Knife mini-mode, you toggle the Knife's ability to perform this kind of cut through the mesh.

WARNING

The Knife's cut-through feature works regardless of whether you can actually see the other side of your mesh (such as when in wireframe viewport shading or when you have Toggle X-ray enabled). For this reason, it's always a good idea to check the other side of your mesh after doing a cut to make sure you get your intended results.

REMEMBER

In Blender's interface, you'll sometimes see the abbreviations LMB (left mouse button), MMB (middle mouse button), and RMB (right mouse button). Throughout this text I'll default to using the longer form.

TIP

Just like with the Inset Faces tool, you can also access the operator behind the Knife tool regardless of what tool is currently active in the Toolbar by using a hotkey. In the case of the Knife tool, you can get to the Knife operator's mini-mode by pressing K. From there, Blender acts just as if you'd clicked on the Knife tool in the Toolbar and started cutting.

Bisecting

If you long-press the button in the Toolbar that you use to enable the Knife tool, a menu expands from there, giving you access to another cutting tool, the Bisect tool. Whereas the Knife tool operates only on the surface of your mesh (unless you enable the cut-through feature by pressing C), the Bisect tool is meant to cut through by default.

REMEMBER

Unlike the Knife tool, the Bisect tool works only on selected edges and faces in your mesh. So if you only have disconnected vertices or nothing selected, Blender will give you a warning if you try to use the Bisect tool. So before you use the Bisect tool, most of the time, you'll want to select all the components of your mesh by pressing A.

With your components selected and your Bisect tool active, you use the tool by left-clicking and dragging your mouse cursor across your mesh. When dragging your mouse cursor, Blender draws a straight line from where you first click to where your mouse cursor is currently located. This line is your bisecting line. When you release your left mouse button, there's a cut that goes all the way through your mesh, with all the necessary edges and vertices required to make that cut. Furthermore, you have the ability to adjust your bisecting cut with a gizmo that appears, as shown in Figure 1-7.

The controls for the Bisect tool's gizmo are fairly straightforward. Left-click and drag the yellow arrow to adjust the placement of your cut. Left-click and drag the light blue circle to rotate your cut.

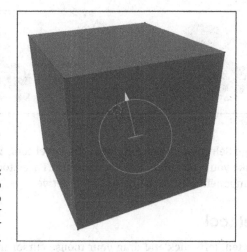

FIGURE 1-7:
The Bisect gizmo
allows you to
adjust your
bisecting cut after
you've made it.

REMEMBER

The Bisect tool's gizmo is placed at the first place you click when you draw your bisecting line, so all rotations of your cut are relative to that point. If you need to rotate that cut relative to a specific location, pay close attention to where you make your first click.

TIP

Like the Inset Faces tool and Knife tool, there is a direct-access operator for the Bisect operator. However, unlike those other operators, there's no default hotkey bound to the Bisect operator. To access it, you need to choose Mesh ⇨ Bisect. From there, you can either assign your own hotkey or add the Bisect operator to your Quick Favorites menu. For more on setting your own hotkeys and managing the Quick Favorites menu, see Book 1, Chapter 2.

Rounding your corners by beveling

I mention earlier in this chapter that nothing in nature has a perfectly sharp corner. Sure, knives are sharp and glass broken at right angles can cut you, but if you zoom in close enough, even those edges are rounded, just on a much finer scale. Barring exceptions like those, just about everything else in nature is going to have a rounded corner that you can see. If you want to make detailed 3D models with realistic geometry, you need to add that kind of rounding to the corners on your meshes. The Bevel tool is designed exactly for this purpose.

Like a few of the tools in Blender's Toolbar, the Bevel tool's gizmo is pretty simple, so when you activate the Bevel tool, there's just this lollipop-looking gizmo sticking out from your selection. Also, similar to the Bisect and Inset Faces tools, you need to have some components selected on your mesh. Figure 1-8 shows a simple mesh on the left and that same mesh beveled in a few different ways to its right.

FIGURE 1-8:
The Bevel tool gives you the ability to add realism to your models by rounding their corners.

TIP

I suggest you use Edge Select when working with the Bevel tool. You don't need to switch tools to make your selection. Just like the Inset Faces tool, you can use left-click to select components while the Bevel tool is active.

Using the Bevel tool

With your edges selected, left-click and drag your mouse cursor in the 3D Viewport, and you'll enter the Bevel tool's mini-mode (like that of the Knife and Inset Faces tools). If you look at the status bar at the bottom of your Blender window, you can see that the Bevel tool's mini-mode gives you the following options:

>> **Width:** With your left-mouse button held down, you can drag your mouse cursor on the circular part of the lollipop gizmo to adjust the width of the bevel you're adding to your selection. When you're pleased with how the bevel looks on your selected edges, just release the left mouse button to confirm the operation.

>> **Cancel (Esc/right-click):** Of course, if you don't like the way the bevel is looking, you can always cancel with right-click or Esc.

>> **Mode (M):** You can choose an assortment of modes or *width types* for controlling the behavior of your bevel. Basically, these modes define how the width of your bevel is measured. For the most part, the default mode of Offset should suit you just fine, but you can cycle through these options by pressing M if you need more precise control:

TECHNICAL STUFF

- **Offset:** In the simplest case of a bevel, you're creating two new edges where before there was only one. With the Offset width type, the bevel width is the distance of each of those new edges from the original edge. For bevels with multiple segments, the offset width is the two outermost edges of the bevel.

- **Width:** This type is simpler to explain. It's the overall width of your bevel. Nice and easy.

- **Depth:** When you create a simple bevel, your two new edges create a face between them. The perpendicular distance between that new face and the location of the original edge is the bevel depth. That bevel depth is the measurement you're using if you choose this width type.

- **Percent:** The Percent width type is wacky and somewhat difficult to explain. It's the percentage of the length of adjacent edges when sliding. What this means is when you bevel one edge on a cube, your two new edges slide this distance along their neighboring faces. If you set the percentage width to 50%, each of your new bevel edges are exactly halfway down their neighboring faces. At 100%, your bevel turns a cube into a ramp. Of course, this is all assuming that you're beveling a single edge. When beveling multiple edges, this mode is a bit more difficult to predict by the numbers.

» **Segments (S/scroll wheel):** As far as the Bevel tool is concerned, a *segment* is a face between newly created edges of the Bevel operator. The default number of segments in your bevel is 1. The fastest way to increase the number of segments in your bevel is to use the scroll wheel on your mouse. However, if you're already holding down the left mouse button (or you're using a drawing tablet), it can be awkward to scroll the mouse wheel. So your alternative choice is to press and release S (while still keeping the left mouse button held down). After pressing S, moving your mouse cursor no longer adjusts the width of your bevel and instead that movement adjusts the number of segments in your bevel.

» **Profile (P):** Like the S hotkey for adjusting the number of segments in your bevel, you can adjust the *profile* or curve shape of your bevel by pressing and releasing P while in the Bevel tool's mini-mode.

» **Clamp Overlap (C):** In the description of the Inset Faces tool, I explained that the tool could occasionally give you ugly geometry with overlapping edges and faces. The Inset Faces tool doesn't have an automatic way of handling that problem, but the Bevel tool does. If you notice that your bevel is generating overlapping faces, you can tell Blender to just stop making your bevel width larger. Toggle this feature on by pressing and releasing C.

» **Affect (V):** By default the Bevel tool operates on selected edges in your mesh. You also have the ability to bevel just the vertices of your selection. Toggle this behavior by pressing and releasing V.

» **Outer Miter (O)/Inner Miter (I):** The *miter* of a bevel is a corner where two or more bevel edges meet, like wrapping around the top of a cube. When you have more than one segment on your bevel, there are a few different ways the edges of those segments can be routed. Use the O and I toggles to cycle through the different miter types for inner and outer miters.

» **Harden Normals (H):** The default behavior for the new faces of your bevels is for Blender to shade them flat, so you see all the facets of the new faces. If you press H, you can toggle the Harden Normals feature, effectively making your bevels look smoother with fewer additional segments.

» **Mark Seam (U)/Mark Sharp (K):** The Bevel tool does what's known as a destructive operation. The name sounds scarier than it is. A *destructive* *operation* is an operation that you perform on a mesh that cannot easily be removed. Yes, you always have the Undo feature, but if you do a few other modeling operations after beveling, it's much more difficult to undo. In contrast, Blender has other modeling features, called *modifiers*, that are non-destructive. There's more on modifiers in the next chapter, but a number of them work on edges that you mark in Edit mode. The U and K toggles while Beveling allows you to mark your new bevel edges as seams (for UV unwrapping; see Book 3, Chapter 2) or as sharp (for the Subdivision Surface modifier, covered later in this chapter).

Taking the hotkey-and-tweak approach to beveling

TIP

You may have noticed from the preceding section that the Bevel tool has a whole mess of options. Those many options are difficult to keep in your brain and on a small computer screen, you might not even be able to see the whole list of options in the status bar while you make your bevel. For that reason, I prefer to take a slightly different approach when I bevel. For one, I like to directly invoke the Bevel operator by pressing Ctrl+B. You get into the same Bevel mini-mode, but you don't have to move your mouse to the Toolbar and change to the tool. Furthermore, you don't have to hold down your left mouse button while beveling, so it's less stressful on your joints during long modeling sessions.

Also, I don't think too hard on any of the details of my bevel. I just make sure I select the edges I want, press Ctrl+B, adjust the bevel width to something close to what I want, and left-click or press Enter to confirm. The reason I don't think too hard on the details is because of the second half of this approach: I use the Last Operator panel. Whether you use the Bevel tool or you call the operator like I do, at the bottom left of your 3D Viewport, you should see the Last Operator panel with the word Bevel on it. It's collapsed by default, but if you expand it, you see all your bevel options right there, clearly labeled, and it's easy to make live adjustments. Figure 1-9 shows the bevel options available in the Last Operator panel.

Spiraling new geometry into existence with the Spin tool

If you're familiar with the traditional meatspace skills of machining or wood-working, you may know about a tool called a lathe. If you've never worked with a lathe, you're missing out on a whole bunch of fun. A *lathe* is a machine that you use to spin a length of material around an axis, and while it's spinning, you use various tools to dig in and cut away material from what's being spun. Lathes are used to make everything from bowls to baseball bats, and they're prized for their ability to turn flat objects into round, cylindrical objects.

Bevel

Affect	Vertices | **Edges**
Width Type	Offset
Width	0.383 m
Segments	1
Shape	0.500
Material Index	-1
	☐ Harden Normals
	☐ Clamp Overlap
	☑ Loop Slide
Mark	☐ Seams
	☐ Sharp
Miter Outer	Sharp
Inner	Sharp
Intersection Type	Grid Fill
Face Strength	None
Profile Type	**Superellipse** | Custom

FIGURE 1-9:
The Last Operator panel gives you all the necessary controls for tweaking your bevel, clearly labeled and easily adjusted.

In 3D computer graphics, there's a similar tool. In fact, on some other 3D applications, they even call it a lathe tool. In Blender, however, it's the Spin tool. Like extruding, there are a few important differences between how you spin geometry in 3D space compared to how you do it on a lathe in meatspace. The most important difference is that lathes work subtractively. They achieve a round shape by removing material. In contrast, Blender's spin tool takes a given profile and extrudes it radially to generate that round shape. Figure 1-10 shows a rough profile of a wine glass and the resulting mesh when you use the Spin tool.

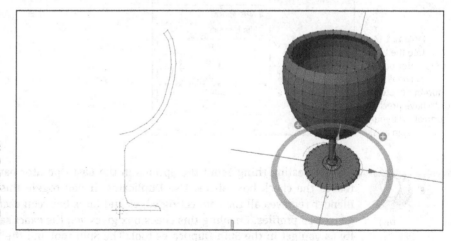

FIGURE 1-10:
Using the Spin tool, you can turn flat profiles into beautiful cylindrical shapes.

Like most of the other tools discussed in this chapter, the Spin tool also has an operator that you can access through a menu. You can find it in Mesh ⇨ Extrude ⇨ Spin. If you'd like, you can assign a hotkey to that operator as described in Book 1, Chapter 2, and you can tweak using the Last Operator panel in the same way I described for the Bevel tool. That said, you're still probably best off using the Spin tool and Spin Duplicates tool from the Toolbar rather than trying to take a hotkey-based approach. The gizmos for those tools give you quite a bit more control.

When you select the Spin tool from the 3D Viewport's Toolbar, Blender provides you with a handy little blue arc-shaped gizmo with plus symbols on either side of it. Left-click and drag on either of the plus symbols and you start spinning your selected geometry around a single axis. If you hold down Ctrl while spinning, the gizmo gets little white tic marks, and your spin steps in fixed increments. When you release your left mouse button, the gizmo gains additional move-and-rotation controls that you can use to tweak the axis about which you did your spin.

When you first do a spin operation with the Spin tool, the results might appear a little bit rough. That roughness is because the default setting for the Spin tool is only to use 12 steps divided by however many degrees you're spinning. To smooth things out, expand the Last Operator panel from the bottom of the 3D Viewport and increase the Steps value. Figure 1-11 shows what the Spin tool's Last Operator options are.

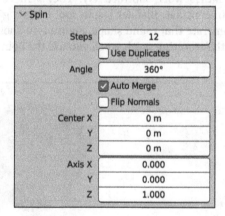

FIGURE 1-11:
Use the Last Operator panel to tweak the number of steps or to have precise control over your spin axis.

One interesting thing about the options in the Last Operator panel for the Spin tool is the check box labeled Use Duplicates. If you toggle this check box on, Blender removes all the connecting edges and faces between each of your newly generated profiles. Enabling this check box gives you the exact same functionality as you get in the Spin Duplicates tool. The Spin tool and the Spin Duplicates tool work exactly alike. The only difference is whether this check box is enabled by default.

Working with Loops and Rings

Regardless of whether you're box modeling or point-for-point modeling, understanding the concepts of *loops* and *rings* definitely makes your life as a modeler a
lot less crazy.

Understanding edge loops and face loops

Generally speaking, an *edge loop* is a series of edges that connect to form a path
where the first and last edges connect to each other — well, that's the ideal case
anyway. I like to call this kind of *closed edge loop* a "good" edge loop.

Of course, then you probably want to know what a "bad" edge loop is. Well, you
can have a path of edges that don't connect at the beginning and end of the loop,
but calling these loops bad isn't really accurate. It's better to refer to edge loops
that stop before reconnecting with their beginning as *terminating edge loops*.
Although you generally want to avoid creating terminating edge loops in your
models, you can't always avoid having them, and sometimes you actually need
them for controlling how edges flow along the surface of your mesh.

To get a better understanding of the difference between closed edge loops and
terminating edge loops, open Blender and add a UV sphere (Add ⇨ Mesh ⇨ UV
Sphere). Tab into Edit mode or switch to the Modeling workspace on the sphere
and Alt+left-click one of the horizontal edges on the sphere. This step selects an
edge loop that goes all the way around the sphere like the latitude lines on a globe,
as shown in the left image of Figure 1-12. This loop is a closed edge loop. Press
Alt+A to deselect all and now Alt+left-click a vertical edge. When you do, you select
a path of vertices that terminates at the top and bottom *poles*, or junctions of the
sphere, as shown in the right image of Figure 1-12. That's a terminating edge loop.

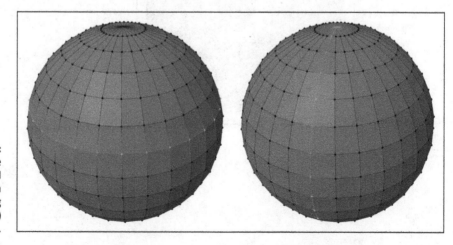

FIGURE 1-12:
A closed edge
loop (left) around
a sphere and a
terminating
edge loop (right)
on a sphere.

The vertical loop doesn't go all the way around because, technically speaking, edge loops rely on *four-point poles*, or a vertex that's at the junction of four edges, to understand which way the loop flows. Imagine that following an edge loop is like driving through a city (one with a proper grid of city blocks). The four-point pole is like a four-way stop, where you have the option of going left, right, or straight. Well, to properly follow the loop, you keep traveling straight. However, if you come to a fork in the road (a three-point pole) or a five-way (or more) intersection, you can't necessarily just go straight and be sure that you're following the loop. Therefore, the loop terminates at that intersection. That's why the horizontal edge loop in Figure 1-12, which is made up entirely of four-point poles, connects to itself, whereas the vertical loop stops at the top and bottom of the sphere, where all the edges converge to a single junction.

 In addition to edge loops, you can also have face loops. A *face loop* consists of the faces between two parallel edge loops. Figure 1-13 shows horizontal and vertical face loops on a UV sphere. In Blender, you can select face loops when you're in Face Select mode (in Edit mode, press 3 on the row of numbers at the top of your keyboard or use the Face Select button in the header of the 3D Viewport) the same way you select edge loops in Vertex Select or Edge Select modes: Alt+left-click a face in the direction of the loop you'd like to select. For example, going back to the UV sphere, to select a horizontal face loop, Alt+left-click the left or right side of one of the faces in that loop. To select a vertical face loop, Alt+left-click the top or bottom of the face.

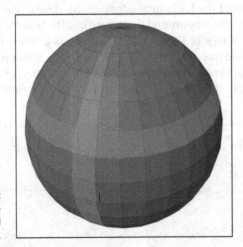

FIGURE 1-13:
Some face loops selected on a sphere.

TIP

In some Linux window managers, the Alt key manipulates windows, which supersedes Blender's control of it and prevents you from doing a loop select. Most window managers allow you to remap that ability to another key (like the Super or Windows key). However, if you use a window manager that doesn't offer that remapping ability, or you just don't feel like remapping that key, you can still select loops by using Shift+Alt+left-click. This key combination is actually for selecting multiple loops, but if you have no geometry (vertices, edges, or faces) selected, it behaves just like Alt+left-click.

Selecting edge rings

Say that instead of wanting to select an edge loop or a face loop, you'd like to select just the edges that bridge between two parallel edge loops, as shown in Figure 1-14. These edges form an *edge ring*. You can select edge rings only from Edge Select mode (in Edit mode, press 2 on the row of numbers at the top of your keyboard or use the Edge Select button in the header of the 3D Viewport). When you're in Edge Select mode, you can select an edge ring by using Ctrl+Alt+left-click. Trying to use this hotkey sequence in Vertex Select or Face Select mode just selects a face loop.

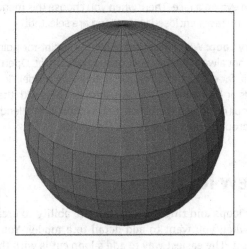

FIGURE 1-14:
An edge ring selected on a UV sphere.

Being able to use rings and loops for selecting groups of vertices in an orderly fashion can be a huge benefit and timesaver for modeling. More importantly, when creating organic models like humans or faces, using edge loops effectively to control your topology makes the life of a character rigger and animator a lot more pleasant. (You can find out more on this topic in the section "The importance of good topology," later in this chapter.)

If you're more comfortable working from menus, you can select both edges and loops from the Select menu in the 3D Viewport. The key to using these menu items is that you need to have a base selection to start with first. So, for example, if you want to select an edge ring, follow these steps:

1. Select one of the edges in the ring you want to select.

2. Choose Select ⇨ Select Loops ⇨ Edge Rings.

The Select ⇨ Select Loops submenu actually has some extra selection options that are pretty handy. When you navigate to this menu, you have the following options (these choices work best from Edge Select mode):

» **Edge Loops:** Just like the preceding example, first select an edge that's on the loop you want, and then choose this menu option to select the whole loop.

» **Edge Rings:** This choice is the one described in the preceding example. Select an edge on the ring you want and then pick this option from the menu.

» **Select Loop Inner-Region:** This menu option requires that you already have a closed loop of edges selected. It doesn't have to be a full edge loop; it just needs to be a closed loop of some sort that connects to itself, like a trace of edges around an eye on a face. Then, when you choose this menu item, all the vertices, edges, and faces enclosed in that loop are selected.

» **Select Boundary Loop:** When modeling (especially point-for-point modeling), your mesh may not always be fully enclosed, or *water-tight*. Open meshes can be problematic if, for example, you're 3D printing your model. So you want to close those holes or *boundaries*. This menu item can help with that. Select all the vertices in your mesh and then choose this menu item. Blender selects the edge loops around any boundaries you may have.

Creating new loops

The ability to select loops and rings is nice, but the ability to create new loops is even more helpful when you want to add detail to a model. You can detail with what's called a *loop cut*. The easiest way to add a loop cut is with the Loop Cut tool, as described earlier in this chapter. When in Edit mode, follow these steps:

1. Enable the Loop Cut tool in the 3D Viewport's Toolbar.

Alternatively, you can simply press Ctrl+R to access the Loop Cut operator directly. Regardless of how you choose to make a loop cut, when you run your mouse cursor over your model, a yellow line is drawn on the mesh, indicating where you might want to add your edge loop.

2. **After you decide where you want to cut, left-click and drag to place your newly created edge loop. Left-click and release places the new edge loop at the exact midpoint between its neighboring loops.**

If you're using the Ctrl+R hotkey combination, left-click and release (right-click cancels the whole operation if you're using the Ctrl+R hotkey combination). Then Blender automatically enables the Edge Slide operator on your new loop. With *edge slide*, you can move your mouse around, and your loop travels along the surface of the mesh between its neighboring loops, allowing you to place it precisely where you want it to go when you left-click, just like the Edge Slide tool.

TIP

If you want your new loop cut to sit at the exact midpoint between its neighboring loops with the Ctrl+R hotkey, right-click after the Loop Cut operator drops you into edge slide.

TIP

When doing a loop cut, you can actually do multiple parallel loop cuts at the same time if you use the Ctrl+R hotkey. When you activate the Loop Cut operator (Ctrl+R), scroll your mouse wheel, and you'll be able to add multiple loops all at the same time. If you don't have a scroll wheel on your mouse or you simply prefer to use your keyboard, you can adjust the number of loops in your cut by pressing Page Up and Page Down. To do the same thing with the Loop Cut tool, you need to make use of the Number of Cuts value in Tool Settings at the top of the 3D Viewport or by using Last Operator panel after you make your loop cut.

REMEMBER

If you ever want to use edge slide without creating a new loop, select the edge loop (or portion of an edge loop) that you want to slide and use the Edge Slide tool. Alternatively, you can use the even faster hotkey sequence G ⇨ G.

The importance of good topology

If you listen to modelers talk or if you visit some of the web forums where 3D modelers hang out, you'll hear the words *topology* and *edge flow* pretty often. These concepts are very important for a modeler, particularly if your model is destined to be animated. These terms refer to how the vertices and edges of your mesh lay out across its surface. Even when sculpting (see Book 2, Chapter 3), 3D modelers will often use a base mesh that has good topology as their starting point. Or, when they're done sculpting, they'll take the model through a process known as *retopology* to give it a clean edge flow that's usable in animation. To that end, whether you're sculpting or just straight modeling, keep a few key guidelines in mind:

>> **Use quads.** Try to avoid triangles and ngons in your final mesh whenever possible. They're fine to use as stand-ins while your work, but four-sided polygons look better when subdivided, and they also tend to deform more cleanly when an armature is used to animate them.

>> **Minimize the use of poles that don't have four edges.** Remember that a pole is where multiple edges join at a single vertex. The UV Sphere mesh has two large poles at its top and bottom. Poles are harder to avoid than triangles, but you should do what you can to minimize their use because they can terminate edge loops, and they don't deform as nicely as four-edged poles. If you're forced to use a pole, try to put it in a place on the mesh that won't deform a lot when it's animated.

>> **Holes such as mouths and eye sockets should be encircled by concentric edge loops.** This guideline is particularly important for character models that may be animated. Having concentric edge loops makes it easier to deform and animate these highly expressive parts of the face.

>> **All faces in the mesh should be somewhat similar in size.** Basically, you should try to avoid making long, thin faces unless you have a particular reason to have them, like when trying to form a crease.

>> **Edges should follow anatomy (at least on the face).** Following the flow of anatomy — particularly musculature — is important on face models because doing so yields cleaner, more natural deformations. For example, the crease from the side of the nose flows around the mouth. For limbs, following musculature is less imperative; tube-type topology usually should be fine.

If you're aiming for anatomical realism in your models, following these little rules really makes the lives of riggers and animators much easier (and it helps make the final animation look better).

Chapter **2**

Simplifying Your Life as a Modeler with Modifiers

Working with meshes can get complicated when you have complex models consisting of lots and lots of vertices. Keeping track of these vertices and making changes to your model can rapidly become a daunting and tedious task, even with well-organized topology. You can quickly run into problems if you have a symmetrical model where the left side is supposed to be identical to the right, or if you need more vertices to make your model appear smoother. In these times, you really want the computer to take on some of this tedious additional work so you can focus on the creative parts.

Fortunately, Blender actually has a feature called *modifiers* that helps tackle the monotony. Despite their rather generic-sounding name, modifiers are an extremely powerful way to save you time and frustration by letting the computer assume the responsibility for grunt work, such as adding smoothing vertices or making your model symmetric. Another benefit of modifiers is that they're *non-destructive*, meaning you can freely add and remove modifiers to and from your object. As long as you don't apply the modifier, it won't make any permanent changes to the object itself. You can always return to the original, unmodified mesh.

Accessing Blender's Modifiers

You can access modifiers for your mesh in the Modifiers tab of the Properties editor (its button has an icon of a blue wrench). Left-click the Add Modifier button to see a list of the available modifiers. Figure 2-1 shows the Modifiers Properties with the list of available modifiers for meshes.

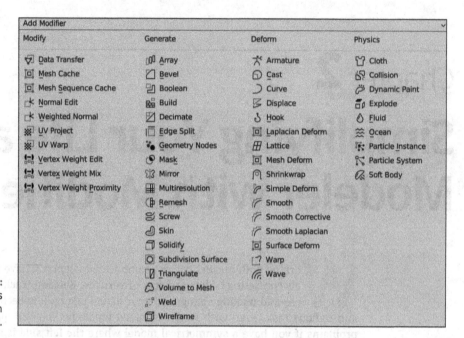

Modify	Generate	Deform	Physics
Data Transfer	Array	Armature	Cloth
Mesh Cache	Bevel	Cast	Collision
Mesh Sequence Cache	Boolean	Curve	Dynamic Paint
Normal Edit	Build	Displace	Explode
Weighted Normal	Decimate	Hook	Fluid
UV Project	Edge Split	Laplacian Deform	Ocean
UV Warp	Geometry Nodes	Lattice	Particle Instance
Vertex Weight Edit	Mask	Mesh Deform	Particle System
Vertex Weight Mix	Mirror	Shrinkwrap	Soft Body
Vertex Weight Proximity	Multiresolution	Simple Deform	
	Remesh	Smooth	
	Screw	Smooth Corrective	
	Skin	Smooth Laplacian	
	Solidify	Surface Deform	
	Subdivision Surface	Warp	
	Triangulate	Wave	
	Volume to Mesh		
	Weld		
	Wireframe		

FIGURE 2-1: All the modifiers you can use on mesh objects.

NEW FEATURE

In Blender 4.0, the Add Modifier menu looks quite different. Rather than being a huge menu with multiple columns, it's a multi-level menu. You have all the same categories of modifiers as shown in Figure 2-1, you just need to drill into submenus to get to the modifier that you need.

Because of space constraints, I can't give an extensive description on every modifier in the list, but I briefly describe each later in this section. That said, all Blender's modifiers share some of the same controls. Figure 2-2 shows the Modifiers section with two modifiers added, Array and Bevel.

The first thing to notice is that the modifiers are stacked one below the other. This stacking is by design. What's more, the order in which the modifiers appear in the stack is important because one modifier feeds into the next one. So the second modifier — Bevel, in this case — doesn't operate on the original mesh data. Bevel actually operates on the new mesh data provided by the first modifier, Array, in this example.

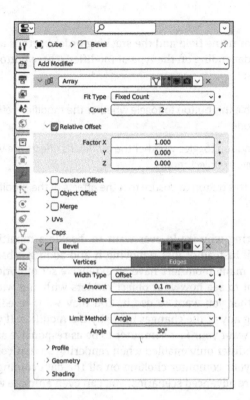

FIGURE 2-2:
The Array and
Bevel modifiers
in Modifiers
Properties.

WARNING

The stacking order for modifiers is a little bit counterintuitive if you think about it in terms of layers, where one builds on top of another. Blender's modifier stack doesn't work like that. Instead, you're better off thinking of Blender's modifier stack as a snowball rolling down a hill. Each modifier you hit on the way down the hill adds something or changes something about your snowball, modifying it more and more as it comes to the base of the hill. The topmost modifier is the first modifier and operates on the original mesh data. The modifier immediately below it works on the data that comes from the first modifier, and so on down the line.

In the preceding example, the object is first made into an array. Then the mesh created by the Array modifier has its edges beveled so that they're not as sharp-cornered. You can change the stacking order by clicking and dragging the "grip zone" on the top right side of each modifier block.

Alternatively, if you click the down arrow at the end of the block of buttons at the top of the modifier's panel, a drop-down menu appears. At the bottom of that menu are Move to First and Move to Last options that move the modifier to the top or bottom of the stack, respectively. The downward triangle to the left of each modifier's name collapses and expands that modifier block when you left-click it. Collapsing the modifier block is useful for hiding a modifier's controls after you've decided upon the settings you want to use.

Between the modifier name field and the stacking order buttons are three or four additional buttons, depending on the type of modifier. Three buttons are common among all modifiers:

>> **Edit Mode:** Enable this button to toggle whether the modifier's effects are visible in Edit mode.

>> **Realtime:** This button toggles whether the modifier's effects are visible in the 3D Viewport while in Object mode.

>> **Render:** Enable this button to ensure that the effects of the modifier appear when rendering.

You may be wondering why you'd ever want to disable a modifier after you've added it to the stack instead of just removing it and adding it back in later. The main reason is that many modifiers have an extensive set of options available to them. You may want to see how your object renders with and without the modifier to decide whether you want to use it. You may want to edit your original mesh without seeing any of the changes made by the modifier. If you have a slow computer (or if you want your fast computer to be as responsive as possible), you want to have the modifier only enabled when rendering so that you can still work effectively without your computer choking on all the data coming from Blender. Furthermore, in more advanced scenarios, you can even animate whether a modifier is enabled.

Some modifiers, like the Array modifier shown in Figure 2-2, have an additional fourth button with an inverted triangle icon at the end of the button block. Its tooltip says "On Cage," and that enabling this button will "adjust edit cage to modifier result." The edit *cage* is the input mesh, prior to any influence by the modifier. Enabling this button means that not only are the effects of the modifier visible in Edit mode, but you can also select and perform limited changes to the geometry created by the modifier.

A few more options are common among all modifiers, accessible from the drop-down menu to the right of the aforementioned visibility toggle buttons:

>> **Apply:** Choosing the Apply operator takes the changes made by the modifier and directly applies them to the original object. Applying is a *destructive* operation and actually creates the additional vertices and edges in the original mesh to make the mesh match the results produced by the modifier and then removes the modifier from the stack. Although modifiers themselves are non-destructive, meaning that they don't permanently change the original object, the Apply button is the one exception.

The Apply button works only if the object you're working on is in Object mode.

REMEMBER

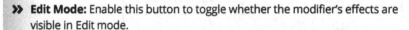

>> **Duplicate:** The Duplicate operator creates a duplicate version of the modifier and adds it to the stack after the modifier you're duplicating. You probably won't be using this function very often, but it's useful when you need to double up a modifier, such as if you want to use one Subdivision Surface modifier with simple subdivisions to get more raw geometry and then use a second Subdivision Surface modifier to smooth or curve that additional geometry.

>> **Copy to Selected:** The third operator in that drop-down menu is grayed out and inaccessible unless you have multiple objects selected. If you do have multiple objects selected, then clicking this operator copies the modifier and its settings from your active object to all the other selected objects.

>> **Move to First/Last:** Normally you can re-order the position of modifiers in the stack by clicking and dragging the grab regions in the upper right of each modifier panel. However, if you know you want to move a modifier all the way to the top or bottom, you can use these menu items.

Understanding Modifier Types

The list of modifiers that you have available in Blender is long. At the time of this writing, there are 54 modifiers available for you to use on mesh objects. A subset of modifiers also works on other object types like curves and text objects (see Book 2, Chapter 4 for more on other non-mesh object types). Grease Pencil objects and Volume objects have their own set of modifiers (see Book 4, Chapter 6 for more on Grease Pencil objects). However, Blender's modifier stack is primarily designed to handle mesh data, so that's where you have access to the largest number of modifiers.

This section gives you a brief summation of each modifier; at the end of this chapter, I show some detailed information on working with a few specific modifiers. I encourage you to play with each modifier on its own to get a real feel for how they work.

Modify modifiers

The first column of modifiers is somewhat of a hodge-podge; it's a bit of a dumping ground for modifiers that don't really fit anywhere else. The main common feature across these modifiers is that they affect vertices or vertex data. With the possible exception of the UV Project modifier, these modifiers are more commonly used in the complex scenes that a more advanced Blenderhead may have, so don't sweat too much if you don't see an immediate-use case for them.

NEW FEATURE

In Blender 4.0, these modifiers are in a menu named Edit.

The modifiers in this column are:

>> **Data Transfer:** When you're working on large projects, it's common to have multiple versions of a mesh that's worked on by multiple people or different meshes that have similar types of internal data like vertex groups, UV maps, or vertex colors. You might want to simplify your life by transferring that data between meshes, so you don't have to redo work that's already been done. Saving that time is what the Data Transfer modifier is here for.

>> **Mesh Cache:** This modifier replaces all your mesh's geometry with new data from a mesh cache file. In large-scale animated productions, it's common practice to take completed character animation (set up with a complex animation rig; see Book 4, Chapter 3) and "bake" it into the vertex data before moving on to lighting and rendering. This modifier facilitates that workflow.

>> **Mesh Sequence Cache:** The Mesh Sequence Cache modifier is very similar to the Mesh Cache modifier but it's arguably more powerful because it uses an incredibly versatile open source file format called Alembic. This is the same file format used by large production studios to help with final adjustments after animation is complete.

>> **Normal Edit:** If you're working in video game development or architectural visualization, you often work with models that have a much lower vertex count than those used in, for example, film animation. When working with fewer faces in your mesh, you tend to pay a lot more attention to how the normals on those faces point so you can better hide the faceted nature of your models. The Normal Edit modifier gives you the ability to procedurally adjust the normals on your model and mix the results back in.

REMEMBER

To make use of the Normal Edit modifier or the Weighted Normal modifier, you need to enable the Auto Smooth check box in the Normals panel of Object Data Properties.

>> **Weighted Normal:** This modifier is similar to the Normal Edit modifier but it gives you a different set of controls and the results override your mesh's normals instead of mixing back with them.

>> **UV Project:** Think of the UV Project modifier as a video projector or a slide projector. It produces a similar effect to an object-mapped texture (see Book 3, Chapter 2), though it's more flexible.

>> **UV Warp:** The UV Warp modifier is similar to the UV Project modifier, as it modifies your mesh's UV coordinates (see Book 3, Chapter 2 for UV coordinates). The difference, however, is that the UV Warp modifier gives you the ability to rig and deform your UV coordinates for animation much like you would rig the vertex data of your mesh.

- **Vertex Weight Edit/Mix/Proximity:** As their names imply, these three modifiers manipulate vertex weights. Vertices in a mesh can belong to one or more vertex groups (I cover vertex groups in detail in Book 4, Chapter 3). For each vertex, you can define a *weight* (a numeric value from 0.0 to 1.0) defining how much a vertex belongs to a particular group. These modifiers give you more control over those vertex weights. (They're particularly useful in complex animation rigs.)

Generate modifiers

The Generate category of modifiers contains the most commonly used modifiers in a Blender modeler's arsenal. They're a procedural means of adding — and in some cases removing — geometry in your mesh. And because they're modifiers, they can be stacked to produce pretty complex models from simple base objects . . . and then the parameters in that stack of modifiers can be animated! The list of available modifiers in this category is extensive. The following is a quick run-through of each:

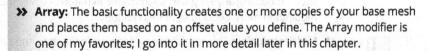

- **Array:** The basic functionality creates one or more copies of your base mesh and places them based on an offset value you define. The Array modifier is one of my favorites; I go into it in more detail later in this chapter.

- **Bevel:** Nothing in the real world has perfectly sharp corners or edges. They're always slightly rounded, even if a little bit. The Bevel modifier helps you add that little touch of realism to your object. This modifier is the non-destructive version of the Bevel tool described in Book 2, Chapter 1, and a lot of the same options from that tool can be used in this modifier.

- **Boolean:** The Boolean modifier allows you to mix two meshes together, adding, subtracting, or intersecting a separate mesh with your current one.

  This modifier can sometimes generate some pretty ugly topology.

WARNING

- **Build:** With this relatively simple modifier, the individual faces in your mesh appear over time. You can also reverse the effect to have your mesh slowly disappear over time, one face at a time.

- **Decimate:** Occasionally you will need to reduce the amount of geometry in your model (for example, your model might need to be used in a video game, a segment of the 3D computer graphics field renowned for having tight geometry budgets for each object). The Decimate modifier can give you a head start in reducing your model's geometry.

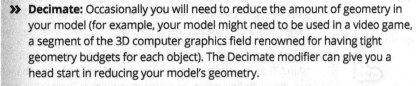

- **Edge Split:** When modeling, you can define whether a face in your mesh gets rendered as smooth or flat. More often than not, you'll want it to appear smooth. However, in doing this, you lose definition at hard edges in your model. You could add a Bevel modifier to fix this, but if you're trying to keep your face count down, that may produce more geometry than you want. The Edge Split modifier lets you keep sharp edges without adding a significant amount of geometry.

 » **Geometry Nodes:** On its own, the Geometry Nodes modifier doesn't look like it does very much. However, this is the entry point for using Blender's Geometry Nodes feature on your object. Select the node group you want to use, and you're off to the races! Book 2, Chapter 5 has more on Geometry Nodes.

In Blender 4.0, Geometry Nodes is a whole menu unto itself since that feature has continued to expand. Since Geometry Nodes are now capable of doing things in any of the modifier categories, it makes sense for them to have their own home.

 » **Mask:** The Mask modifier gives you the ability to define some vertices in your mesh as being hidden from view, depending on either their membership in a vertex group or their relation to an armature bone.

 » **Mirror:** This modifier duplicates the geometry in your base mesh and flips it along one or more of your object's local axes. It's extremely useful when you're modeling anything that's symmetric in nature. I cover the Mirror modifier in more detail later in this chapter.

 » **Multiresolution:** This modifier subdivides your mesh by the same rules used in the Subdivision Surface modifier (covered later in this section). The difference is that Multiresolution can be applied multiple times, and you can use Sculpt mode to freely edit the generated vertices at any of the subdivision levels you generate. I cover the Multiresolution modifier in more detail in Book 2, Chapter 3.

 » **Remesh:** There are times when the topology of your mesh just is not salvageable (such as when doing heavy sculpting or using Booleans). The Remesh modifier can give you a more reasonable starting place for a mesh with cleaner topology (or at least evenly spaced faces for more detailed sculpting).

» **Screw:** The Screw modifier duplicates the geometry of your mesh one or more times and rotates those duplicates about one of its local axes. You can use this to create helix shapes (like springs and, well, screws) as well as a way to generate an object from a simple profile, similar to what you can do with Blender's Spin tool (described earlier in this chapter). There's a tutorial that covers this technique on this book's website (www.blenderbasics.com).

 » **Skin:** Using the Skin modifier, the vertices and edges in your mesh are given a "skin." That is, new geometry is generated around them, based on a radius you define in Edit mode. In a way, it's similar to increasing the Bevel value on a curve object as described in Book 2, Chapter 4. This modifier gives you a fantastic way to generate base meshes for sculpting or sprawling organic shapes like vines and other vegetation. As an additional bonus, this modifier can also generate an armature object with properly defined vertex weights so you more easily deform and animate your mesh.

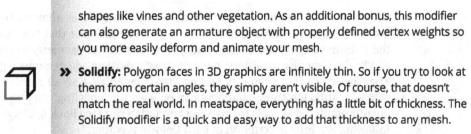

>> **Solidify:** Polygon faces in 3D graphics are infinitely thin. So if you try to look at them from certain angles, they simply aren't visible. Of course, that doesn't match the real world. In meatspace, everything has a little bit of thickness. The Solidify modifier is a quick and easy way to add that thickness to any mesh.

>> **Subdivision Surface:** This modifier is one of the most useful (and frequently used) in Blender. Simply put, the Subdivision Surface modifier adds vertices to your mesh by subdividing each edge and face. (I cover it in more detail later in this chapter.) This behavior allows for more detail and smoother surfaces on your mesh. It's especially useful for organic models like plants and animals.

>> **Triangulate:** Some game engines (the code "under the hood in a video game") require that all meshes consist of only triangular faces. Quads and ngons aren't allowed. Using this modifier, you can get an idea of what your model looks like with all triangular faces, without prematurely committing to that topology.

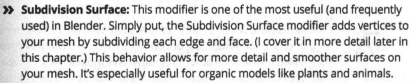

>> **Volume to Mesh:** If you have volumetric data, like clouds imported from OpenVDB files (see Book 2, Chapter 4) or a smoke simulation (see Book 4, Chapter 5), you may want to convert that data into a mesh object. You might want to have such a conversion if you want to use cartoony materials on that volumetric object, or perhaps you want to use sculpting tools on that form. Whatever your reason, the Volume to Mesh modifier allows you to convert a grid component of a volume object into a connected set of mesh data. Incidentally, there is a corresponding Mesh to Volume modifier for volume objects.

>> **Weld:** In a way, the Weld modifier is similar to the Decimate modifier, though it has far simpler controls. Basically, if two vertices in your mesh are within a particular distance from each other, they're merged into being a single vertex.

>> **Wireframe:** The Wireframe modifier is somewhat like the Skin modifier in that it creates geometry around each of the edges in your mesh. The controls and purpose of this modifier are different, however. Instead of being used to generate a base mesh as a starting point, the Wireframe modifier is most useful in generating renderable wireframes of your mesh so you can cleanly show its topology to your peers.

Deform modifiers

In computer graphics, the word *deform* doesn't carry any kind of negative connotation. When something is deformed in computer graphics, it means that subcomponents of that thing have been moved. In the case of 3D computer graphics, those sub-components are the vertices, edges, and faces that make up your mesh's geometry. Knowing that, it isn't hard to figure out that the modifiers in the Deform category are used to change the position of geometry in your mesh. Unlike the Generate modifiers, none of these modifiers add or remove geometry. They just move that geometry around, based on either a set of rules or external controls. Although these modifiers can be used for modeling, they're more frequently employed as tools for creating animation rigs (see Book 4, Chapter 3). The following is a brief description of each Deform modifier:

>> **Armature:** When it comes to animation rigs, the Armature modifier is the tool of choice for associating or *skinning* a mesh to a control armature, sometimes called a *skeleton* in other programs. This modifier is the mechanism that binds your mesh to an armature object and allows the bones of that armature to control the geometry in that mesh.

>> **Cast:** Simply put, this modifier pushes the geometry in your mesh to match one of three primitive forms: a sphere, a cylinder, or a cube.

>> **Curve:** The Curve modifier is similar to the Armature modifier, but it uses it as a curve object rather than the bones of an armature object to define your mesh's deformation. This is useful if you're rigging something that has a naturally curved change in shape, like a cartoon fish or hoses.

>> **Displace:** Using a grayscale image often referred to as a *height map* (lighter pixels represent high areas, darker pixels represent low areas), the Displace modifier can offset individual vertices from their initial location. This modifier can be a handy way to add bumpy detail or even model some terrain.

>> **Hook:** This modifier binds one or more vertices in your mesh to an external object. Hooks are useful for bulging or stretching part of your mesh. They're also useful for controlling curve objects. Book 4, Chapter 3 has a whole section dedicated to hooks and the Hook modifier.

>> **Laplacian Deform:** The deformation capabilities of hooks and armatures are very powerful, but they can occasionally "fuzz out" the details in your model or create excessive distortion that doesn't preserve the volume of your base mesh. The Laplacian Deform modifier helps to alleviate that problem computationally (as opposed to the more manual methods using lattices or the Mesh Deform modifier).

>> **Lattice:** Lattices are special objects in Blender that consist of a boxy network of interconnected control points. When a mesh has a Lattice modifier, you can use one of these lattice objects to perform broad deformations. In cartoony character animation, lattices can be particularly useful for giving characters convincing squash and stretch effects.

>> **Mesh Deform:** In its simplest explanation, the Mesh Deform modifier allows you to use a regular mesh to achieve some of the same deformation effects

that a lattice can give you. There are trade-offs, of course, but that gets into a much more advanced discussion on rigging.

>> **Shrinkwrap:** Using the Shrinkwrap modifier, you can snap the vertices of your current mesh to the surface of another mesh, as if you wrapped that other mesh in shrinkwrap. As an example, if you're doing a cartoon-style animation that involves the cliché of a bulge of water traveling along a water hose, you can achieve that effect with this modifier. Additionally, some modelers use this modifier to help get a starting point when they retopo a sculpt (see the next chapter).

>> **Simple Deform:** This modifier gives you the ability to twist, bend, taper, or stretch your mesh relative to its local Z-axis.

>> **Smooth:** Sometimes you have a model with a lot of hard edges and creases, but you need a version that's generally much smoother. Unlike the Weighted Normal modifier or the Auto Smooth feature in Blender, which adjusts how light reflects off your object to give the illusion of smoothness, this modifier tries to achieve smoothness by actually moving the vertices in your mesh so that they're evenly distributed along the mesh's surface. If your mesh geometry is already evenly distributed, though, this modifier is unlikely to help as much as other solutions.

>> **Smooth Corrective:** Typically speaking, most people refer to this as the Corrective Smooth modifier rather than "Smooth Corrective." In older documentation, you may see it referred to by the original algorithm name, "Delta Mush." The current naming is different just so it can be more conveniently grouped with the other smooth modifiers. The Corrective Smooth modifier is especially useful in character rigs where the armature or lattice might cause some funky deformations. The Corrective Smooth modifier can help automatically clean up some of that nastiness. It's also handy for generating more natural deformations in character rigs by giving the impression of muscle or fat on a character.

>> **Smooth Laplacian:** Like the Corrective Smooth modifier, the naming here is a bit different from what we call it. It's just named Smooth Laplacian in the modifier menu to group it with the other smooth modifiers. The Laplacian Smooth modifier does essentially the same thing as the Smooth modifier, but it uses a different smoothing algorithm. Generally speaking, the Smooth Laplacian modifier is slower than the Smooth modifier, but on complex meshes, this modifier usually gives more appealing results. The Smooth Laplacian modifier can be particularly useful for cleaning up meshes from 3D scanners or the Remesh modifier.

>> **Surface Deform:** Think of the Surface Deform modifier as a variation of the Mesh Deform modifier. The difference, however, is that the Mesh Deform modifier typically makes use of a mostly enclosed mesh, whereas the Surface

Deform modifier only deals with a mesh's surface, so it works well using open meshes. One of the most typical use cases for this modifier is if you do a cloth simulation on a plane and you want to transfer the movement of that plane to a more complex mesh, like chainmail.

» **Warp:** Using the location, orientation, and scale of any two reference objects, you can use the Warp modifier to distort your mesh, stretching its vertices from the origin of one object to the origin of the other.

If you're familiar with proportional editing, as described in Book 1, Chapter 4, think of this modifier as a way to give you that capability without directly selecting any vertices.

» **Wave:** If you apply the Wave modifier to a somewhat heavily subdivided plane, it gives an appearance similar to dropping a pebble in a still pond. Of course, you don't have to use a subdivided plane; the Wave modifier works on any mesh. Fair warning: If your mesh has only a few vertices in it, you will not see the wave effect. It will just appear like your whole mesh is moving up and down as a single unit.

Physics modifiers

The last column of modifiers contains the Physics modifiers. With a couple of exceptions (Explode, Ocean, and Particle Instance), you almost never add or adjust the settings in these modifiers from the Modifiers tab of the Properties editor. They get automatically added to your mesh when you add a particle system from the Particles tab of the Properties editor or add a physics simulation from the Physics tab of the Properties editor. However, for these physics effects to work on your mesh, they need to be associated with the mesh in some way. The modifier stack is how that association is made. This approach also allows you to control if you're doing physics simulations on the original base mesh or geometry generated from another modifier farther up the stack. It's an advanced topic, but Book 4, Chapter 5 has a bit more detail on using particles and physics simulations from within Blender.

» **Cloth:** The Cloth modifier serves as a container for cloth-based physics simulations in Blender. The only time you'd ever really mess with this modifier in Modifiers Properties is to move it up or down the stack.

» **Collision:** In order to support interactions between objects — especially objects with physics simulations — there needs to be a mechanism to handle collisions between those objects. The Collision modifier is that mechanism. Like the Cloth modifier, this is a container for properties that you adjust in the Physics tab of the Properties editor.

>> **Dynamic Paint:** Blender's Dynamic Paint feature is kind of a hidden gem within the application. With this feature, you can adjust the color (or other material properties) of one mesh, based on whether it's made contact with another mesh. Dynamic Paint is frequently used to generate "wet maps" on a mesh to indicate water splashing upon it or to create displacement when a character walks across a deformable surface like packed sand. The Dynamic Paint add-on is how you tell Blender where in the modifier stack to apply this effect, which is defined in the Physics Properties tab.

>> **Explode:** The Explode modifier helps do exactly what's in its name, blow up your mesh! Unlike most of the other Physics modifiers, this one doesn't actually get added from the Physics tab. You add it in the Modifiers tab. However, in order for it to work, you need to set up a particle simulation so the modifier knows where to send the pieces of your blown-up mesh.

>> **Fluid:** Fluid simulations encompass everything from water to smoke and fire. Even though you and I see those as very different things, as far as physics is concerned, all three are fluids, and their movement can be generalized with the same mathematical models. When you add a fluid simulation from Physics Properties, that simulation is added to the modifier stack with this modifier.

>> **Ocean:** Like the Explode modifier, the Ocean modifier is something that you add and control right from the Modifiers tab of the Properties editor. It has the ability to deform the geometry of your existing mesh or create a whole new mesh altogether in an effort to re-create the appearance of a large surface of water, such as the ocean or a lake.

>> **Particle Instance:** The Particle Instance modifier is an interesting little modifier that duplicates your mesh at the location of every particle in a referenced particle system. In a way, you can think of it as a crazy variation of the Array modifier in that you get a bunch of copies of your mesh. The placement of those copies in your scene, however, is a bit more complex to control because you need to set up a particle system.

>> **Particle System:** If you want the geometry of your mesh object to generate particles, then you need to add a Particle System modifier to your mesh. If you create a particle system in the Particles tab of the Properties editor, this modifier is automatically added for you.

>> **Soft Body:** In physics simulations, *soft bodies* are a specific kind of object that deform when they come into contact with other objects. The Soft Body modifier is how you provide that kind of behavior to your mesh objects. Like most of the other modifiers in the Physics column, this one is added when you create the corresponding physics simulation in the Physics tab of the Properties editor.

Working with Commonly Used Modifiers

As the preceding section shows, Blender mesh objects have a *lot* of modifiers that you can use to do all kinds of interesting nondestructive adjustments to your base mesh. Going through and creating a working example of each and every one of these modifiers is, sadly, more than I have available pages for, even in an All-in-One book! However, this section gives you some examples and explanations for some of the most commonly used modifiers in Blender. Hopefully they're enough to whet your appetite and get you to understand the power of modifiers enough to experiment with the other modifiers on your own.

Doing half the work (and still looking good!) with the Mirror modifier

When I was first learning how to draw the human face, I used to have all sorts of problems because I'd draw half the face and then realize that I still needed to do nearly the exact same thing all over again on the other side of the face. I found it tedious and difficult to try to match the first half of my drawing. Without fail, the first couple of hundred times I did it, something would always be off. An eye would be too large, an ear would be too high, and so on. I'm not embarrassed to say that it actually took me quite a long time to get drawings that didn't look like Sloth from *The Goonies*. (Some of my friends and colleagues might argue that a few of my drawings still look that way!)

Fortunately, as a 3D computer artist, you don't have to go through all that trial and error. You can have the computer do the work for you. In Blender, you use the Mirror modifier (Modifiers ⇨ Add Modifier ⇨ Mirror). Figure 2-3 shows the buttons and options available for this modifier.

The Mirror modifier basically makes a copy of all the mesh data in your object and flips it along its local X-, Y-, or Z-axis, or any combination of those axes. The Mirror modifier also has the cool feature of merging vertices along the center seam of the object so that it looks like one unified piece. By changing the Merge Limit value, you can adjust how close vertices have to be to this seam in order to be merged.

When you first look at the controls in the Mirror modifier, it can be pretty overwhelming to see a bunch of buttons in there, all labeled X, Y, and Z. Those letters correspond to each axis in your mesh's local coordinate system, but it's not immediately clear what each of them do and how they're different. For the most part, the ones you want to pay the most attention to are the first row of axis buttons next to the label, Axis.

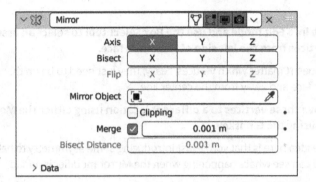

FIGURE 2-3:
The Mirror
modifier.

The X, Y, and Z Axis buttons dictate which axis or axes your object is mirrored along. For most situations, the default setting of just the local X-axis is all you really need. I also almost always enable the Clipping check box. This option takes the vertices that have been merged — as dictated by the Merge value — and locks them to the plane that your mesh is being mirrored across. That is, if you're mirroring along the X-axis, then any vertices on the YZ plane are constrained to remain on that plane. This feature is great when you're working on vehicles or characters where you don't want to accidentally tear a hole along the center of your model while you're tweaking its shape with proportional editing (O) enabled. Of course, if you do have to pull a vertex away from the center line, you can temporarily disable this check box. The Clipping option also prevents inner faces from being created along the center line of your model when extruding.

The other two rows of axis buttons have more specialized functionality. Say you have a mesh that you want to mirror along the X-axis, but it has geometry on both sides of the YZ plane. Now, you could go into Edit mode on your mesh and remove that extraneous geometry, but that's a destructive act. It would be better if that geometry could be removed procedurally with a feature built into the Mirror modifier. That behavior is exactly what you get with the X, Y, and Z buttons in the second row, next to the Bisect label. In this example, if you enable the X Bisect button and the X Axis button, the Mirror modifier knows to get rid of your extra geometry before mirroring. You can adjust the Bisect Distance slider to remove more vertices beyond those on the YZ plane.

What if you want to use the geometry from the other side of the mesh? Good news! That's what the X, Y, and Z buttons on the Flip row are for. As an example, open a new Blender session and perform the following steps:

1. **Select the default cube and delete it (Delete).**

2. **Add a monkey mesh (Add ⇨ Mesh ⇨ Monkey).**

    This is Suzanne; you meet her in Book 1, Chapter 4.

3. **Tab into Edit mode and use the Box Select tool to select an assortment of vertices from the left side of Suzanne's face.**

   It doesn't matter which vertices, really; they just need to be on that one side of her face and away from the center line.

4. **Move those vertices to a different location using either the Move tool or by using the G hotkey.**

   The idea here is that you're just introducing some asymmetry to her face so you can see what's happening when the Mirror modifier is added.

5. **Tab into Object mode and add a Mirror modifier (Properties editor ⇨ Modifiers ⇨ Add Modifier ⇨ Mirror.**

   You should see your change mirrored on both sides of Suzanne's face. However, you've got double geometry because Blender is mirroring both sides along the X-axis.

6. **In the Mirror modifier's panel, left-click the X button next to the Bisect label.**

   Enabling this button should get rid of the changes you made on the left side of Suzanne's face. You're only mirroring the geometry from the right side.

7. **Still in the Mirror modifier, left-click the X button next to the Flip label.**

   Now you should see your change mirrored across both sides of Suzanne again. However, this time, there's no double geometry because now you've bisected away the unedited side of Suzanne's face.

Figure 2-4 shows each version of Suzanne: unmirrored, mirrored with bisect, and mirrored with bisect and flip.

Instead of mirroring relative to the object's origin, you can also mirror relative to another object in your .blend file. Use the Mirror Object datablock field below the axis buttons. By default, the Mirror modifier uses the object's origin as the basis for what to mirror. However, by clicking in this field and choosing the name of any other object in your scene, you can use that object's origin as the point to mirror across. With the Mirror Object feature, you can use an Empty (or any other object) as a kind of dynamic origin. With a dynamic origin, you're able to do fun things like animate a cartoon character splitting in half to get around an obstacle (literally!) and joining back together on the other side.

TIP

Blender's text fields have integrated search, which means that you can type the first few letters of an object's name, and if the name is unique, Blender displays a list of objects in your scene that match what you've typed.

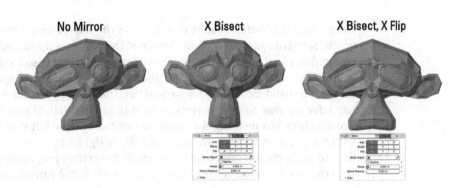

FIGURE 2-4:
On the left, an asymmetric Suzanne with no mirror modifier. In the middle, the mirror modifier is applied with the X Bisect button enabled. On the right, the mirror modifier has both X Bisect and X Flip enabled.

No Mirror   X Bisect   X Bisect, X Flip

At the bottom of the Mirror modifier is a subpanel named Data. The controls in this panel give you more granular control over how the Mirror modifier affects not just the position of the vertices in your mesh but also the data associated with those vertices (such as UV coordinates and vertex groups). I want to call special attention to the check box labeled Vertex Groups. As mentioned in the previous section, you can assign vertices in a mesh to arbitrary groups, known as *vertex groups*, which you can designate in the Object Data tab of the Properties editor, as shown in Figure 2-5.

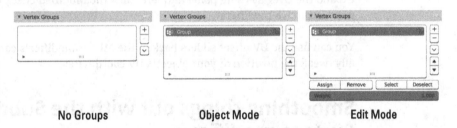

FIGURE 2-5:
Vertex groups are created within the Object Data tab of the Properties editor.

No Groups   Object Mode   Edit Mode

Book 4, Chapter 3 covers the actual process of creating vertex groups and assigning individual vertices to a group. However, the most basic way uses the following steps:

1. **Left-click the plus (+) icon to the right of the list of vertex groups in the Object Data tab of the Properties editor.**

    A new vertex group named Group appears in the list box.

2. **From Edit mode, select some vertices in your mesh and press the Assign button below the vertex group list.**

    You now have a vertex group with a set of vertices assigned to it.

Here's how the Vertex Groups check box in the Mirror modifier works: Say that you've selected some vertices and assigned them to a group named Group.R, indicating that it's the group for some vertices on the right-hand side. And say that you've also created another group called Group.L for the corresponding vertices on the left-hand side, but because you have not yet applied the Mirror modifier, you have no way to assign vertices to this group. Well, if you have the Vertex Groups check box enabled, the generated vertices on the left side that correspond with the Group.R vertices are automatically assigned to Group.L. You don't even have to apply the modifier to get this result! This effect propagates to other modifiers that are based on vertex group names, such as the Armature modifier.

Referring to Figure 2-3, the Mirror U and Mirror V check boxes within the Data subpanel of the Mirror modifier do the same kind of thing that the Vertex Groups check box does, but they refer to texture coordinates, or *UV coordinates*. You can find out about UV coordinates in Book 3, Chapter 2. The simplest explanation, though, is that UV coordinates allow you to take a flat image and map it to a three-dimensional surface. Enable these check boxes on the modifier to mirror the texture coordinates in the UV Editor and possibly cut your texture unwrapping time in half. To see the results of what these buttons do when you have a texture loaded and your model unwrapped, open the Sidebar in the UV Editor (View ⇨ Sidebar or N) and look in the View tab. Within the Display panel of that tab, expand the Overlays sub-panel and left-click the Modified check box. Hooray for nondestructive modifiers!

You can use the UV offset sliders back in the Mirror modifier's controls to manually tweak the position of your object's UV coordinates.

Smoothing things out with the Subdivision Surface modifier

Another commonly used modifier, especially for organic models, is the *Subdivision Surface* modifier. Old-school Blender users may refer to the Subdivision Surface modifier as the *Subsurf* modifier. If you have a background in another 3D modeling program, you may know subdivision surfaces as *sub-ds* or *subdivs*.

If you're not familiar with subdivision surfaces, the concept goes something like this: Blender takes the faces on a given mesh and subdivides them with a number of cuts that you arbitrarily decide upon (usually one to three cuts, or *levels of subdivision*). Now, when the faces are subdivided, Blender moves the edges of these faces closer together, trying to get a smooth transition from one face to the next. The end effect is that a cube with a Subdivision Surface modifier begins looking more and more like a ball with each additional level of subdivision, as shown in Figure 2-6.

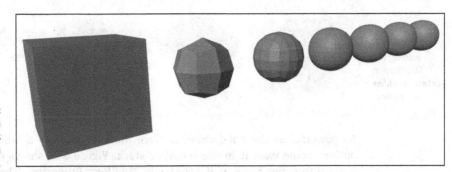

FIGURE 2-6:
A cube with
increasing levels
of subdivision
from 1 to 6.

Now, the really cool thing about subdivision surfaces is that because they're implemented as a modifier, you get the smooth benefit of additional geometry without the headache of actually having to edit all those extra vertices. In the preceding cube example, even at a subdivision level of 6, if you tab into Edit mode, you control that form with just the eight vertices that make up the original cube. This ability to control a lot of vertices with a relative few is a very powerful way of working, and nearly all high-end 3D animations use subdivision surfaces for just this reason. You have the smooth organic curves of dense geometry with the much more manageable control of a less dense, or *low poly* mesh, referred to as a *cage*.

For a better idea of the kind of results you can get with the Subdivision Surface modifier, break out Suzanne and apply it to her with the following steps:

1. **Add a Monkey mesh (Add ⇨ Mesh ⇨ Monkey).**

    Ooh! Ooh! Ooh!

2. **Set smooth rendering on the monkey (Object ⇨ Shade Smooth).**

    At this point, Suzanne is pretty standard. She looks smoother than the faceted look she had when first added, but she's still blocky looking.

3. **Add a Subdivision Surface modifier to the monkey (Modifiers⇨Add Modifier ⇨ Subdivision Surface or use the Ctrl+1 hotkey combo).**

    Now *that's* Suzanne! Instantly, she looks a lot more natural and organic, even despite her inherently cartoony proportions. Feel free to increase the Viewport Levels number in the Subdivision Surface modifier to see how much smoother Suzanne can be. I caution you not to go too crazy, though. Setting subdivisions above 3 might choke your computer a bit if it's too slow.

4. **Tab into Edit mode and notice that the original mesh serves as the control cage for the subdivided mesh.**

    Editing the components of the cage directly influences the appearance of the modified mesh within the cage.

Figure 2-7 shows the results of each step.

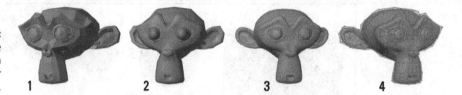

FIGURE 2-7:
Adding the Subdivision Surface modifier to Suzanne.

1   2   3   4

As powerful as the Subdivision Surface modifier is, only a limited number of options come with it in the modifier stack. Figure 2-8 shows the Subdivision Surface modifier block as it appears in Modifiers Properties. The first option is a choice between Catmull-Clark subdivision or Simple subdivision. The former is the default, subdividing and smoothing your mesh as expected. The latter works more like using the Subdivide operator while in Edit mode. It gives you more vertices in your meshes, but not the same kind of organic smoothness that the Catmull-Clark method provides. The Simple subdivision method is good for some situations, though, so it's nice that the option is available.

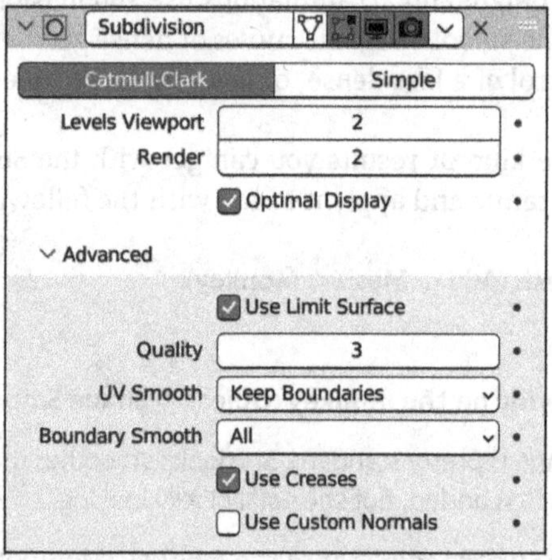

Subdivision		
Catmull-Clark	Simple	
Levels Viewport	2	
Render	2	
☑ Optimal Display		
⌄ Advanced		
☑ Use Limit Surface		
Quality	3	
UV Smooth	Keep Boundaries	
Boundary Smooth	All	
☑ Use Creases		
☐ Use Custom Normals		

FIGURE 2-8:
The Subdivision Surface modifier.

The next set of values, labeled Levels, allow you to set the level of subdivision that you see on your model. The first value is labeled Viewport. This value dictates the number of subdivision levels your mesh uses in the 3D Viewport. The Viewport value can be set to any whole number between 0 and 6. Typically it's set to a lower value than the Render value (described next) because you usually want smoother, higher-quality models in your final render than in the 3D Viewport. Don't go too crazy with setting this value. Because I like to keep my 3D Viewport fast and responsive, I tend to keep this number down at 1. Occasionally, I push it up to 2 or 3 to get a quick idea of what my model might look like in final output, but I always bring it back to 1 or 0 after that.

Beneath the Viewport value is a similar input, labeled Render, that dictates the number of subdivisions your mesh uses when rendering your model to a finished image. The Render value has the same range as the View one. On most of my work, which can get pretty detailed, I rarely use a Render Level higher than 3.

The Optimal Display check box, located below the Levels values, is something I typically like to leave turned on all the time. Optimal Display hides the extra edges created by the modifier when you view the model in wireframe viewport shading. On a complex scene, hiding the edges can definitely help you make sense of things when working in wireframe.

Like the Mirror modifier from the preceding section, the Subdivision Surface modifier has its own additional subpanel. In the case of this modifier, that subpanel is labeled Advanced. For the most part, the defaults in this subpanel are fine, but pay attention to the value field labeled Quality. This field has the same range as the Viewport and Render fields, but its use is slightly different. Basically, the algorithm that's used to make the smooth subdivisions in your mesh can be tuned for accuracy. Higher Quality values give you more accurate results that may take longer to calculate, whereas lower Quality values are faster, but might not be as accurate in the placement of subdivision components.

The Subdivision Surface modifier automatically subdivides your UV texture coordinates for you as well (see Book 3, Chapter 2). However, you do get some additional control over *how* those UV coordinates are subdivided with the drop-down menu next to the Boundary Smooth label. From this menu, you can choose your UV coordinates to be smoothed (the default), or kept sharp at the boundaries.

When working with the Subdivision Surface modifier, I typically like to have the Optimal Display option enabled, along with the On Cage button at the top of the Subdivision Surface modifier panel. Everyone's different, though, so play with it on your own and see what works best for you.

TIP

Using the power of Arrays

One of the coolest and most-fun-to-play-with modifiers in Blender is the Array modifier. In its simplest application, this modifier duplicates the mesh a specified number of times and places those duplicates in line, evenly spaced apart. Have a model of a chair and need to put lines of chairs in a room to make it look like a meeting hall? Using a couple of Array modifiers together is a great way to do just that! Figure 2-9 is a screenshot of Blender being used to create that sort of scene.

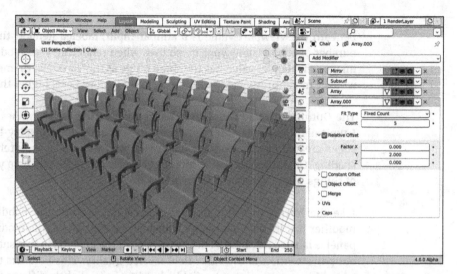

FIGURE 2-9:
Filling a room
with chairs by
using the Array
modifier.

TIP

You're not limited to using just one Array modifier on your object. I achieved the effect in Figure 2-9 by using two Array modifiers stacked together, one for the first row of chairs going across the room and the second to create multiple copies of that first row. Stacking multiple arrays is an excellent way to build a complex scene with just one object.

Blender's Array modifier is loaded with all kinds of cool functions that you can use in lots of interesting ways. Some ways facilitate a desire to be lazy by making the computer do as much of the repetitive, tedious tasks as possible. (For example, you can use the Array modifier to model a staircase, a chain-link fence, or a wall of bricks.) However, you can also use the Array modifier to do some really incredible abstract animations or specialized tentacles or even rows of dancing robots!

The bulk of the power in the Array modifier lies in how it handles *offsets* or the distances apart that the duplicates are set relative to one another. The Array modifier offers three different sorts of offsets, all of which you can use in combination with one another by enabling their check boxes:

>> **Relative Offset:** Think of the Relative Offset as a multiplication factor, based on the width, height, and depth of the object. So no matter how large or small your object is, if you set the Z value to 1.0, for example, each duplicated object in the array is stacked directly on top of the one below it. This type of offset is the one that's used by default when you first add the Array modifier.

>> **Constant Offset:** This offset adds a fixed distance to each duplicated object in the array. So setting the X value beneath this check box to –5.0m shifts each of the duplicates 5 meters in the negative X direction. The same behavior happens in the Y- and Z-axes when you set the values for those offsets as well.

» **Object Offset:** The Object Offset is my personal favorite offset because of its incredible versatility. It takes the position of any object you pick in the Object field — I prefer to use Empties for this purpose — and uses its relative distance from the mesh you added to Array as the offset. But that's just the start of it! Using this offset also takes into account the rotation and scale of the object you choose. So if you have an Empty that's 1 meter away from your object, scaled to twice its original size, and rotated 15 degrees on the Y-axis, each subsequent duplicate is scaled twice as large as the previous one and rotated an additional 15 degrees. Now you can make a spiral staircase like the one in Figure 2-10. And if you feel inclined to create an animation of a staircase where the stairs can be collapsed into each other and hidden, it's as simple as animating the offset object!

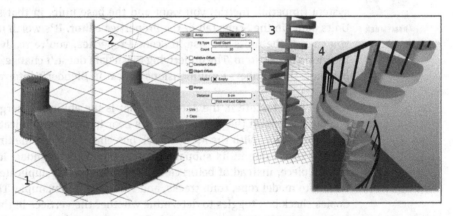

FIGURE 2-10:
(1) Model the step. (2) Add an Empty for Object Offset and rotate in Z. (3) Add the Array modifier. (4) Make it pretty.

You also have a lot of control over how many duplicates the Array modifier creates, thanks to the Fit Type drop-down menu at the top of the Array modifier panel. By default, the Fit Type is set to Fixed Count, and you explicitly enter the number of duplicates in the Count field below it. Fixed Count isn't your only Fit Type option, however. You actually have three:

» **Fixed Count:** This option lets you explicitly enter the exact number of duplicates you would like to create, up to 1,000.

TIP

The maximum value of 1,000 for the Fixed Count value is what's known as a "soft maximum" in Blender. This means that if you adjust that value using the mouse, it caps out at 1,000. However, if you click in that field, you can manually type numbers much larger than 1,000. Blender will use that manually entered number.

>> **Fit Length:** This option creates the proper count of duplicate objects to fit in the distance that you define. Bear in mind that this length isn't exactly in whole units. It uses the local coordinate system of the object that you're making an array of, so the length you choose is multiplied by the scale of that original object, as shown in the 3D Viewport's Sidebar (N).

>> **Fit Curve:** If you choose this option, you can choose the name of a curve object in the Object datablock field below it. When you do, Blender calculates the length of that curve and uses that as the length to fill in with duplicated objects. Using this option together with a Curve modifier is a nice quick-'n-dirty way of creating a linked metal chain.

REMEMBER

Blender has support for real units. Blender defaults to using meters as its base unit of measurement, but you're not limited to that. You can explicitly set the unit system (imperial, metric) you want and the base units in that system from the Units panel in the Scene tab of the Properties editor. It's worth noting that when you change the units you use in Scene Properties, you're really only modifying Blender's grid system. The underlying mesh data doesn't change. The only change is in how the numbers for dimensions appear in Blender's interface.

Another cool feature in the Array modifier is the ability to merge the vertices of one duplicate with the vertices that it's near in another duplicate, similar to the Mirror modifier. With the Merge check box enabled and some fine adjustment to the Distance value in its subpanel, you can make your model look like a single unified piece, instead of being composed of individual duplicates. I've used this feature to model rope, train tracks, and stair rails, for example. The First and Last Copies check box toggles to determine whether the vertices in the last duplicated instance are allowed to merge with the nearby vertices in the first object of the array. Use merging with Object Offset, and you can create a closed loop out of your duplicates, all merged together.

Say that you're using the Array modifier to create a handrail for your spiral staircase, and you don't want the handrail to simply stop at the beginning and end. Instead, you'd like the end of the handrail to have ornamental caps. You could model something and try to place it by hand, but that process can get problematic if you have to make changes or animate the handrail in the future. (Hey, this is computer graphics. Handrails that move and are animated make complete sense!) So another way to place ornamental caps on a handrail is to use the Cap Start and End fields in the Caps subpanel of the Array modifier. After you model what you want the cap to look like, you can pick or type the name of that object in these fields, and Blender places it at the beginning and the end of the array, respectively. Pretty slick, huh?

Chapter **3**

Sculpting in Virtual Space

O ver the years, as computers have gotten more powerful and more capable of handling dense models with millions of vertices (sometimes called *high-poly* meshes, an abbreviation of high-polygon meshes), computer graphics artists have wanted more and more control over the vertices in their meshes. Using a Subdivision Surface modifier is great for adding geometry to make models look more organic, but what if you're modeling a monster and you want to model a scar on its face? You have to apply the modifier to have access and control over those additional vertices. And even though the computer may be able to handle having them there, a million vertices is a lot for you to try to control and keep track of, even with all the various selection methods and proportional editing. Fortunately, Blender supports *multiresolution meshes* and a Sculpt mode that allows for dynamic topology.

Without the advent of digital sculpting, it would be much, *much* more difficult to achieve high detail 3D models like the one in Figure 3-1 as quickly as we have them these days. In the past, all that detail would have to be faked with textures or left out entirely. Or a single model with really high detail would take months to create, and only the most powerful computers of the time would be able to read such geometry, let alone edit it. Now, 3D artists regularly produce this kind of work in "speed sculpting" sessions over their lunch breaks. Living in the future is awesome.

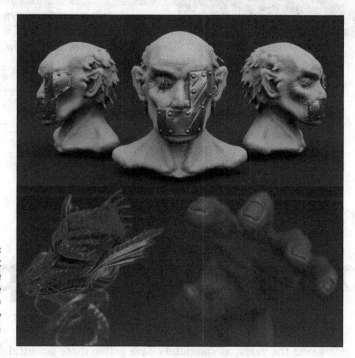

FIGURE 3-1:
Blender's sculpt
tools give you the
ability to create
highly detailed 3D
models as quickly
as you could with
traditional media.

Adding Background Images in the 3D Viewport

Before going headlong into the process of sculpting, it's worth it to take a moment and consider reference material. In meatspace media, artists use reference material all the time. Sometimes they work from a live reference like a model or still life, and sometimes they work using photographic reference. Why would it be any different when working with digital art? Of course, computers capable of doing high-level sculpting aren't quite as portable as most people would like in order to work from live reference (But it's getting there! There are a lot of folks who do rough sculpting in apps on their tablet devices.). So the majority of digital artists work from photographic or image references.

When working with meshes or any other type of 3D object in Blender, reference images are often helpful for getting proper proportions and scale. It's certainly possible to use a separate application (and even a separate monitor) to display your reference material while you work. However, you can use a reference more directly by loading an image into the background of the 3D Viewport. To do so, I suggest you add a Background image object to your scene by following these steps:

1. **Add a Background image object (Add ⇨ Image ⇨ Background).**

   Blender opens a File Browser where you can find your reference image on your hard drive. I suggest you use the Thumbnails display mode to more easily search for your image visually.

2. **Find your reference image and click the Load Background Image button in the lower right-hand corner.**

   Double-clicking also works. Either way, you return to the 3D Viewport and your selected image is loaded at the location of the 3D cursor, oriented to match whatever angle you're currently looking at in the 3D Viewport.

TIP

If you want to get an image quickly in your 3D Viewport, you can also drag and drop it from a File Browser right into the 3D Viewport. You can do this from both Blender's native File Browser *as well as* the one that's built into your desktop operating system (such as Explorer in Windows or Finder in macOS). It should be noted, though, that if you use this technique, the image you add doesn't behave like a background image by default. You need to make some adjustments to that image object. There's more on making those adjustments in the next few sections.

Mastering the types of image objects

You might notice that Blender offers you two types of image objects in the Add menu: Reference and Background. Actually, there are three. Look at the bottom of the Add ⇨ Empty menu and see that there's an Empty type named Image. Now here's a little secret: All three of them are the same thing. The Reference and Background image types are just Image Empties with some additional settings already set for your convenience.

Figure 3-2 shows all three image objects in the same 3D scene with a simple object crossing in front of each so you can have an idea of how they work.

The following list gives a quick rundown of the differences between each image object:

>> **Image Empty (Add ⇨ Empty ⇨ Image):** All three of the objects in this list are basically Image Empties, just with different default behaviors. When you add a basic Image Empty like this one, it's added like a regular object in your Blender scene, oriented to match the world axes with its face pointing along the Z-axis. There is no image preloaded. You need to choose an image separately from the Object Data tab of the Properties editor.

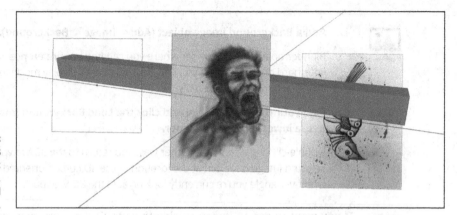

FIGURE 3-2:
The three kinds
of image objects:
Image Empty,
Reference, and
Background.

>> **Reference (Add ⇨ Image ⇨ Reference):** When you add a Reference image object, Blender first opens a File Browser (like the example in the preceding section) where you can immediately pick the image you want to load. After picking your image, it's oriented to match your viewing angle in the 3D Viewport, and its size is set to 5m. Other than that, all its settings are just like loading a regular Image Empty.

>> **Background (Add ⇨ Image ⇨ Background):** The process for loading a Background image is exactly the same as loading a Reference image. The difference, however, is that some of the settings in Object Data Properties are changed. In particular, the Depth buttons are set to Back and the Side buttons are set to Front. These settings ensure that the Background image object behaves like an actual background image.

Changing image object properties

So by knowing how these image objects work, you can make any one of them act like another with a few changes in Object Data Properties, shown in Figure 3-3.

The following is a quick run-down of the properties you have available for all Image Empties:

>> **Display As:** At their core, Image Empties are just like any other Empty object and can, therefore, be changed into any other Empty type from this drop-down menu.

>> **Size:** Use this value field to change the visible size of the Image Empty in the 3D Viewport. The next section shows you a more visual way of adjusting size.

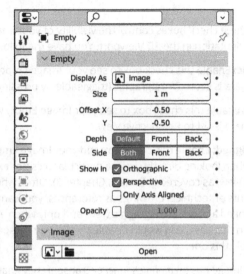

FIGURE 3-3:
The Object
Data tab of the
Properties editor
is where you
can modify the
properties of
Image Empties.

>> **Offset X/Y:** Using these values, you can adjust the position of your image relative to its origin in the 3D Viewport. The next section covers a more visual way of adjusting these values.

>> **Depth:** The Depth property gives you control over how your Image Empty is shown in the 3D Viewport relative to other objects in the scene. You have three options:

- **Default:** This is (appropriately) the default behavior for Image Empties and Reference images. They act just like any other object in the scene. If your image object is behind another object in the scene, it's occluded. If it's in front, it blocks the visibility of that other object.

- **Front:** Choose this option and your image object is treated like it's always in the foreground, regardless of its location in 3D space. If you have this option enabled, you'll probably want to enable the Opacity check box and adjust your image object's opacity.

- **Back:** This option is the default for Background images. Regardless of where the image object is located in your scene, all other objects appear in front of it.

>> **Side:** The three choices for the Side property control which side of the Image Empty shows your image data. The default behavior for Image Empties and Reference images is for the image to be visible on both sides of the image plane, whereas the default behavior for Background images is to be visible only on the Front side.

>> **Display:** These three check boxes control the visibility of your Image Empty based on your orientation in the 3D Viewport. You have the following options:

- **Orthographic:** Enable this check box to see your Image Empty when your viewport camera is set to Orthographic (toggleable by pressing Numpad 5).

- **Perspective:** Enable this check box to see your Image Empty when the viewport camera is set to Perspective view.

- **Only Axis Aligned:** Enable this check box and your Image Empty will be visible only when looking directly down a particular axis (for example, Top, Side or Front view, as covered in Book 1, Chapter 3). Often when you're using blueprints or technical drawings as references, you want them visible only when looked at from orthographic view, and only when aligned to the correct axis. In that case, you would disable the Display Perspective check box and enable this one.

>> **Opacity:** If your image has an *alpha channel* or transparency enable this check box, and that transparency will be used when the image is displayed in the 3D Viewport. But even if the image itself doesn't have an alpha channel, if you want to reduce the overall opacity of your image, enable this check box and use the Color slider to the right of it.

You can always change the image that's displayed with an Image Empty using the controls in the Image panel. For animation reference, you can also choose to load a movie file or image sequence.

Adjusting your image objects

Whether you're using a plain Image Empty, a Reference image, or a Background image, you may not want that image object to be where Blender puts it by default. Fortunately, Blender also gives you some handy visual controls for modifying an Image Empty. Of course, you still have access to all the basic transform tools described in Book 1, Chapter 3. However, wouldn't it be nice if you had visual controls for the Size and Offset controls in Object Data Properties? Luckily, you do!

With an image object in the 3D Viewport, move your mouse cursor over the edges of that image object. You should see that edge of your Image object and the one on the opposite side turn bright yellow with a thicker region in the middle. Likewise, if you move your mouse cursor over the corner, square control points appear at each corner. All these bright yellow shapes are *handles* that let you control the size value of your Image Empty. If you click and drag anywhere on these handles, you can visually change the size of your image object. Whichever side or corner that you click, the opposite side or corner acts as the reference relative to that which you're resizing.

Now, move your mouse cursor to somewhere near the center of your image object. You should notice that there's an X-shaped set of crosshairs at the center. If you click and drag those crosshairs, you can visually change the X and Y offset values for your image object.

However, what if your image object is rotated to face the wrong direction, and you want to fix that? Well, the Image Empty is still a 3D object, so standard rotation controls still work. If you need the Image Empty to face along one of the world axes, you just need to clear rotation (Alt+R or Object ➪ Clear ➪ Rotation) and then use the Rotate tool (or hotkeys) to rotate the object 90 degrees on whichever axis you need.

TIP

If you need your image object to be oriented to match some arbitrary viewing angle that you're using, there's a handy set of steps you can perform:

1. **Orient the 3D Viewport to the angle you want to work from.**

2. **In the header of the 3D Viewport, change the Transform Orientation dropdown to View.**

3. **Select your image object.**

4. **In the 3D Viewport's header, choose Object ➪ Transform ➪ Align to Transform Orientation.**

And just like that, your image object is facing you!

TIP

If you find that you're frequently adjusting your background image to match your viewport, you can add the Align to Transform Orientation to your Quick Favorites menu by right-clicking it in the menu and choosing Add to Quick Favorites. Then you can get that operator quickly by pressing Q.

REMEMBER

There's one other way to have reference images when you work. Camera objects can have their own background images that you can only see when looking through the camera (Numpad 0). You can activate and control camera background images from the Object Data tab of the Properties editor when you have a camera object selected. Book 5, Chapter 3 has more on using camera background images.

Setting Up Your Sculpting Workspace

There are a few different ways that you can access Blender's Sculpt mode:

>> **Change modes.** As you might expect, you can jump over to Sculpt mode from any 3D Viewport by using the Mode drop-down in the 3D Viewport's header. You can get there even faster using the Ctrl+Tab hotkey.

>> **Use the Sculpting workspace.** If you're using the General workflow template (File ⇨ New ⇨ General), the Sculpting workspace is available on the third tab from the left. Pop on over to that tab, and Blender automatically has you set up in Sculpt mode with a 3D Viewport already configured to get out of your way so you can get on with sculpting.

>> **Use the Sculpting workflow template.** Navigate to File ⇨ New ⇨ Sculpting. You have fewer workspace tabs in this template and Blender starts you with a sphere that's an already subdivided cube.

That said, although it's handy to know that Sculpt mode is always available, most people who do 3D sculpting don't typically start with a cube like what you have in the General workflow template. Sculpting usually requires more geometry to push around to get the detail you want, so most sculptors want to start with a more dense mesh. You could go through the process of subdividing and smoothing a cube every time you want to sculpt, but the last option in the preceding list, the Sculpting workflow template, is the recommended way to get started with sculpting in Blender. Figure 3-4 shows what you should see when first loading this workflow template.

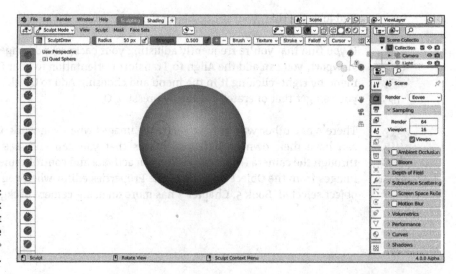

FIGURE 3-4:
The default work environment when you choose File ⇨ New ⇨ Sculpting.

When you create a new sculpting session, there are only two workspace tabs at the top of the Blender window, Sculpting and Shading. Their layouts are just like their corresponding workspaces when you have a new General workflow template. However, one big difference is that instead of starting with just a cube as your starting primitive in the 3D Viewport, there's a high-poly sphere ready and waiting for you to start sculpting in Sculpt mode.

TIP

Referring to Figure 3-4, you may notice that Sculpt mode has quite a few more tools in the Toolbar available when compared to the Edit mode tools described in Book 2, Chapter 1. For this reason, if you're just starting out with 3D sculpting in Blender, I recommend that you expand the Toolbar so it's large enough to display the names of each tool as shown back in Chapter 1 of this book, Figure 1-2. To expand the Toolbar, move your mouse cursor to the right edge of the Toolbar until the cursor icon changes to a set of arrows pointing left and right. Then left-click and drag to the right to expand the Toolbar. At first, you see the tool icons switch to a two-column configuration, and then eventually as you expand further, the tool names get revealed.

Understanding Matcaps: A Display Option for Sculpting

When sculpting in Blender, you may find that the material for your object and lighting settings in the 3D Viewport doesn't give you a good enough sense of the detail you're adding to your mesh. To get around this, you might set up a specific lighting environment and material for sculpting, or you might try adjusting the Studio Lights from the Lights section of Preferences. However, both of those options can be time-consuming to set up, and they aren't necessarily easy to tweak while in the process of sculpting.

Enter *matcaps,* short for *material captures.* A matcap is an image that encapsulates all the properties of a material, including lighting. By mapping that material to the face normals of a mesh, you can make that mesh appear to have the material and lighting captured by the matcap.

Blender ships with 23 preset matcaps that you can quickly and temporarily map to all visible objects in the 3D Viewport. To use them, you need to be in Solid viewport shading. From there, expand the Viewport Shading roll-out and choose Matcap from the Lighting type. Upon enabling matcaps, the ball in the lighting preview changes to display a ball with a matcap material. This is your currently active matcap. If you left-click that preview, it expands as shown in Figure 3-5 to let you choose one of the other available matcaps.

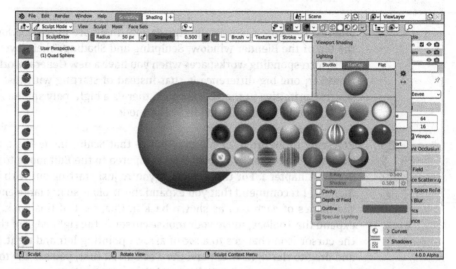

FIGURE 3-5:
The available
matcaps that
come with
Blender are easily
accessible from
the Viewport
Shading roll-out.

Of course, it's worth noting that if you choose to use matcaps in the 3D Viewport, the matcap is applied to all objects visible from the 3D Viewport, whether you're sculpting them or not. Fortunately, this is easy to get around using collections or local view (Numpad+Slash [/]).

All told, matcaps are a fantastically useful feature for 3D sculptors and modelers. It's worth it to take advantage of them as part of your modeling process.

Sculpting a Mesh Object

For each of the available tools in the Tool bar, they work by left-clicking with the brush cursor over the mesh and dragging your mouse cursor around the 3D Viewport. Due to this brush-style of editing, using a drawing tablet can be very beneficial.

Most tools feature a circular "brush cursor" that follows your mouse cursor as you move it around the 3D Viewport. When you bring the brush cursor near the surface of the object you're sculpting, it rotates to conform with that surface. This style of viewing the brush cursor is particularly important when sculpting because you often need to know how your sculpting tool is oriented in space.

In the default Sculpt workspace, the tool properties for all tools have the option to activate symmetry (mirroring) along any of your sculpt object's local axes. Once enabled, you can tell that symmetry is working because on the opposite side of your mesh, a small dot mirrors the position of the brush cursor as you move it over your mesh.

Regardless of the tool that you have active, if it has a brush cursor, you can quickly adjust the radius of that cursor by pressing F. When you press that hotkey, the brush cursor stops in place and snaps to face you. Then, as you move your mouse cursor towards and away from the center of the brush cursor, you can visually adjust the radius of your brush tip.

Likewise, you can also visually adjust the strength of your brush by pressing Shift+F. As you move your mouse cursor closer to the center of the brush cursor in this scenario, you increase the strength value of your brush.

Understanding sculpt tool types

Each type of tool in the Toolbar serves a different purpose when sculpting. The first thing you may notice is that there's a kind of color coding for each tool. These colors serve to help you categorize each tool so you can find what you're looking for more quickly. Granted, it's worth noting that because many brushes have the ability to invert their behaviors, these color categories serve mostly as guidelines rather than strict delineations. The organizational categories are as follows:

>> **Blue:** Generally speaking, tools with blue in their icons are tools that add material to your sculpt and make it larger in the spots where you use that tool. I call these *additive tools*.

>> **Red:** The tools with red in their icons are typically used to remove material from your sculpt and dig in on the surface. I refer to these as *subtractive tools*.

>> **Yellow:** The yellow-icon tools tend to get used for moving the parts of your sculpt around. I think of these as *move tools*, though because the Rotate tool is among them, you might think of them as transform tools.

>> **Purple:** The purple-icon tools are meant for ones that use simulation. In the base set of tools for sculpting, there's only one *simulation tool*, the Cloth tool.

>> **White:** The tools in this category don't really change the shape of your sculpt. They're more used in concert with the other tools that you have available or to adjust the color on your sculpted mesh. I call these tools *helper and paint tools*.

In addition to these base tools, there are another set of tools that I refer to as *mask and filter tools*. These tools are best used in your sculpting workflow to isolate or otherwise focus your workspace to be only what you're working on. Colorwise, their icons are kind of all over the place, ranging from white to multicolored.

NEW FEATURE

There have been a whole slew of new tools added to Sculpt mode since the last version of this book. Enjoy all the new features!

TIP

You always have fast access to any tool in the Toolbar by using the Shift+Spacebar hotkey combination in the 3D Viewport.

Additive tools

If you're starting with a raw sphere as your sculpting primitive, you're often going to go to the additive tools first to rough in the general shape of whatever it is you're sculpting. The following is a brief description of each of these tools:

>> **Draw:** The Draw tool is the default sculpting tool and it basically pulls the surface of your mesh outward. It can also push geometry inward if you enable the Subtract direction in the Brush panel within the Tool tab of the Properties editor (as with most of the additive tools, you can subtract on the fly as you sculpt by holding down Ctrl). By default, the Draw tool works with an even falloff, so the raised areas you draw tend to flow smoothly back into the rest of the mesh.

>> **Draw Sharp:** This tool is a bit of an exception to the "additive tool" paradigm I introduced in this section because by default it digs into the mesh you're sculpting on. That said, it's kind of nice that it's near the top of the Toolbar because it's a handy tool to have available for cutting into your sculpt and defining details like wrinkles and the start of creases. Hold Ctrl to draw a sharp peak on your mesh.

>> **Clay:** The Clay brush is pretty unique among Blender's sculpt tools. Its primary purpose is to make large changes, adding or subtracting volume from your base mesh so you can deal with details later.

Unlike the Draw tool, which just moves vertices along their local normals, the Clay tool uses a reference plane that you can customize from this brush's settings. The Clay tool is also useful for merging unlinked meshes within the same object.

>> **Clay Strips:** This tool behaves similarly to the regular Clay tool, but the technical difference is that it uses a cube to define the brush area rather than a sphere like the Clay tool.

In practice, you should find that the Clay Strips tool feels more like you're building up layers of clay as you work and often yields a textured surface with a bunch of wrinkles and ridges. This is one of my go-to tools when roughing in the form of my sculpts.

>> **Clay Thumb:** The Clay Thumb tool behaves as a kind of mix between the Clay tool and the Thumb tool covered in the Move tools section of this chapter. It has the features of the Thumb tool, but it uses a reference plane like the Clay tool.

>> **Layer:** The Layer tool is like using the Draw tool with a maximum height that it pulls vertices up to, basically creating a raised mesa on the surface of your

mesh. For a simple mnemonic, remember that the Layer tool relates to the Draw tool in the same way that the Clay Strips tool relates to the Clay tool.

>> **Inflate:** When you run the Inflate tool over your mesh, vertices move outward along their own local normals. If the Subtract direction in the Brush panel of your Tool Properties is enabled (or you're holding Ctrl while sculpting), the vertices move inward. This tool is good for fattening or shrinking parts of a model. The difference between this tool and the Blob tool is that Blob inflates vertices in a distinctly spherical way, whereas the Inflate tool works purely based on vertex normals.

>> **Blob:** When you sculpt with the Blob tool, vertices under your stroke are pushed outward or inward in a spherical shape.

This tool is good for adding or removing large forms to or from your mesh when creating rough starting sculpts.

>> **Crease:** In a way, the Crease tool is the opposite of the Blob tool. Instead of pushing vertices away from the center of the brush cursor, the Crease tool pulls vertices closer, sharpening indentations and ridges alike. In contrast to the Pinch tool described in the Move tools section, the Crease tool uses a reference plane, much like the Clay tool does.

Subtractive tools

In traditional sculpting or carving, you spend a lot of time digging into the surface of your sculpture. You define your shape by removing material from it. In digital sculpting, you can do the same thing. That said, you often use subtractive tools in the digital realm for adding detail after you've roughed in the general shape. The following are the subtractive tools that Blender has available:

>> **Smooth:** If you have jagged parts of your mesh or undesirable surface irregularities created while sculpting, using the Smooth tool cleans up those bumpy parts and makes the surface of your mesh, well, smoother.

TIP

You can choose the Smooth tool quickly by pressing and holding Shift while you sculpt. This way you can have quick access to the Smooth tool at any time, regardless of your current active tool. This quick-access feature makes for a very fast sculpting workflow.

>> **Flatten:** The Flatten tool lowers or raises vertices to an average height in an attempt to get them to be as flat, or *planar*, as possible. If you're sculpting a landscape and you decide to remove a hill, this tool is the one to use. The other setting for this tool, Contrast (accessible from the Brush Settings panel in Tool Properties or by holding Ctrl while sculpting), pushes vertices up and down *away* from that average height, increasing the overall distance between them.

>> **Fill:** Using the Fill tool, you can (depending on the tool settings) raise recessed vertices on your mesh as if filling a ditch, or you can deepen that ditch without having an effect on the vertices that are at "sea level."

>> **Scrape:** The Scrape tool is the logical opposite of the Fill tool. Whereas Fill raises or lowers only the vertices that are below "sea level," the Scrape tool works only on vertices that are above sea level. In practical application, you use this tool to flatten mountains or grow them larger.

>> **Multi-plane Scrape:** Sculpt tools are used for more than just organic models. You can also do hard surface sculpts, like architecture or machine parts. These parts often have corners you need to sharpen. You could use the regular Scrape tool on each side of a corner to clean it up, but the Multi-plane scrape tool gives you the ability to do both sides of a corner in a single go. You can control the size of the angle between the two scraping planes from Tool Properties.

Move tools

In sculpting, there are times when you need to make dramatic changes to your mesh. You may need to pull a whole section to one side, or perhaps you need to rotate the limb of a character. These use cases are where the tools in this category really excel. The following is a description of each tool with yellow in its icon:

>> **Pinch:** If you choose the Pinch tool, vertices are pulled toward the center of your brush cursor as you move it over the surface of the mesh. Pinch is a great way to add ridges and creases to a model, though perhaps with a bit less control than you have with the Crease tool, which more consistently pushes topology inward or outward.

>> **Grab:** When you left-click and drag your mouse cursor on a mesh with the Grab tool activated, the vertices within the tool cursor's circle are moved to wherever you drag your mouse. Grab is like selecting a bunch of vertices in Edit mode and pressing G.

On a related note, if you're using Dyntopo (covered later in this chapter), the Grab tool is one of the few that doesn't add or remove vertices to your mesh. It just moves them around. If you want to add and remove vertices while moving them around, try the Snake Hook tool, also covered in this section.

>> **Elastic Deform:** An exciting new addition to Blender's sculpting tool suite is the Elastic Deform tool. When you first choose this tool, it seems a lot like the Grab tool, but there's so much more to it. Based on research done at Pixar, the Elastic Deform tool is a Grab-style tool that preserves volume and proportions on your model as you work with it. And if you look through the tool settings for Elastic Deform, you'll find additional deformation controls for

grabbing on just one or two axes, plus twist and scale deformations. You can use this tool like you would the Grab brush, but it really shines when sweetening the look of an already developed model (like shape keys for additional expressiveness when animating).

» **Snake Hook:** The Snake Hook tool is similar to the Grab tool except it gives you more control over what you can do when you pull the vertices away from the main portion of your mesh. This is especially true if you're sculpting with Dyntopo enabled because the Snake Hook tool generates new geometry, whereas the Grab tool doesn't. With enough geometry, you can actually sketch in 3D with the Snake Hook tool. It's useful for making things like spines, tentacles, and dreadlocks.

» **Thumb:** To think about the Thumb tool effectively, imagine you're working with real clay. If you put your thumb on the clay surface and massage it in a particular direction, the area under your thumb also flattens out. That's the basic effect of the Thumb tool. It's like the Nudge tool (described later in this section) with the additional feature of flattening the area that you push.

» **Pose:** Sometimes when you're sculpting a character, you may want to adjust that character's pose. Maybe you're doing a "pure sculpt" that isn't intended for animation, so you don't need the traditional T-pose for rigging (see Book 4, Chapter 3). Or perhaps you *are* sculpting for animation, but you want to check a test pose without going through the full process of rigging. These scenarios are ideal use cases for the Pose tool. It's a great, fast way to rotate parts of your model with an offset radius, much like rotating a bone in a rigged character.

» **Nudge:** Using the Nudge tool, you can push vertices a bit at a time in the direction of your tool stroke. Think of it as a much more nuanced version of the Grab tool.

» **Rotate:** The Rotate tool, as its name indicates, is a tool for rotating vertices in your mesh. When you left-click and drag your mouse on your mesh, the tool remains stationary and the position of your mouse cursor determines how much the vertices within the area of your tool rotate. It can feel a little unwieldy to work with at first, but the Rotate tool can be exceedingly useful once you master its wily ways.

» **Slide Relax:** Sometimes while sculpting (particularly when sculpting directly on a mesh or when using the Multiresolution modifier covered later in this chapter) you need to shuffle some of your vertices over to another area of the mesh to get more detail. You can certainly remesh the whole model, as covered in Sculpting with Voxel Remesh later in this chapter, but that is often overkill if you just need to tweak one area of your sculpt. This scenario is where the Slide Relax tool really shines. Using it, you can slide vertices along the surface of your mesh and Blender tries to keep the general shape of your sculpt intact, much like the Edge Slide tool in Book 2, Chapter 1.

» **Boundary:** The Boundary tool only really works on *open meshes*, or meshes that don't form a completely closed, water-tight shape. When you choose this tool and move it over the surface of your object, open boundary edges are highlighted in yellow. If you click and drag the tool's brush, an edge either flares out or bends in, allowing you to create nice tapers at the boundaries of your open meshes. This tool is particularly useful when you're doing hard surface sculpting, but you can also use it to flare out the base of a tree if you're sculpting that.

Simulation tools

As of this writing, Blender only has one simulation tool in Sculpt mode. However, it's a doozy. The Cloth tool uses Blender's cloth simulation feature (see Book 4, Chapter 5) to give you the feeling of pushing the surface of your 3D model around like it's a piece of cloth. Say you're sculpting a character's clothes and you need that wrinkle in their shirt that forms at the armpit and grows down to a kind of crumple zone at the waist line. Using the Cloth tool, you can build that wrinkle just as if you were pushing around that character's shirt in meatspace. It's an incredibly powerful tool that's a ton of fun to play with. Functionally, it performs a lot like the Thumb or Nudge tools, but it creates wrinkles instead of smearing your geometry around. In fact, with some tweaks to the default settings of the Cloth tool, you can pretty easily age an existing character by giving them wrinkles. Figure 3-6 shows an example of a cushion that was quickly sculpted using the Cloth tool.

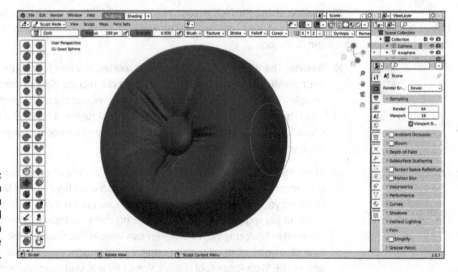

FIGURE 3-6:
The Cloth tool gives you quick, controlled access to cloth simulation while you sculpt.

Helper and paint tools

Sculpting isn't just about adding and subtracting material from digital clay. Sometimes you need to make changes to an underlying mesh structure or protect parts of your mesh when sculpting details nearby. These are the scenarios where the helper tools are, um . . . helpful. Also, since so many of those activities feel like painting on your mesh, you can use that same approach to modify the vertex colors on your mesh (there's more detail on vertex colors in Book 3, Chapter 1). The following tools are what Blender offers to help you while you sculpt:

>> **Simplify:** Of the helper tools, the Simplify tool is the only one that isn't for hiding or isolating parts of your mesh. Instead, you use it to reduce the amount of geometry in your mesh while sculpting. Because this tool actually changes the *topology*, or the number of vertices and how they're connected, on your mesh, it works only when you have Dyntopo enabled. Read more about Dyntopo later in this chapter in the section entitled "Freeform sculpting with dynamic topology (Dyntopo)."

>> **Mask:** There are occasions in sculpting when you want to preserve a part of your mesh and prevent accidentally sculpting those vertices. The Mask tool was created specifically for that purpose. Enable the Mask tool (you can do so quickly by pressing M), and you can paint the vertices on your mesh that you want to protect. Hold Ctrl while painting, and you can erase the mask. If you want to clear the mask altogether, you can choose Sculpt ➪ Clear Mask or use the Alt+M hotkey combination. I like to think of this as the Mask Painting tool because that's how it behaves. Also, Blender has a few other masking tools available, covered in the next section.

>> **Draw Face Sets:** The concept of *face sets* is like a more powerful variation of masks. While masking is incredibly powerful, you only get one. Either your mesh is part of the mask, or it's not. And when you create a new mask, the old one is either replaced or modified. With face sets, you're able to build multiple masks that are more persistent as you work. With the Draw Face Sets tool enabled, you can click and drag along the surface of your mesh, and Blender paints those vertices with a random color. That colored region is a face set. The following are the basic ways to edit and modify your face sets:

- **Draw a new face set** by left-clicking and dragging on your mesh. Each time you click and drag, you create a new face set.

- **Extend an existing face set** by Ctrl+left-clicking and dragging within an existing face set.

- **Isolate a face set** by hovering your brush cursor over that face set and pressing H. Shift+H hides the face set under your brush. Press H again to unhide the face set.

- **Expand a new face set along your mesh's topology** using Shift+W. The result here is much like the Anchored stroke method covered later in this chapter.

Once you have face sets defined, you can either isolate them for sculpting, or you can enable the Face Sets Auto-Masking check box in the Advanced subpanel in Tool Properties for most sculpt tools, and the tool will only work within the face set that you start working in.

>> **Multires Displacement Eraser:** There's a sculpting workflow that takes advantage of the Multiresolution modifier discussed later in this chapter. This tool, and the next one, only work when you're using that specific sculpting workflow. Basically, using this tool you can selectively remove any additional sculpting you've done on a multiresolution level, putting the mesh back to what it would look like if you just used the Subdivision Surface modifier.

>> **Multires Displacement Smear:** Like the previous tool, the Multires Displacement Smear tool works only when you're sculpting with the Multiresolution modifier on your mesh. I like to think of this tool as being similar to the Slide Relax tool, but tuned to work better with multiresolution meshes.

>> **Paint:** It's possible to do vertex painting while in Sculpt mode. Book 3, Chapter 1 covers more on vertex painting, and Blender actually has a dedicated Vertex Paint mode for mesh objects. However, when you're working on meshes that are as dense as Sculpting meshes, that mode can start to get pretty sluggish. The Paint tool in Sculpt mode tends to have better performance for high-poly meshes. One small note: the Paint tool does not work if you're sculpting with a Multiresolution modifier on your mesh.

>> **Smear:** This tool also works on vertex colors that you've painted on your mesh. Like the Paint tool, the Smear tool tends to have better performance on high-poly meshes when compared to its counterpart in Vertex Paint mode. Also, the default settings for the Smear tool in Sculpt mode tend to feel a bit more natural, like smearing paint with your fingers.

Mask and filter tools

Blender's sculpting tools are incredibly powerful, sometimes too powerful. What I mean by that is that because you're sculpting a 3D object using a 2D interface of a mouse cursor on a flat screen, it's possible that your sculpting strokes won't be as precise as you would like. You'll end up accidentally sculpting on parts of your mesh that you don't want to change at all. You can prevent those kinds of accidents by using masking and face sets. The preceding section covered the base Mask and Draw Face Sets tools, and they give decent control, but you're limited to a painting-based interface. Sometimes your sculpting workflow is better if you have other ways to define your masks and face sets. These tools give you those mechanisms:

» **Box Mask:** If you need to mask off large regions of your mesh while you sculpt, it can be tedious to manually paint every part of the mesh you want to mask. The Box Mask tool comes to the rescue. Using it, you draw a box (like with the Box Select tool in Object mode and Edit mode). Any geometry in that box gets masked. You can use the Box Mask tool to subtract an existing mask by holding Ctrl while drawing your box.

A key thing to remember about the Box Mask tool (and the Lasso Mask tool described next) is that it always works through your mesh. That is, if you're sculpting the head of a character and you use the Box Mask tool on the eye from the front view, the back of that character's head will also have a box-shaped mask.

» **Lasso Mask:** The Lasso Mask tool isn't visible by default. You need to long-click the Box Mask tool icon to reveal it. However, once you activate the Lasso Mask tool, it works as you expect. Draw an enclosed shape over your mesh and anything within that shape gets masked. Like the Box Mask tool, the Lasso Mask always works all the way through your mesh.

» **Line Mask:** Imagine that you want to mask off a whole chunk of your model, but at an arbitrary angle. Technically, you could rotate your mesh so you can use the Box Mask tool to get that angle, but since there's the Line Mask tool, that's not necessary. Enable this tool (long-click Box Mask to reveal it), and you can draw a line across your mesh. Blender puts a gradient on one side of that line; that's the side that gets masked. If you want the opposite side to be masked instead, press F to flip the masked side over your line while you draw it.

» **Box Face Set:** This tool mixes the functionality of the Draw Face Set tool covered in the preceding section with the Box Mask tool listed above. Two things are important to note about this tool:

- Like Box Mask, the default behavior is to create the face set all the way through your mesh. You can change this behavior by enabling the Front Faces Only check box in Tool Properties.

  - Unlike Draw Face Sets, the Box Face Set tool creates only new face sets. It doesn't expand or subtract from an existing face set.

» **Lasso Face Set:** Like the Lasso Mask tool, this tool isn't visible by default. You find it by long-clicking the Box Face Set tool. And like the Box Face Set tool, the Lasso Face Set tool is a mix of the Draw Face Set tool and the Lasso Mask tool. And also like the Box Face Set tool, the Lasso Face Set tool creates face sets all the way through your mesh and creates only new face sets.

>> **Edit Face Set:** A bit further down the list of Sculpt mode tools is the Edit Face Set tool. With this tool, you can make adjustments and modifications to face sets on your sculpted mesh. Choose this tool and then click inside the area of a face set on your sculpt. By default, clicking will grow the existing face set, but using the drop-down menu in Tool Properties, you can choose any of the following behaviors:

- **Grow Face Set:** With this option chosen, clicking in the area of a face set increases its size at its borders.

- **Shrink Face Set:** This is the inverse of the preceding option. Clicking in a face set reduces its size from its borders.

- **Delete Geometry:** If you want to remove the vertices and faces that make up your face set, choose this option and click on the face set. It's like hiding, but permanent.

- **Fair Positions:** Choose this option to flatten the geometry in the face set that you click on. In a lot of ways, it's like using the Flatten tool, but all in one shot across a face set.

- **Fair Tangency:** This option is similar to Fair Positioning, but instead of flattening, this option tries to smooth out the geometry in the face set and maintain some of its overall curvature.

>> **Mask by Color:** This option works effectively only if you've already set some vertex colors on your mesh using Vertex Paint mode or Sculpt mode's Paint tool. If you have, then you can use this tool to create a mask based on those colors, much like the "magic select" or "fuzzy select" tools in 2D image editors.

As you sculpt on a mesh, there are times when parts of your mesh just shouldn't be there anymore. Either those parts are in the way and need to be temporarily hidden so you can work on another part of your mesh, or you want to remove those parts altogether. The next set of tools are in Sculpt mode to help address those needs:

>> **Box Hide:** The Box Hide tool works just like the Box Mask tool, but instead of merely masking off parts of your mesh, this tool hides them altogether. There are two main reasons why you'd want to hide parts of your mesh rather than mask them:

- **Part of your mesh is in the way.** By hiding the bit that's in the way, you can get to hard-to-reach parts of your mesh and sculpt them.

- **Performance.** When you sculpt, the vertex count of your mesh can skyrocket. On really large or detailed sculpts, you can easily get millions (or tens of millions) of vertices in your mesh. If you have an older computer or a not-so-great video card, that amount of geometry can bring your machine to its knees. By strategically hiding parts of your mesh, you can ensure that Blender is working only with a limited amount of geometry and get the 3D Viewport to be a bit more responsive.

It's worth noting that the Box Hide tool is the only tool in Sculpt mode that doesn't adhere to any Symmetry setting you choose. There's more on Symmetry later in this chapter.

>> **Box Trim:** What if you don't want to hide part of your mesh? What if you want to remove it? That action is what the Box Trim tool is for. It works just like the other Box tools in Sculpt mode (and it respects symmetry). Only instead of masking or hiding geometry, the Box Trim tool deletes the geometry, adds an ngon face where the removed geometry once was, and sets that ngon as a new face set.

>> **Lasso Trim:** Activate the Lasso Trim tool by long-clicking on the Box Trim tool. This tool operates like the other Lasso tools in Sculpt mode and, like Box Trim, removes geometry, replacing it with a face set.

>> **Line Project:** In some ways, the Line Project tool is like a mix between the Trim tools and the Line Mask tool. In terms of interface, it works just like Line Mask. You draw a line over your mesh and the shaded side of the line is what gets operated on. Unlike the Trim tools, however, the Line Project tool doesn't remove any geometry. Instead it flattens the existing geometry to match the line you drew, much like using the Fair Position option on the Edit Face Set tool. Also unlike the Trim tool, the Line Project tool does not create any face sets.

There is one more class of tools in this section: the Filter tools. Basically, these tools operate on your entire mesh (or at least the unmasked parts of your mesh) to make quick changes across the whole thing. Functionally, they work by clicking and dragging left and right on your mesh. Dragging right increases the influence of the filter, whereas dragging left decreases it. There are three filter tools:

>> **Mesh Filter:** The Mesh Filter tool is a great, quick way to apply a general modeling adjustment to your sculpt. By default, the filter type is set to Inflate, but you also have the choices of Smooth, Scale, Sphere, Random, Relax, Relax Face Sets, Surface Smooth, Sharpen, Enhance Details, and Erase Displacement.

>> **Cloth Filter:** Use this tool to apply cloth simulation across your whole mesh. A handy approach for this tool is to set masks at specific points to "pin" those parts of the mesh in place, then use it to let the mesh sag down from those parts, like a sheet on a clothesline.

>> **Color Filter:** The Color Filter tool does the work of the Paint tool, but across your whole mesh. If you need to quickly set the color of your mesh or make color adjustments to your existing vertex colors, use the Color Filter tool.

REMEMBER

It's worth remembering that although the Filter tools affect your whole mesh, they do still respect any masks you've created with the masking tools described in the preceding bullets. So you can actually control where on your sculpt the Filter tools work.

Understanding the difference between tools and brushes

If you're familiar with other digital sculpting applications, Blender's way of handling tools and brushes may seem a little odd. Whereas in other programs, the terms *tool* and *brush* can almost be used interchangeably, that's not the case with Blender. In Blender, a sculpt tool can encapsulate one or more brushes. The tool is the thing you click in the 3D Viewport's Sidebar. The brush is a datablock that you can select from Tool Properties.

The primary advantage of this approach is organization. Even in 2D digital painting application, brush libraries can explode to be a massive wall of little brush icons that you have to scroll through to try to successfully find the one you're looking for. It's almost as bad as trying to find the right font when doing typographical work. By having tools with the ability to load their own individual brush datablocks, you can have a much more organized approach, and you're more likely to be able to find the brush you're looking for.

Tweaking brush properties

Regardless of the tool you have selected while working in Sculpt mode, all the settings for each tool are located in the Tool tab of the Properties editor. If you prefer to work with a maximized 3D Viewport (Ctrl+Spacebar), you also have access to your tool settings from the Tool tab of the 3D Viewport's Sidebar. And for quick access to frequently used tool settings, you can use the Tool Settings region in the 3D Viewport's header. In most other workspaces, I often keep the 3D Viewport's Tool Settings region hidden, but it can be pretty handy for sculpting and painting. For the sake of not pointing to all three locations every time I mention a setting, I'll spend the bulk of this chapter referring to how the tool settings are organized in the Tool tab of the Properties editor.

As you work your way down Tool Properties, you get finer and finer control of the settings for your sculpting tool. In fact, the first panel, Brushes, just contains a brush datablock, which serves as a means of storing for all the subsequent settings in that tool. By default, each tool only has a single brush datablock assigned to it. Within a tool, you can create as many different brushes as you'd like to save the presets that you like the most. Switch your brushes by clicking on the brush icon above the datablock and choose the preset brush you're interested in.

The Radius and Strength sliders below the list of brush datablocks control the size and strength of the brush you're currently using. As I describe earlier in this chapter, you can use hotkeys for changing these values while in the 3D Viewport so that you don't have to constantly return to the Tool Properties:

>> To change brush radius, press F, move your mouse until the brush cursor is the desired size, and left-click to confirm.

>> To adjust the brush strength, press Shift+F and move your mouse cursor toward the center of the circle that appears to increase the strength or away from the center to decrease the strength. When you're at the strength you want, left-click to confirm.

Related to the Radius value, there are also buttons to switch between the kinds of units you're using for defining your brush radius. The default behavior is to use View units. That is, the brush radius is defined by how many pixels it covers on your screen. However, if you're working more like a traditional sculptor, it may make sense to use real-world units for your brush size. If that's the behavior you want, then switch the Radius Units to use Scene units instead.

Additionally, if you happen to have a drawing tablet, you can bind the Radius and Strength values to the pressure sensitivity of your tablet. Each value slider has a button to its right with an icon of a pen with circles radiating from it. Left-click this toggle button on either slider, and Blender recognizes the pressure information from your tablet.

In the Tool tab of the Properties editor, there is another button to the right of the pressure sensitivity toggle buttons on Radius and Strength. This button is for toggling unified brush settings. If you want the size or strength of your brush to persist regardless of the sculpt tool you choose, enable these toggles. By default, the Radius value has its Use Unified Radius button enabled. The unified settings buttons are visible only in the Tool tab of the Properties editor; they're not shown in the Tool Settings region of the 3D Viewport.

The next set of important controls available while in Sculpt mode are a pair of buttons in the Brush panel. Depending on which sculpt tool you're using, these labels may be named Add and Subtract, Flatten and Contrast, Inflate and Deflate, or they may not be there (for move tools like Grab, Snake Hook, and Rotate). Regardless of what they're named, if they're available, pressing Ctrl while using the tool does the opposite behavior of what's selected. For example, if you're using the Draw tool with Add enabled, the normal behavior creates a small hill wherever you draw with the brush cursor. If you Ctrl+left-click and drag, you sculpt a small valley instead.

When working with additive tools like Draw, Inflate, or Layer, an additional check box, labeled Accumulate, appears in the Advanced sub-panel in the Brush Settings panel. By default, when you use these tools, they move the faces on your mesh relative to the normals that they have when you start making your stroke, regardless of how many times you paint over them in a single stroke. This default behavior is helpful because it prevents your mesh from quickly expanding uncontrollably. However, if you want the tool to continually affect your geometry each time the brush cursor runs over it in a single stroke, then you should enable this check box. Among the subtractive tools, the Flatten tool is the only one with the Accumulate option, and is enabled by default.

Refining control of your tools

The rest of the panels in Tool Properties are available for each of Sculpt mode's tools. With a few exceptions, each set of properties you set is specific to the brush datablock that you've got active, and you can use them when building your own custom brushes. The next section gets into custom brushes in more detail. The following describes each panel in Tool Properties:

>> **Brush Settings:** As the name of this panel implies, the settings here are all of the various settings for the brush you're using on your tool. The most important of these settings are covered in the previous section. However, there are additional sub-panels here that can give you even more control over your brushes:

- **Advanced:** This sub-panel gives you more refined control over your brush, such as whether it affects only face sets or the type of sculpt plane that the brush uses. For the most part, you can leave these settings at their defaults.

- **Texture:** You can create brush textures in Blender and use them to influence your brushes. The Texture panel is where you assign a texture to your current brush. It's the same system that's used for Texture Paint mode in Blender. See Book 3, Chapter 2 for more information on creating textures and Texture Paint mode. If you already have textures created in your .blend file, left-clicking the texture icon gives you the ability to choose which one you want to use on your active brush.

- **Stroke:** The Stroke panel holds settings that dictate what happens when you're dragging the brush over your mesh. The most valuable setting in this panel is Stroke Method. The options in this menu dictate how your brush movement influences your mesh. For fun, choose the Layer brush and set the Stroke Method to Anchored. When you left-click and drag your brush over your model, you get a neat mesh tsunami that originates from the location you clicked.

- **Falloff:** Within this panel are settings for adjusting how the influence of your brush changes from its center to its extremities. You can use an assortment of curve presets, or you can use the curve editor interface to make your own custom falloff profile.

- **Cursor:** The Cursor sub-panel has controls for how the brush cursor appears in the 3D Viewport as you sculpt. You can control the color of the brush cursor itself, whether it's visible at all, and the transparency of your brush as you adjust its size and strength.

» **Dyntopo:** If you choose to enable Dyntopo for dynamic topology sculpting, your controls for Dyntopo behavior are in this panel, as covered in detail later in this chapter.

» **Remesh:** The settings in the Remesh panel give you the ability to redefine the topology of your mesh as you work. This workflow is often used as an alternative to Dyntopo, and it's covered later in this chapter in the section entitled "Sculpting with Voxel Remesh."

» **Symmetry:** This panel controls how the sculpt brushes modify your mesh relative to the object's local axes. For example, if you left-click the X button next to the Mirror label, anything you do on the left side of the mesh automatically also happens on the right side. Symmetry is an excellent timesaver for doing involved tasks like sculpting faces. The X, Y, and Z lock buttons in this panel prevent your sculpted vertices from moving along any of those axes if they're enabled.

WARNING

As of this writing, the Symmetrize operator in this panel does not respect any masking that you've painted on your mesh. So if you've painted a mask in the hope that Symmetrize will only have an effect on the unmasked vertices of your mesh, you're a bit out of luck. Symmetrize will happily mirror your mesh regardless of the mask, removing or changing those vertices that you wanted to preserve.

» **Options:** The Options panel is kind of a dumping ground for miscellaneous brush properties that you may want to set while you work. By default, the Fast Navigate check box is enabled. This option works only if you're sculpting with the Multiresolution modifier on your mesh. With Fast Navigate enabled, Blender drops the resolution of your mesh while you navigate around it. This feature helps prevent your computer from slowing down on really heavy meshes.

Creating custom brushes

Using the controls in Tool Properties while in Sculpt mode, you can create your own custom brush datablock for your currently active sculpt tool. Follow these steps:

1. **Create a new brush datablock by clicking the Add Brush button in the brush datablock.**

    The Add Brush button doesn't have any text; it has an icon that looks like two pieces of paper, as shown in the left margin. Adding a new brush datablock in this manner duplicates the current active brush.

2. **Name your new brush by typing in the datablock field.**

Now you can go about customizing your brush. When you save your `.blend` file, the brush datablock is saved with it.

Using Blender's texture system to tweak brushes

In the Texture panel, you can pick a texture to influence the behavior of your brush. Any texture made in Texture Properties or the Texture Node Editor can be used as a brush when you sculpt. Textured brushes are an excellent way to get more details added to your mesh while sculpting. Choose an existing texture by left-clicking the texture square in this panel and picking from the thumbnail images that appear. (See Book 3, Chapter 2 for more information on creating and loading textures in Blender.) Figure 3-7 shows the Texture panel in Tool Properties.

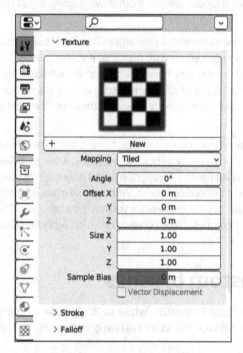

FIGURE 3-7:
Use the Texture panel in Tool Properties to make use of a texture on your active sculpt tool.

REMEMBER

You may want to enable the Rake check box beneath the Angle value when you've loaded a texture. With this option toggled on, the texture is rotated as you sculpt to match the motion of the brush. Using Rake helps you avoid creating unnatural patterns from your textures when you sculpt. The Rake option isn't visible by default because the default Mapping value is set to Tiled. If you set Mapping to View Plane, Area Plane, or Random, Blender makes the Rake check box available.

TIP

If you're sculpting with the Multiresolution modifier (see the next section) and you have a high level of subdivisions, it can be taxing on your computer, using a *lot* of memory to store all those additional vertices. If you use too many levels of subdivision, your computer may run out of memory, and Blender may lock up or crash. This can also happen if you're sculpting with Dyntopo and adding a lot of fine details to your sculpt. In an effort to prevent a crash and give themselves more vertices to play with, some 3D sculptors in Blender often go to the System section of Preferences (Edit ⇨ Preferences) and disable Global Undo as well as change the number of undo steps from the default value of 32 down to 0. This modification removes the safety net of undo, so it's best to do this only if performance starts to get sluggish while sculpting.

Sculpting with the Multiresolution Modifier

The default Sculpting workspace gives you a fairly high-density starting mesh to play with Sculpt mode, but if you're working with just that mesh, you'll quickly discover that you need more geometry to get enough detail in your sculpt. You could subdivide the mesh in Edit mode or add (and apply) a Subdivision Surface modifier, but that workflow is destructive and gives you more geometry at the expense of performance.

Multiresolution (or *multires*) meshes address the problem of having to apply the Subdivision Surface modifier before you can directly control the vertices that it creates. With a multires mesh, you can freely move between a level 1 subdivision and a level 6 subdivision, just like with the Subdivision Surface modifier. However, the difference is that you can directly control the vertices of the level 6 subdivision just as easily as the level 1 subdivision by using Blender's Sculpt mode. And you can see changes made in either level — to varying levels of detail, depending on the level you're looking at. (If you make a very fine detail change in level 6, it may not be readily apparent at level 1.)

Creating a multires mesh is just like adding any other modifier to a mesh object. Go to Modifiers Properties and choose Multiresolution from the Add Modifier menu. Figure 3-8 shows what the Multiresolution modifier's controls look like after being added to your selected object.

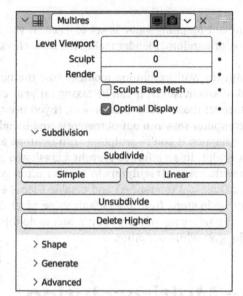

FIGURE 3-8:
The
Multiresolution
modifier block.

The Multiresolution modifier is similar in appearance to the Subdivision Surface modifier, covered in Book 2, Chapter 2. By default, the Multiresolution modifier starts with zero subdivisions on your mesh. Use the Subdivide button to increase the level of subdivision that you want to add to your mesh. Subdividing increments the values for all three level types, Viewport, Sculpt, and Render. Like the Viewport and Render values in the Subdivision Surface modifier, these values control how many levels of subdivision you see in the 3D Viewport, both while sculpting and when your model is rendered, respectively.

However, unlike with the Subdivision Surface modifier, you don't have exactly six levels of subdivision to switch between. In the Multiresolution modifier, the number can be as low as zero and as high as your computer's processor and memory can handle. And before adding a level, you have the option of choosing Catmull-Clark Subdivision or Simple Subdivision, like you can with the Subdivision Surface modifier.

REMEMBER

You can't freely change between subdivision types on a given level with the Multiresolution modifier. Changing from Catmull-Clark to Simple (or vice versa) has an effect on all multires levels.

TIP

If you have a Subdivision Surface modifier on your mesh, I recommend applying it to your mesh or removing it from the modifier stack before adding the Multiresolution modifier. Because the Multiresolution modifier uses the same process to create subdivision levels, you really don't need to have both active at the same time.

After you add a level, you have some additional options available. Clicking Delete Higher removes all subdivision levels greater than the level you're currently in. So if you have five levels of subdivision and you're at level three, clicking Delete Higher effectively kills levels four and five.

Enabling the Optimal Display check box does the same thing that the corresponding check box does in the Subdivision Surface modifier: It prevents Blender from showing subdivided edges in the 3D Viewport. Some 3D modelers who use sculpting tools like to overlay the model's wireframe on the mesh as they work so that they can have an idea of how their topology looks. (See Book 2, Chapter 1 for more information.) Without Optimal Draw enabled, the 3D Viewport of your model can quickly get cluttered, so enabling this check box simplifies the display for you.

Now, if you try to tab into Edit mode on a multires mesh, you still see only the vertices available to you in the cage provided by the base mesh. So how do you actually edit all those additional vertices created by the Multiresolution modifier? The answer: Sculpt mode.

When working in Sculpt mode and using the Multiresolution modifier, the general workflow is to start at low levels of subdivision to block out the rough shape of your model, and then proceed to higher levels of subdivision for more detailed elements of your model. The process is very much like traditional sculpting in meatspace, as well as box modeling in the CG world. The only difference in this case is that the Multiresolution modifier allows you to move between high and low levels of subdivision, so you don't have to block out your whole model in a single go.

Nothing says that you're required to use the Multiresolution modifier when sculpting in Blender. In fact, Sculpt mode works just fine without any Multiresolution modifier at all. That said, the Multiresolution modifier uses some acceleration structures that make Blender capable of sculpting meshes with millions of vertices without breaking a sweat. If you try to sculpt on meshes that large without the Multiresolution modifier, performance can often be orders of magnitude worse.

Freeform Sculpting with Dynamic Topology (Dyntopo)

One of the most loved features among Blender's sculpting community is the ability to have dynamic topology (Dyntopo for short) while in Sculpt mode. Simply put, when you enable Dyntopo, your sculpting brush can add or remove geometry from your mesh on the fly. Need more detail in just one part of your model? There's no need to use the Multiresolution modifier and bump up the vertex count for your whole mesh. Just enable Dyntopo and add that detail exactly where you need it.

To use Dyntopo, you need to be in Sculpt mode. While in Sculpt mode, look at the Tool tab of the Properties editor. A panel there is named, appropriately, Dyntopo. Left-click the check box at the top of the panel and you're off to the races, sculpting with dynamic topology. Alternatively, you can also enable Dyntopo with Ctrl+D while in Sculpt mode. Figure 3-9 shows the Dyntopo panel in Tool Properties.

For such a powerful feature, there are relatively few options specific to Dyntopo. The following is a quick rundown of the options available in the Dyntopo panel:

>> **Detail Size:** Dyntopo works by modifying edges within the area of your brush cursor. The Detail Size field defines a value that lets Dyntopo decide whether a specific edge gets modified, based on its length. This value can either be in screen pixels or a percentage, depending on the detail type method that you choose (I cover detail types in this list).

>> **Refine Method:** Dyntopo can subdivide edges in your mesh and *collapse* them, removing additional detail. The options in this drop-down menu allow you to control which behavior you want your sculpt brush to use:

- **Subdivide Edges:** If an edge within your brush cursor is longer than the detail size, it's subdivided. This refine method is great for fine details, creases, and sharp peaks.

- **Collapse Edges:** When you choose the Collapse Edges option, short edges get collapsed into a single edge. In the case of Dyntopo, a short edge is defined as being two-fifths (2/5) the length of the detail size. This option is great for evening out your topology and removing long skinny triangles that may render weirdly. However, the trade-off is that it also removes any fine details smaller than the detail size.

- **Subdivide Collapse:** The Subdivide Collapse option is the default. With this refine method, edges within the area of your brush cursor are subdivided *and* collapsed, relative to the detail size. This behavior makes the Subdivide Collapse option well-suited for quickly roughing the general forms of your sculpt.

» **Detailing:** When sculpting, it's common for artists to arbitrarily navigate around their model as they work, orbiting, panning, and zooming to get the best view of the section that they're sculpting.

Zooming specifically presents an interesting challenge for Dyntopo because sometimes you want the detail size to remain the same regardless of how much you zoom in or out from your model; other times, you want to do more detailed work as you zoom closer. The options in this drop-down menu let you choose:

- **Relative Detail:** This is the default setting. Choose this option to define detail size relative to the pixels on your screen. If you zoom out far enough, all the edges in your mesh become smaller than the detail size. If you zoom in, you only subdivide smaller edges.

- **Constant Detail:** Choose the Constant Detail option if you want the detail size to remain the same, regardless of how much you zoom in or out from your model. With this option, detail size is defined as a percentage of the base unit you define in the Scene tab of the Properties editor (the default is 1 meter). Additionally, the Detail Size field at the top of the Dyntopo panel gets an eyedropper button. Left-click that button to sample the geometry in your mesh. This means that you can click the eyedropper on a part of your mesh, and the Detail Size field is set to match the edge lengths in that region.

- **Brush Detail:** If you pick Brush Detail, then the Detail Size is determined by the percentage of your brush cursor. Increase the radius of your brush cursor and you increase the edge length. Reduce the brush radius, and you generate more detailed topology.

- **Manual Detail:** Choose this value and edge length is fixed based on the Resolution value you set at the top of the Dyntopo panel. Higher Resolution values mean you sculpt with more detail, regardless of brush size or how close you're zoomed in on your mesh.

» **Smooth Shading:** The Smooth Shading check box toggles between smooth shading and flat shading for your entire mesh while sculpting. This is mostly a personal preference, though some sculptors claim to have a more responsive 3D Viewport with Smooth Shading disabled.

Of course, the power that a feature like Dyntopo presents also necessarily comes with a few caveats:

>> You can't have Dyntopo and a multires mesh at the same time. It's kind of difficult to have fixed subdivision levels if the underlying topology is constantly changing.

>> Because Dyntopo dramatically changes your mesh topology, it will not preserve additional mesh data like vertex groups, UV coordinates, or vertex colors. Also, if you have some faces on your mesh set to smooth shading and others to flat shading, that also gets changed so all faces are either one or the other, depending on whether you toggle the Smooth Shading check box in the Dyntopo panel.

>> Although you can reduce vertices using Dyntopo, it's not currently possible to sculpt a hole in your mesh. You can make holes using the Trim tools covered earlier in this chapter, but they require you to have Dyntopo disabled.

>> It's not possible to use Blender's remesh feature (covered in the next section) while Dyntopo is enabled.

>> Unless your model is being used in a still image and never rigged for animation, it almost always will be necessary to retopologize a mesh that's been sculpted with Dyntopo enabled. This chapter ends with a primer on doing retopology in Blender.

Caveats and trade-offs aside, Dyntopo is an extremely powerful tool for modern 3D modelers. I daresay most of the complex models you see on films, television, and the Internet are made with sculpting techniques rather than traditional modeling techniques. In terms of workflow, it goes something like this:

1. **Start with a base mesh.**

   Depending on what you're modeling, the base mesh could be as simple as a sphere like you get in the default Sculpting workspace, or a somewhat more complex rough form for the model, such as a 3D stick figure to start a character model. In the ideal case, whatever your base mesh is, it should have evenly distributed faces (that is, all the faces on your base mesh should be roughly the same size).

2. **Sculpt with Dyntopo.**

   With Dyntopo enabled, use the various sculpting tools to produce your impressive 3D sculpt.

3. **From Object mode, create a new mesh.**

   It doesn't much matter what kind of mesh it is. When you get into Edit mode, you'll need to initially delete all the geometry in it so you can start the next step.

4. **Retopologize the sculpt using the newly created mesh.**

   At this point, you're basically using the sculpt as a 3D reference model to which you can snap your clean topology vertices. The process of retopology is covered later in this chapter.

5. **Finalize and polish the retopologized mesh.**

   This is where details are re-added using traditional modeling techniques. In this step, you may also bake some of that additional detail from the high resolution sculpt into a texture that you apply to your retopologized mesh. Book 3, Chapter 2 has more on baking textures from your geometry.

Sculpting with Voxel Remesh

In addition to multires sculpting and sculpting with Dyntopo, there's another popular approach to sculpting in 3D that Blender supports: *remeshing*. Like Dyntopo, the remeshing workflow is a destructive modeling workflow, meaning that you're directly affecting the position of real geometry on your mesh. Where Dyntopo and remeshing differ is that Dyntopo only affects vertices that are directly within the radius of your tool's brush. Remeshing is applied to the entire mesh object.

Recall that in the preceding section, the sculpting workflow described talks about starting with a mesh that has evenly distributed faces across its surface. When you use Blender's sculpt tools, that even distribution of faces is eventually going to be a lot less even. Even without Dyntopo, you'll start having more vertices and smaller faces in regions where you have more detail, whereas you'll have fewer vertices and larger faces in low detail parts of your mesh. This kind of situation can not only bog down your computer's performance, but it can often be a hint that you're starting to work on details in your sculpt too early.

As with so many things in 3D art, an ideal workflow involves starting with big, low-detail modifications to the model. Then as those areas start to get the correct general form, you can go in and add higher levels of detail as you go. The remesh workflow for sculpting reinforces this approach, and all of the controls for it live in the Remesh panel in Tool Properties while you're in Sculpt mode, as shown in Figure 3-10.

TIP

The Remesh panel is also available in a couple other places, including the Tool tab of 3D Viewport's Sidebar, and even when you're in Object mode, you can remesh using the Remesh panel in the Object Data tab of the Properties editor.

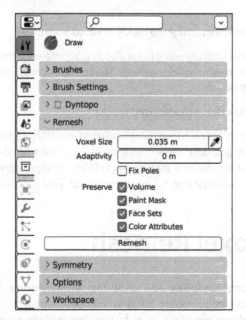

FIGURE 3-10:
The Remesh panel in Tool Properties while in Sculpt mode is where all your remeshing controls live.

In principle, the options available in the Remesh panel are the same as those in the Remesh modifier (see the previous chapter for more on modifiers). The difference is that when you run the Remesh operator — that's the button at the bottom of the panel — it's a destructive operation, permanently replacing all the geometry in your mesh with new geometry based on a *voxel*, or volumetric pixel. The settings in the Remesh panel dictate how Blender creates that new, voxel-based geometry. A description of each parameter follows:

>> **Voxel Size:** This is probably the most important setting in the Remesh panel. The Remesh operator works by building a grid, similar to a Lattice object (see Book 2, Chapter 4) that encases your object. That grid is composed of voxels. Each place where that voxel grid intersects with your object's mesh, Blender creates vertices and faces. The Voxel Size setting controls how fine that grid is. Smaller voxels give you higher detail with a more dense mesh. Larger voxels give lower detail and a less dense mesh,

>> **Adaptivity:** Think of the Adaptivity setting as having the benefits of Dyntopo (covered in the preceding section) built in to the remeshing process. That is, Blender tries to use more geometry in places with more detail and less geometry where there's less detail. This feature will likely introduce triangles into your mesh because your voxel grid is basically varying across your mesh. If you have Adaptivity set to 0m, it's essentially turned off.

>> **Fix Poles:** Enable this check box to try to reduce the number of poles generated by the Remesh operator. Fewer poles should result in cleaner edge flow. However, the process of fixing poles can be computationally intensive, so you may not want to enable this feature if you're remeshing a lot while you sculpt. Also, if you have the Adaptivity slider set to anything other than 0m, the Fix Poles feature is disabled.

>> **Preserve:** Even though the Remesh operator is replacing all the geometry in your mesh, it can do it's best to try to keep certain bits of mesh data that you already have, including the mesh's volume, masks, face sets, or vertex colors. By default, all these check boxes are enabled. If you disable them (particularly the Volume check box), the Remesh operator will likely go faster at the cost of losing that data.

>> **Remesh:** The big Remesh button at the bottom of the panel is what actually triggers the Remesh operator. Click this button and all the geometry in your mesh is replaced.

TIP

Although you can move back and forth between your sculpt and this panel, there's a faster way to work. While in Sculpt mode, press R to quickly adjust the Voxel Size setting in the Remesh panel. Aside from speed, the biggest benefit of this hotkey approach is that Blender draws a visualization of the voxel grid next to your mesh so you can get a more clear understanding of the detail size you're using. Figure 3-11 shows an image of this grid visualization in action. Confirm the Voxel Size that you want by left-clicking or pressing Enter. Then, you can quickly run the Remesh operator by pressing Ctrl+R.

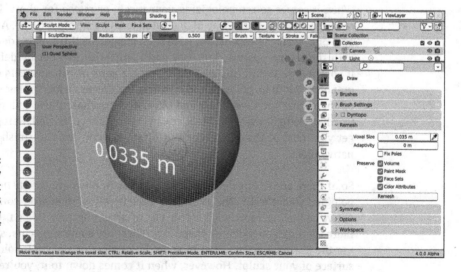

FIGURE 3-11:
The R hotkey while in Sculpt mode gives you a handy visualization of how detailed your voxel grid is.

Using these hotkeys, you end up with a really fast sculpting process that looks a bit like this:

1. **Sculpt the rough form on your object.**

2. **Adjust your Voxel Size (R) to something smaller.**

3. **Remesh (Ctrl+R).**

4. **Sculpt more refined details.**

5. **Repeat Steps 2 to 4 (sometimes increasing your voxel size if you get too detailed, too early) until you're happy with your finished sculpt.**

For myself, I like to use a bit of a mix between all three processes: Dyntopo, remeshing, and multires. I'll often block out the base form using Dyntopo, but the resulting mesh topology from that is often an absolute mess and can be a bit unwieldy for detailed parts of the sculpt. So, I'll start sculpting with remesh to work in those details. And since remeshing gives a more even distribution of vertices on my mesh, I can then add the Multiresolution modifier and use that for working in the highest detail components of my sculpt. From there, if the sculpt is going to be rigged and animated, I'll retopologize the mesh, as covered in the next section.

Understanding the Basics of Retopology

When it comes to retopologizing your mesh, or *retopo* for short, Blender doesn't really have much in the way of dedicated tools built into it (yet!). A few very useful add-ons, such as RetopoFlow, have been created by third-party developers to help with the retopo process, but they don't ship with Blender by default. That said, if you find that sculpting and modeling are your favorite aspects of 3D computer graphics, you'll be going through the retopo process a lot. In that situation, I recommend that you investigate and ultimately purchase those add-ons. But it's still worthwhile to know what Blender can do on its own as well. Retopo add-ons can get you most of the way there, but often you still need to finish with Blender's native tools.

So, if there aren't any dedicated retopo tools in Blender, exactly how do you retopologize your mesh? The answer is deceptively simple. You combine Blender's native modeling tools with clever use of snapping (see Book 1, Chapter 3 for a more thorough overview of snapping). There are some shortcuts, such as trying to use the Shrinkwrap modifier to snap the vertices of a clean topology mesh to the surface of your sculpt. However, when it comes down to it, you're really going to need to do point-for-point modeling. One of the best tools for that purpose is the Poly Build tool in Edit mode.

Once you finish your 3D sculpt, follow these steps as the basic process for retopologizing:

1. **From Object mode, create a new mesh (Add ⇨ Mesh ⇨ Plane).**

In this example, I'm using a plane, but it could be any mesh, as you'll see in the next step. In fact, some modelers use an add-on that creates a zero-vertex mesh object for exactly this kind of thing.

2. **Rename your new mesh object to something that makes sense.**

It could be something like Character.retopo, for example, as long as it's anything other than the primitive mesh's name.

3. **Tab into Edit mode on your new mesh.**

4. **Select all the vertices in this new mesh and delete them (Select ⇨ A, Mesh ⇨ Delete ⇨ Vertices).**

Now you have a mesh object with no data inside.

5. **In the Snap Element drop-down menu in the 3D Viewport's header, set it to use Face Project snapping.**

This step is important; it's what makes the rest of the retopo process possible. You can also enable snapping by toggling the button with the magnet icon, but because of the idiosyncrasies of how the Poly Build tool works, I prefer to just enable snapping on the fly by pressing Ctrl.

6. **Activate the Poly Build tool.**

This is the tool that you're going to use to generate the retopologized version of your sculpt.

7. **Ctrl+left-click on the surface of your 3D sculpt.**

This creates the first vertex of your retopo mesh. By holding down the Ctrl button when left-clicking, you're telling Blender to snap your new vertex right on the surface of your sculpt mesh.

8. **Ctrl+left-click again on the surface of your 3D sculpt.**

Now you have an edge between the vertex you created in Step 8 and this vertex.

9. **Ctrl+left-click a third time on the surface of your 3D sculpt.**

With this move you have three vertices and two edges. Now is where the strength of the Poly Build tool really starts to kick in.

10. **Hold Ctrl and move your mouse cursor near the "corner" vertex that's connected to both edges (don't click anywhere just yet).**

You should see a concave quad like the one in Figure 3-12. When you hold down Ctrl, you get a preview of the geometry that the Poly Build tool is going to create for you.

FIGURE 3-12:
Beginning to
model with the
Poly Build tool.
You start with
three vertices and
you can pull a
face from that.

11. **Still holding Ctrl, left-click and drag your mouse from that corner vertex to form a quad.**

Because you're holding down Ctrl, your new vertex snaps to the surface of your sculpt. If you want to adjust the position of any vertex, left-click and drag that vertex around (press Ctrl while dragging to keep it snapped to the surface of your sculpt).

12. **Repeat the process of Steps 10 and 11 along one of the edges of your newly formed quad to pull out a triangular face from it.**

Don't worry too much about this being a triangle. You'll turn it into a quad in the next step.

13. **Repeat Steps 10 and 11 again along the longest edge of your new triangle to pull it into a quad.**

Now you have two connected quads snapped to the surface of your sculpt! Figure 3-13 shows the general process to get this far in a more visual step-by-step format.

FIGURE 3-13:
Using the Poly
Build tool to start
retopologizing
your sculpt.

14. Continue using the Poly Build tool along with the rest of Blender's built-in mesh editing tools to lay out the vertices of your retopologized mesh.

Remember the basic guidelines outlined in Book 2, Chapter 1 as you work. This step comprises the somewhat tedious and time-consuming process of retopologizing your mesh. However, when you've already made your sculpt, you have a clear plan that shows what your final mesh should look like. At this point, you're basically playing "connect the dots" on the surface of your 3D sculpt. Once you get up to speed, this is a much more effective way of modeling than the traditional box modeling or point-to-point modeling methods described in Book 2, Chapter 1.

Figure 3-14 shows a mesh sculpted using Dyntopo and that same model after it's been retopo'd.

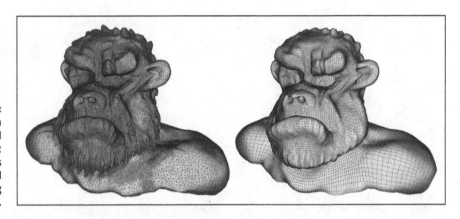

FIGURE 3-14: On the left, a model sculpted with Dyntopo; on the right is the same model after being retopologized.

TIP

To help you better see your retopologized mesh as you build it, you can enable the Retopology check box in the Shading section of the Viewport Overlays roll-out (in Blender 4.0, this check box appears in the Mesh Edit Mode Overlays roll-out). With that check box enabled, you can adjust the offset slider to control the visualization of your retopo mesh while you work. This approach is much better than the classic approach of using the In Front visualization for objects when retopologizing.

Chapter 4

Using Blender's Non-Mesh Primitives

Although polygon-based meshes tend to be the bread and butter for modelers using Blender, they aren't the only types of objects available to you for creating things in 3D space. Blender also has curves, surfaces, metaball objects, and text objects. These objects tend to have somewhat more specialized purposes than meshes, but when you need what they provide, they're extremely useful.

Curves and surfaces are nearly as general purpose as meshes; they're particularly handy for anything that needs to have a smooth, non-faceted look. They're also important for models that require mathematical precision and accuracy in their appearance. Metaball objects are great at creating organic shapes that merge into one another, such as simple fluids. You can also use them to make a roughly sculpted model from basic elements that you can detail further in Sculpt mode. Text objects are exactly what they sound like: You use them to add text to a scene and manipulate that text in all three dimensions. This chapter tells you more about working with all these types of objects. You might also notice that there are more objects available in the add menu above the first break; specifically I'm referring to volume objects and Grease Pencil objects. You see more on volumes in Book 4, Chapter 5 and all of Book 4, Chapter 6 is about Grease Pencil objects.

Using Curves and Surfaces

So, what's the biggest difference between curves and surfaces when compared to meshes? *Math!* Okay, I'm sorry. That was mean of me; I know that math can be a four-letter word for many artists, but don't worry; you won't have to do any math here. What I mean to say is that curves and surfaces can be described in the computer as a mathematical function. You describe meshes, on the other hand, using the positions of all the individual vertices that they're composed of. In terms of the computer, curves and surfaces have two advantages:

>> **Curves and surfaces are very precise.** When you get down to it, the best that a mesh can be is an approximation of a real object. A mesh can look really, really good, but it's not exact. Because curves are defined by math, they're exactly the correct shape, which is why designers and engineers like them.

>> **Curves and surfaces take up less storage memory.** Because the shape is mathematically defined, the computer can save that shape by saving the math rather than all the individual points. Complicated curves and surfaces can often take up quite a bit less hard drive space than the same shape made with meshes.

Of course, these advantages come with some caveats, too. For one, curves and surfaces can sometimes be more difficult to control. Because curves and surfaces don't have vertices for you to directly manipulate, you have to use *control points*. Depending on the type of curve, control points can sit directly on the shape or float somewhere off of the surface as part of a control *cage*.

Even though curves and surfaces are perfect mathematical descriptions of a shape, the computer is actually an imperfect way of displaying those perfect shapes. All 3D geometry is eventually tessellated when the computer processes it (see Book 2, Chapter 1). So even though curves and surfaces can take less memory on a computer, smoothly displaying them may take more time and RAM for the computer to process. To speed up things, you can tell the computer to use a rougher tessellation with fewer triangles. As a result, what you see in Blender is an approximation of that perfect curve or surface shape. Do you find yourself thinking, "But hey, I thought curves were supposed to be perfect mathematical descriptions of a shape. What gives with these facets?" Well, the curve *is* perfect. It's just hard for the computer to show it to you directly.

But despite these minor disadvantages, using curves and surfaces is a smart move in quite a few cases. For example, most designers like to use curves for company logos because curves can scale in print to any size without looking jagged or *aliased* around their edges. As a 3D artist, you can easily import the curves of a logo design and give the logo some depth, dimension, and perhaps even some animation.

And speaking of animation, curves have quite a few handy uses there as well. For example, you can use a curve to define a path for an object to move along. You can also use curves in Blender's Graph Editor to display and control the changes to an object's properties over time. For modeling purposes, curves are great for pipes, wires, and ornate organic shapes. Figure 4-1 shows a park bench. Only curves were used to model its sides.

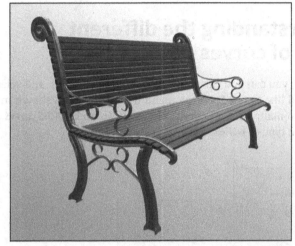

FIGURE 4-1: With the exception of the slats for the seat and back, this entire park bench was modeled with curves.

A set of curves used to define a shape in three dimensions is a *surface*. In some ways, curve surfaces are very similar to meshes that have the Subdivision Surface modifier applied because they both have a control cage defining the final shape that's created. The difference is that the curve surface has space and precision benefits that meshes don't have. Also, surfaces can often be easier to add textures to because you don't have to go through the additional step of *unwrapping* or flattening the surface, so you can apply a two-dimensional texture to it. When you use a surface, you get that unwrapping for free because it's already done for you.

REMEMBER

For these reasons — especially the precision — architects, industrial designers, and engineers prefer to work with surfaces. Someone designed just about everything in your house, including your water faucet, coffee maker, television, car, and even the house itself. If an item was manufactured within the last 30 years, chances are good that it was designed on a computer and visualized with surfaces. Also, before the advent of subdivision surfaces, early characters for computer animations were modeled using curve surfaces because they were better at achieving organic shapes.

Of course, if you're seen using curves to build a character these days, you may be viewed as a bit of masochist . . . especially if you try to do it in Blender. Even though you can do a lot with Blender's curves and surfaces, the toolset for working with them is quite a bit smaller than what a designer might expect if they're familiar with an application that has more dedicated support for curves and surfaces. I personally wouldn't recommend Blender if you're trying to do that kind of CAD-style design. That's a recipe for frustration.

Understanding the different types of curves

In Blender, you can add curves by choosing Add ➪ Curve and selecting the type of curve you'd like to use from the menu that appears. As shown in Figure 4-2, you can use two main kinds of curves: *Bézier curves* and *NURBS curves*. (The Path curve is a specific type of NURBS curve.)

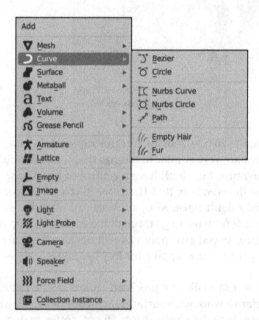

FIGURE 4-2:
The Add ➪
Curve menu.

You generally use Bézier curves more for text and logos. Bézier curves work in three dimensions by default, but you can get them to lock to a single 2D plane if you need to. You can tell that you're using a Bézier curve because if you tab into Edit mode to look at it, each control point has a pair of handles you can use to give additional control over the curve's shape.

NURBS stands for *Non-Uniform Relational B-Spline*. The control points in NURBS curves don't have handles like Bézier curves do. By default, NURBS control points don't normally even touch the curve shape itself. Instead, the control points are *weighted* to influence the shape of the curve. Control points with higher weights attract the curve closer to them. Figure 4-3 shows the same curve shape made with Bézier curves and with NURBS curves.

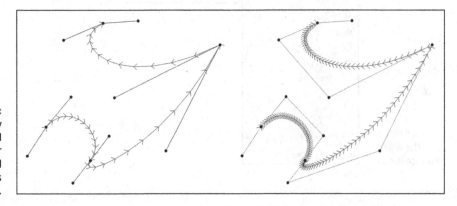

FIGURE 4-3: An arbitrary shape created with Bézier curves (left) and NURBS curves (right).

 Although curves can work in three dimensions and can even create three-dimensional shapes like the park bench in Figure 4-1, you can't arbitrarily join them to create a surface like you would if you were connecting vertices and edges to make a face on a mesh. If you want to create a surface, you need to navigate to the Surfaces menu (Add ⇨ Surface), as shown in Figure 4-4. Notice that NURBS Curve and NURBS Circle are also options on this menu. Be aware, however, that Blender treats these types of NURBS differently than the NURBS curves available in the Curve menu. In fact, Blender doesn't even allow you to perform a Join (Object ⇨ Join) between NURBS curves and NURBS surface curves. This limitation is a bit inconvenient, I know, but the situations where you'd want to do something like that are rare enough that you don't need to worry about it that much.

The anatomy of a Bézier curve

Before you go headlong into making all manner of cool things with Bézier curves, it's worth taking a moment to understand the parts of a curve. There are three parts to a curve:

>> **Control points:** The control points define the shape of the curve. They're like vertices in mesh objects. On Bézier curves, the curve always intersects a control point.

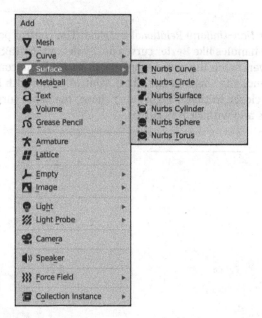

FIGURE 4-4:
The Add ⇨
Surface menu.

>> **Control point handles:** Every control point has a pair of handles that you can use to control the rotation of that control point.

>> **Curve segments:** These appear between two control points and are mathematically defined by the location and rotation of the control points.

In its simplest form, a complete curve consists of two control points and a segment between them. And unlike meshes, curves don't "fork." A control point can have at most one segment going into it and one segment going out. There's no such thing as a control point that connects three or more segments.

Working with curves

Surprisingly few specialized controls are specific to curves. Blender's transform tools (move, scale, and rotate) work as expected. However, there are much fewer tools available in the Toolbar, and they all have different icons. I get into a few of these tools later in this section, but here's a quick rundown of what's available:

>> **Draw:** When you select the Draw tool, your mouse cursor changes to look like a pencil as a signal that you can draw your curves in 3D space, much like you can with the Annotate tool or Grease Pencil objects. There's more on using this tool later in this section.

>> **Curve Pen:** If you've used a vector drawing application like Inkscape, Adobe Illustrator, or Affinity Designer, then the Curve Pen tool should be familiar to you. If you've never used any of those programs, don't worry. This tool gives you point-for-point control over creating your curve. By default, left-clicking adds a new control point connected to an existing point. If you left-click and drag an existing point, you can move it around. Ctrl+left-clicking a control point deletes it, and Ctrl+left-clicking the segment between two points adds a new point there.

>> **Extrude tools:** Although the tool icons are different, the functionality of these extrusion tools is similar to their counterparts in mesh tools (see Book 2, Chapter 1). One important difference to note, however, is that the extrude operator works only on the *end points* (the first and last control points of the curve). If you try to extrude a control point that isn't an end point, Blender just creates a new control point.

- **Extrude:** This tool works like it's counterpart in mesh tools; it even has the same yellow gizmo with a big plus sign on it. Left-click and drag that plus sign to extrude a new control point from the end of your curve.

- **Extrude to Cursor:** This tool provides you with similar functionality to the Curve Pen tool, but built into extruding. It works like the Extrude to Cursor tool for mesh objects. Left-click in the 3D Viewport and a new control point is added, connected to the last end point on your curve.

>> **Radius:** Each control point in a Blender curve has its own radius value. There's more on what this radius value is used for later in the section called "Extruding, beveling, and tapering curves," but the main thing to remember here is that Radius tool is a quick way of visually adjusting the radius of one or more control points in your curve.

>> **Tilt:** Similar to the radius value, every control point on a curve also has a tilt value that controls how much the control point is rotated along the axis of its handles, similar to the roll angle of bones (see Book 4, Chapter 3). This tool gives you visual control over that tilt value.

>> **Shear:** Shearing is the act of moving components parallel to each other, but in opposite directions. For that reason, if you try to use the Shear tool with only one control point selected, it's not going to look like you're doing much. You need more than one. When you make a selection, you get a control widget that looks a bit like the widget used for transform or scale. The difference is that a kind of plus-sign-shaped control appears at the end of each axis. Click and drag these controls to shear your selection along that direction.

>> **Randomize:** It's not likely that you're going to need the Randomize tool frequently, but when you do, you'll be glad it exists. When you select this tool, you can add some randomness to the placement and rotation of your selected control points by left-clicking and dragging your mouse cursor left and right.

When using the various curve tools from the Toolbar, it's important to remember that these tools operate on your current selection. If you don't have anything selected, you're not going to see much results from these tools. Fortunately, even with any of these tools active, you can still make selections on your curve with left-click. The only exception to this is if you have an end point on your curve and you want to select another end point. To do that, you must first deselect everything (Select ⇨ None); otherwise, you'll make the curve cyclic, or closed, as covered next.

If you start with the Circle primitive (Add ⇨ Curve ⇨ Circle), you should notice that it's a *cyclic*, or closed curve. In contrast, the Bézier curve primitive is a *non-cyclic*, or open curve. Regardless of the primitive you start with, you can always toggle any given curve between being cyclic and non-cyclic with any control point selected (not just the start or end) by choosing Curve ⇨ Toggle Cyclic in the 3D Viewport's header or using the Alt+C hotkey. Figure 4-5 shows a cyclic (closed) and non-cyclic (open) Bézier curve.

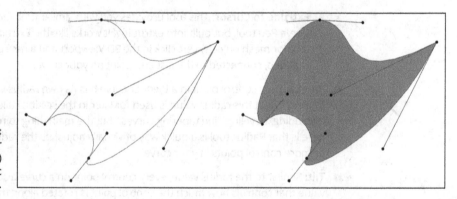

FIGURE 4-5:
The same Bézier curve, cyclic (left) and non-cyclic (right).

If you make a 2D curve cyclic, it creates a flat plane in the shape of your curve. And putting one cyclic curve within the borders of another curve creates a hole in that plane. However, this trick doesn't work with 3D curves because they aren't planar. In those situations, you should use a surface. There's more detail on 2D and 3D curves in the section entitled "Changing 3D curves into 2D curves."

Drawing curves

When you get right down to it, Blender's curve objects aren't all that different from paths and curves that you might be familiar working with in 2D vector drawing applications. Sure, Blender's curves have the ability to exist in three dimensions rather than two, but the basic concepts are essentially the same. For that reason, it shouldn't be surprising that Blender has a tool that allows you to draw curves directly in the 3D Viewport.

To start using the curve's Draw tool, you first need a curve object. Unlike Grease Pencil objects (see Book 4, Chapter 6), there's not a default empty object. If I'm about to draw a custom curve, I typically perform the following steps:

1. **Add a Bézier curve (Add ⇨ Curve ⇨ Bézier).**

2. **With the new curve still selected, tab into Edit mode.**

3. **Delete all the control points (X or Del).**

Now you have an empty curve object that you can start drawing in.

Using the Draw tool for curves is deceptively simple. All you have to do is click and drag in the 3D Viewport and Blender converts that stroke to a curve. That process is a great start, but of course, there are some additional (and helpful!) features built into this tool. A lot of the power of the Draw tool comes from its tool settings. You can find the tool settings for the Draw tool in the Tool tab of the Properties editor. They're also available in the Tool tab of 3D Viewport's Sidebar (for those times when you're working with a maximized 3D Viewport) as well as the Topbar in the 3D Viewport's header. Figure 4-6 shows the Draw tool's settings.

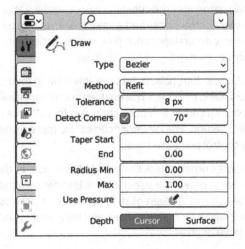

FIGURE 4-6:
The Draw tool's settings give you a lot of additional power when creating curves.

Like I said, the Draw tool is deceptively simple. There are a lot of controls and options that you have the ability to customize. The five options at the top of the Draw tool's settings give you basic controls:

» **Type:** There are two different ways that Blender can generate curves based on the stroke you draw:

- **Bézier:** The Bézier draw type is the default setting. When you have this type chosen, Blender attempts to generate smooth curves with only as many control points as is necessary to produce the shape of your curve. All the other settings for the Draw tool are available when you choose this draw type.

- **Poly:** Choose this draw type for a true "what you see is what you get" drawing experience. Blender will create a lot of control points with straight segments between them in an effort to exactly match whatever shape you draw. The Poly draw type is less computationally expensive than the Bézier type, but it results in a curve with a *lot* more control points, and you don't get any of the additional tool settings described in this section.

» **Method:** The choices in this drop-down menu dictate the algorithm that Blender uses to generate curves from your strokes. There are two choices:

- **Refit:** This is the "higher quality" choice and the default behavior. This choice does a better job of matching the stroke you draw at the expense of using more computational power.

- **Split:** This approach is faster to compute, but is less accurate. If you find that your computer is having a hard time keeping up with your strokes as you draw, then you may want to try choosing this curve generation method.

» **Tolerance:** When drawing with the Bézier draw type, you can use this setting to tune how Blender generates the curve from your stroke. Larger Tolerance values give you fewer control points and a smoother resulting curve. Smaller Tolerance values more accurately match your stroke at the expense of having more control points to manage.

» **Detect Corners:** Curves don't have to be smoothly flowing things; they can have sharp corners. Keep this check box enabled and Blender will attempt to detect when you draw a corner and put a control point with free handles at that corner (see the section "Editing Bézier curves" for more on the different kind of handles a control point can have).

If you have the Detect Corners check box enabled, the slider to the right of it is the angle you have to draw your stroke before Blender recognizes it as a corner. The default value of 70 degrees is a good place to start, but if you're drawing something with a lot of right angles, you may want to set this value to a bit higher than 90 degrees.

There are a few more tool settings in the Curve Stroke sub-panel that you can make use of while drawing your curves. Below the Detect Corners check box, you can adjust the following settings:

» **Taper Start/End:** Even if you're not using a pressure-sensitive drawing tablet, you can still take advantage of organic changes in curve radius. By adjusting the Start and End Taper values, you make your curves have smoother fall-offs at the start or end of your stroke.

» **Radius Min/Max:** If you use Blender with a drawing tablet like those that Wacom makes, Blender can take advantage of the pressure sensitivity of that device while drawing curves. Enable the Use Pressure button below these values (it has an icon like the one to the left) and as you draw your curve, Blender registers the pressure of your pen on the tablet as a change in radius. The harder you push down, the larger the radius. See the section entitled "Extruding, beveling, and tapering curves" for more on making use of the radius on control points.

» **Use Pressure:** Click this button if you have a pressure-sensitive drawing tablet connected to your computer and Blender will recognize pressure input from that device while drawing curves.

» **Depth:** The two options next to the Depth label work as radio buttons; only one is available at a time:

- **Cursor:** This is the default setting. Imagine that there's a plane located at the 3D cursor and rotated to match the orientation from which you're looking at the 3D Viewport. That imaginary plane is where Blender generates the curve from your stroke.

- **Surface:** The Surface option for Depth is super cool. When you enable this option, you can draw curves on any surface in your scene. A simple example would be if you wanted to model vines growing up the side of a tree. A more complex example might be like what's in Figure 4-7, where it looks like a sculpture made by wrapping wire around an invisible Suzanne.

When you enable the Surface option for Depth, you get a few additional options to control how that projection works. The **Offset** value defines how far off the surface the curve is generated. If you want that Offset to remain persistent with changes to the curve radius, enable the **Absolute Offset** check box. If you only want to use the target object's surface as a starting point, enable the **Only First** check box and Blender will only use the depth of the first place your stroke hits the mesh as its reference point for generating curves (as if you chose Cursor projection and placed your 3D cursor somewhere on the surface of the target object).

Changing 3D curves into 2D curves

Curves are initially set to work in three dimensions by default. Working in three dimensions gives you the ability to move curve control points freely in the X-, Y-, or Z-axes. You can optionally lock the points in your curve object to be constrained to its local XY plane.

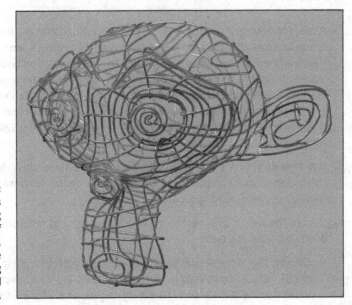

FIGURE 4-7:
Using the curve's
Draw tool along
the surface of
another object,
you can make
some interesting
and detailed
models.

You can still transform a 2D curve in three dimensions, but you have to do that from Object mode.

To lock the curve to working only in two dimensions, go to Object Data Properties (see Figure 4-8) and left-click the 2D button.

All curves have direction, even cyclic ones. The direction of a curve isn't normally all that important unless you're using the curve as a path. In that situation, the direction of the curve is the direction that the animated object is traveling along the curve. To see the direction of your 3D curve objects in Edit mode, expand the Overlays roll-out menu from the 3D Viewport's header and look at the bottom (in Blender 4.0, look in the Curve Edit Mode Overlays roll-out). A slider appears there labeled Normals. Enable the check box next to that slider and you should see that the curve now has a bunch of little arrows spaced along it. These arrows are *curve normals* and indicate the direction of the curve as well as the curve's radius (see the next section). To adjust the visible size of these curve normals, adjust the value in the Normals slider. In 2D curves, curve normals aren't displayed. You can switch the direction of the curve by choosing Segments ⇨ Switch Direction from the 3D Viewport's header.

Figure 4-8 shows the Object Data tab of the Properties editor when a curve is selected.

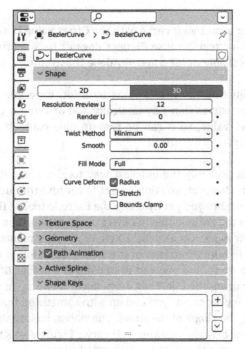

FIGURE 4-8:
The controls for
editing curves.

The controls in Object Data Properties are relevant to all curves, regardless of type. Some of the most important controls are in the Shape panel. You've already seen what the 2D and 3D buttons do. Below them are the Resolution Preview U and Render U values. These values define the resolution of the curve. Remember that Blender shows you only an approximation of the real curve. Increasing the resolution here makes the curve look more like the curve defined by the math, at the cost of more processor time. That's why you see two resolution values:

>> **Preview U:** The default resolution. It's also what you see in the 3D Viewport.

>> **Render U:** The resolution that Blender uses when you render (see Book 3, Chapter 4 for more on rendering). By default, this resolution is set to 0, which means Blender uses whatever value is in Preview U.

Extruding, beveling, and tapering curves

A little further down in Object Data Properties, the controls in the Geometry panel pertain primarily to extruding and beveling your curve objects. The Offset value is the exception to this rule. It's pretty interesting because it allows you to offset the curve from the control points. The effect of the Offset value is most apparent (and helpful) on cyclic curves. Values less than 1 are inset from the control points, whereas values greater than 1 are outset.

TIP

The ability to inset or outset your curve with the Offset value is a quick way to put an outline on a logo or text because Blender doesn't have a stroke function for curves like what's available in Inkscape or Adobe Illustrator.

WARNING

Be careful when adjusting the Offset value by a lot, especially on curves with acute angles. Blender curves don't dynamically add or remove control points as you adjust the Offset value, so it can be easy to give yourself some ugly self-intersecting geometry.

The Extrude value is probably the quickest way to give some depth to a curve, especially a 2D curve. However, you don't want to confuse the curve Extrude value with the extrude capability you get by using the Extrude tool or the E hotkey. The Extrude value affects the entire curve in Object mode, rather than just the selected control points in Edit mode. On a cyclic 2D curve, the flat planar shape that gets created extends out in both directions of the local Z direction of the curve object, with the caps drawn on it. And you can even control whether Blender draws the front or back cap by using the Fill Mode drop-down menu up in the Shape panel. If you extrude a non-cyclic curve, you end up with something that looks more like a ribbon going along the shape of the curve. The ribbon look is also what happens when you increase the extrude value on a 3D curve. Figure 4-9 shows some of the different effects that you can get with an extruded curve.

FIGURE 4-9:
Some of the different things you can do with an extruded curve.

Of course, one drawback to extruding a curve is that you get a sharp edge at the corners of the extrusion. Depending on what you're creating, harsh edges tend to look "too perfect" and unnatural. Fortunately, Bevel can take care of that for you. To give an extruded curve more natural corners, simply increase the Depth value within the Bevel sub-panel and you get a result similar to what happens when you use the Bevel tool on meshes (see Book 2, Chapter 1) or the Bevel modifier (see Book 2, Chapter 2). You can adjust the roundness of the bevel by increasing the Resolution value. Like the Preview U and Render U values, this value increases the resolution of part of the curve. In this case, it's the resolution of the bevel, like the Segments value on the Bevel tool for mesh objects. Increasing the Resolution value makes a smoother, more rounded bevel. Beveling works on both cyclic and non-cyclic curves.

But say that you want something more ornate, kind of like the molding or trim you'd find around the doorway on a house. In that case, you want to use a *bevel object.* Using a bevel object on your curve basically means that you're going to use the shape of one curve to define the bevel on another.

To get a better idea of how you can use bevel objects, follow these steps:

1. **Create a Bézier circle (Add ⇨ Curve ⇨ Circle).**

In the Object Data tab of the Properties editor, make sure that the circle is a 2D curve.

2. **In Edit mode, use the Scale tool (or the S hotkey) to scale up the circle nice and large so that you can see what's going on.**

Tab back to Object mode when you're done.

3. **Create a Bézier curve (Add ⇨ Curve ⇨ Bézier).**

For simplicity's sake, this curve should be a 2D curve, too.

4. **Tab into Edit mode and edit your new curve a bit to get the bevel shape that you want.**

Keep the curve non-cyclic for now.

5. **When you're done editing, tab back out to Object mode.**

6. **Select your Bézier circle and look to the Geometry panel in Object Data Properties. In the Bevel sub-panel, click the Object button.**

This button reveals the controls for treating another curve object as your bevel shape.

7. **Find the name of your Bézier curve object in the Object field.**

If you didn't rename your curve (although you should have!), it's probably called something like BezierCurve or BezierCurve.001. After you select your bevel object, it looks like you've spun the shape of your Bézier curve around your Bézier circle. Now for fun, follow the next step.

8. **Go back to your bevel object curve, tab into Edit mode, and make it cyclic (Curve ⇨ Toggle Cyclic).**

Now you have an enclosed, water-tight shape that follows the main Bézier circle's path. Even better, any edits you make to this Bézier are automatically shown in real time on the circle.

9. **For extra kicks, select the Bézier circle and tab into Edit mode; select any control point and use the Radius tool to shrink or fatten the beveled shape around that control point.**

If you're prone to hotkeys, you can change the radius without using the tool by pressing Alt+S. Slick, huh?

Figure 4-10 shows the results of these steps.

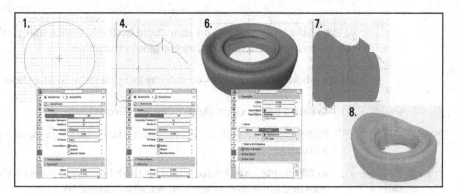

FIGURE 4-10:
Having fun by
adding a bevel
object to a
Bézier circle.

TIP

For a more simple bevel shape, you can instead click the Profile button in the Bevel sub-panel, and use the curve widget there to define a bevel profile for your curve.

If you're using a curve to model anything roughly cylindrical in shape such as a pipe or a tube, you don't need to use a bevel object curve at all. You can get the same effect by just beveling the curve using the Round bevel type. Follow these steps:

1. **Add a new curve object (Add ➪ Curve ➪ Bézier).**

2. **Adjust the Fill Mode property for your curve.**

   Look in the Shape panel of Object Data Properties. For a 2D curve, set the Fill Mode to None. For a 3D curve, set it to Full.

3. **In the Geometry panel, go to the Bevel sub-panel and make sure the Round button is enabled.**

   The Round bevel type is the default setting, so you shouldn't have to click anything.

4. **Increase the Depth value within the Bevel sub-panel.**

   You just beveled without needing to add another object to your scene. Hooray! One less bevel object to hide!

5. **Thicken or make thinner your new tube-y pipe at different points along its length by selecting individual control points in Edit mode and using the Radius tool.**

   You can also adjust a control point's radius from the Sidebar of the 3D Viewport (N). It's the Radius value within the Item tab.

In the preceding examples, I show that you can use the Radius tool on individual control points to shrink or fatten the thickness of the extrusion (or bevel). However, perhaps you'd like to have more control along the length of the curve. This situation is where you'd use *taper object*s. Like bevel objects, the taper objects use one curve to define the shape of another. In this case, you're controlling the curve radius along the length of the curve, and it uses the same workflow as bevel objects: Create a separate curve that dictates the taper shape, and then choose that curve in the Taper Object field of the curve you'd like to control. Figure 4-11 shows how a taper object can give you complete control of a curve's shape along its length.

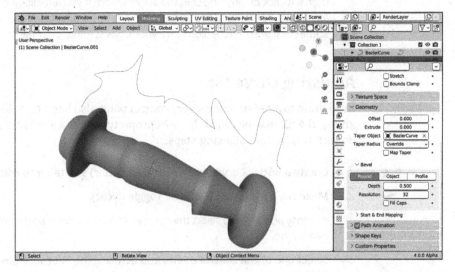

FIGURE 4-11:
Using a taper object to control a curve's lengthwise shape.

TIP

I prefer to create my bevel object and taper object curves in the top view (Numpad 7) along the X-axis. This way, I have a good frame of reference for the curve's center line. That's important because bevel objects use the center line to define the front and back of a curve's extrusion. You can think of taper objects as a kind of profile that revolves around its local X-axis. Bringing your control points to the center line makes the tapered curve come to a point, whereas moving them away from the center line increases the thickness.

TIP

The datablock drop-down menus for Taper Object and Bevel Object can get crowded in a complex scene. Scrolling through all the curve objects can be tedious; even if you did a good job of using sensible naming, it can be annoying or time-consuming to type in or search for that name. Fortunately, Blender offers

Using Blender's
Non-Mesh Primitives

two shortcuts that make filling these fields (and any other fields like them) very convenient:

>> **Drag and drop:** If you're using the Layout workspace, then you have an Outliner in the area above your Properties editor. If you navigate to your object in the Outliner, you can left-click it in the Outliner and drag it to the Taper Object or Bevel Object field in Object Data Properties.

>> **Object eyedropper:** If the Taper Object or Bevel Object fields are empty, there's an eyedropper on the right-hand side of it. If you left-click that eyedropper icon, your mouse cursor becomes an eyedropper and you can then left-click on any object in the 3D Viewport. If you left-click a curve object, its name automatically populates this field. This is a fantastic tool for complex scenes or if you (ahem) didn't give your objects good, clear names.

Adjusting curve tilt

In addition to a radius value, every control point also has a *tilt* value. In other programs, the tilt may be called the *twist* property. To get a good idea of what you can do with tilt, try the following steps:

1. **Create a Bézier Curve (Add ⇨ Curve ⇨ Bézier) and tab into Edit mode.**

2. **Make the curve cyclic (Curve ⇨ Toggle Cyclic).**

You may also want to select the handles and rotate them so there's a cleaner arc.

3. **Select one of the control points and activate the Tilt tool from the Toolbar.**

4. **Click and drag in the circular widget around your selection in the 3D Viewport, moving your mouse cursor around the selection in a clockwise fashion.**

Watch how the Tilt value in the 3D Viewport's header changes.

5. **Confirm completion by releasing your mouse button.**

If you increase the Extrude and Bevel Depth values in Object Data Properties, you should now have something that looks a bit like Figure 4-12.

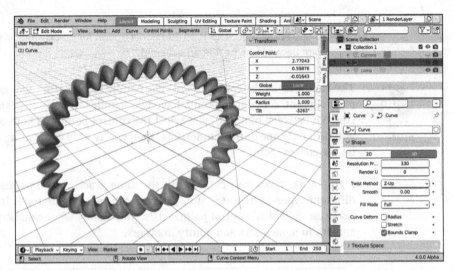

FIGURE 4-12:
Fun with the tilt function! Mmm-mmm . . . twisty.

Editing Bézier curves

The most defining aspect of Bézier curves are the handles on their control points. You can switch between the different types of handles by choosing Control Points ➪ Set Handle Type from the 3D Viewport's header menus or by using the V hotkey. Handles on Bézier curves are always tangential to the curve and come in one of four varieties in Blender. The following is what's available in the Set Handle Type menu; use it with one or more handles selected:

>> **Automatic:** These handles are set by Blender to give you the smoothest possible result in the shape of your curve. They appear in orange in the default theme and generally form a straight line with equal lengths on either side. If you try to rotate an Automatic handle, it immediately reverts to an aligned handle.

>> **Vector:** Vector handles are not aligned with each other. They point directly to the next control point. The shape of the curve is an exactly straight line from one control point to the next. Editing a handle on a vector control point turns it into a free handle.

>> **Aligned:** Aligned handles are locked to one another, always forming a straight line that's tangential to the curve. By default, they appear in a pinkish color. If you move one handle on a control point, the other moves in the opposite direction to balance it out. You can, however, have aligned handles of differing lengths.

>> **Free:** Free handles are sometimes referred to as *broken* handles. They appear red in the default theme and don't necessarily have to be aligned with one another. Free handles are best suited for giving you sharp corners that smoothly flow to the next control point.

>> **Toggle Free/Align:** This is an additional option for quickly toggling a control point between being free and aligned.

REMEMBER

The handle is *not* the control point. The handle is the "arm" that extends from the control point. All control points have two handles. If you select the control point (the dot between handles), you select the control point and both of its handles. If you click only one of the handle dots, then you're only controlling that one handle on the control point.

Figure 4-13 shows four curves with the same exact control points, but each with different types of handles. And, yes, you can mix handle types in a single curve (even on individual control points). It's quite handy when you need a figure to be smooth in some parts and pointy in others.

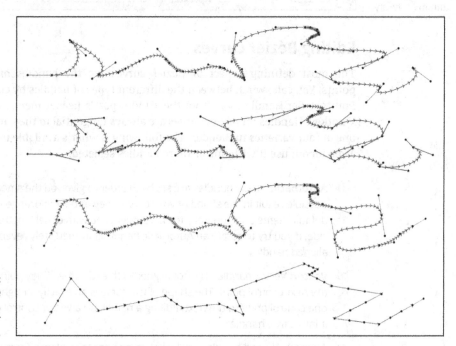

FIGURE 4-13:
The same curve with aligned, free, auto, and vector handles.

As you work with curve objects, you may find that you want to add a new control point in the middle of a segment. Or perhaps you find you have too many control points and you want to remove one. In 2D vector drawing applications, this is often built into some kind of pen tool. In Blender you can use the Curve Pen tool as described earlier in this chapter. However, you also have the same basic operations that are available when editing meshes (see Book 2, Chapter 1).

Say you want to add a control point in the middle of a curve segment. With meshes, one of the easiest ways to accomplish this task is to subdivide. The same goes for curves! Select the control points on either side of a segment and choose Segments ⇨ Subdivide from the 3D Viewport's header menu. You can have even faster access from the right-click context menu. And just like editing meshes, once you subdivide, you can look to the Last Operator panel to quickly add more subdivision cuts. If you need a control point exactly in the middle of a segment or if you need a series of evenly spaced control points, this technique is faster and more accurate than using the Curve Pen tool.

If you want to remove one or more control points, select them and choose Curve ⇨ Delete ⇨ Dissolve Vertices. There's an option in that menu to just delete vertices, but I find that the Dissolve Vertices operator does a better job of preserving the curve shape after deleting.

You can also remove segments while keeping control points in place using the same menu. Select the two control points on either side of the segment you want to remove and choose Curve ⇨ Delete ⇨ Segments.

TIP

For faster access to the delete operators, use the X hotkey.

Editing NURBS curves and surfaces

NURBS are a different kind of beast in terms of controls. They also have control points, but NURBS curves are conspicuously without handles.

REMEMBER

Blender treats a NURBS curve differently than a NURBS surface curve. With that caution in mind, though, whether you're dealing with a curve or a surface curve, the following things generally apply to all NURBS:

>> **Each control point has a weight.** The weight, which is a value greater than zero, influences how much that control point influences the curve. In Blender, you set the weight in the Transform panel of the 3D Viewport's Sidebar within the Item tab. There, for any selected control point, you have the ability to directly modify the X, Y, or Z location of the control point as well as its weight, indicated by the W value. The value in the W field is averaged across all selected control points. (Note that the W field weight value affects the curve differently from the value in the Weight field below it. The latter refers to actual weight for purposes of simulating physics. Book 4, Chapter 5 touches on physics simulation in Blender.)

>> **NURBS have knots.** In math terms, *knots* are vectors that describe how the control points influence the resulting curve. In Blender, you have three settings that you can assign to knots from the Active Spline panel in the Object Data tab of the Properties editor:

- **Cyclic U:** Enabling this check box is the same as choosing Curve ⇨ Toggle Cyclic from the 3D Viewport's header menu.

- **Bézier U:** Enable this check box and the NURBS curve starts to behave like a Bézier curve with every control point working like a free handle on a Bézier curve. Every three control points act like the center and two handles on a Bézier curve's control points. In order for this feature to work, you need to have the Cyclic U check box disabled and the Order U property (described momentarily) must be a value of 3 or 4.

- **Endpoint U:** Endpoint knots, in contrast to the default disabled setting, bring the curve all the way to the last control points, regardless of weight. If you toggle this check box on, the Cyclic U check box needs to be disabled.

» **NURBS have an order.** An *order* is another math thing. What it means, though, is that the lower the order, the more the curve directly follows the lines between control points. And the higher the order, the smoother and more fluid the curve is as it passes the control points. You can also change the values for order in the Active Spline panel below the Bézier U and Endpoint U check boxes.

Figure 4-14 shows the influences that curve weights, knot types, and order can have on a NURBS curve.

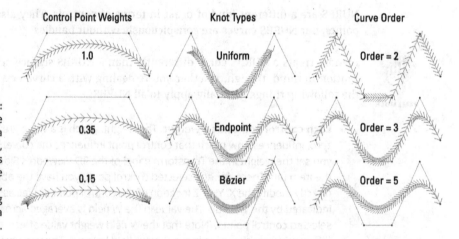

FIGURE 4-14:
Decreasing curve weights on a control point, differences between the three knot types, and increasing the order of a curve.

REMEMBER

If you're using a NURBS surface, you might notice in the Active Spline panel that you can independently set the knot, order, and resolution controls for a U or a V value. If you're dealing with just a curve, the U direction is all you need to worry about and, therefore, all that Blender shows you. However, a NURBS surface works in two directions: U and V. If you add a NURBS Surface (Add ⇨ Surface ⇨ NURBS

Surface), you can visually tell the difference between the U segments, which are reddish, and the V segments, which are yellow.

One cool thing you can do easily with NURBS surfaces that's difficult to do with other types of surfaces is a process called *lofting*. (Other programs may call it *skinning*, but because that term means something else for rigging, I use lofting here.) Basically, lofting is the process of using a series of NURBS surface curves with the *same number of control points* as a series of profiles to define a shape. The cool thing about lofting in Blender is that after you have the profiles in place, the process is as simple as selecting all control points (A) and choosing Control Points ⇨ Make Segment. The classic use for lofting is modeling the hull of a boat, as you see in the following steps and in Figure 4-15:

1. **Add a NURBS surface curve (Add ⇨ Surface ⇨ NURBS Curve) and tab into Edit mode.**

2. **Select All and Rotate –90 degrees around the X-axis.**

   You can use the Rotate tool or use the hotkey sequence R ⇨ -90. In either case, the bottom of your boat is started.

3. **Model a cross-section of the boat's hull.**

   There are no handy Extrude or Draw tools for Blender's NURBS surface objects, so you have to rely on the 3D Viewport's header menu (particularly the Control Points menu) or with hotkeys. You can add more control points using extrude (Control Points ⇨ Extrude Curve and Move) and move them around with the Move tool or the G hotkey.

   TIP

   When modeling your cross-section, it is a good idea to make the curve cyclic in the U direction. You can use the menu (Surface ⇨ Toggle Cyclic ⇨ Cyclic U) or the check box in the Active Spline panel of Object Data Properties. Try to keep the cross-section as planar as possible, like the "ribs" used in the construction of an actual boat. I like to work from an orthographic front view (Numpad 1) when creating that cross-section.

4. **Select all control points in your cross-section (Select ⇨ All).**

5. **Duplicate your hull profile along the Y-axis.**

   Whether you're duplicating from the menu (Surface ⇨ Add Duplicate) or using the Shift+D hotkey, you should press Y immediately after to constrain your movement to the Y-axis.

6. **Make adjustments to the new cross-section to suit your tastes, but *do not add or remove any control points*.**

   Lofting requires that each cross-section has the exact same number of control points. If you add or remove control points from a cross-section, it doesn't work.

7. **Repeat Steps 5 and 6 until you're satisfied.**

8. **Select everything in your NURBS surface object (Select ⇨ All) and connect them together (Control Points ⇨ Make Segment).**

   You've made a canoe!

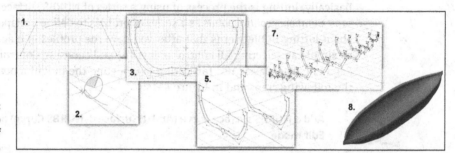

 You might begrudge the fact that I glazed over adding a couple other options in the Add ⇨ Curve menu, like Path curves and Fur curves. The reason for not discussing Path curves is that you can turn any curve into a path. By default, when you add a path, it's a shortcut for adding a straight NURBS curve. Any curve can behave as a path, though. You just need to enable the check box at the top of the Path Animation panel in Object Data Properties. By enabling this check box, Blender understands that a curve is a path that you can use to control the movement of an animated object. As for Fur curves, that's covered in more detail in Book 4, Chapter 5.

Understanding the strengths and limitations of Blender's surfaces

When compared to other tools that work with NURBS surfaces, Blender admittedly falls short in some functions. You can extrude surface endpoints, do lofting, and even *spin* surface curves (sometimes called *lathing* in other programs) to create bowl or cup shapes. However, that's about it. Blender currently doesn't have the functionality to do a ton of other cool things with NURBS surfaces, such as using one curve to trim the length of another or project the shape of one curve onto the surface of another.

However, there's hope. It's been slow coming, but Blender makes a little progress on the integration of better NURBS tools from time to time. Unfortunately, that progress ultimately is excruciatingly slow. If you want to work exclusively with NURBS, your only real choices are to wait with the rest of us or use a different program.

Using Metaball Objects

Metaball objects are cool little 3D surfaces that have been part of computer graphics for a long time. Sometimes metaball objects are referred to as *blobbies*. The principle behind metaball objects is pretty simple: Imagine that you have two droplets of water, and you begin moving these two droplets closer and closer to each other. Eventually, the two droplets are going to merge and become a single, larger droplet. That process is basically how metaball objects work, except you have complete control over when and how much the droplets merge, and you can re-separate them if you'd like.

You can also do something that's more difficult in the real world: You can subtract one droplet from the other rather than add them together into a merged object. They're a ton of fun to play with, and there are some pretty neat applications for them. Figure 4-16 shows two metaballs being merged.

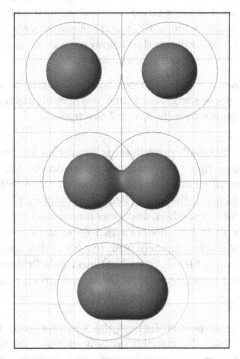

FIGURE 4-16: Merging two metaballs.

Meta-wha?

Metaball objects are a bit like curves and NURBS in that their entire existence is defined by math. However, unlike NURBS or even meshes, you can't control the surface of a metaball object directly with control points or vertices. Instead, the shape of their surface is defined by a combination of the object's underlying structure (a point, a line, a plane, a sphere, or a cube) and its proximity to other metaball objects. There are five metaball object primitives:

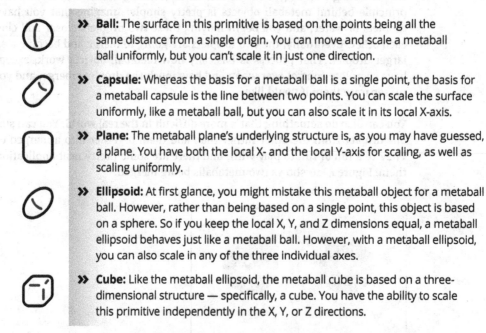

>> **Ball:** The surface in this primitive is based on the points being all the same distance from a single origin. You can move and scale a metaball ball uniformly, but you can't scale it in just one direction.

>> **Capsule:** Whereas the basis for a metaball ball is a single point, the basis for a metaball capsule is the line between two points. You can scale the surface uniformly, like a metaball ball, but you can also scale it in its local X-axis.

>> **Plane:** The metaball plane's underlying structure is, as you may have guessed, a plane. You have both the local X- and the local Y-axis for scaling, as well as scaling uniformly.

>> **Ellipsoid:** At first glance, you might mistake this metaball object for a metaball ball. However, rather than being based on a single point, this object is based on a sphere. So if you keep the local X, Y, and Z dimensions equal, a metaball ellipsoid behaves just like a metaball ball. However, with a metaball ellipsoid, you can also scale in any of the three individual axes.

>> **Cube:** Like the metaball ellipsoid, the metaball cube is based on a three-dimensional structure — specifically, a cube. You have the ability to scale this primitive independently in the X, Y, or Z directions.

A cool thing about metaball primitives is that they're actually primitive components in their own right. The options available in the Add menu are just a starting point. A metaball object can consist of one or more metaball primitives that behave as components of the object. Because they're each full-fledged components (kind of like vertices, edges, and faces on meshes), you can select them as individual pieces while in Edit mode. Furthermore, while you're in Edit mode, you can change one metaball component primitive to another metaball type on the fly. To do so, use the Active Element panel in Object Data Properties. Figure 4-17 shows each of the primitives along with the default settings for them in the Active Element panel.

The Active Element panel always displays the Stiffness value for the selected metaball component. This value controls the influence that the selected metaball component has on other metaball components. The Stiffness value is indicated visually in the 3D Viewport with a green ring around the metaball component's origin. You can adjust the Stiffness value here in the panel, or if you select the green ring, you can use the Scale tool (or the S hotkey) scale to adjust the Stiffness visually. By selecting the reddish, pinkish ring outside of that green ring, you can select the actual individual metaball component.

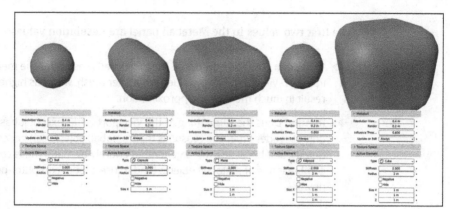

FIGURE 4-17:
The five metaball object primitives.

And depending on the type of metaball component primitive you're using, other values of X, Y, and Z may appear in the Active Element panel while you're in Edit mode. You can adjust these values here or in 3D Viewport by scaling as described in Chapter 3. At the bottom of the panel are buttons to either hide the selected metaball component or give it a negative influence, subtracting it from the positive, and therefore visible, metaball components.

When you tab back out to Object mode, you can move your combined metaball object (a meta-metaball object?) as a single unit. Note, however, that even though you've grouped these metaball components into a single Blender object, they don't live in a vacuum. If you have two complex Blender objects made up of metaballs, bringing the two of them together causes them to merge. Just keep that as something you may want to bear in mind and take advantage of in the future.

 As a single Blender object, though, you can control a few more things using the Metaball panel, as shown in Figure 4-18. This panel is always available to metaball objects, whether in Object mode or Edit mode, and it sits at the top of the Object Data tab of the Properties editor.

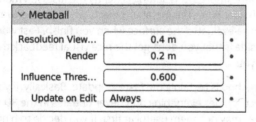

FIGURE 4-18:
The Metaball panel.

The first two values in the Metaball panel are Resolution values:

>> **Viewport:** Controls how dense the generated mesh is for the metaball object in the 3D Viewport. Lower values are a finer mesh, whereas higher values result in much more of an approximation.

>> **Render:** Does the same thing as the Viewport value, except it has an effect only at render time. The reason is that metaball objects can get complex quickly, and because they're generated entirely by math, these complex combinations of metaball objects tend to use a lot of computer-processing power.

TIP

Working at a larger Viewport size in the 3D Viewport helps keep your computer responsive while you work, whereas a finer Render value keeps things pretty on output.

The Influence Threshold value is an overall control for how much influence the metaballs in a single Blender object have over each other. This value has a range from 0 to 5, but in order for a metaball object to be visible, its individual Stiffness value must be greater than the Threshold value.

At the bottom of the Metaball panel is a drop-down menu labeled Update on Edit that controls how the metaball objects get updated and displayed in the 3D Viewport. You have four choices:

>> **Always:** The slowest and most accurate, this setting is the default. Every change you make in the 3D Viewport happens instantly (or as fast as your computer can handle it).

>> **Half:** This option reduces the resolution of the metaball object as you move or edit it, increasing the responsiveness of the 3D Viewport. When you finish transforming the metaball object, it displays in full resolution again.

>> **Fast:** As the name implies, this setting is nearly the fastest. When you enable this button, Blender hides the metaball objects when you perform a transform and then re-evaluates the surface when you finish. Fast works nicely, but the downside is that you don't get the nice visual feedback that Always and Half give you.

>> **Never:** This method is certainly the fastest update. Basically, if you try to edit a metaball object, it hides everything and never updates in the 3D Viewport. Although Never may not seem useful at first, if you decide to bind your metaball object to a particle system as a way of faking fluids, turning this setting on definitely increases performance in the 3D Viewport.

What metaball objects are useful for

So what in the world can you use metaball objects to make? I have two answers to this question: all sorts of things, and not much. The reason for this seemingly paradoxical answer is that you *can* use metaball objects to do quick, rough prototype models, and you *can* also use them with a particle system to generate simple fluid simulations. However, with the advent of advanced modeling tools like sculpting and subdivision surfaces, metaball objects don't get used as often for prototyping. And with more advanced fluid simulation and rendering technology, metaball objects are also used less for those applications as well. They have a tendency to use a lot of computer-processing power and don't often give good topology by themselves.

That said, even though metaball objects are used *less* for these purposes, that doesn't mean that they're never used. In fact, not long ago, I used a set of metaballs with a glowing halo material to animate the life force being forcefully pulled out of a guy in a scene for a local filmmaker. I could probably have used a particle system or fluid simulator to do this effect, but using metaballs was faster to set up, and I had more direct control over where everything was placed on the screen.

Furthermore, if you're a 3D sculptor and you like to use Blender's Dyntopo feature (see the previous chapter), I'd definitely encourage you to try out metaballs as a means of giving yourself a base mesh to start sculpting upon. Just glom together a bunch of metaball components into the rough base shape you want and convert to a mesh (Object ⇨ Convert ⇨ Mesh) for sculpting. So don't count metaball objects out just yet. These little suckers still have some life left. Besides, they're fun to play with!

Adding Text

Over the years, working with text in Blender has come a long, long way. The way you work with text in Blender has quite a few differences from what you might expect of word-processing software like LibreOffice or Microsoft Word. What you may not expect is that Blender's text objects share a few features in common with desktop publishing programs like Adobe InDesign or Affinity Publisher.

Blender's text objects are a specialized type of curve object. Nearly all the options I describe for curves also apply to text. (See the section "Using Curves and Surfaces," earlier in this chapter.) For example, you can quickly bring text objects into the third dimension using the Extrude, Bevel, and even the Bevel Object and Taper Object fields. Figure 4-19 shows an example of the interesting things you can do with a single text object in Blender.

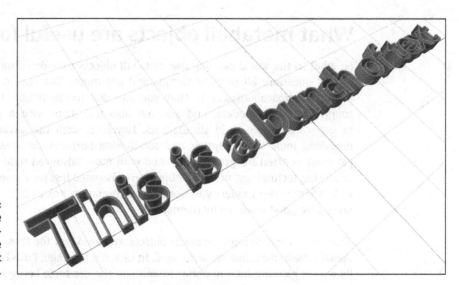

FIGURE 4-19:
Taking advantage
of the curve-
based nature
of Blender text
objects.

Adding and editing text

You add a text object in Blender the same way you add any other object. Choose Add ⇨ Text, and a text object appears at the location of your 3D cursor with the word "Text" as its default content.

To edit the text, you tab into Edit mode. After you're in Edit mode, the controls begin to feel a bit more like a word processor, although not exactly. For example, you can't use your mouse cursor to highlight text, but if you press Shift+← and Shift+→, depending on where the text cursor is located, you can highlight text this way.

TIP

Shift+Ctrl+←/→ highlights whole words at a time. Backspace deletes text and pressing Enter gives you a new line.

Aside from just typing, there are other ways to add text to your text object. If you happen to have a relatively large chunk of text, Blender's text objects support copy and paste. Simply highlight the text you want in another application and copy it (the universal hotkey combination for this is Ctrl+C, but you can usually also do this from a right-click menu). Then, in Blender with your text object in Edit mode, paste the text from your system clipboard by either using Edit ⇨ Paste from the 3D Viewport's header or using the Ctrl+V hotkey combination.

If you have a *lot* of text — like, say, the credits for a short animated film — Blender has another handy feature. In the 3D Viewport's header menu, choose Edit ⇨ Paste File. Doing this, Blender provides you with a File Browser that you can use to pick any text file on your hard drive. The entirety of that text will be added to your text object. Super handy!

Controlling text appearance

Whether you're adding text by typing or pulling from a text file, the default look of Blender's text object is not what you're probably going to want to use. More often than not, you're going to want to use a custom font with customized spacing and placement of the letters in the text you're adding. This section covers how to make your text look really nice. It all starts from Object Data Properties, as shown in Figure 4-20. The first set of controls should look familiar if you already understand how curve objects work. For text, however, there are additional formatting controls.

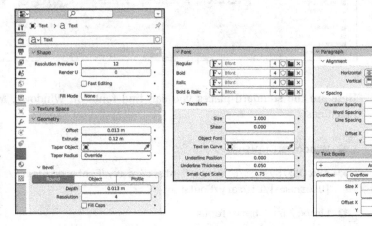

FIGURE 4-20:
The Object Data tab of the Properties editor, sometimes referred to as Text Properties.

Changing fonts

An important thing that's different about Blender's text objects is the way they handle fonts. If you're used to other programs, you may expect to see a drop-down menu that lists all the fonts installed on your computer with a nice preview of each. Blender has that ability, but it is not accessed in quite the same way. What you need to do is left-click the Load button to the right of the Regular Font datablock in the Font panel of Text Properties. Blender then shows you a File Browser where you can track down the actual font file for the typeface you want to use.

When you call the File Browser from any font datablock, it has the Thumbnails display mode automatically enabled (see Book 1, Chapter 4 for more information on using the File Browser). Now, when you navigate to a fonts folder on your hard drive, you should see something like what's shown in Figure 4-21.

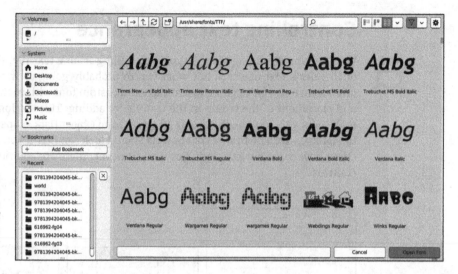

FIGURE 4-21:
Blender's File
Browser can give
you previews of
what the fonts on
your computer
look like.

Here are the standard places you can find fonts on Windows, Mac, and Linux machines:

>> **Windows:** `C:\Windows\Fonts`

>> **macOS:** `/System/Library/Fonts/Library/Fonts,` or `/Users/ [Username]/Library/Fonts`

>> **Linux:** `/usr/share/fonts`

After you load a font, it's saved with your `.blend` file, making it available whenever you want it from the font datablock list. You always have Blender's built-in font available as well.

Fonts in Blender are datablocks just like meshes or materials. That means if they're not actively used in your scene, they won't be saved to your `.blend` file, and when you re-open your file, any unused fonts will need to be reloaded. So if you load a lot of fonts and want to have them available the next time you open this `.blend` file, I would recommend that you give your font datablock a fake user by clicking the shield icon to the right of the datablock.

Now you would think that after you have a font loaded, you should be good to go, right? Well, not quite. Blender's method of handling bold and italic in text is *also* kind of unique. You load a separate font file for each one (hence the four separate Font datablocks: Regular, Bold, Italic, and Bold & Italic). Typically, you use these datablocks to load the bold and italic versions of the font file you choose in the Regular datablock. However, that's not a hard-and-fast requirement. You can use a different font altogether. Although the ability to choose different fonts in the Bold and Italic datablocks is perhaps a mild abuse of the terms, that ability does provide a pretty handy workaround. Technically speaking, Blender doesn't allow you to arbitrarily change fonts in the middle of a text object. However, using the different font datablocks, you can get around that problem by making your Bold or Italic font the other fonts you want to use. Choosing a font file for any style of font is pretty straightforward:

1. **In the Font panel of your text object's Object Data Properties, left-click the Load button on the font datablock you want to change.**

   By default, the built-in font, Bfont, is chosen for all four datablocks.

2. **Navigate your hard drive using the File Browser and choose the font you want to use.**

3. **Use your chosen font in your text object.**

   As an example, say that you chose a new font for the Bold datablock. You can assign that font to characters in your text object with the following steps:

   (a) *From Edit mode (Tab), highlight the text you want to change (Shift + ← or Shift + →).*

   (b) *Toggle Bold (Font ⇨ Toggle Bold or press Ctrl+B in the 3D Viewport).*

Figure 4-22 shows the results of using multiple fonts in a single text object.

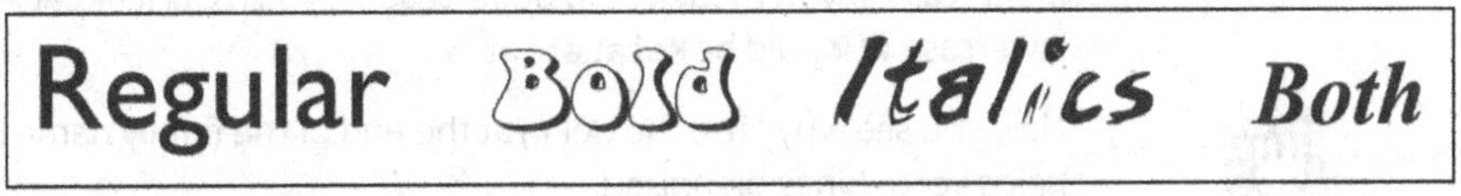

FIGURE 4-22: Using the Bold and Italics fonts to use widely different fonts in a single text object.

Regular ʙᴏ𝖑𝖉 *Italics* **Both**

You may find that while you're typing, you need certain special characters like the copyright symbol or the upside-down question mark for sentences written in Spanish. For these situations, you have three options:

» If the special character is common, you may find it in Edit ⇨ Special Characters.

» You can memorize the hotkey combination for various commonly used special characters as listed in Blender's online documentation. For example, you can insert the copyright symbol (©) by pressing O ⇨ Alt+Backspace ⇨ C.

» If the character is rare or just not in the menu, but you have it in a text file outside of Blender, you can use copy and paste or the Edit ⇨ Paste File operator as described earlier to get that character into your text object.

Some fonts don't always include glyphs for every special character possible. So if you use one of the preceding methods to add a special character and you don't see that character appear in Blender, you may need to try a different font.

Another unique feature that Blender's text objects have is the ability to use any other Blender object as a font character. So if you want to use Suzanne the monkey every time the uppercase S character is used, you can do that. If you want to model letters with metaball objects and spell something with them, like in Figure 4-23, you can do that. With your text object selected, have a look in Object Data Properties. Within the Font panel, there's a Transform sub-panel with a field labeled Object Font. Just follow these steps:

1. **Type the name of your font "family" in Object Font.**

   You can choose any name you like. I like to end my name with a dot (.) so I can differentiate my characters later. For example, you could use MetaLetter. (ending in the period) in this case.

2. **Model a character you want to use.**

   In this example, I'm using metaball objects, so I use Add ⇨ Metaball ⇨ Ball as my starting point and work from there.

3. **Name this object with the family name plus the character it will represent.**

   In this case, if you modeled an uppercase W, you'd call it MetaLetter.W. A lowercase W would be MetaLetter.w.

   Now you see why I use the dot (.) at the end of the family name in Step 1. It helps keep things organized.

4. **Repeat Steps 2 and 3 for each character you need.**

5. **Select your text object and enable vertex instances (from Object Properties, Instancing ⇨ Vertices).**

6. **Adjust size and spacing to fit.**

   And *poof*! You've got metaletters!

7. **To finish, move the original font text to another (hidden) collection so that it's out of the way of your metaletters.**

One detail to note here is that your metaletters don't merge into each other like you might expect. This is a shortcoming within Blender. The same letter will merge with itself, but different letters won't. To my knowledge, a good workaround currently doesn't exist. In fairness, though, this example is a bit contrived and isn't something that people frequently do.

FIGURE 4-23:
Wheeeee!
Metaletters!

 Looking back at the Object Data tab of the Properties editor for your text object, there are a few more handy settings in the Transform sub-panel within the Font panel. There's a block of fields to control how the text appears in the selected text object:

>> **Size:** This field allows you to adjust the font size on a scale from 0.010 to 10. Changing the font size value is generally a better way to change the size of your text instead of simply scaling the text object. Think of it like you would think about scaling a mesh or curve object in Edit mode.

>> **Shear:** Shearing is a quick-and-dirty way to fake italic on a font. Values between 0 and 1 tilt characters to the right, whereas values between –1 and 0 tilt them all to the left.

>> **Object Font:** As described in the preceding text, using this field, you can define Blender objects as characters in a font.

>> **Text on Curve:** If you need your text to flow along the length of a curve object, use this datablock field to choose that particular curve object.

 Either choose your curve object from this field or click the eyedropper icon to use an eyedropper for picking an object from the 3D Viewport (as I described earlier in this chapter for Taper Objects and Bevel Objects).

TIP

>> **Underline Position:** Adjust this value to control the position of the underline, if enabled (Font ➪ Toggle Underline or Ctrl+U on highlighted text). This value has a range from –0.2 to 0.8.

>> **Underline Thickness:** From this field, you can control the thickness of the actual underline, if enabled (Font ➪ Toggle Underline or Ctrl+U on highlighted text). You can set this value between 0 and 0.8.

>> **Small Caps Scale:** If you enable the Small Caps toggle that's among the other formatting buttons in the Font panel (Bold, Italic, Underline), this value controls how small your small capital letters are relative to regular capital letters.

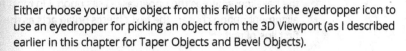

Adjusting paragraph styles

The Paragraph panel consists of two sub-panels, Alignment and Spacing. The Alignment sub-panel has a pair of settings to help you align your text relative to the origin of the text object. For Horizontal alignment, you have the following options:

- >> **Left:** Aligns text to the left. The text object's origin serves as the left-hand guide for the text.

- >> **Center:** All text is centered around the text object's origin.

- >> **Right:** Aligns text to the right. The text object's origin serves as the right-hand guide for the text.

- >> **Justify:** Aligns text both on the left and on the right. If the line is not long enough, Blender adds spacing, or *kerning*, between individual characters to fill the space. This option requires the use of text boxes. (See the next section, "Working with text boxes," for more details.)

- >> **Flush:** This option works similar to the way Justify does, but with one exception: If the line is the end of a paragraph, it forces the text to align both sides. Like Justify, this option requires the use of text frames.

In addition to the preceding Horizontal alignment options, Blender also offers a few Vertical alignment options (they're especially worth thinking about if you have multiple lines of text):

- >> **Top:** Choose this option and your text object's origin acts as the top of your block of text. All text flows beneath it.

- >> **Top Baseline:** This is the default alignment. The *baseline* of text is the line upon which text is written. As an example, the lowercase letter g goes below the baseline, whereas the uppercase G sits upon it in most fonts. With this alignment option chosen, the text object's origin acts as the baseline for the first line of text.

- >> **Middle:** If you choose Middle vertical alignment, the origin of your text object is at the vertical center of your block of text.

- >> **Bottom Baseline:** If you only have one line of text, this choice looks exactly like the default setting of Top Baseline. However, it's pretty easy to notice a difference with multiple lines of text. Choose this vertical alignment option and the baseline of the last line of text is in line with your text object's origin.

- >> **Bottom:** This choice is the inverse of Top alignment. The text object's origin acts as the bottom of your block of text. All text that you add is above the origin.

From the Spacing sub-panel, you can customize the amount of spacing between characters and lines in your text. You have the following four values available to adjust:

>> **Character Spacing:** The global distance between all characters in your text object, also known as *tracking*. This value has a range from 0 to 10.

>> **Word Spacing:** Globally defines the space between words in your text object. This field also has a range from 0 to 10.

>> **Line Spacing:** Line distance, also referred to as *leading* (pronounced "leding"). This value defines the distance between lines of text in your text object and it also has a range from 0 to 10.

>> **Offset:** These values offset the text object from its default position. X values less than zero shift it left and Y values less than zero shift down, whereas values greater than zero shift it right (X) or up (Y).

TECHNICAL STUFF

If you're familiar with typography, you may notice two things right off the bat. First, the terms used here are not the standard typography terminology, and second, the values are not in your typical percentage, point, pica, or pixel sizes. These differences exist for two primary reasons. First, Blender is a 3D program intended for 3D artists, many of whom may not be familiar with typography terms and sizes. The second reason dovetails with the first one, but it's a bit more on the practical side. Blender text objects are 3D objects that can be just about any size in virtual 3D space. Sizes like points, pixels, and picas don't mean anything in 3D because there's not a frame of reference, like the physical size of a printed piece of paper.

Working with text boxes

Both the Flush and the Justify horizontal alignment options in the Paragraph panel require the use of something called *text boxes*. The Left, Center, and Right align options all work relative to the location of the text object's origin. However, if you want to align your text on both the left and the right side, you need more than one reference point. Text boxes are a way of providing those reference points, but with a couple of additional benefits. Basically, text boxes are a rectangular shape that defines where the text in your text object lives. Text boxes are similar to the *frames* you might use in desktop publishing programs. They're also one of those things that you normally don't see in 3D software.

To work with text boxes, you use the Text Boxes panel. By default, Blender gives you a single text box, but all its dimensions are zeroed out. That means that the text box dynamically adjusts to whatever you type in your text object. To get the most out of text boxes, you need to adjust the Size X and Y fields to a specific size (determined by whatever base units you set in the Scene tab of the Properties editor). The Offset X and Y fields determine where the top-left corner of the text box is located. As you adjust these values while in Edit mode, you should see a dashed rectangle in the 3D Viewport.

You should also note that you can control *overflow*, or what happens when the text in your text object takes up more space than the text box allows. The Overflow drop-down menu offers you three choices:

» **Overflow:** This the default setting. The width of your text box is respected, but if you have text that runs longer than the height of your text box, that text will just run past (or overflow) the borders of your text box.

» **Scale to Fit:** Choose this option and Blender will scale the letters in your text object so all of them will fit within the space of your text box.

» **Truncate:** This option is arguably the most brutal. If your text doesn't fit within the space you define for your text box, Blender just hides it.

Now, the cool thing about text boxes is that you can define more than one and place them arbitrarily in your scene. Add a text box by left-clicking the Add Textbox button in the Text Boxes panel. If you have more than one text box defined, the text can overflow from one box into another. Using multiple text boxes is an excellent way to get fine control over the placement of your text. You can even do newspaper-style multi-column text this way, as shown in Figure 4-24.

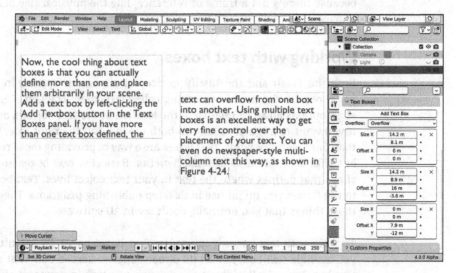

FIGURE 4-24:
Using text boxes to get multi-column text layouts.

TIP

If you're working with a lot of text, you may find that Blender doesn't perform as speedily as you'd like while editing. If you left-click the Fast Editing check box in the Shape panel, Blender uses just the outline of the text in the 3D Viewport while in Edit mode. This adjustment gives Blender a bit of a performance boost so that you're not waiting for characters to show up seconds after you finish typing them.

Deforming text with a curve

Another powerful thing you can do with Blender's text objects is have the text flow along the length of a curve. This way, you can get text that arcs over a doorway or wraps around a bowl or just looks all kinds of funky. The key to this feature is the Text on Curve field in the Font panel (look in the Transform sub-panel). To see how this feature works, follow these steps:

a **1. Create a text object (Add ⇨ Text).**

Feel free to populate it with whatever content you want.

2. Create a curve to dictate the text shape (Add ⇨ Curve ⇨ Bézier).

This curve is your control. You're using a Bézier curve here, but a NURBS curve works fine as well. Also, I like to make my curve with the same origin location as my text object. Granted, that's just my preference, but it works nicely for keeping everything easily manageable.

a **3. Select your text object and choose the name of your control curve in the Text on Curve field.**

Blam! The text should now follow the arc of the curve. If you select the curve and tab into Edit mode, any change you make to it updates your text object live. Figure 4-25 shows 3D text along a curve.

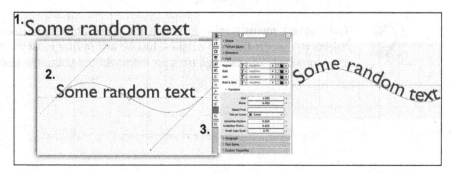

FIGURE 4-25:
Text on a curve.

REMEMBER

You should keep your curve as a 2D curve. Because the text is technically a special type of 2D curve, trying to get it to deform along a 3D curve won't work. For text to follow a 3D curve, you're going to need to convert the text into a mesh. You can do that conversion explicitly, as described in the next section, or you can do it implicitly by giving the text object a Curve deform modifier. Modifiers work on curve objects, but internally those curves are converted to meshes. In simple cases, this may work just fine. More often than not, you'll want the control of explicitly doing the conversion yourself.

Converting to curves and meshes

Of course, although Blender's text objects are pretty powerful, curves and meshes just do some things better. Fortunately, you don't have to model your text by using meshes and curves unless you really, really want to. Instead, you can convert your text object into a curve or a mesh by choosing Object ⇨ Convert ⇨ Curve or Object ⇨ Convert ⇨ Mesh. If you're curious as to some specific cases why you'd want to make this conversion, here are a few:

» Custom editing the characters for a logo or a specific shape (convert to a curve)

» Needing to share your .blend file, but the license of your font prevents you from legally packing it into the .blend (convert to a curve)

» Getting extruded text to follow a 3D curve (convert to a mesh)

» Rigging the letters to be animated with an armature (convert to a mesh or curve)

» Using the letters as obstacles in a fluid simulation (convert to a mesh)

» Using the letters to generate a particle system (convert to a mesh)

TIP

The Convert menu is also available for curve objects, surfaces, and metaball objects to convert them to meshes. Just be aware that most of these conversions are permanent. You can't go back on them without using the undo operator.

IN THIS CHAPTER

» Understanding the benefits and trade-offs with procedural modeling

» Getting familiar with the Geometry Nodes workspace

» Discovering the concept of node-based workflows

» Using nodes in Blender

» Exploring common approaches to modeling with geometry nodes

» Understanding how to think like a procedural modeler

Chapter **5**

Getting Procedural with Geometry Nodes

I n Chapter 2 of this book I cover Blender's modifier stack and introduce the concept of taking a non-destructive approach to creating your 3D models. In the releases of Blender since the last edition of *Blender For Dummies*, the Blender development team has taken that concept and "dialed it up to eleven" with a new feature called *geometry nodes*, or *geonodes* for short. Simply put, geometry nodes are a way for you to build your own modifiers by chaining together a series of smaller operations. Those operations are contained in visual blocks referred to as *nodes*. Blender uses this same node-based concept in other features, such as shading (see Book 3), compositing (see Book 5, Chapter 2), and hair (see Book 4, Chapter 5), so even if you decide that you don't want to use geometry nodes, it's still worthwhile to go through this chapter because a lot of the same base concepts are used elsewhere in Blender.

And really, there's an incredible amount excitement around geometry nodes (and nodes in general) within the Blender community. This feature in Blender gives you the ability to do things that in the past could only be done with Python scripting or directly editing Blender's source code. Sure, those options are still available, but a lot of people find the concept of nodes to be more accessible and fun to work with. In fact, the Blender community even started a month-long event called "Nodevember," where each day there's a prompt for people to try to make something using only Blender's node-based tools. The original concept started with just using shader nodes and then exploded in popularity when geometry nodes were introduced.

In fact, there's so much excitement around nodes that there's a plan to expand their use even more in future versions of Blender, for everything from particles and simulation to constraints and rigging. Now, if you're just starting out, Blender's geometry nodes can seem a bit intimidating. With a tool as powerful and flexible as geometry nodes, it's easy to get overwhelmed when first jumping in. However, by understanding the general workflow and the tools you use to create these node networks, they become a lot less daunting. Hopefully, by the time you finish this chapter, you'll get a sense of why this feature has caught everyone's attention . . . and perhaps feel a little bit of that excitement yourself.

Discovering the Differences between Destructive and Procedural Modeling

The process of using nodes to build flexible, adjustable models is known as *procedural modeling*. Conceptually, it's best to think of procedural modeling as an extension to the non-destructive modeling techniques that I introduce in Chapter 2 of this book with modifiers. Blender isn't the first 3D application to have procedural modeling. This way of creating models has been a common workflow in computer-aided design (CAD) for a long time, where it's important to have a model that can quickly be modified with a few subtle adjustments.

As an example, consider someone who designs footwear. Say you've designed an incredible-looking shoe and you want to make that shoe available to everyone. Well, each person has differently sized feet, and those differences can't always be accommodated by simply scaling the shoe in Object mode. Often, there are a series of smaller parameters to adjust to ensure that the sole remains the correct thickness, the arch keeps its shape, or the toe box has enough space to be comfortable.

If you modeled the shoe using a destructive approach like sculpting or traditional box modeling, you'd need to remodel the whole shoe for each size variation that you want to offer. Sure, you could take some shortcuts with templates, but you're still essentially rebuilding the model each time. But what if you modeled the shoe procedurally? What if you had a "shoe modifier"? You could adjust parameters for foot size, arch height, and toe box size and the model would automatically update to accommodate those adjustments. That's the kind of power and flexibility that you get with procedural modeling.

Now, this example had a bit of a CAD focus because there's where a lot of this procedural approach has been used in the past, but you're not limited to that kind of use. In a program like Blender, which has a much more art-driven focus, procedural modeling opens all kinds of interesting doors. You can use nodes to create a pebble modifier that creates little rocks of all shapes and sizes. You could also have your own custom terrain modifier that generates ground planes with all manner of size and topography. Then, because they're both essentially modifiers, you can chain them together so you have a whole bunch of pebbles scattered over the surface of your terrain.

Or perhaps you've been asked to make a model of a sword for a character in a game or animated short and the sword needs to look more aged, worn, and chipped over time. You don't have to model (and keep track of) multiple versions of that same sword. Instead, you can make an age or damage parameter on your sword model. Then you can adjust as needed with just a slider or two.

When you start thinking procedurally, the list of possibilities is virtually limitless.

Of course, it's important to remember that procedural modeling techniques are not meant to be a replacement for traditional destructive approaches to modeling. Sometimes you just need a "thing" and it's faster to jump into Sculpt mode or Edit mode and get that thing built. What's cool is that you don't have to choose. Procedural techniques are meant to be used *with* destructive techniques. You can have your traditionally modeled sword and just use procedural tools for adding the wear and tear to it.

Alright, that's enough theory. It's time to get into how to actually go about doing this procedural modeling thing.

Using the Geometry Nodes Workspace

Blender ships with a workspace that's dedicated to building and testing your geometry node networks. That workspace — conveniently named Geometry Nodes — is available as a tab in the General workflow template when you start a new Blender session (File ⇨ New ⇨ General). It should be the second-to-last tab in Blender's top row. When you switch to this workspace by clicking its tab, your Blender window should look something like what's shown in Figure 5-1.

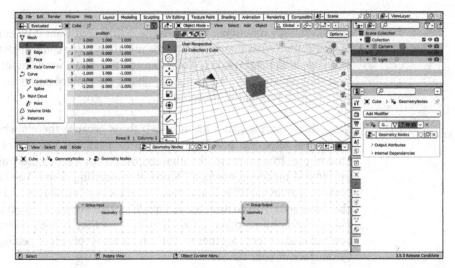

FIGURE 5-1:
The Geometry
Nodes workspace
is where you
go to build
your awesome
geonodes
networks.

In a lot of ways, the Geometry Nodes workspace is not all that different from the Layout workspace. You still have the Outliner and Properties editor along the right side of the window. And you have the 3D Viewport near the middle. The difference, however, is that you have two new editors in this workspace. The largest amount of screen real estate is dedicated to the Geometry Node Editor. This editor is where the majority of your geonodes work gets done. Secondarily, the upper left of the workspace is dominated by Blender's Spreadsheet editor. The Spreadsheet is there to help you understand (and debug) what's going on in your node network. This section goes into each of these editors in more detail.

Meet the Node editor

Regardless of whether you're working with geometry nodes, shader nodes, or compositor nodes, Blender shares the same basic node editor interface. Using the Geometry Node Editor as the example, when you first look at it, the node editor is deceptively simple and barren. There are two nodes in there, input and output, connected by a single link, or *noodle*. That said, it's best to think of this editor as being a blank canvas that you can use to start your procedural modeling adventures.

For the most part, the node editors in Blender conform to the same user interface behavior that's in the rest of the program. You select nodes by left-clicking, you can get a context menu by right-clicking, and you can delete selected multiple nodes by pressing X or Delete. You can reveal a Toolbar on the left by navigating to View ⇨ Toolbar or pressing T. And there's a Sidebar you can show by choosing View ⇨ Sidebar or pressing N. With all these parts expanded, your Geometry Nodes Editor may look more like what's shown in Figure 5-2.

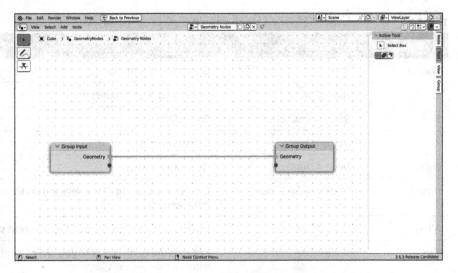

FIGURE 5-2:
Like many
other editors
in Blender, the
Geometry Nodes
Editor has a
Toolbar and a
Sidebar that
you can use
for additional
functionality.

Of course, there are a few differences specifically related to node editors. The Blender development team has worked hard to keep things consistent, though. So where there's a mental model similar to what's in the 3D Viewport, they've tried to use the same menu items and hotkeys. For example, the concept of nodes groups in node editors is pretty similar to objects and collections in 3D space. *Node groups* are bundles of nodes that perform a specific task (that you decide). So to create a node group, you can use the same Ctrl+G hotkey combination that you use to create a collection. Likewise, because you can drill into node groups and edit the components within, it's much like switching to Edit mode on a 3D object. So the same Tab hotkey is used in the node editors to drill into groups. That said, node editors have a few unique concepts, like the ability to mute a node and disable its functionality (Node⇨Toggle Node Mute or press M) or the ability to hide unused node sockets (Node⇨Toggle Hidden Node Sockets or Ctrl+H). Have a look at Table 5-1 to get a sense of the most common hotkeys and menus used in node editors.

Likewise, there are a bunch of mouse actions that should feel quite similar to behaviors in other editors within Blender. For example, you can pan the whole view by middle-clicking and dragging anywhere in the node editor. Likewise, you can use your scroll wheel to zoom in and out on parts of your node network. However, just like with hotkeys, there are functions that don't really have a parallel in 3D space, such as cutting links between nodes or quickly attaching a Viewer node to a particular node's output socket. Table 5-2 shows most of the frequently used mouse actions in the node editors.

TABLE 5-1 **Commonly Used Hotkeys in the Node Editors**

Hotkey	Menu Access	Description
Shift+A	Add	Opens toolbox menu.
G	Node ⇨ Move	Grabs a node and moves it.
B	Select ⇨ Box Select	Box-selects.
X	Node ⇨ Delete	Deletes node(s).
Shift+D	Node ⇨ Duplicate	Duplicates node(s).
Ctrl+G	Node ⇨ Make Group	Creates a group out of the selected nodes (see the next section).
Alt+G	Node ⇨ Ungroup	Ungroups the selected group (see the next section).
Tab	Node ⇨ Edit Group	Expands the node group so you can edit individual nodes within it (see the next section).
M	Node ⇨ Toggle Node Mute	Toggles the selected nodes between being bypassed (muted) within the node network, or enabled.
H	Node ⇨ Hide	Toggles the selected nodes between expanded and collapsed views.
Ctrl+H	Node ⇨ Toggle Hidden Node Sockets	Toggles the visibility of unconnected sockets on a node. Handy for cleaning up your node network so it's easier to read.
Numpad-dot (.)	View ⇨ Frame Selected	Moves the view (without zooming) so your selected node is centered in the node editor.

REMEMBER

It's a good idea to keep the Sidebar visible and set to the Node tab when you're working in the node editor. Most nodes can have their settings directly adjusted right in the node itself. However, sometimes the tiny space afforded by a node isn't enough room to show all its available options and parameters. Those settings are available in the Properties panel within the Node tab of the node editor's Sidebar. That same tab also gives you the ability to give custom labels and colors to your nodes so you can keep your node networks organized.

Spreadsheets? In a 3D Program? Yes.

The other editor in the Geometry Nodes workspace is the Spreadsheet editor. I can hear the questions already, "A spreadsheet? Blender is supposed to be a creative program! Why in the world is there a spreadsheet editor in there?" Well, if Microsoft can put a flight simulator in Excel, why can't a 3D tool like Blender include a spreadsheet?

TABLE 5-2   **Commonly Used Mouse Actions in the Node Editors**

Mouse Action	Description
Left-click	Selects a node. Click and drag to move the node around.
Shift+left-click	Selects multiple nodes.
Left-click and drag in empty space	Box-selects nodes.
Left-click (on a socket)	Attaches or detaches a noodle to/from the socket you click on. Click and drag to the socket you want to connect to. If you release the mouse button in empty space, Blender provides a search menu to help choose a node for you to add and automatically be connected to.
Left-click+drag the left or right side of a node	Resizes the node.
Alt+left-click and drag a node	Disconnects a node from the network.
Shift+Ctrl+left-click a node	Connects the active Viewer node to the output of the clicked node. If there is no Viewer node, one is automatically created. Continuous Shift+Ctrl+left-clicks iterate through the multiple outputs of the node.
Middle-click	Pans compositor work area.
Scroll wheel	Zooms compositor work area.

In seriousness, the Spreadsheet editor in Blender is an incredibly powerful tool for helping you understand what's going on. It actually has quite a few different and handy uses all over Blender, not just for geometry nodes. Any time you need to get an understanding of what's going on with large segments of data, the Spreadsheet editor is there to help you make sense of things. For example, in Book 4, Chapter 3, I talk about weight painting your mesh to control influence of vertex groups on your mesh's vertices for the purposes of rigging. The Spreadsheet gives you the ability to see the weight assignments of a bunch of vertex groups on multiple vertices all at once. Likewise, when you're working on procedural modeling with geonodes, you have a lot of geometry you need to manage and keep track of. The Spreadsheet editor is your tool for that kind of task.

REMEMBER

It's critical to keep in mind that unlike spreadsheets that you might be used to (such as LibreOffice Calc or Microsoft Excel), Blender's Spreadsheet editor doesn't really give you the ability to directly edit the values that it displays. Because you're working procedurally, it doesn't make a lot of sense to directly modify values from the Spreadsheet, because most of those values are generated by the configuration of your node network. If you were able to make a change like that in the Spreadsheet, that would be a destructive edit, which doesn't jive with the whole procedural modeling way of thinking. It's best to consider the Spreadsheet as a "read-only" tool for viewing the state of the data in your object.

Still, there's a lot that the Spreadsheet editor can do for you. As an example, I've taken the default cube and added a vertex group to it named "Carl", then I used Blender's Weight Paint mode to assign a bunch of different weights to vertices in the cube to see their influence by the Carl group (you can find out more about vertex groups and weight painting in Chapters 2 and 3 of Book 4). You can use the Spreadsheet editor to quickly see those weight values. Furthermore, if you enable the Show Only Selected button in the Spreadsheet's header and hop into Edit mode in the 3D Viewport, the Spreadsheet displays the vertex weight on Carl for the selected vertices in the cube. Furthermore, if you expand the Spreadsheet's Sidebar, you can add a filter to only show the vertices with a weight greater than a certain value (like, say, 0.30). These kinds of filtering and visualization tools can go a long way towards helping you debug your models in Blender. Figure 5-3 shows the Spreadsheet editor, showing all vertex weights in this example and filtering to show vertices with a weight greater than 0.30.

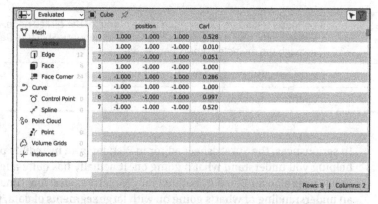

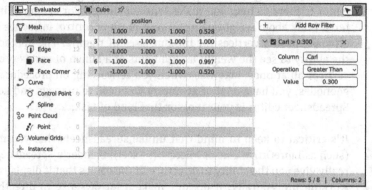

FIGURE 5-3:
The Spreadsheet editor gives you tools for filtering and checking data on your objects. At the top is the Spreadsheet displaying the weights for vertices in the default cube with a vertex group named Carl. At the bottom, the Spreadsheet is filtering this view for the vertices with weights greater than 0.30.

Relative to working with geometry nodes, there's another useful feature of the Spreadsheet for checking on your work. In the Spreadsheet's header, there's an Object Evaluation State drop-down menu that's defaulted to Evaluated as its setting. This setting tells the Spreadsheet to display the result of your object's data after it is processed by your whole modifier stack, including every modifier and geonode network in that stack. This default is particularly good for most situations, but you have other options available:

>> **Evaluated:** As stated, this option is the default and it shows what Blender sees as the output of your modifier stack.

>> **Original:** If you want to have an understanding of the base data that you're starting with before entering your modifier stack, choose Original from the Object Evaluation State menu. With this choice, you can compare your starting data against what your modifier stack creates. It's particularly useful for noticing if there's a vertex group or attribute that's missing at the start.

>> **Viewer Node:** To get a sense of what's going on within a geometry node network in your modifier stack, use the Viewer Node setting from this menu. If you have a Viewer Node in your geonode network, choosing this view gives you insight into the state of your object up to that point in the network. This choice is particularly useful for isolating part of your work and debugging it on its own without disconnecting it from the rest of the network.

Understanding Nodes

In order to effectively work with nodes in any context, it's important to have a good mental picture of how the process works in a general sense. One of the best ways to understand the power of nodes is to imagine an assembly line, like in a manufacturing plant. In these kinds of assembly lines, each step in the process depends on the step immediately preceding it, then feeds directly into the following step. This is the model that's used for Blender's modifier stack. It's also similar to the layer-based approach used in many image-manipulation programs such as Photoshop and GIMP. Each layer has exactly one input from the previous layer and one output to the following one. Figure 5-4 illustrates this idea.

FIGURE 5-4:
An assembly line
approach, similar
to Blender's
modifier stack
and layers
in GIMP or
Photoshop.

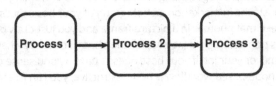

That approach works well, but you can enhance the assembly line a bit. Say that some steps in the process produce parts that can go to more than one subsequent step, and that other steps can take parts from two or more earlier steps and make something new. Then take the idea a bit further by saying that you can duplicate groups of these steps and integrate them easily to other parts of the line. You then have an assembly *network* like that depicted in Figure 5-5. This network–like approach is what you can do with nodes.

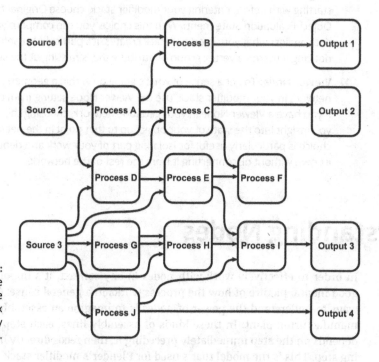

FIGURE 5-5:
Turning a simple assembly line into a complex assembly network.

In the end, what does this all mean? Why is it so great to work with nodes when doing your work? For me, it comes down to the following points:

>> **Nodes are non-destructive.** A *non-destructive* edit is one where the original source material doesn't get changed over the course of working on it. If you draw a moustache in marker on a photograph of your boss, that's a destructive change. If that photo is in a picture frame and you just draw on the cover glass, that's non-destructive (at least for the photo; I can't say what it means for the frame, or your job if your boss doesn't have a good sense of humor). Because a node-based workflow is non-destructive, you can freely make changes that propagate to your end result, but you're not reliant on using Undo to take those changes away. You can make a series of iterative changes, or you can toss out all your changes to try a completely different approach.

Either way, your source material remains pristine, and it's easy to make controlled changes.

» **Node networks are easy to reuse.** So much about working in 3D is about finding ways to work smarter and more efficiently. If you find that you're doing the same modeling steps over and over on every model you make, maybe those steps are a good candidate for being turned into a geonode network. In the context of compositing (which also uses nodes), most compositing work happens on moving images. When working with video and animation material, you need to be able to apply the modifications you make to every frame in the shot that you're working on. In that way, a node network is really like a set of instructions or a recipe that shows how to make the same changes on any image. Likewise, a geonodes network is a set of instructions on how to modify data in an object. With that in mind, that also means you can easily take a portion of your node network (or all of it) and reapply it on a completely different object. This way of working helps ensure that you get consistent results every time you use your node network.

» **Working with nodes is fun!** Because nodes are non-destructive and easy to reuse, you as the artist have a lot of freedom to play with your resulting object. You can easily swap nodes or change connections to get the results you're looking for (or just randomly connect nodes to see what happens). And you can do it all without worrying about damaging your source material.

Working with Nodes

All of Blender's node editors operate by the same basic set of rules. You connect nodes together from the output socket of one node to the input socket of another. In doing so, you provide Blender with a set of instructions on how to get a particular result. In the case of geonodes, that result is a 3D model. In shader nodes, your result is a particular material effect on an object. And in compositing, the result is a processed image or sequence of images. Whatever the final dish is, the node editor is where you make your recipe. Then Blender does the cooking for you.

In Figure 5-1, there's a wire that connects the Geometry socket of a Group Input node to a corresponding Geometry socket on a Group Output node. In Blender, this wire is referred to as a *link*, but among Blender users, we tend to call it a *noodle*. The noodle indicates that data is traveling from the socket on one node to one on another node. In the default case, there's nothing in the middle of the noodle, so the same object data going into the network is passing all the way to the output. If you disconnect this noodle by clicking the green Geometry socket on the Group Output node and moving your mouse cursor away from it, the default cube disappears from the 3D Viewport. The object isn't hidden. It's just that, as far as Blender is concerned, there's no geometry to display from your object. You can reconnect the nodes by clicking the Group Input node's Geometry socket and dragging your mouse cursor to the corresponding socket on the Group Output node.

That's how you connect nodes together within the node editor, but how does your object even know to use this node network of yours? Unfortunately, although Blender's default startup file is great for helping you get started with geometry nodes, it's not exactly the best at helping illustrate what's going on. For that, it's more useful to start from scratch. Follow these steps:

1. **Start a new Blender session using the General workflow template (File ⇨ New ⇨ General).**

2. **Delete the default cube (X or Delete).**

3. **Add a Suzanne mesh (Add ⇨ Mesh ⇨ Monkey).**

4. **Switch to the Geometry Nodes workspace (press Ctrl+PageUp twice).**

   In contrast to the default cube, you should notice that the Geometry Nodes Editor is completely empty with no nodes in it at all. The next step will fix that.

5. **In the header of the Geometry Nodes Editor, click the New button in the geonodes datablock widget.**

   The node editor should immediately be populated with the familiar Group Input and Group Output nodes with a noodle connecting the two of them. However, you should also look to the right of the workspace. In the Modifers tab of the Properties editor, it appears that a new modifier has been added to the stack. However, this isn't one of the modifiers that comes with Blender, as described in Chapter 2 of this book. This is your own custom modifier, based on the geometry nodes network you just added.

6. **From the geonodes datablock in the header of the Geometry Node Editor, rename your geonodes network to something sensible.**

   For this example, I'm calling it My Modifier. That name should also update in your geonodes modifier in the modifier stack. Now it's time to do something interesting.

7. **In the Geometry Nodes Editor, add a Subdivision Surface node (Add ⇨ Mesh ⇨ Operations ⇨ Subdivision Surface) and drag it over the noodle between the Group Input and Group Output nodes.**

   When you click to place your new Subdivision Surface node, it's automatically connected in-line between the Group Input and Group Output nodes. Furthermore, in the 3D Viewport, you should notice that Suzanne is immediately subdivided as if you gave her a Subdivision Surface modifier with a viewport level of 1. If you adjust the Level property in your Subdivision Surface node, you can see your Suzanne model update to correspond to those subdivision levels. That's great within the node network, but what if you don't want to go into your geonode network every time? What if you want to make that change from the modifier stack?

8. **Click and drag a noodle from the Level input socket on the Subdivision Surface node to the unnamed blank socket at the bottom of the Group Input node.**

   WHAMMO! A new Level output socket is added to the Group Input node and, more importantly, when you look at the modifier stack, you should see a numeric control there for adjusting the subdivision levels on Suzanne. As a bonus step, how about you rename this control?

9. **Select the Group Input node and expand the Sidebar in the Geometry Nodes Editor.**

10. **Switch to the Group tab and in the list of inputs, double-click the Level input, and rename it to "Subdivision Levels".**

   You should see the socket name on the Group Input node change, as well as the property in the modifier stack, as shown in Figure 5-6.

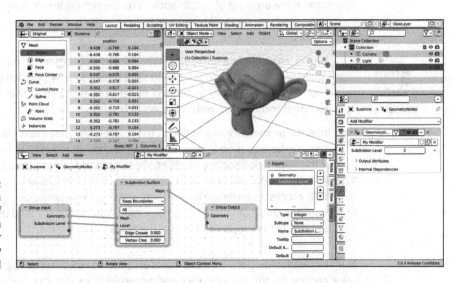

FIGURE 5-6:
Re-creating a simple version of the Subdivision Surface modifier using geometry nodes!

Congratulations! You just created your own simplified version of Blender's Subdivision Surface modifier using geometry nodes. How cool is that?

Identifying the parts of a node

As you continue working with nodes, it's useful to understand the anatomy of a node. This understanding makes it much easier to communicate with other people about how things work, and also makes it easier to get a sense of what kind of data your working with and what the node itself is intended to do. Refer back to the Subdivision Surface node in Figure 5-6 and recognize that it consists of the following parts:

» **Header/Label:** At the top of every node is a header that contains a label with a name for the node. By default, this label corresponds with the type of node that it is, but you can customize the label from the Node tab in the Geometry Nodes Editor's Sidebar. Also, there's a downward-facing arrow at the left of the header. Click this arrow to collapse and expand the node, useful in complex node networks where you need to optimize your space usage.

» **Input sockets:** Along the left side of the node are *sockets*, or places that you can connect noodles between nodes. These sockets usually correspond to a parameter of the node itself. Not all nodes have input sockets. For example, none of the nodes in the Add ⇨ Input menu have input sockets because they're meant to be inputs to your network.

» **Output sockets:** Corresponding with the Input sockets on the left of the node, there are a set of output sockets on the right side that serve a similar purpose when connecting nodes together. Similarly, not all nodes have output sockets.

REMEMBER

The placement of input sockets on the left and output sockets on the right is significant. In Blender, node networks are meant to flow from left to right. So if you find yourself trying to connect nodes in reverse of that flow, chances are good that you'll end up with unexpected results.

» **Internal properties:** In addition to the "socketable" parameters on a node, many nodes also have additional properties that you can set. In the example of the Subdivision Surface modifier, these internal properties are the UV Smooth and Boundary Smooth menus that control the behavior of how the node processes incoming data. In some nodes, these properties aren't always readily available or visible in the node itself. You need to expand the Sidebar and look in the Properties panel of the Node tab to see them.

Also, because node networks can work on all kinds of different data, Blender uses color coding on the node header and on sockets so you can get a better understanding of what's going on. For sockets, you can visually see what kind of data is expected by that socket. Likewise, for node headers, the coloring gives you a sense of what kind of data the node is working on. It's possible to customize these color codes to your liking in your Blender theme from Preferences, but the following is a description of each type of node with a key for the default colors used in their headers:

- » **Attribute nodes (Dark Blue):** Attributes are bits of data that can be associated with geometry components in your object. These nodes give you the ability to use or create attributes in a procedural way.

- » **Color nodes (Yellow):** These nodes process color data. They're more commonly used in shader and compositor node networks, but you do sometimes see them in geonodes.

- » **Converter nodes (Cyan):** These nodes are usually general purpose nodes that do utility work, like math nodes and mapping nodes. These nodes tend to be specific to compositor nodes.

- » **Distortion nodes (Teal):** Like the matte nodes, this kind of node is more common in compositor nodes than in geometry nodes. These nodes adjust image data, like flipping the image or moving it around.

- » **Filter nodes (Violet):** The filter nodes are available only in Blender's compositor nodes. These nodes can be used to add image processing effects like blurring and pixelation to an image.

- » **Geometry nodes (Turquoise):** As the name indicates, these nodes process geometry data. The majority of nodes in the Geometry Nodes Editor have this greenish color as their header color, and you're unlikely to see this header color in the other node editors.

- » **Group nodes (Green):** Group nodes have a green header. They're covered in more detail later in this chapter, but think of these nodes serving as containers for a collection of nodes that perform a specific task. As a bonus, once you build a group node, you can reuse it in other networks.

- » **Group socket nodes (Black):** General group nodes have inputs and outputs. These inputs and outputs are represented by group socket nodes with a black header. It's worth noting that a geometry node network is really just a special kind of group node that ties to the modifier stack. That's why the Group Input and Group Output nodes in your network have black headers rather than pink and burgundy for input and output nodes, respectively.

- » **Input nodes (Red):** These nodes should be treated as constant values that come into your node network. If the whole node network is a recipe, I like to think of input nodes as being my ingredients.

- » **Matte nodes (Brick):** These kinds of nodes aren't common in geometry nodes, but show up frequently in compositor nodes. They're used to build masks, called *mattes*, over image data.

>> **Output nodes (Burgundy):** Output nodes. Use output nodes to give a view of your node network from a specific socket. The Viewer node in geometry nodes and compositor nodes is a particularly handy node for spot-checking the output of your node network without disconnecting from the main output.

>> **Script nodes (Dark Green):** Script nodes are a feature that's specific to Blender's shader nodes. You can write a script using Open Shading Language (OSL) syntax to create shader behaviors that don't come with Cycles by default.

>> **Shader nodes (Bright Green):** Like geometry nodes mentioned previously, nodes with this color header are exclusive to being used in shader node networks. See Book 3 for more on using Blender's shader nodes.

>> **Texture nodes (Orange):** Texture nodes are nodes that create procedural textures for your node networks. The really cool and interesting thing about texture nodes is that many of them are 3D textures, so they can also be used for volumetric data.

>> **Vector nodes (Blue):** The vectors that these nodes work on are mathematical vectors. That is, by the mathematical definition, a *vector* is geometric information that has a magnitude and direction. With respect to their use in Blender, vectors are typically three-dimensional data with values for X, Y, and Z axes. The numeric value for each of these is the magnitude, and direction is determined by whether that value is positive or negative. Usually this information relates to geometric normals.

In addition to the types associated with nodes, the sockets on your nodes also have types and expect certain types of data to be fed to them. And like node types, socket types are color coded to help indicate their type. The following is a list that describes each type of data that gets fed to the node:

>> **Boolean values (Pink):** Mathematically speaking, a *boolean* value is either a true (1) or false (0) logical value.

>> **Collection datablock (White):** For some nodes, you need to feed a collection to it, typically for generating instances of that collection.

>> **Color (Yellow):** Color nodes. Specifically, this socket relates to color in the output image across the entire red/green/blue/alpha (RGBA) scale.

>> **Geometry (Turquoise):** These sockets are the main sockets you see on geometry nodes. As their name implies, they handle geometry data.

>> **Floating point numbers (Gray):** Numeric values, specifically "real numbers" in the mathematical sense. *Floating point numbers* are numbers that incorporate a decimal point (the floating point). Whereas the yellow sockets

technically get four values for each pixel in the image — one for each red, green, blue, and alpha — this socket gets or receives a single value for each pixel. You can visualize these values as a grayscale image. These sockets are used mostly for masks. For example, the level of transparency in an image, or its *alpha channel*, can be represented by a grayscale image, with white for opaque and black for transparent (and gray for semitransparent).

>> **Image datablock (Light Orange):** Similar to the collection datablock sockets, these sockets expect you to connect an image datablock. These sockets differ from color sockets because they're not just the pixels in the image, they're the whole datablock with all the associated metadata that comes with it.

>> **Integer numbers (Green):** These numeric values are numbers without decimals.

>> **Material datablock (Salmon):** Like the collection and image datablock sockets, the material datablock sockets expect to be fed one of Blender's material datablocks. And like how image datablocks differ from color datablocks, material datablocks encapsulate more information than the raw information from shader sockets.

>> **Object datablock (Orange):** Sticking with the set of datablock sockets, the object datablock socket expects to be fed an object, which is a container for geometry data.

>> **Shader (Bright Green):** Shader sockets are exclusively found on shader nodes and available only in the Shader Node Editor.

>> **String values (Light Blue):** A *string* is a series of text characters. These light blue sockets expect that kind of data.

>> **Texture datablock (Magenta):** These sockets are pretty rare to see in any of Blender's node editors, but they expect to receive texture datablocks, like the textures you can build in Blender's Texture Node Editor for sculpting and painting brushes.

>> **Vector values (Blue):** These sockets are pretty special and are related to the vector nodes described earlier. They send and receive information that pertains to the 3D data in the scene, such as speed, UV coordinates, and normals. Visualizing these values in a two-dimensional image is pretty difficult; it usually ends up looking like something seen through the eyes of the alien in *Predator*.

As you work with the various node editors in Blender, there's one further distinction about node sockets in the Geometry Nodes Editor that you don't see in other node editors. In all the other node editors, sockets on nodes are all circles. For the Geometry Nodes Editor, however, sockets come in a few different shapes. Those socket shapes give you one further hint about the kind of data the node expects as input or is sending as output. Sockets in the Geometry Nodes Editor can have the following shapes:

>> **Circle:** For geometry nodes, circular sockets represent "regular data." These sockets should send and receive a single real value, like a set of geometry or a color or a numeric value.

>> **Diamond:** Diamond-shaped sockets are meant to send and receive field data. In geometry nodes, a *field* is a chunk of data that gets processed so the result isn't necessarily uniform. Imagine that your feeding a bunch of selected faces to a node. Each face has its own set of information related to its orientation or the direction of the normal on that face. That's a field of data because your operation calculates results for every one of those selected faces instead of operating on them as a single group. Mentally, you can think of it as the difference between scaling a bunch of objects to a single median point versus scaling each of them on their individual origins.

>> **Diamond with dot:** This kind of socket is most typically seen on node inputs. It means that the socket can accept a field of individual values, but currently there's a single value being applied uniformly.

REMEMBER

A good rule of thumb is, "sockets with the same color and shape can be connected." It may be possible to connect sockets with different colors and shapes, implying a conversion from one type to the other, but the results might be unpredictable or Blender may color the noodle red, indicating that no implied conversion is possible.

Adding nodes to your network

There are two primary ways you can add nodes to your network: The Add menu and by something I've started calling the "pull and search" approach. As I show earlier in this chapter, you can add new nodes by using the Add menu in the node editor's header or by using the Shift+A hotkey combination. Of course, the list of possible nodes you could add is enormous, so at the top of the menu is a search option where you can start typing the name of the node you want. Once you add your node in the editor, you can start connecting sockets with noodles.

TIP

Earlier in this section, I describe how you could click and drag a node's sockets to connect and disconnect the noodles between them. And in the example, you see that it's possible to insert a node on an existing noodle in a single step by dropping the node right on the noodle. As you move a selected node around, noodles get highlighted when it gets near to indicate that you can drop the node and make an automatic connection. If there's not enough space for your inserted node, Blender automatically shifts the downstream nodes in your network to make space for your freshly added node.

If you're not dropping a node in-line (like when creating a branch in your network), then there's a slightly faster way to add a node. Click the socket you want to connect to (it could be an input or an output socket) and drag the noodle out over open space in the node editor. As you move your mouse cursor around, you should notice that there's a little plus (+) symbol next to it, indicating that you can add a node. If you release your mouse button, Blender provides you with a search menu where you can type the name of the node you want to add. As you type, Blender updates the search results live and includes the socket names on the nodes it finds. When you find the node and socket that you want to connect to, choose it from the menu and Blender immediately adds the node, automatically connected to the desired socket. This approach is a really fast way to start building out your node network, especially if you already know the name of the node you want. Figure 5-7 illustrates this way of working.

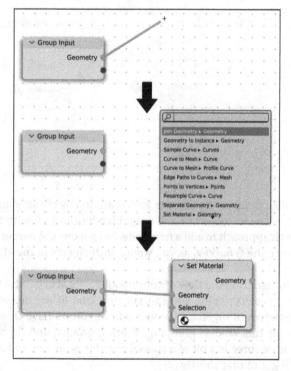

FIGURE 5-7: Using the "pull and search" approach to add a new node by dragging a noodle from an existing socket.

Keeping your nodes organized

As you continue building out your node networks, it's likely you'll find that things can quickly get really complicated. You're going to need some organizational tools in your node editor so you can keep your network organized and easy to understand. One of the easiest things you can do is control the flow of your noodles. By default, noodles connect by a straight(ish) line directly from a socket in one node to a socket in another. When you have a lot of nodes, though, it can get pretty easy to lose a visual sense of the flow since sometimes you'll have nodes sitting on top of noodles that they're not connected to.

Fortunately, Blender's node editors come with a special "node" called Reroute to help you keep an understanding of how one node connects to another. I put the word node in quotes because Reroute isn't so much a node as it is a socket that you can freely move around the node editor and connect noodles to. You add the Reroute socket by choosing Add⇨Layout⇨Reroute and then you can place the socket anywhere you want in the node editor. I typically like to insert the Reroute socket on an existing noodle and then move the socket so it creates a more clear flow path in the network. Figure 5-8 shows how you can use the Reroute socket to clean up the flow in your node network.

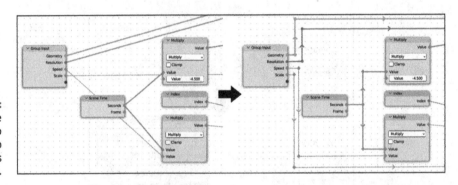

FIGURE 5-8:
Use Reroute sockets to help keep your noodles organized.

REMEMBER

It's not possible to move the Reroute socket around by clicking and dragging. You can select it, but when you click and drag, Blender thinks you're trying to use the pull and search approach to add a new node. So to move the Reroute socket around, you need to use the G hotkey, as you would with objects in the 3D Viewport.

In addition to rerouting the flow of your noodles, it's also helpful to organize your nodes themselves. Typically, you can get this kind of organization by grouping parts of your network together. Blender's node editors have three different tools you can use for this kind of grouping: frames, groups, and the simulation zone. The last of those three is a bit of a special case for geonodes and a fairly advanced topic, but I'll get to that shortly.

Organizing nodes with frames

The simplest kind of organizational block in Blender's node editor is the Frame "node". Like Reroute sockets, a Frame really isn't so much a node as it is a rectangle that you can name, colorize, and put nodes in. You can use the Add menu to add your Frame, but there's a better way:

1. **Select the nodes that you want to collect together.**

2. **Choose Node ⇨ Join in New Frame or press Ctrl+J.**

After you choose that menu item, you should see a dark rectangle wrap around all your selected nodes. That dark rectangle is the Frame, and you can think of it as being the parent of the nodes that you included in it. If you click and drag the Frame (click near the borders) to move it around, all the member nodes travel with it. In fact, if you want to add other nodes to your frame, you can use the same steps you would use in the 3D Viewport for parenting: Select the node, Shift+select the Frame, and press Ctrl+P. Alternatively, you could click and drag your node into the Frame's area and the Frame will expand to include it. You can remove a node from being a member of a Frame by choosing Node ⇨ Remove from Frame or pressing the Alt+P hotkey combination.

For even more organizational control, you can also name and colorize your frame from the Node tab in the node editor's Sidebar. Type a value in the Label field and that text shows up at the top of the frame. Enable the check box on the Color sub-panel, and when you expand that sub-panel, you can use the color picker to choose a desired color for your frame. Figure 5-9 shows how Frames can be used to help organize and label parts of your node network.

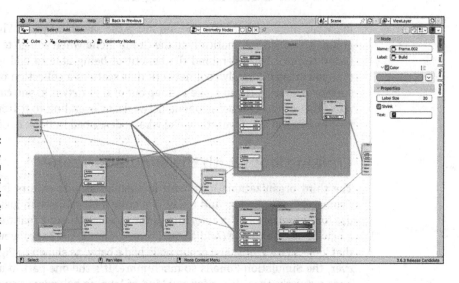

FIGURE 5-9:
Using Frames, you can color-code and label parts of your node network so it makes sense the next time you come back to it.

Building reusable blocks with groups

Earlier in the chapter, I mention that you can group nodes together and that, in fact, you can actually consider geonode networks to be node groups. If frames are like parenting in the 3D Viewport, node groups are like Collections. The ability to make a group of nodes is actually one of the really powerful features of all Blender's node editors. You can box-select a complex section of your node network and choose Node ⇨ Make Group (or press Ctrl+G) to quickly make a group out of that section.

When you create a node group, all the nodes you hadn't selected appear to be hidden, so you're focused only on those selected parts of noodles automatically routed to Group Input and Group Output nodes. I like to think of this as if you're working in Edit mode for the group. Similarly, you can pop out of this group Edit mode by pressing Tab or navigating to Node ⇨ Edit Group. When you're no longer editing the content of your node group, the node editor returns you to your larger node network and your node group is represented by a single node with a green header.

Group nodes have a few really nice benefits. First, there's the obvious benefit of simplifying the look of your node network so that it's not a huge mess of noodles (spaghetti!). More than simplification, though, node groups are a great organizational tool. Because you can name groups like any other node, you can create groups that serve a specific purpose. For example, you can have a specialized subdivision group or a decorative chair leg group.

But wait, there's more! (Do I sound like a car salesman yet?) When you create a group, it's added automatically to the Group menu when you go to add a new node (Add ⇨ Group). To understand the benefit of being able to add groups, imagine that you created a really cool network that scatters a collection of objects on the surface of a mesh. If you make a group out of that network, you can now instantly reuse that group in other geonode networks or even link to it from other .blend files in a linked asset workflow like what's described in Book 6, Chapter 1.

Creating loops with the simulation zone

The third organizational structure in Blender's node editors is specific to the Geometry Nodes Editor. And really, it's quite a bit more than just something you use for organization. I'm referring to the Simulation Zone feature. When you add a new Simulation Zone (Add ⇨ Simulation ⇨ Simulation Zone), you get something that looks like a Frame and group node had a baby, as shown in Figure 5-10. However, the Simulation Zone is so much more. It's the one part in any of Blender's node networks that allows for any kind of looping behavior. Any data that comes into the Simulation Zone by way of the Simulation Input node is used as a starting point, or *initialization* value. Then, as you step forward in time, the values in the Simulation Output node are fed back to the input.

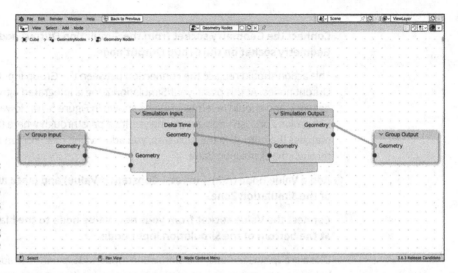

FIGURE 5-10:
The Simulation
Zone in the
Geometry Nodes
Editor is used to
create looping
logic in your node
network.

As an example to illustrate this concept, you can build a simple frame counter by following these steps:

1. **Start a new Blender project in the General workflow template (File ⇨ New ⇨ General).**

2. **In the 3D Viewport, select the default cube and tab into Edit mode.**

3. **Merge all the vertices in the cube to a single one (Mesh ⇨ Merge ⇨ At Center).**

   Now you have only a single vertex in your mesh. With one vertex, it's easier to see what's going on in later steps.

4. **Tab back to Object mode.**

5. **Switch to the Geometry Nodes workspace by clicking its tab at the top of the Blender window or by pressing Ctrl+PageUp twice.**

6. **In the Geometry Nodes Editor, add a Simulation Zone (Add ⇨ Simulation ⇨ Simulation Zone).**

   Unlike regular nodes, you can't just drop the Simulation Zone on the noodle between the Group Input and Group Output nodes and have the noodles automatically hook up for you. You need to connect them yourself.

7. **Connect the Geometry socket from the Group Input node to the Geometry socket on the Simulation Input node.**

8. **Connect the Geometry socket from the Simulation Output node to the Geometry socket on the Group Output node.**

This action should replace the connection between the Group Input and Group Output nodes. At this point, your Simulation Zone is integrated into your node network, and should resemble the one shown in Figure 5-10. However, the Simulation Zone isn't doing anything yet. It's a passthrough where the input matches the output. In the next step, you add a value that you can monitor through the Simulation Zone.

9. **Add a Value node (Add ⇨ Input ⇨ Constant ⇨ Value) and place it to the left of the Simulation Zone.**

10. **Connect the Value socket from your new Value node to the blank socket at the bottom of the Simulation Input node.**

Like a group socket node, the Simulation Input node expands to add a new Value input socket as well as a Value output socket. You should also see Value input and output sockets appear on the Simulation Output node.

11. **Connect the new Value output socket on the Simulation Input node to the corresponding Value input socket on the Simulation Output node.**

Now you can monitor that Value as it leaves the Simulation Zone. It's still just a passthrough at this point, but at least you can see it.

TIP

You can quickly check the output of a socket by hovering your mouse cursor over that socket and waiting for the tooltip to appear. In the next step, you can use a Viewer node to give yourself a more persistent monitor.

12. **Connect a Viewer node to the output sockets of the Simulation Output node by Shift+Ctrl+left-clicking twice.**

Clicking twice connects both the Geometry output socket and the Value output socket to the Viewer node. Now you just need to adjust the Spreadsheet so you can monitor what's going on.

13. **In the Spreadsheet's header, change the Object Evaluation State drop-down menu from Evaluated to Viewer Node.**

Now you should see a single line in the Spreadsheet that shows your single vertex in what was the default cube along with the number coming from the Value socket; it should currently be 0.000. Great! You have a way to monitor changes to that value as it goes through the Simulation Zone, but it's still a passthrough. It's not yet changing.

14. **Back in the Geometry Nodes Editor, add a Math node (Add ⇨ Utilities ⇨ Math ⇨ Math) and drop it on the Value noodle between the Simulation Input and Simulation Output nodes.**

You might not know it yet, but you just built your first simulation. Have a look at the next step.

15. **Step forward in time (right arrow), one frame at a time while watching
the numbers change in the Spreadsheet.**

You should see that every time you move forward in time, the Viewer value
shown in the Spreadsheet increases by 0.5. That's because the Math node you
added defaults to doing an Add operation and the second value in that node is
0.5. Because I started this example saying this is a simple frame counter, make
one more small change.

16. **In your Math node (labeled Add), change the bottom Value from
0.5 to 1.0.**

Now when you step through time, the Viewer value should match your current
frame number. You've just made a simple simulation. Your Blender window
should look something like what's shown in Figure 5-11.

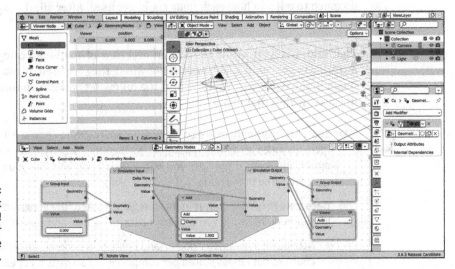

FIGURE 5-11:
Your first
simulation!
A frame counter
using the
Simulation Zone.

REMEMBER

You might find yourself wondering, "How exactly is this a simulation?" It's
important to understand that in the context of geometry nodes, simulation isn't
necessarily always physics simulation like what I describe in Book 4, Chapter 5.
The definition is much more simple. *Simulation* is the change in a system's state
over time. So in the preceding example, the "system" is everything within the
Simulation Zone, and the state that's changing over time is that numerical value.
Of course, with more time and more nodes, you can grow this simulation to be
much more complex, perhaps even to the level of realistic physics. But at the core,
it's the change in state over time.

Getting Familiar with Commonly Used Geometry Nodes

The process of building node networks in geometry nodes is the equivalent of using a visual programming language to create your own custom modifiers. In a *visual programming language*, you use a bunch of component blocks (in our case, nodes) to piece together your final result. The smaller those blocks are, conceptually speaking, the more flexibility you have in connecting them together and the closer you can be to the data that you're working on. Of course, the trade-off is that you end up with a *lot* of those blocks. This is all to say that the Add menu in the Geometry Nodes Editor has an enormous amount of nodes for you to choose from. There's not enough space in this chapter for a comprehensive description of each node and, really, that kind of piece-by-piece description doesn't necessarily do much to tell you how each node could get used. After all, the power of a node-based workflow comes from how you connect them together.

That said, it's worthwhile to have an overview of the broad categories of nodes available to you, with a few notes about where they are used. If you look at the Add menu in the Geometry Nodes Editor, the following breakdown corresponds to the divisions within that menu:

>> **Search:** Because there are so many different nodes to choose from, the Add menu includes an item to quickly access Blender's search feature. Click this option and Blender provides you with a search popover that you can use to type the name of the node that you're looking for.

>> **Data category:** The menus in this category relate to the general data handling in your node network. You can store data, bring it in, and send it out.

- **Attribute:** In geometry nodes (and Blender in general), an *attribute* is a chunk of data that's stored per component of an object. For example, you can think of vertex groups as a kind of attribute. Each vertex can belong to one or more vertex group at a different weight assignment. With attribute nodes, you can create and manage your own custom attribute groups.

- **Input:** As the name implies, these nodes represent data coming into your node network. They can be constant values or they can be general input from your scene, such as the current frame or information about a specific object.

- **Output:** There are only two nodes in this menu: Group Output and Viewer. I describe both of these nodes elsewhere in this chapter, but these nodes are how you get results of your node network out to the rest of Blender.

>> **Geometry category:** Looking at the name on this menu item, you might find yourself saying, "Wait . . . aren't *all* of these geometry nodes?" Yes. However, the nodes in this category are all about accessing, creating, and managing geometry data like vertices, edges, and faces, as well as properties of that data.

>> **Object data category:** The menus in this category correspond to the kinds of objects you can put into your scene using the Add menu in the 3D Viewport. If you're modeling with geometry nodes, you need the ability to create and manage primitives as part of modeling process. These menus give you those tools. The really cool thing is that you're not restricted to using primitives of a particular kind or type. That is, even though your object in the 3D Viewport is a mesh object, you can create and use data from other object types like curves and volumes within your geometry node network. This way, you can get the best of both worlds!

- **Curve:** Curve data tends to get used quite a bit in geonode networks. Because curves have directionality and are mathematically defined, they're really useful for creating procedural geometry.

- **Instances:** One of the most powerful capabilities of geometry nodes is the ability to take advantage of *instancing*, or reusing data without making a copy of it. With instancing, you can get really complex and interesting results with efficient use of computational memory and time.

- **Mesh:** Just like with curves, mesh data gets used a lot in geonode networks. Although meshes can be somewhat less procedural than curves because they consist of a bunch of specific vertices, edges, and faces, they can be a lot easier to control. Furthermore, because so much of Blender is optimized for working with mesh data, it's good to have your geonodes network generate this data so other features in Blender can access it.

- **Point:** Sometimes when you're working, you don't need all the connected parts of geometry data like edges and faces. Sometimes you just need a bunch of vertices, or *points* in space, such as when trying to re-create a particle effect. For those kinds of situations, point data is extremely helpful.

- **Volume:** Most of the 3D data in Blender is known as *surface geometry*. Meshes and curves are, at the end of the day, empty shells that represent a whole solid object with volume. However, there are times when you need to do something with that volumetric data within the shell, or you need to convert volumetric data (like clouds) to a shell to create a specific visual effect. These are the scenarios where the two nodes in this menu can be very helpful.

>> **Simulation category:** As I cover in the preceding section, the Simulation menu has one item in it: the Simulation Zone. This organizational block is used

to manage the change in state of your node network from one animation frame to the next.

>> **Utility category:** This set of menus is a little bit of a dumping ground, organizationally speaking. The nodes that you access from these menus are used to either connect your node network to materials, create textures, or perform more generalized operations on data in your node network.

- **Material:** Nodes in this menu are used either to set materials on parts of your geonodes network or to select materials already linked to your object from the Materials tab in the Properties editor.

- **Texture:** These nodes correspond to the same base texture nodes available in the Shader Node Editor and the Texture Node Editor. It's often useful to control the behavior of geometry using a procedural texture, so these nodes are your means of creating such a texture without leaving the Geometry Nodes Editor.

- **Utilities:** Because they're so general-purpose, the nodes and sub-menus in this menu are some of the most frequently used nodes you come across in geonodes networks. These nodes do mathematical operations, manage color, and control the flow of data within your network. These nodes are also some of the most core building blocks in any network, so for that reason, they're really your best friend.

>> **Organizational category:** As I cover in the preceding section, the nodes in the Group and Layout menus are incredibly helpful for keeping your node network organized and preventing it from looking like a giant messy noodle bowl.

>> **Hair category:** The Hair menu is kind of a specialized menu in Blender. As I cover in Book 4, Chapter 5, Blender ships with an assortment of preset node groups focused on the task of creating and managing hair and fur. Most of the time, you use those node groups on their own, accessing them from the Asset Browser. However, if you ever need to build your own custom node groups or add these groups to your existing node network, you can use the items in the Hair menu to access them.

Thinking Procedurally: Model Like a Rigger

As I mention in the preceding section, the true power of geometry nodes doesn't come from any one individual node. The power comes from connecting those nodes together in a novel way to get some specific result. To that end, it makes sense to walk through a small example that uses geometry nodes. Earlier in this chapter, you see a simple re-creation of the Subdivision Surface modifier and a very simple simulation example. How about something slightly more practical? What about re-creating Blender's vertex instancing feature, but with some customized flexibility?

TIP

Vertex instancing, formerly known as *Dupliverts*, is a handy little feature that I cover in previous editions of the book, but didn't include in more recent editions as they can be pretty unwieldy to control. The supplemental website for this book (blenderbasics.com) has an example file you can play with, but the basic idea of the vertex instancing feature is that you're placing an instance of one object at the location of every vertex of another object. To get the feature to work, you need to first make your duplicated object a child (Object➪Parent➪Object) of the one that has the placement vertices. Then, on the object with the placement vertices, you go to the Object tab of the Properties Editor and click the Vertices button within the Instancing panel. After you do that, an instance of your duplicated object appears at every vertex.

Vertex instances are a great quick-and-dirty feature, but if you want to do anything more sophisticated (for example, put instances only on specific vertices defined by a vertex group) this approach can start to feel limiting. If you build the feature using geometry nodes, you can give yourself the additional controls that you need.

In this example, you're going to use geometry nodes to create your own vertex instance modifier. The modifier can get reused anywhere after you create it, but when making something reusable, it's always best to have a visual goal in mind. In this case, you're going to make a kind of punk rock Suzanne, with spikes at each vertex on her mesh, similar to what's shown in Figure 5-12.

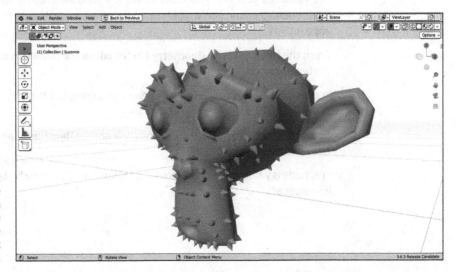

FIGURE 5-12:
The goal: Create your own vertex instance modifier to make a punk-rock Suzanne.

Follow these steps:

1. Start a new Blender session in the General workflow template (File ⇨ New ⇨ General).

To build this geometry node network, you're going to need two objects to start with: The modified object (in this case, Suzanne) and the instanced object (in this case, a cone mesh).

2. Switch to the Geometry Nodes workspace (press Ctrl+PageUp twice).

3. Delete the default cube (X or Delete) and add two new mesh objects to your scene:

- Suzanne (Add ⇨ Mesh ⇨ Monkey)
- Cone (Add ⇨ Mesh ⇨ Cone)

4. From the Outliner, hide the Cone mesh and disable it from being renderable.

Because you're making instances of this mesh, it doesn't actually need to be visible by itself in your scene. This feature has one benefit of your geonodes implementation over the default vertex instancing feature. With vertex instancing, if you hide the instanced object, all the instances get hidden, too. That's not the case when you're working with geonodes.

5. Back in the 3D Viewport, select Suzanne.

Now you're ready to get started.

6. In the Geometry Nodes Editor, go to the header and click the New button in the datablock widget.

You've started your new geonodes network. If you look in the Modifiers tab of the Properties editor, you should see your new geonodes-based modifier appear there.

7. From the header of the Geometry Nodes Editor, rename this datablock to Vertex Instance.

You can, of course, choose whatever name you want, but this choice seems to make the most sense for what you're doing.

8. Add an Object Info node (Add ⇨ Input ⇨ Scene ⇨ Object Info) and place it near the Group Input node.

This node is what you're going to use to tell your modifier which object to make instances of.

9. **Connect a noodle from the Object input socket on the Object Info node to the blank socket on the Group Input node.**

   When you make this connection, you should see an Object datablock appear in your modifier in Modifiers Properties. This datablock widget is what you're going to use to tell your modifier which object to make instances of. In fact, go ahead and do that.

10. **In your geonodes modifier in Modifiers Properties, choose the Cone object using your new object datablock widget.**

    At this point, nothing in the 3D Viewport has changed because your input geometry is being routed directly to the output. To verify that the Object Info node is working, you can wire its Geometry output socket to the Geometry input socket on the Group Output node. The result should look something like Figure 5-13.

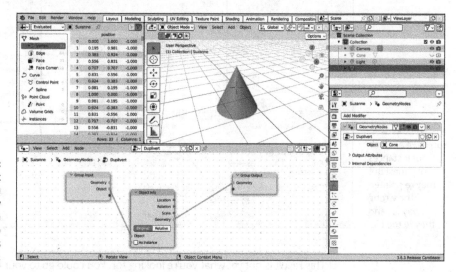

FIGURE 5-13: With the Object Info node, you can pull any object from your scene into your geonodes network.

11. **Add an Instance on Points node (Add ⇨ Instances ⇨ Instance on Points) to the right of your Object Info node.**

    The Instance on Points node is a handy little node that's going to do most of the heavy lifting in this node network.

12. **Connect a noodle from the Geometry socket on Group Input to the Points socket on your Instance on Point node.**

    This action tells Blender that you want to use Suzanne's mesh (or whatever your base mesh is) as the source of vertices for creating new instances.

13. **Connect a noodle from the Geometry socket on your Object Info node to the Instance input socket on the Instance on Points node.**

Now you've told Blender that you want a Cone object to be placed at every vertex in Suzanne's mesh. Of course, you can't see the results of this yet because your Instance on Points node isn't routed to the output of the network.

14. **Connect the Instances output socket on the Instance on Points node to the Geometry socket on the Group Output node.**

Now you should see some results in the 3D Viewport. However, those results are ugly; it's a bunch of huge cones all pointing in the same direction, as shown in Figure 5-14.

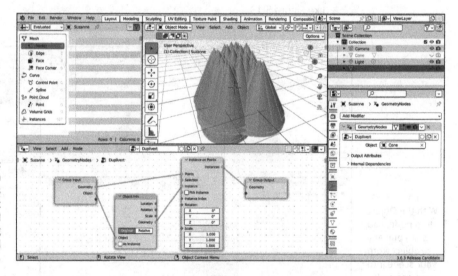

FIGURE 5-14: You have a bunch of instances of cones! But they're pointed the wrong way . . . and they're too big.

This result is not yet what you're looking for. You could go to your Cone object and scale it in Edit mode to fix the scaling issue, but that would be a destructive edit. There's a better, more procedural way. Notice that the Instance on Points node has a Scale input socket. You can adjust the X, Y, and Z values next to this socket to control the size of your instances, but it would be nice if this kind of control were available in the modifier. However, instead of controlling the scale on each axis independently, add a control to control them all at once.

15. **Add a Math node (Add ⇨ Utilities ⇨ Math ⇨ Math) to the left of your Instance on Points node and use the drop-down menu in the node to change it to a Multiply function.**

16. **Connect the Value output of your new Math (now labeled Multiply) node to the Scale socket on your Instance on Points node.**

This connection implies that you're assigning a single value to each axis vector on that Scale socket. Right now, it's multiplying both the input values (0.5) together, so you're setting the scale on your cones to 0.25 their original size. In the next step, you put that control in your modifier.

17. **Connect the top Value input socket on your Multiply node to the blank socket in Group Input and set the bottom Value input socket's value to 1.0.**

You should see the cones double in size because now the math is 0.5 x 1.0. More importantly, you have a control visible in your modifier. Unfortunately, its current name (Value) isn't particularly descriptive.

18. **Select the Group Input node and expand the Sidebar (N) and from the Group tab, double-click the Value name in the Input list to rename it to Scale Factor.**

Now your modifier makes a bit more sense. And when you adjust the Scale Factor value from your modifier, you should see the size of your cone instances change with it. If you drop the Scale Factor to something more reasonable like 0.05, your Blender session should look something like Figure 5-15.

You can control the size of your cones, but in doing so, you should notice that something is missing. You're no longer seeing Suzanne. It's just a bunch of cones. The plan was to instance the cones on the Suzanne mesh. You need to make Suzanne visible again.

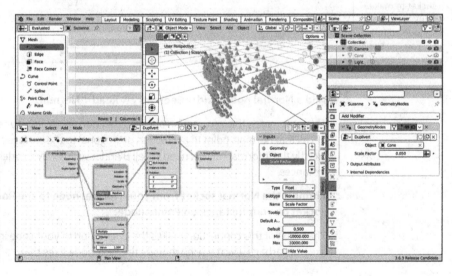

FIGURE 5-15: You can control the scale of your cone instances. Of course, they're the wrong size . . . and where's Suzanne?

19. **Add a Join Geometry node (Add ➪ Geometry ➪ Join Geometry) and drop it on the noodle between the Instance on Points node and the Group Output node.**

The Join Geometry node does exactly as its name implies. You can connect a bunch of noodles to its Geometry input socket and Blender combines them into a single mesh, much like the Object ➪ Join operator in the 3D Viewport. Of course, you've just added the node in-line, so it's not joining anything yet.

20. **Connect the Geometry socket from the Group Input node to the Geometry socket on the Join Geometry node.**

Now you've joined the original mesh data (Suzanne) with the instances, and you should see something like Figure 5-16. Now to fix the orientation of those cones so they point away from her face.

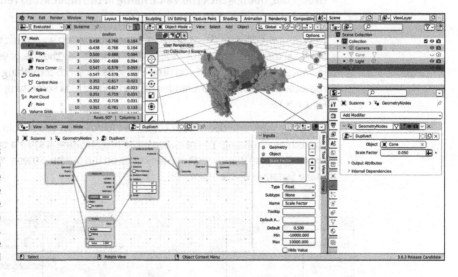

FIGURE 5-16:
With the Join Geometry node (a little Reroute socket to make things pretty in the node editor), you can see Suzanne again!

21. **Add a Normal node (Add ➪ Geometry ➪ Read ➪ Normal).**

This node reads the information about vertex normals from your source mesh. Recall that normals point in a direction orthogonal to the surface of an object, exactly the information you need to tell Blender which way to orient your cone instances.

22. **Connect the Normal socket from your Normal node to the Rotation socket on your Instance on Points node.**

The result of this connection makes the orientation of your cone instances look like hot garbage. Don't worry, though; the next node fixes that.

23. **Add an Align Euler to Vector node (Add ⇨ Utilities ⇨ Rotation ⇨ Align Euler to Vector) and drop it on the noodle between the Normal node and the Instance on Points node.**

The Align Euler to Vector node takes vector data (like the normals on your mesh) and aligns X, Y, and Z rotations (Euler rotations) to match that vector. The results still look horrible, but at least you have controls for fixing that.

24. **In the Align Euler to Vector node, click the Z axis button.**

BOOM! All your cone instances should now face outward from Suzanne's face! The only thing left to do is give your modifier the ability to use a vertex group to control which vertices have the privilege of receiving a cone.

25. **Connect the Selection socket from the Instance on Points node to the blank socket on the Group Input node.**

The Selection socket tells the Instance on Points node which vertices to use for instancing. However, you may have noticed that all your cone instances are gone. Also, if you look at your modifier in the Modifiers tab of the Properties editor, it's just a single check box. There's no way to choose a vertex group . . . yet.

26. **Select the Group Input node and, in the Group tab of the Sidebar, click the Selection item in the Input list.**

You need to make some modifications to this input so it can be correctly used.

27. **Double-click the Selection item to rename it to Vertex Group and change the Type dropdown below the input list to Float.**

By changing the socket type to Float, you're ensuring that the weight assignment to your vertices gets used. In Modifiers Properties, your Vertex Groups value changes from a check box to a numerical input, but there's still not a way to choose a specific vertex group.

28. **In the Modifiers tab of the Properties editor, click the spreadsheet icon to the right of your Vertex Groups value.**

Now you have a place to enter a vertex group. Of course, your cone instances are still missing. That's because you haven't yet added any vertex groups to your Suzanne mesh.

29. **Create a vertex group named "spikes" and assign some vertices to that group.**

If you need a refresher on how to do that, follow these steps:

a. Go to the Object Data tab of the Properties editor.

b. In the Vertex Groups panel, click the Plus (+) button to the right of the list box to add a new vertex group. Double-click the new group's name in the list to rename it to "spikes".

c. In the 3D Viewport, Tab into Edit mode and select the vertices that you want to include in the vertex group.

d. Back in the Properties editor, click the Assign button within the Vertex Groups panel to assign the selected vertices to your new group.

e. Tab back into Object mode.

30. **With your new vertex group created, jump back to the Modifiers tab and, in your vertex instance modifier, choose your new spikes vertex group (Point ⇨ spikes) from your Vertex Groups field.**

And like that, you have made your own vertex instance modifier with additional controls. Your Blender session should look something like what's shown in Figure 5-17.

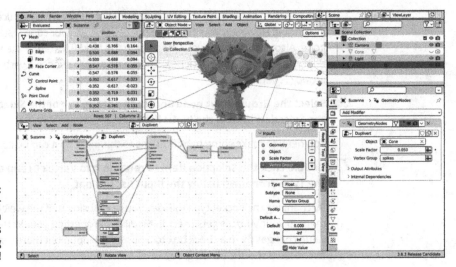

FIGURE 5-17:
You made your own version of a vertex instance as a modifier using geometry nodes!

Now the really cool thing is that you can mark this node network as an asset (see Book 3, Chapter 4), and then you're able to reuse it on any other model in your scene. As an additional bonus, you could make it part of your global asset library and it's available in any Blender session you're in. Of course, if you're going to make it that general purpose, you may want to add a few nice features, like using the actual vertex weights to influence the scale of your instances, giving a check box to let you decide if you want to align to the surface of the object, and control whether your instances are smooth shaded. With those features, your node network may look like what's shown in Figure 5-18. There's not quite enough room in this chapter to add all those parts, but using the information covered here, you should be able to re-create this for yourself.

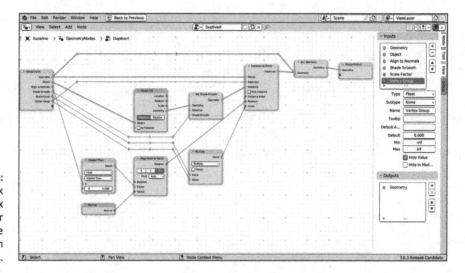

FIGURE 5-18:
A node network
for a vertex
instance modifier
with a few more
nice configuration
options.

**NEW
FEATURE**

The use of nodes is going to continue to expand in future releases of Blender. In fact, in Blender 4.0, there's a new feature that allows artists to create their own tools using geometry nodes. Up until this point, geometry nodes have only been a way for you to create custom modifiers. But in Blender 4.0, those same node networks can be used to create single-run tools that perform destructive edits on your object. And the expansion will continue. A prototype of a node-based particle system already exists, for example. Another avenue that's ripe for "nodification" is the Blender constraint system. So you can look forward to having the flexibility of nodes when rigging characters for animation, too. I don't expect that the future of Blender involves being exclusively made with nodes; however, I do expect that there's likely to be a node-based component of every part of Blender. So watch this space . . . it's going to get bigger.

3

Working with Colors and Materials

Contents at a Glance

Chapter **1**

Changing That Boring Gray Default Material

As you work on your models in Blender, you're eventually going to get tired of that plastic gray material that all Blender objects have by default. Nothing against neutral colors — or plastic, for that matter — but the world is a vibrantly colorful place, and you may occasionally want to use these colors in your 3D scenes. Sure, it's helpful to add matcaps to your objects while sculpting (see Book 2, Chapter 3), but that's just a temporary thing meant to help you while you work. Eventually, you're going to want to add something more specific to your model. To add colors to your scenes and models, you use materials and textures. Think of a *material* as a collection of instructions that you give Blender to describe the appearance of your 3D object. What color is it? Is it see-through? Is it shiny enough to show a reflection? In some ways, Blender's way of adding materials and textures to an object is one of the most confusing parts of the program. It can be a pretty big challenge to wrap your brain around its full functionality.

This chapter is intended to give you the skills to know enough to be dangerous with Blender's materials. Hopefully, with a little practice, you can become lethal. Well, *lethal* might be the wrong word: I don't think I've ever heard of anyone killed by excessively sharp specular highlights. (Don't worry if you don't get the joke right now. After you finish this chapter, you'll realize how horrible a pun this is.)

Understanding Materials and Render Engines

Before you throw yourself down the rabbit hole of working with materials, it's worth it to stop and consider the type of image you're trying to produce. Are you trying to achieve photorealism? Do you want a more cartoony look? Is your image (or animation) meant to have the appearance of a technical illustration? It's helpful to ask the questions before you start working on your materials, because the answers can dictate the render engine that you choose. A *render engine*, or renderer, is what you use to convert the 3D data in your scene to a 2D image (or series of images, for animation). As you might imagine, there are all kinds of ways to convert 3D data into an image. Each has its own strengths and weaknesses. More importantly, every render engine has a different way of going through this conversion, so each has its own preferred way to work with materials and textures. So it's best to know the final look you're trying to attain and, by extension, the most suitable renderer to get there before you start to seriously add materials to your objects.

 Blender supports a wide array of render engines, but three are built in. To pick the render engine you want to use, go to the Render tab of the Properties editor and look at the Render Engine dropdown at the top of that tab. You have three choices:

>> **Eevee:** Eevee is the newest render engine added to Blender. In fact, if you're working in Blender, you're already using Eevee. Eevee is what's known as a *real-time* render engine and uses technologies similar to those found in modern video games to get very realistic results in fractions of a second.

   The benefit of Eevee is that it's very fast while still maintaining an ability to produce very real-looking images because it supports PBR (*physically based rendering*) materials that model the behavior of real, meatspace materials. Furthermore, one of the aims of Eevee is to have materials that behave as similar to Cycles (discussed further on) as possible. That said, don't make the mistake of thinking Eevee is just limited to realism. Eevee also supports an NPR (*non-photorealistic rendering*) approach for cartoon-style rendering. Just about the only real drawback to Eevee is that it still uses a lot of tricks to get the results it does, as opposed to using a fully accurate model of how light works. So there are some materials and lighting scenarios that are difficult for it to pull off realistically.

>> **Workbench:** This one is meant for fast previews while modeling and animating. In fact, it's basically the same as what's used for Solid viewport shading mode in the 3D Viewport, regardless of the render engine you choose for

output. The Workbench engine isn't actually meant to be used as an output renderer, but you're fully free to do so if it's got the look you need (like for cartoony renders).

>> **Cycles:** For images that need to appear as realistic as possible, Cycles is the best Blender renderer for the job. The reason is because Cycles is a *ray-trace renderer*, meaning it calculates how light rays bounce around your scene as its means of generating a final image. Sure, you *can* achieve a level of realism using Eevee, but that process can sometimes be at the expense of a lot of time and confusion. The material system that Cycles uses can be a bit intimidating for first-timers, but it's extremely powerful. Like Eevee's materials, Cycles' materials are PBR materials, meaning that they also have a strong relationship to materials in the physical world. This increase in realism does come at the expense of rendering speed, but that cost is mitigated by two facts:

- **Artist time versus computer time:** If a realistic look will take more time, it's less costly (both financially and mentally) to have that time absorbed by a computer churning through rendering than by an artist sweating over hacky tweaks in every shot.

- **GPU acceleration:** Cycles can take advantage of additional processing power on the graphics processing unit (GPU) of some video cards. Of course, Eevee uses the GPU to draw to the screen too, but in a slightly different way compared to how Cycles does it. Using GPU acceleration, a Cycles render process can often be ten times faster than rendering on the CPU alone.

REMEMBER

One of the things that makes Blender unique is the fact that it has a real-time render engine (Eevee) that uses the same structures for defining materials as its ray-trace render engine (Cycles). In most other tools, there's a pretty arduous process to try to convert real-time materials to ray-trace materials. In Blender (with a few minor exceptions that I cover in this chapter), you just change the render engine from a drop-down menu.

You can find more detailed information on the differences between Eevee and Cycles in Book 3, Chapter 4. I used to recommend that if you don't know what final look you're trying to achieve, you should render with Cycles. However, that answer has changed a bit over the years. Cycles is a more mature render engine than Eevee, but Eevee is faster and honestly gives some pretty solid results. At this point, I'd suggest that you default to rendering with Eevee, and if you find that you need more realistic or physically accurate results in your rendered images, switch over to Cycles. Figure 1-1 shows the same model rendered in Workbench, Eevee, and Cycles.

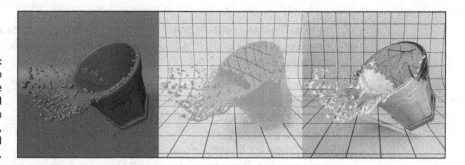

FIGURE 1-1:
From left to right, the same 3D model rendered in Workbench, Eevee, and Cycles.

TIP

It *is* actually possible to take advantage of features in both render engines, but the process is a bit advanced. The short version goes something like this (assuming all your modeling and animation is done, and you just need to do materials, lighting, and rendering):

1. **From the Scene datablock at the top of your Blender window, name your current scene according to its current renderer (for example, Scene. Eevee).**

2. **Make a linked copy of your current scene (left-click the Plus[+] button next to the Scene datablock and choose Linked Copy).**

3. **Name your new scene according to the other render engine (for example, Scene.Cycles).**

4. **In your new scene, change the render engine to the other render engine (for example Cycles, if the original scene used Eevee).**

5. **Create a new empty scene (Scene datablock Plus[+] ⇨ New) and name it Composite.**

6. **In the Composite scene, combine render layers from your Eevee scene with those from your Cycles scene using the Compositor.**

   This is the advanced part. See Book 5, Chapter 2 for more on render layers and compositing.

It's worth noting that by using the Linked Copy method of creating a new scene, the objects in your Cycles scene share the same materials as those in your Eevee scene because, technically speaking, they *are* the same objects and therefore, the same materials. If you want to have different materials based on your chosen render engine, you can use multiple Material Output nodes, each one dedicated to a different render engine using the Target drop-down menu in each node. That's a bit of an involved process, so I've included an example on the supplemental website for this book, blenderbasics.com.

Quick 'n' Dirty Coloring

By default, all newly added objects in Blender share a gray, plastic-like material, whether you're using Eevee or Cycles. Unless your model is a rhinoceros or a stretch of sidewalk, you may be wondering how you change the material's color. There are quite a few ways to make that change, and they vary a bit depending on what your final goal is in your image. This chapter starts with the simple methods and builds up to some of the more advanced ones.

Setting diffuse colors

The simplest way to set an object's color is from the Material tab of the Properties editor. If your object doesn't have a material, follow these steps to add a new material:

1. **Left-click the Plus(+) button next to the list box at the top of the Material tab of the Properties editor.**

   This step adds a material slot (covered in more detail in the next section) to the list box that you can populate with a new material. Technically speaking, this step isn't required because the next step automatically does this for you. However, it's helpful to go through this process the first time you add a material to an object in Blender so you know what's going on when things are automated for you.

2. **Left-click the New button in the materials datablock below the material slots list box.**

Figure 1-2 shows the default settings available when you add a new material.

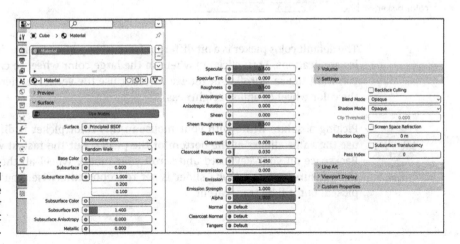

FIGURE 1-2: The Material tab of the Properties editor with a single basic material added.

In Blender 4.0, the default shader got a bit of an upgrade and looks quite a bit different. The basic behavior of the shader is the same and similar names appear in both versions, but if you're using a newer version of Blender and it doesn't match the screenshots in this book, that's the reason.

Although there's an almost overwhelming number of settings when you add a new material to your object, defining the primary color for your material is really quite straightforward with the default material that comes on an object in Blender. For this simple case, you only need to set the diffuse color for the material. A *diffuse color* is the color that a material reflects when light hits it. In Figure 1-2, you should notice that there's a color swatch labeled Base Color. Left-click on the color swatch and Blender's color picker pops up. Figure 1-3 shows what the color picker looks like.

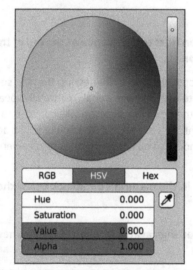

FIGURE 1-3:
Blender's
color picker.

The default color picker is a bit different from what you might find in other graphics applications. Left-click anywhere in the large color wheel to choose the color you want to use. Scroll your mouse wheel or use the vertical slider to the right of the color wheel to adjust brightness.

Picking absolute white with your mouse in this color picker is difficult. You can use the value sliders at the bottom of the picker, but the fastest way is to press Backspace on your keyboard and scroll your mouse wheel all the way up. After that, ensure that the Alpha slider is set to 1.000; otherwise, you'll have a color picked, but it'll be transparent.

Another cool feature is that the color picker gives you a sampler. Left-click the Sample button below the value slider (its icon is an eyedropper), and your mouse pointer changes to an eyedropper as well. The next place you left-click is sampled for color, making it your selected color. You can sample any color in Blender's interface, including the buttons and icons, if you want to.

In fact, when working in design, it's often best to work with a limited and consistent color palette. So some artists will paint an image (or set up objects in the 3D Viewport) with blobs of the exact colors they want to limit themselves to. Then, whenever they need that color, it's readily available to be sampled with the eyedropper.

If you find Blender's current color picker to be a bit disorienting, you have the ability to choose other color pickers in Preferences (Edit ⇨ Preferences) in the Interface section.

TIP

Assigning multiple materials to different parts of a mesh

Using the same material across an entire object is great for objects that are the same uniform material, but what if you want to use multiple different materials on the same object? For that situation, you want to use material slots. Basically, you create a *material slot*, sometimes referred to as a *material index*, by defining a set of object subcomponents — faces in meshes, individual characters in text, and control points in curves and surfaces — and assigning them to a material.

You create material slots directly from the top of Material Properties. In fact, if you added a diffuse color (as described in the previous section), you've already added one material slot. You add more material slots the same way: left-click the Plus(+) button next to the material slots list box to create an empty material slot and then left-click the New button in the materials datablock below the list box. However, to actually make use of those new materials in your material slot, you have to be in Edit mode.

For an idea of how this process works, say you want to model a beach ball and give it the classic primary-colored panels. Follow these steps:

1. **In the 3D Viewport, set your viewport shading to Material Preview by clicking its icon in the upper right.**

   As described in Book 1, Chapter 2, Material Preview viewport shading is meant to be used for defining and refining the materials on your objects. It's a good habit to get used to using the Material Preview viewport shading mode for steps in this chapter. In fact, if you work from the Shading workspace (accessed with the tabs at the top of your Blender window), it's already configured to use Material Preview viewport shading.

2. Add a UV sphere mesh (Add ⇨ Mesh ⇨ UV Sphere).

Using the Last Operator panel or the F6 pop-up panel, edit the UV sphere to have 12 segments, 12 rings, and a radius of 1m. You may also add a Subdivision Surface modifier (Ctrl+1) and set the faces to render as smooth (Object ⇨ Shade Smooth).

3. Tab into Edit mode and switch to Face Select mode (Tab, 3).

4. Add a new material using the material datablock in Material Properties.

Left-click the New button to add a new material, or choose an existing material from the datablock drop-down menu.

5. Use the datablock text field to name your material.

For this example, name it White.

6. Change the base color to white as described in the previous section.

The entire ball turns white. All the faces are currently assigned to this material slot.

7. In the 3D Viewport, use face loop select to select two adjacent vertical face loops.

The easiest way to select a face loop is by Alt+left-clicking an edge perpendicular to the face loop you want to select. Shift+Alt+left-click the neighboring edge to get the adjacent loop. See Book 2, Chapter 1 for more on selecting mesh components.

8. Back in Material Properties, add another new material slot.

Left-click the button with the Plus (+) icon in the upper left of the materials list box. An empty material slot appears at the bottom of the materials list box. That new slot is automatically selected when you add it.

9. Left-click the New button in the material datablock.

You should get a material named something like Material.001.

10. Change the material name to Blue.

11. Change the base color to blue like in Step 6.

After you change the color of this swatch, you might expect the faces that you have selected to automatically change to match this color. That's not quite how it works: Even though you have these faces selected, they're still assigned to the White material slot. Perform the next steps to remedy that situation.

12. **Assign the selected faces to the current material slot, Blue, by clicking the Assign button beneath the material list box.**

The moment you left-click the Assign button, the selected faces all change to the blue color you picked in Step 11.

13. **Using the process in Steps 7 through 12, work your way around the sphere, creating and assigning colors for the other panels.**

If you create a beach ball like the one in Figure 1-4, you should end up with four material slots, one for each color on the ball.

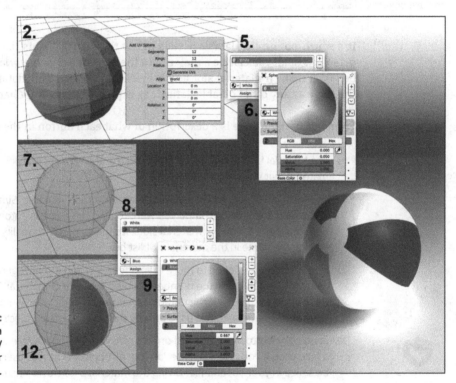

FIGURE 1-4:
Creating a beach ball with a UV sphere and four material slots.

Material slots aren't limited to being used only by meshes. You can also use them on curves, surfaces, and text objects. The process is similar to meshes, with one main exception. Meshes, as shown in the preceding example, allow you to assign individual faces to different material slots. This exception isn't the case with curves, surfaces, and text objects, which only assign material slots to discrete closed entities. So you can assign individual text characters and curves to a material slot. However, you can't set the material slot of an individual control point or a portion of a text character. Figure 1-5 shows material slots working on a curve, surface, and text object.

FIGURE 1-5:
Material slots on
curves, surfaces,
and text objects.

It's worth noting the datablock field below the material slots list box. From this datablock field, you can tie a material to the current active material slot in the list box (you make a material slot active by clicking on it). This datablock functions the same as any other datablock field, as explained in Book 1, Chapter 4.

From left to right, here is a description of what each button in the datablock does.

>> The Material button on the left gives you the ability to choose any existing material that you've already created.

>> The text field allows you to give your material a custom name. Simply left-click in the field and type the name you want to use. The name is automatically updated in the list box of material slots. It's the same functionality as double-clicking the name in the material slot list box.

>> If your material is linked to more than one object, it has a numbered button next to it, representing the number of objects using this material. Left-clicking this button ensures that the datablock has only a single user — it creates a copy of the material that is used only by the current active object.

>> Enable the button with a shield on it to give your material a *fake user*. Without a fake user, if you unlink a material from all objects, it has no users and won't be saved in your .blend file. Giving the material a fake user ensures that your material sticks around when you save. Fake users are great if you want to create a .blend file as a material library, and you're not interested in building a library with the Asset Browser, as covered in Book 3, Chapter 4.

>> Clicking the New Material button adds a new material datablock and assigns it to your active material slot. If there's already a material datablock chosen when you click this button, your new material is actually a duplicate of that material.

>> The X button disconnects the material datablock from the active material slot in the list. It's important to remember that clicking the X button doesn't necessarily delete the material from your .blend file. That only happens if your material has no users and you reload your .blend file after saving.

To the right of the material datablock is a small drop-down menu with a mesh icon on it. This is the Link menu. The Link drop-down menu after the node button is a pretty unique control. Using these menu options requires recalling information about how .blend files are structured. Chapters 2 and 4 in Book 1 detail how .blend files are structured, but basically Blender objects are just containers for the low-level data (mesh, curve, and so on). Now, here's how this information relates to materials. By default, Blender's materials link to the low-level data, as indicated by the Link drop-down menu in the Context panel being set to Data. However, you also have the option of linking the material to the object as well, as shown in the schematics of Figure 1-6.

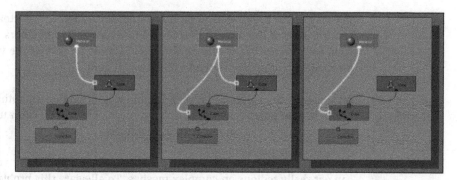

FIGURE 1-6: A schematic showing a material linked to a mesh and to an object.

Why is having the ability to link a material to either the mesh or the object a useful option? Well, say that you have a bunch of objects that are linked duplicates (Objects ⇨ Duplicate Linked), sharing the same mesh information. If the material is linked to the mesh, all your linked duplicates have the exact same material. If you want to have a different material for each duplicate, you can link the material to the object datablock rather than the mesh datablock. Figure 1-7 shows a set of linked duplicate Suzanne heads, each with a different material.

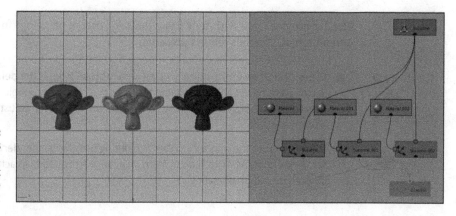

FIGURE 1-7: Linked duplicates of Suzanne, except they don't share the same material.

Using vertex colors

One downside to material slots is that, although they make defining multiple colors and materials on a single mesh easy, there's a very distinct line between materials. The color of one material doesn't smoothly transition into the next. For example, if you want to create a car with a paint job that's light blue near the ground and smoothly transitions to a bright yellow on its roof and hood, you can't effectively do this color graduation with material slots. You could use a texture, as described in the next chapter, but that might be overkill for a simple object. There is another technique that gives you an effective way to quickly color a mesh without the hard-edged lines that material slots give you: vertex colors.

The way vertex colors work is pretty simple. You assign each vertex in your mesh a specific color. If the vertices that form a face have different colors, a gradient goes from each vertex to the others; the color is most intense at the vertex and more blended with other colors the farther away it gets.

Although vertex colors are a very flexible way of adding smoothly transitioning colors to your object, they work only on mesh objects. You can't use vertex colors on other objects like curves, text, or metaballs.

Of course, trying to explicitly set the color for each and every vertex in a mesh can get really tedious on complex meshes. To alleviate this problem, Blender has a Vertex Paint mode. You activate Vertex Paint mode by selecting the mesh object that you want to paint in the 3D Viewport and then pressing Ctrl+Tab to reveal Blender's mode switching pie menu. You can also use the mode drop-down menu in the 3D Viewport's header.

When you enter Vertex Paint mode, your mouse cursor changes to include a paint brush circle similar to the one you see when in Sculpt mode, and the Tools tab available in the Toolbar changes to show paint-related tools, as shown in Figure 1-8.

Blender provides you with four basic tools for vertex painting (in addition to the Annotate tool, which is always present):

>> **Draw:** The Draw tool (ironically using a paintbrush icon) is the default tool for vertex painting. Of all the available tools, it's the only one capable of adding new color to your vertices. All the other tools are meant for adjusting colors already present.

>> **Blur:** Similar to the blur tool in digital painting programs, Blender's Blur tool for vertex painting mixes colors from adjacent vertices to help achieve a smooth transition of colors.

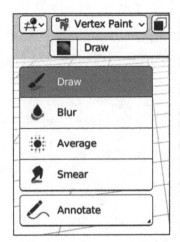

FIGURE 1-8:
The paint tools in
the Toolbar.

>> **Average:** The Average tool is similar to the Blur tool in that it attempts to smooth the transition between colors. This tool just uses a slightly different algorithm. Instead of factoring colors from adjacent vertices, this tool factors in only the colors that are within the circle of the brush size. Oftentimes, I'll roughly get the smooth transition with this tool and then make refining adjustments with the Blur tool.

>> **Smear:** Blender's Smear tool for vertex painting is also very similar to the corresponding tool in 2D digital painting programs. When you click and drag the brush circle around your mesh, you can pull color from one region into another, as if smudging or smearing it with your finger.

Of course, the primary tool for vertex painting is the Draw tool. With this tool active, the Tool tab of the Properties editor has a veritable flood of options available, as shown in Figure 1-9.

TIP

If you want to keep the Properties editor on another tab (like the Object or Material tabs), I'd recommend that you use the Tool tab of the 3D Viewport's Sidebar to work with all the Draw tool's settings. It's faster to access (especially if you're working with a full screen 3D Viewport), and it has all the same settings that are available in the Tool tab in the Properties editor. You can get even faster access with the Tool Settings in the 3D Viewport's header.

The most relevant options for vertex painting with the Draw tool are in the Brush Settings panel. Here, you set the color you want to use and control how that color is applied to the selected object. You can choose the color you want by adjusting the embedded color picker in the Color Picker sub-panel.

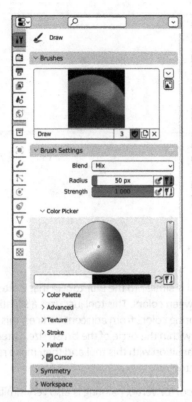

FIGURE 1-9:
The Tool tab of
the Properties
editor gives you a
bunch of settings
for the Draw
tool when vertex
painting.

Using the tool in the 3D Viewport goes pretty much how you would expect. Left-click and drag over the geometry on your object and you assign those vertices the color you've chosen in the color picker. If you're not seeing your vertex colors being assigned in the 3D Viewport, be sure that you're using Solid viewport shading.

Painting controls are similar to the sculpting controls described in Book 2, Chapter 3. (In fact, the Paint tool in Sculpt mode is another way you can edit the vertex colors on your mesh and is particularly useful for high-poly meshes.) The Radius and Strength sliders in Tool Properties control the size of your brush tip and how much influence your chosen color has, respectively. If you're working with a pressure-sensitive drawing tablet, you can enable the pressure sensitivity toggles for each of these values.

Of course, the fastest way to adjust the radius and strength of the Draw tool is with hotkeys. Press and release F to visually resize the radius of your brush (left-click to confirm when you get the size you want). Use Shift+F to change the brush's strength.

The Unified brush check boxes on the far right of the Size and Strength sliders let you keep the same brush settings across each of the different tools available in Vertex Paint mode.

Above the Radius and Strength sliders in the Brush panel is a drop-down menu labeled Blend. Typically, the option chosen in this menu is pre-set, depending on the specific brush you've chosen. However, by adjusting blending modes manually, you can have direct control over how the paint color is applied to your vertices. If you've ever used a 2D digital painting application like Krita or Photoshop, these blending mode options should look familiar to you. The following are your choices; I've broken them down by general classification:

>> **Mix:** Mix simply blends the defined color with the color that the vertex already has assigned, according to whatever value is set by the Strength slider. In most cases, this is the setting you want to use for the Draw tool.

>> **Darken modes:** These modes include Darken, Multiply, Color burn, and Linear burn. All these choices take the dark values of the color you've chosen in the color picker and make any vertices you paint over darker by that value. So if you paint with a light color (like white), your painting will have no effect on any vertices that are already dark. The specific differences among each of these blend modes is really in the mathematical algorithm used to figure out how much darker things will be. If you want to get to black by darkening, I'd recommend you use the Multiply blend mode.

>> **Lighten modes:** Consider these modes as the opposite of the darken modes. Your choices here are Lighten, Screen, Color dodge, and Add. The lightness of your chosen color is added to the color on vertices that you paint. Like the darken blend modes, the differences among these modes is in the algorithm used. If you want to get to white by lightening, I'd suggest using the Add blend mode.

>> **Mixing modes:** In contrast to the actual Mix mode (which is more like a "Replace" mode), these blending modes have algorithms that define how your chosen color combines with the existing colors on your vertices to arrive at a new color. Your options in this section are Overlay, Soft light, Hard light, Vivid light, Linear light, and Pin light.

>> **Inversion modes:** These modes include Difference, Exclusion, and Subtract. In short, use these blend modes to flip the current color on a vertex to its opposite value on the color wheel. Green colors turn red, white turns black, yellow turns violet.

>> **Color modes:** Pick these modes to tweak the influence of color on the vertices you paint over. Typically when you use these blend modes, your chosen paint color will be grayscale — typically either white or black — signifying how much influence you're painting. Your choices here are Hue, Saturation, Color, and Value.

» **Alpha modes:** In this last block of blend modes, you have two options that aren't really blend modes that affect color like the other modes. These choices, Erase Alpha and Add Alpha, are blend modes that exclusively affect the *alpha*, or transparency, of your colors. Typically, if you're painting with these blend modes, your chosen color will be grayscale, like with the color modes.

TIP

As a handy shortcut, if you right-click in the 3D Viewport, you get a small pop-over that gives you quick access to a color picker and sliders for adjusting the Draw tool's radius and strength. Figure 1-10 shows an image of this pop-over.

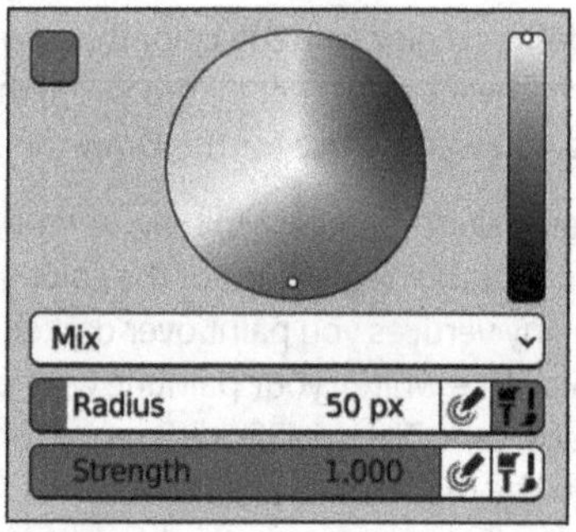

FIGURE 1-10:
Right-click in the 3D Viewport for quick access to color and brush settings.

As you paint, you may want to have a better idea of where the vertices you're painting actually exist on your mesh, especially on *low poly meshes*, or meshes that don't have a lot of actual geometry. In those cases, it's helpful to have Blender overlay the object's wireframe in the 3D Viewport. To do so, navigate to the Geometry section of the Overlays rollout and left-click the check box next to the Wireframe slider. Blender adds the wireframe over the surface of the object, making it much clearer where each of the vertices of the mesh lies. Adjusting the Wireframe and Opacity sliders control how much of your mesh's wireframe you actually see.

TIP

By default, the base vertex color for an object is a flat white. If you would rather start with a different base color for your whole object, choose Paint ⇨ Set Vertex Colors (Shift+K) from the 3D Viewport's header. Doing that sets all the vertices in your mesh to have the color you defined in the Vertex Paint color picker.

Vertex colors are a special class of additional data attached to your mesh called *attributes*. Specifically, vertex colors are known as *color attributes* and it's possible to have multiple sets of them. Over in Object Data Properties, there's a Color Attributes panel with a list box in it. When you enter Vertex Paint mode for the first time, this list box automatically gets a vertex color layer, named

`Attribute`, added to it. You can rename the layer by double-clicking it. New vertex color attributes can be added by left-clicking the Plus (+) button next to the list box. Figure 1-11 shows the Color Attributes panel in Object Data Properties with a few color attributes in the list.

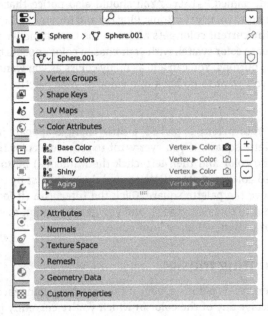

FIGURE 1-11:
You can add multiple color attributes to a single mesh object from the Color Attributes panel within Object Data Properties.

REMEMBER

Although you can have multiple color attributes, it would be a mistake to think of them as layers as you might in a traditional image editing program. You can set only one color attribute as being active for painting. To make a color attribute active for painting, left-click the color attribute's name.

Defining color palettes

In the "Setting diffuse colors" section of this chapter, I mention that it's a common practice for artists and designers to work with a palette of very specific colors. If you're painting the walls of your house blue and green, you want to make sure that if you run out of paint, you get the exact same blue and green. Otherwise, your walls are going to look all kinds of hideous. Likewise when vertex painting, if you choose a particular color, it's good to have a way to come back to that color later if you need to. Fortunately, in Blender's painting system, you have this capability built-in. Conveniently, they're called *palettes*.

Look below the color picker in the Brush Settings panel (if you need to, refer to Figure 1-9). Notice a sub-panel named Color Palette? That's where you can create, transfer, and reuse palettes in Blender, the same as any other datablock.

To create a new palette, left-click the New button in the palette datablock. A new palette is created, named Palette. You should also notice that below the color picker, there are now two new buttons: Plus (+) and Minus (-). Left-click the Plus (+) button, and the current color gets added to the current active palette. You can tell because a square color swatch with your chosen color appears beneath the Plus (+) and Minus (-) buttons. You can add as many colors as you want to your palette. As you work, if you want to go back to a color in your palette, just left-click its square swatch.

When a color in your palette is picked, a little triangle appears in the upper left corner of the palette square. If you ever want to remove a color from the palette, simply choose the color and then left-click the Minus (-) button. You can also move the selected color in your palette up and down the list by using the up and down arrows above the palette square. Click the filter icon (it looks like the one in the margin next to this paragraph), and you get the option to sort your palette colors by hue, saturation, value, or luminance.

Creating painting masks

Occasionally when vertex painting, your mesh may have some faces on it that you don't want to receive any of the color in which you're currently painting. In this case, you define face selection masking by left-clicking the Paint Mask or Vertex Selection buttons in the 3D Viewport's header. They have icons like Face Select and Vertex Select in Edit mode.

When you enable the painting mask, a set of selection tools becomes available in the 3D Viewport's Toolbar (Tweak, Box Select, Circle Select, and Lasso Select). Using those tools, you can select faces of your mesh. After you do, these faces are the only ones affected by your painting. This is an excellent method of isolating a portion of your mesh for custom painting without changing the color of the faces around that area.

The difference in behavior between Paint Mask and Vertex Selection relates to the "hardness" of your painted edge. By using Paint Mask, you get the hard-edged color changes that you get with material slots. With Vertex Selection, you're painting only vertices, so it automatically creates a gradient between your painted vertices and their unselected neighbors.

Making vertex paint renderable

Now, just because you've gone and painted some fun colors on the vertices in your object, that doesn't mean they actually show up when you render, not by default. If you pop back into Object mode, you may be surprised that you can no longer see all your meticulously painted vertex colors, even if you're using Material Preview viewport shading. Don't worry; your vertex paint is still there. It's just not being used by your object's material. You need to tell Blender that the base color for your object shouldn't be a solid color but rather one of your vertex paint layers.

The steps to get your vertex colors visible isn't as complex as it sounds. For this example, everything happens in the Material tab of the Properties editor:

1. **In the Surface panel, ensure that the Use Nodes button is enabled.**

    All new materials in Blender have this toggle enabled by default, but sometimes you may run across a material where it isn't enabled (especially on files that may have originated from older versions of Blender). The material system for both Eevee and Cycles is node-based. For all but the most simple of materials, you should use the Shader Editor to tweak and customize your materials. There's more on that later in this chapter. Fortunately, for this example, it can stay pretty simple. You don't actually need to work in the Node Editor right now.

2. **Left-click the connector button (its icon is a small yellow circular dot) to the left of the color swatch and choose Color Attribute from the (exceedingly large) menu that appears (hint: Color Attribute is in the Input column).**

    This tells Blender that, rather than use the color defined by the swatch, you want to connect some attribute (in this case, the vertex colors you've painted) to control the color. After you choose Color Attribute, the color swatch is replaced with an empty datablock drop-down menu. Click this datablock and choose the name of the color attribute associated with your vertex colors.

That should do the trick. Now when you render (Render ⇨ Render Image) or use either Material Preview or Rendered viewport shading, your vertex colors should be visible on your object. Figure 1-12 shows what your Surface panel in Material Properties should look like. The figure also shows the corresponding node configuration that Blender automatically creates for you.

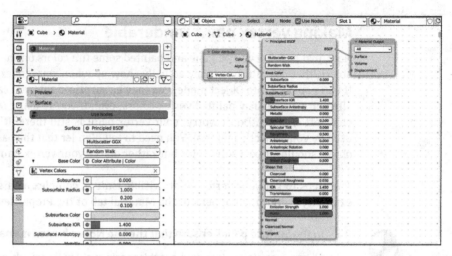

FIGURE 1-12:
On the left, the
Surface panel of
the Material tab
of the Properties
editor when you
use vertex colors
on your mesh.
On the right is
the node graph
that Blender
automatically
creates as a
result.

Setting Up Node Materials

As covered in the preceding "Making vertex paint renderable" section, it's entirely possible to work with Cycles materials from the Material tab of the Properties editor. However, working that way can be a bit clunky, and it doesn't take full advantage of the power afforded by Cycles. When Cycles was first integrated into Blender, the developers decided that they would take full advantage of Blender's node editing capabilities. Although this section details parts of the node editor specific to materials — specifically the Shader Editor — see Book 2, Chapter 5 for a broader overview of node editing in general. That chapter covers node editing in the context of Geometry Nodes, but the interaction and navigation work the same for materials as well.

Adjusting your workspace to work with materials

The best workspace in Blender for working with materials is the Shading workspace, as shown in Figure 1-13.

While the right side of the Blender window remains large — the same as the Layout workspace, with an Outliner and Properties editor — everything to the left of that is quite a bit different. There's still a large 3D Viewport in the middle of the window, but by default it's set to Material Preview viewport display.

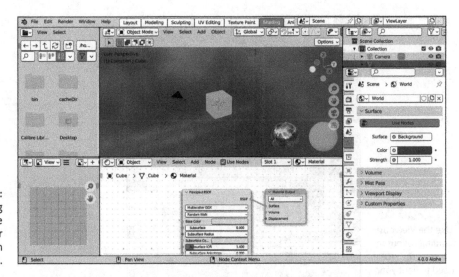

FIGURE 1-13:
The Shading
workspace
is ideal for
working with
node materials.

TIP

If Blender pauses a bit when switching to the Shading workspace, don't worry. Nothing is broken. Chances are good that you haven't used Material Preview viewport shading in your current Blender session, and Blender needs a second or two to get shaders prepared for showing in the 3D Viewport.

In addition to the other differences between the Shading workspace and the Layout workspace, the Toolbar is hidden and there are two strange-looking spheres in the bottom right corner of the 3D Viewport. Those two spheres are your HDRI preview spheres. Recall from Book 1, Chapter 2 that Material Preview viewport display is intended to help you set up materials for your objects in all manner of lighting scenarios. So in the Shading workspace, the 3D Viewport is configured to use a *high dynamic range image* (HDRI) as its source of lighting. The left HDRI preview sphere shows what a mirror ball would look like in that lighting, whereas the right HDRI sphere shows what a ball with a plain white material would look like in the same lighting.

Blender ships with a handful of HDRIs that you can use for lighting. If you expand the Viewport Shading rollout in the 3D Viewport's header, you should see something like what's shown in Figure 1-14. Notice that you see the same mirror ball in this rollout as the HDRI preview sphere. Click the mirror ball in the rollout and Blender provides you with six different HDRIs that you can choose from to test your materials in different lighting scenarios.

TIP

If you have your own HDRIs that you want to use for Material Preview viewport shading, you can configure Blender to recognize them from the Lights section of Preferences (Edit ⇨ Preferences). A great resource for free HDRIs is a website called Poly Haven (https://polyhaven.com).

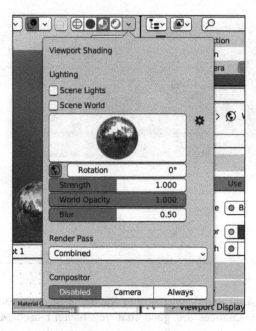

FIGURE 1-14:
Use the Viewport
Shading rollout to
change the HDRI
used to light your
scene in Material
Preview viewport
shading.

The second most important editor in the Shading workspace is the Shader Editor that's beneath the 3D Viewport. When you're working with Blender's node-based materials, this editor is really where you spend the majority of your time. The 3D Viewport is mostly there so you can see the results of your work.

Working with nodes

Earlier in this chapter (see the section titled "Making vertex paint renderable"), I mention the Use Nodes toggle in Material Properties and the fact that it's enabled by default. Likewise, in the header of the Shader Editor, there's a corresponding Use Nodes check box that's also enabled by default. If you happen to have a .blend file with materials made prior to Blender 2.80, you need to enable this toggle (in either the Shader Editor or Material Properties) to make use of the Eevee or Cycles render engines.

When the use of nodes is enabled on your material, the default node network you have is very simple: a Principled BSDF shader node connected to a Material Output node. All materials need to have a Material Output node. The Material Output node is how material properties get mapped to your object; if your material node network doesn't have this node, then the render engine doesn't know anything about your material.

The Principled BSDF shader is sometimes referred to as an "ubershader," meant to give you enough settings to replicate the behavior of most natural materials. In a way, you can think of it as a massive shader network that's been bundled into a single node that's more convenient to work with than rewiring your own custom network. I go into more detail on the Principled BSDF shader later in this chapter.

If you refer back to Book 2, Chapter 5, you may notice that material nodes sockets for color data (yellow), vector data (blue), floating point numbers (gray), and shader (green). As you might expect from the name, shader sockets are specific to shaders and materials in Blender. They're exclusive to shader nodes, which are covered in the next section.

Understanding shaders

The workhorses of Blender's materials are the shaders. A *shader* is a computer algorithm that dictates how a material behaves and what colors it sends to the camera. Shaders control reflectivity, transparency, and general color. By intelligently mixing shaders with each other (often using textures — see the next chapter), you can create some very striking and convincing materials in your 3D scene. To see the shaders available to you, choose Add ⇨ Shader in the Shader Editor. Figure 1-15 shows the list of shaders.

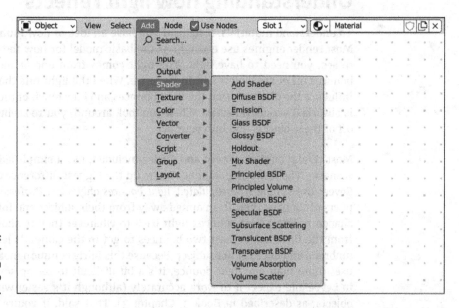

FIGURE 1-15: From the Shader Editor you can add shaders to your material.

TECHNICAL STUFF

Many of the shaders, like the Principled BSDF, have "BSDF" at the end of their names. BSDF is an abbreviation for *bidirectional scattering distribution function*. That's a fancy way of saying "mathy description of how light interacts with a surface." Due to length limitations for this book, I can't give a thorough description of all the things that can be done with node-based shaders and materials. Complete books can be (and have been!) written on that topic alone. My website for this book, www.blenderbasics.com, gives a practical example that should give you a clear idea of how to proceed.

Playing with Materials in Blender

Building materials for 3D objects (sometimes referred to as *surfacing*) is an intricate and detailed art in its own right. The well for that area of study runs deep. Within the confines of the pages of this book, there's no way I could give you an exhaustive rundown of every possible shader scenario you could find yourself encountering. However, what I *can* do is give you a sensible overview of the tools and how they work. Armed with that fundamental understanding, you should be able to sit down at Blender and get results that look good. Furthermore, you should be able to simply play with the Shader Editor to run it through its paces and really get a sense of what's possible.

Understanding how light reflects

To understand materials, it helps if you have an idea of how human sight works. Most render engines use eyesight as the basic model for how they work. In order to see, you need to have light. The light comes from one or more sources and bounces off of any object within its range. When the light hits these objects, they influence the direction that the light bounces and how much of the incoming light is absorbed versus reflected. When you look around, you're seeing light bounced off of these objects and into your eyes.

Most render engines, Eevee and Cycles included, use a simplified version of this scenario. The following sentence sums up the biggest difference as it pertains to Eevee: *Unless otherwise stipulated, light bounces only once.* Professional photographers often have their flash aimed away from their subject and into an umbrella-shaped reflector that bounces light back to whatever they're shooting. The light from the flash has at least two bounces to get to the camera's lens; once off the umbrella and once off the subject. Because this fairly common meatspace scenario uses more than one light bounce, it's a bit difficult to set up something similar in Eevee and expect it to work accurately (although it's easier with a light probe objects, as described in Book 3, Chapter 3). That said, if you're rendering with Eevee, you might be better off directly lighting your scenes so that your materials themselves control that one bounce of the light into the 3D camera.

Exceptions to this rule do, of course, exist, as do ways to cheat around them. You can use techniques covered throughout this chapter and the next one to implement those cheats. Or you could render using Cycles.

Demystifying the Principled BSDF

It's somewhat ironic that the Principled BSDF is meant to simplify the surfacing process for artists. One glance at the bevy of sliders, values, and color swatches in that node, shown in Figure 1-16, could get a person to scream, "*This* is the easy way?!"

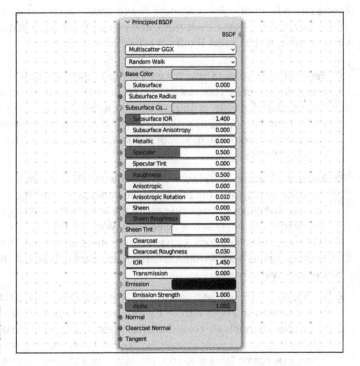

FIGURE 1-16:
The Principled
BSDF node makes
our lives as artists
easier.

**NEW
FEATURE**

In fairness, the appearance of the Principled BSDF node has a much more simple and approachable appearance in Blender 4.0. However, despite the change in appearance, the fundamentals covered in this section still remain the same.

And the answer, strangely enough, is yes. Materials in meatspace are deceptively complex things with all manner of exotic surface properties. If you wanted to make a node network that gives you all the flexibility and possibilities wrapped in the Principled BSDF node, you'd have an enormous tangled mess of nodes and noodles that could be even more difficult to parse yourself, let alone share with others. And even then, that "noodle soup" shader network isn't likely to respond to light in as physically correct a way as the Principled BSDF.

If you break down the Principled BSDF node, it's actually quite a bit more manageable than it seems. This section is a rundown of the most useful and relevant controls on this enormous node. Note that I've organized this section differently than the order of controls as they appear in the node. I've structured it this way to make explaining things a bit easier.

Color inputs

As far as I'm concerned, one of the primary functions of a material is to give your objects some form of color. Colorless renders with gray materials — sometimes called *clay renders* — have their place and can be made to look quite nice, but life is full of color. It'd be great if our art reflected that life.

>> **Base color:** As covered near the start of this chapter, the base color is where everything starts for your material's color. It can be the color you choose from the swatch in the node, or you can connect a color (like vertex colors via the Attribute node) input to its socket. The next chapter has a lot more on giving your materials color variation with textures, and a big part of that is wiring textures to this socket.

>> **Emission:** You can actually use the Principled BSDF as a light source by setting this color swatch (near the bottom of the node) to any color other than black. Do note that although this works out of the box when rendering with Cycles, you need to use a light probe object if you want emission values to work as a light source in Eevee. Book 3, Chapter 3 has more on lighting. That said, emission values are still useful in Eevee if you want to have flat-shaded, cartoon-style coloring.

>> **Alpha:** When working with color in digital applications, you typically have four color channels you work with: red, green, blue, and alpha (RGBA). The first three color channels are color primaries when dealing with additive color (like light, as opposed to subtractive color, like paint). The fourth color channel, alpha, may not be familiar to you. The *alpha* color channel relates to the opacity of the color. Higher values are more opaque, whereas lower values are more transparent.

REMEMBER

If you're rendering with Eevee, adjusting the Alpha value won't give you any visible results the way Blender is configured by default, other than making your material black if you dial it all the way down to zero. To enable transparency in your Eevee renders, go to Material Properties and scroll down to the Settings panel. Change the Blend Mode drop-down menu from Opaque to either Alpha Blend (higher quality, slower to render) or Alpha Hashed (lower quality, faster to render). Figure 1-17 shows the Settings panel in Material Properties.

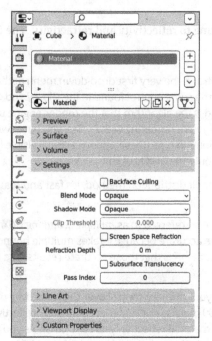

FIGURE 1-17:
Use the Settings panel in the Material tab of the Properties editor to configure the transparency of your material when rendering with Eevee.

Another thing to remember is that if you're trying to get physically correct transparency, like with glass, then you don't actually want to mess with the Alpha value. There's another control in the Principled BSDF, Transmission, that's better suited for that kind of transparency (more on that control later in the next section). Alpha transparency is more useful for masking with textures, like if you want to use an image of a leaf on a plane instead of modeling the whole leaf. See the next chapter for more on using textures.

Reflection and refraction inputs

Reflectivity is a material property that describes how much light that material bounces away from it. A perfect mirror is fully reflective and, therefore, bounces back 100 percent of the light rays that hit it, whereas black velvet has very low reflectivity. *Refraction* is how much light bends when traveling through a transparent or semitransparent material. Refraction is what makes eyeglasses work to correct people's vision or why a straw looks broken when put into a glass of water.

A common challenge of 3D computer graphics is making your materials reflective and refractive in a physically correct way. Fortunately, adding those properties to your materials in Blender isn't too difficult when using the Principled BSDF. Quite a few of the Principled BSDF node's inputs are dedicated to material features that could be classified as relating to reflectivity and refractivity. The following are the most relevant ones:

» **Distribution:** This control is the very first drop-down menu at the top of the node. This property is the same control found in the Glossy and Glass BSDFs. The *distribution* method is the algorithm that the render engine uses to generate reflections. If you're rendering with Cycles, you have two choices when it comes to distribution type (these options are still visible if you're rendering with Eevee, but only GGX is used):

- **GGX:** GGX is the default distribution method. It's fast and reasonably accurate.

- **Multiscatter GGX:** Also referred to as *multiple-scattering GGX,* this distribution method is more accurate because it takes multiple bounces of light into account. The trade-off is that those accurate results take longer to generate.

» **Metallic:** This input is your primary control over the reflectivity of your material. A value of 1.00 makes your material completely reflective, whereas a value of 0 makes your material reflect only its base color. As you play with this value, you may find yourself wondering why at a value of 1.00 your material doesn't seem as perfectly reflective as the HDRI mirror ball. That's because of the input mentioned next in this list, Roughness.

TECHNICAL
STUFF

If you talk to enough people who do surfacing frequently, you'll sometimes hear them refer to a material's *dialectric,* or non-metal component. In meatspace, a material is either metallic or it isn't. The Metallic input on Blender's Principled BSDF gives you the ability to cheat a bit and make materials that are partially metallic and partially dialectric (like maybe dirty metal).

» **Roughness:** Think of the Roughness value of the Principled BSDF as the amount of polish you have on your material. A silver spoon is highly reflective and can have a mirror-like finish on it. However, if that spoon is tarnished, the reflections get blurred out to the point that the surface of the spoon almost starts behaving like a diffuse material. The default value for this input is 0.500. If you drop it down to 0 with a Metallic value of 1.00, you get the mirror finish you'd expect.

» **Specular:** As I mention elsewhere in this chapter, think of the specular value as being a kind of reflectivity, but only for your light sources. Technically speaking, it's the reflectivity of dialectric materials. The specular value doesn't account for any color input from the environment around your material. Specularity is also generally less computationally expensive to calculate in a render engine like Eevee. Say, for example, you're trying to replicate the shininess of polished black leather shoes. Although you could tweak the

Metallic and IOR inputs to get results that look good, you can usually get there faster with more physical accuracy by just dialing up the Specular value and leave the Metallic input alone (unless you have chrome shoes, of course).

>> **IOR:** IOR is an abbreviation for *index of refraction*, or a numerical representation of how much a material bends light. This input is most relevant for materials that you can see through, like glass or water. The cool thing is that because Eevee and Cycles are meant to be physically correct render engines, IOR values match their real-world counterparts. The IOR of air, for example, is 1.00, meaning that light appears unbent. The default IOR in the Principled BSDF is 1.45, about halfway between the IOR of water and the IOR of glass. There are look-up tables on the Internet for the IOR values of all manner of materials. Generally speaking, realistic materials won't have an IOR greater than 2.00.

>> **Transmission:** I mention in the preceding section that if you want a material like glass, you don't want to adjust the Alpha value of your Principled BSDF. Instead, this value, Transmission, is the one you want to work with. It's called Transmission because it's a value that describes how much light is *transmitted* through your material. A Transmission value of 1.00 tells Blender that your material is completely see-through. The result looks like a material with an Alpha of 0, but the difference is that things seen through your material are distorted, as if looking through a lens.

REMEMBER

Being a ray-tracing render engine, Cycles has support for reflection and refraction "for free" because that's just how that kind of render engine works. Eevee is not a ray tracer, so it needs to rely on a few cheats to get decent results. If you're working with a material in Eevee and you need good reflection and refraction behavior, there are a few settings you should adjust so the results are visible in your renders (and the 3D Viewport):

>> In Render Properties, enable the Screen Space Reflections check box.

>> In Material Properties, go to the Settings panel and enable the Screen Space Refraction check box for each refractive material in your scene.

In both these scenarios, enabling each check box makes Eevee render slower. However, if you need reflection and refraction but you don't want to break out the heavy guns of Cycles, that small speed hit is necessary.

Subsurface scattering inputs

Subsurface scattering is basically what you see on the back of your hand when you hold a flashlight against your palm. It's the effect of light being distributed through a volume of material, be it wax, skin, or orange juice. The Principled BSDF has a set of controls for subsurface scattering right at the top of the node.

TIP

If you're using Eevee as your render engine, you may want to enable the Subsurface Translucency check box from the Settings panel in the Material tab of the Properties editor. It's not critical to enable this value, but doing so can give you more accurate results.

» **Subsurface method:** This control is the second drop-down menu at the top of the node. With this drop-down menu, you have a choice of the algorithms Blender uses to generate the subsurface scattering effect:

- **Christensen-Burley:** In computer graphics, a lot of algorithms get named after the people who came up with them. The Christensen-Burley subsurface scattering method is one such algorithm. It's a decent general-purpose choice that works in both Eevee and Cycles, although it's not as accurate as the other subsurface methods.

- **Random Walk (Fixed Radius):** If you want more accurate results on closed, watertight meshes (especially for thin and curved surfaces), I'd suggest you try the Random Walk algorithm. This "fixed radius" version assumes that the radius of the subsurface scattering effect is the same throughout the mesh, regardless of any other features in the shader. As a result, it's more accurate than Christensen-Burley (and slower), but has a tendency to make surface details somewhat waxy and less noticeable than the other variation of Random Walk, covered next.

- **Random Walk:.** This subsurface method is the default setting. This variation of the Random Walk algorithm varies the subsurface scattering radius based on what you set for the Base Color, Anisotropic, and IOR values. It's the slowest of the available choices but the results tend to be a lot better than the others.

» **Subsurface:** This slider controls how much subsurface scattering you have in your object. For realistic subsurface scattering, typical values for this setting are generally pretty low (less than 0.5).

» **Subsurface radius:** This control is one of the more difficult ones to understand. Notice that the input socket for this control is blue, indicating a vector input (see Book 2, Chapter 5 for more on socket colors for nodes). However, it's a bit more complex than that. Each of the three values is the distance that light scatters through the material, broken up by red, green, and blue color channels. The reason for this strangeness is because one of the most common uses for subsurface scattering is for skin, and in skin red light tends to scatter more deeply. That's why the default values for this control are 1.00 for red, 0.20 for green, and 0.10 for blue. If you're making a material that isn't skin, you'll probably want to change these values. That said, radius values are in Blender units where 1 Blender unit equals 1 meter. For realism, a penetration of 1 meter for red is probably too high.

> **» Subsurface color:** This color socket is the base color for your subsurface scattering effect. Typically the color will be pretty close to the base color you've chosen, though perhaps with a higher saturation value. For example, if you're making a skin material, you'll probably make this color red. Of course, that's assuming you're making human skin. If it's alien skin, you'll probably choose a different color altogether.

Combining shaders with the Mix Shader node

If you've never had experience with a node-based workflow, Blender's material system may seem needlessly complicated to you. You could even find yourself thinking that if everything was a Principled shader of some sort, we wouldn't need nodes at all. Of course, that's not true. As shown in Book 2, Chapter 5, there's an enormous amount of power that you get by having the flexibility to mix components together. Whether you're mixing geometry as in that chapter, images like in Book 5, Chapter 2, textures like in the next chapter, or shaders as covered in this chapter, the ability to mix is one of the best core features of a node-based workflow. To give you a taste of what's possible with shaders, I'm going to suggest that you have a look at the deceptively unassuming Mix Shader node.

As Figure 1-18 shows, the Mix Shader is a fairly simple thing: three input sockets and a single output. And only one of those input sockets, Fac, has a value you can manually adjust. Despite its sparse dressing, though, the Mix Shader is one of the most helpful nodes available when working on materials for your objects.

FIGURE 1-18:
The Mix Shader node doesn't look like much, but there's a bucket full of awesome in those four sockets.

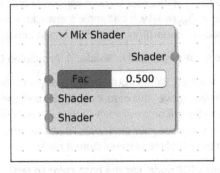

Say you have a model, and you want it to be half one material and half another. Admittedly, this is a bit of a contrived example, but bear with me. Sure, you could use the model's geometry and material slots to do the material separation, but what if you need the separation of materials to follow a line that doesn't match your geometry? Heavily modifying your mesh topology just to account for arbitrary material changes is a lot of extra work. Plus, when you use that approach, it's difficult to make changes in the future. Furthermore, what if you want to animate the change in material? Maybe you have a cartoon character whose face needs to grow red from bottom to top, like a thermometer, as they get angry. This is the sort of thing for which having node-powered materials really excels.

Continuing on this example, I'd like to walk you through the steps of building a fairly simple node network that produces the effect described in the preceding paragraph. For this example, I'm going to use Suzanne, but you're welcome to use any object you'd like (for simplicity, I'd recommend a mesh-based model). From a new general Blender session (File ➪ New ➪ General), switch to the Shading workspace and work through the following steps:

1. **Delete the default cube (X ➪ Delete).**

2. **Add Suzanne (Add ➪ Mesh ➪ Monkey).**

While you're here, I would recommend that you set Suzanne's shading to smooth (Object ➪ Shade Smooth) and give her a Subdivision Surface modifier with two subdivisions (Ctrl+2).

3. **Give Suzanne a new material.**

You can do this from Material Properties, or click the New button in the Material datablock in the Shader Editor's header. While you're here, I'd suggest you name your material something sensible. I named mine HotFace.

4. **Tweak the material on Suzanne to taste.**

In the simplest case, just give her a Principled BSDF base color, like maybe some form of blue. So far, so good. Your Blender window should look something like what's shown in Figure 1-19. It's a simple scene with a Suzanne model that has a basic two-node material (Principled BSDF and Material Output).

5. **Add a new Principled BSDF node (Add ➪ Shader ➪ Principled BSDF).**

When your new node is added, Blender puts it wherever your mouse cursor is in the Shader Editor. As you move your mouse cursor around, the node moves with it. Place the node in the editor area by left-clicking. It's not overly important where in the editor you place your new node; I'd just recommend you place it somewhere to the left of the Material Output node.

6. **In your new Principled BSDF node, set the base color to red.**

Left-click the Base Color swatch in the node and use the color picker to set that color as red. As you make this change, nothing should happen in the 3D Viewport. Nothing is happening because even though you're modifying a shader node, that node isn't connected to anything else in the node network. So none of your changes are visible in the material . . . yet.

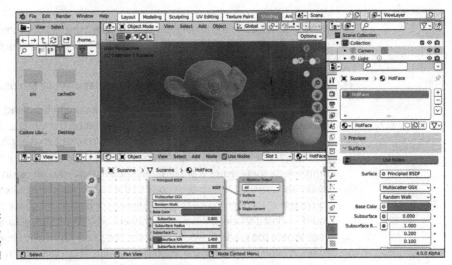

FIGURE 1-19:
Suzanne is here,
ready to be made
angry!

7. **Add a Mix Shader node to your new, red Principled BSDF by clicking and dragging from the BSDF output socket.**

When you drag from that socket, you should see a little plus (+) icon. When you release your mouse button, Blender provides you with a search menu that lists a few available nodes to choose from. Among that list is the Mix Shader node. Click that menu item, and you'll get a Mix Shader node that moves with your mouse cursor, just as in Step 5. Drag the Mix Shader node near the noodle between your original Principled BSDF and the Material Output node. You may need to shuffle the Material Output node to the right a bit to make some room for your Mix Shader node.

8. **Wire the BSDF output socket of your original, blue Principled BSDF node to the bottom Shader socket on the Mix Shader node.**

9. **Wire the Shader output socket of the Mix Shader node to the Surface input socket on the Material Output node.**

It doesn't matter that you already have a noodle connected to that socket; that noodle will be disconnected. If you used blue and red base colors, you should notice that Suzanne is now a lovely shade of purple.

Pause a moment while you're working through these steps to wrap your head around what's happening here. You've run two Principled BSDF nodes through a single Mix Shader node and routed that node's Shader socket to the Material Output node. The result is an even mix of your two Principled BSDFs. If you adjust the Fac slider in the Mix Shader node, you can control the influence of each shader. Dragging the Fac slider left and right, you can change Suzanne from blue to red and back again. That's already pretty cool, and it shows the basics of what can be done with the Mix Shader node, but it's not exactly the change described in the initial example. You want the red color to grow from the bottom of Suzanne's chin to the top of her head. For that effect, you need to add a few more nodes.

10. **Add a Gradient Texture node to the Fac socket on your Mix Shader node.**

You could do this from the Add menu (Add ⇨ Texture ⇨ Gradient), but the faster approach is to click and drag the Fac socket on the Mix Shader and choose Gradient Texture ⇨ Color from the search menu that appears. The next chapter has a lot more on textures, but the Gradient Texture node is a simple node that creates a procedural gradient that you can use in your materials. By wiring this texture node to the Fac socket on the Mix Shader, you're telling Blender to use that gradient to control the influence of each of your Principled shaders. Where the gradient would be black, your Suzanne is blue. Where the gradient would be white, she's red. And in the various gray states in between, you have a smooth transition of colors through purple from one ear to the other. Of course, although that smooth transition is nice, it's not quite like the thermometer effect described in the example. You want the transition from blue to red to be much more abrupt than that.

11. **Add a Color Ramp node (Add ⇨ Converter ⇨ Color Ramp) along the noodle between your Gradient Texture node and the Mix Shader node.**

When you add this node, you can drag the Color Ramp node over the noodle until it's highlighted, and when you place the node by left-clicking, Blender automatically routes the noodle through your node. The Color Ramp node maps incoming grayscale values (on its Fac input socket) to a color ramp you define. When you first add this node to your shader network, it shouldn't appear that anything has changed in the 3D Viewport. That makes sense because at this point, the Color Ramp node is a simple black-to-white gradient; you're mapping the values of your Gradient Texture node to an identical linear gradient. The next step is where you seize control of that texture.

12. **In the Color Ramp node, change the Interpolation from Linear to Constant by clicking the drop-down menu on the right side of the node.**

Yikes! Your whole Suzanne is now red! That's not what you wanted, either. But wait . . . it actually *is* what you want. Notice that instead of being a linear gradient, the whole color ramp is now black. At each end of the color ramp there's a little house-shaped controller called a *color stop*. The left one has a little black rectangle under its roof, and the right one has a white rectangle. If you've worked with gradient editors in image editing programs before, these color stops should be familiar. They represent a point on the color ramp where you define a specific color. If you click and drag the white color stop (the one on the right) to the left, you should see the 3D Viewport update, so one-half of Suzanne's face is blue and the other is red. By dragging the color stop left and right, you can control exactly where her face changes from blue to red, as shown in Figure 1-20.

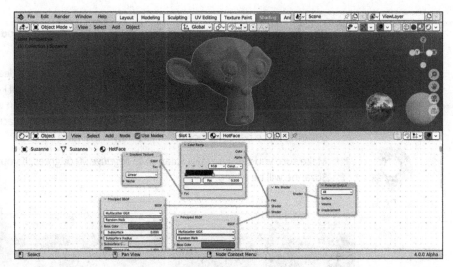

FIGURE 1-20:
With the Color
Ramp node,
you can control
what parts of
Suzanne's face
are red or blue.

Of course, most thermometers don't work from side to side. They get red from the bottom up. To accommodate that feature of your material, you need to rotate how your gradient is mapped to your mesh.

13. **Add a Texture Coordinate node and wire its Generated socket to the Vector socket on your Gradient Texture node.**

As with in Step 10, the easiest approach is by clicking and dragging the Vector socket on your Gradient Texture node and choosing Texture Coordinate ⇨ Generated from the menu that appears. Generally speaking, texture coordinates are how 3D software maps two-dimensional elements (like most textures) to a three-dimensional surface. When you wire up this noodle, there should be no visible change in the 3D Viewport. The reason is because the Gradient Texture node defaults to using Generated texture coordinates when nothing is connected to its Vector input socket. However, in order to rotate your effect, you need to modify how those coordinates are mapped to your mesh. The Mapping node (added in the next step) doesn't have a default coordinate system, so you need the Texture Coordinate node to provide that input.

14. **Add a Mapping node (Add ⇨ Vector ⇨ Mapping) along the noodle between your Texture Coordinate node and the Gradient Texture node.**

No change should be visible in the 3D Viewport because all the values on the Mapping node are at their defaults. You've added the node, but you haven't yet changed any mapping. That happens in the next step.

15. **Choose Texture from the Type drop-down in the Mapping node and change the Y-axis rotation value to -90 degrees.**

Clicking the Texture button in the Mapping node tells it that it's dealing with texture coordinates (the Mapping node can be used to remap all kinds of values, not just texture coordinates). Changing the Y-axis rotation value is the key, though. Once you make that change, the vertical transition across Suzanne's face becomes horizontal, as shown in Figure 1-21.

TIP

Make sure you set the Y-axis rotation to *negative* 90 degrees. If you just do 90, Suzanne will be all red.

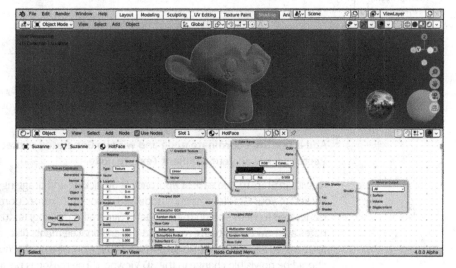

FIGURE 1-21:
The temperature is rising and Suzanne is getting angry. You wouldn't like Suzanne when she's angry.

TIP

As a bonus, you can animate the position of that color transition by keyframing the position value of the white color stop in the Color Ramp node. Simply move the color stop to one place, right-click the Pos field, and choose Insert Keyframe from the menu that appears. Then move forward in the time, adjust the position of that color stop again, and insert a new keyframe. Boom! Suzanne with animated cartoon anger.

And there you have it! So much of the power that you get from Blender's node-based material system comes from the Mix Shader node. Furthermore, because you're mixing shaders, it's not just about mixing colors. You can have half of Suzanne be transparent. Or maybe you want to mix shaders so part of her face looks metallic and another part is glass. This power and flexibility is what you get when you start finding creative ways to mix materials in the Shader Editor.

TECHNICAL STUFF

It's also possible to do shader mixing with the Add Shader node, but that node is less flexible than the Mix Shader node. And if you're concerned about realism, the Add Shader node can be problematic for non-emitting materials because it doesn't adhere to the concept of *energy conservation*. One of the laws of physics is that matter cannot be created or destroyed. The same is generally true for energy, and light is a form of energy. So unless you intend for your material to be a source of light, it shouldn't be adding any energy to your scene. So, as a general rule of thumb, use the Mix Shader for regular materials and the Add Shader for sources of light.

Playing with the Shader to RGB node

With all this talk of realism and physically correct materials, it's sometimes easy to forget that we're working in the digital realm. It's our imaginations, powered by electricity! Why aim for realism when you can literally make anything you want? Just because the sky is blue and grass is green in meatspace, that doesn't mean you have to faithfully replicate that in your work. You can make the sky and grass purple and orange if you want. And a cloudless sky doesn't have to be a smooth gradient at all. It can be textured or painterly or some wild thing that I can't imagine or put into words.

This mindset is the heart and spirit of *non-photorealistic rendering,* or NPR for short. NPR materials are a whole segment of the computer graphics world that, in my humble opinion, doesn't get focused on enough. Artistically speaking, the whole world is open to you. Practically speaking, a large portion of the community of artists that work with NPR materials tends to focus on making 3D artwork that looks like it was drawn, painted, or cartoony. And Eevee has a node that's a powerful tool for that kind of artist: the Shader to RGB node.

REMEMBER

The Shader to RGB node only works when you're rendering with Eevee. Being a ray tracer, it's more difficult to make Cycles do some of the crazy non-photorealistic things that are possible with Eevee.

If you add a Shader to RGB node to your Shader Editor (Add ⇨ Converter ⇨ Shader to RGB), you may note that there is not much to it. As shown in Figure 1-22, the Shader to RGB node is even sparser than the Mix Shader node. There's not even a Fac slider. Just a single Shader socket input and two output sockets, one for color and one for alpha.

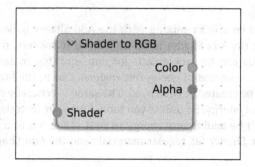

FIGURE 1-22: The lowly Shader to RGB node. Just wait until you see what this thing can do!

The power of the Shader to RGB node is all in what it can do. To give you just a taste of what's possible, open up a new general Blender scene (File ⇨ New ⇨ General) and switch over to the Shading workspace. Then, work through the following steps:

1. **Delete the default cube (X ⇨ Delete).**

   The cube is nice and all, but this example calls for something a little more exciting.

2. **Add Suzanne to your scene (Add ⇨ Mesh ⇨ Suzanne).**

   As with the example in the preceding section, give Suzanne smooth shading (Object ⇨ Shade Smooth) and a Subdivision Surface modifier with 2 subdivisions (Ctrl+2).

3. **Give Suzanne a new material.**

   The easiest way to give her a material is to left-click the New button in the Material datablock within the header of the Shader Editor. Be sure to name your material something that makes sense, like Cartoon Monkey.

4. **Select the Principled BSDF in your new material and delete it (X).**

   For this example, the Principled BSDF is a bit overkill.

5. **Add a Diffuse BSDF to the Surface input socket of the Material Output node.**

   Remember that although you can use the Add menu (Add ⇨ Shader ⇨ Diffuse BSDF), it's faster to click and drag from the Surface socket on the Material Output node and choose Diffuse BSDF ⇨ BSDF from the menu that appears. At this point, things are pretty dull. You have a Suzanne in your scene with a material that looks a bit like unbaked clay. The next few steps are where you start to see something cool.

6. Add a Shader to RGB node (Add ➪ Converter ➪ Shader to RGB) and wire it inline between your Diffuse BSDF node and your Material Output node.

REMEMBER

You can add a node inline by dragging it over an existing noodle and placing it when the noodle gets highlighted.

You may find yourself disappointed with the results here. After all, you just did it. You added the "incredible" Shader to RGB node. Rainbows of unimaginable awesomeness should be shooting out of the back of your computer now, right? Well, not quite. There are still a few steps to go. See, right now you have a yellow Color socket from the Shader to RGB node wired to the green Surface socket on the Material Output node. That's two different kinds of data. The Material Output node expects shader data to be connected to that Surface socket. So, you should give it that.

7. Add a new Emission shader node (Add ➪ Shader ➪ Emission) and place it inline between your Shader to RGB node and the Material Output node.

In performing this step, you've at least gotten all your matching sockets properly connected to one another. The result, however, is still that boring clay monkey.

TECHNICAL STUFF

Let me pause a moment to explain what's going on. Working from the left of your shader network to the right, your first Diffuse BSDF is taking all the lighting data from your scene (in Material Preview viewport shading, that's the light in the scene and the HDRI image connected to the 3D Viewport's world environment). By wiring that Diffuse BSDF to the Shader to RGB node, you're telling Eevee to take that lighting information and interpret it as color data mapped to the surface of Suzanne, kind of like a texture (see the next chapter). Then, by wiring your Shader to RGB node to an Emission shader, you're telling Eevee to use that color data as a kind of texture for that Emission shader before sending the shader data to the Material Output node.

So, in short, the Shader to RGB node lets you treat shader data (light, basically) as if it were a texture that's dynamically mapped to your mesh. This means that you now have the ability to do fun texturing and image processing tricks to shader data. To see what I mean, go on to the next steps.

8. Add a Color Ramp node (Add ➪ Converter ➪ Color Ramp) inline between your Shader to RGB node and your Emission shader node.

Again, the immediate results may appear somewhat lackluster. However, things are about to change.

9. In the Color Ramp node, left-click the Plus (+) button above the color ramp gradient.

Blender should add an additional color stop at the halfway point of the Color Ramp node's gradient. The color at that color stop should be 50% gray.

10. **Change the Color Ramp's Interpolation drop-down menu from Linear to Constant.**

Now, things are starting to get interesting. Instead of having a drab clay kind of look, Suzanne now has a bold shadow that looks like it was filled with a heavy ink pen. If you add more color stops and tweak their positioning in the Color Ramp node, your Blender session could look something like what's shown in Figure 1-23.

FIGURE 1-23:
The Shader to RGB node can give you Suzanne with cartoony or comic book lighting.

And that's it! Sure, this is a fairly rudimentary example, but if you combine the Shader to RGB node with the tools I describe in the next chapter, you can generate some very interesting and complex non-photorealistic materials for your models while still having them react correctly to your scene lighting. Play with this node network. Mess around with it! Add things! Maybe you'll come up with something you never imagined was possible.

Chapter **2**

Giving Models Texture

I f you want a more controlled way of adjusting the look of your object than what's described in the preceding chapter, then using material shaders alone won't get you there. You can use vertex colors, but if you're working on a model you intend to animate, the additional vertices you add to get the details you want with vertex colors can cause you to have a lot of extraneous vertices. Those vertices end up slowing down the rigging, animating, and even rendering processes. Also, you may want to have material changes that are independent of the topology and edge flow of your mesh.

For those sorts of scenarios, you're going to want to use textures, which is the focus of this chapter.

Adding Textures

Generally speaking, a *texture* is a kind of image that you stretch or tile over the surface of your object to give it more detail without adding more geometry. Not only can textures influence the color of your object, but they can also allow you to make additional adjustments, such as stipulating the shininess of some specific parts of the model. For example, on a human face, skin tends to be shinier across the nose and forehead, and somewhat duller around the eyes. With textures, you can control these sorts of things. If you've read through Book 3, Chapter 1, then you've seen some examples of that using the Gradient Texture.

When it comes to textures that are applied to your material, textures are just other nodes that you add to your node network. It's possible to add a texture from the Material tab of the Properties editor from the connector button to the left of any property (it's button with a small circle icon). However, you have a lot more control if you do it from the Shader Editor by pressing Add ⇨ Texture and choosing your desired texture node from the menu. In all but the most simple of use cases, you should use the Shader Editor to add textures to your materials. For this reason, just like in the preceding chapter, the "home base" for working with textures and materials in Blender is the Shading workspace. Figure 2-1 shows the textures available when you open this menu.

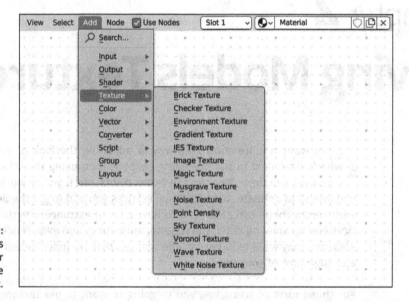

FIGURE 2-1:
You add textures directly in your material node network.

REMEMBER

You might notice that the Properties editor has a Texture tab and that there's also a specific Texture Node Editor that you can put in any area. Those specific controls aren't for material textures. You can make procedural textures that can be used when painting, sculpting, and drawing with Grease Pencil. Those textures are referred to as Brush textures and I get into them more later in this chapter.

Discovering Procedural Textures

Blender offers two kinds of textures: image-based textures and *procedural textures*. Unlike image-based textures, where you explicitly create and load an image (or sequence of images) as a texture, procedural textures are created in software with a specific pattern algorithm.

The advantage of procedural textures is that they're *resolution independent*; they don't get blurry or pixelated when you zoom in very close. They can be a quick way to add a level of detail to your objects without doing a lot of manual painting or repainting for different levels of detail.

Of course, procedurals can be a bit more difficult to control than image-based textures. For example, if you have a character with dark circles under their eyes, getting those circles to show up only where you want can be pretty tough, maybe even impossible if you're only using procedurals. So, the ideal use for procedural textures is as broad strokes where you don't need fine control. Or you may make a procedural texture and mix it with an image-based texture that you use as a mask to dictate where that procedural texture appears. Procedural textures are also great for creating a foundation or a base to start with, such as providing the rough texture of an orange rind's surface.

The following is a list of textures available; note that most of them are procedural:

>> **Brick texture:** As its name implies, this procedural texture node creates a simple brick texture. This may seem like an awfully specific texture to generate procedurally, but I've also used it to create grid patterns and stripes.

>> **Checker texture:** Similar to the Brick texture, this procedural texture's name explains exactly what it does. Many times, it gets used as a placeholder or test pattern, but it's also useful for quickly making textures for race flags, plaid, picnic blankets, and — yes — checkerboards.

>> **Environment texture:** The Environment texture is an image-based texture (and therefore not procedural) typically connected to the Color socket of the Background node for the World shader network. See the next chapter for more on setting up your World environment.

>> **Gradient texture:** The Gradient texture is one of the unsung heroes in Blender's procedural texture arsenal. This texture may seem like a simple gradient, but with the right mapping, it's really quite versatile. I use Gradient textures for mixing two other textures together, creating simple toon-like outlines for meshes, and adjusting the color along the length of hair strands. You can see the real power of the Gradient texture when you use it with a Color Ramp node, as with the example near the end of Book 3, Chapter 1.

>> **IES texture:** The IES texture requires that you use a text-based data file called an IES profile. An *IES profile* describes how the intensity of a light source varies based on direction from its source. It's used for Light objects and is most frequently used in architectural visualization for lighting interior scenes with very specific kinds of lights.

>> **Image texture:** The Image texture is not a procedural texture, but I'm including it in this list because it's visible in the Texture menu. Quite a bit of the rest of this chapter is devoted to working with image-based textures.

>> **Magic texture:** At first glance, the Magic texture may seem to be completely useless — or at the very least, too weird to be useful. However, I've found quite a few cool uses for this eccentric little texture. If you treat the Magic texture as a bump map or a normal map, it works well for creating a knit texture for blankets and other types of cloth. If you stretch the texture with your mapping controls, you can use it to re-create the thin filmy look that occurs when oil mixes with water. And, of course, you can use it to make a wacky, wild-colored shirt.

>> **Musgrave texture:** This procedural texture is extremely flexible and well suited for organic materials. You can use the Musgrave texture for rock cracks, generic noise, clouds, and even as a mask for rust patterns. As a matter of fact, with enough tweaking, you can probably get a Musgrave texture to look like nearly any other procedural texture. Of course, the trade-off is that this texture can sometimes take a bit longer to render than most of the others.

>> **Noise texture:** The Noise texture is a good general-purpose texture. You can treat the Noise texture as a go-to texture for general bumps, smoke, and cloud-like effects.

>> **Point Density:** The Point Density texture is used primarily with Blender's particle system to generate volumetric textures. These kinds of materials are well suited for creating smoke and clouds. (See Book 4, Chapter 5 for more on Blender's particle system.)

>> **Sky texture:** The Sky texture is similar to the Environment texture in that it's typically used in the node network for the World shader. The difference is that the Sky texture is not image-based. It's procedural and can be tweaked to give your scene the feeling of a wide array of external environments. See the next chapter for more on how to use this node.

>> **Voronoi texture:** The Voronoi procedural texture is best thought of as a family of textures in a single node. A lot of the control comes from the Feature Output drop-down menu (it's the second drop-down menu in the node). Like the Musgrave texture, the Voronoi texture is pretty versatile. You can use it to create scales, veins, stained glass, textured metals, or colorful mosaics.

>> **Wave texture:** At its core, this texture can be used to make nearly any striped effect. You can have everything from simple stripes to more turbulent stripes like in polished marble. With a little bit of creativity, you can even use the turbulence in this texture as a fire texture.

>> **White Noise:** White Noise is one of the simplest procedural textures in Blender. Aside from its Dimensions drop-down menu, this texture has no custom controls of its own; it's simply raw noise, which means that you'll never get the same results twice using this texture. Each time you render it, the noise pattern is different. This lack of predictability may be annoying if you're looking to do a bump map. However, if you're looking to have white noise on an old TV screen, this texture is perfect.

Figure 2-2 shows each of these textures applied to a smooth sphere.

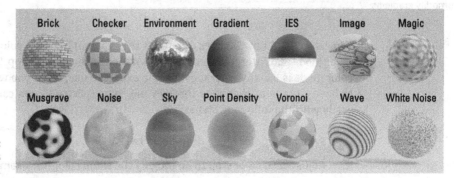

FIGURE 2-2: Blender's texture nodes.

Using Color Ramps

A powerful and under-recognized tool in Blender is the *ramp*. A ramp is a gradient, and its editor interface is used in a few different places in Blender's interface. In Blender's color-related node editors (Shader Editor, Compositor, Texture Node Editor), you can add Color Ramp node by choosing Add ⇨ Converter ⇨ Color Ramp. In the Geometry Nodes Editor, it's a bit harder to find (Add ⇨ Utilities ⇨ Color ⇨ Color Ramp), but it's there. Figure 2-3 shows a detailed view of the Color Ramp node, which is where you most frequently use ramps.

Ramps are a great way, for example, to adjust the color of the stripes in a Wave texture or determine which colors you want to use for your Gradient texture. Book 3, Chapter 1 has an example of using the Color Ramp node with the Shader to RGB node to create cartoon-style and hand-drawn materials. The ramp editor works much like gradient editors in other programs. By default, it starts with a *color stop* positioned at either end of a *colorband* bar, and the color smoothly transitions from one side to the other. The color can be any value in the RGB spectrum, and, using the color picker, you also can control its transparency with the alpha value.

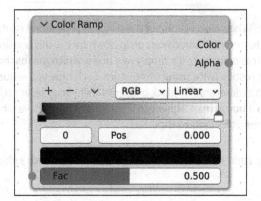

You can control how Blender calculates the gradient between color stops with the Color Mode and Interpolation drop-down menus above the ramp. The default RGB color mode is usually what most people expect to use, but if you want a quick way to have a gradient that runs through the color spectrum, you can do that pretty easily with the following steps:

1. **Switch the Color Mode drop-down to HSV.**

2. **Adjust each color stop to be roughly the same color (for example, red).**

3. **Change the Color Interpolation drop-down to Far.**

And just like that, you have a full rainbow to work with. When the Color Mode drop-down is left to RGB, the Interpolation drop-down lets you control the rate of change between color stops with a set of different algorithms. The default of Linear is most frequently used, but you should also check out the Constant and Ease interpolation settings to see how they work.

To change the position of a color stop, first select it by left-clicking its position in the colorband. Then drag it left and right on the colorband or adjust the Pos value in the number field below the colorband. Color stop positions count up from left to right, starting at 0. So, with the default arrangement, the black color on the left is 0, and the white color on the right is 1. After you select the color, you can change its value by left-clicking the color swatch and using the color picker.

To add a new color stop, left-click the Plus (+) button. A color stop appears at the halfway point in the colorband. You can delete any color stop by selecting it and left-clicking the Delete button.

It may not seem like much, but mastering ramps and knowing when to use them makes your workflow for adding materials and textures much faster.

Understanding Texture Mapping

After you create your texture, be it procedural or image-based, you're going to have to relate that texture to your material and, by extension, the surface of your object. This process is called *mapping*. Mapping consists of relating a location on a texture to a location on the surface of an object. This section walks you through the process of texture mapping in Blender.

Making simple adjustments with the Texture Mapping panel

If you reveal the Shader Editor's Sidebar (N), Blender gives you controls for your material. More importantly, the Node tab shows specific controls for the active node that you have selected. For most of Blender's texture nodes, there's a panel at the bottom of the Node tab labeled Texture Mapping. Figure 2-4 shows the Texture Mapping panel for the Gradient texture.

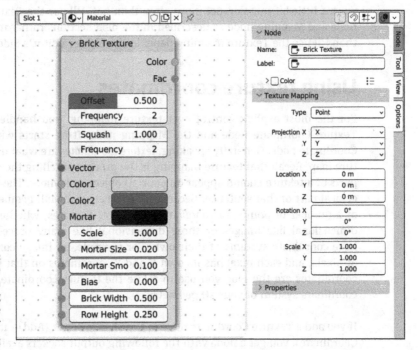

FIGURE 2-4: Most texture nodes have a Texture Mapping panel in the Node tab of the Shader Editor's Sidebar.

REMEMBER

The only texture nodes that don't have a Texture Mapping panel are the IES, Point Density, and White Noise textures.

Near the end of Book 3, Chapter 1, there's an example of using a Gradient texture with a Color Ramp node to mix two materials on Suzanne's face to make it look like she gets more angry. The last few steps of that example involve using a Mapping node to rotate the texture so the gradient is horizontally oriented rather than vertically oriented. Technically speaking, the Mapping node wasn't necessary for that example. You could perform the same rotation directly from the Texture Mapping panel of the Gradient texture. Change the mapping Type from Point to Texture and adjust the Y rotation to -90 degrees.

One of the big advantages of using the Texture Mapping panel as opposed to an explicit Mapping node is that it can dramatically simplify the appearance of your node network. With fewer nodes in the Shader Editor, it's easier to get a high-level understanding of what the node network is doing because there's less clutter.

TIP

That said, you're also hiding details, especially if, like me, you often work in the Shader Editor with the Sidebar collapsed. If you're coming back to a material that you haven't worked with for a long time or you're collaborating with other artists, it may not be immediately clear why your texture is rotated or scaled a particular way. For myself, I tend to err on the side of clarity, even if it makes my node network a little bit messier. So, more often than not, I'll use the Texture Coordinate node and Mapping node as described in the next sections rather more frequently than I'll use the Texture Mapping panel in the Shader Editor's Sidebar.

Using texture coordinates

For the most explicit control over texture mapping, you handle that with the Texture Coordinate node and the Mapping node. It all starts with the Texture Coordinate node. Generally speaking, *texture coordinates* are what define your texture map. Recall that texture mapping is the process of telling the computer what parts of a texture should appear on your 3D object and where. The "where" is the critical part of that sentence. Because 3D geometry is, well, geometry, it consists of a number of points, or *coordinates*, in space. Textures, whether they're two-dimensional like images or three-dimensional like many procedural textures, have coordinate systems of their own. For example, an image consists of a grid of pixels, and each pixel has its own X and Y coordinates on that image. Texture coordinates are the glue you use to relate the texture coordinate system to the coordinate system of your 3D geometry.

If you add a Texture Coordinate node in the Shader Editor (Add ⇨ Input ⇨ Texture Coordinate), you get a node with the following output sockets available:

>> **Generated:** This socket is the default for procedural textures, and it generates texture coordinates based on the object's local coordinates. The Generated

coordinate system works fine for most situations, especially when you're using procedural coordinates on a deforming animated object.

>> **Normal:** Choosing this socket causes the texture to be mapped according to the normal vectors along the surface of the object. This coordinate system is helpful for effects that require textures to react to the viewing angle of the camera.

>> **UV:** UV coordinates are probably the most precise way of mapping a texture to an object. NURBS surfaces have UV coordinates by default. For meshes, however, getting UV coordinates requires you to go through a process called unwrapping, covered later in this chapter in the "Unwrapping a Mesh" section. UV coordinates are the default coordinates for image textures.

>> **Object:** This neat option allows you to use a different object's location as a means of placing a texture on your object. To tell Blender which object you want to use, pick or type its name in the Object field at the bottom of the node. For example, you can load an image texture of a logo and place that logo on a model of a car by using the location, size, and orientation of an Empty. If you have no object selected in the Object field, then the Object coordinates socket refers only to *that* object's coordinates and not those of another object.

>> **Camera:** Camera coordinates are a way of getting a somewhat precise mapping based on the location and orientation of the camera.

>> **Window:** This coordinate system uses the coordinates from the finished render window. In other words, it uses the camera's coordinates. But unlike Camera coordinates, which keep the texture undistorted, this option always stretches the texture to fit the window's dimensions.

>> **Reflection:** The Reflection coordinate system uses the direction of a reflection vector to map your texture to the object. You can use this option with an environment map texture to get fake reflections when you don't need the accuracy of Cycles' ray tracing or Eevee's screen space reflections.

The basics of using the Texture Coordinate node work like this:

1. **Add a Texture Coordinate node (Add ⇨ Input ⇨ Texture Coordinate) to your material in the Shader Editor.**

2. **Connect the socket of your desired texture coordinate system to the Vector input socket on your chosen texture node in your material.**

   The texture node could be any of the ones available in the Shader Editor when you press Add ⇨ Texture. All of them have a blue Vector input socket on their left sides.

3. Optionally, add a Mapping node (Add ⇨ Vector ⇨ Mapping) and wire it on the noodle between your Texture Coordinate node and your texture node.

The Mapping node is what gives you more control over the texture coordinates on your object. They're the exact same controls available in each texture node's Texture Mapping panel in the Item tab of the Shader Editor's Sidebar. The difference is that because you're using a node, the results of the Mapping node can be shared with multiple texture nodes at the same time.

4. Connect the Color output socket on your texture node to the Color input socket on your desired shader node.

If you want your texture to influence the color of your diffuse shader, you explicitly connect it to the Diffuse BSDF node's Color socket or the Base Color socket of the Principled BSDF node. Want your grayscale texture to influence the roughness of your glossy shader? Connect it to the Roughness socket on a Glossy BSDF or the Principled BSDF. In a way, using nodes is a much more direct way of mapping and applying textures to a material, because you can zoom out on the node network and get a really complete understanding of the material all at once.

Figure 2-5 shows a simple node network that maps a single image to the surface of a sphere using Camera coordinates and the Mapping node.

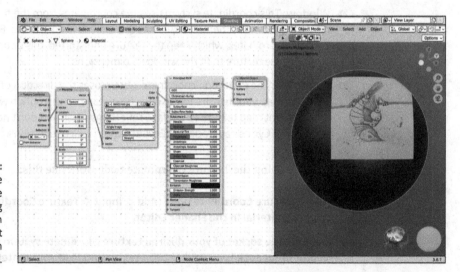

FIGURE 2-5:
Using the Texture Coordinate node and the Mapping node to put an image texture at a specific location on your object.

You may be reading all this and find yourself saying, "Great, but how do I fake having more detail with a bump map or a normal map?" Fortunately, that's also easy. If you have a texture (like the Noise texture) that you want to use as a bump map, all you need to do is wire it to the Displacement socket of the Material Output node, as shown in Figure 2-6. Easy!

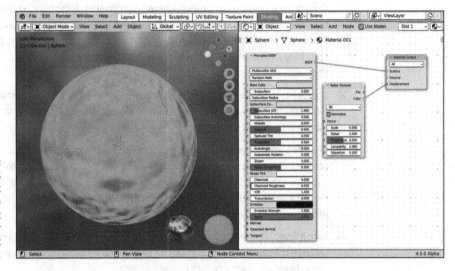

FIGURE 2-6:
Bump mapping is easy. Just connect your texture to the Displacement socket of your Material Output node.

TIP

If you want to have different bumps on different shaders in the same material, that's also possible, though a bit more complex. Rather than wire your Noise texture to the Displacement socket on the Material Output node, add a Bump node (Add ⇨ Vector ⇨ Bump) and wire your texture to its Height socket. Then wire the Normal output socket of your Bump node to the Normal input socket of any shader node. And voilà! Custom bumpiness on any shader!

Looking back at the Texture Coordinate node, if you have experience with other 3D software, you may notice that quite a few of the coordinate systems you might expect to find appear to be missing. Fortunately, the coordinate systems you're looking for are actually available; you just need to use a different node. Specifically, you need to use the Geometry node. This is for organizational reasons. Some coordinate systems have more to do with object geometry than they do with the texture. They're really independent of the texture. For that reason, Blender's developers felt it made more sense to organize them in the Geometry node (not to be confused with the Geometry Nodes covered in Book 2, Chapter 5). If you add it by pressing Add ⇨ Input ⇨ Geometry, you have the following sockets available:

>> **Position:** Choosing this socket uses the scene's coordinates to define the texture space. So if you have an animated object with a texture mapped this way, the texture will seem to be locked in place as the object moves across it. Global coordinates produce kind of a strange effect, but it's helpful in a few situations, such as faking shadows on a moving character.

>> **Normal:** At first, this may appear to be the same as the Normal socket in the Texture Coordinate node. However, the difference is in coordinate systems. This vector uses world-space coordinates, whereas the one from the Texture Coordinate node uses object-space coordinates. What this really means is that these normals always point the same way relative to the world, whereas Texture Coordinate normals move and rotate with your object. Generally speaking, most of the time you're going to want normals from the Texture Coordinate node.

>> **Tangent:** In some ways, this option is similar to Normal coordinates. However, instead of using the surface normal, it uses a tangent vector to map the texture coordinates.

>> **True Normal:** If your object is using smooth shading (most organic objects are) or bump mapping, that effect is achieved by manipulating the normals of a mesh. However, there are occasions where you want the "true" normal — the geometry's normal *before* those additional manipulations. The vector from this socket gives you that normal.

>> **Incoming:** The vector from this socket points back toward the camera. You can use this socket to influence the effect of a texture based on whether the underlying geometry points to the camera.

>> **Parametric:** This socket is typically for much more advanced use. It gives the actual world space coordinates of the *shading points* or the places on the surface of your object where a ray tracer's rays intersect it.

>> **Backfacing:** This is one of two non-vector sockets on the Geometry node. It's an array of 1s and 0s; 1s for the side of a face in your object that point along the same direction as the surface normal, and 0s for the sides that point in the opposite direction of the surface normal.

>> **Pointiness:** This socket is available only if you're rendering with Cycles (it's visible if you render with Eevee, but not functional). Like the Backfacing socket, this one is also not a vector value. Think of it as a grayscale value related to how curved the surface geometry of your object is. With this socket, you can procedurally control the placement of a color or material based on how concave your mesh is. Pointiness values are immensely useful if you want to darken concave parts of your mesh without using ambient occlusion (as described in Book 3, Chapter 3). You can also use it to show aging or wear on objects. Figure 2-7 shows an example of using the Pointiness values of a mesh's geometry to put rust in the creases.

>> **Random For Island:** Like the Pointiness socket, this one only works if you're rendering with Cycles. It's a pretty handy input, though. What it provides is a random value between 0 and 1 for each set of linked vertices in a mesh object (see Book 1, Chapter 4 for more on linked components within a mesh). Using this input, you can provide subtle variations to instances generated by the Array modifier (see Book 2, Chapter 2) or letters in a Text object (see Book 2, Chapter 4).

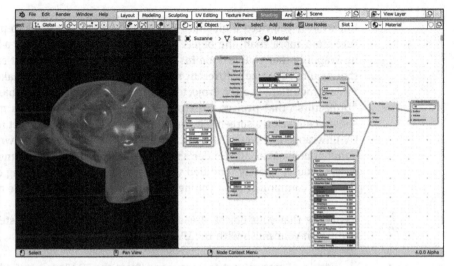

FIGURE 2-7:
Using the
Pointiness
socket, you can
procedurally add
rust on an object
in its creases,
where it's likely to
grow first.

Understanding Object coordinates and the UV Project modifier

Object coordinates are a funky set of coordinates to wrap your brain around. One typical use case is as I described in the preceding section: using the coordinates of one object to map them to your selected object. If you don't include a specific object to use for your mapping, then the data from the Object coordinates socket are primarily useful for getting undistorted procedural textures applied to your object.

REMEMBER

There are two main differences between Generated coordinates and Object coordinates (without a separate target Object):

» Generated coordinates "stick" to your object and Object coordinates do not. If your object is deformed by an animation rig, such as with an armature or lattice, and you're using Generated coordinates, the texture will move and deform with your object. If you're using Object coordinates, those deforming parts of the object will appear to slide under the texture — not usually the desired effect.

» Generated coordinates stretch a texture to the bounding box of your object, whereas Object coordinates impart no such distortion. This point is especially important if you're creating a procedural material that needs to look nice and unstretched, regardless of your object's size.

So there's a bit of a trade-off here. Fortunately, this trade-off isn't a frequent problem. If an object uses deforming animation (see Book 4, Chapters 3 and 4), you typically don't use procedural textures, so it's less common to use Object mapping on them.

But what if you need a bit more flexibility? Maybe you want to project the texture from more than one object, or perhaps you want to take advantage of UV unwrapping that you've done instead of mindlessly using Object coordinates. For that, you need to use a different method. Namely, you should make use of the UV Project modifier. The UV Project modifier treats one or more objects as external "projectors" that project a texture on your object much like a movie projector shows a movie on a screen. The only limitation is that your object must already be UV unwrapped. If you're working with a NURBS surface, the unwrapping is done automatically. Also, all Blender's mesh primitives come already unwrapped. However, if you've heavily modified your mesh object with modeling or sculpting — the more common case — you need to unwrap manually (see the next section).

Assuming that your object already is unwrapped, follow these steps to project a texture on your mesh with the UV Project modifier:

1. **Add an Empty object to your scene (from the 3D Viewport, Add ➪ Empty ➪ Plain Axes).**

   This Empty object is what you'll use as your "projector." The image texture will appear to project along the Empty's local Z-axis. I recommend giving this Empty a custom name like Projector, but you can leave it with its default name. Just remember that name.

2. **With your object selected, add a UV Project modifier from the Modifier tab of the Properties editor.**

   I know I'm drilling the point, but again, make sure that your object is already unwrapped.

3. **Fill in fields on the UV Project modifier.**

   (a) *(Optional) If your mesh has more than one UV unwrapping, use the UV Map field to choose the UV layer on which you want the UV Project modifier to work.*

   (b) *In the Object field below the Projectors value, pick the name of the Empty you're using as a projector. In this example, that Empty is named Projector.*

4. **Set up your material to use UV textures in the Shader Editor.**

   (a) *Add an Image Texture node (Add ➪ Texture ➪ Image Texture) and load an image texture from your hard drive.*

   By default, UV-mapped image textures *tile*, or repeat, when they reach the end of the image. If you don't want this repeating behavior, click the Extension drop-down menu in the Image Texture node (it's the third one down) and change it from Repeat to Clip.

   (b) *Connect the Color output socket of the Image Texture node to the Color input socket of the Principled BSDF node.*

With those steps complete, you should be able to move the Empty around and see the texture slide around the surface of your object in the 3D Viewport.

Figure 2-8 shows what your Blender screen layout might look like.

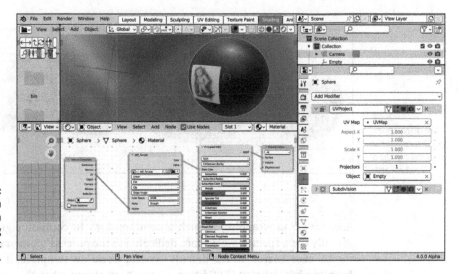

FIGURE 2-8: Positioning a texture on an object using the UV Project modifier.

If you create a separate UV layer in the UV Maps panel within Object Data Properties, you can apply the UV Project modifier on that layer. Then, using those modified UV coordinates (covered in the next section of this chapter), your decal texture is mapped without any need for that projector empty to remain in the scene.

TIP

You can use the same texture with multiple projectors by increasing the Projectors value in the UV Project modifier. When you increase the number of Projectors, you get additional projector object fields beneath it.

Unwrapping a Mesh

The most precise type of mapping you can use is UV mapping. UV mapping also allows you to take advantage of other Blender features, such as Texture Paint mode, the UV Project modifier (see the preceding section), and texture baking. With NURBS surfaces, you get UV coordinates for free as part of their structure. However, Blender is predominantly a mesh editor, and in order to get proper UV coordinates on your mesh objects, you must put those meshes through a process known as unwrapping.

To understand this process, think about a globe and a map of the world. The map of the world uses the latitude and longitude lines to relate a point on the three-dimensional surface of the globe to the two-dimensional surface of the map. In essence, the world map is an unwrapped texture on the globe, where the latitude and longitude lines are the UVs. Figure 2-9 shows a visualization of this process.

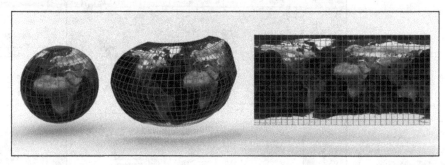

FIGURE 2-9:
UV unwrapping a 3D mesh is like making a map of the Earth.

NASA/Public domain

Because UV unwrapping is such a common task in computer graphics, Blender actually has a specific workspace dedicated to the process of unwrapping and editing UV coordinates. In the default General workflow template, it's the fourth tab from the left, labeled UV Editing. Figure 2-10 shows what this workspace screen layout looks like.

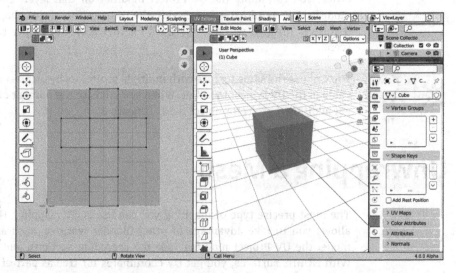

FIGURE 2-10:
The UV Editing workspace is, as you might expect, for editing UV coordinates.

REMEMBER

When you switch to the UV Editing workspace, Blender automatically switches your selected objects into Edit mode so you can get right to work with fewer button presses.

The UV Editing workspace is the Modeling workspace with two areas covering the majority of the Blender window. On the right, closest to the Outliner and Properties editor, is the familiar 3D Viewport, with your selected objects in Edit mode. On the left, there's a UV Editor. The UV Editor is where you edit the UV coordinates of your mesh.

Marking seams on a mesh

The basics of unwrapping a mesh in Blender is a two-step process of selecting all vertices (Select ⇨ All) in Edit mode and choosing UV ⇨ Unwrap from the 3D Viewport's header menu (or by using the U hotkey).

The UV menu has a variety of options, but unless your mesh is simple or a special case, you should use the first menu item, Unwrap. Blender has very powerful unwrapping tools, but to take full advantage of them, you need to first define some seams. Remember that you're trying to flatten a 3D surface to a 2D plane. To do so, you need to tell Blender where it can start pulling the mesh apart. This location on your mesh is a *seam*. If you were unwrapping a globe, you might choose the prime meridian as your seam. I like to think about seams for unwrapping in terms of stuffed animals, such as a teddy bear. The seam is where the bear is stitched together from flat pieces of cloth.

To add a seam to your mesh, follow these steps from the 3D Viewport:

1. **Tab into Edit mode and switch to Edge Select mode (Tab ⇨ 2).**

   You can also add seams from Vertex Select mode, but I find that it's easier in Edge Select.

2. **Select the series of edges you want to make into a seam.**

   Using edge loop selection (Alt+left-click) can really be helpful here. Everyone has their own tastes when it comes to defining seams, but a good general rule is to put the seams on parts of the mesh that are easier to hide (for example, behind the hairline on a character, the undercarriage of a car, and so on).

TIP

   Though edge loop selection can be helpful, it sometimes selects more edges than you want. So, a handy feature in Blender is Select ⇨ Select Linked ⇨ Shortest Path in the 3D Viewport's header menu (you can also get to this operator by searching for it using Blender's integrated search

Giving Models Texture

when pressing F3). For an even faster way, you can just use the mouse with the following steps:

(a) *Select one vertex or edge.*

(b) *Ctrl+select another vertex or edge.*

With the Select Shortest Path feature, if you select two vertices or edges, Blender will select the shortest path of edges from one to the other. That path often works very well as a seam for unwrapping.

3. **Choose Edge ⇨ Mark Seam to mark your selected edges as a seam.**

Seams on your mesh are highlighted in red. If you mistakenly make a seam with the wrong edges, you can remove the seam by selecting those edges and choosing Edge ⇨ Clear Seam.

With your seams defined, you're ready to unwrap your mesh (UV ⇨ Unwrap).

Adding a test grid

The next thing you need is an image for mapping to your mesh. Using a *test grid* — an image with a colored checkerboard pattern — is common practice when unwrapping. A test grid is helpful for trying to figure out where the texture is *stretched*, or unevenly mapped, on your mesh. To add a test grid, go to the UV Editor and choose Image ⇨ New or press Alt+N. A floating panel like the one in Figure 2-11 appears. Name the image something sensible, such as Test Grid, and choose either Color Grid or UV Grid from the Generated Type drop-down menu. Leave the other settings at their defaults for now and click OK. The UV Editor updates interactively.

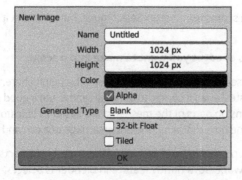

FIGURE 2-11:
The New Image floating panel for adding a test grid image.

TIP

You can unwrap your mesh without adding a test grid, but a test grid gives you a good frame of reference to work from when unwrapping.

Also, note the height and width of the test grid image. The most obvious thing is that it's square; the height and width are equal. When you create the image, you can make it non-square, but UV texturing is often optimized for square images (particularly in some game engines), so consider where your 3D model will be used; if it makes sense, keep its image textures square.

Another tip that helps performance when working with UV textures (especially for video games) is to make your texture size a *power of two* — a number you get by continually multiplying 2 by itself. The default size is 1,024 pixels square, or 2^{10}. The next larger size is 2,048 (2^{11}) pixels, and the next size down would be 512 (2^9) pixels. This strange sizing is because computer memory is measured and accessed in values that are powers of two. So even if you're not using your 3D model in a video game, it's still a good idea to stick to the power of two guideline. It's an easy guide to stick to, and every little bit of performance optimization helps, especially when you start rendering (see Book 3, Chapter 4).

Generating and editing UV coordinates

After marking seams on your mesh and adding a test grid for reference, *now* you're ready to unwrap your mesh. From Edit mode, unwrapping is pretty simple:

1. **Select all vertices (Select ⇨ All).**

2. **Unwrap the mesh (UV ⇨ Unwrap).**

    Poof! Your mesh is now unwrapped! If you used a Suzanne to practice unwrapping, you may have something that looks like Figure 2-12.

TIP

    Technically, Suzanne and all the other mesh objects in Blender are already UV unwrapped by default. They just don't have any seams marked.

REMEMBER

If you look at your object in the 3D Viewport, you might be surprised that you don't see your test grid in Material Preview or Rendered viewport shading. The reason you don't see the image is pretty simple: Even though you loaded the image in the UV Editor, you never added that image as a texture on your object. From the UV Editing workspace, you can still do this pretty quickly:

1. **Quickly change the UV Editor to a Shader Editor.**

    You can use the Editor Type menu in the UV Editor's header, but you can make this switch more quickly by using the Shift+F3 hotkey combination and cycle through each of the different node editors until you get to the Shader Editor.

Giving Models Texture

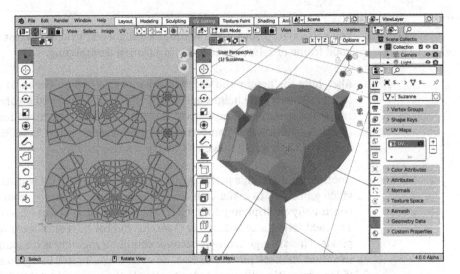

FIGURE 2-12:
An unwrapped
Suzanne head.

2. **In your Shader Editor, drag an Image Texture node from the base color of your main shader node.**

   Recall from the previous chapter that clicking and dragging from a socket gives you a menu where you can search for the node you want (in this case, Image Texture ⇨ Color). If you have a simple material with just a Principled BSDF, you just wire the Image Texture node to the Base Color socket.

3. **Choose your test grid image from the Image datablock in the Image Texture node.**

   If you named your test grid something sensible (like Test Grid), then it should be pretty easy to find. Once you choose your test grid image, the 3D Viewport should update to show your image on your mesh (assuming you're using Material Preview or Rendered viewport shading).

4. **Switch the area with your Shader Editor back to being the UV Editor.**

   Again, you can use the Editor Type menu in the header, or you can get there more quickly by switching over to the Shading workspace using the tabs at the top of the Blender window.

From this point, you can edit your UV layout to arrange the pieces in a logical fashion and minimize stretching. You can tell a texture is stretched with your test grid. If any of the squares on the checkerboard look distorted or grotesquely non-square-shaped, stretching has taken place.

Just like in the 3D Viewport, the UV Editor has a Toolbar along its left side with a similar set of tools. In fact, the first seven tools on the Toolbar are identical to those in the 3D Viewport. The only minor difference is that the UV Editor has a

2D cursor, rather than a 3D cursor like in the 3D Viewport. Furthermore, the Grab (G), Rotate (R), and Scale (S) hotkeys all work as expected, as well as the various selection hotkeys for Box select (B) and Circle select (C).

REMEMBER

Unlike the tools in the 3D Viewport's Toolbar, the UV Editor's Toolbar tools don't have their properties appear in the Tool tab of the Properties editor. Instead, you need to use the tool settings in the Topbar of the UV Editor's header. Alternatively, you can use the Tool tab of the Sidebar (N).

In addition to the familiar tools, there are also four more tools that give you more brush-like control when editing your UV coordinates:

» **Rip Region:** With the Rip Region tool, you can select a series of components (edges, vertices, or faces) and then left-click and drag anywhere in the 3D Viewport to separate, or *rip*, that selected region to be its own island. The Rip Region tool does this without adding any geometry to your object in the 3D Viewport. It can do this ripping operation because, as far as your computer is concerned, every vertex that has more than one edge connected to it is actually a collection of vertices living in the same space. You treat them all as a single vertex in the 3D Viewport. However, in the UV Editor, you have the ability to rip them into islands if that makes the unwrapping result more pleasant.

» **Grab:** In a way, this tool is like the Move tool with Proportional Editing enabled. The difference is that because this tool behaves more like a brush, it gives you a much more fluid editing experience. In addition to that, the settings for this tool (visible in the UV Editor's Sidebar) allow you to enable pressure sensitivity if you happen to be working with a pressure sensitive drawing tablet. The other two tools in this list also support pressure sensitivity.

» **Relax:** This tool is similar to the Smooth tool when sculpting (see Book 2, Chapter 3), but it's not exactly the same. Basically, any vertices that are within the brush area for this tool get pushed out to the brush edge. The Relax tool can be very helpful in reducing UV stretching. When using this tool, you may want to enable the Lock Borders check box in its tool options. That option prevents the outer borders of UV islands from being moved by this tool.

» **Pinch:** The Pinch tool is also very much like its doppelganger in Sculpt mode. Its behavior is the inverse of the Relax brush. Vertices that fall within the brush area get pulled in towards the brush's center.

If you're trying to fix stretching, you may notice that moving some vertices in your UV layout to fix stretching in one place distorts and causes stretching in another. To help with this problem, Blender offers you two features: vertex pinning

Giving Models Texture

(UV ⇨ Pin) and Live Unwrap (UVs ⇨ Live Unwrap). They actually work together. The workflow goes something like these steps:

1. **In the UV Editor, select the vertices that you want to define as *control vertices*.**

   The control vertices are usually the vertices at the top and bottom of the center line of a character mesh and some corner vertices. I tend to prefer using vertices that are on the seam, but sometimes using internal vertices is also helpful.

2. **Pin these selected vertices (UV ⇨ Pin or use the P hotkey).**

   The vertices now appear larger and are a bright red color. If you want to unpin a vertex, select it and choose UV ⇨ Unpin or press Alt+P.

3. **Turn on Live Unwrap (UVs ⇨ Live Unwrap).**

   If a check mark appears to the left of this menu item, you know it's currently enabled.

4. **Select one or more pinned vertices and move them around.**

   As you edit these pinned vertices, all the other vertices in the UV layout automatically shift and adjust to compensate for this movement and help reduce stretching.

REMEMBER

When using pinned vertices and Live Unwrap, selecting and moving unpinned vertices isn't normally going to be very helpful. The moment you select and move a pinned vertex, any manual changes you made to unpinned vertices are obliterated.

TIP

If your computer seems to be performing slowly while editing UV coordinates, you can disable Blender's live updating feature. You can toggle it from the UV Editor's header menu by choosing View ⇨ Update Automatically.

Painting Textures Directly on a Mesh

If you followed the earlier sections in this chapter, you have an unwrapped mesh and a texture on it that doesn't stretch. Woohoo! But say that, for some crazy reason, you don't want your object to have a checkerboard as a texture, and you want to actually use this UV layout to paint a texture for your mesh. You can either paint directly on the mesh from within Blender or export the UV layout to paint in an external program like Substance Painter, Krita, or Photoshop. I actually prefer to use a combination of these methods. I normally paint directly on the mesh in Blender to rough out the color scheme and perhaps create some bump and specularity maps. Then I export that image along with an image of the UV layout to get more detailed painting done in an external program.

Preparing to paint

After you have an unwrapped mesh, the starting point for painting textures on it is Blender's Texture Paint workspace. The Texture Paint workspace is one tab to the right of the UV Editing workspace (you can get there quickly by pressing Ctrl+PageDown). When you switch to the Texture Paint workspace, Blender automatically switches your selection to Texture Paint mode. Figure 2-13 shows an unwrapped Suzanne in the Texture Paint workspace, ready to paint.

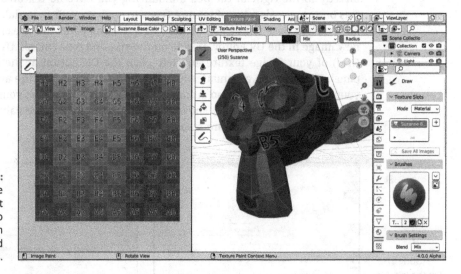

FIGURE 2-13:
You can use the Texture Paint workspace to paint textures on your unwrapped meshes.

Of course, you aren't required to paint from the Texture Paint workspace. You can activate Texture Paint mode from any workspace with a 3D Viewport by left-clicking the mode button in the 3D Viewport's header. Alternatively, Texture Paint mode is available from the pie that appears when you press Ctrl+Tab.

TIP

If you happen to try to enter Texture Paint mode on an object that doesn't have any UV layers, Blender will let you know in the Tool tab of the Properties editor. There may be a warning that says "UV Map Needed." In that case, Blender offers a button, Add Simple UVs, that quickly unwraps your mesh for you without seams.

REMEMBER

Although it's tempting to use this means of unwrapping rather than the steps covered in the preceding section, I don't recommend it (especially if you intend on finalizing your image texture in an external painting program). That said, Blender's texture painting tools have gotten a lot more powerful over the years.

So, if you plan to paint your textures *only* within Blender, the simple UV unwrap you get from clicking this button may be sufficient for your needs. As always, it's about knowing what you want and accepting certain trade-offs based on that knowledge.

Even with your mesh unwrapped, if your material doesn't feature any Image Texture nodes, the Texture Slots panel of Tool Properties will state that you have "No Textures." This warning appears because you need an image texture (even a blank one) so Blender knows what you're painting on.

You can add an image texture to your material as described in the first section of this chapter, but there's also a convenience button labeled with a Plus (+) symbol directly to the right of the box announcing you have no textures. Left-clicking this button reveals a list of texture types to apply to your material. After you pick one (such as Base Color), Blender shows a floating panel like the one for adding a new image in the UV Editor. Decide on the size and type (Blank, UV Grid, or Color Grid) of your image texture and left-click the OK button at the bottom of the panel. Blender then automatically generates your image texture and applies it to your material. (Blender also automatically connects sockets to your shader in the Shader Editor.) Figure 2-14 shows Tool Properties in Texture Paint mode before and after these warnings are resolved.

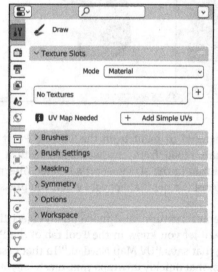
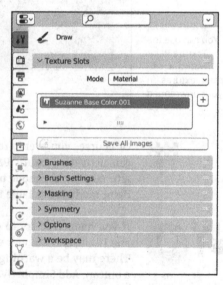

FIGURE 2-14:
On the left, the Tool tab of the Properties editor in Texture Paint mode if your material has no UVs or textures applied to it. On the right is the same tab after resolving those issues.

TIP

After you add your first paint slot, you can add additional ones from that Texture Slots panel instead of adding images in the Shader Editor. Many Blender artists tend to use these slots like layers in a 2D painting program such as Krita or Photoshop.

Working in Texture Paint mode

From here, things are pretty similar to Vertex Paint mode (see Book 3, Chapter 1), but with more that you can do. There are more tools in the Toolbar, and Tool Properties has a much wider array of options. In fact, the controls for Texture Paint mode share even more similarities with Sculpt mode than Vertex Paint mode (though Texture Paint mode has a lot fewer tools than Sculpt mode does).

For Texture Paint mode, you have the following tools available in both the 3D Viewport *and* the Image Editor:

>> **Draw:** As with Vertex Paint mode, described in the previous chapter, the Draw tool allows you to paint a chosen color on your image texture. Unlike Vertex Paint's Draw tool, it doesn't matter what's going on with the underlying geometry. You paint in the 3D Viewport or the Image Editor, and your color shows up right where you click and drag.

>> **Soften:** The Soften tool blurs your image texture wherever you paint with it. This tool works just like blur brushes in other digital painting programs.

>> **Smear:** With the Smear tool you can smudge your image texture. If you've ever worked with traditional painting or drawing tools in meatspace, this tool is the equivalent of using a smudge stick, or rubbing your thumb across wet paint.

>> **Clone:** If you're familiar with clone brushes in digital painting software, this tool works the same way. Rather than painting with a specific color, you're painting with colors sourced from some kind of reference. That reference could be from the same texture you're working on (for example, you may want to replicate skin colors in another part of your image) or a separate reference image altogether. The key is in how you define that reference. Depending on whether you're using the Clone tool in the 3D Viewport or the Image Editor, there are different ways to set your reference:

- **From the 3D Viewport:** If you're cloning in the 3D Viewport, you use the 3D cursor as your Clone tool's reference. Ctrl+left-click on your mesh and Blender will use the pixels under the 3D cursor as the reference for when you paint. Each time you lift your brush and place it down again (or release your mouse button and left-click again if you're using a mouse), the Clone tool resets to that reference point you set with the 3D cursor.

- **From the Image Editor:** Within the Image Editor, the Clone tool works a little differently. You don't set a reference using the 2D cursor. Instead, you explicitly define your image reference. To tell Blender what image you want to reference (even if it's the same image you're working on) expand the Tool tab of the Image Editor's Sidebar and look in the Brush panel. In the Advanced sub-panel of the Brush Settings panel, there's an Image field. By default, it's blank, but if you click that field, you can select an image datablock in your .blend file. Once you choose your image, it will appear superimposed over your actual image texture. Using right-click and drag, you can adjust the position of your reference image. Then, when you paint in the Image Editor, whatever part of the image that's under your brush is what's applied to the image texture that you're painting.

 » **Fill:** The Fill tool in Vertex Paint mode also has slightly different behaviors depending on whether you're painting in the 3D Viewport or the Image Editor.

- **In the 3D Viewport:** If you're using the Fill tool in the 3D Viewport, the default behavior is just to fill your whole mesh with whatever color you have selected according to the Strength value you set in Tool Properties.

 However, if you enable the Paint Mask button in the 3D Viewport's header, you can select individual faces on your mesh, and the Fill tool will only put color in the faces you've selected. The Paint Mask feature also works for the other tools in Texture Paint mode.

- **In the Image Editor:** The Fill tool works differently in the Image Editor. Rather than working within the constraints of your mesh, the Fill tool in the Image Editor works on the pixels of your image, much like the bucket fill tool in Photoshop or GIMP. If you click on a pixel with the Fill tool in the Image Editor, Blender evaluates all the pixels connected to it and any pixels that are a similar color will be filled with the color you pick for the Fill tool. You can control the threshold of how similar colors have to be by adjusting the Fill Threshold slider in the Tool tab of the Image Editor's Sidebar.

 » **Mask:** While you paint, you may find it necessary to temporarily block off parts of your mesh so they don't get messed up while you paint on other parts. You could use the Paint Mask feature just described, but what if you need to mask something out that doesn't follow the flow of your geometry? It's that situation where the Mask tool is incredibly helpful. That said, even though you can select the Mask tool in the Image Editor, it only really works in the 3D Viewport. The workflow goes something like this:

 1. **In the 3D Viewport, enable the Mask tool.**

2. **From Tool Properties, expand the Masking panel.**

3. **Within the Masking panel, enable and expand the Stencil Mask sub-panel.**

The main control you want to pay attention to is the Stencil Image datablock. You can choose any image you want here, but if you haven't yet created a mask, it's best to make a new image like in the next step.

4. **Click the New button in the Stencil Image datablock.**

   In this case, your new image should be all black. Black pixels on your mask image are pixels that can be painted through, whereas white pixels are ones that block painting.

5. **Back in the 3D Viewport, paint your mask.**

   Your paint marks appear as black paint over your mesh. Don't worry, your actual paint job is still there; the mask is just an overlay.

6. **Switch to one of the other Texture Paint tools (such as Draw or Fill) and start painting.**

   If you look in the Image Editor while you paint in the 3D Viewport, you should notice that anything that's under your mask doesn't get affected by your paint strokes.

7. **When you're done using your mask for painting, disable the check box next to the Stencil Mask sub-panel in the Masking panel within Tool Properties.**

   Your paint job in the 3D Viewport should now look just like the results in the Image Editor. Now you're free to continue painting without a mask.

Using textures on your Draw tool

When you have the Draw tool active, you may have moments where you don't want to paint with a perfectly round brush shape. Maybe you want to have a brush that's square, or you want your brush to be uneven and mottled. In digital painting applications, libraries of specialized brushes are often available that give you these specific kinds of brush shapes and effects. In Blender, you can get similar behavior by leveraging Blender's built-in texture system.

Have a look in Tool Properties when you have the Draw tool active. In the Brush Settings panel, there's a Texture sub-panel where you can choose a texture for your brush, so you're not just painting flat colors. It's possible to add a new brush texture from this panel by clicking the New button in the Texture datablock, but doing so creates only a blank image.

The place where you define brush textures is actually in Texture Properties, shown in Figure 2-15. It's the same basic process as using textures for tools in Sculpt mode (see Book 2, Chapter 3). As a matter of fact, you can use these exact same brush textures with both Sculpt mode tools and Texture Paint tools.

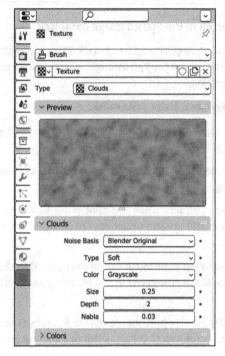

FIGURE 2-15:
Create custom
textures for
painting in
Texture
Properties.

The basic steps for making a custom brush texture are pretty straightforward:

1. **Choose your texture type from the Type drop-down menu at the top.**

   The choices in this menu are almost (but not exactly) identical to the choices
   you have available in terms of texture nodes in the Shader Editor. Here's a
   quick rundown:

   - **None:** No texture at all. You probably won't ever choose this option.
     I never do.

   - **Blend:** This texture type is a Gradient texture. Expanding the Colors panel
     for this texture reveals a built-in color ramp in a sub-panel
     so you can have more control over its gradient.

   - **Clouds:** This texture type is the rough equivalent of what you have
     available in the Noise texture node in the Shader Editor.

   - **Distorted Noise:** The Distorted Noise texture is pretty slick. Actually, strike
     that; this type of texture is best suited to very rough, complex surfaces. The
     way the Distorted Noise texture works is pretty cool, though. You use one
     procedural noise texture, specified by the Noise Distortion menu, to distort
     and influence the texture of your noise basis. With this combination, you
     can get some really unique textures.

- **Image or Movie:** This texture type is the same as loading an Image texture node in the Shader Editor. This is also the default texture type that Blender chooses when you first add a new Brush texture.

- **Magic:** The Magic texture type here is joyously the same as the one in the Shader Editor.

- **Marble:** The Marble texture and the Wood texture (described a little later in this list) are both facets of the Wave texture node in the Shader Editor. The Marble texture has built-in noise among its stripes.

- **Musgrave:** The Musgrave texture type for brushes is nearly identical to its counterpart in the Shader Editor.

- **Noise:** Don't let the naming confuse you too much. This Noise texture type actually has no relation whatsoever with the Noise texture node in the Shader Editor. This texture type is more akin to the White Noise node.

- **Stucci:** Stucci is a nice organic texture that's most useful for creating bump maps. The Stucci texture is great for industrial and architectural materials like stucco, concrete, and asphalt. This texture is also handy if you just want to give your brush a little variety and roughen it up a bit.

- **Voronoi:** Though the brush version of this texture has more built-in controls than its corresponding node in the Shader Editor, the two are roughly the same.

- **Wood:** The Wood texture type is the less noisy, straight-laced cousin of the Marble texture type. As I mention earlier, these two textures together give you the functionality that's mirrored in the Wave texture node within the Shader Editor.

2. **After choosing your texture type, tweak its settings.**

   Most of the time, this step involves adjusting specific properties in the panels below the texture preview. For most of the texture types mentioned in the preceding step, you may want to play with changing the Noise Basis value or tweaking color properties in the Colors panel.

3. **Switch back to Tool Properties and prepare to start painting.**

   If you're using the Tool tab in the 3D Viewport's or Image Editor's Sidebar, no switching is necessary. You can get started painting immediately and keep Texture Properties available so you can tweak your texture as you go.

Technically speaking, once you've created a texture or two, you can get right to painting. If you've created multiple brush textures, you can switch between them by clicking the texture preview at the top of the Texture sub-panel in Tool Properties. That said, there is one more specific control for textures you may want to play around with in the Texture sub-panel of Tool Properties. Specifically, the Mapping drop-down allows you a lot of flexibility in how the brush behaves as you move it over your mesh. It's the same detail as described in Book 2, Chapter 3 for sculpting, so I recommend you refer to that chapter if you need a refresher.

 The controls in Texture Properties should be sufficient for the majority of custom brush textures you want to create. However, if you want to make something truly custom, then the place to go is the Texture Node Editor. Maybe you want a procedural texture that uses a brick or checker pattern. Or maybe you have a killer image texture of dirt you want to use, but you need to do some node-based adjustments to it so it tiles cleanly. That's just a taste of the kinds of things you can do from the Texture Node Editor.

To use the Texture Node Editor, you first need to switch an area to use it. If you're working in the Texture Paint workspace, I would suggest that you temporarily change your Image Editor area to the Texture Node Editor. You can do so using the Editor Type drop-down in the header or by repeatedly pressing the Shift+F3 hotkey combination to cycle through Blender's various node editors.

 When you arrive at the Texture Node Editor, you have just a few small steps to take before you can use it to customize a brush texture:

1. **Use the Texture Type drop-down in the header to choose the Brush texture type.**

    Your texture from Texture Properties should already be visible in the Texture datablock in the Texture Node Editor's header; however, there aren't any nodes visible. You need to tell Blender that you want to use a node network rather than the settings in the Properties editor to define this texture.

2. **Toggle the Use Nodes check box in the header to enable the use of nodes for your chosen texture.**

    After you enable the Use Nodes check box, you should see a pair of nodes in the Texture Node Editor.

Once you activate nodes for your brush texture, you're off to the races. If you've become familiar with the Shader Editor and the Compositor, then quite a few of the nodes here will be familiar. You can create any brush texture that's available in Texture Properties, but that's only the beginning. You have a real node-based interface in front of you with all the power that comes with it to make some truly incredible brush textures.

There's only one caveat to using the Texture Node Editor for brush textures: Performance. If you have an older computer and you make a huge, complex node network to define a brush texture, your machine may not have enough power to let Blender show your paint strokes in real time. You have great power here. Just use it wisely.

Saving Painted Textures and Exporting UV Layouts

Of course, despite the cool things that you can do with Blender's Texture Paint mode, some things are just easier in a graphics program built for painting textures. You could use 2D painting programs like Krita or Photoshop, but these days it's more common for texture artists to work with Substance Painter or Mari. Whichever tool you're using, you need to get the image and UVs out of Blender and into that other program. To work on your image in another program, save the texture you already painted as an external image. You also need to get your UV layout to these other tools.

To save your painted texture, go to the Image Editor and choose Image ⇨ Save As. A File Browser appears, allowing you to save the image to your hard drive in any format you like. I prefer to use PNG because it has small file sizes and lossless compression.

Regardless of whether you're continuing to paint on your texture in an external program, I *strongly* recommend that you save your image file externally anyway. Not only do you reduce the size of your .blend file, but it also serves as a completion milestone that you can always come back to, like a save point in a video game. And from the perspective of a person who's paranoid about data safety (like me), external saving ensures that your texture is preserved if your .blend file becomes corrupt or unreadable. It's a credo I have whenever I do anything with a computer: Save early, save often, save multiple copies.

Even though Blender warns you about this when you save, it's worth emphasizing that if you don't explicitly save your image texture, it *will not* be saved with your .blend file. If you close Blender and then re-open the file, all your painting will be lost. There are only two workarounds for this:

>> **Save your image externally.** As described in the preceding paragraphs, choose Image ⇨ Save As from the Image Editor.

>> **Pack your image in your .blend file.** Also from the Image Editor, choose Image ⇨ Pack. This bundles the image in your .blend file so it will be there when you re-open the file.

In either case, if you continue to paint on your texture in Blender, you will need to continue to either save it externally or repack it to avoid losing your changes.

With your image saved, the next thing you probably want out of Blender for your 2D image editor is the UV layout of your object. The way you go about getting your

UVs out of Blender is going to vary depending on the tool you're using to continue your painting. Most modern tools used for texture painting have the ability to load your 3D model and read your UV layout from that. You just need to export to a format that these programs understand. The two typical go-to's for this are FBX and OBJ. Being the more modern format, I recommend you start with FBX. Export to FBX using File ⇨ Export ⇨ FBX (.fbx). If the FBX file doesn't work for you, try OBJ by navigating to File ⇨ Export ⇨ Wavefront (.obj). In both these exporters, the default settings also include the UV coordinates for your mesh, so you should be good to go there.

If you're using an older workflow or a 2D painting tool that can't load 3D geometry, you need to take a different approach. You need to export your UV layout as an image so you can use that as a reference when painting in 2D. To export the UV layout, you need to be in the UV Editor while in Edit mode. The fastest way to do this is to just switch to the UV Editing workspace with the Ctrl+PageUp hotkey combination. Navigate to UV ⇨ Export UV Layout. This opens a File Browser where you can choose where to save your UV layout on your hard drive.

This UV export feature gives you the option (in the last panel of the left sidebar in the File Browser) to save in the familiar PNG image format as well as two other formats: SVG and EPS. Both SVG (Scalable Vector Graphics) and EPS (Encapsulated PostScript) are vector image formats. If your UV layout is in a vector format, you can scale it to fit any image size you need without losing any resolution. So you can use the same UV layout file to paint both low-resolution and high-resolution textures.

TIP

Most graphics applications should be able to read SVG files just fine. If you run into a problem, though, I recommend opening the SVG in Krita (www.krita.org) or Inkscape (www.inkscape.org). Both applications are powerful open source graphics programs, and freely available to download from their websites. You can edit your UV texture directly in these programs, or you can use them to convert the SVG file to a raster format that your graphics application of choice recognizes, such as PNG or TIFF.

Chapter **3**

Lighting and Environment

I n terms of getting the work you create in Blender out to a finalized still image or animation, having your scene's environment and lighting set up properly is incredibly important. It goes hand in hand with setting up materials on your object (see Book 3, Chapter 1) and the rendering process (see the next chapter). Without light, the camera — and, by extension, the renderer — can't see a thing. You could create the most awesome 3D model or animation in the world, but if it's poorly lit, it won't be turning any heads.

This chapter covers the types of lights available to you in Blender and details some of the best practices to use them in your scenes. In addition to lighting details, I go into setting up the environment in your scene with the settings in World Properties. In many ways, the topics covered in this chapter are what give your scenes that final polish, making them look really good.

Lighting a Scene

Lighting has an incredible amount of power to convey your scene to the viewer. Harsh, stark lighting can give you a dramatic film noir look. Low-angle lights with long shadows can give you a creepy horror movie feeling, and brighter high-angle lights can make things look like they are taking place during a beautiful summer day. Or, you can use a bluish light that projects a hard-noise cloud texture and makes your scene feel like it's happening under water.

Equally important is setting up your environment. Depending on how you set it up, you can achieve a variety of looks. You can set your scene in an infinitely large white space, commonly known as *the white void* in film and television. Or, you can adjust your environment such that your scene takes place outside during the day or somewhere on the moon. When you combine good lighting and a few additional tricks, you can make your scene take place just about anywhere. Figure 3-1 shows a pretty simple scene with a few different environment and lighting schemes to illustrate this point.

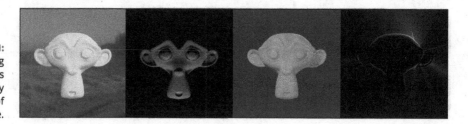

FIGURE 3-1: Different lighting configurations can drastically affect the look of a scene.

Understanding a basic three-point lighting setup

Before I get too deep into how you light a scene in Blender, you should understand some standard lighting setups and terminology. The cool thing is that most of this information isn't limited to use in 3D computer graphics. It's actually pretty standard in professional film, video, and photography. In fact, quite a few photographers and directors like to use 3D graphics as a form of previsualization to test out lighting setups before arriving on set for the actual shoot. (And you thought you were just making pretty pictures on a computer screen! Ha!)

One of the most common ways to arrange lights is called *three-point lighting*. As the name implies, it involves the use of three different sets of lights. It's a common studio setup for interviews, and it's the starting point for nearly all other lighting arrangements. Figure 3-2 shows a top-down diagram of a typical three-point lighting setup.

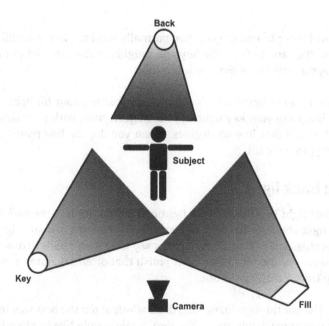

FIGURE 3-2:
A typical
three-point
lighting setup.

Back

Subject

Key

Camera

Fill

The key light

Setting up a three-point lighting scheme starts with placing your subject at the center of the scene and aiming your camera at that subject. Then you set up your main light, the *key light*. The key light is usually the most powerful light in the scene. It's where your main shadows come from, as well as your brightest highlights. Typically, you should set this light just to the left or just to the right of your camera, and it usually should be higher than your subject. This placement is to ensure that the shadows fall naturally, and you don't get that creepy flashlight-under-the-chin look that your friends used for telling scary stories around the campfire.

The fill light

After your key light is established, the next light you want to place is the *fill light*. The purpose of the fill light is to brighten up the dark parts of your subject. The key light is great for putting shadows on your subject, but without any other light, your shadows end up being very dark, obscuring your subject. Unless you're aiming for a dramatic lighting effect, this look is not what you normally want. The fill light tends to be less powerful than the key, but you want it to have a wider, more diffuse fill area. For example, a flashlight has a narrow fill area, whereas fluorescent lights like the ones used in office buildings have a fill area that's wider. You want this wide fill area on your fill because it reduces the amount of highlights and softens the shadows generated by this light. Typically, you don't want hard highlights and shadows from your fill to compete with those from your key. As far as placement goes, you normally want to place your fill on the opposite side of the camera from the key and roughly at the same height as your subject, perhaps a little lower than your key light.

TIP

Here's a way to figure out a good place to position your fill light. Draw an imaginary line from your key light to your subject. Now, with your subject as the pivot point, rotate that line 90 degrees. When you do, the line points right where you should place the fill.

The back light

The last light in a three-point lighting configuration is the *back light* or *rim light*. This light shines at the back of your subject, creating a small edge of light around the profile. That sliver of light helps separate your subject from the background and serves as the nice little bit of polish that often separates a mediocre lighting setup from a really good one.

Now, I've sat through many long discussions about the best way to position a back light (yes, my friends are nerds, too). Some people like to place it directly opposite from the key light, which works well, but sometimes the rim effect competes with the key's highlights. Other people prefer placing it opposite to the camera, which, too, is a good way to go, but if the subject moves, you risk the possibility of blinding the audience. And yet another group of people recommend placing the back light opposite to the fill. This approach can create a nice rim of light that complements the key, but it also has the possibility of looking a bit unnatural. As you can see, everything is a trade-off when it comes to lighting. In fact, the only really consistent thing that people agree on is that the back light should generally point toward the subject. The bottom line is that the best course of action is to play around with your back light and see for yourself where you get the best results. Figure 3-3 shows the effect of different back-light configurations on a simple scene with Suzanne.

FIGURE 3-3:
Suzanne, lit with the back light placed a few different ways.

 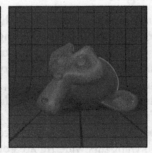 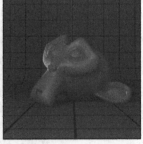

Backlight Opposite Key Light   Backlight Opposite Camera   Backlight Opposite Fill Light

As for the power and fill area, you should typically use a less powerful back light than your key so things appear natural. The fill area can vary because the highlights are all on the opposite side of your subject. I personally like to keep it narrow, but a wide fill area can work nicely for large scenes.

That's basic three-point lighting for you. It works well in computer graphics as well as the "real world," and it's the starting point for most other lighting configurations. Lower the angle of your key to make your subject creepy. Remove or reduce the power of your fill and back lights to get more dramatic shadows. Place your key behind your subject to get a mysterious or romantic silhouette. And that's just the tip of the iceberg!

Knowing when to use which type of light

After you're familiar with the basic principles of three-point lighting, you can use that knowledge to light your scenes in Blender. To add a new light, use Add ⇨ Light and you see the menu shown in Figure 3-4.

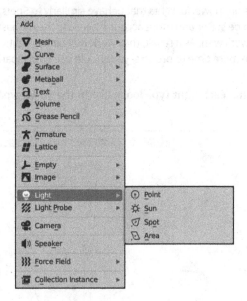

FIGURE 3-4:
Adding a light in the 3D Viewport.

REMEMBER

Although the lights listed in this section are available in both Cycles and Eevee, it's common to use *mesh lights* (that is, using meshes as lights in your scene) than light objects in Cycles. See the section later in this chapter titled "Using mesh lights in Cycles" for more on setting up and using mesh lights. Of course, some lights, like the Spot and Sun lights, are still very useful in Cycles as well as Eevee, so it's worth reading through this section if you've chosen Cycles as your renderer.

The Light menu (Add ⇨ Light) offers you the following types of lights to choose from:

>> **Point:** This type of light is sometimes also referred to as an *omni light,* meaning that the light is located at a single point in space and light emanates in all directions from that point. The default Blender scene has a single light of this type. The Point light is a good general-purpose light, but I prefer to use it as secondary illumination or as a fill light.

>> **Sun:** The Sun light represents a single universal light that comes from a single direction. Because of this single source, the location of the Sun light in your scene doesn't really matter; only its orientation is relevant. This type of light is the only one that affects the look of the sky in your Blender scene's world and is well-suited as a key light for scenes set outdoors.

>> **Spot:** In many ways, the Spot is the workhorse of CG lighting. It works quite a bit like a flashlight or a theater spotlight, and of all the light types, it gives you the most control over the nature of the shadows and where light lands. Because of this control, Spots are fantastic key lights.

>> **Area:** Area lights are powerful lights that behave similarly to Spots; however, the shadows tend to be softer and more accurate because they're based on having a grid of lights to work with. As a result, they work well for key lights, but because they tend to take more time to process, you should use them sparingly.

Figure 3-5 shows what each light type looks like in the 3D Viewport.

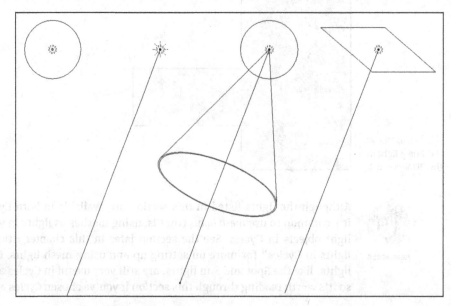

FIGURE 3-5:
From left to right, Point, Sun, Spot, and Area lights.

TIP

Each light has some pretty cool control widgets for adjusting their settings on the fly. If you bring your mouse cursor close to your Point light, the cursor icon changes to look a bit like a compass. Click and drag your mouse from here, and you can adjust the influence radius of the light. On each of the other lights (Sun, Spot, and Area), there's a line coming from them that indicates the direction the light is pointing. Along that line, there's a yellow circle. Using your mouse cursor, you can click and drag that dot to quickly adjust the direction that the light is pointing. And in the case of the Spot light, there's also a cyan arrow you can click and drag to adjust the fill area size of the light. You can, of course, adjust these settings by manually rotating the light or adjusting values in Object Data Properties (more on that later in this chapter), but these widgets give you quick controls so you don't have to leave the 3D Viewport to get the results you want.

Universal light options

When you've chosen a type of light and added it to the scene, the controls to modify these lights are in Object Data Properties. When you have a light selected, the Object Data tab features a light icon (look in the page margin to the left of this paragraph). With a couple of exceptions, all the lights share a few of the same controls. Figure 3-6 highlights the options that are universal for nearly all lights.

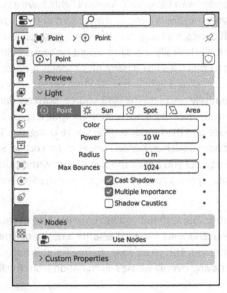
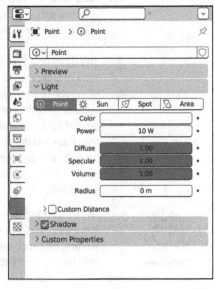

FIGURE 3-6:
Panels and options available for all light types. On the left are the options specific to Cycles, and on the right are properties available when using Eevee.

One cool thing about Blender's lights is that you can instantly change light types whenever you want. Simply select the light you want to work with and choose the type of light you would like it to be in the Light panel. This feature is great for quickly sorting out the type of light you want to use. You can test out different lighting schemes without cluttering the scene by having a bunch of extraneous lights that you have to move to other layers or hide.

Between Cycles and Eevee, only a few options are available to lights in both. In Cycles, the bulk of the properties you want to edit are in the Nodes panel (technically, they're properties of the Emission shader in the Shader Editor). In Eevee, they're in the Light panel of Object Data Properties:

>> **Color:** To set the color for your light, left-click the color swatch and use Blender's color picker.

>> **Power:** The Power value controls the strength of light emitted by the light, measured in Watts, like you might see in light bulbs. If you choose to make your light a Sun light, this value is changed to Strength rather than Power, and although the value is still set to 1000, it's not really comparable to light bulb ratings. For Sun lights, you'll probably want to start with a strength value closer to 1.0.

REMEMBER

It's worth noting that the 1000W light is the default for the scene that ships with Blender. However, when you add a new light using the Add menu, those lights have a power of 10W (and a new Sun light has a strength of 1.0).

>> **Size:** Whether you render with Eevee or Cycles, all lights have a size control of some sort. For Eevee, the size is close to the bottom of the Light panel. If you're rendering with Cycles, it's roughly in the same position, there are just more settings below it. Technically speaking, a light isn't much different from an Empty or a Camera object. It's just a point in 3D space. It doesn't really have any geometry, so scaling a light in the 3D Viewport is pretty meaningless. However, to more faithfully calculate the light source, both renderers need a surface to emit light from, even if it's not technically real. Depending on the type of light you choose and the render engine you're using, the Size property may have a different name, such as Radius, Angle, or (of course, Size). In all cases, that Size property lets you adjust the size of that virtual surface. The section on light-specific options goes a bit deeper into the Size controls for each kind of light.

REMEMBER

The main thing to remember is that if you increase the Size of your light but leave its Power value unchanged, it's still the same amount of light, but it's starting off more dispersed. This gives your shadows softer edges, though with the trade-off of having overall weaker illumination from the light.

REMEMBER

The Eevee render engine does a lot to try and keep its look consistent with Cycles. However, lighting is one of those places where things diverge a bit. Eevee doesn't currently support using nodes to define lights, and it doesn't support mesh lights either. So unless you're using the most simple of light settings, it may be difficult to have Eevee give a true representation of what rendering in Cycles might look like.

That's pretty much it for the truly universal light properties across both render engines. However, after you choose a specific renderer, a few more options are available for all lights. The next two subsections cover those properties. I encourage you to read both sections so you have a firm understanding of what's available to you in each renderer.

CYCLES LIGHT PROPERTIES

The amount of properties available to lights in Cycles is really quite sparse. However, the upside is that those options are very powerful and (for the most part) available to all light types. These options are available with all lights in Cycles:

>> **Max Bounces:** Because Cycles is a ray tracer, it's all about rays bouncing around your scene. It's a bit of a simplified description, but imagine one ray coming from your light. If Max Bounces is set to 0, that ray hits an object in your scene and stops. All it does is illuminate that object (much like simple lighting in Eevee). However, if you increase the maximum number of bounces, you allow that ray to reflect off of objects it strikes.

This reflecting behavior from bounced rays allows for the realistic color bleeding effect that's the hallmark of global illumination. *Color bleeding* is when light reflected from one surface takes on part of that surface's color. So, if you have a bright red object in your scene and Max Bounces is set reasonably high (like the default value of 1024), other objects near your red one will take on a slightly reddish hue from the reflected light.

>> **Cast Shadow:** Cycles' lights have far fewer controls for shadows than their Eevee counterparts. However, they retain the ability to disable shadow casting with this check box. This option is an attractive feature that you don't get with mesh lights.

Why would you want to disable a light's ability to cast shadows? In a three-point lighting setup, you often want your fill light to illuminate the scene without contributing unnecessary shadows. In meatspace, light technicians and cinematographers go through a lot of effort and tricks to do this; usually by trying to make the shadows from the fill light very soft. In CG it's much easier: You just turn shadows off. Neat, huh?

TIP

You can turn off shadows on any object you want, regardless of the type of lights, by going to Object Properties, expanding the Visibility panel, and disabling the Shadow check box in the Ray Visibility sub-panel.

>> **Multiple Importance:** This check box toggles whether the light uses multiple importance sampling. Simply put, *multiple importance sampling* is an algorithm

that allows Cycles to more intelligently choose which rays to use for lighting your scene. Having this kind of intelligence in sampling becomes valuable on larger lights and especially on materials with sharp reflections. Generally, you should leave this check box enabled.

>> **Shadow Caustics:** *Caustic lighting effects* (*caustics* for short) are the result of light bouncing through a material (typically transparent), focusing the light to make bright spots as it leaves the material. If you've ever focused sunlight using a magnifying glass, you were producing a caustic light effect. Generally speaking, caustics are difficult for render engines to do quickly. To help the render engine go a little faster, you can enable this Shadow Caustics check box to activate a technique that approximates caustics when rendering. There are two parts to this feature, though; it doesn't work on its own. In addition to marking a light as having Shadow Caustics, you need to go to any object that receives that caustic effect and, in the Shading panel of Object Properties, enable the Receive Shadow Caustics check box. Only then can Cycles take full advantage of this speed-up technique. Of course, if you don't have any caustics in your scene, it's best to keep this check box disabled.

TIP

If you're rendering with Cycles, you can also apply textures to your lights like you can with materials for objects. This ability is a great way to use lighting to either enhance the environment of your scene or fake certain lighting effects that Cycles takes a long time to produce on its own. One specific example is caustic effects, as described in the previous Shadow Caustics bullet point. As another example, if you have some free time, take a glass of water and shine light through it. Due to the refractive nature of the glass and the water, usually you see a strange light pattern on the table near or around the glass. That effect is an example of caustics and (if you don't need 100 percent accuracy) you can fake it with a Voronoi texture on a Spot light.

On a larger scale, caustics are what make the cool moving patterns you can see on the bottom of a swimming pool. Figure 3-7 shows the node network you'd need on a Spot light to achieve this affect. A key thing to pay attention to here is the Texture Coordinate node. Without that as a reference, Blender doesn't know how to relate the texture to the light. See Chapter Book 3, Chapter 2 for more on textures.

REMEMBER

Technically speaking, you shouldn't have to fake caustics if you're using Cycles, because they're naturally built-in. However, caustic effects tend to take a long time to *converge* or appear cleanly when rendering with Cycles, requiring a lot more samples than you may want to use. For that reason, it still makes sense to occasionally help Cycles along by faking caustics with a texture or approximate caustics using the Shadow Caustics feature.

FIGURE 3-7:
Using a Voronoi texture mapped to a Spot light, you can fake underwater caustics.

The ability to use the Shader Editor with lights in Cycles also allows you to work with IES lights. As covered briefly in the last chapter, IES profiles are text files (often provided by the light's manufacturer) that describe the specific shape of a light's fill area. You know how when you shine a flashlight at the ground, it doesn't always create an evenly distributed circle of light? Sometimes the center of the circle is brighter, or sometimes a bright ring appears around the edge. That behavior can be difficult to fake with regular image textures. Fortunately, IES profiles for all kinds of lights are publicly available for download to make use of in your Blender scene; just wire an IES Texture node to the Strength socket of the Emission node for your light. This feature is especially helpful if you're doing architectural visualization where it's important to have the lights in your scene match their real-world counterparts.

EEVEE LIGHT PROPERTIES

This section details the wide assortment of properties available to lights when rendering with Eevee. On a technical level, even though Eevee is a modern renderer that uses physically based rendering (PBR) techniques, it still tends to use more tricks and fakery than Cycles in how it handles lights and shadows. As a result, there are more controls for you to fidget with.

In addition to Color and Power, there's three additional primary controls available to all lights when rendering with Eevee, known as *reflection factors*. Remember that all light that the camera sees is reflected off of something. So these reflection factors give you additional control over the influence of that reflected light. You have three controls:

>> **Diffuse:** The diffuse reflection factor controls how much the base color of your light affects the objects in your scene. The default value of 1.0 is what

you can consider "full influence" of diffuse values from your light. If you drop the Diffuse value down to 0.0, then your light is only providing highlights and volumetric light. If you set the value greater than 1.0, then you're multiplying the effect, and likely getting a result that looks a bit unnatural.

>> **Specular:** The specular reflection factor relates to highlights on your material. In a render engine like Eevee, reflections from light sources need to be estimated, unlike a ray traced renderer like Cycles. This estimated reflection of light is known as *specularity,* and you can control its influence from your light by adjusting the Specular value. This value is a multiplication factor, so if you want your specular highlights from the light to be twice as strong, set this value to 2.0. If you want them half as strong, use a value of 0.5. If you want no highlights at all (think about your fill light), then drop the Specular value to 0.0.

>> **Volume:** The volume reflection factor relates to how your light influences volumetric materials, like smoke (see Book 4, Chapter 5 for more on volumes and smoke simulation). Like the controls for diffuse and specular reflection factors, the volume reflection factor is a multiplier. Set it to 0.0 and your light doesn't affect volume materials at all. Set it to 1.0 and you have the default full influence. Values greater than 1.0 amplify the light reflected from the volume.

TIP

You might notice that the sliders for the reflection factors stop at 1.0. This behavior is because there's a *soft limit* for those values, set at 1.0. To set any of the reflection factors to a value greater than soft limit, click the value and type the number you want to use.

There's also a Custom Distance sub-panel available for the Point, Spot, and Area lights. It's disabled by default, but if you enable the check box for Custom Distance, you can have customized control over how far your light projects from its origin. The value is in the units defined in the Units panel in the Scene tab of the Properties editor and, if an object is farther away from the light than that distance, it receives no illumination. If you're using a Spot or Area light, you should notice a line extending from your light that gets longer or shorter as you adjust the Distance value. Unfortunately, no such indicator exists for Point lights. That said, if you use the Material Preview or Rendered shading modes for the 3D Viewport, you can see exactly how adjusting the distance value changes the lighting in your scene. If you keep the Custom Distance option disabled, Eevee reverts to using the inverse square law to define a light's falloff like Cycles does.

TECHNICAL
STUFF

Lights in Cycles don't have a Distance value because all light sources (other than the Sun light) in Cycles share a physically correct falloff rate. Incidentally, all natural light follows the *inverse-square law* for falloff. That means that as you get farther from a light source, the strength of its light decreases by the value of $1/distance^2$. So, if the Power value of your light is 100W, when you're 1 meter away, the light's effective strength is 50W. At 2 meters away, the light's effective strength is 25W. And by the time you get just 5 meters away from your light source, the effective strength has dropped to a value of just 4W. So, to make a scene brighter, you need to either make one very strong light source (which may be too bright and overpower the scene) or add multiple smaller lights. The Sun light in Blender is an exception because it's an approximation of the real sun, which is so bright and so far away that we can ignore the inverse-square law at typical scene scales.

When rendering with Eevee, each light has the option of casting shadows. Shadows are enabled by default but could be disabled by clicking the check box at the top of the Shadow panel. If you're using shadows in Eevee, you should be aware of a couple options:

>> **Clip Start:** Consider this value as a secondary control in addition to the Custom Distance value in the Light panel. Objects that appear between the Clip Start and the Custom Distance cast shadows, whereas objects outside of this range do not. Keeping the Clip Start value as close to your shadow-casting objects as possible gives you the most accurate results. Of all the lights, only the Spot and Area lights show a visual representation of the Clip Start value in the 3D Viewport.

>> **Bias:** This value is specific to tweaking how an object *self-shadows,* or how it casts shadows upon itself. Basically, the Bias value offsets the shadow from where it connects to the shadow-casting protrusion on your object. Occasionally, you may get some weird jaggies or *artifacts* in your shadows. Increasing the Bias can help get rid of those artifacts, but you should keep this value as small as possible. If you do have to adjust the Bias, adjust it only as low as it can go before you get artifacts in your renders. Otherwise, your shadows will begin to look very unnatural. A good practice is to do a series of test renders starting with a Bias value of 0.1 and working your way up until you no longer see artifacts.

You also have the ability to enable *contact shadows,* or the kinds of shadows that appear when two objects are touching. This feature is disabled by default, but can be easily turned on by clicking the check box at the top of the Contact Shadows sub-panel. Typically, you should only enable contact shadows if you're having a lot of problems with light leaking (see the section later in this chapter titled "Understanding shadow maps in Eevee"), and other tweaks aren't helping enough. With contact shadows enabled, you get the following control options:

>> **Distance:** Eevee's contact shadows work by guessing where objects intersect or come close to intersecting in the 3D Viewport, similar to how Eevee handles ambient occlusion and screen space reflections (more on this in the section "Setting Up the World"). The Distance value is measured in the units you choose in the Units panel of Scene Properties, and it's what Eevee uses to

estimate those mesh intersections. To work effectively, though, you should try and keep this value pretty low. The larger you make it, the less accurate your shadows will be.

>> **Bias:** This Bias value works exactly the same as the Bias value for regular shadows. It's just specific to contact shadows.

>> **Thickness:** The Thickness value is measured in the same units as your scene. You may want to bump this value up if you have very thin objects in your scene, and they're not being recognized by Eevee as objects that can have contact shadows.

Light-specific options

As you can see back in Figure 3-6, the Point light has options available on nearly every other light but doesn't have much in the way of unique controls. However, the remaining three lights have some interesting options that allow you to optimize their usage to meet your needs.

OPTIONS SPECIFIC TO SUN LIGHTS

The Sun light is incredibly useful because it has the ability to behave more like the real sun. Unlike all the other lights, the distance of the light from the object (or objects) you're lighting doesn't matter when you use a Sun light. For those other lights, if the light is closer, their influences are stronger. Both Eevee and Cycles assume that the light rays from a Sun light are persistent throughout your scene and completely parallel, as opposed to radiating out from a specific point in space. Of course, that's not what's happening with the real sun, but because it's such a far distance from our planet, the approach of the Sun light is a pretty fair approximation of the real thing.

REMEMBER

The only thing that matters is the direction that the Sun is shining. When I use a Sun light, I tend to leave it right at the scene origin, unless it's more convenient to move it someplace else. For me, that placement just makes it easier to find the light later when I'm looking for it.

Object Data Properties contains only a few controls specific to the Sun light. Figure 3-8 shows the full set of options available for Sun lights.

In addition to the Color and Strength values, the Sun light has another primary control: Angle. You might guess that the Angle value has something to do with the angle that your Sun light's rays enter your scene. Surprisingly, that guess would be incorrect. The more complete name for this value is *angular diameter*. In short, it's the Sun light's size. Specifically, it's the measure of the diameter of your Sun in degrees.

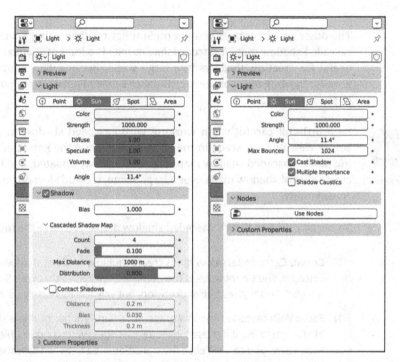

FIGURE 3-8:
Controls for the Sun lights in Eevee and Cycles.

"What? Degrees for distance? How is that even a thing?," you might be saying to yourself. It's actually a unit used in astronomy. If you were to look at the sun (**don't really do this!**), you could imagine a triangle between you and the top and bottom of the sun. If you measure the angle of the corner of that triangle where you stand, that's the sun's angular diameter. It's basically the effective size of the sun, as perceived from your scene. Figure 3-9 tries to illustrate this concept more clearly.

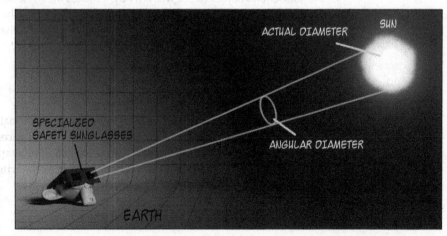

FIGURE 3-9:
The angular diameter of a Sun light is the perceived size of the sun as viewed from your scene.

The other set of controls you get on Sun lights when using Eevee are those for a cascaded shadow map. A *cascaded shadow map* is a kind of shadow map specifically useful for creating shadows in a large scene. Because Sun lights are commonly used for lighting outdoor scenes, it makes sense to have the support of these kinds of shadow maps.

WARNING

Be a little bit careful when working with cascaded shadow maps, especially if you're viewing your scene in the 3D Viewport using the Rendered viewport shading mode. Cascaded shadow maps are continuously updated, and because they can create a lot of shadow maps over a large scene, it could slow down the 3D Viewport considerably.

To tweak your Sun light's cascaded shadow maps, you have the following controls:

>> **Count:** Cascaded shadow maps create multiple levels of shadow maps, called *cascades*. The Count value is the number of cascades that your Sun light uses. A higher Count gives better precision, but will also increase your render times.

>> **Fade:** With cascaded shadow maps, your Sun light has multiple shadow maps. Ideally, you'd like it if those individual cascades weren't noticeable. With the Fade value, you can increase the transition area between cascades and have them overlap a bit. The trade-off of a larger Fade, however, is that your overall shadow map resolution is reduced, so your shadows may be less accurate.

>> **Max Distance:** This value is the maximum distance from your viewing location to use the cascaded shadow maps. If you keep this value low, you have better shadow map resolution because you're using the same number of cascades over a smaller area.

>> **Distribution:** Because you have multiple shadow maps, you have a little bit of control over how they're placed in your scene. Because things in the distance are smaller and harder to see well anyway, it makes the most sense to have the majority of your accuracy closer to your viewing location. Think of the Distribution value as the percentage of resolution you want to have devoted nearer your viewing location.

OPTIONS SPECIFIC TO SPOT LIGHTS

As Figure 3-10 shows, the controls for Spot lights are pretty consistent regardless of whether you're rendering with Eevee or Cycles. The main exception is that the sub-panel with shape controls for Spot lights is labeled Spot Shape when rendering with Eevee, whereas it's called Beam Shape if you're rendering with Cycles.

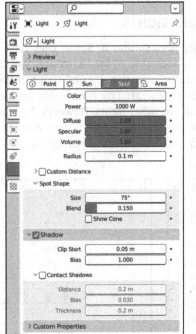 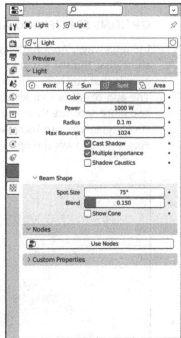

FIGURE 3-10:
The controls for
Spot lights in
Eevee and Cycles.

Regardless of the name of the panel, Spot lights have a handful of settings available for controlling the shape of the Spot light's fill area. Those controls are in the Spot Shape panel:

>> **Size:** This setting controls the width of the Spot's fill area, measured in degrees (kind of like the Angle value in Sun lights). So a value of 180 degrees is completely wide, whereas a value of 30 degrees gives you a narrower cone. Unless I'm doing something special, I like to start with my Spots with a Size value around 60 degrees.

>> **Blend:** The Blend value controls the sharpness of the edges at the boundary where the Spot's cone of influence ends. Lower values give you a crisp edge, whereas higher values soften it, making the light appear more diffuse.

>> **Show Cone:** This feature is incredibly cool and useful. When you enable the Show Cone check box, Blender changes the display of the spot light's cone of influence in the 3D Viewport, allowing you to see its volume more clearly. This feature makes it much easier to see what objects are within your Spot light's influence area.

OPTIONS SPECIFIC TO AREA LIGHTS

In some ways, Area lights are very similar to Spots; they have a direction and a somewhat limited fill area compared to Point lights and Sun lights. The difference is that you have more control over the size and shape of the Area light itself. The end result is that shadows generated by Area lights are generally smoother and more accurate than any of the other lights. However, by adding Area lights to your scene, you can increase your render time dramatically if you're not careful. Figure 3-11 shows the options and settings for Area lights.

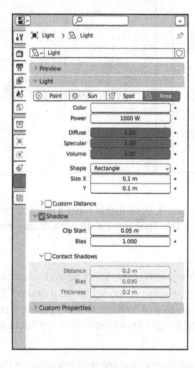
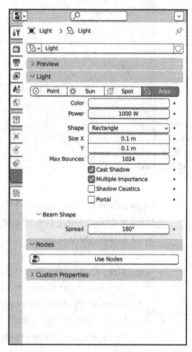

FIGURE 3-11: The controls for Area lights in Eevee and Cycles.

To control the dimensions of your Area light, you first should decide the shape for the light. Using the Shape drop-down menu, you can set your Area light's shape to be a Square, Rectangle (the default), Disk, or Ellipse. If you choose Square or Disk, you get only one size parameter to adjust, whereas if you choose Rectangle or Ellipse, you can control the size of your Area light in both its local X and Y axes.

If you're rendering with Cycles, there's one additional control that you get on Area lights. There's a check box at the bottom of the Light panel labeled Portal. It's a funky name, but it's extremely helpful for lighting interior scenes. If you have an interior scene where the primary light source is outside (like a Sun light or light from an environment texture), then your renders are likely to end up being grainy or having a lot of little bright spots sometimes called *fireflies*. The reason why these interior lighting scenes are so problematic is because you're basically relying only on secondary, bounced light to provide illumination. The majority of your light's rays are lost outside the walls of your scene, and Cycles doesn't have enough rays to quickly converge on a cleanly rendered result. You can try to get around this by pumping up the light samples in Render Properties, but that leads to really long render times. The Portal feature of Area lights is a way to get around that. See the section later in the chapter entitled "Setting up a good interior lighting scene" for more details on using Portals.

Using mesh lights in Cycles

When rendering with Cycles, it's common to use mesh lights, especially if you want the effect of an Area light, but with more control of the light's shape (although Area lights give you more control over beam spread). Part of this is historical — it used to be that you'd get much shorter render times using meshes as lights than by using light objects. The other reason is more practical: Often, lights take on a specific shape that's more complex than the simple look of light objects. Also, if you texture your mesh lights, you can use all the UV coordinate tricks covered in the previous chapter.

NEW FEATURE

Starting in Blender 4.0, all lights have UV texture coordinates available, so you're actually able to use texturing tricks on any light source now!

Making any object a light source in Cycles is incredibly easy. You don't even really need to use the Shader Editor (at least, not for a simple setup). With your object selected, just follow these steps:

1. **In the Material tab of the Properties editor, add a material for your object.**

2. **In the Surface panel of Material Properties, change the Surface drop-down menu to Emission.**

3. **Adjust the Color and Strength values to taste.**

That's it! From the perspective of your material's node network, you've connected an Emission shader to the Surface socket of your Material Output node, as shown in Figure 3-12.

REMEMBER

One side effect of using a mesh to light your scene is that (unlike light objects) meshes are visible objects in your scene, just like they would be in meatspace. The absolute easiest solution is to try to keep your mesh lights off-camera. Sadly, that's not always possible. It would be really nice if you could get the benefits of mesh lights and still keep the mesh object itself invisible from the camera. Fortunately, that's pretty easy to do. Just disable the Camera check box in the Ray Visibility sub-panel of Object Properties (look in the Visibility panel).

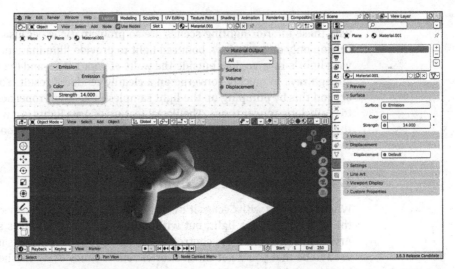

There's another way to get those results. It isn't as simple as a check box and requires a bit of wizardry in the Shader Editor (specifically the Light Path node). However, by using the Shader Editor, you open the door to the possibilities of much more complex and interesting lighting. Assuming you have a mesh light set up like in Figure 3-12, follow these steps in the Shader Editor:

1. **Add a Mix Shader node (Add ⇨ Shader ⇨ Mix Shader).**

    For placement, put the Mix Shader node to the right of your Emission and Transparent BSDF nodes, but to the left of your Material Output node.

    TIP If you drag your Mix Shader node over the noodle connecting your Emission node to the Material Output node, you should notice the noodle get high-lighted. Let go of the Mix Shader node and Blender will automatically connect that node in-line and shuffle the Material Output node to the right to make space for it.

2. **Connect the Emission socket of your Emission node to the upper Shader socket of the Mix Shader node.**

    Perform this step if you didn't follow the tip in the previous step.

3. **Connect a Transparent BSDF node to the lower Shader socket of the Mix Shader node.**

    The easiest way to do this step is by clicking and dragging the lower Shader socket on the Mix Shader node. You should get a noodle extending from the socket with a plus (+) sign close to your mouse. When you release your mouse button, Blender provides you with a search menu where you can type the name of the node you want (in this case, Transparent BSDF). When you select the name of your desired node, it's already connected to your noodle.

If you preview your scene in the 3D Viewport with Rendered viewport shading, you should see that your mesh light object emits light, but is semitransparent. If you adjust the Fac slider in the Mix Shader node to a value of 0, your mesh emits light, but it's completely solid. At a Fac value of 1, your mesh is transparent, but it doesn't emit any light. That's close, but not quite right. The magic happens in the next two steps.

4. **Add a Light Path node with its Is Camera Ray socket connected to the Fac socket on the Mix Shader node.**

As with the previous step, click and drag a noodle from the Fac socket on the Mix Shader node and use the search menu to find Light Path ⇨ Is Camera Ray. Like magic, your mesh object is invisible in the scene, but it's still emitting light.

TECHNICAL STUFF

The technical explanation for what you've done goes something like this: Your mesh object checks each ray that comes in contact with it and determines where that ray came from (the camera, another light source, a shadow, and so on). Then, by wiring the Is Camera Ray socket to the Fac socket on the Mix slider, you're making your material say, "If I'm hit with a camera ray, behave as if I'm transparent, but if I'm hit with any other ray, behave as if I'm a light." And there you go: a mesh light that behaves like a light object.

Figure 3-13 shows what your finished node network should look like.

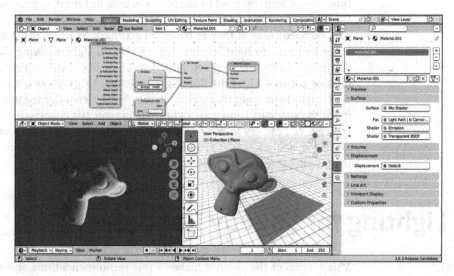

FIGURE 3-13: Getting a mesh light to be invisible in your scene requires playing with the Light Path node.

TIP

While this approach is obviously slower than just disabling visibility in Object Properties, it can also sometimes make your life a bit easier while you work. If you're working on a complex scene, the bulk of your attention is focused on the Shader Editor and the 3D Viewport. It's easy to forget a little check box in the Properties editor when you're trying to figure out why something is or isn't showing when you render.

TIP

It's actually possible to use mesh lights with Eevee too. It's just a little more of a hassle to set up than with Cycles. You set up the emission material for your mesh light the same way you do in Cycles (as covered in this section), but then there's an extra step of adding something called a light probe. See the section "Working with Light Probes in Eevee" later in this chapter for more information.

Understanding shadow maps in Eevee

Eevee is not a ray-traced render engine like Cycles, so it can't use the same techniques for generating shadows in your scene. Instead, it uses a technique called *shadow mapping*. Simply put, Eevee looks at the geometry in your scene and estimates where the shadows will fall. Then it generates a texture of that shadow for all the objects in the scene. That texture is the shadow map, and Eevee can constantly generate this map on the fly several times a second. The shadows aren't quite as accurate as those you'd get from Cycles, but they're generated *very* quickly, and they're often good enough for a lot of images, especially if you're making assets for video games.

As a rendering technique for shadows, shadow maps have been around for a long time. Eevee actually used to support a couple different approaches to generating shadow maps but now relies on a single one. Regardless of the shadow-mapping method used because they're based on estimations, shadows in Eevee can sometimes be prone to light leaking. *Light leaking* is light showing through an object that ought to be blocking (*occluding*) it. Light leaks are particularly common on interior corners when the light is outside and bright, like a Sun light or even a very bright Point light that's close to the object. Generally speaking, the softer you make the shadows from your lights, the greater the chance that you'll have light leakage. You can try to compensate by adjusting the Light Threshold value in the Shadows panel of Render Properties, but often, the better solution is to try to have more lights at a lower power to attain soft shadows.

Lighting for Speedy Renders

This section of the chapter makes a few recommendations and suggestions that have been hotly debated over the years in CG circles, especially with the recent focus on physically correct rendering and greater emphasis on realism. A big part of computer graphics has always been about getting good results quickly. That often results in artists doing little CG "cheats" to get results that look good but may not be entirely accurate to how things work in meatspace. I often tell people that when it comes to computer graphics, if you're not cheating or faking something, you're probably doing it wrong. Even though you can get great results by using ray-traced shadows everywhere with the highest number of samples, these results all come at the expense of high memory usage and lengthy render times. So your scene may look perfect, but if you're taking 16 hours to render every frame in an animation, you could be rendering for a month and not even have two seconds of it done.

Granted, quite a bit of deciding how much you "cheat" depends on who you're working with and who your audience is. If you're collaborating with a bunch of other artists, they may not appreciate having to go through all of your cute tricks to match a particular look you've created. Or, if you're working in architectural or industrial visualization, it may be important that your lighting be as accurate as possible. A lot of people will lean towards physically based, accurate setups that may take longer to render because it saves the artist time (it's cheaper to pay for computers to work than paying an artist for that time).

That said, a large part of being a CG artist is doing everything you can to reduce the amount of work that needs to be done by you *and* the computer while still creating high-quality images. You don't want to be old and gray by the time your first animation is complete. That's why many independent CG artists worry so much about keeping their render times as short as possible and why they make use of tricks and cheats to cut corners where they can.

Working with three-point lighting in Blender

My preferred lighting rig in Blender usually starts with a three-point lighting setup. Here's what I normally start with:

» **Key:** A Spot works well as the key light in Eevee. Keep all settings at their default values except for the size of the spot shape. In the Spot Shape sub-panel, set the Size to 60 degrees. In Cycles, I may use a Spot light as my key, but more frequently, I use a mesh light.

» **Fill:** For a fill light, I may use a large Area light or Sun light. When rendering with Cycles, I'll often disable the Cast Shadows and Multiple Importance options. Occasionally, I may also use a large plane as a mesh light with a low Strength value. When rendering with Eevee, I may drop the Specular reflection factor down to 0.0 to avoid conflicting highlights.

>> **Back:** This is the tricky one. The light is behind the subject, so specularity doesn't matter as much, but if I'm rendering with Eevee, I normally dial the specularity on this light down to zero. Don't get too picky with the location of the back light just yet. Back lighting is a bit of a mystical art with a lot of trial and error per shot; it's one of the rare situations where real-world lights have an easier time yielding the desired effect. For that reason, you end up tweaking the location of the back light a lot, so it's not critical that you get it right the first time in your initial setup. As for types of lights, a Spot light usually can work well as a good back light.

This setup is good for studio lighting, and it works really well for scenes set indoors or for lighting isolated objects. I include an example three-point lighting .blend file on the website www.blenderbasics.com.

Using light portals in Cycles

Like Eevee, Cycles has its own challenges when rendering interior scenes with a primary lighting source coming from outside. In Cycles, though, the issue isn't so much about light leakage as about not getting enough light samples in the room. As I explain previously in this chapter, interior scenes have difficulty converging on a decent result. So for one configuration of render settings, an interior scene might show up really grainy, with a bunch of fireflies, whereas the exact same settings on an outdoor scene my result in a perfect clean rendered image.

The main reason for this difference in results is because of bounced light rays. An interior scene that's illuminated primarily by light pouring through the windows is relying almost entirely on these bounced light rays. And since the primary light is coming from outside the walls of the scene, most of those light rays never make it to your scene camera, meaning that Cycles has overall fewer light rays to calculate a result. So if you're rendering with, say, 100 samples, it's possible that only 10 of those samples actually provide any useful lighting information.

Sure, you could fake it by putting a light right in the window of your scene, but that's not a particularly realistic approach, and doing so negates some of the usefulness you get from using a Sun light or — especially — high dynamic range images (HDRIs) for lighting (more on HDRIs later in this chapter). You could also dramatically punch up the number of samples you use when rendering, but that can make your render times much, much longer. What would be really handy would be the ability to tell Cycles, "Hey! This part of my scene is a window. Prioritize light rays coming through here."

And, in fact, that's exactly what you get with the Portal feature of Area lights. Follow these steps to make use of Portals in your scene:

1. **Set up your scene as you normally would.** If your aim is realism, then you likely should use an HDRI for your world environment texture. The key here is that your main lighting comes from outside your scene through a window or some other opening.

2. **Add an Area light to your scene (Add ⇨ Light ⇨ Area).**

3. **Move your Area light to your window opening and adjust it to match the size of that window.** Change its shape from the Object Data tab of the Properties editor and adjust the size dimensions to match. Don't worry about the Color or Power parameters, but do make sure that the light is pointing into your interior space.

4. **Enable the Portal check box.** And that's it! By adjusting the size of the Area light and enabling the Portal feature, you've let Cycles know that this window opening is the area to focus on the most when looking for light rays.

Figure 3-14 shows a simple scene with and without the use of Portals to help guide the renderer.

FIGURE 3-14: Using Area lights as portals can help reduce overall noise in an interior scene.

WARNING

Understand that Portals aren't a panacea. Each portal you add to your scene will actually increase your overall render times. Usually, you'll need fewer samples to arrive at a good result, but if you add too many portals, you'll negate any benefit that they provide. And if you've already dialed up your Light Paths settings for Cycles (Light Paths panel in the Render tab of the Properties editor) for full global illumination, then Portals can actually make your renders more grainy. There's more on global illumination later in this chapter in the section titled "Understanding ambient occlusion." As with most things, you'll probably need to experiment and play with this feature to get a good feel for when it's the best time to use it.

Using Material Preview to set up lighting

Whether you're working with Cycles or Eevee as your primary rendering engine, you should previsualize your scene as early as possible. That is, in an ideal situation, you want to know what your final render is going to look like before you actually tell Blender to render. In Book 3, Chapter 1, I introduce using the Shading workspace and Blender's Material Preview viewport shading mode. You can use that same workspace and viewport shading mode to get a strong sense of the result your lighting setup is going to give you.

That said, you need to make a few modifications to the default Material Preview viewport shading mode configuration; otherwise, what you see in the 3D Viewport won't quite so faithfully match your final rendered output. Granted, if your final rendered output is with Eevee, then you may as well use the Rendered viewport shading mode. It will be just as fast as Material Preview, and you won't have to make as many changes. However, if you're rendering with Cycles, there's a real benefit to performing the following steps:

1. **Go to the Shading workspace.**

Click on the Shading tab at the top of the Blender window. The large 3D Viewport at the center of the workspace layout should already be in Material Preview viewport shading mode.

2. **Enable Scene Lights and the Scene World.**

The controls for enabling these two options are in the Shading rollout at the top right of the 3D Viewport, as shown in Figure 3-15. Enabling these two check boxes ensures that Blender is using your lights and your world material (see the next section) to generate the results in Material Preview.

3. **(Optional) Enable Screen Space Reflections in Eevee's render settings.**

If your final output is going to be Cycles, you'll need to temporarily go to Render Properties and switch back to Eevee. From there, you can enable the Screen Space Reflections check box. After that, you can switch your render engine back to Cycles. The reason why this is an optional step is because Screen Space Reflects are a bit of an exaggerated approximation of the reflections and bounced light that you naturally get in Cycles with global illumination.

Now, you can quickly test your lighting setup without having to go through a full render or popping over to Rendered viewport shading mode.

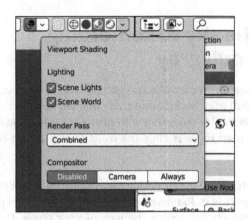

FIGURE 3-15:
To get Material
Preview to
more faithfully
represent your
scene lighting,
enable Scene
Lights and the
Scene World.

Setting Up the World

When you set up your scene for rendering, lighting is really only part of the equation. You must also consider your scene's environment. For example, are you outdoors or indoors? Is it daytime or nighttime? What color is the sky? Are there clouds? What does the background look like? You have to consider these factors when thinking about the final look of your image. Whether you're rendering with Cycles or Eevee, your starting point for setting up your environment is in the World tab of the Properties editor, as shown in Figure 3-16.

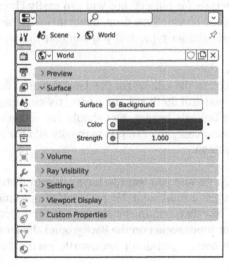

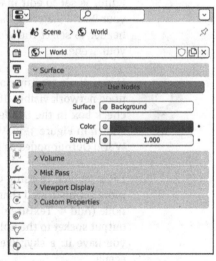

FIGURE 3-16:
World Properties
when the active
renderer is Cycles
(left) and Eevee
(right).

Changing the sky to something other than dull gray

If you've worked in Blender for a while and gotten a few renders out, you might be pretty tired of that dull gray background color that the renderers use by default. Regardless of whether you're rendering with Eevee or Cycles, you can change that color easily. All you need to do is click the color swatch in the Surface panel of World Properties.

An interesting side effect you might notice when changing the World color (especially if the 3D Viewport is in Rendered or Material Preview viewport shading) is that the color dramatically influences the look of your scene. If you change the World color to be blue, everything in your scene (especially the shadows) will start to carry a blue hue. That's because Cycles and Eevee treat the World color as another light source. If you don't want the World color to have any influence at all, drop the Strength value down to zero.

Generally speaking, though, the options available in World Properties seem . . . sparse. This is because these controls are only the most basic available to you. In reality, Eevee and Cycles see the World as just another kind of material. Therefore, most of your customization happens in the Shader Editor.

The best way to see what I'm talking about is to work in the Shading workspace. At the bottom of this workspace is a large Shader Editor. By default, the Shader Editor is set to edit materials for objects, but you can easily change it to modify your World material. Use the Shader Type drop-down menu in the Shader Editor's header to select the World shader type, and you can edit the World material for your scene.

TIP

If you don't see any nodes in the editor, try pressing Home to make your whole node network visible. If you still don't see any nodes, try enabling the Use Nodes check box in the Shader Editor's header. You should see something like what's shown in Figure 3-17. Worst case, you can just manually add the Background and World Output nodes as shown.

Let's say you're using Cycles and you want to have a World material that's a bit more sophisticated than just a solid color. No problem! Simply add a Sky Texture node (Add ⇨ Texture ⇨ Sky Texture) in the Shader Editor and connect its Color output socket to the Color input socket on the Background shader node. And there you have it: a sky. Even better, you don't necessarily need a Sun light in your scene.

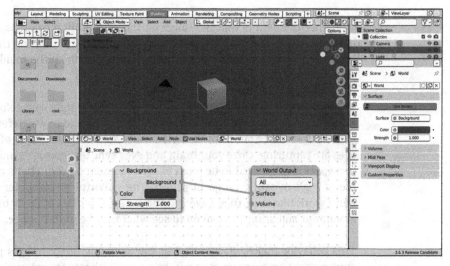

FIGURE 3-17:
Eevee and Cycles treat the World like a material, so most of your modifications take place in the Shader Editor. This is a simple node network for a World material.

Using high dynamic range images (HDRIs) for world lighting

Want to use an image texture for your environment? The Material Preview viewport shading mode has some really cool images for its World material. If you disable the Scene World check box in the Viewport Shading rollout, Blender gives you the choice of eight "chrome balls" to choose as a temporary World material. These chrome balls are actually reflections of images used for your World environment. These images are *high dynamic range images* (HDRIs), and they're used to give your scene the look of real-world lighting by actually using a special high-quality image as a light source.

HDRIs get used a lot in computer graphics, but a lot of people don't take the time to stop and figure out what they really are and why they're helpful, even necessary in some cases. See, computer technology has a bit of an Achilles Heel. Nearly everything in a computer that's a representation of real-world phenomena is an approximation based on a limited number of samples. When it comes to images, this issue becomes *really* apparent. Hold on to your hat, it's going to get a little technical.

TECHNICAL STUFF

Most images you see on the Internet are RGB images with 256 levels for each of the red, green, and blue channels. On the upside, the combination of those values gives you over 16 million possible colors. Pretty good, right? Unfortunately, there are problems. For one, we humans can actually perceive more colors than that.

Lighting and Environment

The other problem is that the range on those 16 million colors is fixed. If a color in the image is black (0,0,0), there's no other color information there, even if the image is of a dark room, and you *know* there's a chair in the middle of it because you could see it.

The reason this is a problem is because we perceive light and color on a dynamic range. Have you ever stepped into a dark room and had to wait a few seconds until your eyes adjust? Your brain is dynamically adjusting the range of light that your eyes are capturing. Once your brain and eyes sync up again, it's much easier to see in a space that seemed to be pitch black a moment before. That's a kind of example of high dynamic range in action. The majority of computer image formats don't work like that; they have a static range. If a pixel is 100% black, there's no amount of adjusting you can do to see what may be in that space.

This behavior makes static range or low dynamic range images problematic for environment textures used as a lighting source because real world environments have a dynamic range. Fortunately, as technology has improved over the years, we have camera sensors, image formats, and graphics applications like Blender that support high dynamic range. Thanks to those advances, we can use HDRIs as light sources in our scenes and create rendered images that have lighting that more accurately resembles what we see in meatspace.

Unfortunately, you don't have quick and easy access to the HDRIs that ship with Blender for Material Preview. That said, there are plenty of great resources for HDRIs that you can download from the Internet. One of my personal favorite places to find HDRIs is on polyhaven.com. That website has oodles of high-quality HDRIs all released for free with the most permissive Creative Commons license available (CC0). In fact, the HDRIs that ship with Blender for Material Preview viewport shading come from that site.

Once you've downloaded an HDRI, it's fairly easy to use it as a texture for your World environment.

1. In the Shader Editor, click and drag the Color socket of the Background node and use the search dialog to find Environment Texture ⇨ Color.

2. Click the Open button for the image datablock in the Environment Texture node and use the File Browser to find your HDRI.

Figure 3-18 shows a simple World setup using an HDRI as an environment texture.

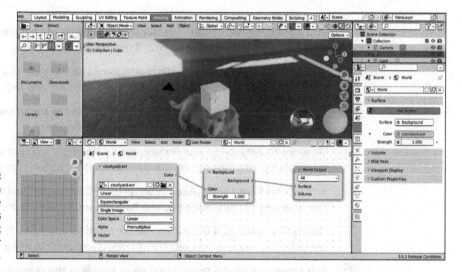

FIGURE 3-18:
You can use high dynamic range images (HDRIs) as an environment texture for your World material.

"But what if I just want a simple gradient as the background without any of this other fancy stuff?" Ironically, getting that effect is less straightforward now than it was in older versions of Blender. A viable cheat (that I've used!) would be to use the Compositor and put your render over a gradient background (see Book 5, Chapter 2 for more on compositing). But say you're a purist, and you want to do it all in your World material. That, too, is still possible. As an example, follow these steps to get a gradient for your World material (these steps assume you're starting with the simple node network in Figure 3-17):

1. **In the Shader Editor, add a Gradient Texture node (Add ⇨ Texture ⇨ Gradient Texture) and wire its Color socket to your Background shader node's Color input socket.**

   As with before, if you click and drag the Color socket on the Background node, you can use Blender's search feature to find the Gradient Texture node more quickly. If you're previewing your scene in the 3D Viewport with Rendered viewport shading, you should see your background become completely black. That's okay. It's supposed to be like that. The problem is that the default texture coordinates don't map in a way that makes your gradient texture easy to see.

2. **Add a Texture Coordinate node (Add ⇨ Input ⇨ Texture Coordinate) and connect its Window socket to the Vector input socket on your Gradient Texture node.**

   Again, click and drag the Vector socket to use the search feature to find your node. Now you should see your gradient, but there's a problem. The gradient goes from left to right, not vertically. You need to tweak your texture coordinates a bit.

3. **Add a Mapping node (Add ⇨ Vector ⇨ Mapping) in-line between your Texture Coordinate node and your Gradient Texture node.**

At this point, nothing in your background should be changed. You still have a black-to-white gradient going from left to right. The next step fixes that.

4. **In the Mapping node, change the Type button at the top of the node to Texture and change the Z rotation value to 90 degrees.**

Woohoo! You've rotated your texture, and it's starting to look like what you want. What you're missing now are controls for the colors in your gradient.

5. **Add a Color Ramp node (Add ⇨ Converter ⇨ ColorRamp) in-line between the Gradient Texture node and the Background shader node.**

On the face of things, it doesn't appear like much has changed. That's because the default gradient in the Color Ramp node is also black to white.

6. **Edit the colors on the Color Ramp node to match the colors you want along the length of the gradient.**

That's pretty much it. But really, with this setup you have even more control than you get with just an image gradient in the background, because with the Color Ramp node you can control the position of the colors and even add more colors to your gradient. It's incredibly powerful. I even would suggest that you add an RGB Curves node to have more control over the rate of change for the gradient. Figure 3-19 shows an example of what your final node network may look like.

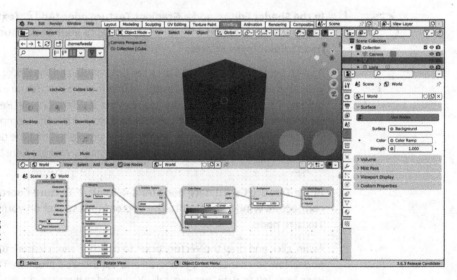

FIGURE 3-19:
A node network for generating a flat gradient background in Cycles and Eevee.

Understanding ambient occlusion

Take a look outside. Now, hopefully it's daytime, or this example isn't going to work, but notice how much everything seems to be illuminated. Even on a bright sunny day, the deepest shadows aren't completely black. The reason is that light from the sun is bouncing off of every surface many times, exposing nearly all objects to at least *some* amount of light. In computer graphics, this phenomenon is often referred to as *global illumination*, or GI, and it's pretty difficult to re-create efficiently.

Another result of GI is that all this bounced light also makes subtle details, creases, cracks, and wrinkles more apparent. At first, this statement may seem like a paradox. After all, if light is bouncing off of everything, intuitively, it would make sense that everything should end up even brighter and seem flatter. However, remember that not only is the light bouncing off of everything, but it's also casting small shadows from all the weird angles that it bounces from. Those small shadows are what bring out those minor details.

The GI effect is most apparent outdoors on overcast days where the light is evenly diffused by cloud cover. However, you can even see it happening in well-lit rooms with a high number of light sources, such as an office building with rows and rows of fluorescent lights lining the ceiling.

The bad news is that the Eevee renderer doesn't have "true" GI capability. Cycles, on the other hand, has that capability. So the quickest way to get GI in your scene is to just render with Cycles. However, there are instances where you need to render with Eevee, so using Cycles isn't an option. Fortunately, Eevee does have a great way of approximating GI, thanks to *ambient occlusion* (AO). Often called *dirty GI* or a *dirt shader*, AO finds the small details in your object and makes them more apparent by making the rest of the model brighter or making the details darker.

 To enable AO in Eevee, left-click the check box next to the Ambient Occlusion panel in the Render tab of the Properties editor. When you enable AO, Blender activates the settings in the Ambient Occlusion panel. This panel gives you all the controls Eevee has available for configuring AO in your scene. Figure 3-20 shows the Ambient Occlusion panel in Render Properties for Eevee.

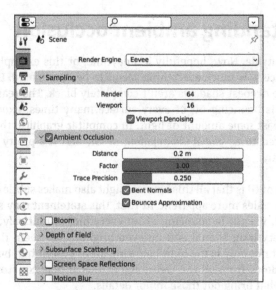

FIGURE 3-20:
You can control the amount of ambient occlusion (AO) in your scene from the Ambient Occlusion panel in Render Properties.

Most of the controls in the Ambient Occlusion panel are fairly straightforward. Here's a description of the options available for AO:

>> **Distance:** In order to approximate those cool AO shadows, Eevee uses the proximity of other geometry to decide if a feature (a crack or crease or wedge) needs the extra shading that AO provides. The Distance value is how you control whether a nearby bit of geometry is used to generate the AO effect. Larger values will get you more shadows, but at the risk of looking less realistic. One common approach is to use a "half a ceiling height" technique. That is, if you set the AO Distance value to half the height of the ceiling in your scene (it doesn't have to be a physical ceiling; it could be the highest that your camera can see), then you can get some pleasant-looking results with AO.

>> **Factor:** The Factor value is the strength of the overall AO effect. The effect generated by the Distance you set is multiplied by this value. Usually it's a good idea to keep this at 1.0, although I recommend that you play with it a bit to see how it affects your scene. It's worth noting that 1.0 is a soft limit. If you want values greater than 1.0, you must type them in manually.

>> **Trace Precision:** If you increase this value, you will have more accurate AO shadows, but renders will take longer to complete and may introduce some noise to your scene.

>> **Bent Normals:** You're probably best off leaving this check box enabled. It limits the calculation of AO shadows to the direction that's least occluded. Why calculate shadows that aren't going to be seen if you don't have to?

>> **Bounces Approximation:** This check box is a little bit of helpful fakery that gives less of a shadowing effect on brighter objects (like shiny plaster). In most cases, there's not a real need to disable this option.

Figure 3-21 shows the same scene rendered with AO enabled, as well as without any AO at all.

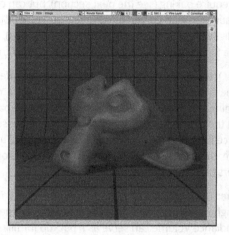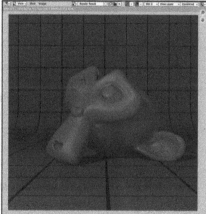

FIGURE 3-21:
From left to right, with their render times: no ambient occlusion and ambient occlusion enabled.

Working with Light Probes in Eevee

Eevee may not have the fully accurate features of global illumination and reflections of a ray-traced render engine like Cycles, but that doesn't mean it can't produce high-quality realistic results. Eevee is a modern renderer with an emphasis on physically based rendering (PBR), so it *can* get results nearly comparable to Cycles with much shorter render times. One of the biggest tricks in getting realistic results in Eevee is the judicious use of *light probes*. Think of light probes as specialized Empties that help feed information about the scene to Eevee for realistic rendering.

The majority of Eevee's features as a renderer are known as *screen space effects*. Features like ambient occlusion and reflections are generated by analyzing only what's within the camera's view. However, if you have an object that's off camera, like a tree casting a shadow or another character standing behind the camera, those objects aren't going to register with a screen space effect. Light probes work by providing additional sampling data that Eevee can use to account for those off-camera objects.

Eevee supports three different kinds of light probes accessible through the Add menu in the 3D Viewport (Add ⇨ Light Probe). Two of the probes are dedicated to reflections, and one is focused on indirect lighting (like global illumination):

>> **Reflection Cube Map:** The Reflection Cube Map light probe is a general-purpose light probe used for generating reflections on objects (or serving as a backup if you're using screen space reflections — enabled in Render Properties). They require baking (see the next section), but can produce decent results on surfaces with curved or complex structures. The map generated by this light probe is sphere-shaped (or box-shaped), and its influence fades in a falloff region as objects reach the limits of that sphere.

>> **Reflection Plane:** Of the different light probes that Blender offers for Eevee, the Reflection Plane is the only one that can be used on the fly. You don't have to bake anything. The simplest explanation is that Eevee basically puts a virtual camera at the location of this light probe and uses those rendered results as the source for mapping a reflection to the surface of an object. Because it's a plane, the ideal use for this kind of light probe is on flat surfaces like mirrors or shiny windows.

>> **Irradiance Volume:** The Irradiance Volume light probe is used for helping to generate indirect lighting effects like global illumination. Like the Reflection Cube Map, the Irradiance Volume can serve as a backup for filling the gaps with screen space effects, and it also must be baked to be of use. When you add an Irradiance Volume light probe, you get a box filled with a grid of sample points. That box and grid are the sample points and area of influence for the Irradiance Volume.

TIP

Earlier in this chapter, I hint that it's possible to use mesh lights with Eevee, but it is a little complicated to set up. Light probes are how you use mesh lights in Eevee.

Figure 3-22 shows each kind of light probe along with its basic settings in Object Data Properties.

To use any of the light probes, the steps are basically the same:

1. **Add the light probe to your scene (Add ⇨ Light Probe ⇨ [your choice of light probe]).**

2. **Use Blender's transform tools to move and rotate the light probe into place.**

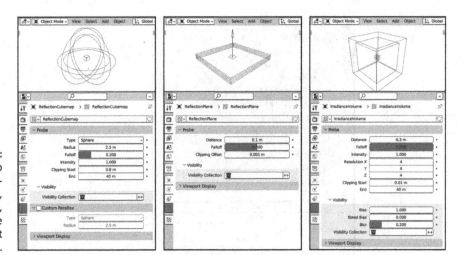

FIGURE 3-22:
From left to right, the Reflection Cube Map, Reflection Plane, and Irradiance Volume light probes.

3. **Use the controls in Object Data Properties to refine control of your light probe's influence area.**

The Falloff value is particularly useful for determining how the light probe's influence area fades away over space. If you're working with an Irradiance Volume, you should pay a lot of attention to the X, Y, and Z resolution values. The higher you make these values, the slower your next step will be.

4. **Bake your indirect lighting if you're using a Reflection Cube Map or an Irradiance Volume.**

See the next section for more details on baking indirect lighting from your light probes.

After you add your light probes with the preceding steps (and bake, if necessary), you're ready to render your scene (see the next chapter).

Baking from your light probes

Light probes are a common trick used in video game render engines because they have the advantage of pre-computing some of your lighting. That computation is saved as a *light cache* by a process called *baking*. If you're only using a Reflection Plane light probe, then you don't need to worry about baking. Reflection Plane data is generated on the fly. However, for Reflection Cube Maps and Irradiance Volumes, you need to bake before they're of any use.

To bake the indirect lighting captured by your light probes, go to Render Properties and expand the Indirect Lighting panel. You should see something similar to what's shown in Figure 3-23.

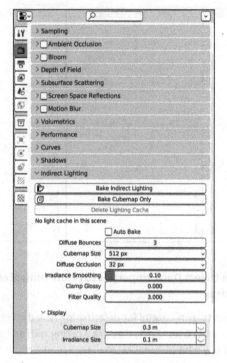

FIGURE 3-23:
The Indirect Light-
ing panel in Ren-
der Properties is
where you bake
indirect lighting
data captured by
your light probes.

The following are the settings you should pay the most attention to in this panel:

>> **Auto Bake:** Enable this check box to automatically re-generate your light cache any time you modify one of your light probes. It's handy when you're setting up light probes but can slow down your workflow if you have it enabled for other steps in your process.

>> **Diffuse Bounces:** Just like with Cycles, the more bounces you have, the more accurate your light cache is going to be. But the trade-off is that the baking process takes longer as well.

>> **Cubemap Size:** Basically, a cube map is just a fancy of texture, kind of like a shadow map. This value controls the size of the cube map in the same way. If your reflections or indirect lighting looks a little jagged at the edges or otherwise appears to be low resolution, try bumping up this value. For the most efficient use of memory, it's recommended to make this value a power of 2 (for example, 512px, 1024px, 2048px, and so on).

>> **Diffuse Occlusion:** Irradiance Volumes contribute light to your scene. Like most things that generate light in Eevee, there's the chance that it could contribute to light leakage on indoor scenes. To combat these leaks, each irradiance sample also stores a shadow map. The Diffuse Occlusion value defines the size of those shadow maps. Larger sizes should help reduce leaks, but will make baking slower.

Once you're happy with the configuration parameters you choose, it's time to get to baking. Baking is performed with one of the two buttons at the top of the Indirect Lighting panel:

>> **Bake Indirect Lighting:** If you have an Irradiance Volume light probe in your scene or a mix of Irradiance Volumes and Reflection Cube Map probes, then this is the button you want to click. When you click this button, Blender bakes the whole light cache for you.

>> **Bake Cubemap Only:** If you don't have any Irradiance Volumes in your scene, then you can click the Bake Cubemap Only button. This choice usually results in a finished bake a bit sooner because it doesn't have to account for all the bounced light in your scene.

REMEMBER

Baking is meant to happen just once *before* you start rendering. So if you find yourself coming back to a file and making changes, you should probably click the Delete Lighting Cache button and re-bake your light cache so all your changes are accounted for prior to rendering.

Understanding the limitations of light probes

Although light probes are a fantastic tool for getting impressive results with Eevee, you're not always going to get renders as accurate as those generated by Cycles. One of the biggest limitations you might discover is when animating. If you've got reflections or bounced light in your scene, and something moves, then the light cache needs to be re-baked to account for that change. Unfortunately, as of this writing, there's currently no easy way (outside of a Python script) to update and re-bake your light cache with each frame change. That means that unless you're really clever about your usage of light probes, you're going to see inaccurate lighting and reflections when you animate, particularly if you animate the lights themselves or large parts of your scene. The first frame of your animation will look fine, but subsequent frames will likely be inaccurate. If you're just animating your camera, though, the effect of the light probes should remain stable.

Another thing to pay attention to is the size of your light probes and their general coverage area. For example, if you place a Reflection Plane in a spot other than your mirror object or if it's rotated slightly differently, you may end up with some distorted-looking reflections. Of course, if you're building a carnival funhouse scene, that might be exactly what you want. But outside of that somewhat limited-use case, you should probably have it match your mirror's placement, size, and orientation.

Also, remember that every light probe you add to your scene can give you slower render times. So don't flood your scene with Irradiance Volumes and Reflection Cube Maps without due consideration.

Don't let this section get you down, though. There are still some incredible results that you can get in Eevee by making smart choices with light probes and mixing them with Eevee's wonderful screen space effects.

Chapter **4**

Exporting and Rendering Scenes

The longer that you work in Blender, the more frequently you'll find that parts of what you create need to be split off from your base .blend file. Sometimes, you'll have a neat little base model or a surface material that you want to reuse in other projects. Other times, you'll find that you need to share your Blender work with other 3D artists who are using different software or building a game. And Still, other times, you may want a printable still image of a scene or a movie of your character falling down a flight of stairs. At their core, all of these activities can be summarized as "getting stuff out of your Blender file." The important distinction is what you intend to do with that "stuff" once you get it out. In the most common scenario, the output isn't 3D at all. It's a 2D image or video that can be viewed anywhere. In other cases, you're defining parts of your file as being reusable assets in other Blender scenes. From there, it's natural to consider getting your 3D data out to other applications. These topics are what's covered in this chapter.

Blender's Render Engines

Rendering is the process of taking the data in your 3D scene (geometry, lights, materials, and so on) and converting it to a 2D image or video. That rendering process is managed by a *render engine*, a set of algorithms that simulate or approximate visual phenomena using your 3D scene as input. Over the years, there have been many different kinds of render engines developed by computer graphics researchers. Broadly stated, there are two approaches to rendering:

>> **Real time rendering:** This rendering approach is most commonly used in video games, where it's critical to generate images in fractions of a second so you can visualize a 3D scene without significant delay. This rendering approach is also used in the 3D Viewport of content creation tools like Blender. As a trade-off for this incredibly fast rendering speed, real time render engines sacrifice a bit of realism because more accurate techniques tend to require a lot of processing power and time to finish.

>> **Offline rendering:** In offline rendering, render time matters a lot less than real time rendering. The emphasis for most offline render engines is a high degree of physical accuracy. Because time is less of a constraint, offline renderers can take advantage of computationally expensive techniques to accurately simulate light behavior in a scene. Of course, the trade-off for this accuracy is that, depending on the complexity of the scene, a single rendered frame can take minutes, hours, and (in extreme cases) sometimes days to complete.

REMEMBER

Whatever the technical differences are between engines, the important difference boils down to trade-offs between artist time and computer time. In real time render engines, the emphasis is on reducing computer time, so sometimes it takes artists longer to set up a scene that looks physically correct. In contrast, offline render engines help optimize artist time, letting them set up scenes quickly at the cost of making the computer work harder to render them.

Blender ships with two render engines, one of each of these types. The real time render engine is called Eevee, while Blender's offline renderer is called Cycles. Typically, because real time and offline rendering techniques can differ so wildly, the way you set up your scene and materials can also be quite different, depending on the kind of rendering you're doing. With Blender, this is not the case. One goal of Eevee is to have as much parity as possible in its materials with those of Cycles. The idea is that you should be able to treat Eevee as a kind of fast preview engine for Cycles. This arrangement allows you to enjoy the best of both worlds without needing to change everything when switching render engines. Of course, you're not prevented from using Eevee exclusively, and many artists do, specifically because it's so fast. There are still a few differences between the two renderers;

the previous chapters in this book all cover some features that are exclusive to either Eevee or Cycles.

Both Eevee and Cycles are considered modern renderers. Ironically, their core technologies are still based on "classic" rendering techniques. Cycles is based on *ray tracing*, an older rendering method that has become more popular as computers have gotten fast enough to use this technique without taking days to output a single frame. A ray tracer works by shooting imaginary lines, called rays, from the camera to the scene. Those rays intersect or bounce off of materials or lights in the scene. Based on where those rays connect, the renderer calculates the correct color and brightness of materials in the scene. Ray tracing can more accurately depict the behavior of light in a scene than the methods used in render engines like Eevee (often called rasterizing renderers). That said, even though Eevee isn't as accurate as a ray tracer, it (like Cycles) is designed to be a *physically based rendering* (PBR) engine. That is, regardless of whether it's using rays like Cycles or "cheats" in screen space like Eevee, both engines try to model light and materials in such a way that they're as accurate as possible to how they work in meatspace. The PBR approach makes it easier for artists to set up lights and materials because you can apply your understanding of the physical world to digital space.

Both render engines can take advantage of the graphics processing unit (GPU) on video cards to accelerate the rendering process, just in different ways. Eevee is the driving force behind everything you see in the 3D Viewport, using a lot of the same technology that video game engines use to show their 3D graphics. If you've modeled or animated in Blender, you've already used Eevee. In contrast, Cycles can take advantage of some of GPUs' ability to do ray tracing calculations (sometimes referred to as GPGPU — general purpose GPU — or GPU compute) much faster than your computer's main CPU. Cycles is still generally slower than Eevee, but it doesn't necessarily have to be.

Technically, Blender also has a third render engine named Workbench. You can choose it from Render Properties, just like Eevee and Cycles. However, as its name implies, it's meant as an engine for the 3D Viewport that's exclusively for working with your 3D geometry, separate from any material or lighting considerations. Although you can do some really cool (and useful!) things with it in the 3D Viewport, the Workbench engine isn't meant as a render engine for final output.

So when do you choose to use one render engine or the other? In an ideal world, you'll use both, actually. If you're just starting out, my recommendation is to focus on the aesthetic. What kind of look are you trying to achieve with your 3D image or animation?

» Are you aiming for the kind of realism you see in a photograph? Cycles usually is a better choice for absolute realism. You could get close with Eevee, but Cycles has the tools to take your image to the next level.

>> You don't care about realism, and you're interested in taking more artistic license with the way things look (leaning toward the cartoony or the abstract)? Eevee may be a better fit for your project because there are a few situations where it's easier to break it out of the PBR mold.

The typical scenario has you using both. Do all your preliminary setup using Eevee, treating it as *lookdev* (look development) for your final output in Cycles. Ultimately, you'll have to decide case by case. In fact, I've used *both* renderers on a project, then composited the results (using the tools covered in Book 5, Chapter 2) to get the best of both worlds.

Whatever you decide, the other chapters in this book (Book 3) cover how to set up materials, lights, and environments in both Eevee and Cycles.

Rendering a Scene

More often than exporting, as covered later in this chapter, you probably want to render your scenes. Again, *rendering* is the process of taking your 3D data and creating one or more 2D pictures from the perspective of a camera. The 2D result can then be seen by nearly anyone using image viewers or movie players.

REMEMBER

Rendering is very much like taking a photograph or a movie in meatspace. If you don't have a camera, you can't take a picture. Likewise in Blender, if there's no camera in your scene, Blender doesn't know what to render, so make sure that you have a camera in there. If there is no camera, you can add a camera (Add ⇨ Camera) and set it as the active camera in the scene (View ⇨ Cameras ⇨ Set Active Object as Camera).

TIP

If your scene is complex, the Outliner is a fantastic place to find and select your camera object. Assuming you haven't renamed your camera object, you can use the Search field in the Outliner's header. Type in `Camera`; if that object exists in your .blend file, it shows up highlighted in the Outliner.

Creating a still image

Rendering single images, or *stills*, in Blender is remarkably easy, regardless of the render engine you choose. Blender actually offers two different ways to do it. The fastest way is to simply press the F12 hotkey. Alternatively, you can choose Render ⇨ Render Image from the top menu. For details on setting up your materials and lighting for each of Blender's renderers, look at Chapters 1, 2, and 3 in this book.

Viewing your rendered images in Blender

Any way you decide to do render, Blender uses its integrated Image Editor to display the rendered output. By default, Blender pops up a new window with a dedicated Image Editor to display your render as it progresses. Of course, some people would prefer a different behavior for displaying renders, especially if they're using the Render workspace that comes with Blender's General workflow template. The default certainly isn't my preferred approach. Fortunately, available options allow you to change that behavior. The control is within the Interface section of Preferences (Edit ⇨ Preferences). Within the Editors panel, there's a Temporary Editors sub-panel. Look for a drop-down menu there labeled "Render In." By default, it's set to New Window.

Figure 4-1 shows the Render In menu and the four different options you have for where to send your renders. I like to use the Image Editor setting or Full Screen. The following is a quick description of what each option does:

» **Keep User Interface:** Blender doesn't display your render at all if you don't already have an Image Editor available. This option can reduce the resources Blender consumes while rendering, but you don't get to see your render as it progresses.

» **Maximized Area:** This option does the same thing as the Image Editor option, except it also maximizes the Image Editor to the entire Blender window.

» **Image Editor:** Blender changes the largest area on your screen to an Image Editor and displays your rendered image there.

» **New Window:** The default. Blender creates a completely new window, populated only with an Image Editor that displays your image.

For any of these render options, you can quickly toggle between your regular Blender workspace and the render view by pressing F11.

TIP

Another cool feature that works regardless of which way you like to see your renders are the render slots (sometimes called *render buffers*). Render slots are useful for comparing how incremental changes you make in your scene affect your final render output. Imagine that you're trying to decide what color works best for a car model, or you're choosing between a few different lighting setups. In those kinds of situations, it's often helpful to quickly toggle between two or more renders so you can get a sense of the change (and whether you like it). You can manually change between render slots using the Slot drop-down menu in the Image Editor's header. Blender offers you the ability to swap between up to eight render slots.

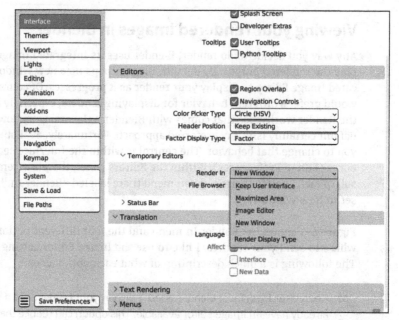

FIGURE 4-1:
To view your
renders, choose
Maximized Area,
Image Editor, or
New Window. If
you don't want to
view your render,
choose Keep User
Interface.

The drop-down menu is nice, but the render slots are most useful when using hotkeys. You can swap back and forth between render slots using the J hotkey. The following scenario is something that I do frequently when rendering my work:

1. **Render once (Render ⇨ Render Image or press the F12 hotkey).**

2. **When you have your render output onscreen in the Image Editor, hover your mouse cursor in that editor and press J.**

   Upon doing so, Blender switches to a different image buffer. The first time, it may seem odd because you just see a blank Image Editor. That's OK, the next step should handle that.

3. **Bounce back to your scene (F11) and make a small change.**

4. **Render again (F12).**

5. **Press J on your render output.**

   It pops back to your previous render.

6. **Press J again, and you're back at your current render.**

   The default behavior is to use J to toggle between two slots, but if you're using more render slots, you can cycle forward and backward by using J and Alt+J, respectively.

Picking an image format

Now, you have your image rendered, but you still haven't saved it anywhere on your hard drive. That image is just in a buffer in Blender; it's not quite available for sharing with other people yet. This, too, is easily remedied, but before you save, you may want to change the file type for your image. Go to the Output tab of the Properties editor and look to the Output panel within it, as shown in Figure 4-2.

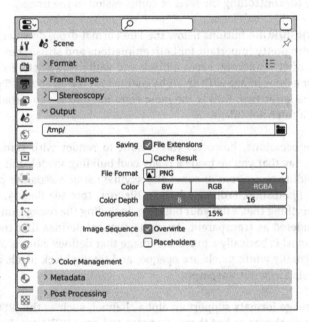

FIGURE 4-2:
The Output panel in the Output tab of the Properties editor.

TIP

When you save with Blender's File Browser, you can also choose the file type for your image from a drop-down menu in the region on the right side.

The file type selector in the File Browser works great if you need to save to a file format that you don't typically save to (sometimes a customer may need both a JPEG and a PNG, for example). It's also handy if you're in a rush and forget to choose your image format ahead of time. In fact, you don't even need to re-render if you change your image format. Internally, Blender stores your renders in the highest possible quality and only compresses when you save to a specific format (see "Saving your still image" in this chapter).

That said, the Output panel in Output Properties is the preferred way because it gives you a few more options for controlling your saved file. The primary control for choosing the format of your file in the Output panel is a File Format drop-down menu. By default, Blender saves renders as PNG (pronounced "ping") images. If you want to render to a different image format, such as JPEG, Targa, TIFF, or OpenEXR, left-click this drop-down menu and choose your desired file type. Depending on the file type you choose, the options at the bottom of the Output panel change. For example, with the PNG file type, the Compression slider is available for controlling the level of compression in the image.

The BW/RGB/RGBA buttons below the File Format drop-down are always visible, and they're pretty important for both animations and stills. They control whether Blender, after rendering, saves a black and white (grayscale) image, a full color image, or a color image with an alpha channel for transparency. Typically, you use one of the latter two. RGB is the most common and is supported by all formats, creating a full color image.

On some occasions, however, you'll want to render with transparency. As an example, say that you've made a really cool building model, and you want to add your building to a photo of some city skyline using a separate program such as GIMP or Photoshop. (You can do it in Blender, too; see Book 5, Chapter 2.) You need everything that's not your building, including the background of your image, to be rendered as transparent. An alpha channel defines that transparency. The *alpha channel* is basically a grayscale image that defines what is and is not transparent. Totally white pixels are opaque, and totally black pixels are transparent. Gray pixels are semitransparent.

REMEMBER

Not all image formats support an alpha channel, such as the JPEG and BMP formats. If you choose one of these file types and have RGBA set, Blender just omits the alpha information when saving. If you want to make sure that your alpha channel is preserved, though, choose one of the following formats: PNG, Targa, TIFF, or OpenEXR.

Setting dimensions for your renders

The Format panel close to the top of Output Properties gives you control over the size of your final render. The X and Y values by the Resolution label set the width and height of your image in pixels. The X and Y values by the Aspect label are for determining the horizontal and vertical aspect ratio of your image. The ability to adjust aspect ratio is for certain circumstances where you want to render your image with rectangular pixels rather than square ones. Typically, rectangular pixels are necessary only for older television formats, so unless you know exactly what you're doing or if you're using a preset, I recommend setting these to the same value. I use 1.000 most of the time.

TIP

Speaking of presets, Blender offers a number of rendering presets for you to use. These presets are available from a drop-down menu at the top of the Format panel. Click the icon that looks like a menu (shown to the left on this page) to see the presets available. Choosing any one of them affects only settings in the Format panel, but they're really handy if you know what your final output should be. You can even add your own preset based on your current settings by clicking the New Preset button at the bottom of the presets menu. Using presets is a great time-saver when you know, for example, that you have to render to high-definition video specifications, but you can't remember the right resolution, aspect ratio, and frame-rate values.

REMEMBER

Whenever you change the resolution or aspect ratio values in the Format panel, you need to render your scene again (F12) to get it to appear (and eventually save) at the right size. If you're just changing your output file type, you don't need to re-render.

Saving your still image

After you've adjusted all your settings, rendered, and chosen your output file format, you have just one thing left to do: Save your still image. Saving is quick and painless. From the Image Editor, choose Image ⇨ Save As, and Blender opens a File Browser. Here, you can dictate where on your computer you want to save your render. That's it!

WARNING

Remember, if you're rendering a still image, it's *not* saved anywhere on your hard drive unless you explicitly save it by navigating to Image ⇨ Save As in the Image Editor. I can't tell you how much time I spent re-rendering images that I forgot to save when I first started using Blender. Hopefully, you can learn from my mistake.

TIP

If you find that you keep forgetting to save your renders or (like me) you just can't be bothered to remember, you can work around it by taking advantage of Blender's Compositor. Book 5, Chapter 2 has a lot more detail on what the Compositor is and the fun things you can do with it. However, for the time being, the main thing you need to know is that the Compositor is used to do automatic modifications to your rendered result. In this case, the "modification" that you're doing is automatically saving by routing your render result to a File Output node. Follow these steps to set up automatic saving (have a look at Book 5, Chapter 2 if any of the terms here seem alien to you):

1. **Switch to the Compositing workspace using the tabs at the top of the Blender window.**

   Your main focus is the large Compositor area in the middle of the window.

2. **Enable the Use Nodes check box in the Compositor's header.**

Two nodes will appear in the Compositor: a Render Layers node and a Composite node.

3. **Add a File Output node (Add ⇨ Output ⇨ File Output).**

The node will be added under your mouse cursor. Left-click to place the node somewhere to the right of your Render Layers node.

4. **Wire the yellow Image socket of the Render Layers node to the yellow Image socket on the File Output node.**

You're almost there. All that remains is a little configuration.

5. **Select your File Output node and click the Node tab in the Compositor's Sidebar.**

6. **In the Node tab, expand the Properties panel and edit the File Output node's settings to taste.**

The most important settings are at the top of the panel, and they should look pretty familiar. They're almost exactly like the Output panel in Output Properties. The key settings you want to adjust are the Base Path (where your file will be saved on your hard drive) and the File Format.

Now, when you render, Blender automatically saves an image to the location on your hard drive that you specified with the Base Path field. The file will be named something like Image0001.png, assuming you rendered using the PNG format and your scene is at frame 1 (that's what the 0001 is there for; if you rendered a JPEG from frame 57, the file would be Image0057.jpg). If you don't want the file name to start with Image, you can change that. In the Node tab where you set the Base Path for the File Output node, there's a list box with only one item named Image. That item corresponds to the Image socket on the File Output node. Double-click that item to rename it something more descriptive, and you'll see the socket on the File Output node update as well. Now, when you render (Render ⇨ Render Image), Blender automatically makes a file on your hard drive that starts with whatever you renamed that socket to be.

The cool thing is that you only have to set up this node network once in your .blend file. After that, any time you reopen this project file, it's already set to save whenever you render.

TIP

If you ever want to disable this automatic saving behavior, you can mute the File Output node by selecting it and pressing M. See Book 5, Chapter 2 for even more information on using the Compositor.

Creating a sequence of still images for editing or compositing

The majority of your controls for rendering animations are in Output Properties, just like for rendering still images. In particular, your main focus should be the Output panel within that tab. Generally speaking, the steps are similar to rendering stills (see preceding section); all the actual file saving happens automatically. The largest consideration is where you intend to store those files on your hard drive. Enter this information in the first field of the Output panel. By default, Blender saves your animations to the temporary directory on your computer. However, you may want to save the animation to a different, more permanent folder on your hard drive. (On most computer operating systems, the contents of the temporary folder are periodically deleted, which is not exactly something you want to happen to your finished images.) Left-click the file folder icon to the right of this text field and use the File Browser to navigate where you want to save your animation.

TIP

When you save a sequence of still images, you should create a specific folder just for these render files. You're going to create a *lot* of files. If the animation is 250 frames long and you render to still images, you're going to get 250 individual images saved to your hard drive. You really don't want to mix all those files with your other project files and assets. For simplicity, I typically make a folder in the same place as my `.blend` file and prefix that folder's name with the word "render-". So if I have an animation of a jumping mongoose, my render path might look like `//render-jumping_mongoose/`. (The `//` is Blender shorthand for a *relative path*, or a location on your hard drive relative to your `.blend` file).

The other consideration when saving an animation deals with the file type you choose. If, for example, you choose a still image format like JPEG, PNG, or OpenEXR, Blender creates an individual image for each frame in your animation. However, if you insist on choosing any of the movie options like AVI or FFMPEG Video, Blender creates a single movie file that contains all the frames in the animation, as well as any sound you use for the animation. See Book 5, Chapter 1 for more on rendering to video.

So, to render animation, the steps are pretty similar to rendering a still:

1. **From Output Properties, set up your render resolution from the Format panel and your File Format from the Output panel.**

   If you've been working on your animation, hopefully, you've set it up already. Although changing the output resolution (the width and height) of the image after you animate isn't too bad, changing to other frame rates after the fact can ruin the timing of an animation, which can be a pain to fix. Set the frame rate from the Frame Rate value in the second block of buttons of the Format panel.

2. **Confirm the start and end frames from the Frame Range panel.**

You probably already made this setting while animating, but double-check these start and end frame values to make sure they're correct. These values also can be set from the Timeline's header.

3. **Verify where you want to save your file in the Output panel.**

4. **Animate by choosing Render ⇨ Render Animation (or use the Ctrl+F12 hotkey).**

Your animation starts the creation process immediately. Now, go get a cup of coffee; rendering an animation can take quite some time.

REMEMBER Unlike rendering a single still image, which does not save anything to your hard drive until you explicitly save it, rendering an animation saves your renders automatically wherever you stipulate in the Output panel. Those files will end up in your folder, named sequentially. So using our jumping mongoose example, if you use your operating system's file browser to navigate to the render-jumping_mongoose folder and you're rendering a sequence of PNG images, that folder will be populated with 0001.png, 0002.png, 0003.png, and so on.

TIP You can add a prefix to each of your render files by typing it at the end of your output path in the Output panel of Output Properties (whew . . . that's a lot of output). For example, if your output path is //render-jumping_mongoose/ and you change it to //render-jumping_mongoose/frame, then when you look in that folder after you're done rendering, you'll have file names that look like frame0001.png, frame0002.png, frame0002.png, and so on.

Rendering a sequence of images versus rendering video

In most situations, rendering out a sequence of still images rather than a single movie file makes a lot of sense. One of the biggest reasons for rendering a sequence of stills is for *compositing*, or combining multiple images together. When you do compositing, there are typically two things that you want on your input images: high quality and (if possible) an alpha channel. With respect to high quality, video compression tends to throw away a lot more information than image compression, so color accuracy and detail is often lost in video. Furthermore, when compositing, you often rely on having an alpha channel that makes everything transparent except for your rendered subject. Most video formats simply don't support an alpha channel, so to accommodate this shortcoming, you render out a sequence of still images in a format that does support alpha, such as PNG.

Another reason that you may want to have a still image sequence rather than a movie file is for *editing*, or sequencing multiple video and animation clips. Many video codecs throw away large chunks of image data from one frame to the next to get smaller file sizes. The result is a small file that plays well but is pretty difficult to edit, because in editing, you may want to cut on a frame that doesn't have very much image data at all. Using a sequence of still images guarantees that all image data for each and every frame is completely there for smooth editing. Book 5, Chapter 1 covers editing in more detail, and Chapter 2 focuses on compositing.

The third reason you may want to render a sequence of still images is largely practical. When rendering to a movie format, what happens if you decide to stop the render and change a small part of it? Or what happens if Blender crashes in the middle of rendering? Or, if an army of angry squirrels invade your office and shut down your computer mid-render? Well, you have to restart the whole render process from the start frame. Starting over, of course, is painful, especially if you have to wait multiple minutes (or hours!) for each frame in your sequence to render. If you render by using a sequence of still images, those images are saved the second they're created. If your render process gets stopped for any reason, you don't have to start rendering again from the beginning. You can adjust the Start value in the Format panel of Output Properties (or in the Timeline) to pick up where you left off and resume the render process.

As an example, imagine that you've got an animation that's 1000 frames long. Your computer has been rendering for three days, and it's at frame 999 when the power goes out. If you rendered directly to a movie file, then POOF . . . you just lost everything, and you've got to spend another three days of rendering. But if you rendered a sequence of images, then all you have to do is render the last frame, and you're all done!

TIP

That said, sometimes it does make sense to render to a movie file. Usually, the recommended time to render to a single movie file is in *post-production*, the time after you've completed your animation and rendered to a sequence of stills. The general workflow is something like this:

1. Work on your animation.

2. Render your animation to a sequence of still images.

3. Post-process those images (video editing to mix with audio, and compositing to mix with other image sequences; see Book 5, Chapters 1 and 2).

4. Render your post-processed output to a video file.

Of course, there are always variations to that workflow. Blender allows you to do compositing tasks before your first render, for example. But the general process of animating to render stills and post-processing to render video is the key thing to remember.

Working with Assets in Blender

As you continue working with Blender, you're going to make a lot of things. Often, you'll want to be able to reuse these things in other projects. In Blender, these "things" are referred to as *assets*. An asset in Blender is essentially a datablock, as described in the second chapter of this All-in-One. With a few exceptions, any datablock can be considered an asset within Blender. That means that objects can be assets, materials can be assets, sculpting and painting brushes can be assets, and even geometry node networks can be assets. The Geometry Node example is covered in more detail when covering hair assets in Book 4, Chapter 5. Assets are even covered in Book 4, Chapter 3 when discussing pose libraries.

Many Blender artists find that with every new project, there's at least one thing in there that they know they want to reuse in future projects. If you're going to do all that work, there are some things you don't want to make from scratch over and over again continually. For example, if you have a really great wood material, that material is the perfect candidate for being an asset that can be used in other projects.

In previous versions of Blender, Blender artists would make special .blend files and use Blender linking and appending features (see Book 6, Chapter 1) to build a kind of makeshift library. This system worked (in fact, it still works); however, this approach isn't necessarily easy to discover, and it's a little kludgy to use as a library. Fortunately, in the releases of Blender since the last version of this book, Blender now has a full-blown asset library that's more tightly integrated and allows for cool features like drag-and-drop of those assets.

Building an asset library

When it comes to building asset libraries, it's important to understand that asset libraries can come in two flavors: local and global. A *local* asset library lives in your current working .blend file and is meant to be used and reused in that active project. A prime example of this kind of asset library is a pose library, as described in Book 4, Chapter 3. Poses travel with a character, so it makes sense to bundle the library in the same .blend file as that character and its rig. A *global* asset library is accessible to all your projects. These are more general kinds of assets and tend to get used across multiple projects. You can set up a third, "middle tier" kind of asset library specific to multiple .blend files in a shared project, but that's a topic deserving of more pages than are available in this section of the book.

To access your asset libraries, you need to make use of Blender's Asset Browser. None of Blender's default workspaces have an area dedicated to the Asset Browser. Instead, you'll need to either create a space for the Asset Browser or switch an existing area to contain the Asset Browser. As an example, follow these steps:

1. **Start a new Blender session with the General workflow template (File ⇨ New ⇨ General).**

2. **In the Layout workspace, click and drag the seam between the 3D Viewport and Timeline to increase the space that the Timeline takes.**

3. **Change the Timeline to an Asset Browser using the Editor Type drop-down in the Timeline's header.**

When you're done with these steps, your Blender window should look something like what's shown in Figure 4-3. This screen layout is particularly helpful if you're blocking out your scene and you're not actively animating.

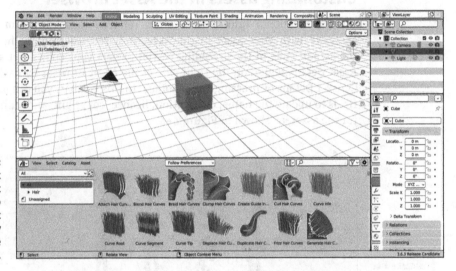

FIGURE 4-3:
You can adjust
the Layout
workspace to
show an Asset
Browser by
changing the
Timeline area.

As of this writing, the default view of the Asset Browser shows a set of geometry node assets used for building and managing hair, as described in Book 4, Chapter 5. The Asset Browser itself is fairly simple in terms of layout. The main body of the Asset Browser is populated with thumbnail images that correspond with the assets in your library. The Source List region on the left side of the Asset Browser shows the categories, or *catalogs*, for your assets, giving you the ability to filter your library by catalog so you can more quickly find the asset you're looking for.

You can make an object an asset from the 3D Viewport by selecting it and choosing Object ⇨ Asset ⇨ Mark as Asset from the header menu. If you do this with the default cube in your base scene, you should see a thumbnail image of your cube immediately added to your Asset Browser. Alternatively, you can right-click the object's name in the Outliner and choose Mark as Asset from the context menu that appears.

TIP

You can tell that a datablock in your `.blend` file is marked as an asset by finding it in the Outliner. If it's marked as an asset, it has an Asset Browser icon (like the one shown in the margin) next to its name.

Now that your cube is an asset, you can immediately add a new one to your scene by clicking its thumbnail image in the Asset Browser and dragging it to the 3D Viewport. In the 3D Viewport, Blender provides you with a placement widget to help you previsualize where the asset is to be placed in your scene. If you drag your mouse cursor over the existing default cube, you should notice that the widget snaps to the faces of the cube so you can place your new one directly on its surface.

Customizing assets in the Asset Browser

There's additional information, often referred to as *metadata*, that you can associate with your asset in the Asset Browser. Continuing the example with the default cube in the preceding section, select your cube asset and expand the Asset Details region on the right side of the Asset Browser by navigating to View ⇨ Asset Details or pressing the N hotkey. In this sidebar, you can use the available fields to update the name, description, license, copyright, and author information for the asset, as shown in Figure 4-4.

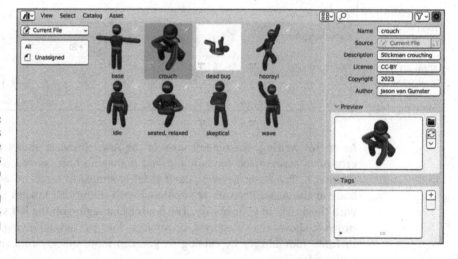

FIGURE 4-4:
The Asset Details sidebar in the Asset Browser is where you can add metadata on your selected asset and update its thumbnail image.

You can also customize the thumbnail image from the Preview panel. Click the refresh icon to have Blender automatically generate a new thumbnail image for you (like if you made a change to the asset), or click the folder icon to choose an image from your hard drive to use as your custom thumbnail image.

From the Tags panel at the bottom of the Asset Details sidebar, you can add text tags to your asset to make it easier to find your asset when you have a lot of them, and catalogs aren't quite enough.

Speaking of catalogs, your example cube asset doesn't yet belong to any catalog. You can confirm this by clicking the Unassigned item in the catalog list on the left of the Asset Browser. You can rectify this situation by clicking the plus (+) symbol next to the category icon in the upper right corner of the category list. However, if you click this icon in the default view of the Asset Browser, nothing will happen. The reason is that Blender doesn't know whether the catalog is local to your current file or part of your global asset library. You need to specify to which asset library to add the catalog by clicking the drop-down menu at the top of the Source List region and select Current File from that menu. Now, instead of seeing all assets in both your global and local libraries, you're seeing only assets local to your current file.

With your current file specified in your Source List, you can now click the plus (+) symbol next to the catalog icon and Blender instantly creates a new catalog named Catalog. Double-click the name, and you can rename the catalog to something more sensible.

After you have your catalog created, you can add assets to it by clicking and dragging their thumbnail image from the Asset Browser to the desired catalog name in the Source List.

There's an asterisk (*) next to your new catalog name. That asterisk is an indication that the catalog name has not yet been saved. Because this is a local asset library, the catalog list travels with it and, therefore, isn't saved until you save your .blend file.

REMEMBER

Creating a global asset library

So far in this chapter, you've been creating a local asset library that stays with your current .blend file. What if you want to populate a global asset library? The first thing to understand is where that global asset library lives. Blender ships with a global asset library named User Library. You can see it by going to the drop-down menu in the Source List region of the Asset Browser and choosing User Library.

When you choose User Library from the Source list, there's a chance that you might see a warning in the main area of the Asset Browser that says the path to your asset library doesn't exist, along with a button that opens the File Paths section of Preferences. At the bottom of that section is an Asset Libraries panel containing a list box that can be populated with multiple global asset libraries. By default, this list has only a single asset library named User Library. Below the list of asset libraries are fields that indicate where on your hard drive Blender is expecting the asset libraries to be saved, typically something like `Blender/Assets` in your computer's `Documents` folder. If you had that error, you can click the folder icon to the right of this field and choose or create a valid path for your global asset library. When you're done, you can close Preferences and go back to your `.blend` file.

Now that you know where your global asset library lives, the process of adding assets to that library is as simple as saving your `.blend` file to that folder. Any object in your file that's marked as an asset will be visible from the Asset Browser in your User Library the next time you open any Blender project.

Exporting to external formats

Exporting takes your 3D data from Blender and restructures it so other 3D programs can understand it. There are two primary reasons why you'd want to export to a 3D file format other than Blender's `.blend` format. The most common reason is to do additional editing in another program. For example, if you're working as a modeler on a large project, chances are good that (unfortunately) Blender is not the only tool in their pipeline, so you'll probably need to save it in a format that fits into their workflow and that their tools understand. Typically, for a lot of production pipelines, common interchange formats are FBX, USD, and Alembic.

Another reason for exporting is for video games. Many games have a public specification of the format they use for loading 3D data. Blender can export in many of these formats, allowing you to create custom characters and sets. In recent years, the glTF format has become one of the more universal interchange formats for interactive applications like games and web apps.

If you've created a model in Blender that you want to use on a 3D printer, then that's another reason you'd be interested in exporting your model to a file format other than `.blend`. Specific to 3D printing, Blender doesn't do *slicing*, or generate print instructions a 3D printer can understand. You need to export to an intermediary format (typically STL or OBJ) and pull that file into dedicated 3D printing software, like Ultimaker Cura, for preparing and slicing.

WARNING

With only a few exceptions, all Blender's exporters are scripts written in the Python programming language. Although all the export scripts that ship with Blender support the basic specifications in their respective formats, they may not support all the features. For example, many of the exporters have difficulty getting armature or animation information out of Blender. So keep this limitation in mind, do a lot of testing with your exported files, and, as many open source programmers like to say, "Your mileage may vary."

To export to a different format, choose File ⇨ Export and select the format you want. A File Browser then appears so you can tell Blender where to save your new file. The left region of the File Browser contains options specific to the exporter you choose.

Most exporters in Blender are implemented as add-ons, the bulk of which are disabled by default. If you're looking for a specific exporter and you don't see it in the File ⇨ Export menu, go to the Add-ons section of Preferences (Edit ⇨ Preferences) and find the add-on that provides the exporter you need. If the add-on is there, enable it, and the exporter should immediately be available in File ⇨ Export. By default, Preferences are automatically saved, so the next time you launch Blender, that add-on will be available without needing to go through Preferences and re-enabling it.

Importing from other applications

Well, if you're working with Blender in a pipeline that you have to export from Blender to other applications, then it stands to reason that you need to be able to import into Blender as well. Fortunately, the process for importing in Blender is very similar to the exporting process. All the importers are written as Python add-ons and available from the File ⇨ Import menu. One consideration to keep in mind is that when you import to Blender, that data is converted to data structures native to Blender. You're now working with Blender data. That means if you make a change to the original, non-Blender file, that change is not going to propagate its way into your Blender file. You'll need to re-import.

One slight exception to this is the Alembic format. The reason for this exception is in how Blender handles the import process. You still use the File ⇨ Import menu, but when Blender does the import, it creates an empty mesh object with a single Mesh Sequence Cache modifier. Alembic is a special kind of file format known as a mesh cache. Basically, in an Alembic file, all the animation and material data is baked down to a sequence of meshes. Using the Mesh Sequence Cache modifier, you can choose an Alembic file and the mesh data of your object is replaced with whatever is in that file. This means that exporting to that same Alembic file from your other application updates it in Blender without needing to re-import.

TECHNICAL STUFF

Technically, the USD format also supports mesh caches and mesh sequence caches. However, as of this writing, Blender's Mesh Sequence Cache modifier doesn't yet support USD mesh caches.

4

Get Animated!

Contents at a Glance

Chapter **1**

Animating Objects

I have to make a small admission: Animation is not easy. It's time consuming, frustrating, tedious work where you often spend days, sometimes even weeks, working on what ends up to be a few seconds of finished animation. An enormous amount of work goes into animation. However, there's something incredible about making an otherwise inanimate object move, tell a story, and communicate to an audience. Getting those moments when you have beautifully believable motion — life, in some ways — is a positively indescribable sensation that is, well, indescribably positive. Animation and the process of creating animation truly has my heart more than any other art form. It's simply my favorite thing to do. It's like playing with a sock puppet, except better because you don't have to worry about whether or not it's been washed.

This chapter, as well as the rest of the chapters in Book 4, go pretty heavily into the technical details of creating animations using Blender. Blender is a great tool for the job. Beyond what this book can provide, though, animation is about seeing, understanding, and re-creating motion. I highly recommend that you make it a point to get out and watch things. And not just animations! Go to a park and study how people move. Try to move like other people so that you can understand how their weight shifts and how gravity and inertia compete with and accentuate those movements. Watch lots of movies and television and pay close attention to how people's facial expressions can convey what they're trying to say. If you get a chance, go to a theater and watch a play. Understanding how and why stage actors exaggerate their body language is an incredibly useful tool for an animator.

REMEMBER

While you're going out there seeing the world like an animator, think about how you can use the technical information in these chapters to re-create those feelings and that motion with your objects in Blender.

Getting Started with Animation in Blender

Before you jump headlong into the world of animating with Blender, it's helpful to understand the general workflow for animation. Then you can see how that workflow applies to Blender. If you recall from Book 1, Chapter 2, Blender has five different editors dedicated to the process of animation. With all those editors available, it might be difficult to guess which one you should be using. Fortunately, this is where knowledge of animation workflows comes in handy. Generally speaking, when you animate, you work in multiple passes, focusing on more detailed movement (and nuances within that movement) with every iterative pass. The basic passes are as follows:

1. **Planning:** This step is frequently done outside of Blender, often with traditional pen and paper. You create a series of drawings that show the key shots in your animated sequence, called a *storyboard*. With a storyboard complete, you have a much clearer understanding of what's going to happen in your animation. You can take the images of your storyboard and assemble them sequentially in a video editor (or Blender's Video Sequencer — see Book 5, Chapter 1 for more on the Video Sequencer) to create a moving storyboard, called an *animatic*. It's also possible to create your storyboard and animatic all within Blender using Grease Pencil objects (see Book 4, Chapter 6) using the built-in Story Pencil add-on, but that topic is a little bit out of scope for this book.

2. **Blocking:** With your plan in place, the next step is *blocking*, where you rough out the biggest movements in your animated sequence. The majority of your time for this step is spent in the 3D Viewport getting things positioned correctly for each major keyframe. The rest of your time is spent in the Dope Sheet, getting the rough timing correct by sliding those keyframes forward and backward in time.

3. **Refining:** With your blocking pass complete, your next step is *refining* your animation. This is the step where you add the little bits of secondary movement that really push life into the objects you're animating. You're still spending a lot of time in the 3D Viewport to work on those keyframes; you're just keying more things and adding more in-between keys to get that refined movement. And again, you're spending the rest of your time in the Dope Sheet where you can adjust the timing on your actions. Often you will have multiple refining passes before you're really happy with the results.

4. **Final Polish:** It's in *final polish* where you really start to use the Graph Editor. This step is where you focus on the nuanced changes between frames. Your focus is tweaking the rate of change, how quickly or slowly the movement happens from one keyframe to the next. Even though this is the final step in the animation process, you often end up spending a *lot* of your time here.

If you're coming to Blender from another 3D animation package, this approach might seem a bit alien. Animators in other software often focus on working exclusively in the Graph Editor. Part of that is because as much as 80 percent of your time as animator is spent in final polish (especially if someone else is doing the planning step). However, another reason, in my opinion, is that the developers of those other packages focused the majority of their attention on the Graph Editors, so their equivalent of the Dope Sheet simply isn't as pleasant to work in as Blender's. And for that reason, many animators choose to spend their time in the Graph Editor in other applications where the more developed tools reside. There's nothing wrong with that workflow, of course, but with all the curves visible in the Graph Editor (regardless of how nice the Graph Editor is), it's often difficult to get a nice high-level understanding of your animation's timing. So it's really beneficial to become friends with the Dope Sheet.

That said, this chapter focuses mostly on the Timeline and Graph Editor because, if you're just starting as an animator, it's helpful to have a visual indicator that something is changing between keyframes, even if you don't know the best way to change it. The curves between your keyframes in the Graph Editor serve this purpose really well, and should help you get a better understanding of how things work in computer animation more quickly. Furthermore, since this chapter focuses on *object animation*, or animating the objects in your scene (rather than controls set up in a rig — see Chapters 2 and 3 in this book for more on rigging), the blocking and refining steps can be done from the Timeline. Then you can jump right to final polish in the Graph Editor. For a more complete look at the animation process, including the use of the Dope Sheet, have a look at Chapter 4 within this book.

Creating the illusion of motion with static images

To effectively do animation, you really need a firm grasp on how moving pictures work. This is the fundamental basis of animation, film, television, and even video games. Without getting into the complex details of psychology and neuroscience, the basics are this: Humans perceive movement as the apparent difference in what we see at two relatively close moments in time.

If you have two images of the same object in different positions, you can create the illusion that the object moves between positions by swapping between those images very quickly. Now, chain a series of those images together and show them in quick succession. Each image is visible only for a fraction of a second before the next one appears. This rapid swapping of images tricks our minds into seeing movement on the screen.

Who said science isn't fun?

Customizing your screen layout for animation

The Blender workspace specifically set up for animation, named — conveniently — Animation, can be chosen from the workspaces tabs at the top of the Blender window or by pressing Ctrl+Page Up or Ctrl+Page Down until you land on the Animation tab. Figure 1-1 shows the default Animation workspace in Blender.

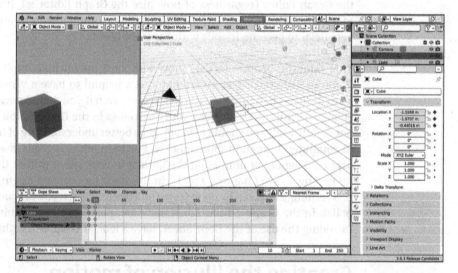

FIGURE 1-1:
Blender's Animation workspace is an excellent place to animate.

This workspace isn't too dissimilar from the Layout workspace, but it does have a few differences. In particular, the 3D Viewport is split to show, on the left, a camera view of your scene with all the non-renderable elements turned off, giving you a clean preview of your animation. The Timeline is compressed at the bottom of the window, so all you see are the playback buttons in its header, and above the Timeline is a Dope Sheet editor. (For a full reminder of what each editor does, refer to Book 1, Chapter 2.)

You may be wondering, however, why this workspace has the compressed Timeline and why it's missing the Graph Editor. Recall from the beginning of this section that the animation workflow that works well in Blender is set up so you shouldn't really need all the different editors visible at the same time. For example, the Timeline and the Dope Sheet have very similar high-level visibility of your animation, and because both of these animation editors have the same scrubbing ability, you only really need the playback buttons from the Timeline. So, in this layout, the Graph Editor isn't really missing. It's just not as necessary when you begin an animation because the workflow typically starts with the Dope Sheet editor.

That said, since this chapter focuses on using the Timeline and the Graph Editor, you may choose to switch the Dope Sheet at the bottom of the Animation workspace to a Graph Editor.

Animating your first scene

It's easiest to understand the animation process by going through a simple example. The following example shows the basic process of animating in Blender and should help explain things more clearly:

1. **Start in Blender with a new General workflow template (File ⇨ New ⇨ General).**

2. **Select the default cube object and switch to the camera view by clicking the camera icon in the upper right of the 3D Viewport.**

3. **Split the 3D Viewport horizontally and change one of the new areas to the Graph Editor (Shift+F6).**

   I like to make the lower one the Graph Editor because it's right above the Timeline in the Layout workspace.

TIP

4. **In the 3D Viewport, make sure that the default cube is selected and choose Object ⇨ Animation ⇨ Insert Keyframe ⇨ Location (you can also use hotkeys for faster access by pressing I ⇨ Location).**

   This step sets an initial location keyframe for the cube. I give a more detailed description of keyframes later in the chapter in the "Understanding keyframes" section. The important thing to notice is that the left region of the Graph Editor is now updated and shows a short-tiered list with the items Cube, CubeAction, and Object Transforms. There's also a keyframe diamond at frame 1 in the Timeline.

5. **Move forward in time by pressing → a handful of times.**

   I'd suggest moving forward about ten frames, or so. You can tell what frame you're on in the 3D Viewport by looking in the upper left corner next to the tool buttons. The second line of text there should say something like (10) Collection | Cube. The number in parentheses is your current frame.

Animating Objects

6. Grab the cube in the 3D Viewport and move it to another location in the scene.

You can either use the Move tool or use the G hotkey to immediately start moving the cube without the need of a transform gizmo.

7. Insert another keyframe (I ⇨ Location) in the 3D Viewport.

A set of colored lines appears in the Graph Editor. These colored lines are *f-curves*. F-curve is short for *function curve*, and it describes the change, or *interpolation*, between two key moments in an animated sequence. Each f-curve represents a single attribute, or *channel*, that's been animated. If you expand the Object Transforms block in the Graph Editor by clicking the triangle on the left side of its name, you can see the three location channels: X Location, Y Location, and Z Location. To see the actual curves a little bit better, move your mouse to the large graph section of the Graph Editor and press Home. Your Blender screen should look something like the one in Figure 1-2.

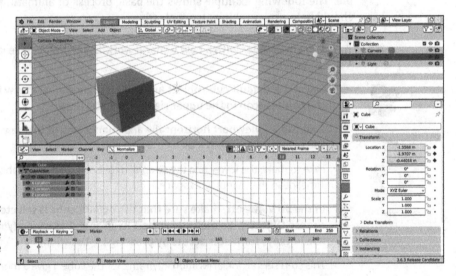

FIGURE 1-2:
Animating the location of the default cube object.

Congratulations! You just created your first animation in Blender. Here's what you did: The largest part of the Graph Editor is a graph (go figure!). Moving from left to right on this graph — its X-axis — is moving forward in time. The vertical axis on this graph represents the value of whatever channel is being animated. So the f-curves that you created describe and control the change in the cube's location in the X-, Y-, and Z-axes as you move forward in time. Blender creates the curves by interpolating between the control points, called *keys*, that you created.

To understand interpolation better, flash back to your grade school math class for a second. Remember when you had to do graphing, or take the equation for some sort of line or curve and draw it out on paper? By drawing that line, you were interpolating between points. Fortunately, you don't do any of that graphing work when animating. That's what we have Blender for!

You can see the result of your work on this example for yourself by playing back the animation. Click the Play button in the Timeline (alternatively, you can press Spacebar from just about anywhere in Blender's interface). A green vertical line, called the *timeline cursor*, moves from left to right in the graph. As the timeline cursor moves between your keyframes, you should see your cube move from the starting point to the ending point you defined in the 3D Viewport.

To stop the playback, you can either press Spacebar again or you can press Esc. If you press Spacebar, the timeline cursor stops in place. If you press Esc to stop, the timeline cursor jumps back to the frame you were on when you first started playing. You can watch the animation in a more controlled way by *scrubbing* in the Graph Editor or Timeline. If you look at the top of each of these editors, you should see a slightly darker region with numbers running horizontally; this is the scrubbing region. To scrub, left-click in the scrubbing region of either the Graph Editor or Timeline and drag your mouse cursor left and right. The timeline cursor follows the location of your mouse pointer, and you can watch the change happening in the 3D Viewport.

Understanding keyframes

As I cover earlier in this chapter, in traditional animation, a whole animated sequence is planned out ahead of time using a script and *storyboards* (drawings of the major scenes of the animation, kind of like a comic book, with arrows to indicate camera direction or character movement). Then an animator goes through and draws the primary poses of the character. These drawings are referred to as *keyframes*, or *keys*. They're the poses that the character must make to most effectively convey the intended motion to the viewer. With the keys drawn, they're handed off to a second set of animators called the *inbetweeners*. These animators are responsible for drawing all the frames between each of the keys to get the appearance of smooth motion.

Translating the workflow of traditional animation to how you do work in Blender, you should consider yourself the keyframe artist and Blender the inbetweener (at least to start). On a fully polished animation, it isn't uncommon to have some kind of key on every frame of the scene. In the quick animating example in the preceding section, you create a keyframe after you move the cube. By interpolating the curve between those keys, Blender creates the in-between frames. Some animation programs refer to the process of having software create these in-between frames as *tweening*.

Inserting keys

To have a workflow that's even more similar to traditional animation, it's preferable to define your keyframes in the 3D Viewport. Then you can use the Timeline, Dope Sheet, or Graph Editor to tweak the change from one keyframe to the next. And this workflow is exactly the way Blender is designed to animate. Start in the 3D Viewport by pressing I to open the Insert Keyframe menu (you can also choose the slower route of choosing Object ⇨ Animation ⇨ Insert Keyframe). Through this menu, you can create keyframes for the main animatable channels for an object. I describe the channels here in more detail:

>> **Available:** If you already inserted keys for some of your object's channels, choosing this option adds a key for each of those preexisting curves in the Graph Editor. If no curves are already created, no keyframes are inserted. Once you start animating, this is often a really good shortcut to have.

>> **Location:** Insert a key for the object's X, Y, and Z location.

>> **Rotation:** Insert a key for the object's rotation in the X-, Y-, and Z-axes.

>> **Scale:** Insert a key for the object's scale in the X-, Y-, and Z-axes.

>> **Transform combinations:** The next set of options insert keyframes for various combinations of the previous three values. Your choices are as follows:

   • Location & Rotation

   • Location, Rotation, & Scale

   • Location, Rotation, Scale, & Custom Properties: This option includes setting keyframes for custom properties that you set on your selected object. Custom properties are covered in more detail in the next chapter, as well as in Book 6, Chapter 2.

   • Location & Scale

   • Rotation & Scale

>> **Delta Location/Rotation/Scale:** The preceding keying options use absolute coordinates for keying animations. *Delta* keys, however, use coordinates relative to your object's current location, rotation, and scale. Delta keys can be useful if you want to have many objects with the same animation, but starting from different origin points. Of course, if you choose Available after choosing Delta keys, Blender is smart enough to know that you want to use relative rather than absolute coordinates.

>> **Visual Transforms:** Insert keyframes for location, rotation, scale, or any combination of these transforms, but based on where the object is visually located in the scene. These options are explicitly made for use with constraints, which I cover in the next chapter.

The basic workflow for setting keyframes in Blender follows these steps, regardless of whether you're animating objects, properties, or controls for an animation rig:

1. **Insert an initial keyframe (I or Object ⇨ Animation ⇨ Insert Keyframe).**

A keyframe appears at frame 1 in your animation (assuming you're at frame 1 when you insert your keyframe).

2. **Move forward 10 frames (press → ten times).**

This puts you at frame 11. Of course, when doing a real animation, your keys aren't always going to be ten frames apart, but this is a good way to rough in your keys. You can go back later and adjust your timing from the Timeline, Dope Sheet, or Graph Editor. To move forward or back one frame at a time, use the ← and → keys. Of course, you can also use the Timeline, Dope Sheet, or Graph Editor to change what frame you are in.

3. **Grab your object and move it to a different location in 3D space using the Move tool.**

Again, this example is assuming that you're animating your object's location. The same steps apply if you're animating rotation, scale, or some combination of transforms.

4. **Insert a new keyframe (I).**

Now you should have f-curves in the Graph Editor that describe the motion of the cube.

You can insert keys in an easier way using a feature called Auto Keying. Like its name indicates, Auto Keying automatically creates keys when you make changes in your scene. To enable the Auto Keying feature, look in the Timeline. To the left of the playback controls in the Timeline's header is a button with a circle icon on it, like the Record button on a DVR. Left-click it to activate Auto Keying. Now, you can simply use the transform tools in the 3D Viewport as you move forward in time and keyframes are automatically inserted for you. Pretty sweet, huh?

By default, Blender uses the Location, Rotation, & Scale keying set (there's more on keying sets later in this chapter) for inserting keyframes when Auto Keying is enabled. This is worth noting because, if you're not careful, Auto Keying can insert keyframes that are unnecessary or (worse) not wanted. It's for this reason that when I use Auto Keying, I like to insert my initial keyframes manually. Then I use the Available keying set for auto keying. The next section covers keying sets and how to choose which one you're animating with.

Animating [almost] anything

A really cool feature in Blender is the concept of "[almost] everything animatable." You can animate nearly every setting or attribute within Blender. Want to animate the skin material of your characters so that they turn red with anger? You can! Want to animate the Count attribute in an Array modifier to dynamically add links to a chain? You can! Want to animate whether your object appears in wireframe or solid shading in the 3D Viewport? Ridiculous as it sounds, that, too, is possible!

So, how do you do this miraculous act of animating any attribute? It's amazingly simple. Nearly every text field, value field, color swatch, drop-down menu, check box, and radio button is considered a property and represents a channel that you can animate. If you look to the right of any of these fields, you should see a small circular dot. Click that dot, and it changes to a larger diamond shape as shown to the left margin. When you do that, the field next to your once-circle-now-diamond icon should change color, indicating that you've just set a keyframe for that value. You can also insert a keyframe for a property by right-clicking it and choosing Insert Keyframes from the menu that appears. Figure 1-3 shows what this menu looks like. If the property is already keyed on the current frame, the right-click menu says Replace Keyframes.

REMEMBER

Don't make the mistake of thinking that a property isn't animatable if it doesn't have a keyframe icon next to it. The keyframe icon is included as a convenience feature for frequently keyed properties. If you want to insert a keyframe for a property and you don't see the keyframe icon, try right-clicking to see if inserting a key is an option.

Whether you use the keyframe icon or right-click the property, after you insert a new keyframe for that property, its color changes to yellow (in the default theme), and a channel for that property is added in the Graph Editor and Dope Sheet. When you scrub forward or backward in time, the color of the control changes from yellow to green and the diamond icon changes from solid-filled to just an outline. The green color and different icon indicate that the property is animated, but you're not currently on one of its keys. Insert another keyframe for that property, and BAM! The field's color turns to yellow, the diamond fills in again, and you now have two keyframes for your animated property.

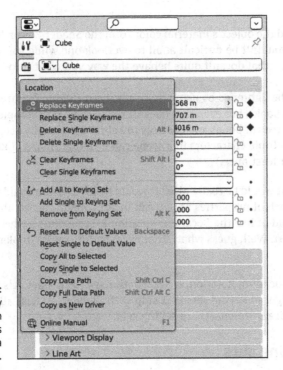

FIGURE 1-3:
Right-click any property in the Properties editor to insert a keyframe for it.

TIP

For an even faster way to insert keyframes on properties, hover your mouse over the property and just press I. This trick even works on the renderability icons (known as the *restrict columns*) in the Outliner if you make them visible. How's that for awesome?

TIP

If you want to insert keyframes on multiple properties at the same time (such as the aforementioned restricted columns in the Outliner), keep holding the I hotkey as you run your mouse cursor over those properties. There you go. One key press, many keyframes. An extremely talented Blender animator I know likes to call this "painting Blender yellow."

Working with keying sets

When working on an animation, you can easily find yourself inserting keyframes for a bunch of different channels and properties at the same time. The troublesome thing is that, on a complex scene, these properties can be located all over Blender's interface. Sure, you can insert keys for an object's location, rotation, and scale by pressing I in the 3D Viewport, but you may also need to key that object's visibility from the Outliner, the influence of a constraint in Constraint

Properties, and the object's material color from the Shader Editor. They're all over the place! It wouldn't be difficult at all to overlook one while you work, resulting in an animation that doesn't quite behave the way you want it to.

This load can be lightened by using more advanced rigging features (see Chapters 2 and 3 in this book), but even that doesn't really solve it. A complex character rig can have hundreds of bones and controls to animate. Manually keeping track of all of them for multiple characters in a scene can be a nightmare. (I know. I've tried. We all have, at least once.)

You know what would be really nice? It would be great if you could make a custom group of a bunch of properties so you can insert a keyframe for all of them at the same time, kind of like the Location, Rotation & Scale option when you press I in the 3D Viewport. Well, guess what? That exact feature exists in Blender. It's called a *keying set*.

Actually, the Location, Rotation, & Scale option *is* a keying set. It's one of a handful of preconfigured keying sets that ship with Blender. In fact, all the options in the Insert Keyframe menu (I) are keying sets.

Using keying sets

To use keying sets, start with a look at the left side of the Timeline's header. The first button after the Editor Type menu is the Playback rollout. For the time being, you don't need to worry about the content of this rollout. The one you *are* interested in, however, is the next one, the Keying rollout. Click this button, and you should see a rollout like the one shown in Figure 1-4.

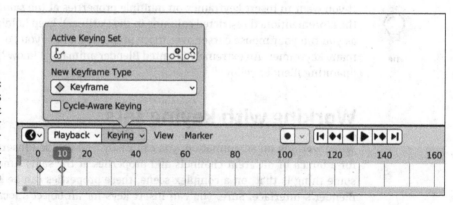

FIGURE 1-4:
The Timeline's Keying rollout has controls for choosing your active keying set and inserting keyframes within that keying set.

For keying sets, the first row in this rollout is the most relevant. The Keying rollout contains three widgets for working with keying sets:

» **Active keying set:** The field for this drop-down menu is empty by default. Left-click it to choose one of the available keying sets to be your active one.

If you have an active keying set, you can make this field empty again by left-clicking the X to the right of your keying set's name.

» **Insert keyframes:** Left-click this button to insert a keyframe at the current frame on the Timeline for every property in the current active keying set. If you don't have an active keying set, a little error pops up to let you know.

» **Delete keying set keyframe:** Left-click this button to remove any keyframes from the current frame that belong to any properties in the active keying set.

If you don't have any keys on the current frame, this button doesn't do anything.

TIP

To quickly choose an active keying set from the 3D Viewport, use the Ctrl+Shift+Alt+I hotkey combination.

REMEMBER

When you choose a keying set, Blender gives preference to the properties in that keying set when you insert keyframes. This means that with an active keying set chosen, you don't get the Insert Keyframe menu if you press I in the 3D Viewport. Blender just quietly inserts keyframes for all the properties in your chosen keying set. This lack of immediate feedback may be disorienting at first, but it makes for a very fast, distraction-free workflow for animating. Also, as mentioned earlier in this chapter, if you have Auto Keying enabled, it uses the active keying set. If you don't have an active keying set chosen, Auto Keying defaults to using the Location, Rotation, & Scale keying set.

Creating custom keying sets

The preconfigured keying sets that come with Blender are handy, but it's also useful to define your own keying sets (especially as your animations become more complex). Keying sets aren't character- or object-specific, so they apply to your whole scene. This means you can use a keying set to insert keyframes for a whole group of characters all at the same time if you want.

Because keying sets are relevant to your whole scene, you can create your custom keying sets from the Scene tab in the Properties editor in the Keying Sets panel. Follow these steps to create a new keying set and populate it with properties to keyframe:

1. **In the Keying Sets panel, left-click the Plus (+) button to the right of the keying set list box.**

The panel should expand with a whole host of new parameters and options you can adjust. The original empty listbox in the panel should be populated with a single entry, named Keying Set.

2. **Adjust your new keying set's settings.**

Double-click its name in the listbox to rename it to something other than the generic Keying Set that you get by default. You can use the Description text field to write a few words that explain the purpose of your custom keying set.

The Keyframing Settings sub-panel contains three toggleable settings under the label of General Override:

- **Needed:** Enable this option to avoid adding extraneous keyframes to your animation. If you have a *hold*, where you've set two keyframes and there's no change between them, then as long as that property doesn't change, it doesn't make sense to add more keyframes within that hold. So by enabling the Needed override, Blender adds keyframes only to the properties that change within a hold. If the property didn't change, no keyframe is inserted, regardless of whether you've pressed I in the 3D Viewport.

- **Visual:** As covered earlier in this chapter, *visual transforms* are the location, rotation, and scale of your object as they appear onscreen, including changes made by constraints. Enable this option and all inserted keyframes in this keying set will use visual transforms for keying.

- **XYZ to RGB:** This option is enabled by default. It dictates that any new f-curves use red, green, and blue for X-, Y-, and Z-axis channels.

REMEMBER

You may notice that there are actually two toggle buttons next to each of these General Override options. One is the familiar check box, and the other has an icon that looks like a pen over a target. Enable this second toggle button to ensure that the associated property overrides the default keying settings in Blender (set in Edit ⇨ Preferences within the Animation section) for cases where the check box is in the on or off state. It's a pretty confusing toggle to think about. However, if you want to change the check box for the property this toggle is associated with from its default state, you need to enable the default override toggle as well. There's more on overrides later in this chapter.

Figure 1-5 shows the Keying Sets panel with a few custom keying sets added in the list box.

REMEMBER

Left-clicking a keying set in the list box of the Keying Sets panel automatically makes that keying set the active one.

At this point, you've created your custom keying set, but it's an empty container. You haven't assigned any properties to it. To add, edit, and remove properties from your active keying set, you need to use the Active Keying Set sub-panel in Scene Properties. It appears within the Keying Sets panel when you have a custom keying set selected in the list box.

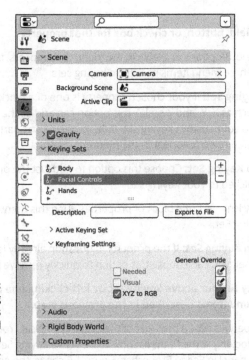

FIGURE 1-5:
The Keying Sets panel is where you add new custom keying sets.

To add a new property to your custom keying set, you need to tell Blender where to find that property. You must give Blender that property's *path*, or the way to navigate through your .blend file's internal structure to your property. It's certainly possible (and sometimes necessary for more obscure properties) to manually add new paths from the Active Keying Set panel by left-clicking the Plus (+) button next to the Paths list box and get more specific from there. However, that can be an excruciatingly tedious process, even if you have a strong working knowledge of .blend file innards.

There's a better, easier way to populate your keying set. Rather than go about the painful, manual way, follow these steps:

1. **In Blender's interface, find the property you want to add to your keying set.**

This could be the material color of your object, just its Y-axis rotation, or its renderability in the Outliner. It can be any property that's capable of being keyframed.

2. **Right-click the field, button, or check box for that property.**

Among all the various options available in the menu that appears, there should be either two or three menu items specific to keying sets:

- **Add All to Keying Set:** If your chosen property is one of a block of properties (such as X, Y, and Z scale), this option can add all the properties in that block to your custom keying set. If the property isn't part of such a block, this option doesn't appear in the menu.

- **Add Single to Keying Set:** Choose this option to add just the property that you've right-clicked to your keying set.

  If the property isn't part of a block of properties, then this menu item reads as Add to Keying Set.

- **Remove from Keying Set:** If the property in question already is in your active keying set, you can choose this option to quickly remove it.

3. **Add the property to your active keying set by left-clicking one of the Add to Keying Set menu items described in the previous step.**

Your chosen property is now a member of the active keying set. You can verify that it's there by looking at the Paths list box in the Active Keying Set sub-panel of the Keying Set panel in Scene Properties. Figure 1-6 shows the Active Keying Set panel with a few paths added.

At the bottom of the Active Keying Set sub-panel is a drop-down menu labeled F-Curve Grouping. This drop-down menu dictates how animation channels are grouped in the Dope Sheet and Graph Editor. You have three choices:

- » **Keying Set Name:** This is the default setting. Animation channels in the Dope Sheet and Graph Editor are grouped according to the name of your keying set.

  It generally works well, but if you have a lot of properties in your keying set, this can make that grouping seem a bit like a grab bag of animated properties.

- » **None:** You have the option of not grouping the properties in your keying set at all. This can lead to pretty messy animation editors, so it isn't an option you'll choose often, but it's nice to know it's available.

- » **Named Group:** This is a very powerful option for organizing a large keying set. If you choose Named Group as your method for f-curve grouping, a text field labeled Group Name appears below the drop-down menu. Type the name of a group in that field. Now, if you choose another property in your keying set and type the exact same group name, both properties are collected together in the Dope Sheet and Graph Editor. This is extremely useful for complex character rigs.

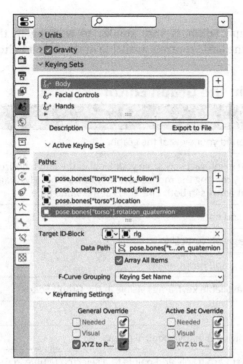

FIGURE 1-6:
The properties of your active keying set are listed in the Active Keying Set panel of Scene Properties.

You may notice in Figure 1-6 that, like the Keying Sets panel, the Active Keying Set sub-panel features the same three buttons for Keyframing Settings, only now they're doubled. You have one set under the label of General Override and another under the label of Active Set Override. By adjusting these settings in the Active Keying Set panel, you override the global Keyframing Settings as defined in the Keying Sets panel, but just for that property.

WARNING

The override behavior in the Active Keying Set panel works only in an additive way. That is, if you have Needed disabled as a General Override, enabling it for a specific property as an Active Set Override will override as expected. However, if that same option is enabled as a General Override, currently there isn't a clean way to do an override that disables it for individual properties in the keying set.

Working in the Graph Editor

After you've added keyframes to your scene, the next logical step is to tweak, edit, and modify those keyframes. You can use the Timeline and Dope Sheet to adjust your general timing by selecting the keyframe diamonds you want to move and dragging them to a different frame in the editor (there's more on that in Chapter 4 of this book). But once you've blocked and refined your animation, the next step is the final polish. In that step, your focus is on the interpolation between keyframes. That editing is done in the Graph Editor.

Working in the Graph Editor is very similar to working in the 3D Viewport. Table 1-1 describes the basic controls available in the Graph Editor.

TABLE 1-1   **Basic controls in the Graph Editor**

Navigation	
Middle-click+drag	Moves around your view of the graph.
Ctrl+middle-click+drag	Allows you to interactively scale your view of the curve horizontally and vertically by moving the mouse vertically or horizontally. Diagonal mouse movement adjusts in both directions at the same time.
Scroll your mouse wheel	Zooms in and out.
Shift+scroll	Moves the graph vertically.
Ctrl+scroll	Moves the graph horizontally.
Home	Makes all available keyframes visible in the Graph Editor.
Editing	
Left-click	Selects individual f-curve control points.
Ctrl+right-click	Allows you to arbitrarily add points to a selected f-curve in the graph. Anywhere you Ctrl+right-click in the graph, a new control point is added to the selected channel.
Left-click and drag in the graph area	Box Select (pressing B also works).
A	Selects all control points.
Alt+A	Deselects all control points.
Region Controls	
Left-click and drag in the scrubbing area	Moves the time cursor.
N	Hides and reveals the Graph Editor's Sidebar (similar to the Sidebar in the 3D Viewport).
Left-click a channel in the left region of the Graph Editor	Selects the channel. You may need to expand the blocks in this region to drill down to the actual animation channels (such as X Location, Y Location, and Z Location).

The Graph Editor also has some handy keyboard shortcuts for hiding and revealing channels. They're particularly useful when you want to manage a complex animation with a lot of keyframes and channels. If you select one or more keyframes, you can use any of these hotkeys:

>> **H** hides the channels that the selected keyframes belong to.

>> **Shift+H** hides all channels *except* for the ones where you've selected a keyframe.

>> **Alt+H** reveals ("unhides") all animation channels in the Graph Editor.

TIP

You can also click the eye icon to the left of each channel to selectively hide or unhide its curve from the Graph Editor.

Editing f-curves

The similarities with the 3D Viewport go even further than those described in the previous section. Not only can you select the control points of f-curves in the Graph Editor, but you can edit them like you would edit a 2D Bézier curve object in the 3D Viewport. The only constraint is that f-curves can't cross themselves. Having a curve that describes motion in time do a loopy-loop doesn't make any sense.

For more detailed descriptions of the hotkeys and controls for editing Bézier curves in Blender, see Book 2, Chapter 4. Selecting and moving control point handles, as well as the changing handle types by pressing V all work as expected (if you want to change handle types using the menus in the Graph Editor rather than the hotkey, choose Key ⇨ Handle Type). However, because these curves are specially purposed for animation, you have a few additional controls over them. For example, you can control the type of interpolation between control points on a selected curve by pressing T or choosing Key ⇨ Interpolation Mode in the Graph Editor's header menu. You get the following choices:

>> **Interpolation:** These three options control the general interpolation from the current keyframe to the next, and they're the ones you'll use most frequently as an animator.

- **Constant:** This option is sometimes called a *step function* because a series of them look like stair steps. Basically, this interpolation type keeps the value of one control point unchanged until it gets to the next one, where it instantly changes. Many animators like to use this interpolation mode when blocking out their animations. This way, they can focus on getting their poses and timing right without the distraction of in-between frames.

- **Linear:** The interpolation from one control point to the next is an absolutely straight line. This option is similar to changing two control points to have Vector handles.

- **Bézier:** The default interpolation type, Bézier interpolation smoothly transitions from one control point to the next. In traditional animation, this smooth transition is referred to as *easing in* and *easing out* of a keyframe. Of course, you can always edit the control handles on your Bézier animation curve to customize that behavior to something else.

>> **Easing (by strength):** The interpolation options in this column are preset, mathematically defined interpolation methods. You can get the same curve profile by manually editing the handles of a curve with Bézier interpolation, but these easing presets are a faster way of getting the same result.

>> **Dynamic Effects:** When things move in meatspace, there isn't always a smooth transition from one pose to the next. When you drop a ball to the ground, it bounces. When you slam on the brakes while driving, the car over-extends, lurching forward before settling back to rest. In many cases, you can (and should) animate this behavior by hand. However, in a pinch, these three Dynamic Effects interpolations can give you a great starting point:

- **Back:** In this interpolation type, the curve "overshoots the mark" set by the keyframe before settling back where you want it. To see what this effect is like, try slapping the surface of a table, but stopping just before your hand makes contact. If you watch carefully, you should notice that your hand goes a bit farther than you want it to before it finishes moving.

- **Bounce:** The Bounce interpolation is a fun one. It makes your object appear to bounce before coming to a rest.

- **Elastic:** Have you ever seen an over-extended rubber band break in half? The loose ends flop all over the place before they stop moving. The Elastic interpolation mode gives your object this kind of effect, like it's stuck to the floppy end of one of those broken rubber bands.

Figure 1-7 shows the Keyframe Interpolation menu.

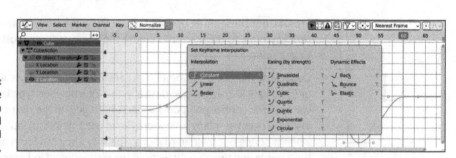

FIGURE 1-7: Changing the interpolation type on selected f-curve control points.

TIP

The interpolation mode options work only on the selected control points in the Graph Editor, so if you want to select all the control points in a single f-curve, select one of those control points and press L or choose Select ⇨ Select Linked in the Graph Editor's header menu. Then you can apply your interpolation mode to the entire curve.

You can also change what a selected f-curve does before and after its first and last keyframes by changing the curve's *extrapolation mode*. You can change a curve's extrapolation mode by selecting an f-curve channel in the left region of the Graph Editor and then pressing Shift+E or choosing Channel ⇨ Extrapolation Mode in the Graph Editor's header menu. When you do, notice four possible choices:

>> **Constant Extrapolation:** This setting is the default. The first and last control point values are maintained into infinity beyond those points.

>> **Linear Extrapolation:** Instead of maintaining the same value in perpetuity before and after the first and last control points, this extrapolation mode takes the directions of the curve as it reaches those control points and continues to extend the curve in those directions.

>> **Make Cyclic (F-Modifier):** This option adds an f-curve modifier (covered in the next section of this chapter) that takes all the keyframes in your animation and repeats them before and after your first and last keyframes.

If you have a looping animation, like a character who never stops waving at you, this option is an easy way to make that happen.

>> **Clear Cyclic (F-Modifier):** If your f-curve has a Cycles modifier, it's possible to remove that modifier from the Graph Editor's Sidebar (N), but this menu option is faster.

Figure 1-8 shows the menu for the different types of extrapolation modes, as well as what each one looks like with a simple f-curve.

If you have lots of animated objects in your scene, or just one object with a high number of animated properties, it may be helpful to hide extraneous curves from view so that you can focus on the ones you truly want to edit. To toggle a curve's visibility (or that of an entire keying set), left-click the eye icon next to its name in the channel region along the left side of the Graph Editor. If you want f-curves to be visible, but not editable, select a channel from the channel region and either left-click the lock icon or press Tab. You can also disable the influence of a specific f-curve or keying set by left-clicking the check box.

TIP

As mentioned previously in this chapter, you can quickly mute/hide animation channels in the Graph Editor by using the H, Shift+H, and Alt+H hotkeys with one or more selected keyframes.

If you need explicit control over the placement of a curve or a control point, the Graph Editor has a Sidebar like the 3D Viewport. You open it the same way: Press N or choose View ⇨ Sidebar. Within the F-Curve tab of the Sidebar, there's an Active Keyframe panel where you can enter the exact value that you'd like to set your selected control point or that control point's handles, as well as modify that control point's interpolation type. Figure 1-9 shows the Sidebar in the Graph Editor.

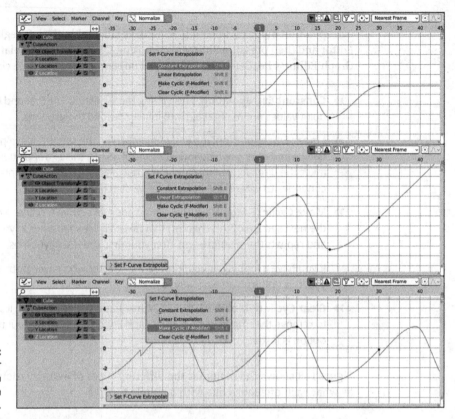

FIGURE 1-8:
The four extrapolation modes you can have on f-curves.

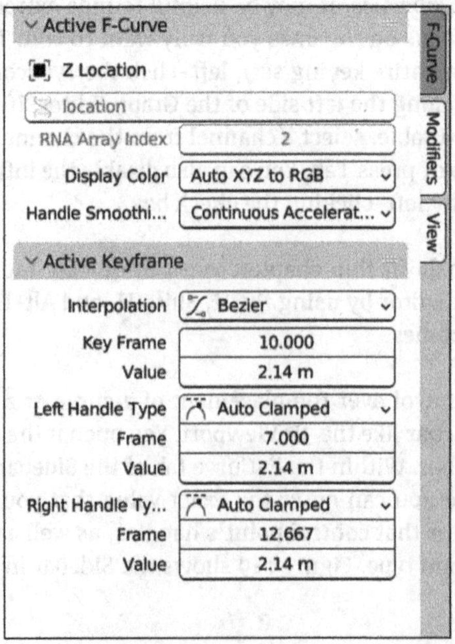

FIGURE 1-9:
The Sidebar (N) in the Graph Editor.

Often, you run into the occasion where you need to edit all the control points in a single frame so that you can change the overall timing of your animation. You may be tempted to try and box-select to select the strip of control points you want to move around. However, a cleaner and easier way is to select just one of the control points on the frame you want to adjust and press K in the Graph Editor or choose Select ⇨ Columns on Selected Keys. All the other control points on the same frame as your initial selection are selected.

Using f-curve modifiers

One of the biggest appeals of computer graphics in general — and computer animation specifically — is the prospect of letting the computer do all the hard work for you. Or, at least you want the computer to handle a big chunk of the boring parts. So if Blender's Graph Editor gives you the ability to procedurally manipulate f-curves with modifiers much in the same way you can with meshes, that's something worth knowing about.

The preceding section addresses modifiers when covering the cyclic curve extrapolation mode (Channel ⇨ Extrapolation Mode). The Cycles modifier described there is one of a handful of f-curve modifiers that you can add. The following is a brief rundown of each of the f-curve modifiers that Blender offers:

>> **Generator:** This modifier generates a new curve based on basic mathematical formulas for lines, parabolic lines, and some more advanced curve shapes. Unless you use additive mode, it completely disregards any existing keyframes on your f-curve.

>> **Built-In Function:** This modifier generates a curve based on a different set of mathematical formulas than the Generator f-curve modifier. The formulas in this modifier are more naturally cyclic, like sine waves and tangent curves. Like the Generator f-curve modifier, this modifier also completely disregards any existing keyframes on your f-curve unless you use additive mode.

>> **Envelope:** Though it can be a bit difficult to control, the Envelope f-curve modifier is extremely powerful. It's like the envelopes in audio processing software. You can add control points to define upper and lower thresholds for your f-curve. Any values in the f-curve beyond those thresholds (outside of the envelope) are attenuated (reduced so they fit within the envelope's bounds). I often couple this modifier with a Noise f-curve modifier to have more control over when the noise influence is added to my f-curves.

>> **Cycles:** This f-curve modifier has nothing to do with the Cycles renderer. Instead, as covered previously in this chapter, this f-curve modifier duplicates your existing keyframes, repeating them over time. This is the modifier that gets added when you choose Channel ⇨ Extrapolation Mode ⇨ Make Cyclic (F-Modifier).

>> **Noise:** With the Noise f-curve modifier, you can add random variation to your f-curve.

Used judiciously, this modifier can bring a lot of life to an animation. For example, you could animate a car rolling along a bumpy road without actually creating those bumps.

>> **Limits:** This f-curve modifier is similar to the Envelope f-curve modifier, except you can't set arbitrary control points. You just have minimum and maximum X- and Y-axis control values for your f-curve. Also, instead of attenuating your f-curve when it exceeds those controls, the Limits f-curve modifier simply clips, or cuts off, the overshot segments of the f-curve.

>> **Stepped Interpolation:** Using the Stepped Interpolation f-curve modifier, you can give your f-curve a stepped appearance as it goes from one keyframe to the next. It would be like using constant interpolation on your f-curve and inserting a keyframe every few frames between the main keyframes of your animation. This can be useful if you want to give your animation a strobed or stop-motion look.

Figure 1-10 shows the panel for each of the f-curve modifiers.

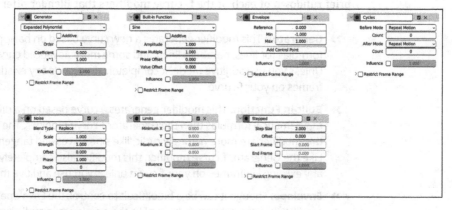

FIGURE 1-10:
Blender offers seven different f-curve modifiers that you can apply to f-curves in your animation.

REMEMBER

Like the modifiers that affect your 3D objects (see Book 2, Chapter 2), you can stack f-curve modifiers so each one contributes to the one before it. For example, you could start with the Built-In Function f-curve modifier on your object's Z location to have your object move up and down sinusoidally. Then you could add a Noise f-curve modifier so it stutters a bit as it moves up and down.

Chapter 2

Adding Controls to Your Scene

O ccasionally, I get into conversations with people who assume that because there's a computer involved, good CG animation takes less time to make than traditional animation. In most cases, this assumption isn't true. High-quality work takes roughly the same amount of time, regardless of the tool. The time is just spent in different places. Whereas in traditional animation, a large portion of the time is spent drawing the in-between frames, CG animation lets the computer handle that detail. However, traditional animators don't have to worry as much about optimizing for render times, tweaking and re-tweaking simulated effects, or modeling, texturing, and rigging characters.

That said, computer animation does give you the opportunity to cut corners in places and make your life as an animator much simpler. For instance, with computer animation, you have the ability to automate the behavior of one part of your animation relative to the movement of another part. As an example, say that you have a pair of wheels and you need to animate their rotations. Rather than go through the process of setting rotation keyframes for both, you can just animate one and have the second one copy the rotations of the first. Congratulations! You've animated two objects in the time it took you to animate one!

These kinds of automated controls are what's covered in this chapter. In particular, there are two Blender features that give you these controls: constraints and drivers. Literally speaking, a *constraint* is a limitation put on one object by another, allowing the unconstrained object to control the behavior of the constrained one. Similarly, a *driver* is a constraint with even more nuanced control (and a slightly greater chance of breaking things). It's not entirely accurate, but I like to think of a constraint as being a more pleasant user interface for common scenarios where you might use drivers.

With automated controls like constraints and drivers, you can do quite a lot without doing much at all. They form the foundation of character rigging, which is covered in the next chapter. Animation is hard work; it's worth it to be lazy whenever you can.

Using Constraints Effectively

The most straightforward way to control the movement of one object with another is by using constraints. In Blender, you do the work of creating and managing constraints from the Constraints tab of the Properties editor. In some ways, constraints are organized similarly to the way modifiers are organized in the Modifiers tab. You add a new constraint by left-clicking the Add Constraint button at the top of the Object Constraints tab. Alternatively, you can choose Object ⇨ Constraints ⇨ Add Constraint (with Targets) in the 3D Viewport's header menu. Either way, you see a menu similar to the one in Figure 2-1.

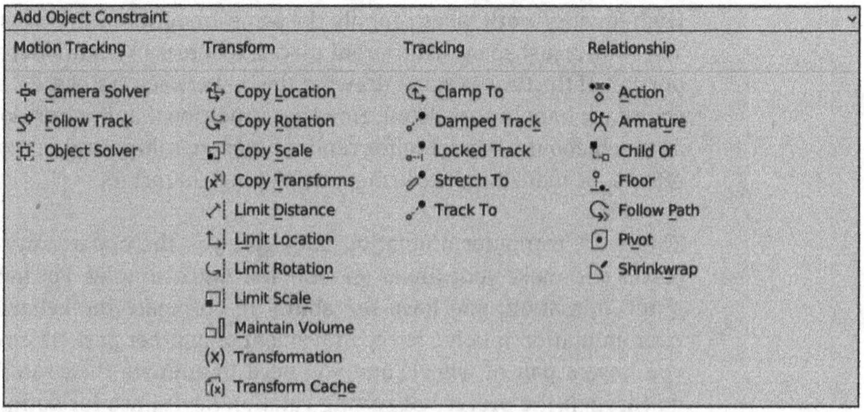

Add Object Constraint			
Motion Tracking	**Transform**	**Tracking**	**Relationship**
Camera Solver	Copy Location	Clamp To	Action
Follow Track	Copy Rotation	Damped Track	Armature
Object Solver	Copy Scale	Locked Track	Child Of
	Copy Transforms	Stretch To	Floor
	Limit Distance	Track To	Follow Path
	Limit Location		Pivot
	Limit Rotation		Shrinkwrap
	Limit Scale		
	Maintain Volume		
	(x) Transformation		
	Transform Cache		

FIGURE 2-1:
The types of constraints available by default within Blender.

When you add a constraint to an object, it gets a new panel added in this tab where you can manage the properties of that constraint. Because the purpose of a constraint is to use the movement or behavior of another object, most constraints have a *target* property as their first property.

If you add another constraint, its panel is added to the bottom of the stack, just like with modifiers. And also like modifiers, you can adjust the order of your constraints by clicking and dragging the little grip area in the upper right of that constraint's panel. Figure 2-2 shows an example of the Constraints panel, populated with a few constraints in its stack.

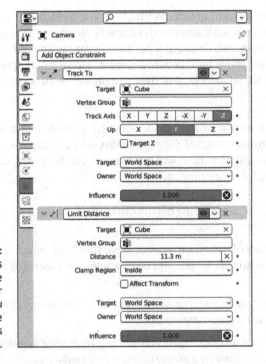

FIGURE 2-2: The Constraints tab of the Properties editor is where you add and manage your object's constraints.

Referring back to Figure 2-1, the Add Constraint menu is organized into a set of columns, much like the corresponding menu in the Modifiers tab. For constraints, they're organized into four categories: Motion Tracking, Transform, Tracking, and Relationship. The next few sections not only give you a brief rundown of the constraints in each of these categories, but they also show you a few practical applications and best practices for constraints.

NEW FEATURE

In Blender 4.0, the Add Modifiers tab is no longer organized into columns, although the Add Constraints menu still keeps the column-based approach.

REMEMBER

In reading though this section, you might notice that I don't cover the constraints in the Motion Tracking column. As the name of the column implies, these three constraints, Camera Solver, Follow Track, and Object Solver, are related to Blender's motion tracking features. In fact, much like the physics modifiers, it's very rare that you would directly add these constraints from the Properties editor.

The preferred (and frankly more straightforward) approach is to use the tools that are part of Blender's motion tracking toolset. I cover all this in more detail in Book 5, Chapter 3.

The all-powerful Empty!

Of all the different types of objects available to you in Blender, none of them are as useful or versatile in animation as the humble Empty. An Empty isn't much — just a little set of axes that indicate a position, orientation, and size in 3D space. Empties don't even show up when you render. However, Empties are an ideal choice for use as control objects, and they're a phenomenal way to take advantage of constraints.

Empties can be displayed in the 3D Viewport in a number of ways. Because an Empty can be used as a control for constraints and animations, sometimes it's useful to have it displayed with a particular shape. The following display types are available in the Add ⇨ Empty menu:

>> **Plain Axes:** Think of this as the default display type. It's just a set of 3D crosshairs.

>> **Arrows:** Occasionally, it's worthwhile to know specifically which axis is facing which direction on your Empty. This display type labels each axis in its positive direction.

>> **Single Arrow:** This display type works great for a minimalist control. The arrow points along the Empty's local Z-axis.

>> **Circle:** If you want an unobtrusive animation control, the Circle display type is a good choice. It allows your Empty to be located inside a volume (like an arm or leg), but still remain selectable because the circle is outside of it.

>> **Cube:** Choose this display type, and your Empty appears like a wireframe cube.

>> **Sphere:** Like the Cube display type, this makes your Empty appear as a simple wireframe sphere.

>> **Cone:** The Cube and Sphere display types can be handy, but they don't naturally give any indication of direction; you don't know which axis is up. The Cone display type draws your Empty like a wireframe cone with the point going along its local Z-axis. It's as large as a cube or sphere, but not as easy to lose as a single arrow.

>> **Image:** With this display type, your Empty appears in the 3D Viewport as a plane with any image you choose mapped to it. This display type isn't particularly useful as a controller for a constraint, but it's extremely useful in modeling. You can have a reference image visible in your 3D Viewport from any direction. Book 2, Chapter 3 has more on using Image Empties as references for modeling.

As a practical example of how useful Empties can be, consider that 3D modelers like to have a *turnaround* render of the model they create. Basically, a turnaround render is like taking the model, placing it on a turntable, and spinning it in front of the camera. It's a great way to show off all sides of the model. Now, for simple models, you can just select the model, rotate it in the global Z-axis, and you're done. However, what if the model consists of many objects, or for some reason everything is at a strange angle that looks odd when spun around the Z-axis? Selecting and rotating all those little objects can get time consuming and annoying. A better way of setting up a turnaround is with the following rig:

1. **Add an Empty (Add ⇨ Empty ⇨ Plain Axes).**

2. **Move the Empty to somewhere at the center of the model.**

   You can use the Move tool or the G hotkey.

3. **Select the camera and position it so that the model is in the center of the view.**

4. **With your camera still selected, click the Add Object Constraint button in the Constraint tab of the Properties editor and choose the Child Of constraint (it's on the right in the Relationship column).**

   A constraint panel is added in the Properties editor for your camera object. You may notice that the name field in your new Child Of constraint panel is bright red. That's because the constraint doesn't yet have a *target* object to constrain to. You'll fix this in the next step.

5. **In the Target field of the Child Of constraint, choose your Empty object.**

   If your scene is relatively simple, you could find your Empty from the drop-down list of objects that appears when you click the Target field. On a more complex scene, I'd recommend that you use the eyedropper at the right of the field. When you click the eyedropper icon, your mouse cursor turns into an eyedropper, and you can click any object in your 3D Viewport or Outliner to choose it as your target object. Of course, if you're organizing your project and naming everything, you can quickly find an object by starting to type its name. The Target field searches your .blend file and updates as you type.

   After you choose your Empty, your Camera is constrained to your Empty. You can tell because there's a light blue dashed line between the Camera and the Empty to show that relationship. If you notice that the camera jumps to a new location once you select your Empty, that's okay. Just click the Set Inverse button in the Child Of constraint's panel in the Properties editor.

6. **Select the Empty in the 3D Viewport and insert a rotation keyframe (Object ⇨ Animation ⇨ Insert Keyframe ⇨ Rotation).**

7. **Move forward in time 50 frames.**

8. **Rotate the Empty 90 degrees in the Z-axis and insert a new rotation keyframe (R ⇨ Z ⇨ 90, I ⇨ Rotation).**

   You can also use the Rotate tool to do your rotation and add your keyframe from the Object menu instead of using hotkeys. In either case, the camera obediently matches the Empty's rotation.

9. **From the Timeline, set the extrapolation mode to linear extrapolation (select the Z Euler Rotation channel, then choose Shift+E ⇨ Linear Extrapolation).**

   You can also switch to the Graph editor and use the Channel menu to do the same thing, but using the hotkey right from the Timeline is faster.

10. **Switch back to the 3D Viewport and set it to use the camera view by clicking on the Camera icon in the upper right corner. Then play back the animation (Spacebar).**

   In the 3D Viewport, you see your model spinning in front of your camera.

In this setup, the Empty behaves as the control for the camera. Imagine that a beam extends from the Empty's center to the camera's center and that rotating the Empty is the way to move that beam.

It's worth mentioning that this arrangement doesn't necessarily require that you use the Child Of constraint. You could also set this up using simple parenting. However, since this section is about constraints, it seemed like a relevant example.

Adjusting the influence of a constraint

One of the most useful settings available to all constraints is at the bottom of each constraint block: the Influence slider. This slider works on a scale from 0 to 1, with 0 being the least amount of influence and 1 being the largest amount. With this slider, your object has the capability of just partially being influenced by the target object's attributes. There's more to it, though.

REMEMBER

You can animate any attribute in the Properties editor by right-clicking it and choosing Insert Keyframe (or pressing I with your mouse cursor hovered over that property). On numerical values, you can insert a key frame by clicking the circular icon to the left of the field. All of this means you can easily animate the influence of the constraint. If you key the Influence value of a constraint, a curve for that influence appears in the Graph Editor, and keyframe indicators are added in the Dope Sheet and Timeline.

Say that you're working on an animation that involves a character with telekinetic powers using their ability to make a ball fly to their hand. You can do that by animating the influence of a Copy Location constraint (see the "Copying the movement of another object" section) on the ball. The character's hand is the target, and you start with 0 influence. Then, when you want the ball to fly to their hand, you increase the influence to 1 and set a new keyframe. KERPLOW! Telekinetic character!

Using vertex groups in constraints

Many constraints (though not all of them) have a Vertex Group field that appears after choosing a valid mesh object in the Target field.

REMEMBER

The Vertex Group option is available only if the target object actually has vertex groups. Meshes, lattices, and Grease Pencil objects all have vertex groups. However, as of this writing, only vertex groups for meshes and lattices are supported by constraints. For the other object types which don't have vertex groups, it wouldn't make sense to have this option available to them.

That said, in the Vertex Group field, you can type or choose the name of a vertex group in the parent mesh. When you do, the constrained object is bound only to those specific vertices. (See the next chapter in this book for details on how to create a vertex group.) After you choose a vertex group from the Vertex Group field of your constraint, the relationship line from the constrained object changes to point to the vertices in that group. Figure 2-3 shows a Suzanne head with a Child Of constraint bound to a vertex group consisting of a single vertex on a circle mesh.

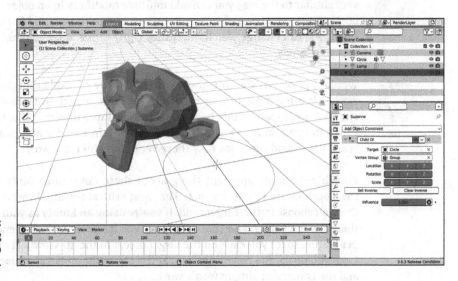

FIGURE 2-3: Parenting an object to a vertex group.

Controlling the location, rotation, and scale of objects with transform constraints

This section is primarily about the constraints in the Transform column, as shown back in Figure 2-1. The nature of these constraints is that they put controls on the location, rotation, or size of the constrained object. In most cases, these constraints are driven by the behavior of another object in your scene, but not always. To try and help a bit more, I've broken down the constraints in this section by the specific purpose that they serve, instead of working through them in order.

Copying the movement of another object

Using simple parenting or even the Child Of constraint (as covered in the example earlier in this chapter in the section titled "The all-powerful Empty!") is helpful in quite a few instances, but it's often not as flexible as you need it to be. With regular parenting, you can't control or animate the parenting influence or use only the parent object's rotation without inheriting the location and scale as well. And you can't have movement of the parent object in the global X-axis influence the child's local X-axis location. More often than not, you need these sorts of refined controls rather than the somewhat ham-fisted regular parenting approach.

To this end, a set of constraints provide you with just this sort of control: Copy Location, Copy Rotation, and Copy Scale.

TIP

You can mix and match multiple constraints on a single object in a way that's very similar to the way you can add multiple modifiers to an object. So if you need both a Copy Location and a Copy Rotation constraint, just add both. After you add them, you can change which order they come in the stack to make sure that they suit your needs.

TIP

Words and pictures aren't always the best way of explaining how constraints work. It's often more to your benefit to see them in action. To that end, the website that accompanies this book has a few example files that illustrate how these constraints work. It's worth it to load them up in Blender and play with them to really get a good sense for how these very powerful tools work.

Probably the most apparent thing about these Copy constraints is how similar their options are to one another. The most critical setting, however, is the object that you choose in the Target field. If you're using an Empty as your control object, this is where you choose that Empty or type its name (or use Blender's eyedropper feature to let you click on the target object in the 3D Viewport or the Outliner). Until you do so, the constraint icon at the top of the constraint block remains red, and the constraint simply won't work.

Below the Target field are a series of three Axis buttons, each labeled to correspond with an axis. The X, Y, and Z buttons here are enabled by default, and control which axis or axes the target object influences. Furthermore, the X, Y, and Z buttons below the Axis buttons, labeled Invert, give you the ability to make your constrained object behave opposite of the target object on the chosen axis. If an Axis button is enabled and the Invert button below it is also enabled, the target object has an inverted influence on the constrained object in that axis. As an example, say you have a Copy Location constraint set up, and you have your constrained object selected. If you disable the X Axis button and then move the target Empty in the X-axis using the Move tool or the G ⇨ X hotkey sequence, the cube remains perfectly still. However, enabling the X Axis button as well as the X Invert button beneath it causes the cube to translate in an opposite X direction when you move the target Empty.

Next up is the Offset check box, which is useful if you've already adjusted your object's location, rotation, or scale prior to adding the constraint. By default, this feature is off, so the constrained object replicates the target object's behavior completely and exactly. With the Offset check box enabled, though, the object adds the target object's transformation to the constrained object's already set location, rotation, or scale values. The best way to see this is to create a Copy Location constraint with the following steps:

1. **Start with a new General workflow template (File ⇨ New ⇨ General).**

2. **Move the default cube to a location other than the world origin.**

3. **Add an Empty (Add ⇨ Empty ⇨ Plain Axes).**

4. **Add the cube to your current selection (Shift+left click) and put a Copy Location constraint on it (Object ⇨ Constraints ⇨ Add Constraint (with Targets) ⇨ Copy Location).**

   Because the cube is the last object you select, it becomes the active object and is therefore the object that the constraint is added to.

5. **From Constraints Properties, put your Empty in the Target field for the Copy Location constraint you just added.**

   The cube automatically snaps directly to the Empty's location.

6. **Left-click the Offset check box in the Copy Location constraint within Constraint Properties.**

   The cube goes back to its original position. However, if you move the Empty, its location influences the cube's location relative to that point.

Another common feature in these constraints is the Target and Owner coordinate system dropdowns. These two drop-down menus give you even more nuanced control. Using this same Copy Location constraint example, rotate your cube about the Z-axis a little bit. Then, in its Location Constraint panel in the Constraints tab of the Properties editor, change the Owner drop-down menu from World Space to Local Space. Now, go back to your Empty and move it along the global X-axis. You should see your cube moving along its *local* X-axis. This feature is incredibly useful when you want to have a control that is always moved along the global axes, but you want corresponding behavior to happen according to the constrained object's local coordinate system.

Now, the Copy Location, Copy Rotation, and Copy Scale constraints are the most simple and straightforward means of having one object copy part of the behavior of another object. But what if you want to have controls that are somewhat more advanced?

>> **Copy Transforms:** If you need a constraint that affects location, rotation, and scale all at the same time (instead of adding those constraints individually), then the Copy Transforms constraint is the one you're looking for. In a way, it's quite similar to the Child Of constraint, except you have a lot more control over which transforms are being copied and when that copying takes place, particularly with the options available in the Mix drop-down menu within this constraint. One thing this constraint can't do, however, is isolate the constraint to a particular axis, like you can with the other copy constraints or the Child Of constraint. So that point is a consideration when choosing which constraint to use.

>> **Transformation:** The Transformation constraint is, in my opinion, one of the most powerful constraints in Blender's arsenal. With this constraint, you can use the transform (location, rotation, or scale) of one object to influence a completely different transform on another object. For example, you could use the local Y-axis location of a car object to control the local X-axis rotation of a wheel object so it spins in the correct direction as your car moves forward and backward. You get this powerful capability by *mapping* one transform to the other using this constraint. Expand the Map From sub-panel to choose the transform (and value range) that you want to use on your target object. Then use the controls in the Map To sub-panel to choose the transform and value range you want to influence on your constrained object. This constraint gives you a lot of the power of drivers (covered later in this chapter) with a much simpler interface.

>> **Transform Cache:** It's rare that you'll ever need to directly apply the Transform Cache constraint. This constraint is added automatically if you import a file in the Alembic or USD file formats (see Book 3, Chapter 4) and there's animation at the object level, as opposed to deformations to mesh data. For example, camera moves or rigid body simulations are often stored in those formats as transform data, so those imported objects will have the Transform Cache constraint added to them.

Putting limits on an object

Often when you animate objects, it's helpful to prevent objects from being moved, rotated, or scaled beyond a certain extent. Say that you're animating a character trapped inside a glass dome. As an animator, it can be helpful if Blender forces you to keep that character within that space. Sure, you *could* just pay attention to where your characters are and visually make sure that they don't accidentally go farther than they should be allowed, but why do the extra work if you can have Blender do it for you?

Here are descriptions of what each constraint does:

>> **Limit Location/Rotation/Scale:** Unlike most of the other constraints, these three don't have a target object to constrain them. Instead, they're limitations on what the object can do within its own space. For any of them, you can define minimum and maximum limits in the X, Y, and Z axes. You enable limits by left-clicking their corresponding check boxes and define those limits in the value fields next to each one.

TIP

The Affect Transform check box that's in each of these constraints can be pretty helpful when animating. To better understand what it does, go to the Sidebar in the 3D Viewport (N). If you have limits and Affect Transform is not enabled, the values in the Sidebar change even after you reach the limits defined by the constraint. However, if you enable Affect Transform, the values in the Sidebar are clipped to the limitations you defined with the constraint.

>> **Limit Distance:** This constraint is similar to the previous ones except it relates to the distance from the origin of a target object. The Clamp Region menu gives you three ways to use this distance:

- **Inside:** The constrained object can move only within the sphere of space defined by the Distance value.

- **Outside:** The constrained object can never enter the sphere of space defined by the Distance value.

- **On Surface:** The constrained object is always the same distance from the target object, no more and no less.

  The On Surface name is a bit misleading. Your object isn't limited to the surface of the target object; it's limited to the surface of an imaginary sphere with a radius equal to the Distance value.

>> **Maintain Volume:** The Maintain Volume constraint is a fun one. In Chapter 4 of this book, I cover the fundamental principles of animation. One of those principles is called "squash and stretch." With the Maintain Volume constraint, you get an automated form of squash and stretch. As an example, add a Suzanne mesh to your scene and give her a Maintain Volume constraint with

the Z button pressed as the Free Axis setting. Now when you scale her mesh (S hotkey or use the Scale tool), she stretches vertically when you scale up while flattening as you scale down.

>> **Floor:** Technically, the Floor constraint is listed as a Relationship constraint, but I tend to think of it more as a limiting constraint. It uses the origin of a target object to define a plane that the origin of the constrained object can't move beyond. So, technically, you can use this constraint to define more than a floor; you can also use it to define walls and a ceiling. Remember, though, that this constraint defines a plane. If your target object is an uneven surface, it doesn't use that object's geometry to define the limit of the constrained object, just its origin. Despite this limitation, this constraint is actually quite useful, especially if you enable the Use Rotation check box. This option allows the constrained object to recognize the rotation of the target object so that you can have an inclined floor, if you like.

>> **Shrinkwrap:** Like the Floor constraint, the Shrinkwrap constraint is also listed in the Relationship column of the Add Object Constraint menu. However, also like the Floor constraint, this one behaves much more like a limiting constraint. With this constraint, you can snap the origin of your constrained object to the surface of another object. In other 3D applications, this is sometimes referred to as a Surface constraint. But in Blender, because its controls are very similar to the Shrinkwrap modifier, this constraint reuses that name.

TIP

When animating while using constraints, particularly limiting constraints, it's in your best interest to insert keyframes using Visual Location and Visual Rotation, as opposed to plain Location and Rotation. Using the visual keying types sets the keyframe to where the object is located visually within the limits of the constraint rather than how you actually transformed the object. For example, assume that you have a Floor constraint on an object that you're animating to fall from some height and land on a floor plane that's even with the XY grid. For the landing, you grab the object and move it 4 units below the XY grid. Of course, because of the constraint, your object stops following the mouse when it hits the floor. Now, if you insert a regular Location keyframe here, the Z-axis location of the object is set to −4.0 even though the object can't go below 0. However, if you insert a Visual Location key, the object's Z-axis location is set to what you see it as: 0. If you enable the Affect Transform check box on all your constraints, you can get similar behavior and just use regular (non-visual) location and rotation keyframing.

Tracking the motion of another object

Tracking constraints are another set of helpful constraints for animation. Their basic purpose is to make the constrained object point either directly at or in the general direction of the target object. Tracking constraints are useful for controlling the eye movement of characters or building mechanical rigs like pistons. All these constraints are in the third column of the constraints menu shown back in Figure 2-1.

Following are descriptions of each tracking constraint:

» **Track To:** Of these constraints, this one is the most straightforward. In other programs, this constraint may be referred to as the Look At constraint, and that's what it does. It forces the constrained object to point at the target object. The best way to see how this constraint works is to go through the following steps:

1. **Load a new General workflow template (File ⇨ New ⇨ General).**

2. **Add a Track To constraint to the camera with the target object being the cube.**

TIP

For a fast way to do this, select your cube, Shift+select your camera, and choose Object ⇨ Constraints ⇨ Add Constraint (with Targets) ⇨ Track To from the 3D Viewport's header menu. When you perform this action, the camera will have a Track To constraint that automatically sets the cube as its target.

By default, this constraint sets the Track Axis to the negative Z-axis (-Z) and the Up axis to Y. In this way, no matter where you move the camera, it always points at the cube's origin. By left-clicking the X, Y, and Z buttons next to the To label and choosing an axis from the Up drop-down menu, you can control how the constrained object (the camera in this example) points relative to the target.

» **Locked Track:** The Locked Track constraint is similar to the Track To constraint, with one large exception: It allows the constrained object to rotate only on a single axis, so the constrained object points in the general direction of the target, but not necessarily directly at it. A good way to think about the Locked Track constraint is to imagine that you're wearing a neck brace. With the brace on, you can't look up or down; you can rotate your head only left and right. So if a bird flies overhead, you can't look up to see it pass. All you can do is turn around and hope to see the bird flying away. This constraint is useful if you need your constrained object to behave kind of like a compass, with the target object as being north.

» **Stretch To:** This constraint isn't exactly a tracking constraint like Track To and Locked Track, but its behavior is similar. The Stretch To constraint makes the constrained object point toward the target object like the Track To constraint. However, this constraint also changes the constrained object's scale relative to its distance to the target, stretching that object toward the target. And the Stretch To constraint can even preserve the volume of the constrained object to make it seem like it's really stretching, similar to the Maintain Volume constraint. This constraint is great for cartoony effects, as well as for controlling organic deformations, such as rubber balls and the human tongue. On a complex character rig, you can use the Stretch To constraint to help simulate muscle bulging.

» **Clamp To:** In a way, the Clamp To constraint is similar to the Follow Path constraint, covered later in this section. It's included among the constraints in the Tracking column because you use this add-on to constrain your object to a curve, as if it were moving along a track. Unlike the Follow Path constraint, however, this constraint does not have the ability to automatically align your constrained object to the direction of the curve. That said, many artists find this constraint much easier to control than Follow Path.

» **Damped Track:** You can think of the Damped Track constraint as being a simpler version of the Track To constraint. If you just need one object to point at another object, but you don't care which way is "up" for the constrained object, then this is the constraint for you. However, if you used this constraint in the camera example at the beginning of this section, you would notice that the camera might sometimes flip upside down while tracking. That's why the Track To constraint is more desirable for that scenario.

There are a couple more tracking-type constraints, namely the Inverse Kinematics constraint and the Spline IK constraint. However, these constraints are available only to bones in an armature object, so they don't appear in the Constraints tab of the Properties editor. You access them from the Bone Constraints tab when you have an armature object selected and set to Pose Mode. The next chapter in this book has more on inverse kinematics and the Inverse Kinematics constraint.

Relationship constraints

It might sound weird to have a specific category of constraints called Relationship constraints. After all, when you add a constraint, aren't you implicitly defining a relationship between two objects? By that logic, all constraints are relationship constraints. Although that may be true, not all constraints can be categorized as transform or tracking constraints. That's why the constraints in the Relationship column of the Add Object Constraint menu (see Figure 2-1) may seem a bit like a dumping ground of leftover constraints. However, don't let that fool you. The constraints in this column are pretty powerful. In fact, I've already covered a few of them, including the Child Of, Floor, and Shrinkwrap constraints. What follows is a quick rundown on the rest of these constraints:

» **Child Of:** This section opened up with an example that uses the Child Of constraint. The best way to think of this constraint is as a more procedural form of parenting. You get the same behavior as parenting, but you have more control over exactly how the parent-child relationship works between your constrained object and the target object.

>> **Action:** The Action constraint is kind of the unsung hero of Blender's suite of constraints. With this constraint, you can control playback of an animated sequence defined in an Action datablock using the transform channel of your target object. As an example, say you have a sci-fi door that opens and closes like a camera iris. Assume you've also rigged it with an armature using the tools covered in the next chapter, and you have an animation of the various bones in that armature to open the door saved as an Action datablock, as covered in Chapter 4 of this book. With the Action constraint, you can use a single Empty (or a bone) to drive the bones in your door rig. This way, you have a single control for opening and closing the door. There is some tedium in setting this up because the constraint needs to be added to each bone, but the time that this kind of rig saves an animator can be huge.

>> **Armature:** Think of the Armature constraint as being the constraint version of the Armature modifier (as covered in the next chapter), but with more control. With this constraint, you can explicitly map vertex groups to armature bones with procedural controls over those influences. In practice, this constraint isn't used all that frequently because most scenarios are covered by the Armature modifier. That said, it does have its uses. The Armature constraint allows you to edit your Armature more easily than if you used bone parenting, and it offers better performance than the Armature modifier on dense meshes, as long as you don't need deformation.

>> **Follow Path:** Using the Follow Path constraint, you can snap your constrained object to a path defined by a curve object, much like the Clamp To constraint, covered earlier in this section. The difference is that all positional control for your constrained object is managed from this constraint's settings. You move your constrained object along the path by adjusting the Offset value. Plus, you have additional controls for adjusting the orientation of the constrained object as it moves along the path. The most useful of these controls is the Follow Curve check box. Enable that curve and your constrained object points along the direction of the curve it's bound to. With this constraint, you can pretty easily rig up a train moving along a railroad track.

>> **Pivot:** Generally speaking, objects in Blender rotate and scale relative to their local origins. As you edit and work, you can certainly have your objects scale and rotate relative to other points in space, including other objects or even the 3D cursor. However, those pivots are transient; they work only while you're editing and not while animation is playing back. For example, say you wanted to animate a cube rolling along the ground. You could certainly do this by carefully animating the location and rotation of your cube so it correctly looks like its rotating around its corners as it moves. However, if you add an Empty to the scene and set the cube up with a Pivot constraint that uses that Empty as a target, you can very precisely control how your cube rolls with fewer keyframes. Figure 2-4 illustrates this example.

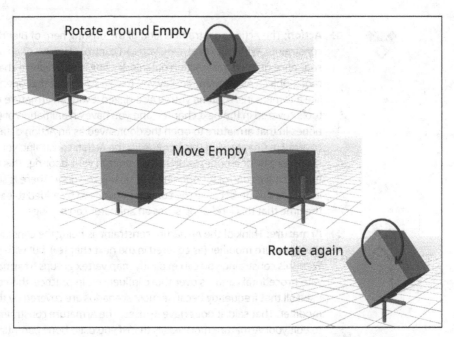

Rotate around Empty

Move Empty

Rotate again

FIGURE 2-4:
Rolling a cube
using the Pivot
constraint.
Rotate, move the
Empty, rotate,
repeat.

Getting Even More Control with Drivers

As powerful as constraints are, they don't give you all the controls that you might need for any given rigging situation or animation situation. Sometimes you need more refined control. For example, you may want to change a shape key based on the position of an Empty. That isn't something that can be done with constraints. To give you this level of refined control, Blender has a system called *drivers*.

Remember that in Blender you can animate just about anything. Any property can have a keyframe applied to it. Likewise, if you can apply a keyframe to that property, that means you can also potentially drive it with some other property. That, at its core, is what's covered in this section.

What are drivers?

Drivers are a little bit more challenging to explain than constraints. In the grossest, simplest explanation, drivers are constraints, but "dialed up to 11." With drivers, you're able to control any animatable property with any other animatable property.

These driven relationships (in other applications, you may hear of them as "driven keys") give you the ability to create all sorts of interesting controls. In a way, using drivers is almost like building a remote control system for different parts of your scene. You can use drivers for animation rigs (see the next chapter in this book for more on rigging), in motion tracking (see Book 5, Chapter 3), and you can even use drivers to add some light interactivity to your scene, kind of like a game.

This is the sort of control that you get with a driver.

With drivers, you take the value of one property and map it to influence another property, either with a graph or a mathematical formula. There only two constraints that come close to giving you this functionality, the Transformation constraint and the Action constraint. However, despite how powerful those constraints are, they don't have the control and flexibility that you can get with drivers.

That said, I will let you know now that the interface for drivers can get complicated. The process for adding and modifying a driver has gotten easier in recent releases of Blender, but it's also easy to get confused pretty quickly. When you have a tool as versatile as drivers, you end up with an interface that is a little bit challenging to work with. That's the trade-off. You get a lot of flexibility and you have a lot of things you can control, but the way to set that up can take more than a couple of mouse clicks.

Fortunately, that's why this book is here. Hopefully, I can help distill this process into something that makes sense and is also manageable.

When to use drivers

A natural question that you may have is, "When exactly do I use a driver?" The short (and probably unsatisfactory) answer is, "When a constraint isn't enough."

Constraints give you a lot of quick access to controlling one object's parameters or properties with another one. However, if you want to do something that's more than just controlling the transforms of an object or limiting those transforms, this is where drivers really excel.

The example at the beginning of this section was driving a shape key with the position of an Empty. Why might you want to do that? That kind of driven relationship is a fairly common practice in rigging (covered in the next chapter). For example, when a character's arm bends, the default mesh deformation at that joint can sometimes look a little bit ugly. To fix that ugliness, you can sculpt or model a specific shape key, often called a *corrective shape key*, to make that deformation look a little nicer (see the next chapter for more on how to create shape keys).

Of course, after making these corrective shape keys, it can be tedious to manually keyframe the influence sliders on them every time your character bends that arm. You can use a driver to help you automate the process. When your character bends their arm, you can use the rotation of that bend to drive the influence slider on a shape key.

Another example would be if you need to have refined control over how one property affects the other. Recall from the previous section that the Transformation constraint can be used to map the transformation property of one object to a different transform on another object. That constraint gives you a lot of flexibility. But the relationship between the properties is linear. What if you wanted to have acceleration and deceleration in the control? That's not possible with the Transformation constraint.

These sorts of situations are where drivers really excel.

Adding a driver quickly

I can hear you saying it already, "Alright, you've convinced me that drivers are useful. How exactly do I add one?"

There are actually two main approaches to adding drivers: a quick way and a more advanced way. This section covers the former of those two. And, really, for most situations where you want to add a driver, the quick way is what you're most likely to use. The general workflow looks like this:

1. **Find the property that you want to be driven.**

    This property can be just about anywhere in Blender's interface, though it's most common to add drivers from the Properties editor.

2. **Right-click the property and choose Add Driver from the context menu that appears.**

    A little pop-over appears (as shown in Figure 2-5) where you can set up your driver.

In the Driven Property pop-over, the most important section to pay attention to is the panel beneath the Add Input Variable button. This panel is a *variable* panel where you tell Blender what your target property is. Drivers work by letting you define some property in your .blend file as a variable that you can then use to affect the driven property. By default, this quick approach to adding a driver automatically adds a variable for you, configured for you to choose the transform channel of another object in your scene. You can use the Type drop-down menu at the top of the panel to choose other sources for your target. The available options are:

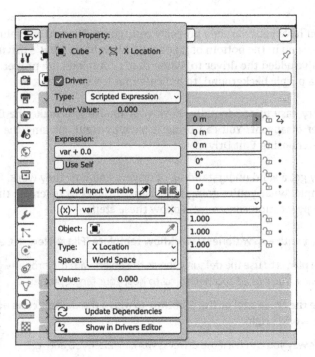

FIGURE 2-5:
The Driven
Property
pop-over is
where you
can quickly
set up a driver
relationship.

 » **Single Property:** If you know the data path to the property you want to target, choose this option to enter that path explicitly. For more on data paths, see the next section, "Understanding data paths."

 » **Transform Channel:** This type of variable is the most commonly used. It also gives you behavior that's most similar to most of the constraints described earlier in this chapter.

 » **Rotational Difference:** With this type of variable, you choose two objects, and the value of your variable is the difference in rotation between those two objects, as measured in *radians* (another way of measuring angles, rather than degrees).

 » **Distance:** Similar to the Rotational Difference variable type, the Distance type gives you the ability to choose two objects, and the value for the variable is the distance between those two objects.

 » **Context Property:** The Context Property type of variable is kind of a special case that's only really used when you're linking a datablock from another .blend file (see Book 6, Chapter 1 for more on linked data). In short, this kind of variable targets a property by context rather than strictly by data path. As an example, you can choose to target whatever the active object is, rather than any one specific object.

After you have your variable properly configured, the current value for that variable shows up in the bottom of its panel. This value is what's driving the property that you've added the driver to. When that's complete, the property field changes to have a purple background, to indicate that it has a driver.

TIP

It's pretty easy to accidentally move your mouse and make the Driven Property pop-over disappear. You can bring it back by right-clicking the property again and now choosing Edit Driver.

To really get a solid understanding of drivers and how they work, it's best to have an example. What you're going to do is use drivers to re-create the basic version of the copy location constraint. Follow these steps:

1. **Start with a new General workflow template (File ⇨ New ⇨ General).**

   The plan is to use the default cube as the object with the property you're driving. You'll need another object to host your target property.

2. **Use the Move tool or the G hotkey to move the default cube away from the world origin.**

   This way you can tell if the driver is working after you add it.

3. **Add an Empty (Add ⇨ Empty ⇨ Plain Axes).**

   You're going to use the X-axis location of this Empty as the target for your driver.

4. **Select the cube and, from the Object tab in the Properties editor, right-click the X-axis location value and choose Add Driver.**

   Blender should show the Driven Property pop-over.

5. **In the Driven Property pop-over go to the variable panel and choose your Empty from the Object dropdown.**

   By completing this step, you're telling Blender that you have a driver on the X-axis location of your cube, and it has a variable that points to the X-axis location of your Empty.

6. **At the top of the Driven Property pop-over, change the Driver Type drop-down menu from Scripted Expression to Averages Value.**

   Choosing this option tells Blender to use the average of all the variable values on this driver. Because you've created only one variable, it's mapped directly to that variable's value. Back in the 3D viewport, you should see your cube jump from its location to align with the X-axis position of your Empty. If you select the Empty and move it along the X-axis, the cube follows along.

Congratulations! You've just created your first driver!

TIP

There's actually an *even faster* way to add a driver. You can navigate to the property that you want to use as your driver, right-click it, and choose Copy as New Driver. Then, go to your driven property, right-click it, and choose Paste Driver. This quickly adds a driver without using the driver interface at all, but it's best to use this approach after you first understand how drivers work and added a few yourself using the other methods covered in this chapter.

Understanding data paths

To really take advantage of drivers to their full extent, you have to have a little bit more of an understanding of how a Blender file is structured. Earlier in this All-in-One book, I describe the Blender file format as being like a database where you can link blocks of data together. That's where the name "datablocks" within Blender comes from.

If you have blocks of data, you need a means of referencing those blocks, just like you would reference files on your hard drive. And kind of like the structure of files on your hard drive, a Blender file has internal paths. These paths serve as a route to each datablock from the root of the .blend file. These routes through a .blend file's internal structure are called *data paths*.

Any property in a Blender file is going to have a path through the internal structure of the file to get to it. Ultimately, this is how drivers reference what they want to drive. Technically speaking, data paths are not only to what you want to drive, but they're also used to tell what's being driven. Fortunately, using the procedure in the preceding section, when you right-click on a property and choose Add Driver, you're implicitly telling Blender that this property you're clicking on is the data path of the driven property.

The Blender developers have tried to make our lives easier by giving us the various different variable types to use for drivers. In fact, if you use the Transform type, you really don't need to know the data path of the target property at all. However, for more esoteric properties, those are a little bit more difficult to find out directly.

This means you need to know the data path to the target property. Fortunately, it's pretty easy to get the data path for any given property. All you need to do is right-click the property and choose Copy Data Path from the context menu.

As with any complex topic, this one is best understood with an example:

1. **Start with a new General workflow template (File ⇨ New ⇨ General).**

   The plan is to use the default cube as the object with the property you're driving. You'll need another object to host your target property.

2. Delete the default cube (Object ⇨ Delete or press the X hotkey).

3. Add a Suzanne mesh (Add ⇨ Mesh ⇨ Monkey).

You may also want to move Suzanne away from the world origin so she's easier to select and see later.

4. In the Modifiers tab of the Properties editor, add a Cast modifier.

Suzanne should look like she's mid-transition into being a sphere. The extent of that transition is controlled by the Factor property within that modifier. You're going to use that Factor value to drive the X-axis location of another object. To do this, you're going to need the data path to that Factor property.

5. Right-click the Factor property in the Cast modifier and choose Copy Data Path from the context menu.

The data path for this property is now stored in Blender's clipboard for use later. Now you need an object that you're driving. For this example, I'm using a torus.

6. Add a torus to your scene (Add ⇨ Mesh ⇨ Torus).

Now it's time to add your driver.

7. With your torus selected, go to Object Properties, right-click the X-axis location property, and choose Add Driver from the context menu.

Blender provides you with the Driven Property pop-over. This is where you use that data path that you copied.

8. In the variable panel within the Driven Properties pop-over, change the variable Type drop-down menu to Single Property.

By default, the Single Property variable type wants you to pick an object. In this case, that object is Suzanne.

9. From the datablock menu labeled Prop, choose Suzanne.

After you choose Suzanne, a new field should appear, labeled Path.

10. Paste the data path you copied in Step 5 into the Path field.

Now, if you go select your Suzanne mesh and go to the Modifiers tab of the Properties editor, you can adjust the Factor value on your Cast modifier and you should see your Torus correspondingly move along the X-axis.

Of course, this example is somewhat contrived. It's not common to use the Factor property in a modifier to drive the position of another object. More frequently, people use custom properties for this purpose. A *custom property* is an extra bit of data that you can tack onto a datablock. Sometimes people create custom properties just to store some additional metadata about whatever they've created, but you can also use them for a more functional purpose. For example, say you want to add a custom property to your Suzanne object so you can use that to control the position of your torus rather than the Factor property in a Cast modifier. Follow these steps:

1. **Select your Suzanne object.**

You can make this selection in either the 3D Viewport or the Outliner, whichever is easiest for you.

2. **In the Object tab of the Properties editor, scroll to the bottom and expand the Custom Properties panel.**

This panel is where you can define a custom property associated with your Suzanne object.

3. **In the Custom Properties panel, click New to add a new custom property.**

By default, the new property is named "prop" and has a value of 1.000.

4. **Click the gear icon to the right of your new property's value to get a Edit Property pop-over and change the Property Name field to something sensible, like "Torus X Location."**

5. **Click OK at the bottom of the Edit Property pop-over when you're done renaming it.**

Now you have a custom property. You can right-click this property and copy its data path just as you had with the Factor value in the Cast node. Then you can replace the data path in the torus' driver with this one. After you do that, you no longer need the Cast modifier; the X-axis location of the torus is controlled with your new custom property on your Suzanne object.

Using the Drivers editor to build complex drivers

In all the examples thus far, you've been using Blender's somewhat simplified Driven Property pop-over to add and configure your drivers. This approach is great for quickly setting up and doing simple edits on a driver. However, if you want to do something more complex or give yourself more control over the driver's behavior, that interface is not exactly the best one to use.

Fortunately, Blender has a dedicated Drivers editor that gives you that ability. That said, none of the workspaces have this editor enabled by default. Now, it's certainly possible to swap any of the areas in your Blender window with a Drivers editor by using the Editor Type dropdown in the header of each editor. However, there's a faster way.

If you right-click any property that already has a driver on it, the context menu has an additional option, Open Drivers Editor. Choose this menu item, and Blender spawns a new window with a Drivers editor dedicated to the driver you're interested in updating. It should look a bit like what's shown in Figure 2-6.

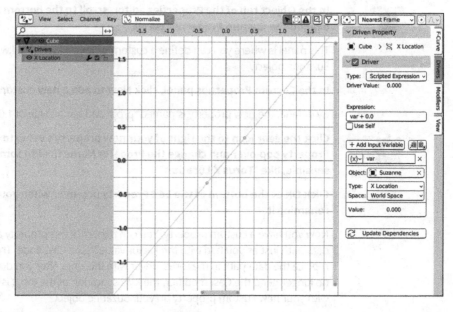

FIGURE 2-6:
The Drivers editor is where you can have complete control over how your drivers behave.

The Drivers editor looks quite a bit like the Graph Editor as described in the previous chapter. The difference is that instead of graphing a change over time, where the X-axis on the Graph Editor is time and the Y-axis is whatever value for your property, the Drivers editor shows a graph of the relationship from one (or more) property to your driven property.

The X-axis in the Driver editor is the property value for the source object, the object that's being driven. At the same time, the Y-axis is the value from the target property. By default, the relationship between these two values is linear, going from 0 to 1 and extrapolating in both directions from there.

Also, a kind of crosshair appears within the graph area of the Drivers editor, indicating the current value of your driver. When you adjust the value of your target property, that crosshair moves to indicate the updated value. As an interesting addition, you can edit the curves in the Drivers editor just like you can edit f-curves in the Graph Editor. With this functionality, you have visual control over your driver's behavior.

Oftentimes, though, you want to have more precise control. Fortunately, those controls are available in the Sidebar of the Drivers editor. From the F-Curve tab, you have numeric inputs for the selected control point on the selected curve, labeled as the Active Keyframe. That gives you one level of control, but if you go to the Drivers tab on the Sidebar, that interface looks just like what you see in the Driven Property pop-over as described in previous sections. The advantage here is that you have a bit more freedom to make your edits to your driver without being worried about losing the pop-over because you moved your mouse cursor away from it.

As you may have guessed, this section on drivers only scratches the surface of what's possible. There are all kinds of exciting things that you can do with drivers, including using scripted expressions in the Python programming language to give mathematical and procedural control over your drivers (see Book 6, Chapter 2). You might have noticed that the uses for drivers are somewhat situational, so it's most useful to have a few existing examples to study and learn from. The biggest thing is knowing how to recognize when a driver would be helpful. After that, it's just about figuring out the best way to get the driver to do what you need.

Chapter **3**

Rigging: The Art of Building an Animatable Puppet

When it comes to character animation, a character is often a single seamless mesh. As a single seamless mesh, it's virtually impossible to animate that character with any detailed movement using the object animation techniques in Book 4, Chapter 1. I mean, you can move the whole character mesh as a unit from one location to another, but you can't make characters smile or wiggle their toes or even bend their arms. You can break the mesh apart and use a complex set of parenting and constraints, but then you lose its nice seamlessness.

What you really want to do is find ways to animate specific parts of the mesh in a controlled manner without tearing the mesh apart. To do so, you need to create a rig for your character. A *rig* is an underlying structure for your mesh that allows you to control how it moves. Rigs are an integral part of modern computer animation, and if done well, they make the life of an animator monumentally easier. Think about it like turning your 3D mesh into a remote-control puppet. This chapter explains the various tools and techniques used to create more complex rigs. Once you understand all the tools, you can create a rig for nearly any object in Blender and have a blast animating it.

Creating Shape Keys

Whether you have to animate a character or a tree or a basketball with any detail, it has to deform from its original shape to a new one. If you know what this new shape looks like, you can model it ahead of time.

As an example, say that you have a cartoony character — maybe the head of a certain Blender monkey. You know that you're going to need their eyes to bulge out, because that happens to all cartoon characters' eyes. One way to create this effect in Blender is by creating a *shape key*, sometimes called a morph target or a blend shape in other programs. A rough outline of the process goes something like this (the next section in this chapter goes into more detail):

1. **Starting with your original mesh, edit the vertices *without creating new geometry* to the new pose you want to use.**

   In the cartoony character example, you'd model the character's eyes all bulgy. (Yes, *bulgy* is a real word. I think.)

2. **Record this new arrangement of your vertices as a shape key to be used later when you animate.**

Creating new shapes

Assuming that you selected an object that supports shape keys (meshes, curves, surfaces, and lattices), you can start adding shape keys in the Shape Keys panel of Object Data Properties.

TIP

Depending on the type of object you're working with, the icon for the Object Data tab will change to match that type of object. That may seem a bit confusing at first, but it can be handy for quickly reminding yourself the kind of object you're working with. Also, in the default theme, it's the only icon in the Properties editor that's green (to match the object data icon in the Outliner).

Figure 3-1 shows three different states for the Shape Keys panel. By default, this panel looks pretty innocent and empty with just a list box and a few buttons to the right of it. However, when you left-click the Plus (+) button, a basis shape is added to the list. The *basis shape* is the original shape that the other shape keys in your object relate to. Left-clicking the Plus (+) button a second time gives you an additional set of options that control the change from the basis shape to a new one, named Key 1.

FIGURE 3-1:
The three different looks that the Shape Keys panel provides.

The best way to see how to create new shapes is to go through a practical example. Staying with the bug-eyed monkey theme, use Suzanne as your test subject, and follow these steps:

1. **Start with a new General workflow template and delete the cube (File ⇨ New ⇨ General, select the cube, then X or Delete).**

2. **Add Suzanne, give her a Subdivision Surface modifier, and set her smooth (Add ⇨ Mesh ⇨ Monkey, Ctrl+1, Object ⇨ Shade Smooth).**

3. **Change to the front view (Numpad 1).**

4. **Add a shape key (Properties editor ⇨ Object Data tab ⇨ Shape Keys ⇨ Plus [+]).**

   Your basis shape is created. The other shapes that you create will be relative to this one.

5. **Add a second shape key (Properties editor ⇨ Object Data tab ⇨ Shape Keys ⇨ Plus [+]) and rename it, if you want.**

   The Shape Keys panel looks like the last one in Figure 3-1. You've created Key 1. If you want, you can rename it by double-clicking its name field. I named mine Eye Bulge.

6. **In the 3D Viewport, tab into Edit mode and change the mesh to have bulged eyes.**

   Make sure that your Eye Bulge shape key is active in the Shape Keys panel before making adjustments. As you modify the mode, be sure that you *do not add or remove any geometry* in the mesh. You should define the shape by moving around the vertices, edges, and faces you already have. A quick way to make Suzanne's eyes bulge is to move your mouse cursor over each eye and press L to select just the vertices there. Then with proportional editing (O) turned on, scale (S) the eyes.

7. **Tab back to Object mode.**

Figure 3-2 illustrates this process.

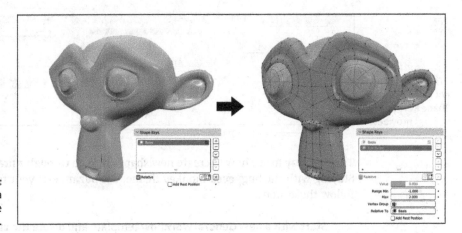

FIGURE 3-2:
Creating a
bug-eyed shape
key for Suzanne.

This process creates two shape keys: Basis and Eye Bulge. With the Eye Bulge shape key selected in the Shape Keys panel, you can use the Value slider to smoothly transition from the Basis shape to the Eye Bulge shape. A value of 0 means that Eye Bulge has no influence and you just have the Basis, whereas a value of 1 means that you're fully at the Eye Bulge shape.

But here's where things get really cool. Notice the Range Min and Max values near the bottom of the panel. The Min is set to 0.000, and the Max is set to 1.000. Just for kicks, change the Max value to 2.000 and pull the slider all the way to the right. Your bulged eyes grow larger than your actual shape key made them. Now change the Min value to –1.000 and pull the slider to the left. Now Suzanne's eyes pinch in to a point smaller than the Basis pose. Figure 3-3 shows the results of these changes. Adjusting the Min and Max Range values is a great way to provide even more extreme shapes for your characters without having to do any additional shape key modeling. How's that for cool?

FIGURE 3-3:
Suzanne with
excessively
pinched and
bulged eyes,
just by changing
the minimum
and maximum
values for a single
shape key.

Mixing shapes

From this point, you can create additional shape keys for the mesh. Say that you want to have a shape key of Suzanne's mouth getting bigger, like she's screaming because her eyes have gotten so huge. The process is about the same as when creating your initial shapes:

1. **Add a new shape key (Properties editor ⇨ Object Data tab ⇨ Shape Keys ⇨ Plus [+]).**

   Feel free to name this key whatever you want. I called mine Scream.

2. **Tab into Edit mode and model the mouth open with the existing vertices.**

   Make sure that you're not touching Suzanne's eyes. You're just editing the mouth to get bigger.

3. **Tab back into Object mode.**

Figure 3-4 shows the results of this process.

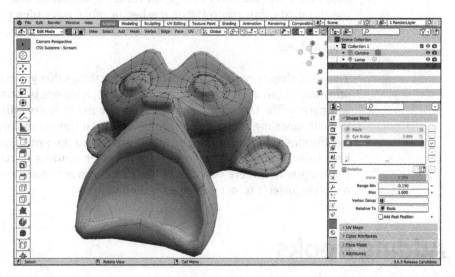

FIGURE 3-4:
Creating a scream shape key.

After you have the Scream shape key created, you can freely mix it with the Eye Bulge shape key, or you can have Suzanne screaming with her regular, bulge-free eyes. The choice is yours. You have the flexibility here to mix and match your shape keys as it pleases you. And animating the mesh to use these keys is really easy.

In Blender, "(almost) everything is animatable," so animating shape keys is as easy as inserting keyframes on the Value slider in the Shape Keys panel. (Click the small dot icon to the right of the Value slider, or right-click the Value field and choose Insert Keyframe from the menu that appears.) Now you can scrub the timeline cursor forward in time and watch Suzanne bulge and scream to your complete delight.

To see another nice little bonus, split off a Graph Editor from your 3D Viewport. If you enable the Show Sliders feature in the Graph Editor (View ⇨ Show Sliders), you can see the numeric values for your shape keys' influences and even key them right there.

Knowing where shape keys are helpful

Now, you *could* do an entire animation using shape keys. But do I recommend it? No. Although shape keys give you very fine control over the placement of vertices in your mesh, the transitioning movement from one shape key to the next is entirely linear from one frame to the next. That is, if you set keyframes for two shape key poses, each vertex moves the shortest distance (a straight line) from one shape key's pose to the other. If you tried to use shape keys for parts of the body that rotate, like arms or legs, the resulting animation looks really funky and unnatural. You can control your meshes in other ways (described later in this chapter) that may give you more natural movement for things like animating arms and legs.

That said, shape keys are the perfect choice for things that you can't do with these other means (or, at least, that are very difficult). A big one is facial animation. The way parts of the face wrinkle up and move around is pretty difficult to re-create without modeling those deformations. Furrowed brows, squinty eyes, natural-looking smiles, and *phonemes*, or mouth shapes for lip-syncing, are where shape keys shine. You can also team them with other controls discussed throughout this chapter to achieve cool effects like cartoon stretchiness, muscle bulges, and morphing objects from one shape to another.

Adding Hooks

Shape keys work well for getting specific predefined deformations, but they can be pretty limiting if you want to have a little bit looser control over your mesh or if you're animating things that move in arcs. For these sorts of situations, you have another control mechanism: hooks. *Hooks* are a special kind of modifier that takes a set of vertices or control points and binds them to be controlled by another object, usually an Empty.

Creating new hooks

The workflow for adding a hook is pretty straightforward. You tab into Edit mode and select at least one vertex or control point. Then you press Vertex ⇨ Hooks ⇨ Hook to New Object. For faster access, you can use the Ctrl+H hotkey combination. An Empty is created at a location that's the median point of all your selected vertices or control points. You also get a Hook modifier added to Modifier Properties.

Tab back into Object mode and transform the hook. All the vertices or control points that you assigned to the hook move with it. And using the options in the Hook modifier, you can control how much influence the hook has over these vertices or control points. The following example gives you a clearer understanding of adding and modifying the influence of hooks:

1. **Start with the General workflow template in Blender (File ⇨ New ⇨ General).**

2. **Select the cube and tab into Edit mode.**

    All the cube's vertices are selected by default. If not, select all vertices by pressing A.

3. **Do a multi-subdivide with four cuts (Edge ⇨ Subdivide, Last Operator Panel ⇨ Number of Cuts: 4).**

4. **Select one of the cube's corner vertices.**

5. **Increase the vertex selection a few times (Select ⇨ Select More/Less ⇨ More, or press Ctrl+Numpad Plus [+]).**

6. **Add a new hook (Vertex ⇨ Hooks ⇨ Hook to New Empty).**

    You can also use the Ctrl+H hotkey combination.

    REMEMBER

7. **Tab back into Object mode.**

    At this point, behavior is as expected. If you select and move the Empty, all the vertices that hooked to it move as if they're parented to it.

8. **With the cube selected, increase the falloff Radius value in the Hook modifier to 1m (Modifier Properties ⇨ Hook-Empty ⇨ Falloff ⇨ Radius: 1m).**

    Now when you select and transform the Empty, the way the vertices follow it is much smoother, kind of like when you're modeling with proportional editing (see Book 2, Chapter 1). For additional kicks, do the next step.

9. **Add a Subdivision Surface modifier to the cube and have it drawn smooth (Ctrl+1, Object ⇨ Shade Smooth).**

    You can also access the Shade Smooth option using the right-click context menu while your cube is still selected. Now the transition is even smoother, as shown in Figure 3-5.

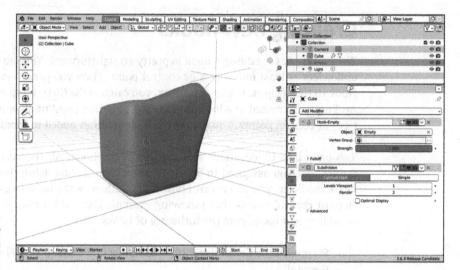

FIGURE 3-5:
A cube smoothly deformed by a hook.

REMEMBER

Vertices aren't just bound to their hook's location. They're also controlled by the hook's scale and rotation. You can really get some wild and complex deformations using this deceptively simple feature.

Knowing where hooks are helpful

The best use for hooks is for large organic deformations. Like shape keys, hooks are nice for creating muscle bulges and cartoony stretching. You can even use them along with shape keys. Because shape keys always use the same shape as the basis for deformation, adding a hook can bring a bit more variety. For example, in the bug-eyed Suzanne example from the "Creating Shape Keys" section, you can add a hook for one of the eyes to make it bulge asymmetrically. These touches give more *character* to your 3D characters.

Using Armatures: Skeletons in the Mesh

Shape keys and hooks are great ways to deform a mesh, but the problem with them is that both are lacking a good underlying structure. They're great for big, cartoony stretching and deformation, but for a more structured deformation, like an arm bending at the elbow joint, the motion that they produce is pretty unnatural looking. To solve this problem, 3D computer animation took a page from one of its meatspace contemporaries, stop-motion animation. *Stop-motion animation* involves small sculptures that typically feature a metal skeleton underneath them, referred to as an *armature.* The armature gives the model both structure and a mechanism for making and holding poses. Blender has an object that provides a similar structure for CG characters. It, too, is called an armature. Armatures form the basis of nearly all Blender rigs.

To add an armature to your scene, go to the 3D Viewport and choose Add ⇨ Armature. Adding an armature creates a single object with a weird shape called an octahedron. Continuing to use the skeleton analogy, that octahedron is referred to as a *bone* in the armature. The wide end of the bone is referred to as the bone's *head* or root, and its narrow end is referred to as the bone's *tail* or tip. Typically, a bone pivots at the head. Figure 3-6 shows a single bone with the head and tail labeled.

REMEMBER

If you're familiar with other 3D animation software, you may be more comfortable with the concept of working with joints. In those applications, the joint is the basic atomic unit of an armature, and the bones are just the incidental connection between joints. I won't say one approach is inherently superior to the other. Either way, you can make a pretty convincing argument in favor or opposition; they're simply two slightly different solutions to the same problem.

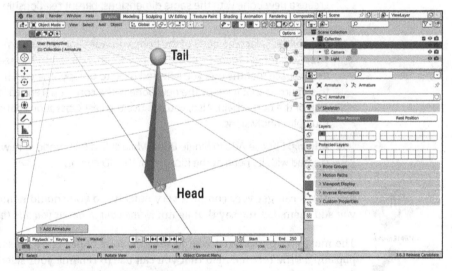

FIGURE 3-6:
An armature object with a single bone. Woohoo!

Editing armatures

You can take a rather inauspicious single bone armature and do something more interesting with it. Like nearly every other object in Blender, you can edit the armature in more detail by selecting it and tabbing into Edit mode or switching to the Modeling workspace (which automatically brings you into Edit mode). In Edit mode, you can select the sphere at the bone's head, the sphere at the bone's tail, or the bone itself. (Selecting the bone body actually selects both the head and tail spheres as well.) You can add a new bone to your armature in five ways:

>> **Extrude:** Select either the head or tail of the bone and press E to extrude a new bone from that point. This method is the most common way to add new bones to an armature. If you add a bone by extruding from the tail, you get the additional benefit of having an instant parent-child relationship. The new bone is the child of the one you extruded it from. These bones are linked together, tail to head, and referred to as a bone *chain*. The Ctrl+right-click extrude shortcut for meshes and curves also works for bones.

If you prefer to use the tool approach, the Extrude tool is the second-to-last tool in the toolbar. With that tool active, you get a relatively simple widget for extruding a new bone and adjusting its length. If you long-click that toolbar button, you can activate the Extrude to Cursor tool, which works by extruding a bone to wherever you click in the 3D Viewport.

>> **Duplicate:** Select the body of the bone you want and choose Armature ⇨ Duplicate, use the right-click context menu, or press Shift+D to duplicate it and create a new bone with the same dimensions, parent relationships, and constraints.

>> **Subdivide:** Select the body of the bone you want and choose Armature ⇨ Subdivide (or get there from the right-click context menu). You see two bones in the space that the one you selected used to occupy. The cool thing about this option is that it keeps the new bone in the correct parent-child relationship of the bone chain. Also, you can use the Last Operations panel and do multiple subdivisions.

>> **Adding:** Choose Add ⇨ Single Bone while still in Edit mode. A new bone is created with its head at the location of the 3D cursor.

REMEMBER

Armatures can get very complex very quickly, so you should name your bones as you add them. Let me say that again: *Name your bones as you add them.*

The most straightforward way to rename your bones is by pressing F2. Blender pops up a little rename field that you can use to rename your selected bone (incidentally, this works for other objects as well). If you don't happen to have F-keys on your keyboard, you can also do it from the Bone tab of the Properties editor while in Edit mode or Pose mode or by navigating to Edit ⇨ Rename Active Item from Blender's top menu. From there, you edit the names of your bones the same way you edit names of other Blender objects. Left-click the name in the Name field and type the name of a bone that makes sense. As an example, if you have a two-bone chain to control a character's arm, you may name one bone arm_upper and the other arm_lower.

Unfortunately, this approach can be really slow if you're in Object mode or if you're trying to name a lot of bones at the same time (because maybe, ahem, you forgot to name your bones as you were adding them). For this hopefully rare case, the Outliner is a good tool for the job. Expand the Armature object to reveal the hierarchy of bones within it. Double-click the name of any bone (or any object, for that matter), and you can rename it right there. Figure 3-7 shows the three places where you can name your bones directly.

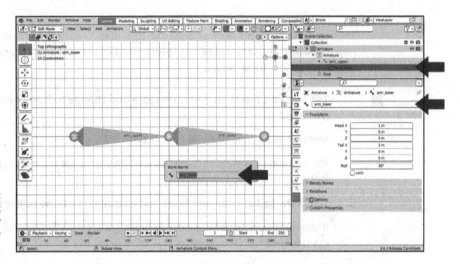

FIGURE 3-7: Three different ways to directly name your bones.

If you really do have a whole bunch of bones that you want to rename, there's an even faster way. You can use Blender's built-in Batch Rename operator. This feature is especially useful if you have multiple bones that you want to rename according to a set of simple rules. For example, maybe you have six bones that make up a character's tail and you were making them quickly, so they're named Bone.001, Bone.002, Bone.003, and so on up to Bone.006. If you select those bones and press Ctrl+F2 (or choose Edit ➪ Batch Rename from Blender's top menu), Blender pops up the Batch Rename floating panel where you can do things like find-and-replace to change all bones starting with "Bone" to "Tail" in one shot. Figure 3-8 shows the Batch Rename panel. This feature actually works for just about any datablock in your .blend file, so you need to use the Type drop-down menu at the top right to specify that you want to just rename bones.

TIP

Blender has a pretty cool way of understanding *symmetric rigs*, or rigs that have a left side that's identical to the right. For these cases, use a .L and .R suffix on your bone names. So in the previous example, if you're rigging a character with two arms, the bones in the left arm would be named arm_upper.L and arm_lower.L. The right arm bones would be named arm_upper.R and arm_lower.R. This naming convention gives you a couple of advantages, but the one that's most apparent when modeling your rig is the X-Axis Mirror feature.

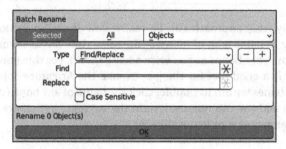

FIGURE 3-8:
Press Ctrl+F2 to
activate Blender's
Batch Rename
operator so you
can change the
names of a bunch
of bones at the
same time.

To better understand how symmetric rigs and X-axis mirroring work, create a new armature at the world origin (Shift+S ⇨ Cursor to World Origin, Add ⇨ Armature) and follow these steps:

1. **Tab into Edit mode on your armature and change to front view (Numpad 1).**

2. **Rename the single bone to** root **(F2).**

   It's common convention in rigging to use this name for the main parent bone in the rig.

3. **Select the tail of your root bone and extrude (E) a bone to the right.**

   If you don't want to use the extrude hotkey, you can Ctrl+right-click or use the extrude tool.

4. **Name this newly extruded bone** Bone.R **(F2).**

5. **Select the tail of your root bone again and extrude (E) another new bone, but this time to the left.**

6. **Name this bone** Bone.L **(F2).**

7. **In the Tool tab of the Sidebar (N), enable the X-Axis Mirror check box.**

8. **Select the tail of** Bone.R **and grab it to move it around by using the Move tool or by pressing the G hotkey.**

   Now, wherever you move the tail of this bone, the tail of Bone.L matches that movement on the other side of the X-axis. You can even extrude (E) a new bone, and a new bone is extruded on both sides of the axis. In this way, X-axis mirroring can speed up the rigging process immensely.

The preceding steps help give you an idea of how the X-Axis Mirror feature works, but it's not exactly a smooth workflow for building a rig. One common practice is to use a few tools built into Blender that take advantage of this naming convention. You can build your rig on one side of your character. Then, you can right-click ⇨ Names ⇨ Auto-Name Left/Right to append the correct L or R suffix to your name, and right-click again and choose Symmetrize to automatically create the bones on the other side of your rig. There's a bit more on this approach later in this chapter in the section titled "Bringing It All Together to Rig a Character."

TIP

When editing bones, it's a good idea to make visible the mesh for which your rig is intended. This way, you get your proportions correct. A good general rule for placing bones is to think about where the character's real anatomical bones would be located and then use that as a guideline.

Parenting bones

One important thing that makes armatures helpful is the notion of how its bones relate to one another. The most important of these relationships is the parent-child relationships between bones. The same hotkeys for parenting and unparenting objects covered in Book 1, Chapter 4 also work with bones, but with a couple additional features. To illustrate the additional features when parenting bones, start a new General workflow template (File ⇨ New ⇨ General), delete the default cube (X), add a new armature object (Add ⇨ Armature), and then tab into Edit mode. Then follow these steps:

1. **Select the single bone created, duplicate it (Armature ⇨ Duplicate or press Shift+D), and place it somewhere in space.**

2. **Add the original bone to your selection (Shift+select).**

3. **Choose Armature ⇨ Parent ⇨ Make or press Ctrl+P to make the original bone the parent of the duplicate.**

    You're given two options:

    - **Connected:** This option moves the entire child bone so its head is in the same location as the tail of the parent, creating a bone chain as if you'd created the second bone by extruding it up from the first.

    - **Keep Offset:** Choosing this option leaves the child bone in place and draws a dashed relationship line between the two bones. They're not connected, but one still has an influence on the other, kind of like regular parenting between objects.

4. **After you create the parent relationship, select just the child bone.**

5. **Clear the parent relationship by choosing Armature ⇨ Parent ⇨ Clear or by pressing Alt+P.**

    You have another pair of options:

    - **Clear Parent:** This option removes any sort of parent-child relationship this bone has. If the bone was connected to the parent bone, it's now disconnected, and you can move it around freely. Note that this *does not* reposition the child bone back to where you first placed it.

- **Disconnect Bone:** This option doesn't actually clear the parent relationship. Instead, if your bones are connected, choosing this option maintains the parent-child relationship, but the child bone can move independently of the parent's tip. The bone behaves as if you made the parent by using the Keep Offset option.

Figure 3-9 shows how two bones in an armature can be related.

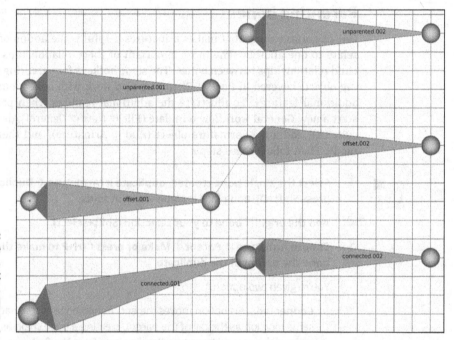

FIGURE 3-9:
Bones that are unparented (top), with an offset parent (middle), and parented with a connection (bottom).

Even with bones parented — connected or otherwise — if you rotate the parent bone, the child doesn't rotate with it as you might expect in a typical parent-child relationship. That's because you're still in Edit mode, which is designed mostly for building and modifying the armature's structure. The parent-child relationship actually works in a special mode for armatures called Pose mode. You access this mode by pressing Ctrl+Tab, choosing Pose Mode from the Mode menu in the 3D Viewport's header, or switching to the Animation workspace with your armature object selected.

When you're in Pose mode, if you select individual bones and rotate them, their children rotate with them, as you might expect. From there, you can swap back out to Object mode by pressing Ctrl+Tab again, or you can jump back into Edit mode just by pressing Tab. The next chapter in this book has more on working in Pose mode.

Armature properties

When working with armatures, the Properties editor has some sections specific to armatures with options and controls that are incredibly helpful. Select your armature and have a look at the Properties editor. In particular, note that in addition to the green Object Data tab with the Armature icon, two more sets of tabs appear when you're in Pose mode: a Bone tab and a Bone Constraints tab. Figure 3-10 shows the contents of these panels.

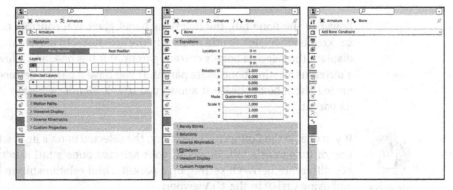

FIGURE 3-10:
Armature-specific tabs in the Properties editor.

NEW
FEATURE

If you're working with this book in Blender 4.0 or later, you may notice that Figure 3-10 doesn't match what you see in Blender. In version 4.0, bone layers and groups are replaced with a bone collections system that's much more like how object collections work in the rest of Blender.

As you may have guessed, the Object Data tab of the Properties editor (I think of this as Armature Properties) provides options for the armature overall, whereas the Bone tab provides options for the currently selected bone. Looking first at the contents of the Bone tab, some options and controls are immediately helpful. The text field at the top lets you rename your bone. The Transform panel (visible only in Edit mode and Pose mode) gives you precise numeric control over the location of the head and tail of the selected bone, as well as its *roll angle,* or the orientation of the octahedron between the head and the tail, while in Edit mode. For the most part, these controls are the same as the transform controls in the Item tab of the 3D Viewport's Sidebar (N). There are a few differences, though. When you're in Edit mode, the Bone tab's Transform panel doesn't show any of the envelope deform options (all of them are available in the Deform Panel, covered later in this section). Another small difference is that the Bone tab's Transform panel has an additional check box labeled Lock when you're in Edit mode on your armature object. Enable this option and Blender prevents you from transforming the bone in Edit mode. The Lock feature is useful when building complex rigs where you have a lot of bones and you need to prevent accidentally editing some critical ones.

The Bendy Bones panel gives you more refined controls over how the bone itself deforms. See, a bone in Blender isn't merely the connection between two joints. It's possible for a bone to have multiple internal segments between the head and tail. Those segments allow additional transformations of the bone like bending and twisting. In a way, you can think of the bone as a simple Bézier curve with controls at the head and tail. The bendy bones feature of Blender's bones give you a lot of built-in functionality that's not as quick to set up in other rigging systems. The Bendy Bones panel gives you control over that functionality. There's more on building a rig with bendy bones at the end of this chapter.

Lower in the Bone tab, the Relations panel gives you controls to define how the selected bone relates to other bones in the armature. In particular, the Parent field displays the selected bone's current parent, if it has one, and allows you to choose a different existing bone as its parent. If you have a parent defined here, the Connected check box beneath it allows you to tell Blender whether it's connected to its parent.

REMEMBER

If you enable the Connected check box, the selected bone's head snaps to the location of its parent's tail. However, your selected bone's tail *won't* move. This is a key difference between setting up a parent-child relationship in Bone Properties and using Ctrl+P in the 3D Viewport.

A series of buttons, known as *bone layers*, appear at the top of the Relations panel. Now, if you are familiar with older versions of Blender, then these buttons should be recognizable. However, if you're new to Blender, then it may not be immediately clear what these bone-layer buttons do. I like to think of them as organizational blocks. Each button in this array represents a single bone layer. Any given bone can belong to one or more bone layers, just like any object can belong to one or more collections in the Outliner. The reason for this dedicated organizational structure for bones is because character rigs can get pretty involved. Using bone layers is a good way to keep your rig logical and organized. Left-click a layer button to toggle your selected bone's membership to that layer. If you'd like the bone to live on more than one layer, you can Shift+left-click the buttons for those layers. To add your bone to a lot of layers all at once, Shift+left-click and drag your mouse cursor over the bone layers.

NEW FEATURE

If you're using Blender 4.0 or newer, there are no bone layers in the Relations panel. Instead, bones can be members of collections, similar to object collections in the rest of Blender. I get into the bone collections features briefly later in this chapter in the section titled "Making the rig more user friendly."

REMEMBER

The options in the various armature-related sections of the Properties editor change a bit between Edit mode (Tab), Object mode, and Pose mode (Ctrl+Tab). What I cover here is available in Edit mode and Pose mode.

Two other important sets of controls are in Bone Properties. The first is the Deform panel. Simply put, the check box for this panel is a toggle that tells Blender whether the selected bone can be mapped to the geometry of your mesh. If the mesh's geometry is mapped, or *weighted*, to the bone, then that bone is considered a *deformer*. Deformers should have the Deform check box in Bone Properties enabled.

Besides deformers, you can also have bones whose purpose is to control the behavior of the deformer bones. These bones are often referred to as *control* bones. To prevent these control bones from inadvertently influencing your mesh's geometry, you should make sure that their Deform check box is disabled in Bone Properties.

From an organizational standpoint, I tend to put my deformer bones on the lower row of bone layers while reserving the upper row of bone layers for my control bones.

Back in Armature Properties (the Object Data tab of the Properties editor), there are two sets of layer buttons in the Skeleton panel. These buttons correspond to the bone layers in the Bone tab. The difference is that *these* layer buttons control which layers the armature is actually displaying in the 3D Viewport. The layer buttons under the Protected Layers label have an effect only if you're linking your rig into a separate scene file. Book 6, Chapter 1 gets more into linking data between .blend files.

The Viewport Display panel contains a set of buttons for controlling how bones in the armature are displayed in the 3D Viewport:

>> **Display As:** This drop-down button gives the choice of four different draw types for your armature's bones in the 3D Viewport. Note, however, that even though the bone display type may not be drawn in the 3D Viewport, its influences are still valid. That is, even if you're displaying Stick bones, they still control the same vertices within the range of the Envelope bones and still make use of the segmentation in B-bones. Figure 3-11 shows examples of each of these bone display types:

- **Octahedral:** The default bone display type, the octahedral shape is great for building a rig because it shows which way a bone points as well as its roll angle.

- **Stick:** This display type draws the bones as a thin stick. I like to animate with my bones in this type so that they stay out of my way.

- **B-Bone:** B-bones are drawn as boxes. The interesting thing, though, is that b-bones can be dynamically subdivided and treated as simple Bézier curves. B-bones are the visualization of choice for bendy bones. To increase a bone's subdivisions, select the bone and switch to the Bendy Bones panel in Bone Properties. In this panel, increase the Segments value, which makes the deformation from one bone to the next much smoother. Even if you don't display the b-bone type, Blender still pays attention to the Segments value. So if your character deforms in an unexpected way, you may want to check the Segments value in Bone Properties.

- **Envelope:** This display type draws the bones with a scalable sphere at each end and a tube for the bone body. Vertices on your mesh that are within the influence area of these bones will have their locations influenced by them. Use Alt+S to adjust the size of selected spheres and tubes in this display type. Armature ⇨ Transform ⇨ Scale Envelope Distance increases the bone's range. For numerical access, all the envelope controls are available in the Deform panel within Bone Properties.

- **Wire:** The wire display type is very similar to stick, but it's thinner and even less obtrusive with a thickness of only one pixel. As an additional bonus, this display type also shoes b-bone bending, so it's especially useful as a "working" display type that animators can use.

➤➤ **Extra display options:** In addition to the bone draw type, there are a series of additional check boxes in the Viewport Display panel of Armature Properties. You can enable all, one, or none of these options in any combination you want.

- **Names:** This check box toggles the display of each bone's name in the 3D Viewport. Names can make selecting bones and defining constraints much easier.

- **Shapes:** To help communicate a bone's purpose to the animator, you can display any bone in Blender as any object in your scene. While in Pose mode, select a bone and go to the Viewport Display panel in Bone Properties. There, you can define the object you want as your bone shape by choosing it from the Custom Object field. With the Shapes check box enabled in Armature Properties, the bone is displayed as your chosen object while in Pose mode, regardless of the bone display type you've chosen.

- **BoneColors:** To help organize bones in an armature for an animator, you can actually define custom colors for bones by using bone groups (see the section later in this chapter called "Making the rig more user friendly"). Set all facial controls to blue, or the left side of the armature in red. Enable this check box so that you can make use of those colors. As a note, if you're using Blender 4.0 or later, color is a property of a bone rather than a group.

- **In Front:** The In Front check box in this panel does the same thing as the In Front check box in the Object tab of the Properties editor. In fact, both check boxes control the same property. It allows you to see the bones of your armature in the 3D Viewport, even if they're technically inside or behind another object. Enabling this feature makes your bones easier to see and select when rigging or animating.

- **Axes:** This option toggles the display of the center axis of the bones. The Axes check box is helpful for understanding the bones' true roll angles. There's a Position slider to the right of this check box that allows you to slide the bone axis along the length of the bone. It's important to remember, though, that this is a visualization of the bone's orientation. Regardless of where you place this visualized axis, rotation for a bone is still about its head.

- **Relations:** The buttons next to the Relations label control how the dashed relationship line between parent and child bones is displayed. The relationship line always connects to the head of the child bone. And by default, that line connects to the tail of the parent. However, if you click the Head button for this option, the relationship line connects to the parent's head instead. As with the Axes controls, this control is only a visualization of the relationship. It doesn't change how the bones behave in relation to one another.

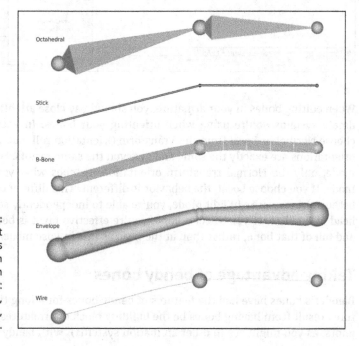

FIGURE 3-11:
The different display types for bones in Blender from top to bottom: octahedral, stick, b-bone, envelope, and wire.

When building a rig, it's not uncommon to find yourself frequently switching between tabs in the Properties editor. In particular, you may find yourself cycling back and forth between the Object Data tab and either the Bone or Bone Constraints tabs. To alleviate the pain of these frequent tab switches, I often split the Properties editor in half so I can have both tabs quickly accessible at the same time. Whether you split it vertically or horizontally depends mostly on what you find most comfortable, but the single-column layout introduced in Blender works surprisingly well with a narrow Properties editor. And since you're not changing between tabs, you can hide the tabs and gain a little extra space by clicking and dragging the border between the tabs and the content of the tabs Figure 3-12 shows an example of what this screen might look like.

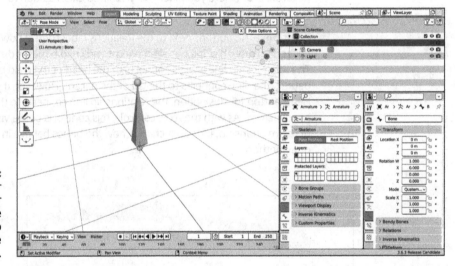

FIGURE 3-12: Splitting your Properties editor can give you the ability to see two tabs open at the same time.

When editing bones in your armature, you should pay close attention to the coordinate systems you're using when orienting your bones. In Pose mode, if you choose Normal or Local from the Transform Orientation roll-out, both transform orientations are exactly the same and give you the same results. However, in Edit mode, only the Normal transform orientation matches what you have in Pose mode. If you choose Local, the behavior is different. This difference in behavior is because when you're in Edit Mode, you're able to independently select the bone's head and tail. So if you select a bone, you're effective pivot is between the head and tail of that bone, rather than at the head as it is in Pose mode.

Taking advantage of bendy bones

Blender's bones have had the features of bendy bones for a long time. These features result from having bones be the building block of armatures (as opposed to joints, as you might see in other animation systems). With bendy bones, you can treat a bone like it's a Bézier curve between the head and the tail. This feature gives you the ability to unlock additional deformation controls without adding a bunch of extra bones to your armature. You can control the properties of this incredibly powerful feature from the Bendy Bones panel in Bone Properties editor, as shown in Figure 3-13.

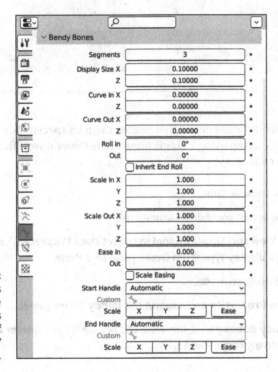

FIGURE 3-13:
The Bendy Bones panel in Bone Properties gives you full control of the "bendiness" of your bones.

TIP

Before working with the Bendy Bones panel, it's most useful to enable the b-bone display type in the Viewport Display tab of Armature Properties. Without changing your armature's display type, you won't be able to easily see the effects of any changes you make in the Bendy Bones panel.

Before going into these controls in detail, it's worth it to take a moment and wrap your brain around bendy bone terminology. Looking back at Figure 3-13, notice that a lot of the controls for bendy bones have variations labeled In and Out. For clarity's sake, it would be much better if you mentally replace "in" with "head" and "out" with "tail" because that's what they're referring to. For example, the Curve In X value controls how much bend the bone has about the X-axis at the head of the bone, whereas Curve Out X controls bending about the X-axis of the bone's tail. Figure 3-14 illustrates this difference on a single bone.

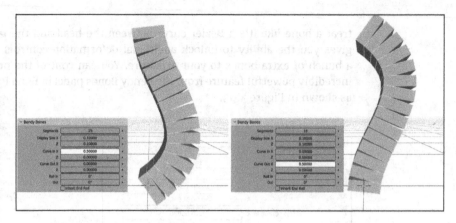

FIGURE 3-14:
Adjusting Curve
In X bends the
bone about the
X-axis of its head
(left), whereas
Curve Out X
bends about the
X-axis of that
bone's tail (right).

So, what is it about bendy bones that makes them so special? It's really easiest to see with a simple setup using a single bone in the General workflow template (File ⇨ New ⇨ General):

1. **Delete the default Cube.**

2. **Add a new armature (Add ⇨ Armature).**

3. **From the Viewport Display panel in Object Data Properties, change the armature's display type from Octahedral to B-Bone.**

4. **Ctrl+Tab into Pose mode.**

5. **Go to Bone Properties and expand the Bendy Bones panel.**

6. **In the Bendy Bones panel, increase the Segments parameter to something relatively large, like 15.**

Your Blender workspace should look something like what's shown in Figure 3-15.

Now you can play with the various parameters in the Bendy Bones panel and get a good visual sense for what each one does. Most parameters have an "in" (head) and "out" (tail) variant. Your basic options are as follows:

» **Display Size:** These two values are the exception to the "in/out" variations. Fortunately, they control only how the bones are displayed in the 3D Viewport and not any kind of behavior. Adjust these values to change the size of how bone segments are displayed. Using these values, you can make your bone larger than your character's mesh to make the bone more easily selectable, or you can make the bone really thin so it's unobtrusive.

» **Curve:** There are four value fields dedicated to adjusting your bendy bone's curve, Curve In X, Curve In Z, Curve Out X, and Curve Out Z. These values bend the bone so it arcs similarly to how handles bend Bézier curves.

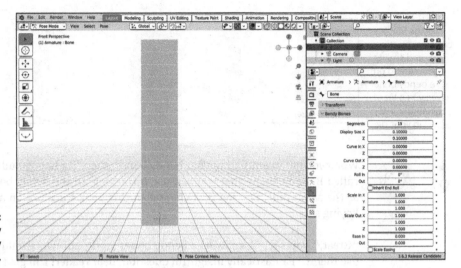

FIGURE 3-15:
A single bendy bone, currently unbent.

>> **Roll:** There are only two Roll values, Roll In and Roll Out. These are the values that control how the bone twists along its local Y-axis, which runs along the length of the bone. There's an additional check box after these fields, labeled Inherit End Roll. Enable this check box if you have a chain of bendy bones and you want this current one to start with the Roll value that its parent bone has.

>> **Scale:** Like the Curve parameters, you have multiple Scale parameters. For each in and out set of values, you can adjust scale along the X, Y, or Z axes. These parameters work as their name advertises. You adjust them and the head or tail of the bone is scaled in that axis.

>> **Ease:** If you adjust the Ease parameters, the results on their own might appear a little weird; you may not be able to tell that anything is happening at all. The easiest way to see the influence of the Ease parameters is by first setting one of the Curve parameters. For example, if you set Curve X In to something like 1.00 and then adjust the Ease In value, you should see the bend result from the Curve In X parameter move up and down the length of the bone. This control is similar to changing the length of a handle on a Bézier curve.

>> **Handle controls:** At the bottom of the Bendy Bone panel are a set of controls related to handles on your bendy bones. *Handles* are basically the equivalent of control points on Bézier curves. These options give you advanced control over those handles and how they behave. For the time being, I recommend leaving the Start Handle and End Handle parameters at their default value of Automatic.

Figure 3-16 shows the influence of each of these parameters in isolation (I only show the results on the X-axis) along with a single example of them all modified at the same time.

FIGURE 3-16:
All the various
bending, twisting,
and scaling
you can do on
a bendy bone
gives you a lot of
dynamic variety
in your rig.

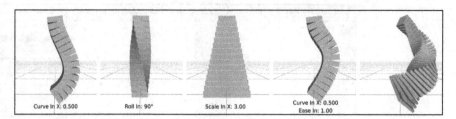

Curve In X: 0.500   Roll In: 90°   Scale In X: 3.00   Curve In X: 0.500
Ease In: 1.00

TIP

When you get to animating your bendy bones, there's a handy built-in keying set called B-Bone Shape that you can use for keying all the bendy bone parameters at the same time. See the first chapter in this book for more on animating with keying sets.

"Great," you say, "I know *how* bendy bones work, but *why* would I ever want to use them?" Fantastically insightful question, dear reader! I'm glad you asked. The most obvious answer to this would be if you had to build a rig for a cartoony character. Bendy bones are a fantastic choice for "rubber-hose" style arms and legs.

However, don't limit your imagination to just cartoony things. Forearm twists are notoriously difficult to rig in non-bendy bone systems. You get it for free with the Roll parameters on bendy bones. Animal tails often require long chains of bones or a curve with hooks for controls. With just a few bendy bones, you can get all the tail movement you could ever want. If you need muscle to bulge out when your character flexes, you can get a simple form of that behavior by animating a bendy bone's Scale and Ease parameters. Facial rigs for characters are often a complicated mix of bones and shape keys (especially for the eyes and mouth). With bendy bones, a lot of that complexity can be removed.

Long story short (too late?), with a little bit of clever ingenuity, you can use bendy bones in a rig to give yourself or another animator a bunch of control over how a character looks when posed.

Putting skin on your skeleton

Armatures and bones are pretty interesting, but they do you no good if they don't actually deform your mesh. When you create your own rig and switch to Pose mode (Ctrl+Tab), you can move, rotate, and scale bones, but the moving bones have no influence whatsoever on your mesh by default. What you need to do is bind the vertices of the mesh to specific bones in your armature. This binding process is commonly referred to as *skinning*. Blender has two primary ways of skinning: envelopes and vertex groups.

Quick-and-dirty skinning with envelopes

Envelopes are the quickest way to get the armature to control a mesh's vertices. You don't have to create anything extra: It's just a simple modifier that seals the deal. To use envelopes to control your mesh, follow these steps:

1. **In Object mode, select the mesh you want to rig and add an Armature modifier to it in the Modifiers tab of the Properties editor.**

2. **Within the Armature modifier, select the armature you created in the Object field.**

    If you named your armature object something sensible, it should be pretty easy to find. Otherwise, you can use the eyedropper from this field to select your armature in the 3D Viewport.

3. **Still within your Armature modifier, enable the Bone Envelopes check box.**

    You can also disable the Vertex Groups check box, if you'd like.

4. **Select your armature and go to the Viewport Display panel of Armature Properties to enable the Envelope bone display type.**

    This step reveals the exact location of the influences for your envelopes.

5. **If some part of your mesh isn't under the influence of an envelope, tab into Edit mode and use the controls from the Deform panel in Bone Properties to adjust the envelope's influence area.**

Figure 3-17 illustrates envelopes in action.

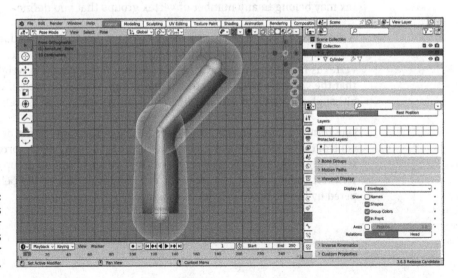

FIGURE 3-17: Using envelopes to control your armature's influence over the mesh.

TIP

There's a handy shortcut for the whole process described in the preceding steps: parenting. If you select your mesh and Shift+select your armature, you can press Ctrl+P and choose Armature Deform from the menu that appears (alternatively, Object ⇨ Parent ⇨ Armature Deform from the 3D Viewport's header menu). This single operation performs Steps 1 through 3 in the preceding description all at once.

Envelopes are great for quickly roughing out a rig and testing it on your mesh or for giving yourself simple controls to pose a sculpt (see Book 2, Chapter 3 for more on sculpting), but for detailed deformations, they aren't ideal. Where the influence of multiple envelopes overlap can be particularly problematic, and there's a good tendency for envelope-based rigs to have characters pinch a bit at their joints. For these cases, a more detailed approach is necessary.

TIP

That said, using envelopes in your armature gives you one distinct control you can't have with armatures otherwise. You can actually use an armature with envelopes to control the deformation of curves and surfaces. As long as a control point is within the influence space of a bone's envelope, you can modify it and, therefore, animate it with the armature.

Assigning weights to vertices

A *vertex group* is basically what it sounds like — a set of vertices that have been assigned to a named group. In many ways, a vertex group is a lot like a material slot (see Book 3, Chapter 1). Besides the fact that vertex groups don't deal with materials, vertex groups have a couple of distinctions that set them apart from material slots. First of all, material slots are based on faces, whereas vertex groups are based on vertices. Secondly, vertex groups aren't mutually exclusive. Any vertex may belong to any number of vertex groups that you define.

A side effect of multiple group membership is another distinction: You can give a vertex a *weight*, or a numerical value that indicates how much that particular vertex is influenced or dedicated to a specific vertex group. A weight of 1.0 means that the vertex is fully dedicated to that group, whereas a weight of 0 means that although the vertex is technically part of the group, it may as well not be.

One thing to note: Vertex groups need to have the exact name of the bones that control them. So if you have a bone called pelvis, you need a corresponding vertex group with the same name. The vertices assigned to that group then have their position influenced by the location, rotation, and scale of the pelvis bone, tempered by the vertices' individual weights.

To adjust the assignments and weights of vertices in their respective vertex groups, you can use the Vertex Groups panel in Object Data Properties for your selected mesh. You create a new group with the Plus (+) button to the right of the list box. To select the vertices that you want to assign to the group, you need to tab into Edit mode. With the vertices selected in Edit mode, you can adjust the value in the Weight slider and then assign them to the vertex group by left-clicking the Assign button.

TIP

If you don't see the Assign button or Weight slider in the Vertex Groups panel, then you're not in Edit mode. Tab into Edit mode and those controls should appear for you. Figure 3-18 shows the Vertex Groups panel with a few different groups added.

FIGURE 3-18:
You can use the Vertex Groups panel to manually create vertex groups from the vertices in your mesh.

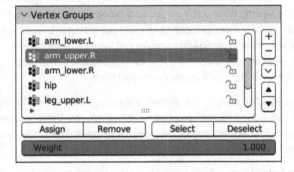

REMEMBER

Something to note about vertex weights is that, when used for armatures, they are *normalized* to 1.000. That is, a vertex can be a member of two vertex groups and have a weight of 1.000 for both. In these cases, Blender adjusts the weights internally so that they add up to 1.000. So in my example, that double-grouped vertex behaves like it has a weight of 0.500 on both groups.

TIP

If you're interested in seeing a numerical representation of your bone weights, you can change one editor in your workspace to a Spreadsheet. From there, you can see each vertex in your mesh and its corresponding weight value for each vertex group.

Of course, on a complex armature, this process of creating vertex groups and painstakingly assigning weights to each vertex can get excessively tedious. Fortunately, Blender has a couple tools to make things less painful. First of all, you don't have to create all the vertex groups by yourself. Refer to the preceding section on the process of skinning with envelopes (a daunting task indeed if you have a rig with hundreds of bones). By parenting the mesh to the armature there, you're presented with a few options. If you worked through the preceding section, you may already be familiar with the basic Armature Deform choice (Object ⇨ Parent ⇨ Armature Deform). For vertex groups, the additional menu items are more helpful.

TIP

The parenting choices in the Object menu are mind-bogglingly extensive. I personally prefer to use the Ctrl+P hotkey for parenting because it provides a menu with a more sane length and more relevant options:

» **Object:** This option is just a simple parenting operation. Your whole mesh becomes a child of the armature object, just as if you'd parented it to another mesh or an Empty. No modifier is applied to your mesh at all.

You may notice that there are three other object parenting choices, labeled (Keep Transform), (Without Inverse), and (Keep Transform Without Inverse). These are slightly more difficult-to-explain parenting relationships, but outside of some very specific scenarios, they're not very commonly used. If you're curious, you can look them up in the official Blender documentation, but it's safe to assume that you'll rarely ever need them.

» **Armature Deform:** As in the envelope skinning example of the preceding section, this option doesn't create any vertex groups, thereby ensuring that the mesh is influenced only by the bone envelopes. There are, however, three additional options that specifically relate to vertex groups:

- **With Empty Groups:** This option creates vertex groups for you using the names of all the bones with the Deform check box enabled in Bone Properties. However, it doesn't automatically assign any vertices to any of those groups. Use this option if you want to manually assign weights.

- **With Envelope Weights:** This option is a bit of a compromise. It first creates the vertex groups based on the bones with their Deform option turned on. Then, it looks at the influence area of the bone envelope for each bone and uses that to assign vertices to each vertex group, with their weights varied accordingly. The advantage of this option is that it gets you weighted vertices. The downside, though, is that if the influence area of your envelopes isn't set up well, the weight assignment can look messy.

An example of a messy assignment would be if you modeled a character with their hands down at their sides. In that situation, the envelope area for the hand may intersect with their thigh. So after assigning vertex weights using envelopes, if you move their hand bone, part of their leg would move with it, as shown in Figure 3-19. Not comfortable at all, and potentially difficult and annoying to clean up. In this scenario, the better choice is to use the next parenting option (With Automatic Weights).

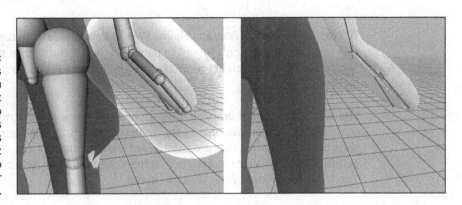

FIGURE 3-19:
Envelope weights
can give you
unpleasant
vertex group
assignments
(left), whereas
automatic
weights tend to
give much better
results (right).

- **With Automatic Weights:** This is my favorite option to use. It works like the With Envelope Weights option, but instead of using the influence area of the bone envelopes to determine weights, it uses a more complex process known as *bone heat* that generally results in better vertex assignments and weights.

  Long story short, *this* is the option that you're most frequently going to use when skinning your mesh to your armature.

REMEMBER

>> **Bone:** This is a simple parenting operation like the Object option. No Armature modifier is applied to your mesh. The only difference here is that rather than parent your mesh to the whole armature object, this option allows you to parent your object to a single bone.

>> **Bone Relative:** This option works like the Bone option, but it doesn't move the child object if the bone is moved in Edit mode. Technically speaking, it's really a shortcut for enabling the Relative Parenting check box in your selected bone's Bone Properties. This option is handy for specific uses, but it isn't frequently used.

Tweaking vertex weights in Weight Paint mode

Regardless of which option you choose for generating your vertex weights, you'll probably still have to go in and manually tweak the weights of the vertices in each vertex group (unless the object you're trying to rig is incredibly simple). Trying to do those tweaks just from the Vertex Groups panel can be pretty tedious and annoying, even with the additional information from the Spreadsheet editor. Fortunately, there is Weight Paint mode. This mode is almost exactly like Vertex Paint mode (see Book 3, Chapter 1), except that rather than painting color on the mesh, you're painting the weight assignment to a specified vertex group.

To access Weight Paint mode from Object mode, select the mesh and choose Weight Paint from the Object Mode drop-down menu in the 3D Viewport's header.

You can also press Ctrl+Tab and choose Weight Paint mode from the pie menu that appears. Even if you don't intend to paint weights, Weight Paint mode is a great way to see how the weights were assigned by Blender if you used the automatic method.

The way that weights are visualized is kind of like a thermal map, where red is the hottest value and blue is the coldest. Extending this logic to work with bone weights, vertices that are painted red have a weight of 1.0, whereas vertices painted blue are either not assigned to the vertex group or have a weight of zero. The 50 percent weight color is bright green.

TIP

If the thermal map color styling isn't your thing (as can be the case if you're colorblind), you can define your own weight paint color range. Open Preferences (Edit ➪ Preferences) and navigate to the Editing section on the left Sidebar. Within that section, is a panel labeled Weight Paint where you can define a custom gradient for visualizing vertex weights.

When in Weight Paint mode, you get a bunch of painting panels in the Tool tab of the Sidebar (N). With a few minor exceptions, these controls are identical to the ones used in Vertex Paint mode.

TIP

When weight painting, it's often useful to enable the Wireframe check box in the Viewport Display panel of Object Properties. Enabling this check box overlays the mesh's wireframe on it. Seeing the wireframe is especially helpful when weight painting because it helps you see where the actual vertices on the mesh are. That way, you're not just painting in empty space where no vertices exist. The only slight hiccup is if you're painting *planar vertices* or vertices that all share the same plane. In this particular case, Blender may try to simplify the wireframe overlay. Although that simplification may be nice in general, it can be problematic when painting. To get around that obstacle, enable the All Edges check box in the same Viewport Display panel of Object Properties.

A handy feature in the Tool tab of the 3D Viewport's Sidebar while weight painting are the symmetry buttons in the Tool Settings header in the 3D Viewport. They're the X, Y, and Z buttons next to the icon that looks a bit like a butterfly (as shown in the left margin). Symmetry painting can literally cut your weight-painting time in half. When you enable one of these axis buttons and enable the Mirror Vertex Groups check box from the Symmetry roll-out, Blender takes advantage of the left/right naming convention discussed earlier in the "Editing armatures" section of this chapter. So, if you're tweaking the vertex weights on the left leg, Blender automatically updates the weights for the corresponding bone on the right leg so they match. If that ain't cool, I don't know what is.

WARNING

Be sure to enable the Mirror Vertex Groups check box from the Symmetry roll-out to properly take advantage of the left/right naming scheme. Without that check box enabled, the symmetry options merely paint the same weight for a single vertex group on both sides of your mesh, but without affecting any of the other vertex groups.

The actual process of weight painting is nearly identical to using vertex paint. However, you need to pay attention to one more thing with weight painting: the need to tell Blender which vertex group you're painting. You can do so in two ways. The slow way, you already know: Select the group from the list box in the Vertex Groups panel in Object Data Properties.

Of course, the kind Blender developers have provided a faster way: You can select the bone that you want to paint weights for, even while in Weight Paint mode on your mesh. Enabling this feature requires a small bit of setup, but it's totally worth it:

1. **From Object mode, select your armature object.**

2. **Add your mesh object to your selection (Shift+left-click).**

   This act also makes your mesh object the active object.

3. **Put your mesh in Weight Paint mode (Ctrl+Tab ⇨ Weight Paint).**

Now, when you Alt+click a bone, Blender automatically activates the corresponding vertex group and allows you to paint. As an added bonus, you can test your weights on the fly by grabbing, rotating, or scaling the selected bone using the transform hotkeys (G, R, and S, respectively) while you're still in Weight Paint mode.

TIP

Because weight paint relies so much on color, if you're reading this book in print or on an e-reader, I highly recommend you look on the web (perhaps on this book's website) for full-color images of meshes in Weight Paint mode to get a better sense of what a weight-painted mesh looks like.

REMEMBER

If you choose to use vertex groups (and in most situations, you should), have a look at the Armature modifier on your mesh. Under the Bind To label are two check boxes: Vertex Groups and Bone Envelopes. By default, only the Vertex Groups check box is enabled. However, both options can be enabled. With both enabled, the mesh is influenced by vertex groups as well as the bone envelopes from your armature. This double influence can be useful in some instances, but most riggers tend to prefer to work with one or the other. This way, you know that the only reason a vertex is deforming improperly is because its weight isn't assigned properly. You don't have to concern yourself with the influence of the bone's envelope.

Bringing It All Together to Rig a Character

As you may have guessed, rigging is a pretty intensive process. You need to be technically minded and creative at the same time. The best riggers I've ever met are the sort of people who fit this description and have an eye for the big picture. Well, regardless of whether you're one of these people, the best way to understand the full process of rigging is to actually create a rig of your own. The examples throughout the rest of this section are done with a simple stick figure character that I like to use for creating quick animations that test body language and timing. I love animating with stick figures, even in 3D. Ninety percent of an animated character's personality comes through in that character's body language. Animating with stick figures allows you to focus on that essential step and keeps you from getting distracted with secondary details.

This stick figure, in both rigged and unrigged versions, is available to download from this book's supplemental website (blenderbasics.com). With them, you have a starting point to practice with, as well as a finished reference. Of course, if you have a character already modeled and want to rig it, that's great. You can use the techniques here for rigging nearly anything.

Building Stickman's centerline

If you load the unrigged stickman file in Blender, the first thing you might notice is his pose. He's standing up with his arms out to his sides. This stance is referred to as a *T pose* because the character looks like the letter T. This pose is probably the most common one that modelers use when they create their characters, and it's the most preferred pose for riggers. Some modelers may also model with the arms at the sides, or sometimes they have the arms somewhere halfway between the T pose and having arms at the side (sometimes called an *A pose*). There are valid reasons people give for any of these poses, but ultimately it really comes down to personal preference.

It's time to get an armature in this mesh. A good way to start is to create the centerline bones first: the body bones, the head, and the hipbone. To create these bones, following these steps:

1. **Add your armature and start with the first body bone (Add ⇨ Armature).**

2. **Enable In Front viewing for the armature (Armature Properties ⇨ Viewport Display ⇨ In Front).**

   This step ensures that you can always see the bones of your armature.

3. **Tab into Edit mode and move this bone up in the Z-axis until it's around Stickman's waistline.**

   You can use Blender's transform tools or the G ⇨ Z hotkey sequence to do this move as well as any of the ones following.

4. **Select the tail of this bone and move it up in the Z-axis until it's at the top of the torso.**

   Remember that the small end of the bone is the tail.

5. **Subdivide this bone into two bones (select the bone, Armature ⇨ Subdivide).**

   You can also subdivide a bone from the right-click context menu.

6. **Name the bottom bone** body.1 **and the top bone** body.2.

   You can quickly rename your bones using the F2 hotkey.

7. **Select the joint between the two bones and move it back along the Y-axis a little bit.**

   This step helps the bones match the natural curvature of the spine.

8. **Select the tail of** body.2 **and extrude it up in the Z-axis to the top of Stickman's head.**

   As explained earlier in the chapter, you can extrude bones using the bone extrude tool, Ctrl+right-clicking, or by using the E hotkey. I tend to be a hotkey kind of guy, so I default to pressing E.

9. **Name this bone** head.

10. **Select the head of** body.1 **and extrude it down in the Z-axis to the bottom of Stickman's pelvis.**

    Remember that the large end of the bone is its head.

11. **Name this bone** hip.

    You have something that looks like Figure 3-20.

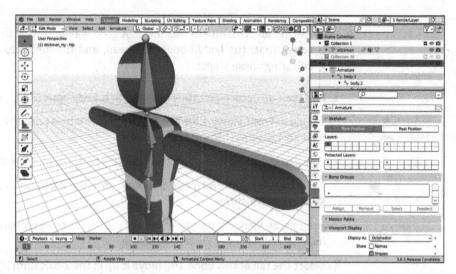

Adding Stickman's appendages

The next step is to create bones for the arms and the legs. You do so by creating bones for half of the rig and then letting Blender do the rest of the work for you by mirroring the bones. First things first, though — you have to create that first half of the rig:

1. **Still in Edit mode, switch to the front view, select the** head **bone, and duplicate it, putting its root at Stickman's left shoulder joint (Numpad 1, select, Armature ⇨ Duplicate).**

   You can also duplicate using the Shift+D hotkey combination. Also note that by working this way, the new bone is an offset child of the body.2 bone.

2. **Name this new bone** arm_upper.L **(F2).**

3. **Select the tail of** arm_upper.L **and move it to Stickman's elbow.**

   If you're using the G hotkey to move things rather than using the transform manipulator, it may help to press Ctrl to guarantee that the bone is perfectly horizontal.

4. **Extrude from this tail to create a new bone along the X-axis that extends to Stickman's hand (Armature ⇨ Extrude ⇨ X).**

5. **Name this new bone** arm_lower.L **(F2).**

6. **From the front view, select the** hip **bone and duplicate it, placing the new bone's head at the top of Stickman's left leg (Numpad 1, select, Armature ⇨ Duplicate).**

   For the time being, this duplicated bone is automatically named hip.001.

7. **Select** `hip.001`'s **tail and move it along the Z-axis to Stickman's feet (select, G ⇨ Z).**

8. **Select the main part of** `hip.001` **and subdivide it into two bones (select, Armature ⇨ Subdivide).**

9. **Rename the top bone from** `hip.001` **to** `leg_upper.L` **and name the bottom bone** `leg_lower.L` **(F2).**

10. **Select the joint between these bones and move it forward in the Y-axis a little bit (select, G ⇨ Y).**

   This step gives the knee a bit of bend, which helps deformation when adding constraints.

11. **Parent** `leg_upper.L` **to** `hip` **(select** `leg_upper.L`**, Shift+select** `hip`**, Armature ⇨ Parent ⇨ Make ⇨ Keep Offset).**

You now have something that looks like Figure 3-21.

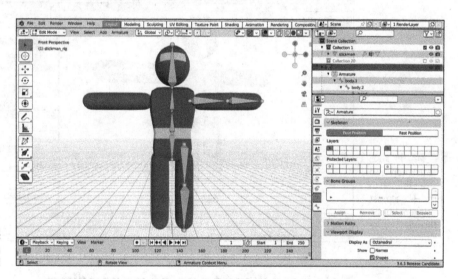

FIGURE 3-21: A half-skeleton Stickman!

TIP

Technically speaking, you don't actually have to add all the `.L` suffixes at the end of your bone names. For example, you could just have `arm_upper` and `arm_lower`, then select them and choose Armature ⇨ Names ⇨ Auto-Name Left/Right to have Blender add the suffixes for you. I appreciate this feature because, before it, I would sometimes get my lefts and rights backwards while rigging. Having Blender handle that for me takes out a lot of guesswork.

Now, for the really cool part of letting Blender do the work for you. You want to select all the bones that aren't on the centerline, duplicate them, and mirror them along the X-axis. Here are the specific hotkeys and steps:

1. **In Edit mode, select all the bones in your armature (Select ⇨ All).**

2. **Make use of the Symmetrize operator (Armature ⇨ Symmetrize).**

   In this one step, all your bones that have the .L suffix are automatically duplicated, mirrored across your armature object's X-axis, and properly renamed with a .R suffix. All the bones along your centerline remain unchanged (and, even better, there are no unnecessary duplicates).

That's it! What was once a six-step process with a lot of complicated selection in previous releases of Blender is now just two steps. Figure 3-22 shows the resulting bone layout.

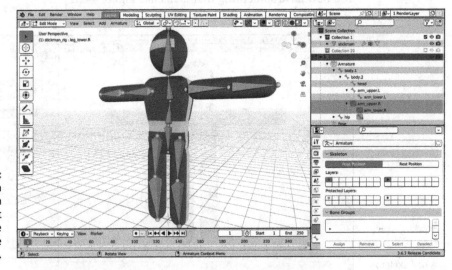

FIGURE 3-22: Stickman with a skeleton in him. He's almost rigged, but he still needs some controls.

Taking advantage of parenting and constraints

What you currently have in place is the basic structure of the rig's armature. The primary function of these bones is to deform the character mesh. Technically, you *could* animate with just these bones after you skin them to the mesh. However, you can (and should) add some additional bones to the armature to make it easier to animate. They work by taking advantage of the parenting set up by the bone chains and combining them with some reasonable constraints.

For example, you currently have a structured skeleton in place, but what happens if you Ctrl+Tab into Pose mode and grab the body.1 bone and move it? Because the entire upper body is directly or indirectly a child of this bone, the upper torso, arms, and head move with the body.1 bone. Unfortunately, the lower half of the body doesn't share this relationship, so you end up tearing Stickman's skeleton in half. Ouch!

To compensate, you need a bone — called a *root bone* — that both the hip and body.1 bones relate to, binding the upper half of the body to the lower half. Moving this bone should move the entire armature. Adding a root bone to the rig is pretty simple:

1. **Tab into Edit mode on the armature and switch to the side view (Numpad 3).**

   You can also use the navigation gizmo in the upper right of the 3D Viewport to align the viewport to the side view.

2. **Select the head of either the body.1 or hip bones.**

   Both heads are located in the same place, so it doesn't really matter which one you select.

3. **Extrude a new bone along the Y-axis (E ⇨ Y) and name it root (F2).**

   Move in the positive Y direction, toward the back of Stickman.

4. **Parent the body.1 and hip bones to the root bone (select body.1, Shift+select hip, Shift+select root, Armature ⇨ Parent ⇨ Make ⇨ Keep Offset).**

   This parent relationship means that you can move the entire armature by just selecting and moving the root bone. Before creating this parent relationship, some people may choose to switch the direction of the root bone (Armature ⇨ Switch Direction) so that they can have the root bone's tip actually connected to the heads of body.1 and hip. It's all a matter of taste, but I prefer not to. Because bones naturally rotate around their head, it's more useful to me to keep the head of the root bone in the center of the character. In my opinion, using this setup helps make bending at the waist look more natural.

5. **Select the root bone and disable the Deform check box in Bone Properties.**

   This bone is intended purely to control the other bones. You don't want any of the mesh's vertices assigned to it.

Another convenient control bone that you may want to add is a head control. Sure, you can rotate the head bone as you want, but using a bone as the head's (or eyes') target is often easier. That way, when you want the character to look at something, you just move the target bone to that something's location. An added benefit is that by building your rig this way, you can successfully create complex moves, such as keeping characters looking at an object as they walk by it. To add a head control to your rig, you use a Track To constraint:

1. **Tab into Edit mode and select the head bone.**

2. **Duplicate the head bone and move it in the Y-axis (Armature ➪ Duplicate ➪ Y) and name it head_target (F2).**

   The idea is that you want the control bone to be far enough in front of the face so that you can have some control without getting in the way of the rest of the rig. I moved mine about 3 meters out.

3. **Clear the parent relationship on the head_target bone (Armature ➪ Parent ➪ Clear Parent ➪ Clear Parent).**

   The Alt+P hotkey gives you faster access to clearing the parent relationship. More importantly, because the head_target bone came into existence by duplicating the head bone, it inherited the parent relationship to the body . 2 bone. You don't want this relationship because you want to be able to move the head target independently of the rest of the rig.

4. **Ctrl+Tab into Pose mode, select the head_target bone, and then also select the head bone (select, Shift+select).**

5. **Add a Track To constraint to the head bone (Shift+Ctrl+C ➪ Track To).**

   If you look at Bone Constraint Properties, you should notice a Track To constraint to the head bone, automatically populated with your head_target bone as its target. The head bone is also colored a nice shade of green. (You could manually add this constraint yourself, but the Shift+Ctrl+C hotkey combination is extremely convenient.) Chances are good that the head bone may be rotated incorrectly. It's difficult to tell but from the default settings for this constraint, your head bone is likely pointing backwards — not the behavior you want. You need to change the alignment axes that the constraint works on.

6. **In the Track To constraint, change the To axis to Z and the Up axis to Y.**

   This step fixes the head bone so that it points in the proper direction. Now, when you select the head_target bone and move it around, the face area of the head bone always points at it.

7. **Select the head_target bone and disable the Deform check box in Bone Properties.**

   Like the root bone, this bone isn't meant to be skinned to a mesh. Figure 3-23 shows what your rig looks like now.

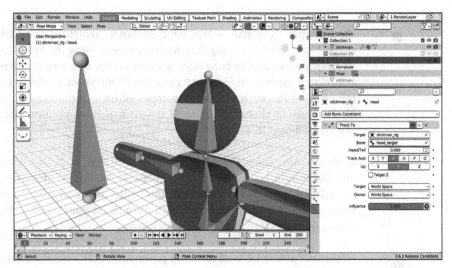

FIGURE 3-23:
The Stickman rig, now with head control!

Your Stickman rig is mostly functional now. However, another constraint is a staple of nearly all character rigs and is monumentally helpful to animators. It's called an *inverse kinematics*, or IK, constraint. The next section goes into what this constraint does, how it works, and how to give your rig its benefits.

Comparing inverse kinematics and forward kinematics

When it comes to animating characters in 3D with an armature, you have two ways to move limbs around: *inverse kinematics* and *forward kinematics*, or IK and FK. *Kinematic* is just a fancy way of saying motion.

By default, your rig is set up to use FK. Say that you have a bone chain, and you want to place the tip of the last bone to a specific location in 3D space. To do so, you have to rotate the first bone in the chain, then the next, and then the next, and so on until you can get that last bone's tip properly placed. You're working your way *forward* along the bone chain, from the head to the tip. Because of the parenting relationships between the bones, you can currently use FK with your Stickman rig.

That's FK. It gets the job done, but it can be awfully difficult and tedious to try to get the tip of that last bone exactly where you want it. It would be nice if you could just grab that tip, put it in place, and let the computer figure out how all the other bones have to bend to compensate. This method of letting the computer figure things out for you, basically, is the essence of IK. You move the tip of the last bone in the chain, and Blender works *backward*, from the tip to the head, along the chain to get the other bones properly placed for you.

To see what IK is like, select your Stickman armature and Ctrl+Tab into Pose mode. Now, select the body.2 bone and move it using the Move tool or the G hot-key. Notice that all the bone does is rotate; it doesn't actually change its location. Cancel that movement (Esc) and go to the 3D Viewport's Sidebar to access the Tool tab (or Tool Properties in the Properties editor). In the Pose Options panel, ena-ble the Auto IK check box. Auto IK isn't a real IK constraint, but it will help you understand how IK works.

Grab and move the body.2 bone again. Notice that, now, this bone moves around, and the body.1 bone rotates to compensate for the locations that you try to put body.2. Selecting the head bone or one of the arm_lower bones results in similar behavior. Click around and play with Auto IK on your rig. It's pretty cool. When you're done, disable the Auto IK check box.

REMEMBER

IK is really awesome stuff and very powerful, but it's not the ultimate solution for animating. See, one of the core principles of animation (as mentioned in the next chapter) is that natural movement tends to happen in arcs. Generally speaking, arcing movement is more believable and, well, natural looking. Things that move in a straight line tend to look stiff and robotic. Think about how a person's arms swing when walking. It doesn't necessarily matter exactly where the hand is. The entire arm rotates and swings back and forth. That is FK movement. If you're ani-mating, you can easily re-create that motion by keying the rotation of the upper arm bone at the extreme ends of the action.

In contrast, IK movement tends to happen in a straight line. You're just keying the tip of the chain, so that tip moves directly from one location to the next and the bones along the chain rotate to compensate. To re-create a swinging arm in IK, you need *at least* three keyframes: one at each extreme and one in the middle to prevent the hand from going in a straight line. And even then, the elbow might flip in the wrong direction, or you might need even more intermediary keys to try to get that smooth arc that you get automatically with FK.

However, where IK shines is when the tip of the bone chain needs to be precisely positioned. A perfect example is feet. When a person walks, the feet must touch the ground (if you can walk without touching the ground, I hear there are a num-ber of superhero organizations with openings). Trying to achieve this effect with just FK usually ends up with feet that look floaty and not locked into place as the character moves.

Another example is if your character is holding on to a fixed object and doesn't want to let go of it, like a climber on the edge of a cliff or a three-year-old with an ice cream cone. You want to keep the hand in place and let the elbow bend natu-rally. In instances like these, IK is really helpful. The most common use, though, is for foot and leg rigs on characters. And to that end, you're going to use the fol-lowing steps to add IK controls to the Stickman rig:

1. **Tab into Edit mode on the armature and select the tip of the** `leg_lower.L` **bone.**

If you have X-axis Mirror enabled in the Pose Options panel of the 3D Viewport's Sidebar, you can actually select either the left or right bone. With X-Axis Mirror enabled, whatever you do on one side of your armature also happens on the other. If X-Axis Mirror isn't enabled, go ahead and enable it.

2. **Extrude a new bone in the Z-axis (E ⇨ Z).**

You don't have to extrude the new bone very far — just enough to know it's there.

3. **Name this bone** `leg_IK.L` **and make sure that the mirrored bone is named** `leg_IK.R` **(F2).**

4. **Clear the parent-child relationship between** `leg_IK.L` **and** `leg_lower.L` **(Alt+P ⇨ Clear Parent).**

5. **Ctrl+Tab into Pose mode, select** `leg_IK.L`**, and add** `leg_lower.L` **to the selection (select, Shift+select).**

6. **Add an IK constraint (Pose ⇨ Inverse Kinematics ⇨ Add IK to Bone).**

You can also use the Shift+Ctrl+C ⇨ Inverse Kinematics hotkey. Both provide the same results: an IK constraint in `leg_lower.L`'s Bone Constraint Properties.

7. **Go to Bone Constraint Properties panel and, in the Inverse Kinematics constraint, change the Chain Length value to 2.**

By default, the IK bone chain goes all the way back to the head of the hipbone. You actually want it to have an influence only up to the head of the upper leg bone. That's a chain length of two bones.

8. **Perform Steps 5 through 7 on** `leg_IK.R` **and** `leg_lower.R`**.**

Sadly, X-Axis Mirror works only in Edit mode, so you have to add your IK constraints on both sides on your own. Alternatively, you can delete all the bones on the left side of the rig and rerun the Symmetrize operator.

> **TIP**
>
> To speed up your workflow, you may want to consider enabling the Copy Attributes add-on. With that, you can copy selected constraints from one bone to another using Ctrl+C. You'll still need to adjust your constraint targets, but if you have a rig with a lot of IK constraints (like on an insect), every little speed-up helps.

9. **Select the** `leg_IK.L` **and** `leg_IK.R` **bones and disable the Deform check box in each of their Bone Properties.**

Like the `root` and `head_target` bones, these control bones should not be used for skinning. You can disable the Deform check box for both selected bones at the same time by Alt+clicking it. At this point, you have a basic IK rig on your character's feet. The rig looks something like what's shown in Figure 3-24.

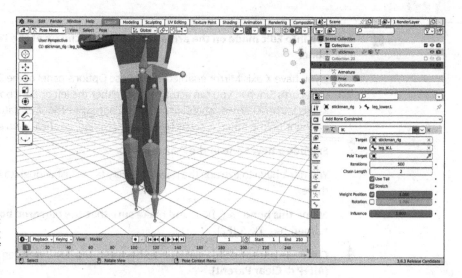

FIGURE 3-24:
A basic IK rig
for the legs of
Stickman.

Test your rig by selecting the root and moving it around, particularly up and down the Z-axis. The leg bones in your Stickman rig should bend all by themselves to compensate for the location of the root bone relative to the IK bones. You can also select each of the leg_IK bones and move them around to control the bending of each leg independent of the other.

In doing so, however, you may notice that on some occasions, the legs don't quite know how to bend. They may randomly flip backward or roll out in odd angles. Aside from slightly bending the rig at the knees when you created the leg bones, you haven't provided the legs with much of a clue as to *how* exactly they should bend. Fortunately, the solution is pretty simple. It's called a *pole target*. To define a pole target, you need to create two more bones, one for each leg:

1. **Tab into Edit mode on Stickman's armature and select leg_IK.L.**

   Again, because X-Axis Mirror is enabled and you're in Edit mode, choosing either leg_IK bone works fine.

2. **Switch to side view, duplicate the bone, and move the new bone to somewhere in front of the knee (Numpad 3, Armature ⇨ Duplicate).**

3. **Name this bone knee.L and make sure that the mirrored bone is named knee.R (F2).**

4. **Switch the direction of knee.L (Armature ⇨ Switch Direction or Alt+F).**

   This step isn't essential. I just like to have my floating bones point upward.

5. **Parent knee.L to leg_IK.L (select knee.L, Shift+select leg_IK.L, Ctrl+P ⇨ Keep Offset).**

6. **Ctrl+Tab into Pose mode.**

7. **Select** leg_lower.L **and in its IK constraint (Bone Constraint Properties), choose your armature object in the Pole Target field and** knee.L **in the Bone field that appears.**

   This step defines knee.L as the pole target for the left leg's IK chain. However, the knee joint for the left leg may instantly pop to the side, bending the leg in all kinds of weird ways. The next step compensates for that problem.

8. **Still in** leg_lower.L**'s IK constraint panel, adjust the Pole Offset value to -90 degrees.**

   This step causes the leg's knee joint to properly point at the knee.L bone. If it doesn't, try adjusting the Pole Offset value until it looks correct. Usually this value is 0, 90, -90, or 180. The default behavior is to point leg_lower.L's local X-axis toward the pole. If the local X-axis isn't forward, adjusting the offset compensates.

9. **Perform Steps 7 and 8 on** leg_lower.R.

   At this point, you have a fully configured IK rig for both of Stickman's legs. You're nearly ready to animate him.

For reference, your rig looks like the one in Figure 3-25.

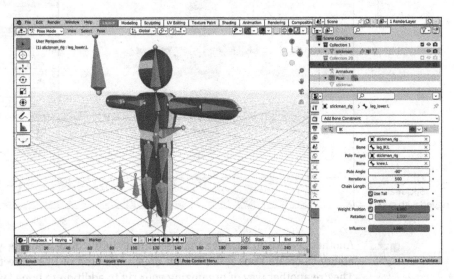

FIGURE 3-25: A completely working Stickman rig.

At this point, skinning the Stickman mesh to your armature should be pretty safe. Using the automatic weights method covered in this chapter gives you the best results, so select the mesh, Shift+select the armature, and press Ctrl+P ⇨ With

Automatic Weights. Now when you move around and pose your rig, the Stickman mesh obediently follows in kind.

Making the rig more user friendly

You have a great basic rig that you can start animating with immediately. However, you can perform a few tweaks that make this rig even more usable.

For one, you can change the way the bones display in the 3D Viewport. Now that you're done with the bulk of rigging, knowing which end of a bone is the head or the tail is a bit less important.

 Go to the Viewport Display panel in Object Data Properties and change the bone type from Octahedral to Stick. Stick bones are the second-least obtrusive bones immediately available to you (the least obtrusive draw type for bones is the Wire type, but I find those bones can be a bit hard to see when animating). Now, you can see more of your mesh while you're animating without as much clutter and geometry in the way. Figure 3-26 shows the Stickman rig with stick bones.

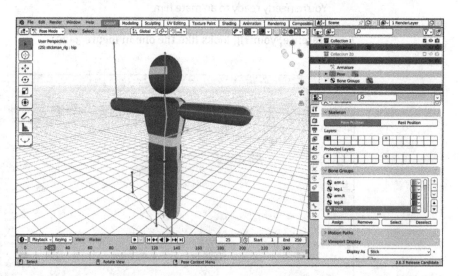

FIGURE 3-26:
Stickman . . .
rigged with sticks!

 Another feature in Blender that is quite helpful for organizing your rigs is the ability to create bone groups. *Bone groups* are kind of like collections for bones. They're another way of organizing your rig in addition to bone layers, as covered earlier in this chapter. To create bone groups, select the bones you want while in Pose mode and choose Pose ➪ Bone Groups ➪ Assign to New Group to group them together. If you try to do this a second time with another set of bones, you have four options:

>> **Assign to New Group:** Choosing this option adds the selected bones to a new bone group. If you have no bone groups already created, this is the only visible option.

>> **Assign to Group:** Choosing this option adds your selected bones to the active group in the list box within the Bone Groups panel of Object Data Properties.

>> **Remove Selected from Bone Groups:** If the bones you have selected are part of any groups, choosing this option removes them from all bone groups.

>> **Remove Bone Group:** Choosing this option removes the group currently selected in the list box within the Bone Groups panel of Armature Properties. This option doesn't remove the bones, just the group that they're associated with.

 You can rename your bone groups in the Bone Groups panel of Armature Properties. I used the bone groups feature to create groups for my main bone chains: `left arm`, `right arm`, `left leg`, `right leg`, `head`, and `body`. Create your own groups as you see fit.

 Beyond organization, bone groups offer an additional benefit. You can define custom bone colors based on the bone groups you have. The controls are also in the Bone Groups panel. Make sure that the Group Colors check box is enabled within the Viewport Display panel and then, in the Bone Groups panel, click the Color Set drop-down menu and choose a theme color set from the menu that appears. I used this feature to make all my left-side bones green and my right-side bones red. It's a good visual trick to let you or another animator quickly identify which bones are being used. Figure 3-27 shows what the Bone Groups panel looks like.

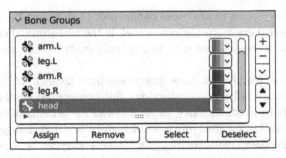

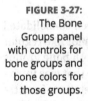

FIGURE 3-27:
The Bone Groups panel with controls for bone groups and bone colors for those groups.

As an additional bonus, when you use bone group colors, those colors also get used in the channel regions of the Graph Editor and the Dope Sheet. So, those colors aren't just good for organizing your rig in the 3D Viewport, they're also extremely useful for staying organized in your animation editors.

Besides groups, another organizational tool for making your rig more usable are bone layers. Bone groups make visualizing and selecting your bones easy. However, bone layers are a faster, more reasonable way of showing and hiding the bones in your rig. The basics of how bone layers work are covered earlier in this chapter.

As an example, have a look at Stickman's legs. Because the legs are using an IK constraint, they're entirely controlled by the leg_IK and knee bones. And because you can see the Stickman mesh, you really don't need to see the leg_upper and leg_lower bones. In some ways, they just get in the way of seeing your character's acting. In that case, moving the bones to a different layer and hiding that layer makes plenty of sense.

To move these bones to another layer, you could go through the tedious process of selecting each one, going to the Relations panel in Bone Properties, and selecting the new layer for it (Alt+clicking affects all selected bones). You could do that, but it's a slow way to work. Instead, use this two-step process to do everything without leaving the 3D Viewport:

1. **Select the bones you want to move.**

   You can Shift+select each one, box select, or press L with your mouse over the leg bones to select the entire leg chain. Use whatever feels fastest for you.

2. **Press M to open a little Change Bone Layers pop-up.**

   The pop-up has a block of buttons that look just like those in the Relations panel of Bone Properties. Only in this case, the change happens on all selected bones. I moved the bones to the first layer in the second block of layers.

Now, if you ever want to see those bones, just go to Object Data Properties and enable the layer there in the Skeleton panel. In the meantime, though, your Stickman rig is much cleaner, and now, you're *really* ready to start animating.

NEW
FEATURE

In the release of Blender 4.0, bone groups and bone layers have been consolidated into a new feature called Bone Collections. Bone collections work a lot like regular object collections in the Outliner, so you have all the benefits of both bone groups and bone layers, but bundled into a single feature. Another change that was introduced was how bone colors are managed. Since a bone can be a member of multiple collections, it doesn't make sense to assign color by collection. Instead, colors are now assigned at the bone level. If you select a bone and go to the Viewport Display panel in Bone Properties, you can choose the bone color theme there, both in Edit mode and Pose mode. If you want to use the same theme across multiple selected bones, Alt+click the color drop-down menu when you choose your color theme to assign.

There's one additional small tweak you may want to make to your character setup, though it has more to do with how your rig is deforming Stickman than anything specific to your rig. Select your Stickman mesh and go to the Modifier tab in the Properties editor. In the Armature modifier's panel, there's a check box labeled Preserve Volume. Enable this check box and the Stickman character will deform a little bit more cleanly when you make poses. The influence of this check box is most apparent at the character's joints. Without it enabled, those parts often pinch or round-off when bent. The Preserve Volume feature helps prevent that from happening.

In addition, on your own characters, you may try adding a Smooth Corrective modifier to the top of the character's modifier stack. That modifier doesn't do much for a simple character like Stickman, but for a more complex character, it can help maintain clean deformations.

Working with Pose Libraries

One of the really exciting new features that's come into Blender since the last edition of this book is the Asset Browser. Most of that feature is covered in Book 3, Chapter 4, but for animators there's one especially useful feature of the Asset Browser. You can use it to store poses for your characters in a visual *pose library*. Now, Blender has had a pose library feature in it for quite a few years already. However, the past versions of the pose library were always a bit kludgy, and there was never an easy visual way to see the poses on your character without actually adjusting the character's rig. With the new pose library feature in the Asset Browser, that's no longer the case.

Building a pose library

To start building a pose library, you need to start with a rigged character. If you're working your way through this chapter, the rigged version of the Stickman character should work rather nicely. You can use your own version that you've been working on, or you can grab the stickman-rigged.blend file from the supplemental website for this book (blenderbasics.com).

The work of creating your pose library starts in the Asset Browser. If you're in the Layout workspace within the General workflow template, my recommendation would be to expand the area containing the Timeline and switch that area to the Asset Browser. By default, you should see your global asset library for Blender. As of this writing, that library is only populated with hair assets (see Chapter 5 of this book for more on hair and fur). Your Blender session should look something like what's shown in Figure 3-28.

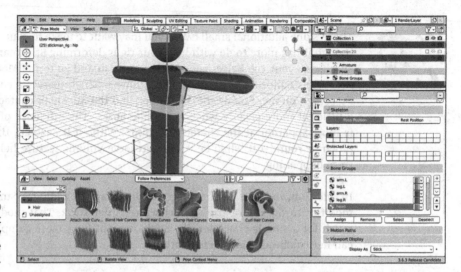

FIGURE 3-28:
A Blender session with an Asset Browser, ready to create a pose library.

With this basic setup, you can begin creating your pose library. Follow these steps:

1. **In the Asset Browser, choose Current File from the Asset Library drop-down.**

   Now, the Asset Browser is displaying assets only for the file you're currently working in.

2. **In the Catalog listbox, click the Plus (+) icon in the upper right to create a new category.**

   This category is where you're going to store the poses for your character. The default name for the catalog is Catalog. Change this to something more clear in the next step.

3. **Double-click your new category's name in the listbox and change it to something that makes sense for your character.**

   In this example for the Stickman character, I'm naming my category Stickman Poses.

4. **In the 3D Viewport, modify the controls in your character rig to define a specific pose for your character.**

   For a simple character like Stickman, you just need to use the transform tools to move and rotate the control bones in the armature.

5. **Select all the control bones in your armature.**

   You can press the A hotkey or choose Select ➪ All from the header menu. It's important to select all your bones because only the selected bones get stored in the pose asset. In more advanced usage, you can create poses for specific parts of your character, like facial expressions or hand positions. Then you can mix and match poses as you need them.

6. **Back in the Asset Browser, choose Asset ⇨ Create Pose Asset from the header menu.**

Congratulations! You've just added your first pose to your pose library. Of course, by default the name of the pose is just the name of your armature object. That won't do.

7. **Expand the Sidebar for the Asset Browser by clicking the gear icon in the upper right corner or by pressing the N hotkey.**

The Sidebar gives you a bunch of different fields that you can populate with information about your selected pose, including giving it a custom thumbnail image. In this case, though, you're just interested in changing its name.

8. **Edit the Name field in the Sidebar to change the name of your selected pose asset.**

And with that, *now,* you have the start of a fantastic pose library.

Now, you can populate your pose library with all manner of poses for your character. With the Stickman example, your Blender session might look something like what's shown in Figure 3-29. If you find that you have a lot of poses, you can even create sub-categories within your main category. This way, you can keep your character nice and organized.

TECHNICAL STUFF

As covered in Book 3, Chapter 4, when you create a new asset category for your .blend file, a text file also gets created on your hard drive in the same folder. That text file holds the names for the asset categories in that file. If you transfer your character file to another computer, be sure that this text file goes with it.

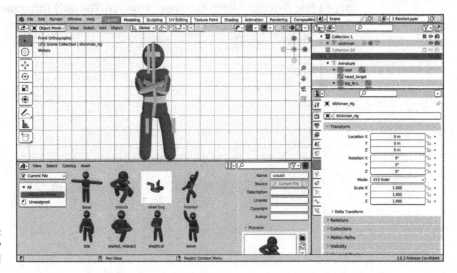

FIGURE 3-29: A pose library for Stickman!

Rigging: The Art of Building an Animatable Puppet

Using pose libraries

Once you have your pose library created, the process for using it is pretty straight-forward. Ensure that your character's armature object is in Pose mode and follow these steps:

1. **In the 3D Viewport, select the bones that you want to be affected by the pose you're about to choose.**

Recall that when you made your pose library, new poses were created using only the currently selected bones. Assigning a pose to your armature works the same way.

2. **From the Asset Browser, double-click the pose you want to use.**

Boom! Pose applied. You can tweak the pose from here to suit your tastes. If you happen to be animating, this would be the time to insert your keyframes for this pose.

NEW
FEATURE

Speaking of animating, there's actually an even faster way to apply poses from your pose library. However, this feature is only in versions of Blender newer than 4.0. In these newer versions of Blender, the 3D Viewport has an additional region at the bottom of it called the Asset Shelf. You can actually see the Asset Shelf back in Figure 3-29. To make the Asset Shelf visible, be sure that your character's armature is in Pose mode and go to View ⇨ Asset Shelf in the 3D Viewport's header menu.

With the Asset Shelf visible, you can use the hamburger menu in it to show tabs for each of your asset catalogs. Assigning a pose using the Asset Shelf uses the steps I just described from the Asset Browser. The only difference in this case is that you need only a single click on the pose thumbnail to choose it rather than a double-click.

Chapter 4

Animating Object Deformations

L ooking at the title of this chapter, you may find yourself wondering how this chapter is different from the book's first chapter. Both chapters cover animation, but this chapter covers the cool things you can do in Blender if you're animating with a fully rigged mesh. Chapter 1 in this book covers what is often referred to as *object animation* — that is, animating the attributes of a single object.

With an animation rig, you have more bits and pieces to manage, keep track of, and control. Managing all that additional complexity can be daunting if you have only the Outliner and the Graph Editor to work with. Fortunately, Blender offers a few more features that help make rigged *character animation* easier to wrap your head around.

Working with the Dope Sheet

So, you have a rigged character that you want to animate. Awesome! With your armature selected, change to the Animation workspace by clicking the Animation tab at the top of the Blender window (you can also press Ctrl+Page Up repeatedly until you land on the correct workspace tab). Once you're in the Animation workspace, your selected armature (or armatures, if you've selected more than one) is automatically in Pose mode, ready to animate.

TIP

After changing workspaces, I suggest you enable the Rotate manipulator in the Viewport Gizmos rollout in the header of the 3D Viewport. I'd also recommend that while you're in the Gizmos rollout, you set the Transform Orientation drop-down menu to Normal orientation. You should switch to Normal orientation because when you're animating with an armature, most of the time, you're animating bone rotations. By setting the Rotation manipulator to the Normal coordinate space, you can have quick, controlled transformation of bone rotations without having the 3D manipulator get in your way too much. This way of working is also a faster way to use transform widgets than constantly switching to the Rotate or Transform tools.

The next thing you need to pay attention to is the Dope Sheet. As nice as the Graph Editor may be, seeing all the f-curves for each object and each bone in your scene can quickly get overwhelming. You need a different editor — one that gives you a big picture of the keyframes for multiple objects and bones in your animation. And, perhaps more important, this editor allows you to edit the timing of bones, objects, and properties individually. The Dope Sheet (Shift+F12) fills those needs.

TECHNICAL STUFF

In traditional animation, the *dope sheet* was where the entire animation was planned out, frame by frame, on paper, prior to a single pencil line being drawn by the animator. In computer animation, it's taken on a slightly different meaning and purpose, but the core notion of being able to see your entire animation all at once is still there. When you have elements in your scene animated, the Dope Sheet shows a channel for each keyed bone, object, and property.

When it comes to editing the overall timing of a character's performance, the Dope Sheet is really *the* tool for the job.

Selecting keys in the Dope Sheet

TIP

Like selecting in other parts of Blender, you can select individual keyframes in the Dope Sheet by clicking the diamond-shaped keyframe indicator. You can select multiple keyframes in a variety of ways:

» **Shift+click** for selecting multiple individual keys.

» **Click+drag** to box-select.

» **A** selects all visible keyframes in the Dope Sheet (Alt+A deselects).

» **Select ⇨ Columns on Selected Keys or pressing K** is an interesting feature. If you have one or more keyframes selected, this operator selects any other key in the Dope Sheet that's on the same frame as your selected key.

>> **Select ⇨ Column on Current Frame or pressing Ctrl+K** gives you similar functionality to Columns on Selected Keys, but using the time cursor rather than your current selection.

REMEMBER

Initially, you may not think either of the column key selection methods is all that useful. However, if you think about the process used for animating — especially cartoon-style animation — it starts making more sense. The workflow for animation usually goes from one pose to the next. At each pose that you key, multiple bones are all keyed at the same time (often with keying sets, as described in Book 4, Chapter 1), forming a column in the Dope Sheet. In fact, unless you're doing some kind of frantic, shaky animations, it's a pretty good practice to make sure that you have nice columns in your Dope Sheet, at least to start. Uneven columns tend to indicate that your timing may be off on a specific part of the rig. Of course, this suggestion is a guideline more than a hard-and-fast rule. As your animation gets closer to being final, your columns will get necessarily messier.

After they're selected, you can move those keyframes around by clicking on them and dragging your mouse cursor left and right. Of course, that kind of moving affects only the one key that you click on. You can move a whole column of keys by clicking and dragging the keyframe icon in the Summary channel at the top.

However, what if you want to move a bunch of different keys on different frames in the Dope Sheet? The Dope Sheet doesn't have manipulator gizmos like the 3D Viewport. You can use the operators in Key ⇨ Transform, but they're faster to access using hotkeys:

>> **Move (G):** I like to think of this as *grabbing* rather than moving as a better way of remembering the hotkey. The operator acts as described. You press G, move your mouse cursor to place the selected keys, and left-click or press Enter to confirm.

>> **Extend (E):** This way of moving keyframes increases the time between two sets of keys without affecting the timing of the keys before or after (assuming those keys are also selected). The most common use for this operator is when you have all the keys in the Dope Sheet selected. From there, you scrub the time cursor to the time that you want to extend and press E. All the keys after the time cursor will move as a single group.

>> **Slide (Shift+T):** I like to think of the keyframe slide operator as the Dope Sheet equivalent of the edge slide or vertex slide operator when working on meshes in the 3D Viewport (see Book 2, Chapter 1 for more on mesh editing). This operator allows you to proportionally tweak the timing between your earliest and latest selected keyframe in the Dope Sheet. It uses the placement of your time cursor as a reference (similar to the 3D cursor in the 3D Viewport), so pay attention to where you place that.

>> **Scale (S):** The behavior of the Scale operator should be familiar to you. Using this operator, you can move your selected keys closer together or farther apart, relative to the location of the time cursor.

REMEMBER

Most frequently, you move (G) and scale (S) selected keyframes. When performing these actions, there's something you should pay attention to. First of all, when you scale, extend, or slide selected keyframes, everything is relative to the position of the time cursor in the Dope Sheet. So if you want to increase the length of your animation by stretching out the keyframes, put your time cursor at frame 1 before scaling. If you place your time cursor in the middle or at the end, the keys at the beginning of your animation are arranged so that they take place before your animation starts — typically that's something you don't want, so be careful.

By default, the Dope Sheet has Nearest Frame snapping enabled. So when moving your keys, they snap to the closest frame to them. If you toggle snapping off by clicking the magnet icon in the Dope Sheet's header, Blender stops this behavior and allows you to place keys between frames. However, you normally don't want to set keys between frames; usually, it weakens the poses that the audience actually sees and makes it hard to replace keyframes without causing jumps while animating.

However, if you do have keys located in-between frames, you can quickly fix that with the Snap Keys operator. Select the keys you want to fix in the Dope Sheet and choose Key ⇨ Snap (you can also invoke the snaps pie menu by pressing Shift+S).

Whether called from the Dope Sheet's header or the pie menu, you have four options in this menu:

>> **Selection to Current Frame:** This option snaps all selected keys to the location of the time cursor in the Dope Sheet.

>> **Selection to Nearest Frame:** Choosing this option takes the selected keys and shifts them to the even frame number that's closest to each of them.

>> **Selection to Nearest Second:** Like the Nearest Frame operation, but this option snaps the selected keys to the nearest frame that's at the start of a second in time.

>> **Selection to Nearest Marker:** Blender's Dope Sheet allows you to place reminders on the Timeline referred to as *markers*. You can add a new marker at the location of the timeline cursor by choosing Marker ⇨ Add Marker in the header menu of any of Blender's time-based editors (Timeline, Dope Sheet, Graph Editor, Nonlinear Animation editor, and the Video Sequencer) or by using the M hotkey. There's more on markers and keyframe indicators in the next section of this chapter. If you have one or more of these markers on your Timeline, choosing this option snaps selected keyframes to the marker that's nearest to them.

Generally, though, it's best practice to use Blender's frame-based auto-snap feature that's enabled by default. You can change the auto-snap method by left-clicking the Modes drop-down menu on the far right of the Dope Sheet's header. This menu has almost all the same options as the preceding list. The only difference is that there's no Current Frame option, because the snap modes are meant to work continuously and not as a single operation.

Working with markers

When animating, it's frequently useful to leave notes to yourself in the Timeline. You may have key timing points noted in your storyboard, or maybe you just need to have an indicator that shows when a character grabs on to something or when there's a camera change. The Dope Sheet doesn't have the ability to have Annotations like the 3D Viewport or Image Editor. And even if it did, you'd want those notes to be maintained in sequence with all your keys, and you'd want them visible in all your time-based editors.

The right tool for the job in this case are *markers*. I mention them briefly in the preceding section, but markers are basically a means of indicating something important is happening during your animation. With a little Python scripting, I've even used markers to update text objects in animation (such as for title graphics in a presentation).

REMEMBER

I'm going to use the Dope Sheet to talk about adding and editing markers, but these same controls also work in the Timeline, Graph Editor, Nonlinear Animation editor, and Video Sequencer.

To add a marker, place your timeline cursor on the frame where you want the marker added and choose Marker ⇨ Add Marker (or press M). At the bottom of the Dope Sheet, a new darkened region is added and there's a little triangle indicator and dashed line in the same location as your time cursor. This is your new marker. By default the marker has a name that corresponds to the frame number where you added it. For example, if you added your marker on frame 35, the text next to your marker's triangle will read F_35.

To rename your marker, select it (left-click) and choose Marker ⇨ Rename Marker or press the F2 hotkey. Upon doing so, you get a little pop-up where you can change the name of your marker to something more sensible to your animation (like "velociraptor explodes here!").

Selecting and moving works much the same way as with keys. The only thing to remember is that if you use the G hotkey to move your markers, you need to be sure your mouse cursor is in the marker region when you do it. Otherwise, you'll move your keys rather than the markers.

To remove a marker, select it and choose Marker ⇨ Delete Marker or press X.

Figure 4-1 shows an example Dope Sheet with a few helpful markers added to it.

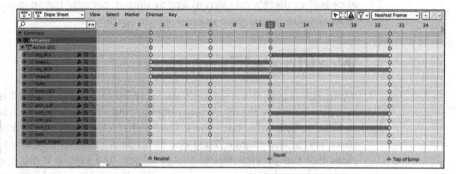

FIGURE 4-1:
Using markers,
you can add
helpful notes to
your animated
sequences.

Recognizing different kinds of keyframe indicators

After working in the Dope Sheet for a while, you might notice that the shapes and colors of individual keyframes may vary a bit. Some of those shape and color changes are handled automatically. They're there to give you an indication of the type of handle on each key, which should give you an idea of how the interpolation between frames appears without the need to look at the Graph Editor. See Book 2, Chapter 4 for more on the types of handles available on curves. You can change the handle types of any selected keyframe by choosing Key ⇨ Handle Type in the Dope Sheet or by pressing the V hotkey. The following is an explanation for each shape you may see for keyframes:

 » **Diamond:** The keyframe has a Free handle type.

 » **Solid Circle:** The keyframe has auto-clamped handles, meaning that the curve doesn't go above or below the value set in the keyframe.

 » **Circle with Dot:** The keyframe has automatic handles, much like curves in the 3D Viewport.

 » **Square:** The keyframe has vector handles (and therefore linear interpolation).

» **Rhombus:** The keyframe has aligned handles, trying to keep the f-curve smooth.

» **Upwards or downwards arrow at the top or bottom of the icon:** This isn't exactly a shape in its own right, more of an overlay on any of the existing keys. To see them at all, you need to enable Show Curve Extremes in the View menu of the Dope Sheet. Once you do that, certain keyframes will have these little arrow overlays. They serve as a way of indicating whether that's the maximum (upwards arrow) or minimum (downwards arrow) value for that f-curve. So, if you have a bouncing ball and you need to know on which frame it hits the ground, you just need to look at the Z Location channel and find the keyframe that has a downward arrow overlay.

The space between frames also helps give you an indication of what's going on between them, interpolation-wise. That space can have basically three states:

» **No bar:** Empty space between keys indicates that the keyframe values are different and that there's change happening between them.

» **Solid gray bar (orange if the keyframes are selected):** A thick solid bar between keyframes lets you know that this is a *hold*. The two keyframes have the same value, and there's no change between them.

» **Thin green bar:** If you've manually changed interpolation (Key ⇨ Interpolation Mode or the T hotkey) to anything other than Bézier interpolation, you have what's known as *fixed* interpolation. That means regardless of what you set as your keyframe handles, it doesn't matter because the interpolation mode takes precedence. In those cases, there will be a green bar between frames to show that keyframe handle settings don't apply.

Other than the shapes and colors Blender automatically sets in the Dope Sheet, you can actually set keyframe types yourself and color-code them. These custom keyframe types don't actually change anything about the shape of your animation f-curves, but they do serve as handy notes to indicate what you mean to be happening in your animation. Think of them like markers but for specific keyframes rather than moments in time. To set a custom keyframe type, select the keyframe you want to modify and choose Key ⇨ Keyframe Type, or press the R hotkey. Either way, you'll invoke a menu with the following choices:

» **Keyframe:** This is the default keyframe type. Just the standard yellow keyframe icon.

» **Breakdown:** Choose this option and your selected keyframes become slightly smaller and cyan in color to indicate that they're breakdown frames. A *breakdown frame* is the moment between extreme poses. In your typical walk cycle, the breakdown frame is the one where the character's legs pass each other.

» **Moving Hold:** The Moving Hold keyframe type is slightly smaller (like the Breakdown keyframe) and more orange in color than the standard keyframe color. If a hold (as described earlier) is where two keyframes are identical and there's no change between them, a *moving hold* is where two keyframes aren't identical, but still really close to one another. In character animation, a moving hold is how you have a character sit still without looking like a robot that was suddenly just turned off.

>> **Extreme:** When you choose the Extreme keyframe type, your selected keys get slightly larger and pink. In animation, an *extreme pose* is a primary pose that shows the character at the limits of that particular action. In a walk cycle, the extremes are where the legs are farthest from one another.

>> **Jitter:** Choose this option, and the keyframe becomes slightly smaller than the default keyframe type and green. Sometimes when you're animating, you add keyframes where there's not a huge change from one to the other, but it's just enough to provide some realism and life to the movement. You may use this keyframe type when animating a camera move to indicate that it should look hand-held rather than like it's smoothly moving along a track.

REMEMBER

Remember that keyframe types don't actually change anything about your animation. They're notes to yourself or other animators that you're working with so everyone knows the intent of those keyframes. The exception to this is the Breakdown type. There are operators in the Pose menu (specifically Pose ➪ In-Betweens) that look for keyframes that you've marked as being Breakdown keys to generate in-between keys for you.

Animating with Armatures

If you're already used to object animation, using armatures to animate in the Dope Sheet extends naturally from the base that I cover in Chapter 1 of this book (planning, blocking, refining, final polish). When I animate, I like to use the following process:

1. **Plan the animation.**

   I can't emphasize this point enough: Know what you're going to animate and have an idea about the timing of the motion. *Act out the action.* If you can, record yourself acting it out. Video reference is key for seeing subtle movements. Sketch out a few quick thumbnail drawings of the sequence. Even stick-figure drawings can be really helpful for determining poses and figuring out camera framing.

 2. **Set your timeline cursor at frame 1 and create the starting pose for your character by manipulating its rig in Pose mode.**

3. **Select all visible bones (Select ⇨ All) and Insert a Location, Rotation & Scale keyframe for *everything* (Pose ⇨ Animation ⇨ Insert Keyframe ⇨ Location, Rotation & Scale).**

Granted, there's a good chance that most of the bones can't be moved or scaled but only rotated, so setting a location or scale keyframe for them is kind of moot. However, setting a keyframe for all the bones is faster than going through and figuring out which bones can be keyed for just rotation and which bones can be keyed for some combination of rotation, location, and scale.

Alternatively, if you've set up a keying set for your character (see Book 4, Chapter 1), you can pick that keying set from within the Keying rollout in the Timeline. Then you can insert keyframes for every property in that keying set just by pressing I.

4. **Within the Dope Sheet, make sure all your recently added channels are selected (they should be by default) and change the interpolation type to Constant (Key ⇨ Interpolation Mode ⇨ Constant).**

This is kind of an optional step, but it's really helpful for the blocking pass of your animation. With Constant interpolation set, you can focus exclusively on your character's poses and the timing between those poses without the distraction of seeing how Blender generates the in-betweens for you.

5. **Move the timeline cursor forward to roughly when you think the next major pose should happen.**

It doesn't really matter which editor you use to adjust the timeline cursor. It could be the Timeline, the Dope Sheet, or the Graph Editor. In fact, using ← and →, you can even adjust the timeline cursor from the 3D Viewport.

6. **Create your character's second pose.**

If the next pose is a *hold*, or a pose where the character doesn't change position, you can duplicate the keys of the previous pose by selecting them in the Dope Sheet and choosing Key ⇨ Duplicate or by pressing Shift+D.

The Shift+D hotkey combination also works in the Timeline.

TIP

7. **Select all visible bones (A) and Insert an Available keyframe (Pose ⇨ Animation ⇨ Insert Keyframe ⇨ Available).**

Again, if you're using a keying set, you can just press I. If you want, you can also switch to the Available keying set in the Timeline before inserting keyframes.

8. **Continue with Steps 5 through 7 until you complete the last major pose for your character.**

9. **Using the Dope Sheet, play back the animation (Spacebar), paying close attention to timing.**

At this point, hopefully your poses are acceptably refined, so you should pay even *more* attention to timing than to the accuracy of the poses.

10. **Go through the keys in the Dope Sheet and tweak the timing of the poses so that they look natural.**

11. **Continuing to tweak, go back and start adding additional poses and keyframes for secondary motions between your major poses.**

Somewhere around here you've migrated from the blocking phase of animation to the refining phase. So at this point, you may want to select all the keys in your animation and switch back to Bézier interpolation (Key ⇨ Interpolation Mode ⇨ Bézier). Now you can focus on perfecting the movement between keyframes.

12. **Continue on this course, refining the timing and detail more and more with each pass.**

One luxury of computer animation is the ability to continually go back and tweak things, make changes, and improve the animation. You can take advantage of this process by training yourself to work in passes. Animate your character's biggest, most pronounced motion first. Make sure that you have the timing down. Then, move to the next pass, working on slightly more detailed parts of the performance. For example, animate your character's arm and hand bones before you get into the nitty-gritty details of animating the fingers. The biggest reason to work this way is time. It's much easier to go in and fix the timing on a big action if you do it earlier. Otherwise, you run into situations where you find yourself shuffling around a bunch of detail keys after you find out that your character doesn't get from Point A to Point B in the right amount of time.

TIP

Don't be afraid to break out a stopwatch and act out the action to find out exactly how long it takes to perform and what the action feels like. Animation is very much like acting by proxy. So, it helps to know what some actions actually feel like when they're performed. If you're fortunate enough to have friends willing to help, have them act out the action for you while you time it or even record it to video. Getting animation to look right is all about having the proper timing.

Principles of animation worth remembering

As you create your animations, try to pull from a variety of sources to really capture the essence of some action, motion, or character expression. My first and most emphatic recommendation is to keep your eyes open. Watch everything around you that moves. Study objects and try to get an idea of how their structure facilitates motion. Then, think about how you would re-create that movement.

Of course, merely gawking at everything in the world isn't the only thing you should do (and you should be prepared for the fact that people will probably look at you funny when you gawk). Studying early animation is also a good idea. Most of the principles that those wonderfully talented pioneers developed for anima-tion are still relevant and applicable to computer animation. In fact, you should remember the classic 12 basic principles of animation that were established by some of the original Disney animators. These principles are a bit of divergence, but if your aim is to create good animation, you should know about them and try to use them in even the most simple animations:

>> **Squash and stretch:** This one is all about deformation. Because of weight, anything that moves gets deformed somehow. A tennis ball squashes to an oval shape when it's hit. Rope under tension gets stretched. Cartoon charac-ters hit all believable and unbelievable ranges of this when they're animated, but it's valuable, albeit toned down, even in realistic animation.

>> **Anticipation:** The basic idea here is that before every action in one direction, a buildup in the opposite direction occurs first. A character that's going to jump bends their knees and moves down first to build up the energy to jump upward.

>> **Staging:** The idea of staging is to keep the frame simple. The purpose of animation is to communicate an idea, a movement, or an emotion with moving images. You want to convey this idea as clearly as possible with the way you arrange your shots and the characters in those shots. A good trick here is to use Solid viewport shading. Using the Shading rollout in the 3D Viewport's header, you can change the Lighting setting to Flat and the Color setting to Single (and set the color swatch that appears to black). If you can still tell what's going on with just a silhouette, then you've got good staging.

>> **Straight-ahead action versus pose-to-pose action:** These are the two primary methods of animating. The process that I discuss near the beginning of this chapter is more of a pose-to-pose technique. Pose-to-pose can be more organized and structured, but it may result in movement that's cartoony or robotic. Straight-ahead action is generally a more open-ended approach and gives more freedom for improvisation, but the action may be less clear and more difficult to tweak on future passes. Most modern animators use a hybrid approach, blocking in the initial poses and then working straight-ahead between them.

>> **Follow through and overlapping action:** The idea here is to make sure that your animations adhere (or seem to adhere) to the laws of physics. If you have movement in one direction, the inertia of that motion requires you to animate

the follow-through even if you're changing direction. When a character throws a ball, their arm doesn't stop moving when the ball is released. The arm follows through with its own momentum.

» **Ease in and ease out:** Ease in and ease out, sometimes known as "slow in, slow out," means that natural movement does not stop and start abruptly. It flows smoothly, accelerating and decelerating. By using Bézier curves in the Graph Editor, you actually get this principle for free, though that doesn't mean you should just take the defaults. Depending on the type of movement, you often have to customize the degree of easing in your animation (for example, a bounce eases in and out very fast in a way that doesn't necessarily look smooth).

» **Arcs:** Along the same lines as the previous two principles, most natural movement happens in arcs. So if your character is changing direction or moving something, you typically want that to happen in some sort of curved, arc motion. Straight lines are generally stiff and robotic (and therefore good for machinery and robots), but they're also very useful for powerful actions like punching.

» **Secondary action:** These actions are those additional touches that make characters appear more real to the audience. Clothing that shifts with character movement, jiggling fat or loose skin, and blinking eyes are just a few actions that can breathe life into an otherwise stiff, empty puppet.

» **Timing:** Timing is, in my opinion, one of the most important of the 12 principles. Everything happens according to time. If the timing is off, it throws off the effect for the whole animation. I'm not just talking about controlling the timing of actions to appear believable. I also mean *story-based timing* — knowing exactly the right time to make a character give a sad facial expression that impacts the audience the most. Think of it like telling a joke. The best punchline in the world will fall flat if you don't say it at exactly the right time.

» **Exaggeration:** Exaggeration makes animation fun. You can do anything with animation, and you're nearly duty-bound to take advantage of that fact. Otherwise, you may as well just work in video or film with meatspace people.

» **Solid drawing:** Solid drawing refers to the actual skill of being able to draw. Computer animators *can* get away with not being experts at drawing, but it's to your benefit to make the effort. Drawing is an extension of seeing. When you draw, you turn on a part of your brain that studies how things look relative to one another. Being able to see the world with these eyes can make all the difference in re-creating believable motion. Besides, with Grease Pencil objects (see Chapter 6 of this book), you can draw in Blender, too!

» **Appeal:** This one is easy. Make things that are awesome. If you're going to animate something boring, what's the point? It needs to be interesting for you to make, and it's nice if it's also interesting for other people to watch.

Those are the basic principles of animation, but not a single one of them is carved in stone. You can effectively break every one of them and still pull off some incredible animation. That said, more often than not, it's in the best interest of your work and your sanity that you at least start within these principles and then later on find where you can break them in the best ways possible.

Making sense of quaternions (or, "Why are there four rotation curves?!")

Even though the bulk of your time animating with armatures is spent working with the Dope Sheet, you still may frequently need to tweak things in the Graph Editor. If you go to the Graph Editor and view the f-curves for a bone with the intention of tweaking rotation, you may run into a particularly jarring shock. The X Rotation, Y Rotation, and Z Rotation channels that you would expect for rotation aren't there: They've been replaced with *four* channels to control rotation, called *quaternions*. Figure 4-2 shows a set of quaternions in the Graph Editor, describing the rotation of some bone.

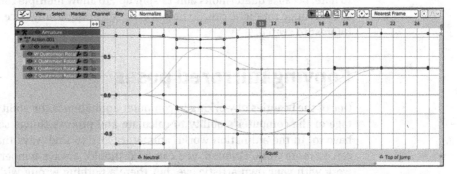

FIGURE 4-2:
Quaternions in action! They're nearly incomprehensible!

TECHNICAL STUFF

Quaternions are a different way of defining rotations in 3D space, and they're quite a bit different from the standard X, Y, and Z rotations called *Euler* (pronounced "oiler") rotations. Quaternions are used in the rotation of bones because Euler rotations can get into a nasty situation referred to as *gimbal lock*, which involves being mathematically unable to compensate for or adjust a rotation because you have only three axes to define it. Having that happen in an armature is unacceptable. Fortunately, quaternions don't suffer from gimbal lock. However, they do suffer from another affliction: They have virtually no intuitive relationship to rotation that non-mathematicians can understand. The best explanation I've ever heard is to imagine a set of springs attached to the object you want to rotate. The W value has a spring that pulls to the original rest position (a value of 1), whereas the X, Y, and Z values each have two springs pulling full rotations in each direction (-1 and 1). This is the reason why the default rotation value for a quaternion is (1, 0, 0, 0). Of course, even with that explanation, it can still be confusing to think about.

To make a long story short, if you're using quaternion rotations, it may be easier for you to tweak a rotation by adding additional keyframes to the rotation. If you're not fond of mathematics, you may very well go crazy trying to figure out how they relate to your bone's rotation.

You aren't stuck with quaternions if you don't want them, though. You can control the rotation mode of any bone in an armature. To do so, select a bone and visit the Bone tab of the Properties editor. At the bottom of the Transform panel is a drop-down menu labeled Rotation Mode. By default, it's set to Quaternion (WXYZ), and in most cases, you want to use this setting. However, in a couple cases where you're sure that you won't run into gimbal lock problems for example, if you rigged a bone to define the rotation of a wheel or you've rigged an elbow, which rotates on only one axis), it may be more helpful to use a different rotation mode like XYZ Euler or Axis Angle. The wheel example is also a good one to note, because quaternions don't "spin up" to allow multiple rotations like Euler or Axis Angle rotations can. So unless your wheel spins only once, it's in your best interest to switch.

Copying mirrored poses

One of the beauties of working in computer animation is the ability to take advantage of the computer's ability to calculate and process things so that you don't have to. In the animation world, animators love to find ways that the computer can do more work. Granted, you can (and should) always temper the computer's work with your own artistic eye, but there's nothing wrong with doing half the work and letting the computer do the other boring, tedious, and repetitive half.

With the auspicious goal of getting the computer to do the work for you, Blender has three incredible operators in the Pose menu of the 3D Viewport. With these operators (available only when you have selected an armature and it's in Pose mode), you can copy and paste poses from and back to the armature:

>> **Copy Pose (Ctrl+C):** Use this operator and the armature's pose is stored in memory.

>> **Paste Pose (Ctrl+V):** This operator takes the coordinates of all the bones you selected when copying the pose and applies them back to your character exactly as you copied them.

>> **Paste Pose Flipped (Shift+Ctrl+V):** This operator does the same thing as Paste Pose, except it takes advantage of Blender's built-in left/right naming convention (see the previous chapter in this book for more details) and pastes the mirrored version of the pose to your character. Pasting a flipped pose is really handy if you're doing something like creating a walk cycle. You can create a left-foot-forward pose and then use Paste Pose Flipped to instantly create a right-foot-forward pose. Figure 4-3 shows a character posed one way and then mirror-pasted to pose the other.

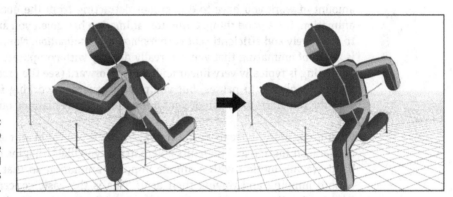

FIGURE 4-3:
All you have to do is put one foot forward, and Blender handles the other for you.

TIP

These copy/paste pose operators work only on your selected bones. So before you use any of these operators, be sure to select the bones you want to copy from or paste to. Often, you're using these operators on all the bones in your armature, but you don't have to.

The typical workflow for using these operators goes like this:

1. **Select all bones (Select ▷ All).**

You can actually get away with selecting just a few bones, but selecting all the bones actually illustrates my point a little better.

2. **Use the Copy Pose operator (Pose ▷ Copy Pose).**

The armature's pose is stored into your computer's memory.

3. **Move to a different location in the Timeline where you'd like your character to resume this pose.**

4. **Paste the pose back to the character with either Paste Pose (Pose ▷ Paste Pose) or Paste Pose Flipped (Pose ▷ Paste Pose Flipped).**

REMEMBER

Note that after you paste the pose, you need to insert a keyframe for that pose at that location. Otherwise, the next time you scrub the Timeline, the pose won't be there, and you'll have to copy and paste it all over again.

Doing Nonlinear Animation

Animation is hard work, really hard work. So, any time you can cut down the amount of work you have to do without detracting from the quality of the final animation, it's a good thing. Computer animation has given you another cool way to effectively and efficiently cut corners: *nonlinear animation*. Nonlinear animation is a way of animating that you can really do only with computers. The process of animating is typically very linear and straightforward (see the preceding section). You may animate in passes, but you're still generally working forward in time with the full start-to-finish of your animation already planned out.

What if you didn't have to work this way? What if you could animate little chunks of character motion and then mix and match as you like? Imagine mixing a simple hand-waving motion with a simple jumping animation so that your character is both jumping and waving their arm? This is the basic concept behind nonlinear animation, sometimes known as *layered animation*. Nonlinear animation takes many of the same principles used in nonlinear video editing and applies them to 3D computer animation. The idea is that you create a library of simple motions or poses and then combine them any way you want to create much more complex animated sequences. Using a library of motions is useful for background characters in larger productions and is also very handy for video games. Instead of trying to pull a specific set of frames from a single unified Timeline, video game developers can now just make a call to one or more of these library animations and let the computer do the rest of the work. Nonlinear animation is also the main approach to tweaking and adjusting animation that comes from motion capture data.

Working with actions

In Blender, the basic building blocks for this library are Actions. *Actions* are collections of f-curves, and they are really cool because they have their own datablock. You can create multiple actions within a single .blend file, share the actions between armatures, and basically build up a library of movements.

TIP

To create a new action, first change the Dope Sheet from the default Dope Sheet editing context to the Action Editor context using the Mode drop-down menu in the header. Then you can use the Action datablock, also in the header of the Dope Sheet, to add a new action, as highlighted in Figure 4-4. This datablock widget is just like the one used for materials, textures, and even objects in other parts of Blender's interface. Create a new action by left-clicking the New button on the datablock (if you've already set keyframes, then you will already have an action here and you won't have to click New). After adding a new action, you can (and should) click in the text area of the datablock and give your new action a custom name.

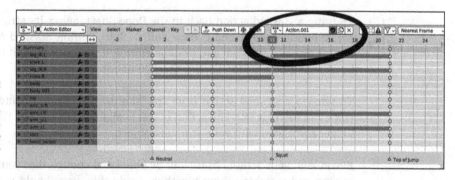

FIGURE 4-4:
Using the Action datablock in the Dope Sheet to create a new action for your armature.

With the new action created, you can create another core animation and start building up your character's action library. Animate waving each arm, a walk cycle, various facial expressions, a standing idle animation, and any other simple action that comes to mind.

WARNING

Before you create a new action, be sure to left-click the Fake User button in the datablock widget for your current action (it's the button with a shield icon on it) so it's enabled. Let me write that again: *Give your actions a fake user.*

Remember the way that Blender's datablocks work. If a datablock doesn't have any users, it gets destroyed when you close Blender or open a different .blend file. So if you go through and create a bunch of actions without giving them users, all those userless actions disappear when you close Blender, regardless of how frequently you saved while working. To ensure that this doesn't happen, you need to make sure that all your actions have users. This is where the Fake User button comes in. When a datablock has that button enabled, it won't be obliterated when you close your file.

Although the effort of making a fake user for each action is a good practice to avoid losing your animation data, a slight problem occurs in that there's not an automatic association between your action and your armature object. The upside is that you can technically reuse the same animation data on multiple objects, but if you're not interested in that feature, you either need to use a clever naming scheme or simply remember which actions belong to which objects. This can get pretty confusing in a complex scene, so there is a slightly better approach: stashing.

Stashing an action is actually pushing your action to the Nonlinear Animation editor (as described in the next section of this chapter), but it's muted and not editable. To stash an action, make sure your Dope Sheet is in its Action Editor context and look to the header of that editor. To the left of the action datablock is a button labeled Stash. Left-click that button and your current action gets pushed as a strip to the Nonlinear Animation editor into a track labeled [Action Stash]. Now your action is stored in a way that's associated with your armature.

 To bring a stashed action back to the Dope Sheet, select its strip in the Nonlinear Animation editor and choose Edit ⇨ Start Editing Stashed Action from the header menu. And when you're done editing it, you can bring it back to its stash by choosing Edit ⇨ Stop Editing Stashed Action.

To remove a stashed action from the Nonlinear Animation editor, left-click its track and delete it (X). The action is still available to the Action Editor, but it's no longer associated with your armature object.

Eventually, your action library will be populated enough that you'll want to start mixing and matching them together. To do this, you should use the Nonlinear Animation editor. Add the Nonlinear Animation editor to the Animation workspace with the following steps:

1. **In the Animation workspace, left-click and drag the seam at the top of the Dope Sheet up, making more room for that editor.**

2. **Split the Dope Sheet area in half horizontally so you end up with two Dope Sheets stacked atop one another.**

   You can split the Dope Sheet's area by clicking and dragging from the area's corner widget or navigating to View ⇨ Area ⇨ Horizontal Split in the Dope Sheet's header menu.

3. **Change the upper Dope Sheet's editing context to be an Action Editor.**

4. **Change the lower Dope Sheet to a Nonlinear Animation editor.**

Your screen layout may look something like Figure 4-5.

Mixing actions to create complex animation

When you have an action loaded in the Dope Sheet's Action Editor, you should notice a bright orange bar in the Nonlinear Animation editor. This orange bar is the current active action on your armature, and you can push that action on the Nonlinear Animation editor stack to build your animation.

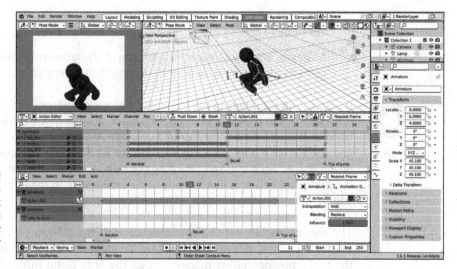

FIGURE 4-5:
An animation
screen layout
with the
Nonlinear
Animation editor
added to it.

To add your actions to the Nonlinear Animation editor:

1. **Push your current action into the stack by left-clicking the button to the right of the active channel in the channel region of the Nonlinear Animation editor (the icon for this button is on the left).**

    A new Nonlinear Animation *track* is created, populated with your current action as another orange *strip*. The text on the strip should match the name of your action. The track itself is also named to match the name of your action, as indicated in the Nonlinear Animation editor's channel region. The track isn't required to have the same name as the action, though. You can double-click that name to rename it to something more descriptive.

    You can also push an action to the Nonlinear Animation editor from the Dope Sheet using the Push Down button in the header while in the Action Editor context. It's just to the left of the Stash button.

    TIP

2. **Add a new strip in the graph area of the Nonlinear Animation editor (Add ⇨ Action Strip).**

    You see a menu of all the actions you created.

3. **Choose the action you want to add to the Nonlinear Animation editor.**

    The action is placed in the Nonlinear Animation editor as a strip in the currently selected track (left-click the track name in the channel region to select a track), and its start position is wherever the time cursor is located.

    If the timeline cursor is in the middle of an existing strip on your selected track, adding a new strip creates a new track named NlaTrack (short for nonlinear animation track). The existing strip doesn't get trimmed or removed.

    REMEMBER

4. **Continue to add actions to the Nonlinear Animation editor.**

Of course, unless you make the last frame of one Action strip match the pose at the head of the next frame, the animation looks pretty erratic.

If your action is already in the Nonlinear Animation editor from being stashed (as described in the previous section), you can't push it down from the Dope Sheet because it's already a strip in the Nonlinear Animation editor. To "unstash" it and make it an active track, all you have to do is enable and unlock its track by enabling the check box and disabling the lock on its track. From there, your formerly stashed action is just like any other action strip in the Nonlinear Animation editor.

The way to smooth out the animation is with the Sidebar (N) in the Nonlinear Animation editor, shown in Figure 4-6. To make the transition from one strip to the next smoother, either make sure that the Auto Blend In/Out check box in the Active Strip panel for each strip is enabled and let them overlap a bit, or manually set the Blend In and Blend Out values in this panel.

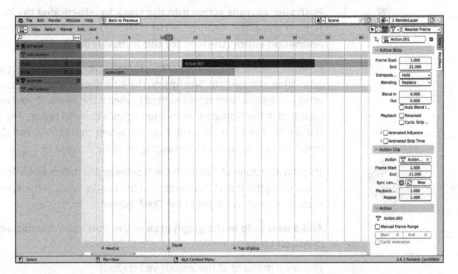

FIGURE 4-6:
Using the Sidebar in the Nonlinear Animation editor.

Taking advantage of looped animation

Another benefit of using the Nonlinear Animation editor is the ability to easily loop any action strip and rescale its timing. In Chapter 1 of this book, I explain how to do looped, cyclic animations using f-curve modifiers, but the Nonlinear Animation editor gives you even more control. You can loop and rescale the timing in the Nonlinear Animation editor from within the Sidebar. The Action Clip panel shows a pair of values at the bottom: Playback Scale and Repeat. The very first is

Playback Scale, with a default value of 1.0. However, you can increase or decrease this value as much as you want to adjust the timing on your action, speeding it up or slowing it down as necessary.

Below the Playback Scale value is Repeat. Like Playback Scale, the default value is 1.0, and you can increase or decrease the value to taste. As you do, you should see the strip increase in length proportional to the increase of the Repeat value. Now, to have an effective looping animation, it's definitely in your best interest to make the first and last poses in the action identical. The easiest way to do so would be to go into the Dope Sheet, column-select the keys in the first frame (column selecting is described earlier in this chapter), and duplicate (Shift+D) it to the last frame of the action. However, you can also use the copy and paste pose operators in the 3D Viewport:

1. **In the Dope Sheet, select the action strip you want to loop from the Actions datablock.**

2. **While still in the Dope Sheet, scrub the time cursor to the first pose in the action.**

3. **In the 3D Viewport, select all bones (A) and use the Copy Pose operator (Pose ⇨ Copy Pose or press Ctrl+C).**

4. **Back in the Dope Sheet, scrub the time cursor to some place after the last keyframe.**

5. **In the 3D Viewport, use the Paste Pose operator (Pose ⇨ Paste Pose or press Ctrl+V).**

6. **Insert a new keyframe (I ⇨ Available).**

   When you get to this step, all the bones should still be selected, so you don't need to reselect anything.

   When you return to the Nonlinear Animation editor, the action strip should automatically be longer to account for the additional frame at the end. Furthermore, the Action strip should also loop seamlessly upon playback (Spacebar).

Figure 4-7 shows the Nonlinear Animation editor with a looped strip.

Be careful when changing the scale of Action strips. More often than not, changing the scale results in a keyframe being placed at what's called a *fractional frame* or *intraframe*, a spot on the Timeline that isn't a nicely rounded frame number. Fractional frames aren't necessarily a bad thing, but animations do tend to look a little bit better if the keyframes fall on full frames so that the audience has the chance to "read" the pose.

WARNING

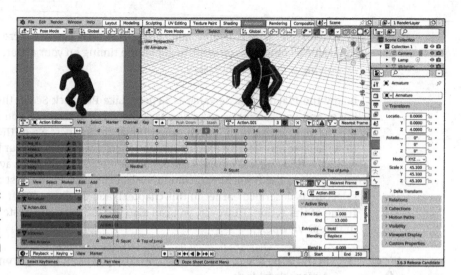

FIGURE 4-7:
Action strips in
the Nonlinear
Animation editor,
looped and
rescaled.

TIP

Many of these animation concepts, especially ones involving the Nonlinear Animation editor, are much easier to grasp if you can see them in motion. After all, this is animation, the art of motion. The `.blend` files on this book's website (`www.blenderbasics.com`) provide a stronger notion of how these things work together.

Chapter **5**

Letting Blender Do the Work for You

When animating, some actions are difficult or very time consuming to get right, such as explosions, fire, hair, cloth, and physics-related actions like moving fluids and bouncing objects. One solution to get these actions to look right is to let the computer do the work and create a simulation of that action. You use variables like gravity and mass to define the environment, and the computer calculates how the objects in the scene behave based on the values you set. Using the computer is a great way to get nearly accurate motion without the need to key everything by hand.

That said, don't make the mistake of thinking simulations always give you a huge time savings in animation. This assumption isn't necessarily true, because some highly detailed simulations can take hours, or even days, to complete. Instead, think of simulations as a way to more reliably animate detailed, physically accurate motion better than you might be able to do by hand alone. If you look at the process while wearing your "business hat," paying for a computer to crunch through a simulation is cheaper than paying for an artist to create it manually.

REMEMBER

This chapter only scratches the surface of what you can do with the simulation tools in Blender, so you should certainly look at additional resources, such as Blender's official online documentation and the wide variety of online tutorials from the community, particularly those on www.cgcookie.com and www.blenderdiplom.com to get a full understanding of how each feature works. But hopefully, this chapter gives you an idea of the possibilities you have at hand.

Using Particles in Blender

Blender has had an integrated particle system from its early beginnings. Over the years, though, it has grown and matured into a much more powerful system for creating particle-based effects like hair, flock/swarm behavior, and explosions. And the particle system gets more and more powerful with every release.

The controls for Blender's particle systems live in the Particles tab of the Properties editor, as shown in Figure 5-1. Initially, this section looks pretty barren, with just a single list box. However, if you have a Mesh object selected and click the Plus (+) button to the right of the list box, a whole explosion of additional panels for controlling particle behavior appear. Adding a particle system in Particle Properties also adds a Particle System modifier to your object. Technically, you can create your new particle system from Modifier Properties as well, but it's better to do it from Particle Properties, because that's where all the particle controls live.

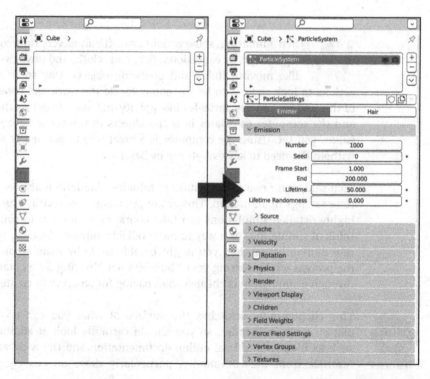

FIGURE 5-1:
Creating a basic particle system.

TIP

If you click the Play button in the Timeline or press Spacebar after adding the particle system to your default cube object, you should see little white particles falling off your cube to the space below it. Press Esc to stop playback.

Knowing what particle systems are good for

Particle systems have a handful of good uses. Each use involves large numbers of individual objects that share some general behavior. Consequently, particle systems are ideal for groups of objects that move according to physics, such as fireworks or tennis balls being continuously shot at a wall. Particle systems are also decent for simulating hair and fur. If the path along which an individual particle travels could be considered a strand, you could use groups of these particle strands to make hair. This technique is exactly what Blender does. That said, the preferred system for hair and fur in the most recent releases of Blender uses curves and Geometry Nodes instead of particles. That's covered later in this chapter.

There's also one other use for particle systems: simple flocking or crowd simulation. Say that you want to have a swarm of gnats constantly buzzing around your character's head. A particle system is a great way to pull off that effect.

After you create your first particle system, the context panel at the top of Particle Properties gives you the simplest controls, allowing you to name your particle system and add additional particle systems to your active object. Objects in Blender can have more than one particle system and can even share the same particle system settings between objects. Beneath the Particle datablock are a pair of buttons that you use to pick which of the two types of particle system behaviors to work with: Emitter and Hair. In most instances, you'll probably use the Emitter type. Hair particle systems are an older way to create manageable hair and fur in Blender and is mostly there so you can load files from older versions.

Customizing Emitter settings

If you choose Emitter, the Emission panel has some of the most important settings for controlling how many particles you have and how long they exist in your scene. Here's a brief explanation for each value:

>> **Number:** As the name implies, this value is the total number of particles created by the system. After the particle system generates this number of particles, it stops. You can get additional particles in more than one way, but the most straightforward (though potentially CPU-intensive) way is to increase this value.

>> **Seed:** Particle systems rely on randomness to look organic and natural, but computer programs themselves are actually incapable of being truly random. Despite some of the quirky behavior you may have experienced with computers, it's true, they can't be truly random. Randomness has to be computationally generated with an algorithm of some sort. This computed randomness is said to be *pseudorandom,* and most pseudorandom algorithms require a *seed* value as a starting point for computing random numbers. The Seed property for your particle system is the number that your particle system uses to generate its randomness.

>> **Frame Start:** This value is the frame where particles start emitting from the source object. By default, the value is set to frame 1, but if you don't want to have your particles start until later in your animation, you can increase the value in this field. You can also set this value to be negative, so your animation starts with the particles already in motion.

>> **End:** This value is the frame where Blender stops emitting particles from the source object. By default, it's set to frame 200. With the default values for Number and Frame Start (1000 and 1.0, respectively), Blender creates five particles in each new frame in the animation (1000 ÷ 200 = 5) up to frame 200 and then stops generating particles.

>> **Lifetime:** The Lifetime value controls how long an individual particle exists in your scene. With the default value of 50.0, a particle born on frame 7 disappears from the scene when you reach frame 57. If you find that you need your particles in the scene longer, increase this value.

>> **Lifetime Randomness:** This value pertains specifically to the Lifetime of the particle. At its default of 0.0, it doesn't change anything; particles live for the exact length of time stipulated by the Lifetime value and disappear, or *die,* at the end of that time. However, if you increase the Lifetime Randomness value, it introduces a variation to the Lifetime option, so all the particles born on one frame disappear at slightly different times, giving a more natural effect.

TIP

One additional option to pay attention to in the Emission panel is the Use Modifier Stack check box within the Source sub-panel. If you're emitting particles from a mesh on which you've used Generate modifiers (such as the Mirror modifier or the Remesh modifier), you may want to enable this check box. Otherwise, only the geometry of your base mesh will emit particles; in many cases, that's not likely to be what you want.

Choosing physics simulation models

You can associate any particle type with one of five varieties of physics simulation models stipulated in the Physics panel with the Physics Type drop-down menu:

» **None:** Very rarely do you have a need to use the None option, but it's good to have in those uncommon situations.

» **Newtonian:** Typically, the default Newtonian setting is the most useful option because it tends to accurately simulate real-world physical attributes, such as gravity, mass, and velocity.

» **Keyed:** Occasionally, you may want to have more explicit control over your particles, such as when you need to direct particles to follow a specific path. This is where Keyed physics come into play. You can use the *emitter object* of one particle system to control the angle and direction of another one.

» **Boids:** The Boids option tells your particles to have flocking or swarming behavior, and you get settings and panels to control that behavior.

» **Fluid:** The last option, Fluid, is a physics-based choice similar to the Newtonian option, but particles have greater cohesive and adhesive properties that make them behave like part of a fluid system.

Creating a basic particle system

To create a basic particle system, follow these steps:

1. **In the 3D Viewport, add a mesh to work as your particle emitter (Add ⇨ Mesh ⇨ Grid).**

   In this example, I use a simple grid, but really any mesh works. The key thing to remember is that, by default, particles are emitted from the faces of your mesh and move away from the face in the direction of that face's normal.

2. **Navigate to Particle Properties and add a new particle system.**

   After you click the Plus (+) button next to the Particles list box, all the options available to particles become visible. If you try to play back the animation now (press Spacebar or left-click the Play button in the Timeline), you see particles dropping from your grid.

TIP

Don't stop the playback of your particle system now. Keep it playing as you work through the rest of the steps in this section. If you do that, you'll be able to see Blender update the particle system live as you edit it. This is a really handy way to work because you can get instant feedback as you modify the properties of your particle system,

While your particles play, look at your Timeline. Along the bottom edge of the Timeline is a red bar. Some of that bar may be solid, whereas the rest is semi-transparent. This is your *particle cache,* or the movement in your particle system that Blender has stored in memory. Working with particle caches is a bit of an advanced topic, but the main thing to know is that when your timeline cursor is not in the solid red area, that moment in time for your particle system has not yet been cached. The result is that it may not be accurate to your final results, and it may play back slower than the cached part. The cache will be updated with any major changes that you make in Particle Properties.

3. **Decide what type of physics you would like to have controlling your particles.**

   Newtonian physics are usually the most common type of particle system used, but I'm also pretty fond of the Boids behavior for Emitter particle systems. It just looks cool, and they're a lot of fun!

4. **Adjust the velocity settings to control particle behavior.**

   You change this setting from the Velocity panel in Particle Properties. For Newtonian physics, you can give your particles an initial velocity. I tend to adjust the Normal velocity first because it gives the most immediate results. Values above 0 go in the direction of each face's normals, whereas values below 0 go in the opposite direction. Boid particles don't have velocity settings; use the Movement sub-panel to control how each Boid particle interacts with its neighboring particle.

5. **Play back the animation to watch the particles move (Spacebar).**

   If you followed the tip in Step 2, you could be playing your particle animation already. If not, press the Spacebar or click the Play button in the Timeline and see what your settings make the particles do. If your particles start behaving in erratic or unexpected ways, it's a good idea to make sure that your timeline cursor in the Timeline is at or before the frame you entered for the Frame Start value in the Emission panel when you start the animation playback.

   Watch how your particles move and behave. You can now either tweak the particle movement during playback or, if it's more comfortable for you, press Esc to stop the playback and adjust your settings before playing the animation again. I usually use a combination of live adjustments and this back-and-forth tweaking to refine my particle system's behavior.

Bear in mind that these steps show a very basic particle system setup, and you're just barely scratching the surface of what's possible. I definitely recommend that you take some time to play with each of the settings and figure out what they do, as well as read some of the more in-depth documentation on particles in Blender's online documentation.

TIP

If you change a lot of settings, it's a good practice to go back to frame 1 and replay your animation to cache your particle system from the beginning rather than from just the previous frame. If you like your particle system results, it's also possible to save your cache to your hard drive using the Cache panel in Particle Properties.

That way, the next time you re-open your `.blend` file, your exact particle movement is still there.

Using force fields and collisions

After you create a basic particle system, you can have a little bit of fun with it, controlling the behavior of your particles. You control this behavior by using forces and deflectors. A *force field* is a controlling influence on the overall behavior of the particles, such as wind, vortices, and magnetism. In contrast, you can define collision objects, or *deflectors*, for your particles to collide with and impede their progress. Generally speaking, forces are defined using specialized Empties, whereas deflectors are created with meshes.

 All the controls for forces and deflectors live in the Physics tab of the Properties editor. For particle force fields, left-click the Force Field button, and a Force Fields panel appears. If you need collision settings, left-click the Collision button, and the Collision panel appears.

 You typically use these panels to add force and collision behaviors to objects already in your scene. You select an object and then, from Physics Properties, add force field and collision properties to that object. For force fields, however, you can add them in a slightly faster way: from Blender's Add menu in the 3D Viewport. If you choose Add ⇨ Force Field, you get a whole list of forces that you can add to your scene. Then, you can just adjust the settings for your chosen force from the Force Fields panel in Physics Properties.

Now, I could go through each and every option available for force fields exhaustively, but things usually make more sense if you have an example to work with. That being the case, follow these steps to create a particle system that generates particles influenced by a wind force that causes them to collide with a wall and then bounce off of it:

 1. **Create a simple particle system.**

   If you need a refresher, follow the steps in the preceding section to create a basic Emitter particle system with Newtonian physics.

 2. **Add a Wind force field (Add ⇨ Force Field ⇨ Wind).**

   Notice that the Wind force field object looks like an Empty with circles arranged along its local Z-axis. This visual cue lets you know the strength and direction of your wind force. Left-click and drag the yellow arrow gizmo to increase the Strength value in the Force Fields panel visually. The larger the Strength value, the larger the space between the four circles of the Wind force field object. Play back the animation (Spacebar) to see how your wind is affecting the movements of the particles. While playing your animation, if you rotate your Wind object or adjust its force field settings (in the Force Field panel; the Strength gizmo disappears when you play your animation), the particles are affected in real time. Neat, huh?

For the remaining steps, you don't have to stop the animation of your particle system. Let it keep playing. This is one of the benefits of Blender's non-blocking user interface philosophy. As you add and change things in your scene, the particle system updates and reacts in real time.

TIP

3. **Add a plane (Add ⇨ Mesh ⇨ Plane).**

This plane is your deflector. Grab the plane (feel free to use the Move tool or the G hotkey) and move it so that it's in the path of the particles pushed by your wind force. Rotate (using the Rotate tool or the R hotkey) the plane to make sure that the particles actually run into it head-on.

REMEMBER

If your particle animation is still playing, you're not able to see any of the control gizmos. For these situations, it's really beneficial to know Blender's hotkeys for grabbing, rotating, and scaling.

4. **Make the plane a Collision object.**

With your plane still selected, add a Collision panel in Physics Properties. Whammo! You made a deflector! If you play back the animation (Spacebar) — or if you've been playing the animation the whole time — your particles should be blown by your wind force into your plane, which they should bounce off of rather than shoot straight through.

Figure 5-2 shows the results of this step-by-step process. And like the preceding section, you're just seeing the tip of the iceberg in terms of what's possible with forces and deflectors. You can use all sorts of cool forces and settings to get some very unique behavior out of your particle systems.

NEW FEATURE

In future releases of Blender, the particle system is likely to have more control using a node-based interface, much like geometry nodes (Book 2, Chapter 5) and shader nodes (Book 3, Chapter 1). Keep an eye on new developments and look specifically for mention of "simulation nodes" to see what new features are coming down the pipe for Blender's particle system.

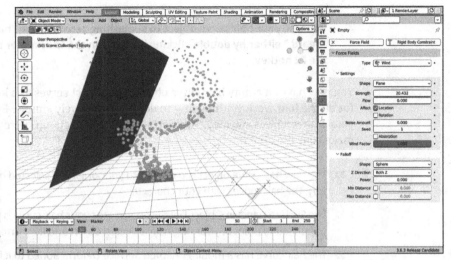

FIGURE 5-2:
Creating a wind force that blows your particles into a plane, which they bounce off of.

Creating hair and fur

NEW FEATURE

In the past, Blender used to use particles as its base tool for its hair and fur system. However, since the publication of the last edition of *Blender For Dummies*, Blender now uses a different system to create hair and fur for your characters. Instead of using particles, Blender's hair system is now based on curves and Geometry Nodes. Geometry Nodes are covered in more detail in Book 2, Chapter 5, and can get very complex, very quickly. This fact is especially true when duplicating and controlling strands in a hair system. Fortunately, even though the new hair system uses Geometry Nodes, you don't actually have to directly interact with any of those nodes to give your characters great hair.

The process for giving your character hair starts with adding an empty hair curve to your scene. Follow these steps:

1. **In the 3D Viewport, select the character (or part of your character) that needs hair.**

    I'll refer to this object as the *source* object throughout the rest of this section. This selection step is important. Unlike when you add other objects to your scene, for hair curves, it's important to have a mesh object selected. This way, Blender knows which object to associate with the new hair curve object.

2. **Add a new empty hair curve (Add ⇨ Curve ⇨ Empty Hair).**

    It won't look like much happens in the 3D Viewport. However, if you look in the Outliner, you should see a new object named Curves added as a child of the object selected in Step 1. This is your new hair curve object.

3. **Rename your hair curve object to something sensible, like "hair" or "beard," either by double-clicking its name in the Outliner or by pressing the F2 hotkey.**

You now have an empty hair curve object. This object serves as a kind of container for all the hair work you're going to do. It's deceptively simple. By adding it with your source object selected, Blender automatically sets up quite a few things to make your life easier:

>> The new hair curve object is parented to your originally selected object. This way, the hair moves with your character.

>> The Surface panel in Object Data Properties for your hair curve is pre-populated to point at your originally selected object and its UV map.

>> The hair curve has a modifier named Surface Deform added to it in Modifier Properties. Technically, this modifier isn't a modifier; it's a Geometry Node network named Surface Deform. However, because it's already made, you only have to interact with it as if it were just like any normal modifier.

Yes. Technically speaking, you could manually do all these steps yourself if you add a hair curve object without first selecting your source object. However, it's faster and more convenient to have Blender do this work for you.

Great. You have an object that's supposed to hold all your hair settings and controls, but your character is still bald. When does it finally get hair? Now.

Working with Sculpt mode on hair curves

The work for adding and controlling hair happens in Sculpt mode for your hair curve object. Like Sculpt mode for other object types, such as meshes (see Book 2, Chapter 3), the Sculpt mode for hair curve objects gives you the ability to control the geometry of your object using a set of tools bound to brushes. For hair curves, I like to think of Sculpt mode as more of a "grooming" mode. You use Sculpt mode for hair curves to grow, customize, and comb your hair curves. Figure 5-3 shows an object with particle hair being combed in Sculpt mode.

You switch to Sculpt mode by using the Mode menu in the 3D Viewport's header or by selecting it from the pie menu option when you press Ctrl+Tab. With your hair curve object selected, switch into Sculpt mode. When you're in Sculpt mode, you have the ability to create and modify hair curves with dedicated tools you can select from the Toolbar. For each tool in Sculpt mode, you have a circular brush cursor like the one used in Sculpting and Vertex Paint modes. You can adjust the brush's size and strength using the sliders in the Active Tool tab of the Properties editor or by pressing F and Shift+F, respectively.

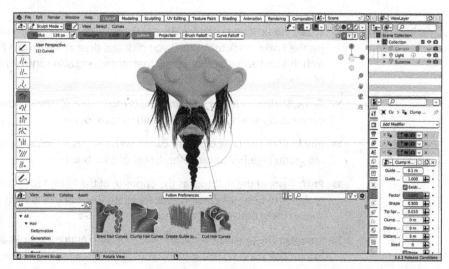

FIGURE 5-3:
Combing hair in Sculpt mode. Suzanne looks so wise with a moustache and beard!

The following is a quick description of each tool you have available in hair curve Sculpt mode:

>> **Paint Selection:** The Paint Selection tool is used to control which hair curves (and what parts of those curves) are affected by other tools in Sculpt mode. This tool works much like the Mask tool in Sculpt mode for meshes. Click and drag the brush cursor over the strands you want to affect and they appear brighter. Dark strands are masked off and won't be influenced by other Sculpt mode tools.

>> **Add:** Use the Add tool to increase the number of hair curve strands where you click. By default the Count setting for this tool is set to 1. Increase that value and Blender adds more hairs within the space of your brush cursor as you work.

>> **Delete:** This tool is the inverse of the Add tool. Hair curves are removed from the places where you click with this tool.

>> **Density:** The Density tool is where I typically like to start adding hair curves because it adds and removes hair curves based on what you define in the tool's Distance Min and Count Max settings. As a handy tip, click the Edit Minimum Distance button in the Tool Settings header of the 3D Viewport and then click on your mesh; Blender provides you with a hand gizmo to visualize the density value you want.

>> **Comb:** This tool is the primary workhorse of Sculpt mode. Use it to coerce your hair curves into behaving. No more bad hair days!

>> **Snake Hook:** If you combine the Comb tool with the Grow/Shrink tool, you get the Snake Hook tool. When you click and drag at the tip of a hair strand with this tool active, you can grow that strand and also control the direction of growth.

>> **Grow/Shrink:** Left-click and drag the brush cursor of this tool over your hair curves and you'll make those affected strands longer.

>> **Pinch:** Click and drag over hair curves with the Pinch tool, and those curves will group together towards the center of your brush cursor.

>> **Puff:** Think of the Puff tool as the opposite of the Pinch tool. Where the Pinch tool tries to bring your hair curves together, the Puff tool is what you use to spread them out and put distance between them.

>> **Smooth:** The purpose of the Smooth tool is to reduce the kinks and pinches in your hair curves. I recommend you use it with a fairly light strength value.

>> **Slide:** If you have a hair curve where you like its shape and length, but its root is located at the wrong part of your source mesh, you can use the Slide tool to change the location of that hair curve's root.

REMEMBER

Technically speaking, the curves that you create in hair curve Sculpt mode aren't necessarily hairs in their own right. Although you can certainly use them that way, the real power is in treating them as *guide curves* that control the direction and flow of other hair strands that are added between these guides. The difficulty, of course, is that if you're really sparse with your guide curves, it's difficult to get an overall sense of how your hair is flowing.

Here's the workflow that I like to use when adding hair:

1. Add your hair curve object as described earlier in this section.

2. Switch to hair curve Sculpt mode (Ctrl+Tab ⇨ Sculpt Mode) and use the Density tool with its default settings to add hair on your model where you want it.

3. Use the other Sculpt mode tools to comb, grow, and otherwise groom the shape of your hair curves to taste.

4. Choose the Density tool again, but in the Curve Shape roll-out, enable these check boxes:

   - Length
   - Shape
   - Point Count

By enabling these check boxes, you ensure that any new hair curves generally follow the shape of the curves already in your hair system.

5. **Adjust the Distance Min value in the Density tool's tool settings to a reasonably small number.**

   You can start by testing with 0.05m, or use the preferred approach of taking advantage of the Edit Minimum Distance button's visualization.

6. **Paint over all of your existing hair curves to dramatically reduce the number of hair curves in your system.**

TIP

Like with Sculpt mode on other object types, you can take advantage of the X, Y, and Z Symmetry buttons in the Tool Settings header of the 3D Viewport to grow and comb hair curves symmetrically.

Generating additional hair strands with hair assets in the Asset Browser

Although it's possible to use the hair curves that you've directly added in Sculpt mode, you miss out on some really helpful procedural features that you can get with the rest of Blender's hair system. The key to this process is the use of Geometry Nodes to generate more hair strands in addition to your base hair curve guides. Then, those procedurally generated strands can be further tweaked using additional Geometry Node networks. Furthermore, managing and displaying hair curves can take up a lot of computing power. When animating, you don't necessarily want to be waiting on Blender to draw all your character's hair in the 3D Viewport. To deal with this problem, you can hide from the 3D Viewport some or all those additional curves generated by nodes.

Of course, setting up a complex node network for generating and managing hair curves can be difficult and time-consuming. Fortunately, Blender ships with a bunch of hair-related Geometry Node networks that are accessible as assets in the Asset Browser. To see all of these different hair assets, you need to make an Asset Browser visible. My preferred approach in the Layout workspace is to increase the height of my Timeline area and then switch that area to being an Asset Browser. If you do so, your Blender session may look like what's shown in Figure 5-4.

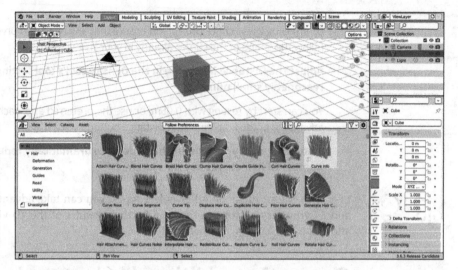

FIGURE 5-4:
Use the Asset Browser to get quick access to helpful pre-configured Geometry Node networks for hair.

Unfortunately, there isn't enough space in the book to exhaustively cover what each hair asset does exactly, but the asset categories on the left side region of the Asset Browser give a decent hint. The categories available to you are the following:

» **Deformation:** The Geometry Nodes assets in this category control how generated hair curves transition between your guide curves.

» **Generation:** The node networks in the Generation category are used to create hair curves. Technically speaking, if you know that your source mesh is supposed to be totally covered in fur, you can use the Generate Hair Curves asset to create all that hair for you without any need to jump into Sculpt mode at all.

» **Guides:** The Guide category assets are incredibly useful for styling your generated hair. You can use these assets to give your hair curls, braids, orclump them together as if they were wet.

» **Read:** The assets in the Read category are most useful if you're going to start building a really customized hair system for your character. You often need these node networks to extract information about generated hair curves so other node networks can make use of that information. For most hair situations, you won't need to use these.

» **Utility:** Like the node networks in the Read category, the assets in this category are typically used for more advanced situations.

» **Write:** The Write category only has a single asset in it by default, Set Hair Curve Profile. With this node network, you can control the general shape of each hair curve when rendered. It's definitely useful to have this asset added to your hair system because different hair can have different kinds of shapes.

Also, if you happen to use the hair system to generate a field of grass, this asset can make your hair strands have a shape that looks more like a blade of grass.

To use a hair asset, click and drag it from the Asset Browser to your hair curve in the 3D Viewport. When you release your mouse button, the hair asset shows in Modifier Properties for your hair curve object. Assuming you've followed the steps to create and groom the shape of your guide hairs, the fastest way to add generated hairs to your hair system is by using the Duplicate Hair Curves asset from the Generation category. When you click and drag this asset from the Asset Browser to your hair curve object in the 3D Viewport, you can then use the Duplicate Hair Curves modifier (it's really a Geometry Node network) in Modifier Properties to adjust the number of generated hair curves for each of your guide curves, as well as their proximity to those guide curves. Another option would be to use the Interpolate Hair Curves asset, but the Duplicate Hair Curves asset is faster and requires less setup.

Once you have generated hairs added, you have a bunch of options on what you can do next. You could go back into Sculpt mode and further refine the grooming on your hair. You can use additional assets like the ones in the Guides category to give your hair system additional features. You could even add a new hair curve object on your mesh to give it a second hair system with different properties (for example, facial hair tends to be thicker and curlier than the hair on a person's head, so it would make sense to use two different hair systems for that).

REMEMBER

There's an important thing to remember as you build out your hair system and add more assets to it from the Asset Browser. It's best to keep the Surface Deform modifier at the *bottom* of the stack, which means that every time you add an asset, it's in your best interest to move the Surface Deform network to the bottom. If you don't, your hair system may give you undesirable results.

Rendering hair in Eevee

With the hair system properly generating your hairs, the only thing you have to worry about now is controlling how Blender renders this hair. Of course, because Blender ships with two render engines, the process depends on the renderer you're using. Here's a quick-and-dirty rundown of the steps I go through to get the hair to render nicely using the Eevee renderer:

1. **In Render Properties, enable Screen Space Reflections.**

    Hair is shiny, and enabling Screen Space Reflections helps your hair material react more naturally to lights in your scene.

2. **Still in Render Properties, go to the Curve panel and switch the Curve Shape to Strip.**

   The default value of Strand gives you thick, full-bodied hair, but it also results in hair tips that are blocky and squared off. You could fix that issue with color ramps, but it's way faster to just change this property. Plus, you get slightly better render-time performance with strips as opposed to strands.

3. **Still in the Curve panel of Render Properties, increase the Additional Subdivision value to 1.**

   This setting is most helpful when doing guided features like curls or braids. Sometimes, it's necessary to push this value up to 2, but beyond that, you don't typically get much more benefit, just more processing time.

4. **Set up the material for your hair.**

   Generally speaking, the Principled BSDF should give you all the controls you need for a relatively decent hair material in Eevee. After setting a base color, the three material properties that I tend to play with the most are the Metallic, Roughness, and Anisotropic sliders in the Principled BSDF node. Since you're working with only a single node, you can perform this step right from Material Properties. For a more involved material, you'll want to use the Shader Editor (and probably the Shading workspace).

Rendering hair using Cycles

If you're rendering with Cycles, the process isn't all that different than with Eevee. To render hair curves using Cycles, follow these basic steps:

1. **In Render Properties, expand the Curves panel and tweak the Curve Subdivisions value.**

   The default value of 2 is probably sufficient, but it's worth it to check what setting you have. And that's pretty much all there is to it. Seriously. The next step is tweaking to taste.

2. **Set up the material for your hair.**

   Because you're rendering with Cycles, you have access to the super-cool Principled Hair BSDF. You can certainly use it like any other shader and directly color your hair, but there's a really cool feature nestled in the Color Parameterization drop-down menu at the top of the Principled Hair BSDF node. Instead of setting it to Direct Coloring, choose Melanin Concentration from that menu. Melanin is the protein in your hair that gives it color. Darker hair has more melanin and lighter hair has less. With this option selected, you have a couple sliders (Melanin and Melanin Redness) that you can use to quickly choose any natural-looking hair color that a character could have!

TIP

Because Eevee (which is what's used for Material Preview viewport shading) doesn't support the Principled Hair BSDF, I recommend that you use Rendered viewport shading while you tweak your hair material for Cycles. This viewport shading mode gives you a very accurate understanding of what your final render will look like.

Figure 5-5 shows the same particle system as Figure 5-3, but rendered in both Eevee and in Cycles.

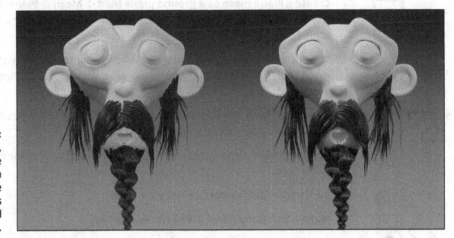

FIGURE 5-5: On the left, bearded Suzanne rendered in Eevee. On the right, she's rendered with Cycles.

Giving Objects Some Jiggle and Bounce

Have you ever sat and watched what happens when a beach ball gets hit or bounces off the ground? Or seen what happens when someone places a plate of gelatin on a table? Or observed how a person's hair moves when they shake their head? When these things move and collide with other objects, they have a bit of internal jiggle that can be difficult to reproduce correctly with regular animation tools. This jiggling is the basis for what is referred to as *soft body dynamics.*

You can simulate soft body dynamics in Blender from the Physics tab of the Properties editor. Left-click the Soft Body button, and a Soft Body panel appears. In that panel, you can make adjustments and tweak the behavior of your soft body simulation.

Just as with particle systems, adding soft body dynamics to an object from Physics Properties also adds a Soft Body modifier to your object. You can verify this addition by looking in Modifier Properties.

What follows is a basic step-by-step process for creating a simple soft body simulation with the default cube object:

1. **Select the default cube and move it up in the Z-axis so that it floats above the 3D grid.**

You can move the cube using the Move tool or more quickly by using the G hotkey. You want to give the cube some height to fall from. It doesn't have to be very high; 3 to 5 meters should be enough.

2. **Create a Plane mesh as a ground plane (Add ⇨ Mesh ⇨ Plane) and scale it larger so that you have something for the cube to hit (S or use the Scale tool).**

This plane is the surface for your jiggly cube to bounce off of. It may be helpful to put your 3D cursor at the origin (Shift+S ⇨ Cursor to World Origin) before adding the plane.

3. **With your plane still selected, add a Collision panel in Physics Properties to give your plane collision properties.**

Doing so makes Blender understand that the plane is an obstacle for your falling cube.

4. **Back in the 3D Viewport, select your cube.**

5. **Make a Soft Body panel in Physics Properties.**

That's all you really have to do to enable soft body physics on your 3D objects. However, in order to get the cube to properly act according to gravity, there's a couple more steps. Notice that adding soft body properties to your cube reveals a bunch of new panels to the Physics tab of the Properties editor.

6. **Disable the Goal check box next to its panel.**

This step disables the default goal behavior of soft bodies. When Goal is enabled, you can define a group of vertices in the object to be unaffected by the soft body simulation. A scenario where you may want to have Goal enabled would be a character with loose skin, like the jowls of a large dog. You may want the dog's snout to be completely controlled by your armature animation but have the jowls that hang off to be influenced by soft body simulation. But because, in the case of this cube, you want the entire object to be affected by the simulation, it's best just to turn it off.

If you play back the simulation now (Spacebar or click the Play button in the Timeline), it mostly works, but you see the cube start to collapse in on itself rather unrealistically. The next step can fix that.

7. **Expand the Edges panel and enable the check box for the Stiffness sub-panel.**

Enabling this check box helps prevent the edges of your cube from collapsing in on themselves like a poorly constructed tent.

8. **Play back the animation (Spacebar) to watch the cube fall, hit the ground plane, and jiggle as it lands again.**

Pretty cool, huh? Figure 5-6 shows this process being completed. As with particles, it's a good practice to make sure that you're at the start frame of your animation before playing back your simulation.

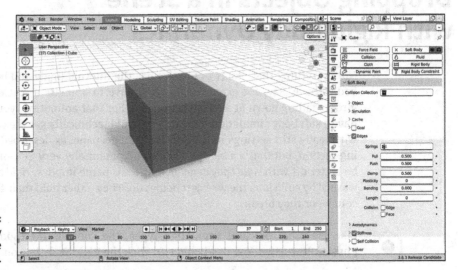

FIGURE 5-6:
Dropping a jiggly cube into the scene.

Now, I have to admit that I cheated a bit in the preceding example by using a cube. If you were to try those steps with another type of mesh, like a UV Sphere or Suzanne, the mesh would collapse and look like it instantly deflated when it hit the ground plane. To get around this issue, you need to adjust one more setting. In the Edges panel is a Bending setting with a default value of 0.00. This value sets the bending stiffness of your object. With a setting of 0, you have no stiffness, so the mesh collapses. However, if you change this setting to a higher value, such as 3.0 or 5.0, the falling mesh retains its shape a little bit better when it collides with the ground plane. If you change this value on your cube, you can disable the Stiffness check box that you enabled in Step 7. The Bending check box gets your mesh to retain its shape even better, but it can also slow down the soft body calculation substantially.

Similar to particles, if you look in the Timeline when you play your soft body simulation, you should see an orange bar along the bottom. If the orange bar is opaque, Blender has cached that part of the simulation. If it's semitransparent, that moment in time has not yet been cached. Cached simulation data plays at a rate closer to real time. To get a good idea of the timing of your simulation, let it play through all the way once, ensuring that the simulation gets cached. When you play it again, you should get a much more reasonable sense of the simulation's timing.

Dropping Objects in a Scene with Rigid Body Dynamics

Not everything that reacts to physics has the internal jiggle and bounce that soft bodies have. Say, for example, that you have to animate a stack of heavy steel girders falling down at a construction site. For that animation, you don't want to have a soft body simulation. I mean, you could technically get the correct behavior with really stiff settings in the Soft Body Edges panel as described in the preceding section, but that's a bit of a kludge and potentially very CPU-intensive. You'd be better off with *rigid body dynamics*. As their name implies, *rigid bodies* don't get warped by collisions the way soft bodies do. They either hold their form when they collide, or they break.

 Like the other physical simulation types, the controls for rigid bodies are in Physics Properties. You need only left-click the Rigid Body button.

Follow these steps to get a simple rigid body simulation with the default cube:

 1. **Select the cube and move it up in the Z-axis by a few units.**

   You can move the cube using the Move tool or more quickly by using the G hotkey. Like the soft body simulation, 3 to 5 meters should be fine.

 2. **Create a mesh plane to act as the ground (Add ⇨ Mesh ⇨ Plane) and scale it larger so that you have something for the cube to hit (S or use the Scale tool).**

 3. **With your plane still selected, add a Rigid Body panel in Physics Properties.**

   Unlike the soft bodies example, your ground plane *should not* get a collision panel. This is unique to how rigid bodies work in Blender.

4. **In your newly created Rigid Body panel, change the Type drop-down menu from Active to Passive.**

   This tells Blender that the ground plane should be part of the rigid body calculations, but that it isn't going to be a moving object. Setting the type to Passive is basically how you set up a rigid body collider.

5. **Back in the 3D Viewport, select your cube.**

6. **Make a Rigid Body panel in Physics Properties.**

   That's the last required step to have your cube drop into the scene. You may want to give the cube a bit of an arbitrary rotation (use the Rotate tool or the R ⇨ R hotkey sequence) so it lands and bounces around on the plane in a more interesting way.

7. **Play back the animation (Spacebar) to watch the cube fall, hit the ground plane, and bounce around a bit.**

   Congratulations! You have a rigid body simulation.

Figure 5-7 shows a breakdown of the preceding steps.

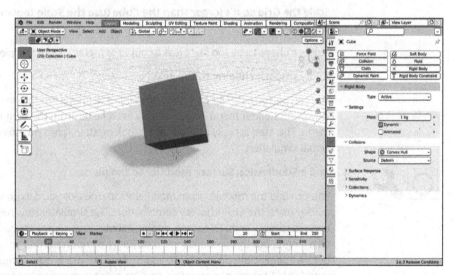

FIGURE 5-7: Creating a simple rigid body simulation.

Simulating Cloth

Cloth simulation and soft body simulation are very similar in Blender, despite a few key differences. Both soft bodies and cloth work on open as well as closed meshes — that is, the mesh could be flat like a plane, or more of a shell like a cube or sphere. However, soft bodies tend to work better on closed meshes, whereas cloth is better suited for open ones.

Also, the cloth simulator tends to work better with *self collisions*. Think about the fabric of a flowing dress. In the real world, if you bunch up part of a dress, it's technically colliding with itself. In computer simulations, you want to re-create that effect; otherwise, the fold of one part of the dress breaks through the fold of another part, giving you a completely unrealistic result. The cloth simulator handles these situations much better than the soft body simulator.

Revisiting the simple default cube (File ⇨ New ⇨ General), here's a quick walk-through on getting some cloth to drape across it:

1. **Create a mesh Grid (Add ⇨ Mesh ⇨ Grid) and move it along the Z-axis so that it's above the default cube.**

    You can move the cube using the Move tool or more quickly by using the G hotkey. This grid is going to be your cloth object. The reason why you're using a grid object rather than a plane is because the cloth simulator needs more vertices to work with than the mere four you get with a simple plane.

2. **Scale the Grid so it's larger than the Cube (use the Scale tool or the S hotkey).**

    It doesn't have to be too high; just a couple of meters should be plenty.

3. **Apply smooth shading to the grid.**

    You can perform this step by choosing Object ⇨ Shade Smooth in the 3D Viewport's header menu, or you can access it faster from the right-click context menu. This step is really just to make it look prettier. It has no effect on the actual simulation.

4. **Add a Subdivision Surface modifier to the plane.**

    You can add the modifier from Modifier Properties, or you can do it more quickly using the Ctrl+1 hotkey combination. The simulator now has even more vertices to work with. Of course, adding subdivisions causes the simulation to take longer, but this amount should be fine. It's important that you do this before adding cloth properties to your mesh. Like many other simulators, cloth is added in Blender as a modifier, and the order in the modifier stack is important.

5. **In Physics Properties, left-click the Cloth button to enable the cloth simulator.**

    The default preset for the cloth simulator is Cotton. That preset should work fine here, but feel free to play and change to something else. You can see the other available presets by clicking the presets hamburger menu on the right side of the Cloth panel's header.

6. **In the Collisions panel, enable the Self Collisions check box.**

This step ensures that the simulator does everything it can to prevent the cloth from intersecting with itself.

At this point, your cloth simulation is all set up for the plane. However, if you were to play the animation with Spacebar right now, the plane would drop right through the cube. You want the cube to behave as an obstacle, so follow the next steps.

7. **Select the cube object and left-click the Collision button in Physics Properties.**

Collision properties appear for your cube. Your simulation is set up.

8. **Press Spacebar or click the Play button in the Timeline to watch the cloth simulate.**

Figure 5-8 shows what the results of this process should look like. It's a good idea to set your time cursor at the start of your animation in the Timeline before playing back the simulation.

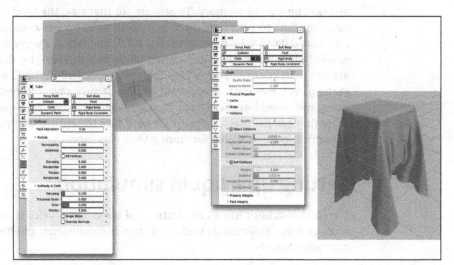

FIGURE 5-8: Creating a simple cloth simulation.

As with the other simulation types in Blender, if you select your cloth grid object and look in the Timeline when you play your cloth simulation, you should notice a bar along the bottom. In the case of cloth simulation, that bar is blue. If it's opaque, Blender has cached that part of the simulation. If it's semitransparent, that moment in time has not yet been cached. To get a good idea of the timing of your simulation, let it play through all the way once, ensuring that the simulation gets cached. On the second time playing, you should get a much more reasonable sense of the simulation's timing.

Splashing Liquids in Your Scene

In my opinion, an especially fun feature in Blender is its integrated fluid simulator. This thing is just really cool and a ton of fun to play with, to boot.

Before running headlong into fluid-simulation land, however, you should know a few things that are different about the fluid simulator. Like most of the other physics simulation controls, the main controls for the fluid simulator are in the Physics tab of the Properties editor. However, unlike particle, cloth, and soft body simulations, which can technically work in an infinite amount of space, the fluid simulator requires a *domain*, or world, for the simulation to take place.

TIP

Another difference is that the fluid simulator actually creates a separate chunk of data for each and every frame of animation that it simulates. Because of the detail involved in a fluid, these blocks of volumetric data can get to be quite large and take up a lot of memory. To account for that size, the fluid simulator actually saves the data to your hard drive in .vdb files. The other simulation systems can also save data to your hard drive, but fluid simulation always does because your whole fluid simulation usually can't be cached in RAM. By default, those files are stored in your temporary files folder (as specified in the File Paths section of Preferences). However, if you want to consistently save and replay your simulations, you should explicitly tell Blender where to save these files. Also because these files can get pretty large, it's a good idea to confirm that you have plenty of hard drive space available for storing your simulation.

Setting up a liquid simulation

The fluid simulator has all the features of the other physics simulators. It recognizes gravity, understands static and animated collisions, and has a wide array of available controls.

Follow these steps to create a simple fluid simulation:

1. **Select the default cube and scale it larger using the Scale tool or the S hotkey.**

    This cube serves as your simulation's domain object. The domain can actually be any shape or size, but I definitely recommend that you use a cube or box shape as the domain. Other meshes just use their width and height, or *bounding box*, so it's essentially a cube anyway. In this example, I scaled the default cube by a factor of 5.

2. **In Physics Properties, left-click the Fluid button and choose Domain from the Type drop-down menu.**

Now, the fluid simulator recognizes your cube as the domain for the simulation. In the 3D Viewport, your cube should now show as a wireframe with a tiny cube in one corner to indicate that it's a domain object.

3. **In the Settings panel, set your Domain Type to Liquid.**

The default domain type is Gas; this setting is more useful for smoke simulation (see the next section). Liquid is the setting that you want for this example. When you choose this setting, your cube changes to being solid rather than a wireframe.

4. **Decide what resolution you want to use for the simulation.**

This value is set with the Resolution Divisions value in the Settings panel. The defaults should work fine for this example, although higher values will look better. Be careful, though. Depending on the type of machine you're using, very large values may try to use more RAM than your computer has (despite saving data to the hard drive). These large values can bring the simulation time to a crawl or even crash Blender itself.

5. **Determine the time scale that you want to simulate the fluid's behavior.**

The Time Scale value in the Settings panel is multiplied by the overall time of your simulation, measured in seconds. By default, the simulator uses a value of 1.000, meaning that the simulation should match real time. However, if you want the simulation to look like it's in slow motion (as if it were captured by a high speed camera), you would reduce the Time Scale value.

6. **In the Cache panel, set the location where simulation meshes are saved.**

By default, Blender sends the .vdb files to their own folder in your temporary files folder. However, I recommend you create your own folder somewhere else on your hard drive to make it easier to re-open and share your simulation. Left-click the folder icon to navigate to that location with the File Browser.

7. **In Object Properties, expand the Viewport Display panel and change the Display As drop-down to Wire.**

Now your domain is displayed as a wireframe again, and you can more clearly see what's going on inside it.

8. **Create a mesh to act as the fluid in your simulation (Add ⇨ Mesh ⇨ Icosphere).**

I typically like to use an icosphere, but any mesh will work. To give yourself some more room, you may also want to move this mesh up the Z-axis to somewhere near the top of the domain cube so that you have some room for the fluid to fall.

9. **In Physics Properties, left-click the Fluid button and choose Flow from the Type drop-down menu.**

This setting lets Blender know that the icosphere is acting as a source of fluids in your scene.

10. **In the Settings panel, choose Liquid from the Flow Type drop-down menu.**

The other flow types in this menu are more related to smoke and fire, which is covered in the next section. At this point, you technically have everything you need for a fluid simulation. Your icosphere serves as the volume of liquid that's simulated in the domain. If you play the simulation (Spacebar), you should see a set of colored particles drop from your icosphere and splat at the bottom of the domain. It's fluid, yes. But it could be more exciting.

11. **(Optional) Change the Flow Behavior drop-down from Geometry to Inflow.**

Your icosphere is now set as the source for continuous liquid entering the domain. Choosing Inflow means that the mesh constantly produces more and more fluid as the simulation goes on. At this point, your simulation is configured. You can play the simulation from the Timeline (or press Spacebar) and watch your domain fill up with liquid.

Making liquids renderable

As you play your liquid simulation, you might notice that it looks an awful lot like the particle simulations covered earlier in this chapter. That's because, strictly speaking, liquid simulations are a specialized kind of particle simulation in Blender. Furthermore, if you try jumping over to the Shading workspace to add cool liquidy materials to your simulation, you'll find that the results aren't quite what you expect. Even if you go back to Object Properties and change the Display As drop-down in the Viewport Display panel to Textured, all you see is a solid cube for your domain, and a bunch of falling particles for your fluid simulation. This result can be really frustrating if you don't know how to fix it.

Fortunately, the fix is pretty simple. In short, you need to convert your fluid simulation from being purely volumetric data to being a mesh that can more properly react to light for the render engine. The work to do that conversion amounts to clicking a single check box. Follow these steps:

1. **Select your domain object.**

2. **In Physics Properties, scroll down to the Liquid panel and click the check box next to the Mesh sub-panel.**

   Immediately, the mesh of your domain object stops being a cube and starts taking a form that matches the shape of your liquid simulation. Now you have a mesh that you can add materials to.

3. **(Optional) In Object Properties, go to the Viewport Display panel and set the Display As drop-down menu to Textured.**

   Now you can see your liquid mesh in Material Preview viewport shading and adjust the materials on your liquid to your heart's content!

Baking liquids

I know that this sounds odd — "Baking liquids? Really? Won't it boil?" — but that's the terminology used. In order to ensure that your fluid simulation replays the same way every time, you want to explicitly save or "bake" your cache to your hard drive. Going through this process is most valuable if you're collaborating with other artists or sending your animation to a render farm to be rendered. You want to have high confidence that your liquid simulation will appear exactly the same way on every single computer.

Technically speaking, Blender is automatically baking the liquid cache to your hard drive by creating those .vdb files. In the previous section, you even specified where Blender should put those files. By that logic, you're already good to go. However, imagine the scenario where you've set up the basic behavior of your fluid simulation to be the way you want, but you need the actual simulation data to be at a much higher resolution. This is where explicitly baking your simulation is most useful.

To bake your liquid simulation, select your domain object and follow these steps:

1. **In Physics Properties, scroll to the Cache panel and change the Type drop-down menu from Replay to All.**

   The default value of Replay just uses playback on your Timeline to execute the bake process. Switching this to All gives you the ability to do a more explicit bake operation. When you choose this option, you should see a Bake All button appear at the bottom of the panel.

2. **Click the Bake All button and watch the progress bar in the status area of the Blender window.**

Alternatively, you may want to go make yourself a cup of tea. Depending on how powerful your computer is, this baking process can be pretty time consuming. I once had a 4-second fluid simulation that took 36 hours to bake. (Granted, it was at a high resolution, and I had a lot of crazy Inflow objects and complex moving obstacles, so it was entirely my fault.) Just know that the more complexity you add to your simulation and the higher the resolution, the more time it's going to take.

3. **Play back the finished simulation with Spacebar.**

   One thing to note here is that your mesh may look faceted. You can easily fix this issue by choosing Object ⇨ Shade Smooth or using the right-click context menu.

And, POW! You have water pouring into your scene! Using these same basic steps, you can add obstacles to the scene that can move the water around as you see fit. In fact, that's basically how I made the cover image for the 4th edition of *Blender For Dummies*, as shown in Figure 5-9!

FIGURE 5-9: Splashing orange juice out of a glass. This image was on the cover of the last version of this book.

Smoking without Hurting Your Lungs: Smoke Simulation in Blender

In addition to all the other cool physics simulation goodies that come bundled with Blender, you can also do smoke and fire simulations. The process for setting up the smoke simulator is similar to the liquid simulator. In fact, if you went through the preceding section, you may have noticed multiple times where you had to tell Blender *not* to do smoke simulation and do liquid simulation instead. However, the similarities end when you get down to trying to render the smoke. All these processes are covered in this section.

Creating a smoke simulation

Before you can render smoke, you need to set up an initial smoke simulation. Follow these steps:

1. **From the default scene, scale the cube up.**

   For this example, scaling by a factor of 5 should be fine. You can use the Scale tool or, to get the job done faster, use this hotkey sequence: S ⇨ 5 ⇨ Enter.

2. **From Physics Properties, left-click the Fluid button to create a Fluid panel.**

3. **In your new Fluid panel, choose Domain as your Type.**

   When you select Domain from the Type drop-down menu, Blender knows to treat your cube as a smoke domain. The cube automatically changes to wireframe display in the 3D Viewport, and you get a whole bunch of additional panels in Physics Properties. For now, you can leave all these settings at their defaults.

4. **Back in the 3D Viewport, add a simple mesh and lower it a bit (Add ⇨ Icosphere).**

   This object will be your smoke source. And your smoke naturally will float up, so it makes sense to lower your object a bit to give the smoke some room to show up.

5. **In Physics Properties, add a Fluid panel for your smoke source.**

6. **In your new Fluid panel, choose Flow from the Type drop-down menu.**

   This establishes your smaller object as your smoke source. There are fewer panels and options for a smoke flow object than a smoke domain, but there's still quite a few. Fortunately, you can leave these settings at their defaults for now.

7. **(Optional) Change the Flow Behavior drop-down from Geometry to Inflow.**

   Just like with the liquid simulation, this change causes smoke to constantly flow into the domain from your flow object.

8. **Play back your simulation with Spacebar.**

   Smoke should start billowing up from your flow object and stop when it reaches the faces of your smoke domain.

9. Tweak your smoke settings to taste.

There's a lot of playing that you can do here. Not only does the smoke simulator make smoke, it can simulate fire, and you can add objects to collide with the smoke in all kinds of interesting ways. You really can lose hours — perhaps days — of your life messing around with all the settings in the smoke simulator.

Those are the basics of setting up a simple smoke simulation in Blender. As Figure 5-10 shows, the 3D Viewport gives you a nice preview of your smoke simulation.

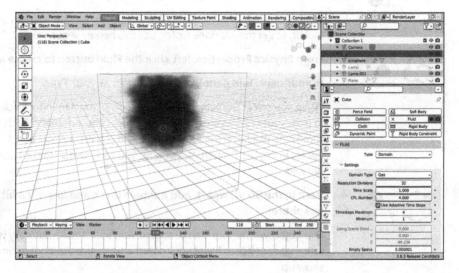

FIGURE 5-10:
A simple smoke simulation displayed in the 3D Viewport.

Unfortunately, if you try to render your smoke simulation as is, you'll be disappointed. Without doing anything further, regardless of whether you're using Eevee or Cycles, all you'll see in Material Preview or Rendered viewport shading is the wireframe shape of your smoke domain. To get your smoke simulation to render, you need to make a few more improvements, as covered in the next section.

Rendering smoke

In 3D computer graphics, smoke and fire fit into a category of materials referred to as *volumetric effects*. In meatspace, there's no such thing as a smoke object (a *smoking* object, yes, but not a smoke object). It isn't a single object. You see smoke because it's a buildup (a *volume*) of millions of small particles floating in the air. They reflect and obstruct light. Unlike solid objects, it just isn't sufficient to render the surface of smoke and fire. The result doesn't look believable. Your renderer must support volumes.

Fortunately, both the Eevee and Cycles renderers have support for volumetric materials. And as a matter of fact, setting up volumetric material in Blender has never been easier, thanks to the Principled BSDF node.

TECHNICAL STUFF

Volumetric data, like smoke simulation, is made up of voxels. A *voxel* is a volumetric pixel. This is how Blender stores your smoke simulation. Voxel data from your simulation is basically treated as a three-dimensional texture for the volumetric shader. Interestingly, Blender stores the volumetric data for your smoke simulation with the same .vdb files used for liquid simulation. All you need to do is tell Blender where the simulation data is and how it influences the material's appearance.

To get your smoke simulation rendered in either Eevee or Cycles, follow these steps:

1. **In the 3D Viewport, select your smoke domain object.**

   Since you're working with materials and shading, I suggest you perform these steps from the Shading workspace, as covered in Book 3.

2. **If your smoke domain doesn't already have a material slot, add one by clicking the Plus (+) icon next to the list box at the top of Material Properties.**

   Your smoke domain should have only one material. If you already have a material slot and material in use, just use that one and skip down to Step 4.

3. **In the Material datablock, left-click the New button to add a new material.**

   Name the material something descriptive, like Smoke. From this point, you *could* continue to work in Material Properties, but it's much easier to see what's going on (and generally good practice) from the Shader Editor.

4. **In the Shader Editor, select the Principled BSDF shader node that's there by default and delete it.**

5. **Add a Principled Volume BSDF (Add ⇨ Shader ⇨ Principled Volume) and wire it to the Volume socket of the Material Output node.**

   And poof! (Pun intended.) You have smoke in your render. From here, you can tweak colors and other attributes of your material to land on the visual effect that you want. For example, you may want to darken or thicken the feeling of your smoke.

6. **Add a Volume Info node (Add ⇨ Input ⇨ Volume Info).**

7. **Wire the Density socket of your Volume Info node to the Density socket on your Principled Volume node.**

   Upon completing this step, you should notice that your smoke gets a little bit fainter. That's because you're actually feeding the same density information to the Principled Volume node twice. Don't worry, though, you'll fix that in the next step.

8. **In the Principled Shader node find the text field next to the Density Attribute socket and remove any text from it.**

   By default, the text here should read density. Because you're populating this with the Volume Info node, you no longer need to tell the Principled Volume node the name of the Density Attribute.

9. **Add a Math node (Add ⇨ Converter ⇨ Math) and wire it inline on the noodle between the Volume Info node and the Principled Volume node.**

   REMEMBER

   Recall that you can quickly put a new node right inline on a noodle by dragging that node until the noodle is highlighted. Your smoke simulation likely hasn't changed the way its rendering all that much yet. That's because you're *adding* 0.500 to your Density value. What you really want to do is multiply.

10. **Change your new Math node to use Multiply rather than Add and increase the bottom Value slider to something larger than 1.**

    In my example, I set the value to 2.500. Once you do that, you have a slider that you can use to control how dense and thick your smoke simulation renders.

Figure 5-11 shows the same smoke simulation rendering in both Eevee and Cycles.

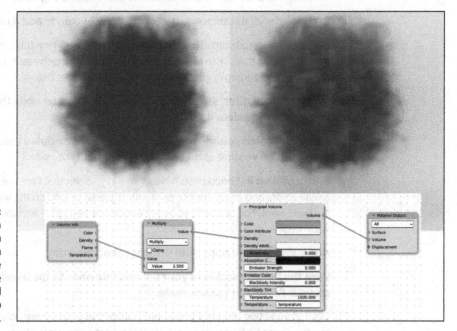

FIGURE 5-11:
On the left, a smoke simulation rendered in Eevee. On the right is the same simulation and material setup in Cycles.

Cheating (in a Good Way) by Using Quick Effects

One of the really cool features in Blender is a set of handy shortcuts for creating various effects with Blender's particle and physics systems. You find them in the Quick Effects submenu by choosing Object ⇨ Quick Effects in the 3D Viewport's header. When you call up this menu, you have four choices:

>> **Quick Fur:** Using Blender's hair and fur system, you can use this Quick Effect to set up fur for your selected object.

>> **Quick Explode:** By combining a particle system with the Explode modifier, you can procedurally break apart a selected object in your scene.

>> **Quick Smoke:** Blender's smoke simulation features require adding some additional objects to your scene to define where the simulation occurs. This Quick Effect sets those objects up for you.

>> **Quick Fluid:** Like the preceding Quick Effect, the fluid simulator also requires some supplemental objects. Choose this Quick Effect to add those to your scene, along with the necessary modifiers and physics controls.

Usage is pretty straightforward. Select the object you want to add the effect to, and then choose Object ⇨ Quick Effects and pick the effect you want to add. Blender then does all the preliminary setup and adds any supplementary objects that the effect requires to get you going. From there you can go about customizing the effect to get the results you want. Using these Quick Effects is a great way to cut corners and get yourself set up more quickly than by going through the process manually, but they're no replacement for knowing what you're doing. My recommendation would be that before you use the Quick Effects options, you work your way through this chapter so you understand how the effect works. That way, when you get to customizing it to your own tastes and needs, you know the best process for going about that.

Chapter 6

Making 2D and 2.5D Animation with Grease Pencil

Being an animator at heart, it's been exciting over the years to see Blender's Grease Pencil feature mature from being a simple means of annotating scenes to blossoming as a full-blown hand-drawn animation tool on steroids. That's right. You can do hand-drawn animation right in Blender! And even if you're not an animator, you can actually draw in Blender. There are so many talented 3D artists whose drawing skills atrophy over years because most 3D tools don't provide the facilities for a good drawing workflow. And at the same time, there are heaps of amazing 2D artists who never get into working in 3D because dealing with vertices and edges and polygons doesn't jive with their sensibilities.

Well, not any more. Blender gives you the best of both worlds with Grease Pencil. You can draw and paint in Blender just like in so many other digital painting programs. But because you're doing it in Blender, you *also* have the full power of an infinite 3D canvas and all of Blender's modeling and animation tools. This isn't a 2D painting application with some basic 3D capabilities bolted on. It's the closest I've ever felt to seeing my drawings come to life in three dimensions. Hopefully, after playing with the features and tools described in this chapter, you'll be as excited about Grease Pencil as I am.

Getting Started with the 2D Animation Workflow Template

It's absolutely possible to work with Grease Pencil objects in any of Blender's workspaces that have a 3D Viewport. However, if you want the absolute best Grease Pencil experience, I recommend using the 2D Animation workflow template that ships with Blender. To get started, choose File ➪ New ➪ 2D Animation and your Blender window should look something like the one in Figure 6-1.

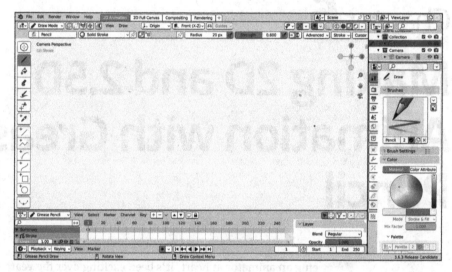

FIGURE 6-1:
Blender's 2D Animation workflow template gives you a super-comfortable environment to start drawing with Grease Pencil.

In contrast to seeing the dark 3D Viewport that you're used to seeing when you work in Blender, the 2D Animation workspace presents you with a fully white 3D Viewport that's more akin to what you'd expect when drawing on a blank canvas or sheet of paper. Furthermore, the default behavior also has you looking through the scene camera object, which is oriented in space to look down the Y-axis of the world. This way, when you render your scene, what you draw is what you get.

In addition to the 2D Animation workspace, there are also three other workspace tabs across the top of your Blender window: 2D Full Canvas, Compositing, and Rendering. I describe the purpose of each of these workspaces in Book 1, Chapter 2. For the most part, though, I recommend doing most of your work in the default 2D Animation workspace. The Compositing and Rendering workspaces are basically the same workspaces you have available when working on a traditional 3D project, and the 2D Full Canvas workspace is best when you've got all your base drawing done and your primary focus is on animation.

Another default that you get with the 2D Animation workflow template is that your scene is pre-populated with Grease Pencil Stroke object, and you're already in Draw mode for that object. This fact brings to light two important things to keep in mind:

>> Grease Pencil objects have a special Draw mode in addition to some of the other standard Blender modes.

>> Unlike other Blender objects, the only Add menu for Grease Pencil is when you're in Object mode.

Because you typically add to a Grease Pencil object by drawing, primitives like the ones you have for mesh objects aren't as helpful. In fact, there are only three Grease Pencil primitives that ship with Blender, plus a few handy shortcuts for the Line Art modifier (I briefly touch on this later in the chapter). If you're in Object mode and choose Add ⇨ Grease Pencil, you see the following choices:

>> **Blank:** In most situations, the Blank Grease Pencil object is what you want to start with. There's nothing already in there. It's just an empty container on which you can switch to Draw mode and get right to drawing.

Of course, if you're going to add a Blank object to your scene, I strongly recommend that you immediately name it something sensible in the Outliner, especially if you don't begin drawing in it immediately. Otherwise, your scene will be littered with blank objects named GPencil and GPencil.001 that you can only find and select in the Outliner.

>> **Stroke:** The Stroke Grease Pencil object is a simple curved stroke. You could use this as a starting point for a Grease Pencil drawing, but unless you're testing Grease Pencil features like modifiers (described later in this chapter), your first move will likely be deleting or erasing that base stroke.

That said, one of the things about the Stroke object that makes it attractive as a starting point is the fact that it comes prepopulated with layers and materials so you can get to work immediately without needing to set all that up. In fact, the default object that you get in the 2D Animation start file is a Stroke object with that first stroke removed.

>> **Monkey:** If mesh objects can have a Suzanne for doing tests and examples, why shouldn't there be one for Grease Pencil objects? Of course, although the Grease Pencil Suzanne retains a lot of the same base attributes of the mesh Suzanne in terms of shape, it's not a mere conversion. The Grease Pencil Suzanne is her own monkey, and she's great for testing out all of Grease Pencil's features.

NEW FEATURE

>> **Line Art Primitives:** In more recent releases of Blender, the developers have added a new Grease Pencil modifier called the Line Art modifier. I get into more details on Grease Pencil modifiers later in the chapter, but the Line Art modifier is notable because it automatically generates Grease Pencil strokes based on 3D geometry in your scene. This modifier is particularly useful for adding outlines to 3D models that you want to render in a cartoony way. The following three primitives give you a shortcut to using this modifier by adding a Grease Pencil object with the modifier already added, along with a few preset settings:

- **Scene Line Art:** Choose this menu item and Blender adds an empty Grease Pencil object with a Line Art modifier that's set to use the whole 3D scene as its source. Every 3D object in the scene receives Grease Pencil strokes.

- **Collection Line Art:** Use this menu item if you want to have a Grease Pencil object that has the Line Art modifier with a single collection as its source. By default, Blender uses the current active collection when you add this Line Art primitive.

- **Object Line Art:** Assume you only want to add Grease Pencil strokes to outline a single object in your scene. Choose this item to make that happen.

Figure 6-2 shows both the Stroke and Monkey primitives for Grease Pencil, along with an Object Line Art primitive that uses a mesh Suzanne as its source.

REMEMBER

One key thing to keep in mind as you work in Draw mode is that the 2D Animation workspace is designed to feel comfortable to artists with a background in 2D digital painting programs. The expectation is that you take much more advantage of the Tool Settings region at the top of the 3D Viewport for changing brushes, adjusting brush settings, and changing the layer that you're working on. Of course, if you don't like working that way, you always have access to adjusting brush and tool settings from the Tool tab of the 3D Viewport's Sidebar or the Tool tab of the Properties editor. However, since it's likely that you'll want to be able to quickly adjust tool settings as well as layers or materials, it makes sense to keep the Properties editor on the Material tab or the Object Data tab and manage your tool settings from the Tool Settings region in the 3D Viewport.

FIGURE 6-2:
The primitives
for Grease Pencil:
Blank, Stroke,
and Monkey
(of course!),
but the Line
Art primitives
allow you to
automatically
generate strokes
for any 3D object.

Working with Grease Pencil Tools

At this point, Grease Pencil objects are nearly as powerful and flexible as mesh objects in Blender. They're truly first-class citizens, with dedicated modes for drawing, editing, sculpting, and even modifiers. Short of creating hyper-realistic images, you can make (and animate!) just about anything you want with Grease Pencil objects.

Blender provides a wide array of modes for working with Grease Pencil objects. When you work with Grease Pencil objects, the general workflow goes something like this:

1. Draw.

Using Draw mode, you flesh out your Grease Pencil object, setting up layers and colors, as well as roughing in your general drawn image.

2. Sculpt.

Grease Pencil objects have a Sculpt mode, similar to mesh objects. You can use the tools in Sculpt mode to massage the line work of your Grease Pencil drawings and tune their shapes after you've already drawn them. Sculpt mode also comes in handy when animating because you can take existing art and nudge it around to give that art movement.

3. Edit.

In a lot of ways, Grease Pencil objects are just like any other object. They have an Edit mode, too! Blender's Edit mode tools are great for really adding that last bit of polish to your drawn artwork. With the tools in Edit mode, you can select the individual control points of your drawing and place elements exactly where you want them in 3D space.

4. **Modify.**

Like working with mesh objects, Grease Pencil objects can have modifiers to help automate some effects or generally make your life easier as an artist. You can even use modifiers to build animation rigs so you can animate Grease Pencil objects more like 3D objects instead of redrawing on every frame.

5. **Animate.**

Some people use Grease Pencil just to make really cool 2D images. In fact, I know of at least two different web comics that are produced with the help of Grease Pencil objects in Blender. However, where Grease Pencil objects really shine is in animation. Animating is what they're made for, and that's where you can really experience everything these little objects have to offer.

Of that workflow, this section covers the tools used in the first three steps.

Drawing with Grease Pencil

Unless you're starting with the Suzanne primitive, everything with Grease Pencil objects starts with drawing; the 2D Animation workspace defaults to putting you in Draw mode on your selected Grease Pencil object. The fundamental unit of a Grease Pencil object is a drawn stroke. The tools in Draw mode are what you use to create those strokes.

TIP

You can also import vector drawings in SVG format as Grease Pencil objects in Blender. So if someone has created artwork outside of Blender in a vector drawing application like Inkscape or Adobe Illustrator, you can import that work and add Grease Pencily goodness to them.

Working with brushes for the Draw tool

As you may guess, the Draw tool is what you spend the bulk of your time using while in Draw mode. In a lot of ways, the Draw tool for Grease Pencil objects is like any of the Sculpt mode tools for mesh objects (see Book 2, Chapter 3 for more on sculpting meshes). The Draw tool has some basic settings, but it serves as a container for a variety of brushes. Unlike the mesh-sculpting tools that default with having only one brush datablock per tool, the Draw tool for Grease Pencil ships with eight basic brushes:

>> **Airbrush:** This brush gives the feeling of working with an airbrush or spray paint on your canvas, with soft edges and accumulated buildup of color. You may want to use it for blocking in your drawing, but I tend to prefer it for soft coloring, subtle shading, and diffuse highlights.

>> **Ink Pen:** In cartoon animation and comic book art, the inking process was what you did after you'd gotten the basic sketch of your drawing complete. In the Draw tool, the Ink Pen brush serves the same purpose. One of the nice things about this brush is that it doesn't stop abruptly when you stop drawing; the stroke nicely tapers at each end of your stroke.

>> **Ink Pen Rough:** One of the nice things about hand-drawn animation in traditional media is the life that your linework can have, due to unexpected and sometimes imperceptible variations in the surface you're drawing on or the pen tip itself. That variation can give your linework a vibrant, organic feel, and the Ink Pen Rough brush tries to replicate that in your Grease Pencil strokes.

>> **Marker Bold:** I've personally never been skilled at drawing or coloring with markers in meatspace, but I stand in awe at the people who can. The Marker Bold brush datablock gives the Draw tool a feel similar to that of drawing and coloring with a round thick-tipped marker.

>> **Marker Chisel:** Think of this brush as if you're drawing with a highlighter or, if you go way back in traditional media, a blue pencil. The Marker Chisel brush is ideal for roughing in the general shape of your drawing, including construction lines and other scribble aids to get your silhouette and proportions right. I like to use this as a kind of sketching brush.

>> **Pen:** The Pen brush behaves similarly to the Ink Pen brush, but with much less line variation. Think of the Ink Pen tool as drawing with a physical brush or calligraphy pen, whereas the Pen brush is more like a ballpoint or rapidograph pen.

>> **Pencil:** The Pencil brush is what Blender defaults to when you first choose the Draw tool. Like the Marker Chisel brush, the Pencil brush is great for sketching and getting the rough form of your drawing in place. At larger brush radii, the Pencil brush is also quite nice for shading.

>> **Pencil Soft:** Speaking of shading, the Pencil Soft brush is the champion of shading when using the Draw tool. You can certainly use fills on your objects, but it depends on the final effect you want to see. If you want a more sketchy or painterly look, the Pencil Soft brush is a huge help.

As for using the Draw tool, if you've used Blender's sculpting (see Book 2, Chapter 3) or painting tools (see Book 3, Chapters 1 and 2), then the interface should be pretty familiar to you. Left-click and drag in the 3D Viewport to add strokes. Press F to visually adjust the radius of your brush cursor. Press Shift+F to visually adjust the brush's strength. And if you're working with a pressure-sensitive drawing tablet, Blender recognizes and takes advantage of that pressure sensitivity for both brush radius and strength. You can toggle pressure sensitivity with the Use Pressure button in your brush's tool settings.

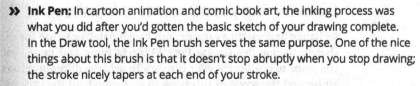

Customizing your Draw tool brushes

As handy and useful as the default brush datablocks are for drawing and creating shapes, as you use Grease Pencil objects more and more, you'll likely find that you want to customize your brushes to achieve different effects with them. It's a bit beyond the scope of this book to go through all the various brush settings and show how to tweak them. However, I can say that the basic steps are the same ones you take to make custom sculpt brushes or painting brushes:

1. **Choose the brush that's the most similar to the one you want to create.**

2. **In Tool Properties, go to the Brush datablock in the Brush panel and click the Add Drawing Brush button.**

   The Add Drawing Brush button looks like two pieces of paper stacked upon one another. Clicking this button duplicates your current brush and gives you a starting point for making your custom brush.

3. **Within the Brush datablock, rename your brush to something that makes sense to you.**

   To further customize your brush, you can go down to the Display panel and give your brush a custom icon. It can be any image you want, but smaller square images tend to work best.

4. **Customize your brush settings to taste.**

As you customize your brushes, you may find yourself wondering how to make textured brushes for Grease Pencil, much like how you would for sculpt or painting brushes. You may also find yourself disappointed that there isn't a Texture panel at all in your brush datablock's tool properties like you might expect.

But worry not, dear Blenderhead! The feature is indeed available! The reason why you can't find a way to add textures to your brushes in your brush settings is because they're actually controlled by Grease Pencil materials. This organization may seem odd at first, but it starts to make sense as you come to understand how Grease Pencil materials work. I cover that later in this chapter in the section appropriately entitled, "Understanding Grease Pencil Materials." In the meantime, you can switch to the Material tab of the Properties editor and have a look at the Stroke sub-panel (it's within the Surface panel). In that sub-panel, there's a drop-down menu, labeled Style. By default, this property is set to Solid, but if you click it, you can change it to Texture. Once you change the Style property to Texture, Blender provides you with an Image datablock that you can use to load an image from your hard drive as a brush texture. Figure 6-3 shows a few examples of customized Grease Pencil brushes that can be made.

FIGURE 6-3:
Blender's default
Grease Pencil
brushes are
great, but it's
even better to
make your own
custom ones!

There are quite a few artists that are loving Blender's Grease Pencil objects more and more. Even better, they're creating and sharing custom brushes that you can use and further customize on your own. One of the best places to start looking for custom brushes is over on the Blender Cloud (studio.blender.org). The site is a subscription-based resource service set up by the folks at the Blender Foundation, but they also provide quite a few free assets (like brushes!) that anyone can download and use. Alternatively, you can also go to Blender Market (blendermarket.com), which is a market place for all kinds of assets and add-ons created in Blender. There are a few really nice brush packs there as well.

Understanding the other tools in Draw mode

Even though you spend a large amount of time in a Draw mode using the Draw tool, you shouldn't forget that there are a bunch of other useful tools available for you to work with. Working down the Toolbar, these are the other tools you can use on Grease Pencil objects while in Draw mode:

>> **Fill:** The Fill tool takes a bit of getting used to. The reason it may feel strange at first is because it depends on the active material slot you have selected in Material Properties. There's more on Grease Pencil material later in this chapter, but the main thing to remember is that the Fill tool only really works if you're using a material that has filling enabled. Once you know that, the Fill tool starts to behave as expected. Left-click anywhere within an enclosed stroke and the Fill tool fills it with your selected material.

If you want to fill an area that isn't fully enclosed, you can Alt+left-click and drag to draw a *boundary line* so you have an enclosed area to fill. You can remove boundary lines later in Edit mode by choosing Grease Pencil ⇨ Clean Up ⇨ Boundary Strokes.

» Erase: As you might expect, the Erase tool does the opposite of what the Draw tool does. Depending on the specific brush datablock that you choose, the Erase tool removes strokes, in part or in whole, from your drawing. Blender ships with four eraser brush datablocks:

- **Hard:** The difference between the Hard Eraser brush and the Soft Eraser is pretty subtle. They both have soft edges where you erase using your brush cursor. The main difference is that the Hard Eraser brush is slightly more aggressive and more likely to remove parts of your stroke and not leave semitransparent bits dangling about.

- **Point:** The Point Eraser brush works on the actual geometry of your stroke. Each Grease Pencil stroke is similar to Blender's curve objects. It consists of a number of control points connected by segments. When you use the Point Eraser, if your brush cursor has a control point within its radius when you click and drag in the 3D Viewport, that whole control point is completely deleted, and the stroke comes to an abrupt end right there.

- **Soft:** The Soft Erase brush is the default datablock that's active when you first choose the Erase tool. As its name implies, think of using it like a soft white eraser when working with traditional media.

- **Stroke:** By far the most aggressive brush in the set that comes with the Erase tool, the Stroke Erase brush flat-out deletes any stroke it comes into contact with. It has the power to obliterate your whole drawing with just a few sweeps of your brush cursor but used judiciously, the Stroke Erase brush is fantastic for cleaning up construction lines and rough sketches.

» Tint: Using the Tint tool, you can paint on existing Grease Pencil strokes, influencing their color with whatever color you have associated with this tool in its Tool Settings.

» Cutter: The best way of thinking about the Cutter tool is to imagine that you've combined the Lasso Select tool with the Point Eraser brush. When you select this tool, you can draw a selection area with your mouse cursor. Blender deletes any control points on your stroke that fall within the area that you draw.

» Eyedropper: The Eyedropper tool isn't used for drawing, but it's extremely handy for creating materials with a consistent color palette. When you click in the 3D Viewport with the Eyedropper tool, Blender adds a new material to your current Grease Pencil object that matches the color you clicked upon.

The preceding list of tools give you controls that feel a lot like painting or drawing. Blender also offers the ability to create shapes more akin to what you could do in a vector drawing program like Inkscape or Affinity Designer. Freeform drawing is fantastic fun, but sometimes you need to get a bit more precise in your drawings. It's useful to have some base shapes with additional controls so you can do more precision work, like for blueprints, technical drawing, or logo design. Fortunately, Blender offers six specific tools in Draw mode to help you.

Generally speaking, after you select the tool, you need to left-click and drag in the 3D Viewport to start drawing the shape you want. Once you release your mouse button, you have the general shape of your stroke with some additional controls. Use those controls to customize the shape, and then press Enter to convert that shape to a finalized Grease Pencil stroke using the brush datablock you pick from your tool settings. You can press Esc to cancel drawing with any of these tools.

The following are the shape tools available:

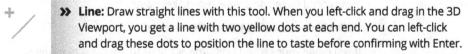

>> **Line:** Draw straight lines with this tool. When you left-click and drag in the 3D Viewport, you get a line with two yellow dots at each end. You can left-click and drag these dots to position the line to taste before confirming with Enter.

>> **Polyline:** Draw multiple connected straight lines using the Polyline tool. Click and drag in the 3D Viewport to start the first segment. Then continue clicking in the 3D Viewport to add subsequent segments to your polyline.

>> **Arc:** Similar to the Line tool, the Arc tool gives you a line with two yellow controls at each end, but it also provides a cyan dot that you can use to control the shape of your arc before confirming with Enter.

>> **Curve:** Continuing the theme of adding a line with additional controls, the Curve tool gives you a line with *two* cyan control dots. With those controls you can tweak the shape of your curve much like you would tweak the shape of a NURBS curve object (see Book 2, Chapter 4).

>> **Box:** Using the Box tool, you can draw squares and rectangles in your scene. When you left-click and drag in the 3D Viewport, you get two yellow controls for adjusting the size of your box. The red dot in the center serves as a frame of reference so you can tell where the center is. If you want to draw a square with the Box tool, you need to hold Shift when you do your initial left-click and drag. Likewise, you can have your box grow around the center point by holding Alt as you draw the square. As of this writing, when you tweak the shape of the square, the Alt and Shift keys don't have an effect.

>> **Circle:** The Circle tool operates with the exact same controls as the Box tool. If you want a perfect circle growing around the center point, hold Shift and Alt as you draw.

There's one further tool in Draw mode that's incredibly useful when you're doing hand-drawn animation with Grease Pencil objects. It's the Interpolate tool at the very bottom of the Draw mode Toolbar. This tool generates strokes interpolated based on the neighboring keyframes on the Timeline. To get a sense of how the

Interpolate tool works, start a new Blender session with the 2D Animation workflow template (File ⇨ New ⇨ 2D Animation) and follow these steps:

1. **Draw a rectangle with the Box tool.**

This drawing is your first keyframe.

2. **In the Timeline, move forward a handful of frames.**

10 frames should be fine.

3. **In the 3D Viewport, use the box tool to draw another rectangle, but in a different location or at a different size.**

This second rectangle is your second keyframe.

4. **In the Timeline, move back a few frames**.

If you made your second keyframe at frame 10, try going to frame 5.

5. **In the 3D Viewport, choose the Interpolate tool and click and drag your mouse cursor from left to right in the 3D Viewport.**

Blender automatically tries to create your in-between, or breakdown, keyframe by interpolating between the keyframes on frame 1 and frame 10. If you keep your mouse button pressed and move your mouse cursor left and right, you can adjust the interpolated result to taste.

The Interpolate tool doesn't always give you perfect results, but often, it can get you a good enough starting point that you can pretty easily tweak and refine the results much more quickly than if you were to redraw them from scratch.

Sculpting Grease Pencil objects

After you have your drawing created in a Grease Pencil object, you may want to go in and do some custom tweaks. Perhaps you want thicker or thinner lines in some places. Or maybe you drew the whole thing with your mouse, and the line-work is all shaky and uneven, so you need to smooth it out. Or it could be that your proportions are slightly off, and you need to push the parts of your drawing around to fix it. Perhaps you did your original Grease Pencil without the benefit of a pressure-sensitive tablet, and you want to add variation to line thickness and opacity after the fact. For those kinds of situations, Blender's Sculpt mode for Grease Pencil objects is perfect.

You can quickly switch between modes by pressing Ctrl+Tab and using the mode switching pie menu.

REMEMBER

When you enter Sculpt mode on a Grease Pencil object, you have the following tools at your disposal:

» **Smooth:** Choose this tool, and you can use it to take the jitter out of any strokes you made while drawing. One thing to note about the Smooth tool is that it affects the control points of your stroke, not really the stroke itself. That means if you created a stroke using the Ink Pen Rough brush in Draw mode, the Smooth tool isn't going to reduce the noisiness of the stroke, just the smoothness of the segments from one control point to the next.

Like the Smooth tool when mesh sculpting, you can quickly access this tool from any other tool by holding down Shift as you left-click and drag in the 3D Viewport.

» **Thickness:** If you find that you're not satisfied with the line width of the strokes in your drawing, you can use the Thickness tool to adjust it. Left-click and drag over a stroke and it gets wider. If you hold Ctrl while sculpting with the Thickness tool, it reduces the width of the strokes your brush cursor touches.

» **Strength:** Think of this as a kind of opacity tool for sculpting. Using this tool you can make semitransparent strokes more opaque and, if you hold down Ctrl, you can soften strokes that are already dark.

» **Randomize:** The Randomize tool is kind of like the evil doppelganger of the Smooth tool. Rather than reduce variation along the length of a stroke, the Randomize brush *increases* variability, ultimately making your linework more shaky and uneven. Used with animation, this sculpt tool could be used to add a bit of "line boil" to your lines so they undulate over time.

» **Grab:** Much like the corresponding tool in mesh sculpting, the Grease Pencil sculpting Grab tool moves the control points of your strokes around, as if you'd selected them in Edit mode and moved them with Proportional Editing enabled.

» **Push:** I tend to think of the Push tool as a kind of cousin of the Grab tool. Functionally, they're similar in that they move around the control points that are within the area of your brush cursor. However, the Push tool relies more on the direction you move that brush cursor. If you've worked with a "liquefy" effect in 2D graphics applications, the Push tool feels very much like that.

» **Twist:** You might think that the Twist tool is like the Rotate tool when mesh sculpting or even the regular Rotate tool. If you do, you're only partially correct. Although this tool does rotate control points that are under your brush cursor, it's more of a cumulative effect; you don't have to move your brush cursor at all. Just hold down the left mouse button and anything within the area of the brush cursor spins around its center. By default, the Twist tool spins things counterclockwise. Hold down Ctrl to twist in the clockwise direction.

>> **Pinch:** When you sculpt with the Pinch tool, any control points within the area of your brush cursor are pulled to its center. By sculpting with this tool, you can pull control points closer to each other. Hold down Ctrl to repel control points from the center of your brush cursor, effectively spreading them apart.

>> **Clone:** The Clone tool allows you to paste copies of a stroke in other parts of the scene. This tool is not at all like the Clone tool when in Texture Paint mode. The only similarity is that you need to select a reference to actually clone. In the case of the Clone tool in Grease Pencil's Sculpt mode, you make that reference by selecting all or part of a stroke in Edit mode and copying it (Grease Pencil ⇨ Copy or Ctrl+C). With a stroke copied, Ctrl+Tab back over to Sculpt mode, and you can use the Clone tool to paste as many copies of that stroke as you'd like.

Editing Grease Pencil objects

Grease Pencil objects are proper 3D objects just like any other in Blender. As such, it makes sense that they should also have an Edit mode where you can manually add, remove, and generally modify the components of those objects. For the most part, the tools in Edit mode should be familiar to you if you've worked with other object types in Blender. The usual transform tools (Move, Rotate, Scale, Transform) are at the top of the Toolbar. The next set of tools are very much like their counterparts in Edit mode for meshes and curves:

>> **Extrude:** With the Extrude tool you have the same extrude widget that's also available for mesh and curve objects. Select one or more control points and then activate this tool. From there you can left-click the yellow plus symbol on the Extrude tool's widget and extrude more control points from your stroke. If you're more comfortable using hotkeys to extrude, you should be happy to know that the E hotkey also works for Grease Pencil objects, regardless of what the active tool is.

>> **Radius:** The Radius tool is Edit mode's corresponding version of the Thickness tool in Sculpt mode. The primary difference in this case is that the Radius tool affects only the selected control points in your stroke. Though you can use various forms of masking to limit the influence of the Thickness tool in Sculpt mode, the Radius tool in Edit mode is much nicer for adjusting the width of your line with more accuracy.

Bend: The Bend tool is useful for performing very simple deformation adjustments to selected parts of your stroke. The thing to remember about the Bend tool is that it always works relative to the location of the 3D cursor; so if you plan to use the Bend tool, you should make the 3D cursor visible from the Overlays roll-out in the 3D Viewport's header.

 Shear: The Shear tool does a shear operation on your selected control points. That is, if your stroke is the shape of a rectangle and you want to change it to a parallelogram, the Shear tool is the right tool for the job. There are two things to remember about the Shear tool:

- It always shears relative to the horizontal or vertical axis that you're viewing your selection from.

- Vertical shearing is the default behavior. You can change between horizontal and vertical shearing by pressing and releasing the middle mouse button while in the middle of shearing.

 To Sphere: To access the To Sphere tool, you need to long-press on the Shear tool's button in the Toolbar. Once activated, you just need to left-click and drag in the 3D Viewport and your selected control points will adjust position to assume a more sphere-like shape relative to the center of that selection.

Transform Fill: The Transform Fill tool works only on selected strokes that have fills in their material. However, if you do have this sort of stroke in your Grease Pencil drawing, you can use the Transform Fill tool to adjust the position, rotation, and size of the fill you have in your material, regardless of whether it's a gradient or a texture.

Interpolate: The Interpolate tool in Edit mode behaves exactly like the Interpolate tool in Grease Pencil's Draw mode.

One thing to remember as you edit and sculpt your Grease Pencil drawings is that even though you're drawing in just two dimensions, these objects exist in all three. You can move control points or even whole strokes closer or farther away from the camera, giving your drawn objects real dimensionality.

Understanding Grease Pencil Materials

One thing to keep in mind as you work with Grease Pencil objects is that despite the amount of flexibility and the generally pleasant drawing experience that they provide, drawing in Grease Pencil is a lot more like working in 2D vector drawing programs like Inkscape or Illustrator than raster-based digital painting programs like Krita or Photoshop. You may be able to have organic brush strokes with a textured appearance and smooth tonal changes, but at the core, you're

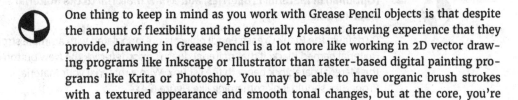

still working with curve-based strokes. The upside of this approach is that it's generally nondestructive, meaning that you have a lot of freedom to go back and make changes to your drawings with the incredible tools described in the preceding sections. The downside is that choosing colors and mixing strokes can be a bit more complicated.

Being 3D objects, Blender's Grease Pencil objects get their color and texture properties not from the brush you use when drawing, but from material properties you define in the Material tab of the Properties editor. If you're coming from a 2D painting application, this approach might feel a little alien, but if you're familiar with how materials work on other 3D objects in Blender, you should feel right at home. Likewise, if you're coming from a 2D animation tool like OpenToonz or ToonBoom, Blender's material-based approach should feel pretty familiar.

To get an understanding of how everything works, it's best to start from scratch. Start a new 2D Animation file (File ➪ New ➪ 2D Animation) and follow these steps:

1. Ctrl+Tab to Object mode and delete the default Stroke object that Blender starts you with.

Generally speaking, the default object you get in the 2D Animation start file is great, but for this example, it's best to get it out of the way and start fresh.

2. Add a Blank Grease Pencil Object to your scene (Add ➪ Grease Pencil ➪ Blank).

The Blank object is truly a bare-minimum starting point. It's just a container for you to start filling with Grease Pencily goodness.

3. Ctrl+Tab into Draw mode and with the Draw tool, choose the Marker Chisel brush.

It could be any brush datablock really, but the Marker Chisel brush gives a nice wide stroke that will make it easier to see changes that you make.

4. Draw any kind of line you want.

It doesn't have to be extravagant or pretty. The idea is that you're going to use this to play with Grease Pencil materials. If you're at a loss of what to draw, just write your name.

5. (Optional) In Material Properties, add a new material to the material slots list box.

By default, the Blank Grease Pencil object is pre-populated with a simple stroke material named Black. If that material doesn't exist, left-click the New button in the Material datablock beneath the list box. With a material your Material Properties should look something like Figure 6-4.

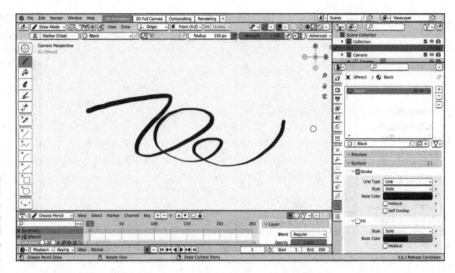

FIGURE 6-4:
Material
Properties with
a single Grease
Pencil material
added to
your object.

The main working area for a Grease Pencil material is in the Surface panel. Within that panel there are two sub-panels, Stroke and Fill. By default the Stroke sub-panel is enabled and the Fill sub-panel is disabled. If you disable the check box at the top of the Stroke sub-panel, your stroke in the 3D Viewport disappears. Likewise, toggling the Fill check box results in Blender trying to fill the stroke you drew (if your stroke isn't an enclosed shape, the result will probably be quite ugly). For the next step, make sure that the Stroke sub-panel is enabled and the Fill sub-panel is disabled.

6. **In the Stroke sub-panel, change the settings for your stroke.**

   As you make changes, you can see your stroke update at the same time in the 3D Viewport. Within the Stroke sub-panel, you have two primary properties:

   - **Mode Type:** From this drop-down menu you can dramatically change the look of your stroke. The default type of Line is great for smooth, continuous lines. However, if you plan to use image-based textures for your strokes, you may prefer the Dots or Squares mode types.

   - **Style:** There are only two options for this property: Solid and Texture. With the Solid style, you get a Color swatch that you can use to change the color of your material. That color material fills the whole space of your stroke, depending on the mode type you choose. If you choose the Texture style, however, you can choose any image file on your hard drive and use that as the texture for your stroke material. From there, you can adjust the spacing of that image along your stroke with the UV Factor value or mix it with a solid color by enabling the Mix Color check box.

   For the sake of simplicity, just change your mode type to Dots and change your stroke color to something fun. Maybe orange. Upon making those changes, your Blender session may look like Figure 6-5.

FIGURE 6-5:
Changing the
Stroke properties
of your Grease
Pencil material
gives you a lot of
control over how
it looks, and you
can watch those
changes happen
in real time in the
3D Viewport.

7. **Back in the 3D Viewport, use the Draw tool to make an enclosed stroke.**

Just drawing a circle should be fine.

8. **In Material Properties, use the Plus button to the right of the material slots list box to add a new material slot.**

You have a new material slot, but you still need to create a material to fill that slot.

9. **Left click the New button in the Material datablock to create a new material.**

At this point, you may have expected your last stroke to adopt the properties of the new material you created. That's not what happened, though. You just created a material. You haven't assigned it to any strokes in your drawing. There's no way to assign materials on strokes you've already created while in Draw mode. To do that, you need to switch to Edit mode.

10. **In the 3D Viewport, Ctrl+Tab to Edit mode and select at least one control point on your enclosed stroke.**

It's not possible to partially assign materials on a stroke. Each stroke is only one material.

11. **In Material Properties, assign your new material to your selected stroke.**

Select the material slot you want to use in the material slots list box and left-click the Assign button beneath the Material datablock. If you selected the control points in your second stroke (the enclosed one), it should immediately switch to using the material in the second material slot.

12. **Still in Material Properties, enable the check box at the top of the Fill sub-panel.**

You drew an enclosed shape; you may as well take advantage of it. Looking at the Style property in the Fill sub-panel, you actually have three different choices for fill styles:

- **Solid:** Plain but reliable, this fill style does as you expect. You fill the enclosed space with a solid color.

- **Gradient:** When you choose the Gradient fill style, you get an array of properties that you can use to control the color, size, and position of your gradient, be it linear or radial. If you choose the Gradient fill pattern, I suggest you change the Mix Factor value from 0.000 to 0.500 so you can see what you're doing.

- **Texture:** Like the Texture style for strokes, the Texture fill style for fills gives you the ability to choose any image on your hard drive as a fill pattern. Choosing this option expands the Fill sub-panel with controls for the size, placement, and orientation of your fill texture.

13. **In the 3D Viewport, Ctrl+Tab back to Draw mode.**

Your Blender session should look something like what's shown in Figure 6-6.

At this point, you've got a single Grease Pencil object with two different materials. The really cool thing now is that each material is completely available to you when drawing new strokes.

FIGURE 6-6:
A single Grease Pencil object with two materials on it, one a dotted stroke and the other a solid enclosed stroke filled with a gradient fill.

14. **Choose the first material in the material slots list box and draw a new stroke in the 3D Viewport.**

Blender draws with that material.

15. **Switch over to your second material and draw another stroke in the 3D Viewport.**

Now you're drawing with the second of your materials!

If you want to create another material for new strokes, it's as easy as adding a new material slot, populating it with a new material, and using that for your next stroke. I like to think of this process like I'm building a palette of stroke types that I can use when drawing in the 3D Viewport. It may seem a bit limiting in the fact that the only looks you can have for your strokes are the ones you define in Material Properties, but the trade-off is that you get an enormous amount of flexibility by using Blender's material system. Have a look at Figure 6-7. With just a few minutes of adjusting just the materials that come with Suzanne, you can get some rather dramatic changes to her appearance.

FIGURE 6-7:
With just a little bit of playing around with materials on Suzanne.

NEW FEATURE

In upcoming versions of Blender (version 4.0 and beyond), changes are planned for how Blender handles materials for Grease Pencil objects. The details of how this new system will work aren't finalized as of this writing, but the plan is for Grease Pencil objects to have the ability to use Eevee materials (and material shader networks) just like any other 3D object in Blender. The downside is that such a system is likely to be quite different from what's described in this chapter. However, the upside is that if you already know how to use Blender's material system for meshes and other 3D objects, then you'll have the tools to use this new system for Grease Pencil.

Mastering Grease Pencil Layers

In addition to being able to work with multiple materials and independently assigning strokes to them, Grease Pencil objects also have built-in layers, similar to the way that Armature objects have built-in layers. The difference, however, is that layers for Grease Pencil objects behave a lot more like layers in digital drawing and painting applications. That is to say, instead of just being mere collections of strokes, the order of layers in Grease Pencil objects actually matters. They're arranged in a stack, with the layers at the top occluding the layers beneath them.

 You manage all the layers in a Grease Pencil object from the Object Data tab of the Properties editor. It's the first panel at the top of that tab and in the Layers roll-out in the Tool Settings region of the 3D Viewport, as shown in Figure 6-8.

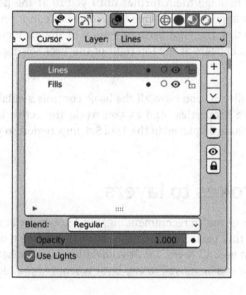

FIGURE 6-8: Use the Layers roll-out in the 3D Viewport's Tool Settings region to quickly change layers so you can keep the Properties editor available for tweaking materials as you draw.

You can organize your layers however you see fit. That said, I like to start off with three layers on my Grease Pencil objects when I start working:

>> **Lines/Ink:** This layer is the topmost layer and hides everything underneath. If I'm creating art in a cartoon or comic book style, this is the layer where I put all my inked linework. Pretty much every stroke on this layer uses only materials with Stroke enabled and Fill disabled.

>> **Fills/Colors:** On this layer is where my drawings get color. Most of the strokes on this layer have materials that have Fill enabled. Workflow-wise, this is the layer that I typically fill in last.

>> **Sketch:** This is the bottom layer and the layer that I actually start working on. Typically strokes on this layer are made with the Marker Chisel or Pencil brush. When I get to final render, this layer is generally hidden.

When you start a 2D Animation project, I suggest that you go ahead and get all your layers set up like this as a starting point. Then as you work in Draw mode, all you have to do is left-click the layer you want to work on and move right along with drawing. Of course, the difficulty is that while you draw, you may want to also switch through different materials as you go. It can get pretty tedious to constantly switch between the Material tab of the Properties editor and the Object Data tab.

TIP

You *could* split your Properties editor horizontally so you have two of them, with one dedicated to layers and the other dedicated to materials, but that eats away at your screen space. Because you've already set up your layers and you typically don't need to manage them further until you're at the polishing stage of your project, a nicer approach is to leave the Properties editor on the Material tab and switch layers using the Tool Settings region of the 3D Viewport. A roll-out panel labeled Layers appears at the top right of the Tool Settings region (refer to Figure 6-8).

From that Layers roll-out, you have all the basic controls available in the Layers panel of Object Data Properties. And as you work, the active layer that you're working on has its name displayed in the Tool Settings region so you always know where you are.

Moving strokes to layers

"I like this layer setup you're recommending, but I got excited and started drawing before reading this part of the chapter. Now I'm doomed and have to start all over!" Hold on a second there. Don't go deleting all your hard work just yet. Any stroke you draw can be moved to any layer whenever you like. The process is pretty easy:

1. **Ctrl+Tab into Edit mode on your Grease Pencil object.**

2. **Select at least one control point in the stroke you want to move.**

   Like with materials, strokes can't be partially on a layer. It's an all or nothing kind of thing.

3. **Move your stroke to the desired layer (Stroke ⇨ Move to Layer, or press the M hotkey).**

   The Move to Layer menu lists the layers in your Grease Pencil object that already exist. Click on one to choose it. If you want to create a new layer for your selected stroke, that option is available to you as well. The layer that has the pencil icon next to it is your current active layer.

4. **Ctrl+Tab back to Draw mode and get back to work.**

See? Easy!

Tweaking your drawings with layer adjustments

The Layers panel in Object Data Properties has a few sub-panels in it that you can use to do more wide-sweeping changes to your drawing on a per-layer basis. Whereas Grease Pencil materials give you the ability to change the look of individual strokes, Grease Pencil layers give you the ability to make more global changes to groups of strokes.

You can get a certain level of control with the Blend property to change how the strokes on one layer interact with the strokes on layers beneath it. And the Opacity slider is pretty handy, too, especially when you need to animate the visibility of a Grease Pencil layer. However, the real power for having a heavy influence over the look of strokes on a layer resides in the Adjustments sub-panel, as shown in Figure 6-9.

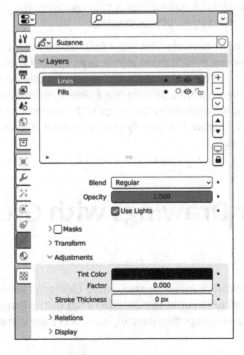

FIGURE 6-9:
The Adjustments sub-panel for Layers lets you modify all the strokes on a single layer at the same time.

It doesn't look like much, but the Adjustments sub-panel gives you a gateway to massive ways to affect your layer. Working through the properties in this sub-panel:

>> **Tint Color:** Using the color swatch in this property, you can give a general color overlay to every stroke on the selected layer. Of course, when you first set this color, it may not look like anything is happening. That's because you need to adjust the next property.

>> **Factor:** The Factor property tells Blender how much your chosen Tint color should influence and ultimately override the color of every stroke on your layer.

>> **Stroke Thickness:** The Stroke Thickness control may seem like something that's only useful if you somehow messed up and made your drawing with strokes that were too thick or thin and you need to have a quick fix. However, there's more to it than that. If you're animating a character that's moving from far away to close up, you may want to animate the thickness of your strokes so they look more natural. For animating, this is an extremely handy feature.

>> **Pass Index:** This property lives in the Relations sub-panel within Adjustments. With the Pass Index property, you can start to get a sense of how you can really supercharge the customization of your layers. Pass Indices get used in compositing to isolate specific parts of the render based on material or object. In this case, it's an isolation by Grease Pencil layer. They also get used in some Grease Pencil modifiers (described later in this chapter) so you can apply a modifier to only certain layers of your drawing.

>> **View Layer:** *This* is the property (also in the Relations sub-panel) that can really facilitate massive modifications to your Grease Pencil layer. View layers are used by Blender's Compositor to do all manner of totally sweet image processing to rendered output. By assigning a Grease Pencil layer to a view layer, you instantly have the ability to use any of the compositing tricks covered in Book 5, Chapter 2 on your Grease Pencil layer. Kaboom. Suddenly, anything is possible.

Automating Your Drawings with Grease Pencil Modifiers

 Like mesh objects (and to a lesser degree, curve objects), Grease Pencil objects have modifiers applied to them in the Modifiers tab of the Properties editor. In terms of granularity and things they control, modifiers have some of the broadest controls over your Grease Pencil objects, and the finest control happens in Edit mode. To visualize the structure a bit, it goes something like what is shown in Figure 6-10.

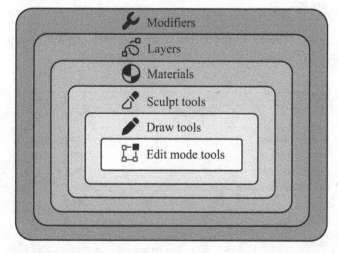

FIGURE 6-10:
A visualization
of the levels of
control Blender
gives you control
of Grease Pencil
objects.

That said, with modifiers, you can have a lot of control over various parts of your drawing throughout that structure. You can add control points to brush strokes or simplify them. You can adjust the thickness of all the strokes on a single layer or material or the overall object. You can color-adjust fills and stroke colors. And even better, because you're making those changes with modifiers, it's all nondestructive and easy to animate. Grease Pencil modifiers represent the same amount of timesaving power that you get with mesh modifiers.

When you go to Modifier Properties and click the Add Grease Pencil Modifier button, you get a menu of modifiers, broken down into four separate categories:

>> **Modify:** The modifiers in the Modify column are best thought of as modifiers that you use to affect the data within your Grease Pencil strokes. For example, you can adjust the UV coordinates of textures on your strokes or give an offset to the keyframes on your whole object.

>> **Generate:** Similar to the Generate modifiers for meshes described in Book 2, Chapter 2, these modifiers are used to change the strokes of your Grease Pencil objects at a fundamental level. Usually it's by adding control points, but in at least one modifier, control points are removed.

>> **Deform:** The Deform modifiers are the "meat and potatoes" modifiers of animation. With these modifiers, you can distort your drawing in a controlled, repeatable way and, therefore, build complex animation rigs for your drawings.

>> **Color:** Yes, you can use the Compositor to do image processing and color correction adjustments to you drawings. However, if you're just tweaking color, you can get much better performance by doing it in real time in the 3D Viewport. Those kinds of color adjustments are what the Color modifiers are for.

Figure 6-11 shows what you see when you click the Add Grease Pencil Modifier button in the Modifiers tab of the Properties editor.

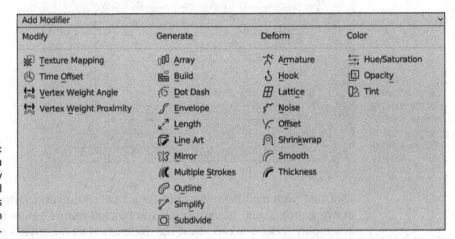

FIGURE 6-11:
Blender gives you almost as many Grease Pencil modifiers as there are mesh modifiers.

REMEMBER

With the exception of the Armature modifier and the Time Offset modifier, there are controls at the bottom of each modifier that allow you to specify a particular material or layer. That means that when you add a modifier to your Grease Pencil object, it doesn't have to affect every stroke in your drawing. With clever use of materials and layers, you can have modifiers affect only portions of your drawing, giving you ultimate flexibility over their look and behavior.

Modify modifiers

The modifiers listed in the Modify column affect the data of your Grease Pencil strokes more than anything else. You have the following modifiers available:

>> **Texture Mapping:** Like regular curve objects, Grease Pencil objects are also curves and therefore get UV coordinates "for free," in that you don't have to UV unwrap them. However, because there's not an explicit UV unwrap process, it can be difficult to control that mapping. The Texture Offset tool in Draw mode helps, but if you need more procedural controls, the Texture Mapping modifier can give them to you.

>> **Time Offset:** Imagine you have an animation completed using a Grease Pencil object, but you've discovered that the timing needs adjustment. Maybe the sequence needs to start a few frames later, or the whole thing needs to be done at 30 fps instead of 24 fps. It's certainly possible to go into the Timeline or Dope Sheet and manually adjust all the keyframes in your animation, but that's an incredibly time consuming (and potentially error-prone) process. You can make those adjustments much faster using the Time Offset modifier. You can't specify control of this modifier down to the material level, but you can isolate specific layers for it. Furthermore, because you can stack multiple modifiers on a single object, you could use a combination of the Time Offset modifier and the Offset modifier to add variety on a simple crowd animation.

>> **Vertex Weight Angle:** Like mesh objects, Grease Pencil objects can have vertex groups, and the control points in a Grease Pencil object can be assigned to those vertex groups with an associated weight value. You can manually paint your weights using Weight Paint mode on your Grease Pencil objects, but you can also get procedural control of your vertex weights using modifiers. The Vertex Weight Angle modifier assigns weights to your control points based on a specified angle in the modifier's settings.

>> **Vertex Weight Proximity:** Like the Vertex Weight Angle modifier, the Vertex Weight Proximity modifier can procedurally assign vertex weights to your Grease Pencil control points. For this modifier, you can use the closeness to another object as the factor that controls the weight assignments.

Generate modifiers

The basic thing to remember with modifiers in the Generate column is that they change the actual geometry of the strokes in your drawing. Generally speaking, these modifiers add control points in one way or another, but they don't necessarily have to. Some of them generate new strokes (sometimes called *derivative strokes*) with fewer control points than the original that you drew.

Breaking down the modifiers in this column, you have the following choices:

>> **Array:** Similar to the Array modifier for meshes, this modifier creates copies of your whole drawing based on the number you set in the Count value and allows you to offset those copies with the controls below that. The Object offset is particularly cool because it lets you use any arbitrary 3D object as the basis for offsetting the location, rotation, and size of each copy.

>> **Build:** The Build modifier is a really fun one because with it you can basically replay the process of drawing your Grease Pencil object over a specified number of frames. The Fade transition type for this modifier is particularly nice for slowly making your Grease Pencil object "undraw" itself over time.

When you first add the Build modifier, you may be startled to see your whole Grease Pencil object disappear. Don't let that frighten you too much. Just scrub the Dope Sheet at the bottom of your Blender window (see Chapter 4 of this book for more on working with Blender's animation editors) and you get to see your drawing show up over time.

 » **Dot Dash:** You can control how strokes are drawn from Material Properties, including whether the stroke is a line or a series of dots. Using the Dot Dash modifier, you can override what you set in your materials.

 » **Envelope:** With the Envelope modifier, Blender adds a mesh-like bit of geometry around your strokes. This envelope geometry gives kind of the appearance of cob webs on your strokes and tends to add a bit of life and jitter to them.

 » **Length:** If you need to increase the length of your Grease Pencil strokes beyond the point where they started or ended, the Length modifier can give you that control while trying to stick to the tangent of the original stroke.

 » **Line Art:** There was already a bit of an introduction to the Line Art modifier at the beginning of this chapter covering Grease Pencil primitives. This modifier can use one or more 3D objects from your scene and generate Grease Pencil strokes based on those objects' position and orientation relative to the active camera. This modifier is incredibly useful for adding outlines to 3D objects that you're rendering in an NPR (non-photorealistic rendering) style.

 » **Mirror:** This modifier can create a single copy of your drawing along each of its local axes. The biggest thing to remember is that all mirroring is relative to your Grease Pencil object's origin. So if you want your drawing to be mirrored across the X-axis, most of your strokes should be on either the left or right side of the origin.

 » **Multiple Strokes:** In a way, the Multiple Strokes modifier is similar to the Array modifier. The difference is that whereas the Array modifier duplicates your strokes as a complete object, the Multiple Strokes add-on adds new strokes offset from the originals.

 » **Outline:** Using this modifier, Blender adds an outline around the strokes in your Grease Pencil object.

 » **Simplify:** The Simplify modifier is the Grease Pencil equivalent of the mesh object's Decimate modifier. Increase the Iterations value and your Grease Pencil object gets made with fewer and fewer control points. This modifier is a nice, nondestructive analog to the Simplify operator in Edit mode (Stroke ⇨ Simplify).

>> **Subdivide:** On the opposite side of the spectrum from the Simplify modifier is the Subdivide modifier. It's useful to mix this modifier with any of the Deform modifiers (covered in the next section) to help provide enough control points to get smooth deformations when you animate.

Deform modifiers

In contrast to the Generate modifiers, the Deform modifiers don't substantively change the control points that make up your Grease Pencil drawing. Instead, these modifiers give you control over the results of those strokes. You can move them around, change their thickness, or give them procedural jitter that changes over time.

Here's a quick rundown of what each modifier can do:

>> **Armature:** Just like the Armature modifier for mesh objects, you can use this modifier to point your Grease Pencil object at the bones of an armature object in your scene and use those bones to deform and animate your drawing. You can even use vertex groups and Weight Paint mode (yes, Grease Pencil objects have vertex groups and weight painting) to refine exactly how the armature object deforms your drawing. The process is exactly like what's described for mesh objects in Chapter 3 of this book. With this modifier, you have the ability to do everything from simple cutout-style animation to fully rigged deformation of your Grease Pencil drawings.

>> **Hook:** The Hook modifier is analogous to its counterpart in mesh objects. However, the workflow for using this modifier is a bit different. There's no convenient shortcut for creating a hook and binding your selected control points to that hook in Edit mode. You're going to need to set up vertex groups to take advantage of that. And if you're going to go through the process of setting up vertex groups, my recommendation would be that you just use an Armature object and the Armature modifier. Or, if you're looking to get more general deformations, I'd suggest you use the Lattice modifier (described next). The only real advantage the Hook modifier has over the Armature modifier is that you can isolate whether the hook affects specific layers or materials. But with vertex groups, you pretty much get the same basic functionality.

>> **Lattice:** Happily, the Lattice modifier for Grease Pencil objects retains the straightforwardness and simplicity of the one used for mesh objects. Simply add a Lattice to your scene in Object mode (Add ⇨ Lattice), add this modifier to your Grease Pencil object, and select the name of your Lattice from the Object menu. From there, you can edit the vertices of the Lattice to squash and stretch your drawing to your heart's content.

» **Noise:** On its own, the Noise modifier doesn't appear to do much for your drawing other than kind of mess it up a bit. However, if you have a layer structure like the one I describe earlier in this chapter, you can apply this modifier to just the ink layer of your Grease Pencil object and get a nice bit of line boil for your object, so it more closely resembles hand-drawn animation in traditional media.

» **Offset:** The Offset modifier is a wily one. When you apply it to your Grease Pencil object, all it does is adjust the transforms of your drawing as if you're using the Transform tools. That in itself isn't particularly useful. However, when you start using this modifier on just specific materials or layers in your object, things start to get a lot more interesting.

As an example, if you load the Suzanne Grease Pencil object in your scene (Add ⇨ Grease Pencil ⇨ Monkey), you may notice that her pupils have their own material. If you add an Offset modifier to her and choose just the Pupils material to be affected by this modifier, you have a quick and dirty way of animating which way she looks without the need of hooks or armatures. Like I said, interesting!

» **Shrinkwrap:** Much like the modifier of the same name for mesh objects, the Shrinkwrap modifier for Grease Pencil objects can snap your strokes to the surface of a target object. If you are hand-drawing outlines (rather than using the Line Art modifier), the Shrinkwrap modifier can help ensure that your strokes are stuck to the mesh to which you're adding lines.

» **Smooth:** Sometimes the deformations of other modifiers can cause the strokes in your Grease Pencil object to distort in awkward ways. Or, sometimes the strokes that you draw just aren't clean enough and you don't want to go through the work of using Sculpt mode to smooth them all out. For both those situations, the Smooth modifier can come to the rescue.

» **Thickness:** When it comes to the drawn line, I'm a huge proponent of varying your line thickness to give the overall drawing more life and energy. Not every drawing should look like a sterile technical blueprint. That said, sometimes that's just the kind of work we end up drawing. With the aid of the Thickness modifier, you can adjust the thickness of each stroke along its length. If you worked with curve objects, as described in Book 2, Chapter 4, this modifier is akin to giving your Grease Pencil strokes a custom taper object. The only difference is that you don't have to add a new curve to your scene; you can enable the Custom Curve check box and modify the curve profile right from within the modifier.

Color modifiers

At first blush, the Grease Pencil Color modifiers may seem out of place. After all, if you want to tweak colors, why wouldn't you do that with layers or materials, or even the Compositor? Why have that kind of thing controlled by a modifier? One answer: linked assets. Because Grease Pencil objects are proper datablocks like any other object in Blender, you can make linked duplicates (Object ⇨ Duplicate Linked, or Alt+D) of as many of them as you'd like. And then when you edit your strokes in Edit mode or Sculpt mode, those modifications propagate to all your linked versions.

But what if you want each of those linked objects to have different color properties? You spent a lot of time getting your layers and materials set up for each object. It would be a pain to unlink each duplicate and then make different variations of each one's materials. Fortunately, you have Color modifiers. With just a few clicks, you can change the color properties of one linked duplicate without affecting any of the others.

The following is a quick description of each Color modifier:

>> **Hue/Saturation:** I like to treat the Hue/Saturation modifier like a quick-and-dirty color adjustment tool because, well, that's what it is. Add this modifier to your Grease Pencil object and you can use the HSV (hue, saturation, value) sliders to override the colors on all or part of your object.

>> **Opacity:** The Opacity modifier is really handy for doing motion graphics work with Grease Pencil objects. If you need to fade all or some of the strokes in your object in and out of view, this is the modifier that can help with that task.

>> **Tint:** Sometimes you just need to make it look like a color layer was laid over the top of your Grease Pencil object. This modifier is exactly the right tool for the job. Over in Book 3, Chapter 1, I describe how to make a 3D Suzanne look like she's gotten a red face from anger. If you want to do something similar to that with the Grease Pencil Suzanne, you can do it with the Tint modifier.

Understanding Grease Pencil Effects

In the same spirit as modifiers, Grease Pencil objects have an additional tab in the Properties editor unique to them: the Effects tab. Grease Pencil effects are similar to modifiers in that they give you procedural control over the look of your drawings. The difference, however, is that modifiers tend to affect the data of your object, whereas effects influence the look of the object, much like filters in a 2D image program or Blender's Compositor. However, because Grease Pencil effects have a stack structure like modifiers, you can build effects one atop another to get your own custom result.

IMPORTANT

As you experiment with Grease Pencil Effects, you may discover that they don't seem to change anything in the 3D Viewport. The reason you're not seeing anything is because Grease Pencil effects are visible only when you use the Rendered viewport shading mode.

To add an effect to a Grease Pencil object, select your object and go to the Effects tab of the Properties editor. Within that tab, click the Add Effect button and choose one of the following effects from the drop-down menu that appears:

» **Blur:** Add this effect to blur the strokes in your Grease Pencil object, much like you would use the Blur node in Blender's Compositor (see Book 5, Chapter 2).

» **Colorize:** Apply this effect to procedurally modify the colors in your Grease Pencil object, using a set of preset color modes including the following:

- Grayscale

- Sepia

- Duotone

- Transparent

- Custom

All the Colorize modes have a Factor slider that you can use to influence the impact of the effect. The Transparent mode is especially useful for animating objects to smoothly disappear without resorting to the Compositor or material tricks.

» **Flip:** Add this effect to quickly mirror your whole Grease Pencil object either horizontally or vertically.

» **Glow:** This effect adds a soft glow to your Grease Pencil object. You can define the color of the glow as well as how it mixes with the colors in your object, if it mixes at all (you can set the glow to be behind the strokes in your object if you want).

» **Pixelate:** Add this effect to give your Grease Pencil object an old school low-resolution look. Using the X and Y Size properties, you can adjust the size of the pixel blocks that make up your drawing.

» **Rim:** Use this effect to quickly fake the lighting on your Grease Pencil drawing so it looks like it has a rim light, as covered in Book 3, Chapter 3. The difference here is that there are no actual light objects providing you with this look. It's all from the effect.

>> **Shadow:** The Shadow effect gives your Grease Pencil object the appearance of having a drop shadow. This effect is particularly useful if you're using Grease Pencil objects to re-create the look of cut-out animation and you need those subtle shadows that appear between the cut pieces of paper in that style of animation.

>> **Swirl:** The Swirl effect is pretty interesting. You define another object in your scene (often an Empty) as being the central point of the effect, and then use the Radius and Angle sliders to control the distance the effect occurs from your chosen object and how much the effect spins your strokes around that object.

>> **Wave Distortion:** Add the Wave Distortion effect to apply either a horizontal or vertical sinusoidal effect to your Grease Pencil object.

Animating with Grease Pencil

At its heart, Grease Pencil objects are built for animating. They are meant to be easy for you to change over time and generate moving pictures. When it comes to actually animating with Grease Pencil objects, there are two basic approaches that you can take: a traditional hand-drawn workflow and a more 3D-like rigged animation workflow. Neither approach is more correct than the other. It really just depends on the aesthetic you want to have when you finally hit render on your work.

This section outlines the general way you come at each of these workflows in Blender. I recommend that you read through both ways and decide afterward which one feels more appropriate to the way you like to work.

Using a hand-drawn animation workflow with Grease Pencil objects

The hand-drawn approach to animating in Blender is simultaneously easy to describe and difficult to do well. Part of the reason is because the process involves repetitively drawing, re-drawing, editing, re-drawing, editing, drawing, and re-drawing. Did I mention drawing? Blender does provide some handy short-cuts and helpers, but animating in a hand-drawn style is exactly what it sounds like: drawing by hand . . . a lot.

I'm going to assume that you've already done all of your preproduction planning and storyboarding for what you're animating, and now you're on the task of actually sitting down to animate (see Chapters 1 and 4 of this book for more detail on the overall animation process). The process of doing hand-drawn animation in Grease Pencil breaks down into the following steps:

1. **Create a new 2D Animation session in Blender (File ⇨ New ⇨ 2D Animation).**

   I suggest that you go ahead and Ctrl+Tab to Object mode and delete the default stroke object. Technically, you don't really have to delete the default stroke; it has included a few nice thing, such as some base materials and layers. However, if you're using a slightly different workflow, it can be a hassle to go in and replace those defaults with your own. Furthermore, if you're starting your Grease Pencil animation outside of the 2D Animation start template or you add other Grease Pencil objects to your scene, they don't have the benefit of those preset materials. So, it's worth it to understand how to work from a truly blank slate.

2. **Add a new Blank Grease Pencil object (Add ⇨ Grease Pencil ⇨ Blank).**

3. **Create a new layer in your Grease Pencil object.**

   You can perform this step in Object Data Properties or from the Layer rollout in the 3D Viewport's Tool Settings region. Either way, name your new layer `Pencil Test`.

4. **On your `Pencil Test` layer, left-click the Onion Skinning icon to enable onion skinning for that layer.**

   When disabled, the Onion Skinning icon looks like a single circle at the far right of the layers list box. When you left-click it to enable onion skinning, the icon appears to have shadow circles radiating from it. This step is critical for giving you a reference when you draw subsequent frames of your animation.

5. **Ctrl+Tab into Draw mode and draw your first frame.**

   You're ready to start drawing your first frame. My suggestion would be to use the Draw tool with the Pencil and Marker Chisel brushes to get the rough shape of whatever you're animating. In this case, you want to pay the most attention to the pose and the silhouette of the thing you're animating. Don't get caught up in details at this point. It's the pose that matters the most.

6. **Move forward in time a few frames.**

   I like going forward 10 frames; it's a nice round number for roughing things in. You can move forward in time by either scrubbing in the Dope Sheet at the bottom of the Blender window or by pressing → ten times.

   At this point nothing much has changed about your drawing. You've just moved forward in time.

7. **Start drawing the next major pose in your animated sequence.**

Immediately when you start drawing, the linework of what you drew in Step 5 turns green to indicate that it's an onion skin of the previous frame, and the linework in your current frame has the correct color for your brushes.

8. **Repeat Steps 6 and 7 for all the keyframes in your animated sequence.**

As you work, you may want to take advantage of the fact that you can move Grease Pencil strokes in Edit mode rather than try to redraw the same shapes over again. The Edit mode and Sculpt mode tools do wonders as timesavers when animating. Just Ctrl+Tab over to either of those modes and when you make a modification to your Grease Pencil object, Blender automatically inserts a keyframe for you. When you finish working through all your key poses, you basically have a rough animated pencil test. You can play the sequence in the 3D Viewport by pressing Spacebar to get a sense of the timing.

9. **Using the Dope Sheet at the bottom of the 2D Animation workspace, adjust the timing of your key poses.**

See Chapter 4 of this book for more on working with the Dope Sheet. Once you're happy with the timing, you're ready to work on your secondary poses. If you're doing a classic "bouncing ball" animation using this technique, then at this point in the process your Blender window may look like what's in Figure 6-12.

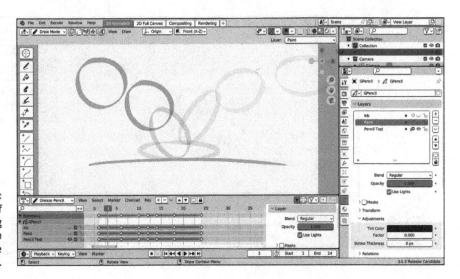

FIGURE 6-12: The first stages of a classic bouncing ball animation with Grease Pencil.

10. **Set your time cursor between two of your key poses and draw an in-between pose.**

Again, you may want to take advantage of Edit mode and Sculpt mode to work with stroke geometry that's already in your scene and give yourself a decent starting place before adding new strokes. You can also use the Interpolate tool to try and rough in the drawing at that frame for you.

11. **Move your time cursor between the next set of key poses and draw another in-between pose.**

As you continue fleshing out your animation, you may want to tweak the properties within the Onion Skinning panel of Object Data Properties. Those controls allow you to see more or fewer of the onion skinned keyframes around your current frame to help you get a better sense of timing and movement.

12. **Repeat Steps 10 and 11 until all your secondary poses are complete.**

At this point, it depends on how detailed (and how long) your animated sequence is. Either you're happy with where you are, or you're going to continue adding more and more in-between poses and adjusting timing until you actually are happy with the sequence. Assuming you're at a happy stage, the next steps get you to start polishing. Continuing with the example of the bouncing ball, your screen may look like Figure 6-13.

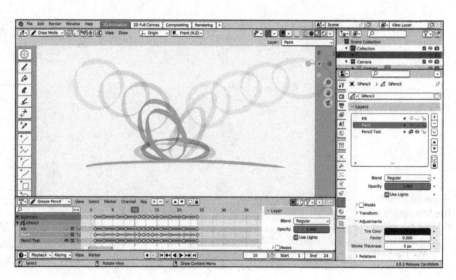

FIGURE 6-13: Bouncing ball pencil test, complete!

13. **Create a new layer for your Grease Pencil object.**

Name this new layer Ink. Whether you enable onion skinning for this layer is up to you. If your Pencil Test layer is detailed enough, you won't have to.

14. **Using an Ink brush, go through each of your frames and redraw them with clean lines.**

This step is time consuming, but it's the step where your animation really starts to come to life. With your line ink complete, the next step is color.

15. **Create a new layer for your Grease Pencil object and put it between your Pencil Test layer and your Ink layer.**

This is the layer that you use to paint the color fills for your animated sequence, so it makes sense to name this layer Fills or Paint. Depending on how comfortable you are with the animated sequence, you may also want to hide your Pencil Test layer.

16. **Using Grease Pencil materials with Fill enabled, begin the process of adding the color fill for your animation.**

As in Step 14, this step can be extremely time consuming. However, when you complete this step, you'll have a fantastic-looking, hand-drawn animation created entirely with Blender's Grease Pencil objects. Figure 6-14 shows what your Blender session might look like with a completed bouncing ball animation using this technique.

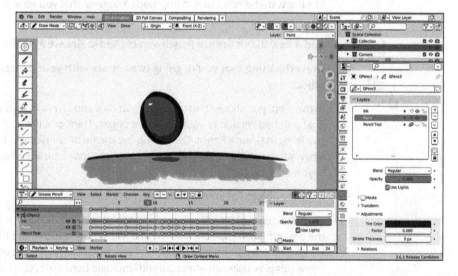

FIGURE 6-14: One bouncing ball animation, ready for render!

Of course, as you grow and mature as an animator, you'll find ways to cut corners on some of these steps and speed up your workflow. Some people even prefer to have a fully fleshed-out drawing with all the necessary colors and layers for the first frame before they start animating. Then their focus becomes more about going through each drawing and less about trying to build materials and layers on the fly. Either way, that's the process of hand-drawn animation: Draw, edit, redraw, edit, draw, and redraw again.

Rigging Grease Pencil objects for animation

Perhaps drawing isn't your thing, maybe you're a long-time veteran of a fully rigged 3D animation workflow, or perhaps you're really into the cut-out animation style of 2D animation. Whatever the reason, you may be looking for an approach to animating that doesn't follow the hand-drawn way of doing things. Fortunately, Blender's Grease Pencil objects also support being rigged for animation just like mesh objects.

The workflow for a rigged approach to animation requires fewer steps, but each step tends to require a bit more technical understanding. The process goes something like this:

1. **Create a new 2D Animation session in Blender (File ⇨ New ⇨ 2D Animation).**

   Just like with the hand-drawn approach, I suggest that you go ahead and Ctrl+Tab to Object mode and delete the default stroke object.

2. **Add a new Blank Grease Pencil object (Add ⇨ Grease Pencil ⇨ Blank).**

3. **Draw the thing that you're going to animate with your Grease Pencil object.**

   In this step, you should create all the materials and layers that you need for the final polished version of your animated object. Think of it like sculpting and modeling in Grease Pencil. Continuing the theme of animating a bouncing ball, when you finish this step, your Blender session may look like what's shown in Figure 6-15.

4. **Rig your object for animation.**

   The full arsenal of Blender objects and tools is at your disposal. In the case of the bouncing ball example, you may have a simple setup where the ball Grease Pencil object is parented to a spherical Empty. Or maybe you have something more complex using an armature with multiple bones for controlling and deforming your Grease Pencil object. For the sake of this example, the rig shown in Figure 6-16 is a fairly simple thing using a couple bones to take advantage of the Armature modifier.

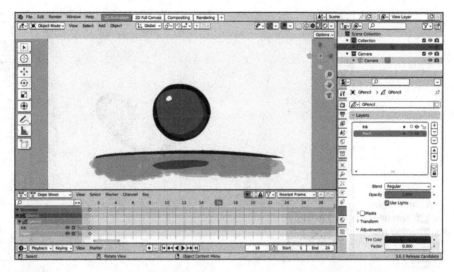

FIGURE 6-15:
One Grease
Pencil rubber
ball, ready to be
bounced.

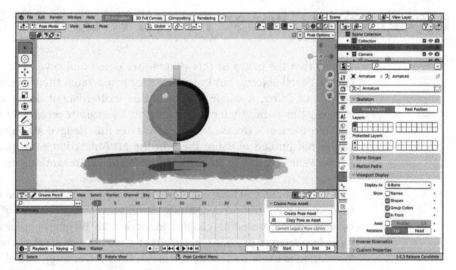

FIGURE 6-16:
It hasn't been
animated yet, but
this ball now has
a rig and can be
animated like any
other 3D object in
Blender.

5. **Using the same processes described in Chapter 4 of this book for animating a rigged character, animate your Grease Pencil object using the rig you created in Step 4.**

   There's an awful lot baked into this one step, but if you've animated in 3D before, it should be familiar to you. Move the controls on your rig, insert keyframes for the attributes you want to animate, scrub forward in time, wash, rinse, repeat. When this step is complete, though, you have a fully animated scene, and you only really had to draw once to get your initial setup established. Figure 6-17 shows what your Blender window may look like as you complete this step.

FIGURE 6-17:
A hand-drawn
ball, drawn once
and bounced with
technology from
the future!

Integrating Grease Pencil with a 3D Scene

I know that the pages of this chapter are dense and cover a lot of ground with Grease Pencil objects, but in reality, they just scratch the surface of what you're capable of doing. A whole book could be written about doing 2D animation in Blender. I'm awfully tempted to write it. I've said it repeatedly throughout this chapter: Blender's Grease Pencil objects are full-fledged 3D objects. That means you're not limited to using them in the 2D Animation workspace. You can use Grease Pencil objects to enhance any 3D scene you're working on.

Say, for example, you have a 3D scene set at a haunted house, and you need a thick knee-level mist around everything. Sure, you could use some of the techniques covered in the preceding chapter to work with Blender's smoke simulator and particle system to provide you with that effect. But as great as the results can be, simulation is computationally intensive, time consuming, and difficult to render. Why not make a textured Grease Pencil material and *draw* the fog into your scene? You can even use Grease Pencil modifiers to animate your fog strokes to give you that living volumetric feel.

Or maybe you need to have a bunch of wires that look like they're running across the surface of an object. You can go to the header of the 3D Viewport while in Draw mode and change the Stroke Placement roll-out to use Surface rather than the default Origin behavior. Then when you draw, all your strokes run along the surface of the 3D geometry in your scene. If you absolutely need those strokes to be 3D geometry, you can easily convert them to curves (Object ➪ Convert to).

And, of course, Grease Pencil objects can be invaluable when compositing, as covered in Book 5, Chapter 2. You can certainly use them to make detailed animated masks, but Grease Pencil objects can also be enormously beneficial when creating motion graphics.

The other really cool thing you can do is swing the pendulum in the other direction. Using Eevee as your render engine, you have a high-powered, non-photorealistic rendering engine right at your fingertips. Using the Shader to RGB node, as described in Book 3, Chapter 1, you can give 3D objects materials that hand-painted look. By combining cartoony Eevee materials with Grease Pencil objects using the Line Art modifier, you can have full 3D scenes that look hand-drawn and seamlessly integrate them with your Grease Pencil drawings.

With a bit of work and cleverness, it really is possible to make just about anything you can imagine.

5

Sharing Your Work with the World

Contents at a Glance

IN THIS CHAPTER

» Taking a look at editing and
compositing

» Editing video and animations with
Blender's Video Sequencer

» Getting your final video output from
Blender

Chapter **1**

Editing Video
and Animation

I n live-action film and video, the term *post-production* usually includes nearly
anything associated with animation; basically anything that doesn't get directly
captured by the camera when they're shooting. Nearly every animator or visual
effects specialist has groaned upon hearing a director or producer say the line,
"We'll fix it in post." Fortunately, in animation, post-production is more specific,
focusing on editing and compositing.

This chapter is a quick guide to editing, using Blender's Video Sequencer.
Compositing is covered in the next chapter. Understand that these topics are large
enough for a book of their own, so the content of this chapter isn't comprehensive. That said, you can find enough solid information here and in Blender's online
documentation (https://docs.blender.org/manual) to figure it out. I explain
Blender's interface for these tools, as well as some fundamental concepts. With
this understanding, these tools can help turn your work from "Hey, that's cool"
to "Whoa!"

Comparing Editing to Compositing

Editing is the process of taking rendered footage — animation, film, or video — and adjusting how various shots appear in sequence. You typically edit using a *nonlinear editor* (NLE). An NLE, like Blackmagic Design's DaVinci Resolve or Adobe Premiere, differs from older *linear* tape-to-tape editing systems that required editors to work sequentially. Footage was captured on tape and editors would play through the footage to find where they wanted to cut, mark that spot (or physically cut it, in the case of film), find the start of the next scene they want, and then splice the two scenes together.

Working that way was okay in the day, but this approach is problematic if you want to go back and refine your edits or tweak your timing. With linear editing, every change affects all the others later in the sequence. Fortunately, with a modern NLE, you can easily edit the beginning of a sequence without worrying too much about it messing up the timing at the end. Blender has basic NLE functionality with its Video Sequencer.

In earlier versions of Blender, the Video Sequencer was called the Video Sequence Editor, or VSE. A lot of long-time Blender users still use this shortened form, so if you go on the web to look for additional help with using the Video Sequencer, I would suggest that you include "VSE" as one of your search terms. You'll get a much larger number of hits with relevant information.

Compositing is the process of mixing animations, videos, and still images into a single image or video. It's the way that credits show up over footage at the beginning of a movie, or how animated characters are made to appear like they are interacting with a real-world environment. Blender has an integrated compositor that you can use to achieve these sorts of effects, as well as simply enhance your scene with effects such as blur, glow, and color correction.

If you were comparing editing and compositing, it may be best to think of editing as putting a sequence of images in order, whereas compositing is more like stacking those images on top of each other. Most post-production consists of doing a little bit of both. Compositing tasks tend to focus on one specific shot in a sequence, whereas editing tasks chain a series of shots together.

Working with the Video Sequencer

 Looking at the workspaces for the General workflow template in Blender, you might notice that there's not an obvious Video Editing workspace. It's not one of the default workspaces visible in the tabs at the top of the Blender window.

Now, you *could* add a new Video Editing workspace by clicking the plus button on the far right of the workspace tabs. However, in the General workflow template, there are already a ton of tabs up there. It's a lot to look at if all you want to do is edit video. The better way to go is to use the Video Editing template that comes with Blender. From a fresh Blender session, choose File ⇨ New ⇨ Video Editing, and you'll load the base template for working with Blender as an NLE. Figure 1-1 shows the Video Editing workspace that you get when you fire up this workflow template.

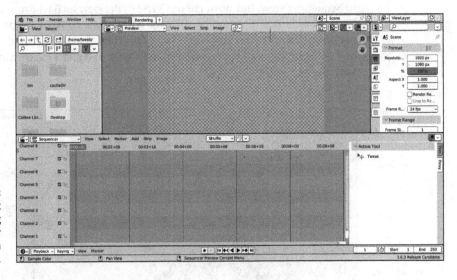

FIGURE 1-1:
The default Video Editing workspace for when you start a project.

The large editor across the middle of the layout is a Video Sequencer in Sequencer view. As a Blender editor, the Video Sequencer actually has three view modes, changeable from a drop-down menu in the header:

 » **Sequencer:** In this view, you can add and modify sequences, called *strips,* in time. The numbers across the top of the Sequencer correspond to time in the Video Sequencer in seconds. The numbers to the left are labels for each of the tracks, or *channels,* that the strips live in.

 » **Preview:** The Preview view of the Video Sequencer shows the footage under the time cursor while you're editing. In the default Video Editing workspace, there's a larger Video Sequencer in Preview view at top center.

 » **Sequencer & Preview:** This view splits the editor area into two parts stacked atop one another to show both the Preview view and the Sequencer view at the same time. You might use this if you're creating your own custom video-editing workspace on a small screen and you don't want as many editor areas in your workspace layout.

TIP

You can quickly toggle between the Preview and Sequencer views by pressing the Ctrl+Tab hotkey combination.

If you're working on a computer with a small screen, the default Video Editing workspace can feel pretty crowded. You can get around this by maximizing Sequencer area (Ctrl+Spacebar or choose View ➪ Area ➪ Toggle Maximize Area from the Sequencer's header) and switching it to Sequencer/Preview view. That's an improvement, but the preview section is still taking up half your screen space. There's another thing you can do instead: With the Sequencer maximized, keep it in Sequencer view. But now, choose View ➪ Preview as Backdrop from the header. When you do this, the preview of your edit shows up right in the Sequencer as a backdrop. Your various strips are simply overlaid above the preview so you can edit and see your video all in the same space. Figure 1-2 shows a maximized Sequencer with the preview set as a backdrop.

FIGURE 1-2: You can edit video and preview it all in the same space using Preview as Backdrop.

The upper left area of the Video Editing workspace is a File Browser. Treat the File Browser as a kind of asset bin for your video footage. This way, you can easily drag and drop footage from the File Browser directly into the Sequencer. The upper right of the workspace is a Properties editor. It's useful to have the Properties editor available when you're doing your initial setup of screen resolution and frame rate, as well as when you're rendering your finished edit. At the bottom is a Timeline, which, at first, may seem odd. However, when editing, as with animating, the benefit of having the Timeline around all the time is that you can use the Sequencer to edit a specific portion of your production, while still having the ability to move the time cursor over the full piece (called *scrubbing* a timeline). The playback controls are also handy to have onscreen.

The Timeline at the bottom of the screen controls how Blender plays your sequence. However, when it comes to editing video, the most relevant button in the Timeline is the Playback roll-out menu. In particular, you'll want to check the Sync drop-down in this menu. By default, it should be set to Sync to Audio for synchronized audio and video. Having Sync set to this value ensures that your audio plays back in sync with your video while editing. You could also set this to Frame Dropping, but I tend to get better results when I choose Sync to Audio. Nothing is worse than doing a ton of work to get something edited only to find out that none of the audio lines up with the visuals after you render. Figure 1-3 shows the options in the Playback roll-out menu of the Timeline.

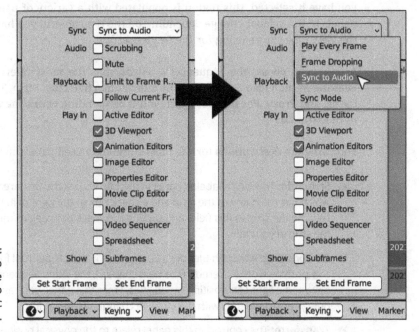

FIGURE 1-3:
Choose Sync to Audio to ensure that your audio plays back in sync with your video.

The settings in the Dimensions panel amid the Output Properties are important for editing in Blender because that's where you set the frame rate, measured in frames per second (fps), and resolution for the project. If you're editing footage that runs at a different frame rate or resolution than the one that is set here, that footage is adjusted to fit. So if your project is at standard HD settings (24 fps and 1920 x 1080 pixels in size), but you import an animation rendered at 50 fps and at a size of 640 x 480 pixels, it's possible for the footage to appear stretched and in slow motion.

When importing video files to the Sequencer, Blender has a number of options available in the Sidebar of the File Browser to try and help mitigate these issues. In fact, with the default settings, you should see no distortion in time or scaling at all. However, it is possible to have imported video change the framerate you've chosen in Output Properties, so be sure to double-check after importing.

Besides your Output Properties, the Sequencer's Sidebar (visible by default on the right side of the Sequencer view; press N to toggle its visibility while the mouse cursor is in the Sequencer) is relevant to your editing process. Because the default layout doesn't have any strips loaded, the Sidebar appears as a blank region on the right side of the Sequencer. However, if you have a strip in the Sequencer and you have it selected, this region is populated with a variety of panels. (The exact panels in the Sidebar change depending on the type of strip you have selected and the view type you're using for the Sequencer.)

As you may guess, the Sequencer's Sidebar has the most relevant options for working in the Video Sequencer. The Sidebar has five tabs: Strip, Tool, Modifiers, Cache, and Proxy. For the most part, you'll be spending your time with the panels in the Strip tab.

Following are descriptions for the most commonly used panels in the Strip tab:

>> **Strip Info:** This isn't a labeled panel in the tab; it's just the first area at the top, which has the name of the strip and a check box to the right of it. You can rename the strip in this field, and clicking the check box toggles the visibility of the strip in your edit.

>> **Compositing:** Although Blender's Compositor is the proper tool for serious compositing work (covered in the next chapter), the Video Sequencer does have some light compositing capabilities. From this panel, you can control how your strip blends with the strips in channels beneath it.

>> **Transform:** The controls in this panel relate to the physical position, orientation, and size of the contents of your strip when on the screen. When you have an audio strip selected, a Sound panel appears where the Transform panel is normally located.

>> **Time:** The buttons in this panel allow you to control which portion of the strip shows up in the Sequencer.

>> **Effect Strip:** This panel appears only for certain effect strips that have editable attributes. I give more detail on some effects that use this panel in the section "Adding effects and transitions," later in this chapter.

WARNING

Before I get heavily into using the Video Sequencer, let me first say that Blender's Video Sequencer is *not* a complete replacement for a traditional NLE. Although a very powerful tool, the Video Sequencer is best suited for animators who want to create a quick edit of their work or when planning larger animation projects using Blender scene strips. Professional video editors may have trouble because the Video Sequencer is missing a number of expected features, such as a listing of available footage, sometimes called a *clip library* or *bin*. You can use the File Browser in thumbnail view to partially emulate the behavior of a bin, but it's still not quite the same. That said, all the open movie projects from the Blender Studio were successfully edited using Blender's Video Sequencer. I find the Video Sequencer more than sufficient for quite a few of my projects, so you ultimately have to decide for yourself.

Adding and editing strips

If you want to use the Video Sequencer to edit footage, you have to bring that footage into Blender. If you're using the default Video Editing workspace I describe in the preceding section of this chapter, you can use the File Browser and navigate to where your footage is. Then you can just drag and drop that file from the File Browser directly into the Sequencer. The ability to drag and drop from the File Browser is an extremely handy feature that even many veteran Blender users don't know about. In fact, you can even drop media files from your operating system's file manager. Alternatively, you can add a strip by using the Add menu in the Sequencer's header. If you're not the type that likes to use header menus, you can hover your mouse cursor in the Sequencer and press Shift+A (just like adding objects in the 3D Viewport) to have the Add menu pop up right by your mouse cursor. Figure 1-4 shows the menu of options that appears.

You can import a variety of strips: scenes, clips, masks, movies, still images, audio, and effects. These strips are represented by the following menu options:

>> **Scene:** Scene strips are an extremely cool feature unique to Blender. When you select this option, a secondary menu pops up that allows you to select a scene from the .blend file you're working in. If you use a single .blend file with multiple scenes in it, you can edit those scenes together to a final output sequence without ever having to first render out those scenes. This handy feature allows you to create a complete and complex animation entirely within a single file. (This feature also works with scenes linked from external .blend files, but that's an advanced use.) Scene strips are also a great way to use Blender for overlaying graphics, like titles, on video.

Add

- Scene ▶
- Clip ▶
- Mask ▶

- Movie
- Sound
- Image/Sequence

- Color
- Text

- Adjustment Layer
- Effect Strip ▶
- Transition ▶
- Fade ▶

FIGURE 1-4:
The Add menu
in the Video
Sequencer.

When expanding the Scene menu, you might notice it just says "No Items Available." That's because you have only one scene in your file, and it's not possible to add the scene that you're using to edit video as a strip. That would be a pretty nasty feedback loop. It's best practice to use separate scenes for animating and editing video. Blender re-enforces that practice.

» **Clip:** Clips relate to Blender's built-in motion-tracking feature. Read more about motion tracking in Chapter 3 of this book. A Clip is similar to a Movie strip (covered two bullets down), except that it's already loaded in Blender in the Movie Clip editor and has its own datablock. In contrast, Movie strips by themselves don't have any associated datablocks; they exist only on the Video Sequencer's timeline.

» **Mask:** To add a Mask strip, you must first create a Mask datablock in the Image Editor. To create a mask, left-click the Editing Context drop-down menu in the Image Editor's header and choose Mask. Masks are pretty heavily used in advanced motion tracking and compositing.

» **Movie:** When you select this option, the File Browser that opens allows you to select a video file in one of the many formats Blender supports. On files with both audio and video, Blender loads the audio along with the video file as separate strips in the sequencer.

WARNING

Pay close attention to the settings in the File Browser's Sidebar when you import. In particular, double-check the Use Movie Framerate check box. If you have that check box enabled, Blender updates the framerate for your whole scene (in Output Properties) to match the framerate of your imported video.

Most of the time this is a helpful convenience, but if you're working with a bunch of video with different framerates, you can end up with some video appearing to play too fast or too slow.

» **Sound:** This option gives you a File Browser for loading an audio file into the Video Sequencer. When importing audio, you definitely want to import sound files in WAV or FLAC (Free Lossless Audio Codec) formats, which gives you the best quality sound. Although Blender supports other audio formats like MP3, they're often compressed and sometimes sound bad when played.

» **Image/Sequence:** Selecting this option opens a File Browser from which you can select one or more images in any of the formats that Blender recognizes. If you select just one image, the Video Sequencer displays a strip for that one image that you can arbitrarily resize in time. If you select multiple images, the Video Sequencer interprets them as a sequence and places them all in the same strip with a fixed length that matches the number of images you selected.

» **Color:** Color strips create an infinitely sized color strip. You can use this handy little type of strip to do fades or set a solid background color for scenes.

» **Text:** Text strips are a relatively new type of strip to Blender's Video Sequencer. They're a very quick way to add text to the screen, such as for adding subtitles or simple text overlays.

» **Adjustment Layer:** Adjustment Layer strips are a bit unique. The cool thing is that Adjustment Layer strips can make simple modifications (*adjustments*) to the look of all strips below them on the Video Sequencer's timeline. If you add an Adjustment Layer strip and look at the mostly empty Sidebar in the Sequencer, you may wonder exactly how you add those adjustments. This is where you can apply Video Sequencer modifiers. In the Modifiers tab of the Sidebar, you can left-click the Add Strip Modifier drop-down menu. Video Sequencer modifiers are relatively simple adjustments, but they're immensely useful in getting your edits to look good. Most of them are used for adjusting the color values in your video:

- **Bright/Contrast:** The Bright/Contrast modifier gives you very simple controls for adjusting the brightness of your image and its overall contrast. It can be a quick and dirty way of making footage shot in dark lighting look a little bit clearer.

- **Color Balance:** This modifier provides the lift, gamma, and gain controls (basically color controls for dark values, midtones, and highlights, respectively) that an experienced color correction artist can use.

- **Curves:** If you're familiar with adjustment curves in image editing programs such as GIMP or Photoshop, the Curves modifier should look pretty familiar to you. You can use it to not only control how much of each color or value is present in your footage, but also the rate of change in that color's influence on the image.

- **Hue Correct:** Sometimes you need to adjust the color on some piece of footage to match another shot. Perhaps the lighting or time of day was slightly different between shots, causing them to be noticeably different. With the Hue Correct modifier, you can adjust the hue, saturation, and value of each pixel using a curve.

- **Mask:** When working with modifiers, you may sometimes have a whole stack of modifiers working together (just like the modifiers you use when working in 3D). When you do this, you may want to have one modifier affecting part of your image, and another affecting the rest — for example, if you have footage of a bright red ball and you want everything else in the picture to be grayscale. With the Mask modifier, you use a mask as created in the Image Editor or the transparency of another strip to control the influence of modifiers above and below it in the stack.

- **Tone Map:** Modern cameras can shoot incredibly high-quality video. In fact, many of them can capture color and brightness ranges greater than most monitors, televisions, or printers can display. These are called *high dynamic range* (HDR) images. This is especially true in 3D renders because you're not limited to the abilities of a camera sensor. Of course, it would be nice if you could show all those beautiful images on regular screens without them looking overly dark or blown-out white. This is where tone mapping and the Tone Map modifier comes in. With this modifier, you can adjust the range of brightness and color in your image (remapping the tones) so everything is clearly visible on screens that don't have HDR capabilities.

- **White Balance:** When professionals shoot video footage, it's a pretty common practice to spend some time white-balancing their cameras before they shoot. *White balancing* is the process of calibrating the video image so everything is relative to a common white value. They'll often shoot a few seconds of footage with a white piece of paper or board to make sure everything is calibrated correctly. Of course, even professionals sometimes forget to do this, and you sometimes end up with footage shot in the same light, but with cameras that have different calibrations. Using the White Balance modifier, you can "fix it in post" and make those different shots look like they were taken by cameras with the same calibration.

REMEMBER

Modifiers don't just have to be used with Adjustment Layer strips. They can be applied to any strip. The difference is that a modifier on an Adjustment Layer strip affects all the other strips below it in the Sequencer, whereas a modifier on any other strip affects only that strip you added it to.

» **Effect Strip:** This option pops out a secondary, somewhat lengthy, menu of options. These strips are used mostly for effects. I cover them in more depth in the next section.

>> **Transition:** When editing video, you're going to have multiple shots that you must cut between. Most of the time, it will look best if you have *straight cuts* with nothing fancy transitioning between them. However, on occasion, you may want to fade to black or show the passage of time with a dissolve. In those cases, Transition strips are a big help. Like Effects Strips, I'll cover these types of strips in more detail in the next section.

>> **Fade:** Fades aren't strips that you add to the Sequencer. Instead, the items in this submenu are a convenient shortcut to adding opacity keyframes to your selected strip. There's a bit more on this in the next section.

When you load a strip, it's brought into the Sequencer so it starts at the location of your time cursor. Table 1-1 shows helpful mouse actions for working efficiently in the Sequencer.

TABLE 1-1   **Helpful Mouse Actions in the Sequencer**

Mouse Action	Description
Left-click	Select strip to modify. Left-clicking the dark region at either end of the strip selects that end of the strip and allows you to trim or extend the strip from that point. If you left-click and drag on the work area rather than a strip, you can border-select multiple strips.
Left-click+drag a strip	If you left-click and drag on a strip, you'll automatically start moving it around the timeline. If you left-click and drag one of the dark regions at the head or tail of the strip, you can extend or shorten the clip from that side.
Left-click time value at the top of the Sequencer	Move the time cursor in the Sequencer. Left-clicking and dragging scrubs the time cursor, allowing you to view and hear the contents of the Sequencer as fast or slow as you move your mouse.
Shift+left-click	Select multiple strips.
Middle-click	Pan the Sequencer work area.
Ctrl+middle-click	Zoom height and width of the Sequencer work area simultaneously.
Scroll wheel	Zoom the width in and out of the Sequencer work area.
Ctrl+scroll wheel	Scroll the Sequencer work area left and right.
Shift+scroll wheel	Scroll the Sequencer work area up and down.

One thing you may notice is that quite a few of the controls are similar to those present in other parts of Blender, such as the 3D View and Graph Editor. This similarity is also true when it comes to the hotkeys that the Video Sequencer recognizes, although a few differences are worth mentioning. Table 1-2 lists some the most common hotkeys used for editing.

TABLE 1-2   **Common Features/Hotkeys in the Sequencer**

Hotkey	Menu Access	Description
G		Grabs/Moves your selected strips. This is particularly useful if you have multiple strips selected at the same time.
E	Strip ⇨ Transform ⇨ Move/Extend from frame	Grabs a selection and extends one (or both, if it's to one side of the time cursor completely) end of it relative to the position of the time cursor.
Shift+D	Strip ⇨ Duplicate Strips	Duplicates the selected strip(s).
X	Strip ⇨ Delete	Deletes the selected strip(s).
K	Strip ⇨ Split	Splits a strip at the location of the time cursor. Similar to the razor tool in other NLEs.
Ctrl+G	Strip ⇨ Make Meta Strip	Combines selected strips into a single *meta strip*, a collection of strips.
Ctrl+Alt+G	Strip ⇨ UnMeta Strip	Separates a selected meta strip back into its original individual strips stacked on different channels.
Tab	Strip ⇨ Toggle Meta	Tabs into a meta strip to allow modification of the strips within it.
H	Strip ⇨ Lock/Mute ⇨ Mute Strips	Hides a strip from being played.
Alt+H	Strip ⇨ Lock/Mute ⇨ Unmute Strips	Unhides a strip.
Ctrl+H	Strip ⇨ Lock/Mute ⇨ Lock Strips	Prevents selected strips from being moved or edited.
Ctrl+Alt+H	Strip ⇨ Lock/Mute ⇨ Unlock Strips	Allows editing on selected strips.
Spacebar		Plays the animation starting from the location of the time cursor (or pauses if it is already playing).

Editing in the Sequencer is pretty straightforward. If you have two strips stacked in two channels, one above the other, when the timeline cursor gets to them, the strip that's in the higher channel takes priority, just like stacking plates. In most video footage, the top strip simply overrides any of the strips below. You can, however, change this behavior in the Compositing panel of the Sequencer's Sidebar (make sure you're on the Strip tab). The drop-down menu labeled Blend controls the *blend mode* of the selected strip. You can see that the default setting is Alpha Over, meaning that if the footage in the strip has any transparency (called the *alpha channel*), the strips below will show in that transparent area. However, if you left-click the Blend drop-down, you get a short list of modes similar to the layer-blending options you see in a program such as Photoshop or GIMP. Besides Alpha Over, the ones I use the most are Replace and Add.

Like almost everything in Blender, most of the strip controls can be animated in the Sequencer. One of the primary animated values for strips is the Opacity slider in the Compositing panel. This slider controls the influence factor that the strip has on the rest of the sequence. For example, on an image strip — say, of a solid black image — you can animate the overall opacity of that strip. Values less than 1.0 make the image more transparent, thereby giving you a nice way to create a controlled fade to black. The Fade items in the Add menu of the Sequencer are shortcuts to quickly adding these keyframes. The same principle works for sound strips, using the Volume slider in the Sound panel of the Sequencer's Sidebar. A value of 1.0 is the sound clip's original loudness, and it gradually fades away the lower you get. Values greater than 1.0 amplify the sound to a level greater than the original volume.

Like animating elsewhere in Blender, all the keyframes you add will show up in the Graph Editor and the Dope Sheet. If you're at the point where you're adding these keyframes, it may make sense to temporarily change the File Browser in the Video Editing workspace to a Graph Editor while you're animating. You'll also see your keyframes show up in the Timeline at the bottom of the workspace. Figure 1-5 shows what this workspace layout could look like.

FIGURE 1-5: You can swap the File Browser with a Graph Editor in the Video Editing Layout to give yourself more control over animated strip values.

By animating values for your strips, you can create some very cool results. Say you have a logo graphic with an alpha channel defining the background as transparent, and you want to make the logo flicker as if it's being seen through poor television reception. To make the logo flicker, follow these steps:

1. Add a logo image to the Sequencer (Add ⇨ Image/Sequence).

Editing Video and Animation

2. Make sure that the logo's strip is selected and, in the Compositing panel, insert a keyframe for the strip's opacity (left-click the keyframe icon to the right of the Opacity field in the Compositing panel, or press I with your mouse hovered over the Opacity value field).

3. In the Graph Editor (again, you may want to temporarily change your File Browser area to show the Graph Editor instead), tweak the Opacity f-curve so that it randomly bounces many times between 1.0 and 0.0 (Ctrl+right-click).

After tweaking the curve to your taste (see Book 4, Chapter 1 for more on working in the Graph Editor), you should now have your flickering logo effect.

Adding effects and transitions

The Add menu in the Sequencer provides you with quite a few options other than importing audio and video elements. A large portion of these options are effects and transitions, and many typically require that you select two strips that are at least partially stacked on top of each other in the Sequencer. When necessary, I point out which effects these are.

TIP

Pay close attention to the order in which you select your strips because it often has a dramatic influence on how the effect is applied. The second strip you select is the *active strip* and serves as the primary controller of the effect.

Here's a list of the available options:

» **Add/Subtract/Multiply:** These effects are the same as the blend mode settings in the Compositing panel of the Sidebar. The main reason you would use these effects is if you want something to happen only between two specific strips and nowhere else. Most of the time, you can get away with using blend modes instead of adding these effect strips. It works just as well and keeps your Sequencer timeline from getting too cluttered. Using these effects requires that you select two strips before adding any of them. The following steps give a quick example of how to use them:

1. Select the strip you want to start with.

2. Shift+left-click the strip you want to mix with.

3. Choose Add ⇨ Effect Strip ⇨ Add.

A new red strip is created, which is the length of the overlap between your two selected strips. On playback (Spacebar), the bright parts of the upper strip amplify the overlaying bright parts of the lower strip.

>> **Over Drop/Alpha Over/Alpha Under:** These effect strips control how one strip's alpha channel relates to another. They're also available as Blending modes, and in most cases the blending modes are sufficient. Just like with Add, Subtract, and Multiply, you use these effects when you need to apply them between two specific strips and no others.

>> **Color Mix:** The previous six effects are set on their own because they can get used pretty frequently. But what if you want to use one of the other blend modes, and it's not enough to just use the blend mode that's built into the strip? For example, what if you want to use the Difference blend mode, but only between two strips and not with the whole stack of channels below one strip? This is where the Color Mix effect comes in handy. You can use it to set a blending mode between any two selected strips.

>> **Multicam Selector:** If you're using Scene strips in the Sequencer and you have multiple cameras in your scene, you can use this effect strip to dictate which camera you're using from that scene. As with most things in Blender, you can animate that camera choice, allowing you to easily do camera-switching in your scene.

>> **Transform:** This effect provides very basic controls for the location, scale, and rotation of a strip. The effect works on a single strip, and you can find its controls on the Effect Strip panel of the Sidebar in the Strip tab. You can use f-curves on this effect strip to animate the transform values. These controls are the same basic ones available in the Transform panel for most types of strips. It's mostly in Blender for supporting older .blend files.

>> **Speed Control:** With the Speed Control effect, you can adjust the playback speed of individual strips. In the Effect Strip panel of the Sidebar, you can choose to influence the Global Speed (1.0 is regular speed; setting it to 0.50 makes the strip play half as fast; setting it to 2.0 plays it twice as fast). You can also have more custom control using the Graph Editor.

>> **Glow:** The Glow effect works on a single strip and is a simple compositing effect to throw on using the full Compositor in Blender. This effect takes the pixels in a given strip and makes the bright points in it glow a bit brighter. Ever wonder how some 3D renders get that glowing, almost ethereal quality? Glow is one way to do it. The Effect Strip panel in the Sidebar lets you adjust the amount of glow you have and the quality of that glow.

>> **Gaussian Blur:** This effect works like a simplified version of the Blur mode in the Compositor (covered in the next chapter). Using the Size X and Size Y values in the Effect Strip panel of the Sidebar, the Gaussian Blur effect gives you the ability to make the images or video in a strip blurry.

Besides adding effects between strips, you can also animate the transition between effects. Sure, it's certainly possible to animate opacity or volume on an individual strip using Fades and tweak the timing with the Graph Editor, but sometimes it's more convenient to use a pre-baked transition effect. That way, you can focus on editing, and you don't have to think as much about animating transitions. The Video Sequencer gives you a few of these preset transitions when you choose Add ⇨ Transitions:

» **Sound Crossfade:** The Sound Crossfade transition can be used only with audio strips. Where two strips overlap, the Sound Crossfade transition reduces the volume of your one strip to zero while increasing the volume from your other strip up from zero to one.

TIP

When you add a Sound Crossfade transition, there doesn't seem to be any obvious change in the Sequencer work area. Unlike with other transitions, no new strips are added. Instead, there's a subtle overlay that visualizes a ramp on each strip where they overlap. Furthermore, if you look in the Timeline, you should notice some new keyframes have been added. The Sound Crossfade menu option is more like a shortcut for automatically adding animation keyframes for the Volume control in the Sound panel of the Sequencer's Sidebar.

» **Cross/Gamma Cross:** These transitions are *crossfades* or *dissolves* between overlapping strips. Like with effects strips, the Cross and Gamma Cross transitions add short red strips that give you some additional controls over the transition. For images and video, Gamma Cross works the same as Cross, but takes the additional step of correcting the color in the transition for a smoother dissolve.

» **Wipe:** Wipe is a transition effect like Cross and Gamma Cross. It transitions from one strip to another like a sliding door, à la the *Star Wars* movies. This effect also uses the Effect Strip panel in the Sidebar to let you choose the type of wipe you want, including single, double, iris, and clock wipe. Also, you can adjust the blurriness of the wiping edge and the direction the wipe moves.

Rendering from the Video Sequencer

To render your complete edited sequence from the Video Sequencer, the steps are largely identical to the ones outlined for creating a finished animation in Book 3, Chapter 4. There are a few minor differences, though. In contrast to what I wrote at the end of Book 3, Chapter 4, the output from an editing session should almost always be a video file rather than a sequence of images. Blender has some presets that make this pretty easy for you. When you're done editing, follow these steps to render out a video file that you can share with others:

1. **In Output Properties, find the Output panel and choose FFmpeg Video from the File Format drop-down.**

   There are two other video choices in the File Format menu (AVI JPEG and AVI Raw). I don't recommend using them because the output file sizes are typically very large and your audio doesn't get bundled in the file. Using FFmpeg Video is a much better choice. Upon making this selection, an Encoding sub-panel will appear. This sub-panel is where you make a few additional choices.

   TECHNICAL STUFF

   What is FFmpeg? Why not just say "Video"? FFmpeg is actually a separate open source program for video encoding that Blender is using as a library when generating video files. It's incredibly powerful. In fact, only a fraction of what it can do is actually exposed in Blender's interface. You can do much, much more with FFmpeg from its command line interface.

2. **Select your container type from the Container drop-down menu.**

   Video files are wacky beasts. All the frames of your video and the audio are bundled into a single file, called a *container*. It's the file type that serves as the bucket that holds all your audio and video data. The default is set to MPEG-4, the most commonly used container format for output video.

3. **Choose a video codec from the Video Codec drop-down menu.**

   You can find this drop-down menu in the Video panel that appears below the Encoding panel. *Codec* is an abbreviation for coder-decoder. It's the algorithm that defines how your video footage is compressed (like JPEG and PNG for still images). A dizzying variety of choices are available to you here. This is where things can get a bit tricky. Even though you can technically use any codec you want, some video players, such as Windows Media Player, don't know how to play all codecs in all the containers they support. There are whole web pages out there dedicated to figuring out which version of which video player supports what combination of container and codec. Unless you're doing something very specific, I'd suggest you choose H.264 or WEBM/VP9 from this drop-down menu. Those are the options most commonly paired with the MPEG-4 container. And in most cases, all the other settings in the Video panel can remain at their defaults.

4. **Choose an audio codec from the Audio Codec drop-down menu.**

   The Audio Codec drop-down menu is in the Audio panel at the bottom of the Encoding sub-panel. Like when choosing a video codec, there are quite a few choices here and not all video players support all combinations of containers and video and audio codecs. The safest choice here is PCM, but that's fully uncompressed audio. For compatibility reasons, your next best choices are probably AAC or AC3.

Figure 1-6 shows the Encode sub-panel in Output properties with commonly chosen settings.

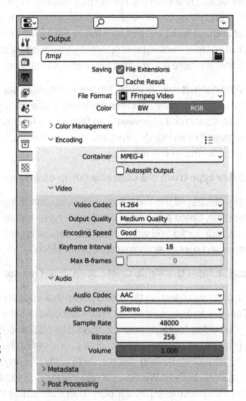

FIGURE 1-6:
Common FFmpeg
settings for
container, video,
and audio.

 Although it's handy to know all the ins and outs of each and every video format out there, most folks just want to get the work done. To help a bit with this, Blender does offer some presets to help you choose some encoding settings quickly. If you look to the top right of the Encoding sub-panel, you should notice an icon there that resembles a little bulleted list. This is how you access the encoding presets. When you click this icon, you can choose H264 in MP4 to get settings for a video that should work in most players. You may still need to choose your audio codec manually, but these presets can help you take a four- to six-step process and do it in two.

 Before you render, make sure your other Output Properties are set the way you want. In particular, double-check the Dimensions panel and ensure you have the correct image size and frame rate and that your start and end frames are where you want them. It's really annoying to be halfway through rendering your video and suddenly realize you've forgotten to include the first 15 seconds of your edit session.

REMEMBER

It's also a good idea to choose an explicit output path for your rendered video file. By default, Blender is going to throw the finished file in your operating system's temporary folder with a filename that's just the start frame and end frame of the sequence (such as 0001–0250.mp4). Use the Output Path field at the top of the Output panel to choose a location and name that makes more sense for your project. Otherwise, you might have a hard time relocating your video file (or worse, you could overwrite another project with the same simple naming scheme).

Once you've set all your output settings for your video file, you should be ready to render out your editing session. Just like with rendering animations, you do this by navigating to the Render menu at the top of your Blender window and choosing Render ⇨ Render Animation.

TIP

One additional thing you should check is in Output Properties, in the Post Processing panel. Make sure that the Sequencer check box is enabled. Activating this check box lets Blender know that you want to use the strips in the Video Sequencer for your final output rather than anything in front of the 3D camera. If you don't enable this check box, Blender just renders whatever the camera sees, which may be just the default cube that starts with Blender or whatever else you might place in front of the 3D camera.

Editing Video and
Animation

Chapter **2**

Compositing Images and Video

Whether you're doing 3D animation, visual effects for film and video, or just making a really cool render of a 3D model you've sculpted, it's natural to start adjusting your output images and mixing them with other graphics. That's the essence of compositing. The art of compositing can happen in many forms. It could be as simple as putting a logo in the corner of a photo or as complex as replacing a live action actor with a fully rigged and animated 3D character. In the simplest form, you're working on a single image, and a lot of compositing work can be done in your photo-editing software of choice. However, when you start working on sequences of images, like video footage or an animated character, that's where a Compositor like the one built into Blender really shines.

Understanding Nodes

Compositing is the process of mixing multiple visual assets to create a single image or sequence of images. By this definition, you may notice that *technically* Blender's Video Sequencer qualifies as a sort of Compositor because you can stack strips over each other in channels and blend them together with effects and transitions. After all, as covered in the previous chapter, the Sequencer contains a panel labeled Compositing that's used for mixing strips. Although this statement is true, the Video Sequencer is nowhere near as powerful as Blender's Compositor for mixing videos, images, and other graphics together.

REMEMBER

As designed, the Video Sequencer is intended for working with multiple shots, scenes, images, or clips of video. It's also meant to play back in real-time (or as near to that as possible). In contrast, the Compositor is intended for working with a single shot, and it's most certainly not meant for working in real-time (though recent advancements in Blender have certainly made things faster). There is a little bit of overlap in the functionality of these two parts of Blender, but depending on the task at hand, one is more suitable than the other.

What makes the Compositor so powerful? In a single word, it's *nodes*. Have a look at Book 2, Chapter 5 for an in-depth description of node-based workflows and the power of working with nodes. If you've read through other books in this All-in-One, you've at least been exposed to some of the incredible things you can do with nodes using geometry nodes, shader nodes, and hair nodes. All that power was actually born in Blender's Compositor. The Compositor was the first node editor in Blender and has continued to be an excellent example of how flexible and powerful nodes are.

In a nutshell, the strength of nodes comes from the ability to link (*noodle*) a bunch of smaller operations together to achieve a larger result. In addition, node networks represent instructions to do work on your inputs instead of working on that data directly, so they're inherently procedural and nondestructive. This feature of nodes means that it's always easy to roll back or remove an operation because your original image data remains unchanged.

Getting Started with the Compositor

The preferred way to do compositing in Blender is from the Compositing workspace. From a new Blender session in the General workflow template (File ⇨ New ⇨ General), it's the third-to-last workspace tab at the top of the Blender window. The same workspace is also available when you use the VFX workflow template (File ⇨ New ⇨ VFX). If you have your own custom set of workspaces in your .blend file, you can add a Compositing workspace by clicking the plus (+) button at the end of the workspaces' tabs and choosing Compositing from the General or VFX submenus.

The majority of your compositing work will take place in the large Compositor area. The rest of the workspace takes its cues from the Animation workspace. The Outliner and Properties editor are located along the right side of the window.

At the bottom, you have a Dope Sheet and a collapsed Timeline. The reason the Timeline is collapsed is because you can scrub time easily from the Dope Sheet. The Timeline is mostly there to give you playback controls.

By itself, the Compositor looks pretty stark and boring, like a lame 2D version of the 3D Viewport. However, toggle the Use Nodes check box in the header and Blender adds some starting nodes to the Compositor: a Render Layers node and a Composite node. The section "Discovering the Nodes Available to You" has more detailed information about these nodes and others available in the Compositor. Figure 2-1 shows what you're greeted with when you choose the Compositing workspace and enable the Use Nodes check box.

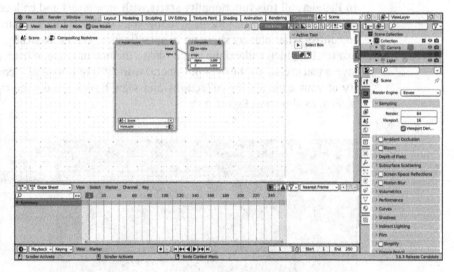

FIGURE 2-1:
The Compositing workspace that ships with Blender is the preferred starting point for compositing work, whether you're starting with 3D assets or compositing a sequence of images.

Rendering in Passes and Layers

Before taking full advantage of nodes, it's worthwhile to take a quick moment and understand what it means to render *in layers*. Assume for a moment that you animated a character walking into a room and falling down. The room is pretty detailed, so it takes a fairly long time for your computer to render each frame. However, because the camera doesn't move, you need to render the room only once. Then, if you render your character with a transparent background, you can superimpose the character on that still image of the room, effectively cutting your final render time to a fraction of what it would be.

That's the basics of rendering in layers. The preceding example had two layers, one for the room and one for the character. In addition to rendering in layers, each layer can contain multiple *passes,* isolated components of that layer that you can use in your composite. For example, if you want to, you can have a render pass that consists of just the shadows in the layer. You can take that pass and adjust it to make all the shadows slightly blue. Or you can isolate a character while they're walking through a gray, blurry scene.

Another thing to understand for compositing 3D scenes is the concept of Z-depth. Basically, *Z-depth* is the representation of the distance between an object and the camera, along the camera's local Z-axis. The Compositor can use this Z-depth to make an object look like it fits in a scene even though it was never rendered with it.

In Blender, all this functionality starts with *view layers* and collections. The same collections that you use for organizing your scenes when animating can be used to control what objects show up in specific view layers. Basically, you can decide arbitrarily which collections you'd like to include or exclude from any of the view layers you create. In the default General workflow template of Blender, the majority of your controls for collections and view layers are on the right side of the screen, as shown in Figure 2-2.

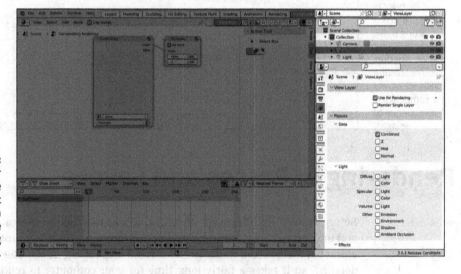

FIGURE 2-2:
Controls for your view layers are all along the right side of the screen when using the Compositing workspace.

TIP

You know you're looking at something relevant to view layers when you see the View Layer icon. It looks like a stack of photographs.

At the upper right is a View Layer datablock, where you control the active View layer you're working on. If you click the datablock's icon, it reveals a drop-down list of all the view layers in your scene. Click the view layer you want to make it active. By default, there's only one view layer, creatively named View Layer. Like any other datablock in Blender, you can rename it by clicking in the text area of the datablock. I strongly encourage you to rename your view layers to things that make sense to you, especially when you have more than one in your scene. View layers can be added and removed from your scene using the add and remove buttons on the right side of the datablock.

The View Layer display mode of the Outliner (which is the default display mode) houses the controls for how your collections relate to your active view layer. The Outliner is where you tell Blender which collections should be included in your active view layer. Click the check box to the right of each collection to toggle its inclusion in your active view layer. For more on collections and how they work, have a look at Book 1, Chapter 4.

You control the passes in your view layer from the View Layer tab in the Properties editor. This tab is where the real magic and power of view layers lies. What's visible in this tab varies a bit, depending on whether you've chosen Eevee or Cycles as your renderer in the Render tab. As shown in Figure 2-3, you have fewer options and panels if you're rendering with Eevee.

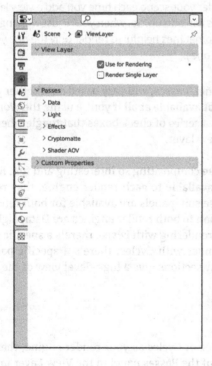
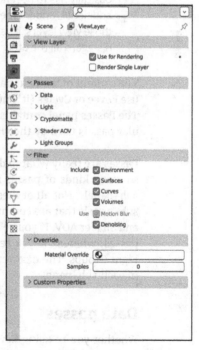

FIGURE 2-3:
View Layer properties with Eevee as your render engine (left) versus that same tab with Cycles as your chosen renderer.

Discovering passes available in Eevee and Cycles

Regardless of the render engine you've chosen, there's always a View Layer panel at the top of the View Layer tab in the Properties editor. In this panel, you have two options:

>> **Use for Rendering:** Enabled by default, this property toggles whether your active view layer is rendered. You might find yourself wondering why you would ever have a view layer that *isn't* used for rendering. After all, it's not called a "don't view" layer. Typically speaking, you wouldn't disable a view render. However, if you're working on a large project that has a lot of view layers and you just make a change to one, it's very useful to be able to toggle off all the view layers you don't need. Interestingly enough, you can animate this property. Another common practice is for artists to set up a "working" view layer where they can freely toggle on and off collections without compromising any carefully configured render layers for compositing.

>> **Render Single Layer:** When doing test renders on your scene, render times can sometimes get pretty long if you have a lot of view layers. Blender basically has to re-render your scene each time you add a view layer. Those additional render times can add up. So, when you're just working on one of those view layers, it's sometimes helpful to render only the one you're in and disregard all the other ones.

The content of the next panel, Passes, will vary based on whether you've chosen to use Eevee or Cycles (it's not available at all if you're using the Workbench engine). The Passes panel contains a series of check boxes that toggle whether that particular pass is used by the view layer.

Passes are really what make compositing so interesting and fun. Because there are so many kinds of passes available to each render engine, they're organized into sub-panels. Not all of these sub-panels are available for both render engines. The sub-panels that are common to both render engines are Data, Light, Cryptomatte, and Shader AOV. If you're rendering with Eevee, there's a specific panel for Effects passes, whereas if you render with Cycles, there's a specific panel dedicated to Light Groups. The next few sections give a high-level view of the passes available in each sub-panel.

Data passes

Whether you're using Eevee or Cycles as your render engine, there's a Data sub-panel available at the top of the Passes panel in the View Layer tab of the Properties editor. These passes consist of data about your scene from the perspective of the render engine. When you render with Cycles, you have quite a few more passes available to you than when you render with Eevee. However, the following four passes are common between both engines and tend to be the most frequently used:

>> **Combined:** The Combined pass is the fully mixed, rendered image as it comes from the renderer before getting any processing. It's enabled by default and there's usually no reason to disable it.

>> **Z:** This pass is a mapping of the Z-depth information for each object in front of the camera. It is useful for masking as well as faking camera effects like *depth of field,* where a short distance of the viewable range is in focus and everything else is blurry.

>> **Mist:** In a way, the Mist pass is similar to the Z pass because it's based on Z-depth information. There are three big differences:

- Values in the Mist pass already are normalized between 0 and 1.

- The Mist pass takes the transparency of your materials into account; the Z pass doesn't.

- Unlike the Z pass, the Mist pass is nicely anti-aliased and doesn't have some of the nasty star-stepped jaggies you may see in the Z pass.

>> **Normal:** The information in this pass relates to the angle that the geometry in the scene has relative to the camera. If you were to look at an image generated by the Normal pass, it looks pretty funky. In an RGB image of a Normal pass, the red channel indicates how much a face of geometry is aimed left or right. The blue channel indicates how much that face is tilted up or down, and the green channel indicates how much that face is pointing at the camera. There are a lot of creative uses for the Normal pass; most commonly, it can be used for additional bump mapping as well as completely altering the lighting in the scene without re-rendering.

Light passes

Although the Light sub-panel of passes is available when you're rendering with either Eevee or Cycles, the contents of this panel vary wildly between the two render engines. A large reason for this difference is that, as different render engines, the way that each of them handles light information is dramatically different. Because these passes all deal with light, they're all related to topics covered in Book 3, Chapter 3, so refer to that chapter if you need a refresher. Still, a few passes are consistent between the two:

>> **Emission:** If any objects in your scene have an Emission shader on them, those materials are going to be caught in this pass if you enable it.

>> **Environment:** If any of your World background is visible, whether it's a solid color or an HDRI, this pass gives you a socket that shows only those visible pixels from that background.

>> **Ambient Occlusion:** The Ambient Occlusion pass includes any ambient occlusion (AO) data generated by the renderer, if you have AO enabled.

For each pass that you enable in the View Layer tab, you should notice that the corresponding Render Layers node in the Compositor expands with an output socket that matches the pass you enable. Figure 2-4 shows a Render Layers node with a variety of additional passes enabled.

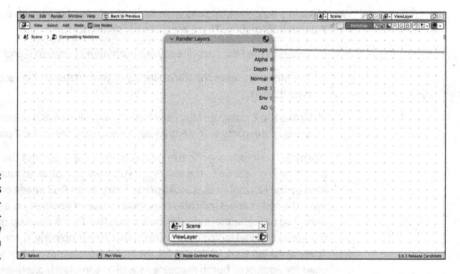

FIGURE 2-4: Enabling passes adds corresponding output sockets on your view layer's node in the Compositor.

REMEMBER

You may notice Blender's interface has parts that refer to View Layers and Render Layers. For the most part, you can use these terms interchangeably. Render Layers are basically what View Layers were in older versions of Blender. Blender's interface has been updated to refer to View Layers throughout most of it, with the one notable exception being the Compositor. There's an input node (typically the main input node in your node network) called Render Layers. You choose that node to specify a view layer from your scene that you want to route into your compositing node network. It's a bit confusing, but hopefully, in future versions of Blender, the developers update the naming and make things a bit more consistent.

Cryptomatte passes

Blender also has support for a specialized feature called *cryptomatte*. Cryptomatte is an open source standard for *mattes* (masks) that the visual effects community has settled upon for compositing. The best way to think of cryptomatte is to consider it like the Object Index and Material Index passes "turned up to eleven." (You can find out more about Object Index and Material Index passes in the section titled "Understanding Cycles-only Passes). Not only do you have the ability to isolate individual objects and materials in a render, but that masking is done automatically; you don't have to go to the Object or Material tab to give each object its own pass index. And even better, cryptomatte has much better support for camera features like motion blur, depth of field, and transparency.

"That's great," you say, "but how do I use the thing?" The first thing you need to do is go to the View Layers tab. As shown back in Figure 2-3, there's a Cryptomatte sub-panel at the bottom of the Passes panel. The only controls you really need to worry about at this point are the three buttons at the top of the sub-panel:

>> **Object:** This option is cryptomatte's version of Object Index passes. The difference here is that you don't have to manually assign any pass indices yourself. Cryptomatte takes care of that for you. Enable this button if you want to make mattes specific to certain objects.

>> **Material:** Enable the Material button if you want mattes specific to materials in your scene. This option is like the Material Index pass, but with the indices all automatically set up for you.

>> **Asset:** There's no real equivalent to Asset mattes elsewhere in the Passes panel. If you have a group of objects sharing the same parent, enabling this option allows you to treat them all as a single unit for making a mask.

Once you enable the type (or types) of cryptomatte you want to use in your compositing session, the Render Layers node in the Compositor for your view layer expands with cryptomatte sockets, three for each type that you've enabled. For example, if you enable Object cryptomattes, you should see three new sockets on your Render Layers node: CryptObject00, CryptObject01, and CryptObject02. You don't really need to use any of them. These sockets are included to support an older, legacy version of the Cryptomatte node, but they're also helpful to remind you that you've enabled cryptomatte on your view layer. In any case, attaching a Viewer node to any of these sockets won't display anything useful. To make use of these sockets, follow these steps (review the next section on working with nodes if any of the terms in these steps don't yet make sense to you):

1. **Add a Cryptomatte node (Add ➪ Matte ➪ Cryptomatte) in the Compositor.**

   You'll need a different Cryptomatte node for each of the cryptomatte types (object, material, and asset) that you enable.

2. **Ensure that the Render button at the top of the node is enabled and that ViewLayer:CryptoObject is selected from the Cryptomatte Layer dropdown menu.**

3. **Add a Viewer node (Add ⇨ Output ⇨ Viewer) and connect it to the Pick output socket on the Cryptomatte node.**

If you haven't rendered yet, you're not going to have any feedback after connecting your Viewer node. Do a quick Render (Render ⇨ Render Image), and your Compositor should look somewhat like what's shown in Figure 2-5.

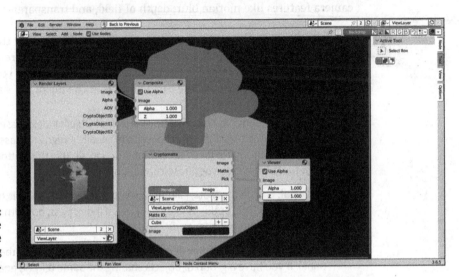

FIGURE 2-5:
Setting up the
Cryptomatte
node for picking
your mattes.

There's a backdrop image in the Compositor much like the backdrop in the Video Sequencer described in Chapter 1 of this book. The backdrop in the Compositor, however, isn't tied to your final output. Instead, it's bound to your active Viewer node. In this case, the backdrop image should show a kind of wacky multicolor version of your render. That's the output of the Pick socket. It's a fun-looking image, but it's not yet doing much for you. If you connect your Viewer node to the Cryptomatte's Matte socket, the backdrop image should be solid black, meaning that you don't have any mattes. That's where the next step comes in. Reconnect your Viewer to the Pick socket before proceeding.

4. **Pick the objects you want to have mattes of.**

In the Cryptomatte node, Plus (+) and Minus (-) buttons appear next to a field labeled Matte ID. Click the Plus (+) button and your mouse cursor changes to an eyedropper. Use the eyedropper to click on the Pick image in the backdrop to choose which objects you want to have mattes of. Likewise, clicking the Minus (-) button gives you an eyedropper that you can use to exclude objects from your matte. You can verify that you've picked correctly by connecting the Matte output to your Viewer node. In this example, I've chosen to make a matte of the cube in my scene. Figure 2-6 shows the resultant matte.

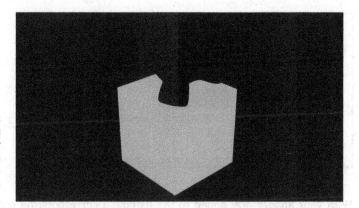

FIGURE 2-6:
Just some objects
I picked for
making a matte
to use elsewhere
in a composite
session.

By using your cryptomattes with the rest of your compositing network, you can ensure that specific effects and adjustments affect only specific parts of your scene. This is how you can change the color of just one leaf on a tree or hide a character that was re-rendered later. Masks and mattes are absolutely fundamental tools in a professional Compositor's toolbox.

Shader AOV passes

There's one further sub-panel in Passes that's available for both Eevee and Cycles, though it's a pretty advanced topic. When building materials as covered in Book 3, you may find certain situations where you want to create your own custom passes. Perhaps you want to specifically debug part of your shader node network, or maybe you need a pass that isn't one of the stock ones that comes with each render engine. Whatever the reason, what you're trying to do is get data out of your material and into the Compositor. In computer science, whenever you pass data from one part of a program to another, you use a variable. In this specific scenario, you need to create an *arbitrary output variable*, or AOV. In the Shader Node Editor, you do this for your material by adding an AOV Output node (Add ⇨ Output ⇨ AOV Output).

The AOV Output node, as shown in Figure 2-7, has two input sockets, Color and Value, as well as a Name property. Type a name that makes sense in the Name field. That's the name of your variable. And the values that travel with that variable are whatever you connect to the Color and Value sockets on the node.

To make use of the AOV from the Compositor, go to the View Layers tab of the Properties editor and expand the Shader AOV sub-panel. Click the Plus (+) button to the right of the listbox in this panel to add a new AOV. By default the AOV is named AOV and is set to refer to color data. Double-click the name to rename it to whatever name you chose in your shader node network, and use the Type drop-down on the right to choose whether you want to use data from the Color or Value socket.

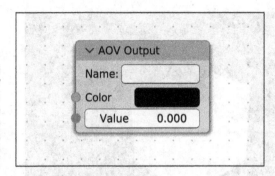

FIGURE 2-7:
Use the AOV Output node in the Shader Node Editor to create a custom pass to send to the Compositor.

 With your Shader AOV added to the listbox, a corresponding socket should also appear in your Render Layers node in the Compositor, and you can use it to your heart's content.

Using Eevee-only Effects Passes

There's one sub-panel in the Passes panel that appears only when you're rendering with Eevee. This panel is the Effects panel, and it holds controls for enabling passes for a couple effects only available in Eevee. As of this writing, only two passes are available in this sub-panel:

» **Bloom:** As noted in Book 3, Chapter 3, emission shaders in Eevee don't really emit light on your scene the way they do in Cycles, so it's difficult to get a nice glowing effect from lights using these kinds of shaders. However, you can hack the look a bit by adding a bit of glow, or *bloom*, to the render. The effect works by finding the bright pixels in the render and blurring them to give a bit of glow. By default, this effect is disabled, but you can enable it from Render Properties. If you do enable this effect, then the Bloom pass is available for you to use in your compositing work. Otherwise, the Bloom check box is grayed out and you can't toggle it.

» **Transparent:** Sometimes it's useful to have a pass that only has your transparent objects in it. Perhaps you want to do a quick colorization on those objects or affect them in some other way. Enable this check box to send that pass to your Render Layers node.

Understanding Cycles-only Passes

A few other passes are (as of this writing) only available when rendering with Cycles. However, they're so handy when compositing your 3D work that they're worth mentioning on their own. I expect that as Eevee matures as a render engine, we're likely to see more of these passes supported there as well:

>> **Vector:** This pass includes speed information for objects moving in front of the camera (meaning that either the objects or the camera are animated). This data is particularly useful for the Vector Blur node, which gives a decent motion blur effect in cases where Cycles' built-in motion blur does not work or takes too long to finish.

>> **UV:** The UV pass is pretty clever because it sends the UV mapping data from the 3D objects in your shot to the Compositor, similar to how the Normal pass works, but with more control. Basically, this pass gives you the ability to completely change the textures on an object or character without the need to re-render any part of the scene (see the end of this chapter for an example of this technique). Often, you want to use this pass along with the Object Index pass or cryptomatte to specify on which object you want to change the texture.

>> **Object Index:** This pass carries index numbers for individual objects, if you set them in the Relations panel of the Object tab in the Properties editor. The Object Index pass allows very fine control over which nodes get applied to which objects. This pass is similar to plain masking but somewhat more powerful because it makes isolating a single object or group of objects so much easier.

To use it, you need to go to Object Properties and expand the Relations panel. At the bottom of that panel is a field labeled Pass Index. By default, it's set to zero, meaning that the pass index is unset. Change the Pass Index value to something else. Then remember that value, because you'll need to use it with the ID Mask node in the Compositor (more on specific nodes in the "Discovering the Nodes Available to You" section). You can give multiple objects the same Pass Index value to make them share, or you can give a unique Pass Index value for each object.

>> **Material Index:** Like with objects, you can assign index numbers to each of your materials (look in the Settings panel of Material Properties). It gives you the same kind of masking control you get with the Object Index pass, but at the material level. Using this pass, you can make quick masks of a character's hair, for example.

To give an individual material its own Pass Index, go to Material Properties and look at the bottom of the Settings panel. The Pass Index field here works the same as the one for objects. In general, pass indices are great for isolating objects, but when you have a complex scene, setting (and remembering) individual index values can be tedious and annoying. For that reason, the easier solution is to take advantage of cryptomattes, as covered earlier in this chapter.

Aside from the main passes available in the Data sub-panel when you have Cycles as your chosen render engine, there are two more sub-panels with even more passes you can make available to the Compositor. The first is the Light sub-panel. These passes specifically relate to how light in your scene interacts with materials on objects in that scene. I already mentioned it a bit in reference to the Emission, Environment, and Ambient Occlusion passes, but with Cycles as your renderer, it doesn't stop there. You get a whole block of material passes that vary based on how light bounces from the object to your scene camera. You should note that these passes closely mirror the kinds of shaders described in Book 3, Chapter 1:

>> **Diffuse:** Think of diffuse color as the "solid" color of an object. If light doesn't go through the object or reflect the environment, the Diffuse passes give you their color.

>> **Glossy:** As its name indicates, the Glossy pass gives you image data for anything in your scene that's reflective.

>> **Transmission:** Transmission is render-engine speak for see-through. If light goes through an object in your scene, that image data gets captured in a Transmission pass.

>> **Volume:** Volumes are shapes without a surface, like clouds or fire. If you have any volumetric materials in your scene, these passes can be used to tweak how they look in the Compositor.

>> **Other:** The passes in this category are a bit of a grab-bag, but the only one that's specific to Cycles is the Shadow Catcher pass, which is used to pass shader information from objects marked as a shadow catcher from the Visibility panel in Object Properties.

With the exception of the Volume and Other passes, all of the aforementioned passes have three possible types that you can enable:

>> **Direct:** As it relates to ray traced light (see Book 3), a Direct pass is the color that your 3D camera sees on a ray directly between the object and the camera. It doesn't bounce anywhere else in the scene. The Direct passes give the color and shading of your object, absent any additional influence.

>> **Indirect:** In a ray traced render engine like Cycles, light rays bounce all over your scene. Color from green grass is going to reflect a bit off a nearby white wall. These bounced colors are what's captured in Indirect passes.

>> **Color:** Occasionally, you just want the color of your object with no consideration whatsoever for its lighting or any bounced light off of it. That's what you get with the Color pass. For anyone familiar with the old Blender Internal renderer in previous releases of Blender, Color passes are similar to what you'd get with a shadeless material. The Volume passes don't have a color option because volumes don't have a surface and, therefore, don't have an implicit color.

One of the really exciting features to come to Blender's Compositor since the last edition of this book is the concept of light groups. With light groups, you can define multiple lighting scenarios for the same scene, but have passes in the Compositor lit as if only using one of those groups. The light groups feature is an extremely versatile one that gives you a lot more flexibility when setting up lights for your scene. As of this writing, light groups are available only when you render using Cycles.

The process of using light groups starts in the View Layers tab of the Properties editor. It's best to understand this feature by working through an example, so follow these steps:

1. **In the View Layers tab of the Properties editor, expand the Light Groups sub-panel.**

   If this panel isn't visible, jump over to Render Properties and ensure that you have Cycles set as your chosen render engine.

2. **Click the Plus (+) button to the right of the listbox in the Light Groups sub-panel to add a new light group.**

   You'll probably want to create more than one light group because the common use for this feature is having multiple lighting passes available to the Compositor. In this example, I made two light groups: Day and Night. In the Render Layers node in the Compositor, you should see a socket added for each light group, prefixed with Combined_ on its name.

3. **Assign your light sources to their corresponding light groups.**

   - You can assign objects (lights objects with emission materials) to the light group from the Object tab of the Properties editor. Expand the Shading panel and look for the Light Group sub-panel. Use the Light Group dropdown to choose the light group you want the object to be part of. An object can only be a member of a single light group.

   - World materials can also be assigned to a light group. The controls for this live in World Properties within the Settings panel. There's a Light Group sub-panel in there that matches the one in Object Properties.

After you've built out your light groups, you can use them from your Render Layers node in the Compositor.

Working with Nodes

After you set up your view layers the way you want, you're ready to work in the Compositor. The Compositor is a node editor, like the Geometry Nodes Editor, Shader Editor, and Texture Node Editor, so it operates by the same basic rules as those editors (see Book 2, Chapter 5). By connecting nodes together from one or more inputs to one or more outputs, you provide Blender with a set of instructions on how to get a particular result. In the case of compositing, that result is a processed image or sequence of images. See Chapters 8, 9, and 10 for details on Blender's other node editors.

As shown back in Figure 2-1, Blender's Compositor starts by presenting you with two nodes, one input and one output. You can quickly tell which is which by looking at the location of the connection points, or *sockets*, on each node. The left node, labeled Render Layers, has sockets on the right side of it. The location of these sockets means that it can serve only as an input to other nodes and can't receive any additional data, so the Render Layers node is an input node. It adds information to the node network.

In contrast, the node on the right, labeled Composite, is an output node because it has no sockets on its right edge, meaning it can't feed information to other nodes. Essentially, it's the end of the line, the result. In fact, when you render by using the Compositor, the Composite node is the final output that appears when Blender renders.

The line connecting the Render Layers node to the Composite node is sometimes called a wire or *noodle*. The noodle indicates that data is traveling from the socket on one node to one on another node. In the default case, it's showing that the Render Layers' image data is being sent to the Composite node. If you disconnected this noodle by clicking the yellow Image socket on the Composite node and moving your mouse cursor away from it, the output render would just be an image filled with black. You can re-connect the nodes by clicking the Render Layers' Image socket and dragging your mouse cursor to the corresponding socket on the Composite node.

Configuring the backdrop

As covered in the previous section on cryptomatte, the Compositor has a backdrop feature, much like the Video Sequencer. It's enabled by default and it displays whatever noodle is currently connected to an active Viewer node.

You might notice that there isn't a Viewer node available at first when you enable nodes in the Compositor. It's easy enough to fix that by adding a Viewer node from the menu (Add ⇨ Output ⇨ Viewer), but there's actually an even faster way. If you Shift+Ctrl+left-click on any node with sockets along its right edge, Blender automatically connects a Viewer node to the first of those sockets. If you don't currently have a Viewer node in your Compositor, Blender will automatically add one for you. Then, each time you Shift+Ctrl+left-click that node, Blender cycles through connecting each socket to your Viewer node. This fast-click access to the Viewer node and the Compositor's backdrop feature make previewing different parts of your composite network very speedy.

TIP

This setup is the way I typically like to work when compositing. In fact, I often take it one step further and press Ctrl+Spacebar to maximize the Compositor to the full window size. This way, you can take full advantage of your entire screen while compositing.

The downside, however, is that if you're rendering at full size, then even with the Compositor maximized, the output image is often too big to be seen completely as a backdrop. Fortunately, there are some features to help with that problem as well. Like the 3D Viewport and most other editors in Blender, the Compositor has its own Sidebar, typically along the right side of the editor. The Compositor's Sidebar contains a series of tabs, and the View tab is of particular interest in this context. The View tab has a panel labeled Backdrop that you can use to control the size and position of the backdrop image. When your backdrop image is larger than the viewing area in your Compositor, adjust the Zoom value. Values less than one make it appear smaller than its original size, whereas values larger than one make it appear larger.

Of course, once the backdrop image is at a manageable scale within your Compositor, there are some easier onscreen controls for the size and position of the backdrop. Click your Viewer node to make it your active node, and you should notice that the backdrop image has a white line around it and a little rectangle at every corner. By clicking and dragging any corner box or white edge line on your backdrop image, you can quickly adjust the Zoom value. And if you click and drag the X at the center of the backdrop image, you can re-position it in the Compositor.

Of course, if you find that the backdrop gets in your way, you can disable it by clicking the Backdrop check box in the View panel or, if that panel is hidden, you can use the Backdrop toggle button in the Compositor's header.

Discovering the nodes available to you

Blender has quite an extensive list of nodes that you can add to your compositing network. In fact, it seems like with every release of Blender, more and more incredible node types are added to the Compositor. Many nodes have a *Fac*, or factor, value that you can usually either set with a value from another node or explicitly set by typing. Values less than one make the node have less influence, whereas values greater than one make the node have more influence than usual over the image. The following list describes each of the node categories available to you in the Compositor (for a more detailed description of each node, see this book's supplemental website, blenderbasics.com):

>> **Input:** The input nodes are one of the two most important node types in the Compositor. If your node network doesn't have any inputs, you don't have

anything to composite. The types of inputs include images, masks, colors, textures, and control values.

>> **Output:** I mentioned that Input nodes are one of the two most important node types in Blender. As you may have guessed, the Output nodes are the other important node types, for a similar reason. If you don't have an output node, Blender doesn't know what to save when it renders. The two most-used output nodes are the Composite node and the Viewer node, but the File Output node is also quite handy (see Book 3, Chapter 4).

>> **Color:** The color nodes have an enormous influence over the look of the final output. These nodes directly affect how colors appear, mix, and balance in an image. And because an image is basically just a bunch of colors arranged in a specific pattern, you can understand why these nodes have so much control.

>> **Converter:** These handy little utility nodes have a variety of purposes, including converting one set of data to another and ripping apart or recombining elements from a rendered image. The ColorRamp and ID Mask nodes in particular get used quite a bit. The ColorRamp node is great for helping visualize or re-visualize numerical values on a scale.

>> **Filter:** Filter nodes can *drastically* change the look of an image and are probably the Number One way to fake any effect in an image. These nodes actually process the pixels in an image and can do things like put thick black lines around an object, give the image a variety of customized blurs, or make bright parts of the image glow.

>> **Vector:** Vector nodes use 3D data from your scene to influence the look of your final 2D image. The usage of these nodes tends to be a bit advanced, but they allow you to do things like change the lighting in a scene or even change the speed that objects move through the scene . . . all without re-rendering! If you render to an image format that understands render passes, like the very cool OpenEXR format (more on this topic in the next section), and you include vector and normal passes, these nodes can be a huge timesaver.

>> **Matte:** The matte nodes are specifically tailored for using color information from an image as a way of isolating certain parts of it. Matting is referred to as *keying* because you pick the main color, or *key color,* to represent transparency. Keying is the fundamental basis for those cool *bluescreen* or *greenscreen* effects used in movies. The filmmaker shoots the action over a blue or green screen (blue is used for analog film, whereas green is typically used for digital footage), and a Compositor removes the blue or green and replaces it with other footage or something built in 3D. This submenu is also where you find the Cryptomatte node as well as a few other nodes that are specific to masking, rather than keying.

>> **Distort:** The distort nodes typically do general-purpose image manipulation operations like Translate, Rotate, Scale, Flip, or Crop.

>> **Group:** When you create a node group (Node ⇨ Make Group), that group is placed in this menu. When you group a set of nodes, you instantly have the ability to reuse that group in other parts of your compositing node network. Also, grouping gives you the ability to share node networks between .blend files. When you append or link a node group from another file, it shows up in this menu.

>> **Layout:** The choices available in the Layout submenu are difficult to classify as nodes in the traditional sense. It's really best to think of them as tools for organizing your node network and making it easy to understand what's going on in a complex set of noodles — especially if you're coming back to a file you haven't opened in a few days (or months).

Rendering from the Compositor

If you're using the Compositor, you hopefully already know all the basic steps for getting a rendered image out of it. Of course, if you skipped Book 3, Chapter 4 and came straight to this section, here's the quick version: Make sure that the Compositing check box in the Post Processing panel of Output Properties is enabled.

That said, you need to know one other thing about rendering from the Compositor. Say that you're working on a larger production and want to save your render passes to an external file format so that either you or another Compositor can work on it later without re-rendering the whole scene. You'd have to save your renders to a file format that understands view layers and render passes. That format is the venerable open source OpenEXR file format, developed and gifted to the world by the cool people at Industrial Light & Magic.

Now, I know what you're thinking: "Using this format is as easy as setting up my view layers and then choosing OpenEXR from the menu in the Output panel of Output Properties." You're actually two-thirds correct. You do set up your view layers and you do go to the Output panel of Output Properties. *However*, choosing OpenEXR saves only the final composite output (not the layers or passes) in an OpenEXR file (extension .exr). In order to get layers and passes, you should instead choose OpenEXR MultiLayer. With this format, you get an OpenEXR file that has all the layer and pass information stored with it.

WARNING

Pay close attention to your hard drive space when you choose to render to OpenEXR with all your layers and passes embedded. Keeping all your render layers and passes is a great way to tweak and make adjustments after rendering. However, the file size for each individual .exr file can be *huge*. Whereas a high definition (HD) frame in PNG format may be only a couple hundred kilobytes, an OpenEXR file on the same single frame with all the passes enabled may be well over 100 *megabytes* — yes, megabytes. And that's just for one HD image. If your animation has a length in minutes, that 100 megabytes per frame starts taking up space quickly, even more so if you're rendering in higher resolution images like 4k. So make sure that you do test saves to get a good benchmark for the file size and see that you have enough hard drive space to store all those frames.

Compositing in Real-Time in the 3D Viewport

As you're working in 3D, you may start thinking, "It would be really nice to see what my final composite shot looks like without doing a full render. What if I could see the result of the Compositor in the 3D Viewport?" As it turns out, you're not the only one with that idea. The fine folks on the Blender development team have actually added real-time compositing in the 3D Viewport. You just need to know where to look to enable it.

For myself, I like to use this feature from the Shading workspace. From that workspace, I can easily swap the Shader Node Editor with the Compositor. In any case, the key to using real-time compositing in the 3D Viewport is ensuring that you're either using the Material Preview or Rendered viewport shading mode. With either of these modes in effect in the 3D Viewport, you can expand the Viewport Shading roll-out from the 3D Viewport's header. At the bottom of this roll-out, as shown in Figure 2-8, is a modest little section labeled Compositor.

The Compositor section of the Viewport Shading roll-out gives you the ability to choose one of three options:

>> **Disabled:** This option is the default behavior; real-time compositing is disabled in the 3D Viewport.

>> **Camera:** Click this option and your real-time compositing results show up only when you're looking at your scene through the camera object in your scene. This option is the best balance between performance and seeing the results of your compositing network. For the most part, you only really care about the results based on your render, so it makes sense to show Compositor results only from the camera view.

>> **Always:** Enable this option to have the Compositor's results appear in the 3D Viewport at all times, regardless of whether you're looking through the camera. This option may be a good choice if you haven't yet locked down where in your scene you want to place your camera.

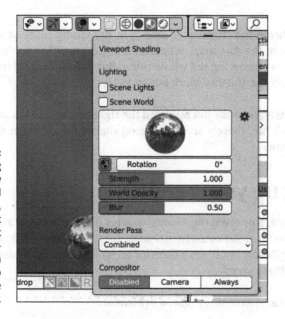

FIGURE 2-8:
When using Material Preview or Rendered viewport shading, the Viewport Shading roll-out includes a Compositor section at the bottom to enable real-time compositing.

WARNING

As of this writing, not all of the nodes in the Compositor are fully supported in real-time in the 3D Viewport. The most common ones are, and with each release of Blender, more are included. However, if you find that a particular node's results aren't showing up in the 3D Viewport or those results look different than after rendering, chances are good that the node isn't yet supported. It's also worth noting that although it's incredibly cool to see results from the Compositor happen nearly instantly in the 3D Viewport, this feature can be taxing on your computer's video card. If you have an older computer, real-time compositing may make your 3D Viewport a bit laggy.

A Simple Example: Replacing a Texture without Re-rendering

As with so many things that involve nodes, it's difficult to understand how to use them without a reference example. To that end, I'm including this section in this chapter to help walk through a simple compositing effect.

Say you have the hypothetical situation where you've spent a long time working on a shot. You've gotten it to the point that you have a sequence of rendered images. And you rendered with Cycles at a high resolution, so each image took about an hour to render. However, on final review, you notice that there's something wrong with your character's texture (see Book 3, Chapter 2 for more on texturing). Maybe the character's scar is in the wrong place or you accidentally forgot to enable the dirt map. Whatever the case may be, you're looking at the possibility of re-rendering the whole thing. But you don't have time for that. You promised to get the finished work out by today.

Well, fortunately, because you rendered the right passes and bundled those passes in an OpenEXR file, there's actually a good chance that you can meet your deadline. Here's how.

Setting up your render

In this example, I'm using the Einar character file that's freely available from the Blender Studio (https://studio.blender.org/characters). By default, this file renders using Eevee, but it's not difficult to get it set up for rendering with Cycles by following these steps:

1. **Open `einar_release_v1.blend` in Blender.**

2. **In the Render tab of the Properties editor, use the Render Engine dropdown to switch from Eevee to Cycles.**

    No only does this change illustrate the hypothetical situation given at the beginning of this section, it also allows the passes necessary to get the rest of the steps in this process done.

3. **(Optional) If your GPU supports it, use the Device dropdown to switch to GPU Compute to save yourself a little bit of time on the initial render.**

4. **In the View Layers tab of the Properties editor, make sure that the following passes are enabled:**

    - UV
    - Diffuse Direct
    - Diffuse Indirect
    - Cryptomatte Object

    You can, of course, enable other passes, but these are the critical ones for this example.

5. **In the Output tab of the Properties editor, go to the Output panel and from the File Format dropdown choose OpenEXR MultiLayer as the file type that you're using to save your renders.**

6. **Save your changes to a new file (File ⇨ Save As).**

    I named my file `einar_release_v1-cycles.blend`.

7. **Render an image (Render ⇨ Render Image).**

This will take a while. On my computer, it took about 30 minutes to finish. Go grab a cup of coffee or take a walk.

8. **When the render is complete, use the Image Editor to save it to your hard drive (Image ⇨ Save As).**

Remember what you named the file. I called mine einar.exr. It will be a large file. My image weighed in at about 246MB. However, when it's done, the rendered image should look like what's shown in Figure 2-9.

FIGURE 2-9: Einar, rendered in Cycles and ready to have his face replaced.

Bringing an image into the Compositor

Now that you have a render with the necessary passes created, you can get started with the actual work of doing texture replacement. In this example, you're replacing Einar's face with a simple UV grid image. However, you can use whatever image you want and, using these same steps in the example, you can replace any texture on this render:

1. **Start a new Blender session using either the General or VFX workflow template (File ⇨ New ⇨ General or VFX).**

Both templates have the Compositing workspace, so either will work. In this example, I'm using the VFX workspace.

2. **In the Compositing workspace, go to the Compositor and enable the Use Nodes check box.**

You should see the (by now) familiar starting view of the Compositor shown back in Figure 2-1 with a Render Layers node and a Composite node.

3. **Select the Render Layers node and delete it (X or Delete).**

    Because you're going to be working from an image you already rendered, you won't need anything from the 3D scene in this .blend file.

4. **Add an Image node (Add ⇨ Input ⇨ Image) and place it to the left of your Composite node.**

5. **From your newly added Image node, click the Open button at the bottom of the node and find your OpenEXR render of Einar.**

    A preview of the image should appear in the node, but there's a chance that you won't see all the passes that were stored with the file. To see those passes, choose View Layer rather than Composite from the Layer dropdown in the Image node.

6. **Add a Viewer node (Add ⇨ Output ⇨ Viewer) and connect it to the Combined output socket on your Image node).**

    As a shortcut, you can do this step all at once by Shift+Ctrl+left-clicking your Image node.

7. **Adjust the Zoom of the backdrop in the View tab in the Compositor's Sidebar so your image is visible.**

8. **In the Output tab of the Properties editor, go to the Format panel and set the X and Y Resolution values to 2048.**

    Your original render of Einar was 2048 x 2048, so you should set the composite output to be the same size.

9. **Save your .blend file (File ⇨ Save As).**

    I named mine uv_replace.blend. At this point, your Blender session should look something like what's shown in Figure 2-10.

Replacing a texture with the Compositor

The pass that has all the data you need for replacing a texture is the UV pass. If you connect the Viewer node to it, the backdrop of the Compositor should look like a kind of weirdly smooth pink and blue version of your Einar render, as shown in Figure 2-11. That's because UV data isn't really an image. It's data that happens to be stored using the structure of an image. The red, green, and blue values for each pixel gives an indication of how much an input image needs to be distorted to map correctly so it matches the original 3D data.

FIGURE 2-10:
Your Einar render loaded in an Image node in the Compositor.

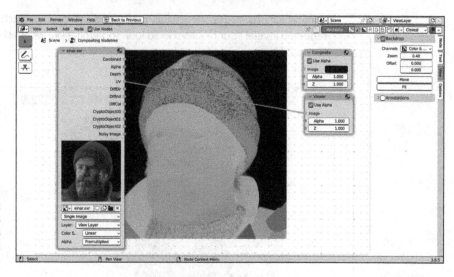

FIGURE 2-11:
The UV pass of a render looks kind of weird and alien.

You're going to use the UV pass with the Map UV node to map another image in place of Einar. Follow these steps:

1. In the Compositor, add a new Image node (File ⇨ Input ⇨ Image) and place it somewhere below your Einar Image node.

This image is your replacement image.

2. **In your new Image node, click the New button to generate a new image and from the pop-over that appears, and Color Grid from the Generated Type dropdown.**

   All the other defaults should be fine. In this example, you're using a generated image from Blender, but you could also have another painted texture of your own.

3. **Add a Map UV node (Add ⇨ Distort ⇨ Map UV) and place it somewhere between your node network's inputs and outputs.**

4. **Connect your Map UV node to the correct sockets on your other nodes:**

   - UV socket on your Einar Image node to the UV socket on Map UV.

   - Image socket on your generated Image node to Image input socket on Map UV.

   - Image output socket on Map UV to Image socket on Viewer.

   Congratulations! You've successfully remapped a texture to match your rendered image! Your results should look something like what's shown in Figure 2-12.

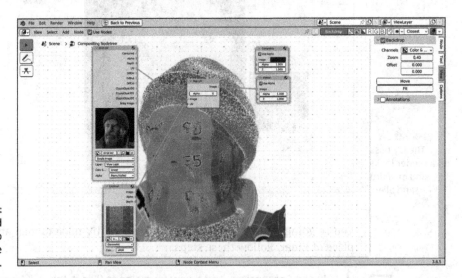

FIGURE 2-12: A color grid remapped to match the UV of Einar.

It may not look like it, but at this point, the bulk of the work is done. Everything else in this example is about isolating the part of the model that you want and mixing this texture in with the correct lighting, and then isolating just the part that you want to replace.

Mixing lights and shadows with the replacement texture

In order to make the texture replacement appear seamless in your render, you need to ensure that it has the same lighting as the rest of it. This is where those Diffuse passes that you enabled come in handy. All the main lighting information from the scene is accessible from the Diffuse Direct and Diffuse Indirect passes. You need to add these passes together and mix them with your remapped texture using the following steps:

1. **In the Compositor, add a color Mix node (Add ⇨ Color ⇨ Mix) and choose Add from the Blending Mode drop-down menu at the top of the node.**

    Now the heading of the node is named Add to reflect the kind of mixing that it does.

2. **Connect the DiffDir socket on your Einar Image node to the top Image socket of your Add node.**

3. **Connect the DiffInd socket on the Einar Image node to the bottom Image socket on your Add node.**

    In this way, you've added together both the direct and indirect lighting results. Now you can apply those results to your remapped image.

4. **Add another Mix node (Add ⇨ Color ⇨ Mix), and this time choose Overlay from the Blending Mode drop-down menu.**

    This node is going to do the work of getting your lighting information mixed with your remapped image.

5. **Connect the Image output socket of the Map UV node to the top Image input socket on your Overlay node.**

6. **Connect the Image output socket of the Add node to the bottom Image input socket on the Overlay node.**

7. **Connect your Viewer node to the Image output socket of the Overlay node.**

    Now you have lighting applied to your remapped texture. Your result should look like what's shown in Figure 2-13.

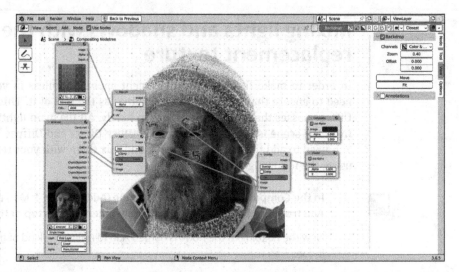

Mixing your remapped image with the original

Of course, so far you've remapped one texture over your whole render. The goal of this example is to replace the texture on just one part of the image. You need to isolate that part and then replace it in the image. To isolate part of an image, you need a mask or a matte. In this case, you can get the job done nicely using cryptomatte, like so:

1. **Using the steps covered earlier in the chapter in the section titled "Cryptomatte passes," create a mask of Einar's face using the Cryptomatte node.**

The important difference from those steps is that, in the Cryptomatte node, you need to click the Render button and then choose your Einar image from the Image datablock in the node. The result should look something like what's shown in Figure 2-14. Now that you have a mask, you can use that to isolate just that part of your remapped image.

2. **Add another color Mix node near the end of your compositing node network.**

This time, you're not going to change the Blending Mode dropdown, but you're leaving it as Mix.

3. **Connect noodles to your new Mix node as follows:**

- Matte output socket from Cryptomatte to Fac input socket on Mix.

- Combined output socket from Einar Image to top Image input socket on Mix.

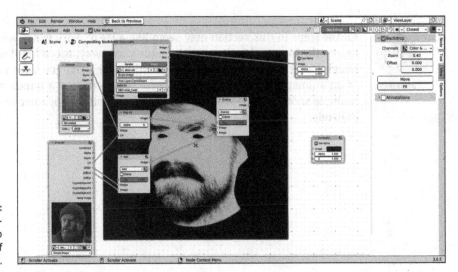

FIGURE 2-14:
Use the Crypto-
matte node to
make a mask of
Einar's face.

- Image output socket from Overlay to bottom Image input socket on Mix.

- Image output socket on Mix to Image socket on the Composite and Viewer nodes.

And with that, you have a node network that replaces a texture on your image without fully re-rendering the image. The result should look something like what's shown in Figure 2-15.

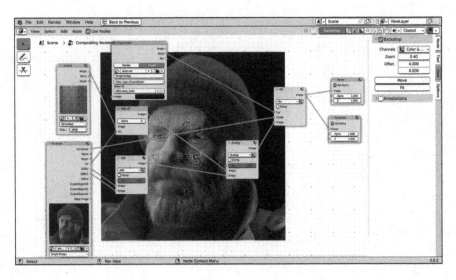

FIGURE 2-15:
Einar has a
new face!

REMEMBER

All the steps in this section may seem like a lot of work when you could just re-render the image with the correct texture. In a way, it *is* a lot of work. However, imagine that this wasn't just a single still image and you have multiple frames of an animation to re-render. Or worse, you rendered a bunch of frames from multiple shots! This is where a reusable compositing node network really comes in handy.

Chapter **3**

Mixing Video and 3D with Motion Tracking

One of the most exciting features in Blender is an integrated motion tracking system. In *motion tracking*, software analyzes video footage and tracks various features in the footage in either two-dimensional or three-dimensional space. With properly tracked footage, an artist can add all kinds of exciting visual effects. Say that you have some video footage of a car driving away from you. With a good motion track (that you can create from right within Blender), you could do almost anything with that footage. It could be as simple as blurring out that car's license plate or as wild and complex as adding rocket boosters to the car and having it cruise into the sunset through a dystopian wasteland populated by ravenous man-eating cacti. Anything you can do in Blender can be added to that footage!

So much of the visual effects process relies on good motion tracking. The previous chapter in this book covered a lot of the things you can do with Blender's Compositor, but most of its focus was using the Compositor on rendered frames that you generate right from within Blender. If you're interested in integrating your 3D work with live video footage, then you're going to want to do motion tracking on that video and use it to correctly position and orient the camera in your 3D scene. With your camera correctly set up in 3D space around a reference wall or ground of some sort, you have enough information to start mixing your 3D assets with that video.

Making Your Life Easier by Starting with Good Video

Before you jump into Blender, you should take a moment and consider your input. Getting good tracking and an accurate camera solve relies heavily on the quality of your source material. There are a few things in source footage that can give any motion tracking software a hard time. Knowing these things in advance can help you avoid them so you're more likely to get a good tracking result. In the live film and video world, this is known as "shooting for the edit" or "shooting for post" (as opposed to just fixing it in post). *Post* is short for post-production, the process of modifying or enhancing footage after it's been shot.

When you capture footage that you intend to use for motion tracking, these are the things you're looking for in good source material:

>> Knowledge of the camera

>> Good, stable lighting

>> "Clean" frames

>> Physical attributes of the scene

The next sections in this chapter go more in depth into each of these aspects of good source material.

Knowing your camera

Conceptually speaking, a camera is a pretty simple machine. Light bounces off objects, enters through an aperture, and strikes with some kind of photosensitive material that captures that light. And unless you're shooting with a pinhole camera, there's also some kind of lens in front of the aperture that's used to focus the light on the material used to capture it. In older film cameras, that material would be an actual piece of light-sensitive film. In modern digital cameras, there's a sensor that collects that light. Figure 3-1 shows a simple illustration that helps visualize the basics of how a camera works.

But why do you need to know this? Well, just like changing the settings on Blender's scene camera can affect the look of your renders, a physical camera works in a similar way. Different lenses can distort your captured footage. Differently sized sensors capture light with varying levels of quality and detail. Some even impart their own little bits of distortion on the captured image. If you know this basic information about the camera that's used to shoot your footage, then your motion tracking software can compensate for these distortions and give you more accurate results. If you *don't* know this information, then it becomes much more difficult to get good results.

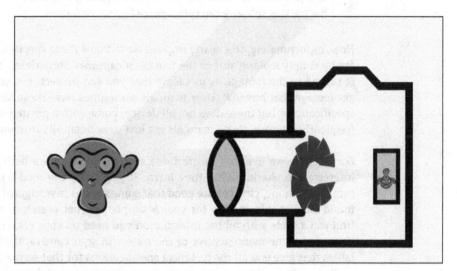

FIGURE 3-1:
A camera captures light bouncing off the environment with a lens and focuses that light on a photosensor.

In general, you want to shoot your video footage with the highest quality camera that you have access to. The cameras on modern mobile phones are pretty good, but many of them incorporate a lot of cheats to try and make the finished image look better than it really may have been. If you can shoot with a dedicated video camera or a high quality digital SLR (an abbreviation for *single lens reflex*) camera, that's ideal. However, if all you have is a mobile phone, you can still get decent results if you know the specifications on that camera.

In particular, these are the specifications that matter most:

>> **Sensor size:** Without the photosensor, the camera doesn't capture any images at all. The size of that sensor has a direct correlation with the quality of those images. Typically speaking, the larger the sensor, the better the captured image. If you can get the exact dimensions of that sensor (typically measured diagonally in millimeters or inches), then your motion tracking software will have a better sense of any distortions that the sensor may have.

>> **Pixel aspect:** Not all pixels are square. Especially in older cameras, video footage could be captured in rectangular pixels to save space in storage and the camera's internal memory. If you happen to shoot footage with one of these cameras, it's extremely helpful to know how much that camera stretches its pixels.

>> **Lens focal length:** Just about every camera used for shooting video has a lens. Lenses, by definition, bend light. So even though cameras use them to focus light on the sensor, each lens contributes a bit of distortion to the final captured image. However, most lenses have a mathematically defined shape, so if you know the dimensions of the lens (typically measured in millimeters), the tracking software can compensate for that distortion.

Now, unfortunately, it's nearly impossible to know these specifications of a camera by simply looking at it or the footage it captures. Sometimes, the information is tagged to the footage as metadata that you can inspect, but you don't always get footage that has that. User manuals sometimes have these kinds of technical specifications, but these days not all devices come with a printed manual (or, as is frequently my case, those manuals get lost or accidentally thrown away).

Fortunately, we live in a future filled with people who are both inquisitive and interested in sharing what they learn. If you know the model number of your camera or phone, chances are good that someone has investigated that device and found all that information for you. A simple Internet search or two can usually find you a table with all the information you need on your camera. For example, if you know the manufacturer of the sensor in your camera, then Wikipedia has tables that give you all the technical specifications for that sensor. Get that information and record it somewhere so you can use it when doing your motion tracking. If you have video that was shot with multiple different cameras, then you may want to tag each bit of footage, so you know the kind of camera that captured it.

Keeping your lighting consistent

One way to think about images shot with a camera is that they are the light captured at that moment in time. This means that the quality of your light is vitally important to the quality of your image. Practically speaking, there are a few things you want to do when shooting video for motion tracking:

>> **Have good lighting.** This guideline sounds a bit nebulous. What is "good lighting" anyway? Fortunately, if you've worked through Book 3, Chapter 3, many of the rules for lighting a digital scene still hold true for lighting a scene in meatspace. Above all, you want to be able to clearly see the subject matter in your scene. Furthermore, it's best to avoid dark scenes. Physical cameras often have a hard time capturing images in low light scenarios, and the resulting footage is often grainy and noisy. If you're shooting footage that you know will be motion tracked and composited, your best course of action is to shoot the scene well-lit and then make everything darker when compositing. That's how "fixing it in post" is *supposed* to work.

>> **Avoid auto-aperture.** To make shooting video easier for people, most cameras have an auto-aperture feature that automatically resizes the aperture of the camera to let in more or less light on the fly while shooting. Though an auto-aperture feature helps to try and keep the captured image at an "ideal" brightness, that same feature can wreak havoc on a motion tracker. Motion trackers rely on pixels in captured images staying relatively consistent, or at least only gradually changing over time. By having the camera constantly adjusting its aperture, that consistency is lost, and when you're compositing, it's much more difficult to match the lighting of the scene. So if you're shooting video for motion tracking and compositing, it's best to disable the auto-aperture feature of your camera. If you can't disable it, my recommendation would be to find another camera where you can.

>> **Have consistent lighting.** This tip is kind of a combination of the two preceding ones. Ideally, you want the lighting in your scene to be stable. If you have a flickering light in the scene, that can cause a lot of problems for getting a good track (and even worse if you happen to have auto-aperture enabled). Of course, flickering lights are common in a lot of dramatic lighting scenarios, so it may be unavoidable. But if you can, it's best to try to add that flickering when compositing and keep clean, consistent light when shooting.

Having images in good focus

Motion trackers work by marking groups of pixels in an image, called *features*, and tracking where those features move from one frame of video to the next. If your source footage is blurry, then those features are fuzzed out and much more difficult to track from one frame to another.

It's more than just focus, though. Any blurring can be problematic for a motion tracker. That includes interlacing, motion blur, and depth of field effects. For that reason, you should follow these tips when shooting footage that you intend to motion track:

>> **Use progressive or deinterlaced video.** *Interlacing* is an effect that's most frequently found in older video cameras. These cameras would capture lower resolution images at faster frame rates and assemble individual frames by interleaving alternating rows of pixels from each captured image. Although a clever way for camera manufacturers to cut corners, interlacing makes it difficult to do motion tracking. Figure 3-2 shows a close-up image of what interlaced footage looks like. Ideally, you can shoot your footage with *progressive frames* or *full frames* and avoid interlacing entirely. If not, then you should run your video footage through a deinterlacer before trying to do motion tracking on it.

>> **Disable auto-focus.** Just like the auto-aperture feature covered in the preceding section, most cameras have an auto-focus feature to try and help people shoot video that's always in focus. Unfortunately, if you have a scene focused long ("long" is shorthand for "far away") and a character walks in front of the camera in the foreground, that person's presence could trigger the auto-focus feature and totally blur out any pixels you're tracking elsewhere in the image (it also just looks bad). As a rule, disable auto-focus on any camera that you're using to shoot video you intend to track.

>> **Avoid motion blur and depth of field.** Motion blur and depth of field are natural parts of good dramatic shots, and taking out these in-camera effects can feel like building a doghouse with only a hammer. As cool as they are though, they both add blurring to a shot and, therefore, make motion tracking that much more difficult. So when you shoot for tracking, you want to reduce these effects as much as possible. On the upside, when you get clean tracking data, you automatically get both depth and movement information for your scene. With some clever use of this tracking data and compositing, you can actually add depth of field and motion blur to your captured footage. The best of both worlds!

FIGURE 3-2:
An interlaced frame is assembled by interleaving neighboring frames in captured footage.

Understanding the scene

Most of the time, when you're motion tracking video you're doing so with the intent of adding 3D elements to that footage. You want to add something to the scene that wasn't there when it was shot. Because you're adding something to that world, it makes sense to know its physical attributes. If you have video footage of a table and you want to put a digital wine glass on it, it's helpful to know the actual physical dimensions of that table. That way, if you need to make a digital proxy for that table, you can model it to its actual size and make your life as a compositor easier.

In addition to the physical size relationships of objects in your captured footage, you should also think about capturing the light in the scene. At the most basic, take note of the locations of the major light sources. If the footage is shot outdoors, where is the sun? If the footage is shot indoors, how many lights are in the scene and where are they located? Understanding this will help you light your 3D scene more accurately so shadows on your digital objects fall the same as they do in the video.

If you're really ambitious, you can actually capture the light of the scene with a high dynamic range image (HDRI). The process for capturing an HDRI reference is beyond the scope of this book, but it typically involves taking a few racked exposures of the scene either as a panorama or on a chrome ball and tone-mapping those images. It takes some work, but the benefit of this approach is that you capture the actual ambient light of the scene, and you can light your 3D stand-ins with the most accurate lighting possible.

REMEMBER

Your best course of action is to record everything you can about the scene. It's very common practice to have a "shot" journal where you log every detail you can, including camera details, the physical distance between objects in the scene, time of day, and so on. If you write it down, you have it available for use when you start motion tracking the footage in Blender.

Getting Familiar with the Motion Tracking Workspace

Just as with 2D animation and video editing (see Book 4, Chapters 6 and Book 5, Chapter 1, respectively), Blender has a workspace specifically tailored for motion tracking; conveniently, it's called Motion Tracking, but it doesn't show as one of the tabs you can access when you start a new Blender session using the General workflow template by choosing File ⇨ New ⇨ General. You *could* add it by clicking the Plus (+) tab at the end of the row of workspace tabs, but there's a better way. Also like with 2D animation and video editing, there's a specific Blender workflow template that you can use. The VFX (short for *visual effects*) Blender workflow template is your best choice for a starting point when doing motion tracking. You can get to it by starting a new Blender session by choosing File ⇨ New ⇨ VFX. When you start a Blender session in this way, your Blender window should look like what's shown in Figure 3-3.

When you start a VFX session, Blender puts you in the Motion Tracking workspace as your starting point. You also get three other workspace tabs along the top of your Blender window. If you've worked in any of the other templates (particularly the General or 2D Animation ones), then the Compositing and Rendering workspaces should be familiar to you. If you click on the Masking workspace, you get a kind of modified variant of the Motion Tracking workspace that's specifically focused to building masks after you've already gone through the process of tracking. The bulk of this chapter is devoted to working in the Motion Tracking workspace.

In the Motion Tracking workspace (shown back in Figure 3-3), the right side of your Blender window looks just about like most other workspaces: an Outliner and a Properties editor. Nearly everything to the left of those editors, however, is different from most of the other workspaces. Sure, like the Animation workspace (covered in Book 4, Chapter 1), there's a Timeline at the bottom that's showing only its header. There's also an empty 3D Viewport in the upper right, but that editor is of limited use until you've gotten to tracking.

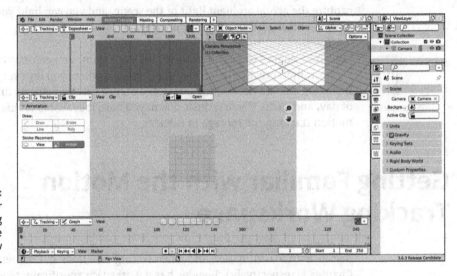

FIGURE 3-3:
Start your
motion tracking
session with the
VFX workflow
template.

The bulk of your Blender window is actually populated with different views of the Movie Clip Editor. Kind of like Blender's Sequencer (see Chapter 1 of this book), the Movie Clip Editor has multiple possible viewing modes. The main difference between the Sequencer and the Movie Clip Editor is in the kind of data they're meant to work on. Whereas the Sequencer is designed to work with and reorder multiple video sequences on the same timeline, the Movie Clip Editor is meant to focus on just one video file (or one portion of one video file) at a time.

The largest area in the Motion Tracking workspace is dominated by a Movie Clip Editor in its Clip viewing mode. This area is where you do the bulk of your tracking work (covered later in this chapter). The other two Movie Clip Editors are primarily for visualizing your tracking data. The upper Movie Clip Editor uses the Dope Sheet display type, whereas the bottom Movie Clip Editor shows the Graph display type. When you become more advanced at tracking, you can use these editors to do control tweaking of your track. For most situations, though, your focus is in the big one in Clip viewing mode.

Tracking Movement in Blender

As with so many things, the best way to understand how to do motion tracking is to actually go through the process yourself. Furthermore, it's not really helpful to study the Movie Clip Editor without first having some footage loaded in it. Otherwise, it's a stark and empty place that doesn't seem all that useful.

Your first step, as already covered in the first section of this chapter, is to capture some video that you intend to use for motion tracking. If you're just starting out, you can probably make do with the camera on a mobile phone. Of course, you'll get better results with a better camera.

TIP

If you don't have access to a camera, don't give up! There are abundant resources on the web. If you need video footage to practice motion tracking, there are quite a few great websites that offer free video footage under a Creative Commons license. A number of these sites even include basic information about the camera and lens that was used to capture the footage. In a pinch, you can even look on the Internet Archive (archive.org) to find something to work with. Most of the time, though, you can get high quality footage to work with if you do a search for "creative commons video footage."

Wherever you get your video footage, you typically use the following steps each time you load a video file to get tracked:

1. **In the main Movie Clip Editor of the Motion Tracking workspace, go to its header menu and choose Clip ➪ Open Clip.**

Blender provides you with a File Browser that you can use to load the video file or image sequence you want for tracking. When you have your file loaded, the Movie Clip Editor shows the first frame of your video, and the Toolbar region of the Movie Clip Editor gets a lot more interesting. Figure 3-4 shows the Movie Clip Editor with a video file loaded.

2. **In the Track tab of the Movie Clip Editor's Toolbar, click the Set Scene Frames button.**

Clicking this button sets your .blend file's frame range to match the length of your video sequence. Of course, if you're interested only in tracking a specific segment of that sequence, you can adjust your frame range to taste from the Output tab of the Properties editor.

TIP

At this point, it's worth mentioning that you often get your best results if the length of the sequence you're tracking is relatively short. Although I'm sure it's possible to motion track all 30 minutes of your brother's wedding, it will be much better for your time and sanity if you just focus on the part of the video that you actually want to add visual effects to. Typically, a single visual effects shot doesn't last more than a few seconds.

3. **From the Output tab of the Properties editor, set your scene's frame rate to match that of your video sequence.**

This step isn't critically necessary for tracking, but if you want Blender to play back your footage at the same rate that it was captured, it's best to perform this step. Blender's default frame rate is 24 fps (frames per second). Although 24 fps is a fairly common setting you can choose on consumer cameras, most default to 25 or 30 fps. If you look in the Footage tab in the Movie Clip Editor's Sidebar, the frame rate for your movie clip is shown at the bottom of the Footage Settings panel.

4. **Back in the Track tab of the Movie Clip Editor's Toolbar, click the Prefetch button in the Clip panel.**

This step preloads into Blender as many frames of your video sequence as your computer's RAM will allow. You can see the amount of frames that Blender preloads by looking at the bottom of the Movie Clip Editor. There should be a semitransparent blue bar there after the Prefetch process completes. If that bar goes all the way across the bottom of your image, then the entirety of your frame range has been prefetched. If the bar goes only halfway across, then you only have enough RAM to store half the length of your frame range.

With the frames of your video sequence preloaded, they're already in memory and Blender has an easier time tracking data on those frames. Otherwise, each frame has to be loaded on the fly and, depending on the speed of your hard drive, that process could be quite a bit slower.

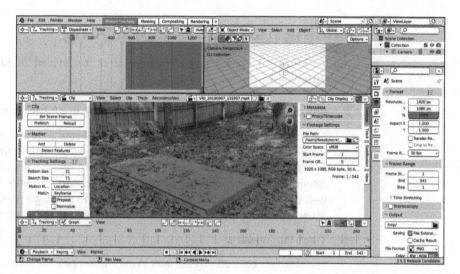

FIGURE 3-4:
With a video sequence loaded, the Movie Clip Editor has a lot more that you can do.

You've got your video sequence loaded into the Movie Clip Editor. Now you're ready to start the process of tracking that footage.

TIP

If you already know that the footage you're loading is blurry or has fast movement (and perhaps some motion blur), then you may want to consider adjusting the values in the Tracking Settings panel within the Track tab of the Movie Clip Editor's Toolbar. The details of this panel are a bit out of scope for this book, but what's really helpful is the fact that Blender ships with some handy presets for specific kinds of footage. Click the presets button at the top of the Tracking Settings panel, and you have the following options:

>> Blurry Footage

>> Default

>> Fast Motion

>> Planar

Most of these settings are self-explanatory. The only one that requires a bit more coverage is the Planar preset. *Planar tracking* is a specific kind of tracking where the features you're tracking in your footage are all on the same plane. If you know this is the case, then the motion tracking can make a few assumptions and get you accurate results faster. Typically speaking, though, I suggest you start with the Default preset and see how good your results are first.

Adding markers and tracking

The workflow for tracking your footage after it's loaded in Blender is pretty straightforward:

1. **Add one or more tracking markers to a feature in a frame in your sequence.**

    A *tracking marker* is a little feature that you add to your sequence in the Movie Clip Editor to tag or *mark* a handful of pixels as a *feature* in the image. A good, trackable feature in your image is usually a set of pixels that are consistently lighter or darker than their neighboring pixels. Corners also work relatively well. One thing you should be sure of is that you're tracking a physical feature in the shot rather than the intersection of features with different depths.

2. **Track that feature.**

    This step gets covered in detail later in the chapter (see the section titled "Tracking your footage").

3. **Evaluate the results of the track and either refine the marker or remove the track if it's inaccurate.**

    Because tracking data is generated automatically, it isn't always 100 percent accurate. If your sequence gets blurry on a frame or two, a marker may lose track of its feature, and you need to reorient that marker or get rid of it altogether if you find that feature becomes difficult to follow.

4. **If the track is accurate, lock the track.**

    You tend to overlap multiple tracking sessions, so if you find a tracker you like, it's a good idea to lock that track so it doesn't get modified on subsequent sessions.

Those are the basic steps, but of course, each step has a bit more detail baked into it. The next few sections cover the preceding steps in more detail.

Manually adding markers

Before manually adding tracking markers to your footage, you need to pick a frame in your sequence as a starting point for tracking. Generally speaking, the first and last frames of your sequence are smart choices. If you have a complicated camera move in the sequence or it's especially long, then you may also want to choose a frame or two in the middle of your sequence.

REMEMBER

Regardless of the frame you choose for adding features, here's the thing to remember: *Always track your footage after you add your markers for a given frame.* Even a simple sequence can involve a large number of markers, and you're likely to do multiple tracks starting at different frames. So it's in your best interest to have them track before you change frames. Otherwise, you run the risk of not remembering which markers have tracking data and which ones don't.

Assume that you've chosen the first frame in your sequence to add tracking markers. The process for adding a tracking marker goes like this:

1. **In the Track tab of the Movie Clip Editor's Toolbar, click the Add button in the Marker panel.**

   It won't immediately be apparent that you've done anything. That's because Blender is expecting you to tell it where to add the tracking marker.

2. **Left-click on a feature in your frame.**

   Remember that a good feature is a distinctive set of pixels in the frame you're working on. It could be that those pixels form a distinctive shape, but more frequently, it's a little grouping of pixels that are lighter or darker than their neighbors.

When you left-click on your frame in the Movie Clip Editor, Blender adds a tracking marker that looks like the one shown in Figure 3-5. It's a simple box with a set of control points at its corners and an additional controller handle extending from its center.

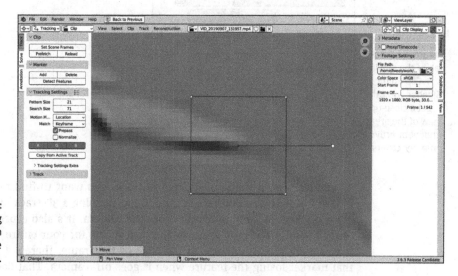

With your marker added in the Movie Clip Editor, you can edit its position, rotation, and shape to refine how it covers the feature in your footage. Left-click and drag a corner of the marker box to move that corner around. Left-click and drag the end of the controller handle to simultaneously modify the tracking marker's scale and rotation.

TIP

As you refine the position of your tracking marker, it's helpful to have the Movie Clip Editor's Sidebar (on the right side of the Movie Clip Editor) on its Track tab. The Track panel in that tab shows an up-close view of your active tracking marker with a little yellow crosshairs at the center so you can place your marker with the utmost accuracy. Figure 3-6 shows the Track tab of the Movie Clip Editor's Sidebar.

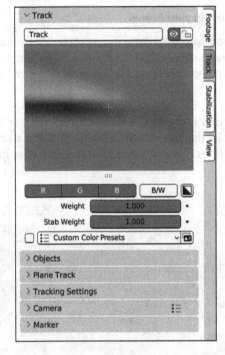

FIGURE 3-6:
From the Track tab of the Movie Clip Editor's Sidebar you can get a close-up view of the area that your active marker covers.

As you work on a frame of footage to track, you want to find multiple features in that frame to add markers to. And if you're doing a 3D track, it's important to place markers at varying depths from the camera. It's also especially important to try to add markers to features that are visible for your entire video sequence. If you mark a feature close to the edge of the frame, there's a good chance of that marker losing the feature when it goes off-camera. That doesn't mean you shouldn't track those features. It just means that you should *also* track features that have more persistence throughout your sequence.

TIP

When adding a lot of markers to a frame, it can be tedious to continually return to the Toolbar so you can click the Add button. Fortunately, there's a faster way. Blender automatically places a marker anywhere you Ctrl+left-click on your frame. Then you can go about refining your new marker as you please.

Automatically placing markers

Even though you know how to manually place a tracking marker in your scene, you may not have to, if you're lucky. Blender can analyze a frame of your footage and find suitable features for you.

Say you've put your time cursor on the first frame of your sequence, and you want Blender to find a feature in that frame for motion tracking. In the Track tab of the Movie Clip Editor's Toolbar is a panel labeled Marker. The bottom button in that panel is labeled Detect Features. Left-click that button and Blender searches the current frame of your sequence and finds what it thinks would be good candidates for features to track. For any of those features, Blender automatically places a tracking marker. Of course, how well this automatic detection works can vary a bit depending on your source footage. On one shot you may have good results, whereas on another the detected features may be horrible choices. It requires a bit of experimentation to test and find what works. After you click the Detect Features button, your Movie Clip Editor may look like what's shown in Figure 3-7.

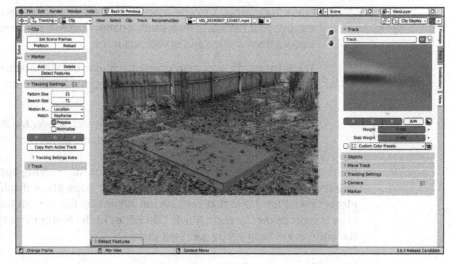

FIGURE 3-7: Have Blender automatically detect features in your footage, and your frame could be instantly covered in markers.

REMEMBER

A small word of warning. Although having more markers in your shot means Blender's tracker has more data to work with, not all tracked shots need an abundance of markers. Sometimes, all you need is eight markers to get the job done. There's no sense in having your computer work harder than it needs to.

Tracking your footage

With markers set on the frame you want to work with, you now get to the actual step that this chapter is named after: tracking motion in your video sequence. Follow these steps:

1. **Select your markers.**

   You can press the A hotkey to select all unlocked markers in the Movie Clip Editor.

2. **From the header menu of the Movie Clip Editor, choose Track ⇨ Track Motion ⇨ Forwards.**

   This step assumes that your markers are on the first frame of your video sequence, and you want to track the features in the sequence through to the end. You actually have four options for tracking:

   - **Track Frame Backwards:** Choose this option to track features within your selected markers a single frame backwards on the Timeline.

   - **Track Backwards:** This operation tracks features in your selected markers through your footage in reverse. It's a handy feature if the frame you're tracking from is at the end of your sequence.

   - **Track Forwards:** As already covered, this uses the markers to track features in your footage forward in time until the feature is lost or Blender reaches the end of your frame range.

   - **Track Frame Forwards:** Choose this option and Blender tracks the features in your selected markers a single frame forward in time.

For convenience, you have quick access to each of the tracking options from a set of buttons in the header of either the Graph or Dope Sheet display views of the Movie Clip Editor. I find that because the Movie Clip Editor with the Graph display view is right below the main Movie Clip Editor in the Motion Tracking workspace, the buttons are most easily accessed there.

When Blender completes tracking the features under your markers, you should notice two things. First, the Graph view of the Movie Clip Editor at the bottom of your Blender window should be populated with a bunch of red and green curves. These curves are plots of the X- and Y-axis locations of each selected marker. Even though these curves are not directly editable, they can give you helpful information about each marker. If the majority of the markers are showing a similar curve profile, and the curves for one marker appear to stray from that standard, chances are good that marker doesn't have a good track, and it should be removed from the set.

Likewise, in the main Movie Clip Editor at the center of your Blender window, you should notice that each marker has what looks like a squiggly red-and-blue worm growing from it. This "worm" is the tracking path for that marker. The red part are the upcoming frames, whereas the blue part are the frames that have already been passed. Just as with the curves in the Graph view of the Movie Clip Editor, if any of the track paths in main Movie Clip Editor don't seem to match the same general movement and shape of the other paths, then it probably has a bad track, and you should remove it from the set.

REMEMBER

Another thing to notice is that at the bottom of the Movie Clip Editor, the semi-transparent blue bar is now two-toned. The bottom half of that bar region is now yellow, indicating how much of your video sequence has been tracked. Ultimately, you want the whole bottom bar to be yellow to indicate that every frame in the sequence has tracking data.

As I've mentioned a couple times already, you get the best results when you track your footage with multiple markers starting in multiple places of your video sequence. For a quick-and-dirty track that gets you good results on a simple scene, try this workflow (assuming your video sequence is already loaded in the Movie Clip Editor):

1. **Go to the first frame of your sequence.**
2. **Use the Detect Feature function on this first frame.**
3. **Track Forward.**
4. **Lock your selected tracks (Ctrl+L).**
5. **Go to the last frame of your sequence.**
6. **Use the Detect Feature function on this last frame.**
7. **Track Backwards.**
8. **Lock your selected tracks (Ctrl+L).**

You may need to scrub through your video sequence and check for any bad tracks, but once you do, you should end up with a Blender window that looks like what's shown in Figure 3-8.

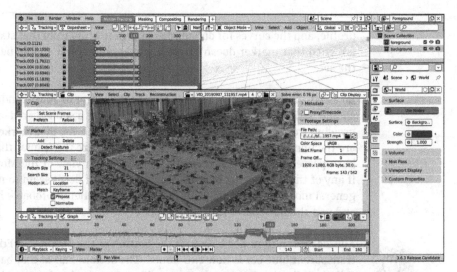

FIGURE 3-8:
With good
tracking data
on your video
sequence, you
may have all
kinds of "marker
worms" all over
your Movie
Clip Editor.

Solving camera motion from tracker data

Blender is tracking a bunch of features in your video sequence, but what can you
actually do with that tracking data? How do you translate a bunch of pixels moving in a sequence of images to locations in a 3D environment? Though we do that
kind of thing all the time with our eyes and our brains, it's a pretty computationally intense problem. And it's for that exact reason the next step in the process is
called *solving*. What you want Blender to do is take all your tracking data and make
a guess at where in space the camera was when shooting that footage. Then, with
that guess, Blender takes the camera in the 3D Viewport and animates it to match.

REMEMBER

It's worth noting that getting a camera solve is just one example of what you
can do with tracking data. There's a bunch of other cool things you can do with
tracking data in the Movie Clip Editor and the Compositor. That said, a solve is a
good way to get tracking data into the 3D Viewport where some of the tools may
be more familiar to you.

In the simplest case, this process is a one-button press in the Movie Clip Editor.
Switch to the Solve tab of the Movie Clip Editor's Toolbar, and you should see
something like Figure 3-9.

Although it's incredibly tempting to just go off and click the big Solve Camera
Motion button in the Solve tab, don't do it just yet. There's a little bit of setup that
you should work through first.

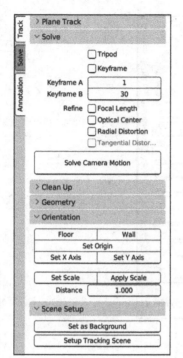

FIGURE 3-9:
The Solve tab of
the Movie Clip
Editor's Toolbar
is where your 2D
footage meets
your 3D scene.

Configuring your camera

Recall that at the beginning of this chapter I say that it's really valuable to know the specifications of the camera that was used to capture your motion tracking shot. This step is where that information gets put to use.

In the Track tab of the Movie Clip Editor's Sidebar, expand the Camera and Lens panels. You should see something like what's in Figure 3-10. In the Camera tab, there's a whole mess of presets available for commonly used cameras. If your camera is one of these, then all you have to do is select that preset and you're good to go. Of course, if you're camera isn't on the preset list, you need to manually enter the correct values for Sensor Width and Pixel Aspect. The Optical Center values you can typically keep at their defaults if you're working with HD video (typical resolution of 1920 x 1080).

Likewise, in the Lens panel, set the correct Focal Length value for the lens that was used on the camera that shot your footage. If you don't have this information, you can keep it at the default values, but know that the resulting camera solve that Blender produces in the 3D Viewport may not be accurate.

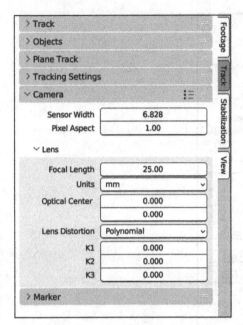

FIGURE 3-10:
Use the Camera
and Lens panels
in the Track tab
of the Movie Clip
Editor's Sidebar
to set values that
match the device
used to cap-
ture your video
footage.

Solving (and re-solving)

Generating, or solving, the camera motion in your 3D Viewport from your tracking data in the Movie Clip Editor is as simple as clicking the big Solve Camera Motion button in the Movie Clip Editor's Sidebar. Left-clicking that button won't appear to have changed anything. You should see a progress bar work in the Status area of the Blender window, but no changes in your 3D Viewport. Rest assured that Blender has generated a solve solution based on your tracking data, but there's nothing yet in the 3D Viewport that lets you know what it's done. To get to that point, you need to set up your tracking scene. There's a useful button at the bottom of the Solve tab in the Movie Clip Editor's Toolbar labeled Setup Tracking Scene. Although it's incredibly tempting to rush forward and hit that button, I suggest you restrain yourself. I cover the function of that button later in the section titled "Setting up your scene for integrating with your video footage." First, however, you need to let Blender know how your scene should be oriented in space. Which way is up? How far away are different features? That's covered in the next section.

REMEMBER

It's not expected that you click the Solve Camera Motion button once and you're done. After you have your tracking scene set up, you might notice some glitches in how that scene lines up with your footage. So the expectation is that you go back to your tracking data, refine your markers further, and then solve again. Ideally, each time you solve, the result should get better.

Defining scene orientation

You've got a camera solve, Blender doesn't yet have a clear understanding of how to properly orient the scene camera to the global coordinate system. You need to tell Blender which way is up. In the Solve tab of the Movie Clip Editor's Toolbar, have a look at the Orientation panel. To correctly guess which way is up in your scene, it's helpful to let Blender's solver know where the floor is or, if your shot doesn't have a convenient floor, maybe where a wall is. With a planar reference like that, Blender's solver will be able to more accurately orient the scene camera so it matches your footage.

Unfortunately, it's not quite as easy as pointing to a part of your footage and saying, "This is a floor." I mean, that's basically what you're doing, but there are specific rules regarding what you used to define that floor. It basically comes down to this:

>> You need to have a successful camera solve already complete (that was covered in the preceding section).

>> You must pick three (*only* three, no more and no less) markers that are on the floor (or wall) in your shot.

>> The markers you pick need to have bundles.

Bundles are tracking data that exist at both Keyframe A and Keyframe B in the Solve panel. Those keyframes are set to 1 and 30 by default, and they're indicated by two green vertical lines at the bottom of the Movie Clip Editor. Basically, you need to select three markers on the floor (or a wall) in your shot whose yellow stripes at the bottom of the Movie Clip Editor cross both of those green lines.

Once you have your three markers chosen, left-click the Floor (or Wall) button in the Orientation panel of the Solve tab in the Movie Clip Editor's Toolbar. Now you've given your camera a reference for orientation.

Of course, at this point, you still don't really know if the results of your camera solve are any good. Frequently, they're not. Most often, the floor or wall you define doesn't quite match up. But how can you tell? And then, how can you fix it? The answers are in the next section.

Setting up your scene for integrating with your video footage

You've got your video sequence tracked and as far as you know, you've been able to successfully generate camera movement based on that tracking data. But you haven't visually verified that the solve Blender generated was worthwhile. You need a frame of reference in the 3D Viewport so you can better see what's going on. Fortunately, at the bottom of the Solve tab in the Movie Clip Editor's Sidebar, there's a panel that can help you out.

The Scene Setup panel has two relatively unimposing buttons that can make your life much more pleasant when motion tracking. In particular, the Setup Tracking Scene button is the most useful. That button is disabled until you click the Solve Camera Motion button at least once (as covered in the previous section). But once you've generated your solve data, the functionality of this button becomes available.

Click the Setup Tracking Scene button and Blender does a whole bunch of handy things simultaneously for you:

>> The 3D Viewport in the upper right of the Motion Tracking workspace gets filled with Empty objects, each one corresponding to a tracking marker in the Movie Clip Editor.

>> The Camera object in the scene is animated with Blender's best guess at its location and orientation in space, based on the floor or wall you defined in the section titled "Defining scene orientation."

>> The scene camera gets your footage in the Movie Clip Editor as a background.

>> A couple scene primitives (specifically a plane for a floor and a reference cube) are added at the origin in the 3D Viewport.

>> A simple node network is added in the Compositor to help you mix the rendered results from your 3D scene with your video footage.

The result should appear like what's in Figure 3-11.

With these updates to your scene in the 3D Viewport, you're able to start getting a sense of how successful your solve data is. By looking at the reference primitives in relation to your footage as a background for the scene camera, you can immediately see whether the solve you created is accurate. If it isn't, you could try reorienting the cube and plane to try and match, but the better approach is to try different markers to get a better reference for a floor or wall in the scene. Sometimes it takes a few tries. In fact, you may find that you need to go back to the tracking markers in the Movie Clip Editor and refine them further. Eventually, though, you end up with those reference objects matching the orientation of objects in your video sequence. As shown in Figure 3-12, you might even put in additional 3D objects (like maybe a certain monkey) to get a better sense of the scene orientation as you scrub the Timeline.

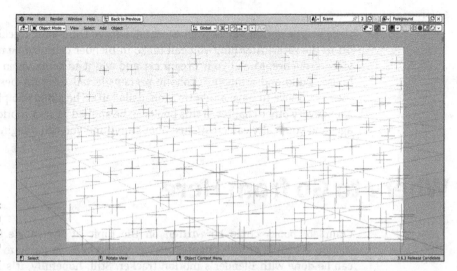

FIGURE 3-11:
Solving camera
motion puts a lot
of information in
the 3D scene.

FIGURE 3-12:
A simple
shot, tracked
and solved,
with Suzanne
added for good
measure.

REMEMBER

It's worth mentioning that the camera background image is a different kind of reference than the reference and background images covered in Book 2, Chapter 3. Instead of being an actual object in your 3D scene, a camera background image is visible only when you're looking at your scene through the scene camera. You can set it manually by selecting your camera and going to Object Data Properties and expanding the Background Images panel. If you click the Add Image button in that panel, you get a sub-panel much like the one you get with Image Empties. Just select the image (or in this case, video) that you want to use and then enable the Background Images check box. Of course, if you use the Setup Tracking Scene feature from the Movie Clip Editor, Blender does all this for you.

Once you've gotten yourself an acceptable solve from your tracking data, you're off to the races! Anything you can make in Blender can now be mixed with your video sequence. Model your dream car and add it to some video footage of your house. Build and animate a robotic prehensile tail for your best friend (or for me . . . I'd love to have a robotic prehensile tail). The skills you pick up from just about every other chapter in this book can be applied to your motion tracked footage, and you really can create just about anything you can imagine!

Where to Go from Here

Complete books could be written on the topic of the Movie Clip Editor and motion tracking, so this chapter isn't a comprehensive guide to everything that can be done with Blender's motion tracker. Still, hopefully, it's given you a fair taste of what's possible. There is an incredible video tutorial series produced by Sebastian Koenig called "Track, Match, Blend" available on the Blender Cloud (http://cloud.blender.org), the Blender Foundation's resource for Blender assets and training. At this point, that specific tutorial is a little dated and it uses an older version of Blender, but it's still one of the best resources available. I highly recommend these tutorials from Sebastian; there's really no better place to discover how to take full advantage of Blender's motion tracking features. After watching "Track, Match, Blend" you can look on YouTube and other resources to transfer that knowledge to the current Blender interface.

6

Getting Technical

Contents at a Glance

Chapter **1**

Working with Linked Data

As you start working with more complex projects that have multiple scenes, your `.blend` files will get increasingly complex. At that point, it starts making sense to begin using a slightly more complex project structure that involves working in multiple files. I touched on this concept briefly in Book 3, Chapter 4 when discussing asset libraries in Blender. Sometimes, though, you need something that falls somewhere between the needs of a local asset library and a global one. You need project-based assets.

As an example, consider the situation where you're working on an animation and you have a character that needs to appear in three or four different scenes. As you work, you suddenly discover, "Oh no, this character is supposed to have green eyes!"

However, the model that you worked with has brown eyes in every scene. With a more naive workflow, you would have to go into every one of your shot files and change the color of your character's eyes. For one change in maybe three or four scenes, maybe that's not such a big deal. But what if it's multiple changes across a dozen or more shots? Handling those kinds of edits can quickly become time-consuming and, really, you probably have better or more interesting ways to spend your time.

Fortunately, if you structure your project intelligently, you'll be able to reuse data. In the example scenario in the previous paragraph, you can change your character's eye color in one file and that change propagates to every shot file where that character is used. This approach is the fundamental basis of working with linked data in Blender.

Of course, sometimes you don't want to link every bit of data between files. Sometimes you want to override what's in the source file or you want to pull a copy of some Blender datablock from one file to another. Those processes are also covered in this chapter.

Appending and Linking Datablocks between Blender Files

To get a sense of how the process of accessing data from external .blend files to use in your current working file works, it's best to start with the concept of appending. In Blender, *appending* a datablock is the process of copying it from one file to another with no reference to the source file. Technically speaking, the easiest way to append data in this way is to use Blender's copy and paste functionality that mirrors the process used in many other programs. For a quick refresher, here's the process:

1. **Open your source .blend file.**

2. **In the 3D Viewport, select the object(s) you want to pull into your target file.**

3. **Copy the object using Object ⇨ Copy Objects from the 3D Viewport's header menu or press the Ctrl+C hotkey combination.**

4. **Open your target .blend file.**

5. **Paste your copied object in the 3D Viewport using Object ⇨ Paste Objects or pressing Ctrl+V.**

This process works pretty well for objects and selected nodes, but what about other kinds of datablocks like collections, materials, mesh data, or sculpting brushes? Sure, you can move to the Outliner and use copy/paste capabilities there, but the disadvantage of this approach is it hinges on leaving your current .blend file and going to another one or launching a second instance of Blender. There's another approach worth going over because the same basic steps are used for linking datablocks between files (which is covered in more detail later in this section).

Appending datablocks

What is appending? As mentioned earlier, appending is literally copying data from one Blender file into another Blender file. You are appending that datablock from the other file to your working file. Once that datablock is appended, that copy of data lives in the file. Any changes you make don't push back upstream to the original file, and no changes in the original file come downstream to you in your working file.

Appending is a great tool for quickly building scenes where you want everything to be self-contained within a single .blend file.

TIP

In addition to the copy/paste method described at the start of this section, there are two ways to append datablocks from one .blend file to another:

>> Use any other arbitrary Blender file.

>> Use the asset library.

Of the two, the most simple approach is to use the asset library, as described in Book 3, Chapter 4. If you have an asset library already built, you can drag and drop assets into your current scene from the Asset Browser. The default behavior for this approach is appending. That asset is copied from the library into your working .blend file.

The asset library approach is fast and works really well, but it also assumes that the datablock that you want is already in your global asset library. That's not always the case. For those situations, you use a method that allows you to append from any arbitrary .blend file. That process uses the following steps:

1. **Open your working .blend file, the one that you want to append to.**

2. **Choose File ⇨ Append in Blender's top menu.**

Upon choosing this menu item, Blender shows you a File Browser.

3. **Using the File Browser, find the location of your source .blend file on your hard drive and double-click it.**

However, when you click on the .blend file, Blender doesn't open the file like it does when using File ⇨ Open. Instead, the File Browser drills into that .blend file, allowing you to see the contents of the file as if it were a regular folder on your hard drive.

4. **Navigate to the data path of the datablock that you're interested in appending to your working file.**

   For example, if you're trying to append a material, you would go to the Material subfolder within the .blend file. At that point, you've hopefully named your material something memorable, or you can use the File Browser's thumbnail view to choose the material datablock you want. Likewise, you can do the same thing for objects or animations, or even brushes for sculpting or painting.

5. **Select your desired datablock and click the Append button in the bottom right of the File Browser.**

At this point, the datablock you selected is pulled into Blender. You can use it in your scene just like any other datablock. Continuing the material example, that material is immediately available as a selectable datablock in Material Properties for any object in your scene. And because you've appended the material, you can make changes to it that stay in your working file.

Linking datablocks

 Now that you're familiar with the process of appending datablocks from one .blend file to another, you can use that same workflow for linking. In contrast to appending, which copies data from one file to another, *linking* points to a data block in another file and refers to that other file's data for display, but doesn't copy that datablock into your working file. If you want to make a change to the source datablock that's linked, you can't do it in your working file without performing overrides (covered later in this chapter). You have to open the source file, make your change there, save it, and then refresh your working file to see the change. That process may seem like a lot of work if you're just linking one datablock to one other file. However, if you're linking that same datablock between multiple work files, having the ability to make your changes in one place and let them update in all other files becomes a huge timesaver. This is the real power of linking.

The actual process of linking datablocks between .blend files uses the same processes covered for appending (with the exception of copy/paste; you can't use copy/paste to create links). You can either use the Asset Browser, or you can link using any arbitrary .blend file.

 To link datablocks using the Asset Browser, there's one small tweak to the process that you need to do before dragging and dropping the asset from Asset Browser to your scene. If you look at the header of the Asset Browser, in the center there's an Import Type drop-down menu. The menu isn't labeled, but is defaulted to Follow Preferences. If you expand this menu, you have four options:

>> **Follow Preferences:** This option is the default behavior for the Asset Browser, where it chooses to import using the approach defined in the Asset Libraries panel of the File Paths section of Preferences. Import types can be different for each custom asset library you add, so this setting has a lot of flexibility. The overall default is Append (Reuse Data), described later in this list.

>> **Link:** Choose this option to ensure that the datablocks you pull into your working file are linked and not copied. For the purposes of this section of the chapter, this is the option you want to pick.

>> **Append:** Choose this option to append, copying all datablocks (and child datablocks) to your working file. This option is the most "data heavy," but it allows you to make local changes to everything without affecting any other assets in your scene.

>> **Append (Reuse Data):** This option is the overall default behavior. It's an append operation, but if you append the same asset multiple times, Blender does its best to reuse child datablocks instead of copying them. For example, if you append an object multiple times, you'll have multiple object datablocks for it, but all of them will share the same material datablock.

To use linked data from the Asset Browser, set the Import Type dropdown to Link.

REMEMBER

What about linking datablocks from an arbitrary `.blend` file? That process uses the same flow as appending. The only difference is where you go in the File menu. For linking datablocks, choose File ⇨ Link. . . . from the top menu. From there, Blender presents you with a File Browser to navigate to your hard drive and the internal structure of `.blend` files, just like when appending.

There is an important thing to note. When you link in an object from another file, it comes into your 3D Viewport with the exact same location, rotation, and scale that it has in the source file. Furthermore, it's not possible to do any transforms or add a modifier on that object in your working file. All properties of that object are linked, so any changes need to be done in the source file.

Fortunately, there are a few different ways around this limitation. One approach is to use library overrides, as described at the end of this chapter. Another approach is to take advantage of collections in your source file. The process looks something like this:

1. **In your source file, select the object (or multiple objects) that you're interested in linking and bundle it in a collection (Object ⇨ Collection ⇨ Link to Collection ⇨ New Collection).**

    Name the collection something memorable. You could also use the Move to Collection operator in the Collection menu, but that moves your selected object(s) from any existing collection into your new one, and that might not be the behavior you want.

2. **Save your source .blend file.**

3. **Open your working .blend file.**

4. **Choose File ⇨ Link. . . and use Blender's File Browser to navigate to your recently created collection in your source file.**

5. **Select the collection and click the Link button on the bottom right of the File Browser to link the collection to your working file.**

An instance of your collection appears at the location of your 3D Cursor.

TIP

You can tell that a datablock is linked by finding it in the Outliner. If that datablock is linked, it will have a chain link icon (like the one shown in the margin) next to its name. This same icon appears on the right side of any datablock widget for this asset. For example, if you've linked an object, you can go to the Object tab of the Properties editor, and the datablock widget at the top of that tab displays the name of your object along with a button to the right with the link icon. If you click this button, Blender unlinks the datablock and makes it local, effectively appending it to your working file.

It's important to understand that this is an instance of the containing collection in your source file rather than a direct link to the object. In fact, if you select your newly linked collection, you can go to the Object tab in the Properties editor and look in the Instancing panel. From there, you can see that what you really have is an Empty that's displaying an instance of your linked collection. You can even add more instances to your scene from the Add ⇨ Collection Instance menu. More importantly, you're able to freely grab, rotate, and scale this instance as much as your heart desires.

Of course, if you want to go into Edit mode and change the geometry of your model or adjust the materials on your object, you still need to make those changes in the source file. That process can be a bit tedious. Fortunately, Blender ships with an add-on that makes the process much easier, covered in the next section.

Taking Advantage of the Edit Linked Library Add-on

So, here's a hypothetical situation for you: You have your character that you've linked to your working file as described in the preceding section and you've started work animating that character. As you work on it, say you run into the situation where you discover that your character is wearing the wrong style of hat.

Now, the normal way you go about fixing this situation is by following these steps:

1. **Save your work in your current working file.**

2. **Open your source file in either the same session of Blender, or open the source file in a second Blender session.**

3. **Make the necessary changes to your character in the that source file (in this case, you're updating the character's hat).**

4. **Save your changes.**

5. **Go back to your working file and reload it to ensure that your changes are updated.**

TIP

Reloading your current file can be done pretty quickly using File ⇨ Open Recent (or the Ctrl+Shift+O hotkey) and choosing the name of your working file from the list.

The steps I just described aren't particularly hard, but if you find yourself doing them frequently, they can be time consuming and pretty annoying to perform each time. Fortunately, Blender does ship with an add-on that makes this process much faster called Edit Linked Library. Full disclosure: I wrote this add-on.

The Edit Linked Library add-on allows you to make edits on linked assets more quickly, reducing the amount of time spent shuffling Blender sessions on your own. Of course, to take advantage of this add-on, you first need to enable it. Although the add-on ships with every version of Blender, it's disabled by default because not everyone works on large projects with a lot of linked assets.

You enable the Edit Linked Library add-on the same way you enable most other add-ons in Blender:

1. **Go to Edit ⇨ Preferences in Blender's top menu.**

2. **In the Preferences window, navigate to Add-ons section.**

3. **Use the Search feature to look for Edit Linked Library.**

4. **When you find the add-on, enable it by clicking the check box next to its name.**

   The add-on is now enabled, so you can close the Preferences window.

After you have enabled the Edit Linked Library add-on, have a look in the Item tab in the 3D Viewport's Sidebar. At the bottom, there's a new panel labeled Edit Linked Library. Expand the panel and, if your active object is a linked asset, the add-on gives you some options on what to do next, as shown in Figure 1-1. If your active object isn't a linked asset, the panel will inform you that the object is local to your working file.

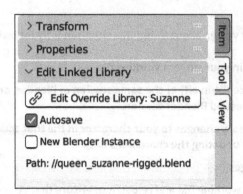

FIGURE 1-1:
The controls provided by the Edit Linked Library add-on are available in the Item tab of the 3D Viewport's Sidebar.

The way the add-on works, you first need to select an object in your working file that is a linked asset. That asset would be an object or collection you linked using the steps in the preceding section. Once you have the object selected, there's an Edit Library button in the Edit Linked Library panel. Click that button and Blender opens the source file for that linked asset so you can make changes to it. In your source file, the Edit Linked Library panel has a button that says Return to Original File. Click that button after making your changes and Blender reopens your working file. All the steps listed at the beginning of this section are boiled down to two button clicks. Woohoo!

In addition to the base functionality, the Edit Linked Library add-on includes a couple useful options that you can take advantage of, shown at the bottom of the Edit Linked Library panel:

» **Autosave:** Enable this check box and Blender automatically saves your work before switching between your working file and your source file (and vice versa). It's enabled by default to ensure that you don't lose any changes you make when switching files.

» **New Blender Instance:** If you enable this check box, the Edit Linked Library add-on spawns a second Blender session instead of closing your current file and opening the source one. Some people prefer this approach so they don't lose their place in their working file.

TIP

The Edit Linked Library add-on also works in Blender's various node editors, so you can use it to work on linked node groups for geometry nodes, compositing nodes, or shader nodes.

This add-on is a really handy feature when you're working in an environment that makes heavy use of linked assets. Of course, I'm a little biased about it, so definitely test it yourself and see if you find it helpful. If you don't, you can always disable it from Preferences.

Working with Library Overrides

Earlier in the chapter, I mentioned two solutions for dealing with the situation where you're unable to make local changes to an object that you've linked from an external .blend file. One solution is to take advantage of Blender's ability to create instances of collections. The other is with a feature called library overrides.

This discussion assumes the hypothetical example where you've directly linked a mesh object from one .blend file to your current working file. As a directly linked asset, all the properties of that datablock are also linked, meaning it's not possible to perform any kind of transform operation (translate, rotate, scale) on the object or add a modifier to it. Now, you could go back to your source file, bundle the object in a collection, and then link that collection into your working file, but for a quick change on a single object, that can be a lot of effort. This situation is where a library override is helpful. A *library override* is a feature of Blender that allows you to make a linked datablock local to your working file so you can make changes while still referencing unchanged data from the source file.

Creating a simple library override

To create a library override, select the linked object in the 3D Viewport and choose Object ⇨ Library Override ⇨ Make from the 3D Viewport's header menu. After you create your override, the chain link icon next to your object's name in the Outliner changes to an icon of a link with an arrow, as shown in the margin.

With your library override created, you are now free to transform your object in the 3D Viewport. If you test this ability out by grabbing your object and moving to a different location, you should notice that after you perform that translation, the X, Y, and Z location values of your object in Object Properties (and the 3D Viewport's Sidebar) change to a teal color to indicate that you've overridden those values in your local file.

The cool thing is that if the mesh in your source file gets modified, that link is still maintained between the two .blend files. Your working file gets updated with the new mesh data from the source file, but that object is positioned where you put it in your working file.

If at any point, you decide that you no longer want to use your library override, the Object ⇨ Library Overrides menu contains some additional options. The following list describes each one:

>> **Make:** This option is the one that was just described. If you have a linked datablock selected, choosing this option creates a library override for you.

>> **Reset:** Choose this option to remove all the local changes you've made to the selected datablock. You can still make changes because your library override is intact. It's just that the values have been set back to what they are in the source file.

>> **Clear:** When you choose the Clear option, Blender removes the library override and reverts the datablock to being a linked asset. After you choose this option, you would need to make a new library override if you want to make any local changes to the datablock.

Making deeper library overrides from the Properties editor and Outliner

An important thing to remember about library overrides is that they try to preserve linked data from your source file as much as possible. This principle also applies to nested datablocks. In the example from the preceding section, the library override was created on the object datablock so you can do local transforms. However, if you try to add custom attributes to the mesh in the Object Data tab of the Properties editor, the plus (+) buttons in that panel are grayed out. The reason is that although you're overriding the object datablock in your working file, the mesh datablock is still linked to the source file. (See Book 1, Chapter 4 for a refresher on how mesh datablocks are associated with object datablocks in a `.blend` file.)

If you want to make local edits to your linked mesh in this example, you need to create a library override for the mesh datablock as well. This kind of "deep" library override is more difficult to do from the 3D Viewport. Instead, the Properties editor and Outliner are better places to create these overrides. To create a deep library override, you first need to select the datablock that you want to override. To do so using the Properties editor, follow these steps:

1. **From the 3D Viewport select the linked object that you want to create a deep override for.**

This step doesn't really have to be from the 3D Viewport (you could also use the Outliner), but it's often easiest to select the object you want from there.

2. **In the Properties editor, go to the tab that has the datablock you're interested in.**

In the example where you want to edit mesh data, you would go to the Object Data tab. For material datablocks, you would go to the Material tab.

From the Outliner, selecting the datablock you want is much easier. You can use the integrated search feature to type the name of the datablock (assuming you've named it something sensible) or that datablock's parent. Then you can expand the containing datablock to find the one you need. Alternatively, you can select the containing object in the 3D Viewport and then, in the Outliner, press Numpad-dot (.) to use the Frame Selected feature to automatically scroll to your selection. Then you can expand and select your desired datablock from there.

Once you have isolated your desired datablock in either the Properties editor or the Outliner, the process for making a library override on that datablock is the same in both. Right-click the name of the datablock and choose Library Override ⇨ Make.

TIP

In the Properties editor, you can also quickly make a library override by Shift+clicking the link button on the right of the datablock widget.

REMEMBER

As of this writing with Blender 3.6 (and even Blender 4.0), deep library overrides for mesh data and materials are still pretty rudimentary. It's not currently possible, for example, to create a library override of your mesh data and make local changes in Edit mode. To make those kinds of changes, you still need to jump back to the source file.

Using library overrides with collections for linked characters

It's important to note that you're not restricted to using just collections for linking or just using library overrides. In fact, the most common use case for these features uses them both together for getting a rigged character into a scene. Typically, you want the character mesh and materials to all live in the source file, but to animate, you need the bones on the character rig to be locally posable.

The most common way to achieve this result is by linking a collection that contains the character mesh and rig and then overriding the armature. As an example, say you want to use the Stickman character from Book 4, Chapter 3 in a shot that you're creating. The first thing you need to do is bundle the character and rig into a collection so you can link it properly. Open your .blend file with your rigged Stickman character and follow these steps (if you don't have this file, you're welcome to download it from this book's supplemental website, blenderbasics.com):

1. **Select your character's armature object (in the example, it's named stickman_rig).**

   Recall that the armature is the parent of your character mesh and, therefore, the root of the character in your scene hierarchy

2. **From the Outliner, right-click the stickman_rig item and choose Select Hierarchy from the context menu that appears.**

   Now you've selected your whole character, including its rig and mesh.

3. **Back in the 3D Viewport, choose Object ⇨ Collection ⇨ Move to Collection from the header menu and choose New Collection from the secondary menu that appears.**

   Name your new collection something sensible, like stickman. You could also Link to Collection from the Object ⇨ Collection menu if you don't want to remove your armature and mesh from an existing collection and you want to also bundle them in a new one. Remember that in Blender, objects can live in multiple collections.

4. **Save your character's .blend file.**

Now that you have your character successfully bundled in a collection, you can open the .blend file you want to use for your shot and link the character to that file using the steps described earlier in this chapter. The important thing is that once you drill into your character's .blend file with the File Browser, you want to go to the Collections sub-folder in the file and choose the collection that holds your character. In this example, that's the collection named stickman you just created.

At this point, you've got your character's collection linked to your working file, and there should be an instance of that collection in your 3D Viewport. You're able to move the whole collection around as an object, but you're not yet able to make any changes to the character in Pose mode. This situation is where library overrides come into play:

1. **In the 3D Viewport, select your newly linked collection.**

2. **Choose Object ⇨ Library Overrides ⇨ Make from the 3D Viewport's header menu.**

When you create a library override on a collection, Blender drills into the collection and also makes library overrides for the objects within that collection. Now you should be able to select the character's armature (in this example, stickman_rig) and Tab into Pose mode. You can now animate Stickman to your heart's content.

REMEMBER

You might notice that the pose library that was built with the Stickman character doesn't come with it when you link the character to your working file. Unfortunately, there's no fast way to pull that pose library into your working file. To get your pose library assets to appear in your Asset Browser, you'd need to make the Stickman file a global asset by saving it to the folder on your hard drive where your global asset library lives, as described earlier in this chapter.

IN THIS CHAPTER

» Getting in the right mindset for automating parts of your art-making process

» Familiarizing yourself with the Scripting workspace in Blender

» Discovering the Python scripting language

» Getting started with scripting

» Making scripts faster using built-in templates

Chapter **2**

Automating Blender with Python Scripting

O ne of the really handy, albeit advanced, features within Blender is its integrated scripting capability using the Python language. What this means is that you can write little snippets of code or full-blown applications all within Blender. The purpose of this capability is to help you work faster and in a way that's more customized to your preferences. It's worth noting that all Blender's add-ons are written in Python using the same methodologies covered in this chapter. This fact includes the add-ons that ship with Blender as well as the ones you can purchase online at places like the Blender Market.

Scripting and coding can be a fairly advanced topic, but it doesn't have to be. Although there are four letters in it, "code" doesn't have to be one of *those* four-letter words. Like so many things in 3D art, quite a large part of this process is about having the right mindset. Even if you've never coded anything in your life before, the main requirement is realizing when automation is helpful. After that, it's just about knowing where to look for the right answers on how to do it (or finding someone else to do it for you).

I should say now that no matter how you shake it, there's still a lot to wrap your brain around when it comes to writing scripts. There are whole books dedicated to just that topic. So I don't have enough pages available in this chapter to give you a comprehensive education on scripting and programming. However, I hope that the content here gives you enough to get curious, get started, and maybe even make your life as an artist a little bit easier.

Understanding the Usefulness of Automation

Now, the question you might find yourself asking is, "Well, if there's a feature that makes my life easier, why doesn't Blender have it already? Why do I have to make it myself?"

There's actually a couple answers to those questions. The first is that Blender is meant to be a general purpose digital content-creation program, and it gets used in all kinds of different contexts. If the Blender developers optimize for one particular way of working, they risk making things more difficult for another. If you happen to be working in industrial visualization, architecture, visual effects, or commercial animation, there are some things that you do that don't apply to any of those other fields. You have things you do that are very specific to the kind of workflow used in your industry.

If Blender supported all these specific use cases equally, its user interface would be even more complex than it is, filled with extra features that only one segment of the user community uses. In fact, this focus on generalization is one of the reasons why Blender has so many add-ons that ship with it, which are disabled by default.

Another answer to the question of why you may need to code your own features is that sometimes you need a little bit of automation that helps with whatever you're doing right now, but isn't easily extended for all situations in which you may need it. For example, you may have a bunch of files with one name, and you realize you misspelled it. You can automate the renaming process, but because it's so specific to that one spelling mistake, you don't need it formalized to a full feature or even an add-on. You just need a script to automate the change on a bunch of objects.

In a creative tool like Blender, the main focus of any block of code should be on making your life as an artist easier. Without software like Blender, working in 3D might look a lot more like accounting, where you manually have to keep track of the locations of vertices and the relationships between them. By giving you a visualization of that 3D data, 3D tools like Blender provide a much easier way to understand all those numbers.

We have software to manage complex and tedious tasks, so we have more time to spend our energy on those unique things that only we can put into our work. So, as a creator, it's in your best interest to be on the lookout for those tedious, repetitive, non-unique tasks. Those tasks are where scripting and automation shine the most. As a personal mnemonic device, I try to mentally step outside of myself while I'm working and look at the specific activities that I'm doing. If I see that I'm doing the same thing more than three times in a row, that's a pretty strong indicator that the task is something that can and should be automated.

Have I convinced you yet? Well, maybe I haven't. But hopefully, by the end of this chapter, you'll have enough ammunition to be able to do a little bit of automation for yourself. Then you'll be able to focus most of your energy on what you're best at, which is probably not coding or doing monotonous things.

Discovering Blender's Scripting Workspace

When it comes to making scripts and automation within Blender, the best place to start is the Scripting workspace. This workspace is available in the General workflow template (File ⇨ New ⇨ General). It is the last tab all the way on the right, labeled Scripting. When you click on that tab, Blender puts you in the Scripting workspace. Your Blender session should look something like what's shown in Figure 2-1.

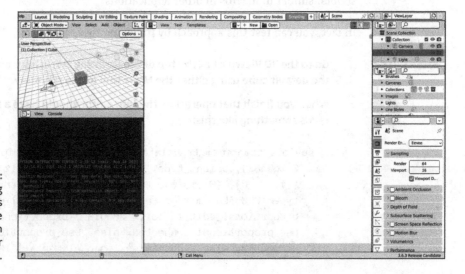

FIGURE 2-1: The Scripting workspace is the best place to start when writing scripts for Blender.

Automating Blender with Python Scripting

The Scripting workspace is actually pretty different from most of the other ones shown in this book. Along the right-hand side you should see the fairly familiar Outliner and Properties editors. One subtle difference is that there are actually two Outliners on the right side, with two different display modes. The top one is set to the familiar View Layer display mode, whereas the Outliner below that is set to the Blender File display mode. The reason this second Outliner exists is because when scripting, it's sometimes helpful to understand the structure of your current .blend file. Having a second Outliner gives you the ability to explore the contents of the file without interfering with the standard View Layers view.

Along the left side of the Scripting workspace you see a 3D Viewport at the top. That area is there mostly so you can how your scripts affect what's going on in your scene. Also, if you're building an add-on with a tool that's activated in the 3D Viewport, you can test it in this space.

Below the 3D Viewport on the left side is an editor called the Python Console. The Python Console is a space where you can write little snippets of Python code and execute them immediately without having to save a file. Think of it as your experimental play space where you can quickly test things out. To facilitate that approach, the Python Console launches with some modules and presets already set up for you.

At the bottom left is an Info editor. The Info editor is a handy little editor that gives you a log of everything that you do within Blender's interface as if it were written with Python. You may not realize it yet, but just about anything you can do in Blender has a corresponding Python call. That means nearly anything you can do through Blender's user interface can also be done using Python. The Info editor gives you a window into that world and provides a handy way to start constructing scripts, similar to macros in other applications.

In fact, you can test this approach by following these steps:

1. **Go to the 3D Viewport at the top of the Scripting workspace and move the default cube using either the Move tool or the G hotkey.**

2. **When you finish that operation, the Info editor should have a line that reads something like this:**

```
bpy.ops.transform.translate(value=(1.09473, 2.81075,
0.269583), orient_type='GLOBAL', orient_matrix=
((1, 0, 0), (0, 1, 0), (0, 0, 1)), orient_matrix_
type='GLOBAL', mirror=False, use_proportional_edit=False,
proportional_edit_falloff='SMOOTH', proportional_size=1,
use_proportional_connected=False, use_proportional_
projected=False, snap=False, snap_elements={'INCREMENT'},
```

```
use_snap_project=False, snap_target='CLOSEST', use_snap_
self=True, use_snap_edit=True, use_snap_nonedit=True,
use_snap_selectable=False)
```

That's a lot of code, but right now you don't need to know what all of it does.

3. **In the Info editor, click the line of code and copy it using the Ctrl+C hotkey.**

4. **In the Python Console, press Ctrl+P to paste your copied code at the prompt.**

5. **Still in the Python Console, press Enter to run the line of code.**

You should see the default cube shift in location again, in the same direction and distance as your initial move.

Congratulations, you've just executed your first function in Python!

REMEMBER

It's important to remember that the Info editor shows you a log of only what you've been doing in your current Blender session. It gets cleared out every time you save and reload your .blend file, so it's not a working history of everything you've done in this file.

The largest space within the Scripting workspace is devoted to a Text Editor. Yes, Blender has an integrated text editor where you can write code or write notes to yourself. In fact, my personal most common use for the Text Editor is the latter. If I need a note on my project file and I want that note to travel along with it, the Text Editor is the perfect place. In the context of this chapter, though, the Text Editor is where you go to write your Python scripts without immediately running them. This is in contrast to the Python Console where the function is run immediately after you press Enter.

The other advantage of writing scripts in the Text Editor is that it gives you the ability to write Python code that can be executed multiple times. And once you have a script that you like, you can save the text to an external file and load it into another Blender project.

There's one further thing you should consider doing when you start writing scripts in Blender. Go to Edit ⇨ Preferences and navigate to the Interface section in the window that appears. In the Display panel, enable the check box labeled Python Tooltips. With this check box enabled, all Blender's tooltips also include the Python function associated with the button, field, or menu you hover your mouse cursor over. As I mentioned earlier, nearly everything in Blender's interface is accessible via Python. This feature, along with the log in the Info editor, is a quick way to give you hints about the functions you should include in your scripts. You can also enable the Developer Extras check box, which lets you see the source code for just about any button in Blender so you can copy and paste that code into your own scripts.

TIP

Getting Familiar with the Python Language

If you're going to be doing any scripting within Blender, you'll have to be at least a little bit familiar with the language that's used for scripting within Blender. That language is called Python. Python is an open source scripting language actually integrated in to all sorts of creative tools these days, and Blender is no exception. Arguably, Blender was one of the first 3D programs to really use Python as a built-in scripting language.

That said, this book is not going to give you a comprehensive understanding of everything that's available within Python or even how to fully code within Python. There are multiple very large books and great online documentation that cover the language in more detail, so I really encourage you to check out those resources. You should find that the basics of the language are actually pretty easy to pick up. I know quite a few people who have been able to start doing simple (but still useful) scripts in Python after just a few days.

Part of the reason why it's often less a struggle to learn than other languages is because at its core, Python, as a language, is designed to be more comprehensible and readable. So, most of its structure can be defined with some pretty basic rules. If you follow those rules and keep them in mind as you work, you can become productive pretty quickly. Of course, your life will be easier if you already know a little bit about programming, but that's not a firm requirement.

In the context of using Python to write scripts in Blender, it's worthwhile to work through a Blender-flavored example. Nearly every Blender-related Python script is going to include the following line of code (usually at the beginning):

```
import bpy
```

This little line of code tells Python to pull in (*import*) a bunch of Blender-specific functions from a library, or *module*, called bpy. Think of a module as a package that someone else has already written that you can use to do stuff in Python. The bpy module is such a package, and it's filled with things you can do in Blender. The Blender development team put together a set of these modules, and together, they're referred to as Blender's Python API, or *application programming interface*. When you begin your script with import bpy, you're telling Python, "Hey, there's a whole bunch of Blender going on that I want to use to do cool stuff."

Of course, Python has a bunch of modules you can also import that are not specific to Blender, and many of them can be quite handy for quickly putting together scripts. However, when it comes to scripts made for Blender, the most important module is bpy.

The Python Console on the left side of the Scripting workspace already has the bpy module imported, so you don't have to write that import statement there.

Another common practice when writing scripts is creating variables. A *variable* is a name assigned to some kind of data so you can refer to it again later. You make this assignment by typing the name, followed by an equals symbol (=) and then the data. The following lines of code are examples of a few different variables being set:

```
some_number = 732
my_string = "This is a bit of text."
ob = bpy.context.active_object
```

If you look at each of these lines, there are some critical things to pay attention to. First and foremost, notice that each variable assignment happens on its own line. With rare exception, Python is set up such that one line of code corresponds to exactly one action. In this case, that action is assigning data to a variable. The next thing to notice is that none of the variable names have spaces in them. As a general rule of thumb, programming languages don't like spaces. If you have a variable that consists of two words, put an underscore (_) between those words instead of a space. The second thing to notice is that the second variable, my_string, has a chunk of text assigned to it. That chunk of text (known as a *string* in coder-talk) does have spaces. To make sure the spaces are recognized, and to let Python know the data is a string, you wrap the text in quotation marks ("). The last variable assignment is a little bit more complex, but what's happening there is something that's very Blender-specific. It's using the bpy module to assign your active object in the .blend file to a variable named ob (the variable shouldn't be named object because that word has special meaning in the Python language). The important thing to notice in that assignment, is that you can drill into a Python module to access its components by using the period (.) character.

So, to sum up some Python-related rules:

>> Variables are assigned with the equals (=) symbol.

>> One line of Python code corresponds to one action.

>> Don't use spaces in variable names.

>> Strings are wrapped in quotes.

>> The period (.) character is used to access parts within a Python data structure.

Another important thing to understand about Python is how it defines scope. When it comes to coding, *scope* is the concept of a block of code with information that's relevant only to that code. Think of it as a kind of data sandbox. The kids (variables and functions) within the sandbox (scope) can interact with each other, but the kids outside of the sandbox have only limited, if any, access to the kids inside. Scope is an important concept to understand so you can have nicely organized and properly functioning code.

Now, relative to some other programming languages, Python is considered a bit funky in the way it defines scope. In other programming languages, scope is often defined with things like brackets or parentheses or curly braces. In Python, you use indenting. If you indent, you're "in scope." When you remove the indent, you're "outside the scope." As an example, have a look at the following lines of code (don't focus too much on what it does; this is just for illustrating the concept of scope):

```
if book_done:
    author_says = "Woohoo!"
```

In this example, there's an if statement, and you can tell that the author_says variable is within the scope of that if condition because it's indented. By standard, the indent to define scope should be four spaces. Scope gets used for all kinds of things, including function definitions, loops, conditionals, and defining complex data structures like dictionaries. I cover some of those things later in this chapter.

REMEMBER

The biggest thing to remember is that scope is defined by indenting. You want to make sure that you indent with spaces, and each indent is about four spaces long. In Blender's text editor, the Tab key is defaulted to inserting four spaces for you as a handy little shortcut.

These rules are the basic building blocks of the Python scripting language. Of course, there's a lot more, but these are the basics. The rest is easier to understand by working through some real examples. Fortunately, that's what the next section is for!

Writing Your First Blender Script

In this section, you write your first Python script in Blender. Actually, it will be your first two scripts, but more on that in a moment. The standard example for any programming language is known as the "Hello World" example. Basically, you write a little chunk of code that outputs "Hello world" somewhere, typically somewhere on-screen. In this section, you're going to do a couple variations of the "Hello World," one just in Python, and the other one a bit more Blender-y.

Writing code in the Python Console

To start, the simplest way to execute Python code in Blender is from the Python Console in the Scripting workspace. In the Python Console, type the following text:

```
print("Hello world!")
```

After you've typed that code, press Enter. Immediately after you press Enter, the Python Console should have additional text that reads Hello world! like what's shown in Figure 2-2.

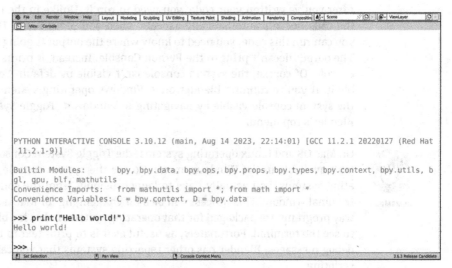

FIGURE 2-2: Your first Python script in Blender. Hello world!

So what's going on here? Based on what's covered in the preceding section, you can see that there's a string wrapped in quotes that reads "Hello world!" Wrapped around that string is a set of parentheses, and to the left of that is text that reads print. What you're doing in this line of code is calling a function called print(). A *function* in Python is a name for a block of code that performs some action, based on some kind of input. You can tell when something is a function because a function name is always followed by parentheses. Within those parentheses is whatever input that's being fed to the function. In this example, you fed a string to the function, and the action was displaying that string on-screen.

Of course, because you typed and executed that function in the Python Console, it's kind of ephemeral. It isn't really saved anywhere. For that, you need to have the code saved to a text file. If you're working in a text file, the place you want to be is Blender's Text Editor.

Automating Blender with Python Scripting

Coding in the Text Editor

To start creating your script in the Text Editor, you need to create a new text document. In Blender's Scripting workspace, go to the Text Editor and from its header menu, choose Text ⇨ New. You can also click New in the center of the Text Editor's header. Now you can start writing your script.

In the Text Editor, type the same code that you put in the Python Console in the preceding section, like so:

```
print("Hello world... again!")
```

After you've written your code, you need to run it. Unlike in the Python Console, the code doesn't automatically execute when you press Enter. However, before you can run this code, you need to know where the output is going to be displayed. The output doesn't print to the Python Console. Instead, it prints to your system console. Of course, the system console isn't visible by default. You have to enable it. If you're running Blender on a Windows operating system, you can make the system console visible by navigating to Window ⇨ Toggle System Console in Blender's top menu.

REMEMBER

On Mac OS and Linux operating systems, the Toggle System Console functionality isn't available in the Windows menu. To see the system console on these operating systems, you actually have to launch Blender from the command line in a terminal window. This process can be a bit challenging for Mac users because the way programs are packaged for that operating system makes it a bit more difficult to see the terminal. Fortunately, as useful as it is to print text to the terminal for debug messages, Blender has other reporting systems that you can use for actual scripting.

Once you have a system console visible, you can run the script from the Text Editor by choosing Text ⇨ Run Script or by clicking the Run Script button in the header. Either way, when you run the script, you should see Hello world... again! show up in the system console.

Writing a more Blender-y "Hello World"

The previous sections covered simple examples of the standard Python "Hello World," but what about something more Blender-y? For that, you're writing a script that changes the name of the default cube from Cube to Hello world. To work through this example, start a new Blender session with the General workflow template (File ⇨ New ⇨ General) and switch to the Scripting workspace. Then add a new text file in the Text Editor (Text ⇨ New). Now you can start writing your script. The text of that script should read like the following:

```
import bpy

bpy.data.objects["Cube"].name = "Hello world"
```

If you run this script (Text ⇨ Run Script) and look in your Outliner, you should see that the default cube has been renamed to Hello world.

Congratulations! You've done a simple script that renames the default cube!

Of course, on the face of it, that doesn't seem very useful, does it? You could've just as easily double-clicked the name in the Outliner and changed it there. Although that's true for one object, think about the scenario when you need to rename a lot of objects.

For example, say you haven't followed any of my advice throughout this book about naming the objects you add to your scene. Say you've built a scene, and now perhaps you have 25 cubes in your scene. Sadly, each of these cubes is named Cube.XXX, where the XXX is some number.

This is a problem. It would be best if you named all these objects something that makes more sense. Perhaps you want to name them all "building," "desk," "bunny," or "Frank." This scenario is where a script can save you a lot of time.

REMEMBER

Yes, technically speaking, you can use Blender's built-in batch renaming feature by pressing Ctrl+F2 and get the same thing done. However, this example shows you how to do it with Python, and you can use it to work on other types of data in Blender.

As a hypothetical example, say you have a scene with 50 Suzanne monkeys, and they're all named Suzanne. The problem, though, is that Suzanne no longer wants that to be her name. She now wants her name to be Susie. You should be able to make this example file pretty quickly yourself, but if you don't want to, I have a .blend file you can use on this book's supplemental website, blenderbasics.com.

So, with your file with 50 Suzannes opened in Blender, switch to the Scripting workspace and create a new text file in the Text Editor using Text ⇨ New. Now you can start writing your script. The script you're writing looks like this:

```
import bpy

for monkey in bpy.data.objects:
    if monkey.name.startswith("Suzanne"):
        monkey.name = "Susie"
```

It's a few lines of code, with a few pieces you haven't seen before, so the next bit of text walks through each line in the script. The first line should look familiar. Because you know you're going to be using Blender's Python API, the first line is import bpy, as covered earlier in this chapter.

The next line of code is known as a *for loop*. In programming, a *loop* is a language feature where all the code within the scope of that loop is repeated until some condition is met. In this example, you have a for loop, which is a special kind of loop that iterates through items in a list. The list that you're walking through is the list of all objects in your .blend file, indicated by bpy.data.objects. You're using the Blender Python API from the bpy module to go through each object in your file. And each time the script gets to an object, the for loop temporarily assigns that object to a variable named monkey. Translated from Python to English, for monkey in bpy.data.objects: means, "For each object in my .blend file, let's call that object 'monkey' and then do the following stuff with it:"

In the next line of code, if monkey.name.startsiwth("Suzanne"):, you're within the scope of the for loop, and now you're at something called an *if statement* or a *conditional*. Think of conditionals as tests. If some condition (in this case the current monkey's name starts with "Suzanne") is true, then jump into the scope of that statement. Since you're "inside" the for loop, you're now only dealing with one object at a time, and you're testing to see if that object's name starts with the text, "Suzanne."

For the final line of code in your script, monkey.name = "Susie", you're assigning the string "Susie" to the name variable within your monkey object. I have to admit that we're cheating here a little bit. In a more rigorous Python script, you may want to only change the prefix of your object names and leave the suffix untouched. In this example, you're relying on the fact that Blender doesn't allow two objects to share the same name, so they get numbers added to them automatically.

Now that you have an understanding of how the script works, you can run it from the Text Editor by navigating to Text ⇨ Run Script. Immediately after running the script, if you look in the Outliner, you should see that all the objects with names formerly starting with "Suzanne" now have names that start with "Susie."

Well done! You've renamed Suzanne to Susie 50 times. And as a bonus, you should have a pretty general understanding of how Blender's Batch Rename operator works under the hood.

Taking Advantage of Templates and Documentation

You don't necessarily have to write all your code yourself and become a Python expert to build tools that help you work faster. One of the really nice things that the Blender developers have done to make things easier to start scripting is include a large number of templates that ship with Blender. You can use these templates as a starting point for creating your own scripts and add-ons within Blender. Furthermore, you can also use these templates to get more familiar with Python and understand how scripting works in Blender.

You access the Python scripting templates from Blender's Text Editor. Navigate to the header menu and choose Templates ⇨ Python, and you should see a menu like what's shown in Figure 2-3.

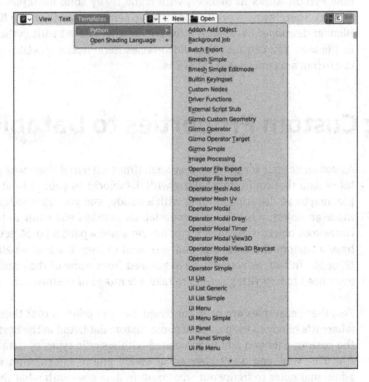

FIGURE 2-3:
A large assortment of templates for Python scripts are available from the Templates menu in Blender's Text Editor.

If you select one of the templates from this menu, Blender loads a Python template with some example code that shows you how to create a particular kind of script in Blender. Most of these templates are functional, too. For example, if you pick the first template, Addon Add Object, and then immediately run that script with Text ⇨ Run Script, the script creates and enables an add-on called New Object. You can tell that the add-on is working because if you choose Add ⇨ Mesh in the 3D Viewport, there's a new entry at the bottom of that menu named Add Object. If you choose that menu item, a plane is added at the location of the 3D cursor. Now you can make a modification to the template script (such as changing the name of that menu item from "Add Object" to "Add A Plane Named Carl" — you can do that by changing line 67 in the template). Then if you run the script again, that change shows up in Blender's interface.

In addition to the templates that ship with Blender, I highly encourage you to check out the official Blender Python API documentation at `https://docs.blender.org/api`. This documentation is a fantastic resource for understanding how Python works in Blender, with some really solid examples to help you get started. There's also a pretty handy video series available on the Blender Cloud by Blender developer Dr. Sybren Stüvel on getting started with Python and scripting in Blender. You can find that video series here: `https://studio.blender.org/training/scripting-for-artists`.

Adding Custom Properties to Datablocks

As you write your scripts, you may sometimes wish that there was some extra little bit of data that could travel along with datablocks in your `.blend` file. For example, maybe you're collaborating with a buddy, and you want to keep track of who made an object, a brush, or a material. Or perhaps you want to track how many times your object-renaming script has renamed a particular object. Or, maybe you have a custom character rig, and you need to keep track of whether a limb is in IK or FK. In fact, as you may have guessed from some of the examples, you don't even need to be writing scripts to take advantage of custom data.

Yes, these examples are little contrived, but the point is that there are situations where it's handy to keep track of some custom data. And in the best-case scenario, the custom data you add is associated with specific types of data in your `.blend` file. This way, you don't have an unwieldy pile of information where you need additional notes to figure out what custom data goes with what thing in your file.

Fortunately, Blender has a feature to give you this exact functionality. They're called *custom properties*, and you can associate them with just about any kind of datablock in a `.blend` file. The question, then, concerns how you add this data. The best way to understand custom properties is by going through an example and adding one yourself. Follow these steps:

1. **Start a new session using the General workflow template (File ⇨ New ⇨ General).**

2. **Go to the Object tab of the Properties editor and, at the bottom, expand the Custom Properties panel.**

   The contents of the panel should be pretty stark, just a single button, labeled New.

3. **Click New in the Custom Properties panel.**

   Congratulations! You've just created your first custom property. Currently, that property is named "prop." It's a floating point (decimal) number, and it's associated with your default cube object (because that's the object selected when you first launch Blender). Now you can edit that property.

4. **Click the gear icon to reveal an Edit Property pop-over.**

   From the Edit Property pop-over, you can refine the attributes of your custom property and give Blender a sense of the kind of data that the custom property should store. First, though, you should give your custom property a sensible name.

5. **In the Property Name field, change the name of your property to "Customized."**

   You're going to make this property a simple indicator that helps you remember if you customized it. However, to do that, a floating point number doesn't make a lot of sense. It would be better if you had a boolean value, something you can toggle with a check box.

6. **Use the Type dropdown to change your custom property's type to Boolean.**

   Boolean values are either true or false. You'll leave the other settings at their default values.

7. **Click OK at the bottom of the Edit Property pop-over to finalize your changes.**

   After clicking OK, you should see that you have a check box in Custom Properties labeled Customized. By default, it's off. But if you click it, it's toggled on. And if you save your `.blend` file, the next time you open it, that property and its toggle value will still be associated with the cube in that file. Even better, if you link or append that cube to another file, the custom property goes with it. Figure 2-4 shows a brief overview of the process described in these steps.

Automating Blender
with Python Scripting

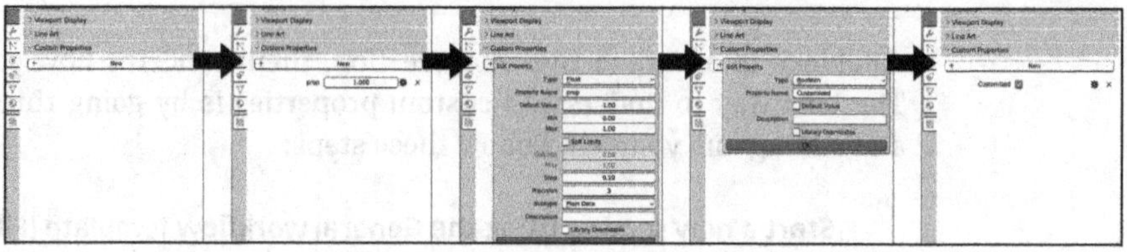

FIGURE 2-4:
Adding a custom property to the default cube.

TIP If you want to remove a custom property, click the X icon to the right of it.

Now if you explore each of the tabs in the Properties editor, you should notice that most of them have a Custom Properties panel at the bottom. Scenes, view layers, objects, materials, textures, object data (meshes, curves, and so on) . . . all these datablocks support having custom data assigned to them. Even better, these custom properties work just like any other property in Blender. You can keyframe and animate them (see Book 4, Chapter 1). This means that you can also use them as control values in drivers (see Book 4, Chapter 2), which, in turn, makes them incredibly useful when building custom rigs for animation. And, of course, because these custom properties can be used as drivers means they have a data path. Since each custom property has its own data path, you can also access them (and modify them) using Python scripts. And with that, a whole world of possibilities is at your fingertips. Happy Blending!

Index

About the Author

Jason van Gumster is an independent creative with a particular interest in open source tools. Very nearly everything that he produces — stories, animations, designs, videos, podcasts — are all made using free and open source tools, from applications all the way down to his choice of operating system. Jason has run an animation studio, written all previous editions of *Blender For Dummies*, co-authored *GIMP Bible*, and helped "fight bad guys with art" by designing anti-counterfeit technology for banknotes. Most recently, as Director of Special Projects and Marketing at Autotroph, Jason has been focused on expanding the use of Blender by artists, studios, and toolmakers.

He does all this while living and traveling full-time in an RV with his wife, two children, and two dogs. When Jason isn't working on his own creative projects, he's drinking coffee and trying to be awesome. The former, he's pretty much gotten down to a science. The latter . . . well, every now and then, he succeeds at that one and makes it look like it wasn't an accident.

To my family. I can't wait to see the adventures ahead.

Author's Acknowledgments

My biggest thanks has to go to my family. My wife and children have been so graciously patient with me as I've spent countless hours with my nose buried in my computer as I write this book. You indulge in letting me do all these projects and I can't thank you enough for that. But I'm going to try every chance I get . . . like now. Thank you!

And, as with all previous versions of this book, I need to give a huge thanks to all the Blender developers around the globe, both part of the core development team and all the volunteer developers scratching their own itches. Without your regular commits and patches, Blender wouldn't be the incredible creative juggernaut that it is. Of course, I also need to thank the community of Blender users at large as well. We help each other get better, both as artists and as people. I've said it many times before: This community is Blender's strongest feature. You're what takes the 1s and 0s that make up Blender and transforms it into something truly special.

And finally, a hearty thank you goes out to the team at Wiley. For each edition of *Blender For Dummies*, you've continued to be a patient source of guidance and discipline. To Steve Hayes, thank you for reaching out for this latest edition and getting the page count bump to support the ever-growing list of features available in Blender. Maureen and Scott Tullis, as editors, you've done a great job keeping me on track and ensuring I'm not just dumping words on a page but instead giving useful information in a way that's easy to follow and makes sense to the reader. To Bassam Kurdali, you've been the technical editor for every edition of *Blender For Dummies*, and your expertise is the thing that's elevated this book beyond the drafts you've reviewed. And finally, Murari Mukundan, you've been huge in guiding me despite the timeline delays I've introduced. Thank you to you all.

And ever continuing in the tradition of previous editions of this book, I maintain my thanks to the brilliant human that first filtered water through ground coffee beans. You made a drink that is dark and bitter, so I don't have to be.

Thank you.

Publisher's Acknowledgments

Executive Editor: Steve Hayes

Project Editor/Copy Editor: Scott Tullis

Technical Editor: Bassam Kurdali

Production Editor: Tamilmani Varadharaj

Managing Editor: Murari Mukundan

Project Manager: Maureen Tullis

Cover Image: Compliments of Jason Van Gumster